Basic Cookery

Fundamental Recipes and Variations

Second Edition

Richard E. Martland

Principal Lecturer in Catering Studies,
North Warwickshire College of Technology and Art

Derek A. Welsby

Formerly Senior Lecturer in Hotel and Catering Studies,
Henley College, Coventry

Heinemann Professional Publishing

Heinemann Professional Publishing Ltd
Halley Court, Jordan Hill, Oxford OX2 8EJ

OXFORD   LONDON   MELBOURNE   AUCKLAND   SINGAPORE
IBADAN   NAIROBI   GABORONE   KINGSTON

First published 1980
Reprinted 1982, 1984 (twice), 1985
Second edition 1988
Reprinted 1988

British Library Cataloguing in Publication Data
Martland, Richard E.
Basic cookery. – 2nd ed.
1. Cookery
I. Title   II. Welsby, Derek A.
(Derek Andrew), *1942*–
641.5

ISBN 0 434 92234 X

Illustrations drawn by Christopher Ake and Frances Tomlinson

Printed in Great Britain by
Redwood Burn Limited
Trowbridge

Contents

Preface   xi
Acknowledgements   xiii
Introduction   1

SECTION ONE – RELATED STUDIES

1 KITCHEN ATTIRE   11
Equipment and Organization
Protective clothing – Chefs' knives – Manual kitchen
equipment – Cooking vessels in general use – kitchen
organization

2 MODERN KITCHEN EQUIPMENT   38
Micro-wave and Convection ovens – High pressure steamers –
Pressureless convection steamer – Liquidizer – Vertical
cutter/mixer – Bratt pans – Régéthermic regenerating ovens –
Computerized fryers

3 THE COOKING OF FOOD   55
Heat and heat transfer – Cooking methods listed and discussed
– Reasons for cooking food – Effects of cooking on foods
(changes in texture, flavour, colour and odour)

4 THICKENING AND BINDING MECHANISMS   67
Starch gelatinization – Protein coagulation and gelation –
Emulsification

5 ENTRÉES AND RELEVÉS   77
Definition and menu examples

SECTION TWO – LARDER WORK

6 COLD SAUCES – DRESSINGS AND DIPS   83
Introduction – Salad dressings – Mayonnaise and derivatives –
Dips

7 SALADS   91
   Introduction – Rules for salad making – Classification – Salads
   – Contemporary trends – Simple salads – Compound salads –
   Warm salads

8 COLD HORS D'OEUVRE   106
   Introduction – Classification – Cocktail canapes, à la russe –
   Hors d'oeuvre Moscovite – Presentation – Examples of hors
   d'oeuvre

9 SANDWICHES   127
   Introduction – Preparation of sandwiches – Types, hot and
   cold – Varied examples of sandwiches

10 COLD PIES   134
   Introduction – Categorisation – Service – Production factors –
   Typical menu examples

11 TERRINES – PÂTÉS – GALANTINES   139
   Introduction – Definitions – Comments on preparation –
   Typical menu examples

12 COLD BUFFET: RUDIMENTARY CONCEPTS   147
   Introduction – Layout – Types of buffet – Garnish and
   decoration – Sauces and aspics

SECTION THREE – KITCHEN: STOVE WORK
13 BASICS OF CULINARY PRACTICE   161
   Practical applications of thickening and binding agents – Basic
   flavourings – Stocks, essences and glazes – Sauces, foundation
   and miscellaneous – Garnishes and other basic preparations –
   Ancillary larder/pastry preparations

14 SOUPS: LES POTAGES   204
   Soup classification explained; purées, creams, veloutés,
   thickened brown, bisques, broths, consommés and unclassified
   soups

15 EGG COOKERY AND EXTENSIONS   228
   Introduction – Poached, boiled, en cocotte, sur le plat, fried,
   scrambled, omelets

16 FARINACEOUS COOKERY AND EXTENSIONS   242
   Introduction – rice, pasta, gnocchi preparations

17 THE PRINCIPLE AND PRACTICE OF BOILING   257
   Boiling explained – applied to: fish, butcher's meat, offal,
   poultry and vegetables – garnishes and accompaniments

18 THE PRINCIPLE AND PRACTICE OF POACHING 277
Poaching explained – applied to: fish, poultry, offal – garnishes
and accompaniments

19 THE PRINCIPLE AND PRACTICE OF STEAMING 289
Steaming explained – applied to: fish, butcher's meat, offal,
poultry, vegetables – garnishes and accompaniments

20 THE PRINCIPLE AND PRACTICE OF FRYING 293
Deep frying explained – safety factors – organizational factors
– fats and oils used – frying temperatures – protective coatings
for food – applied: fish, poultry, butcher's meat, offal,
vegetables – garnishes and accompaniments. Shallow frying
explained – applied as above to include, game and application
as a quick method of re-heating foods

21 THE PRINCIPLES AND PRACTICE OF STEWING AND BRAISING 335
Stewing explained and applied: fish, butcher's meat, offal,
poultry, game, vegetables, fruits for breakfast cookery –
garnishes and accompaniments.
Braising explained – applied as above to include comments on
ancillary larder work

22 THE PRINCIPLE AND PRACTICE OF ROASTING 282
Roasting explained – analysis chart – applied: butcher's meat,
poultry, game, vegetables – carving – garnishes and
accompaniments

23 THE PRINCIPLE AND PRACTICE OF POT-ROASTING 396
Pot-roasting explained – applied: butcher's meat, poultry,
game, offal – modes of service – garnishes and accompaniments

24 THE PRINCIPLE AND PRACTICE OF BAKING 401
Baking explained and applied: fish, butcher's meat, poultry,
game, vegetables, garnishes and accompaniments,
miscellaneous preparations

25 THE PRINCIPLE AND PRACTICE OF GRILLING 417
Grilling explained – comments on ancillary larder preparations
– applied: fish, butcher's meat, offal, poultry, vegetables –
garnishes and accompaniments

26 COMBINED METHODS OF COOKERY: MEAT AND FISH 435
Introduction and explanation – applied: fish, butcher's meat,
offal, poultry, game – garnishes and accompaniments

27 COMBINED METHODS OF COOKERY: VEGETABLES AND
POTATOES 457
Introduction and explanation – applied: diverse vegetable and
potato preparations

28 SAVOURIES AND HOT HORS D'OEUVRES   464
   Introduction – applied: diverse preparations in common use –
   garnishes and accompaniments

29 BREAKFAST COOKERY   471
   Breakfast cookery explained – applied: English and Continental
   preparations

SECTION FOUR – PASTRY WORK
30 BASIC PASTRIES   475
   Introduction – Classification outlined
   Short pastries – Introduction – Ingredient principles – Various
   short crust pastries – applications – crumbles
   Choux pastry – Introduction – Ingredient principles –
   Production method – Applications
   Puff pastries – Introduction – Ingredient principles –
   Production factors – English, French/Continental, pastries –
   Application
   Suet pastry – Introduction – Ingredient principles – suet pastry
   – applications

31 CAKES, BISCUITS, GATEAUX AND TORTEN   511
   Introduction – Aeration factors – Ingredient principles
   Typical applications of cakes and biscuits – Gateaux and
   Torten defined – Composition and assembly – Typical
   examples

32 STEAMED AND BAKED PUDDINGS   527
   Introduction – Ingredient/production principles, Pudding
   moulds – Typical examples

33 FERMENTED/FERMENTED LAMINATED GOODS   534
   Introduction – Commodity factors – Production factors –
   Typical examples

34 MILK PUDDINGS   546
   Introduction – Ingredient principles – Production principles –
   Production methods, baked and boiled – Typical examples

35 BAKED EGG CUSTARD SWEETS   549
   Introduction – Ingredient/production principles – Basic
   mixture and extensions

36 POACHED AND STEWED FRUITS   555
   Introduction – Ingredients/production criteria – Applications –
   Typical examples

37 PANCAKES, FRITTERS AND SWEET OMELETS   558
   Introduction – Batter production – Pancakes – Soufflé
   pancakes – Fritters – Sweet omelets

38 HOT SWEET SOUFFLÉS   566
    Introduction – Ingredients criteria – Examples of dry baked
    soufflés – Examples of pouding soufflés

39 SWEET FLAMBÉS   573
    Introduction – Flambéing techniques – Fruit flambés – Crêpes
    Suzette

40 RICE BASED COLD SWEETS   576
    Introduction – Ingredient/production principles – Rice Condé
    – Other menu examples

41 BAVAROIS (BAVARIAN CREAMS)   580
    Introduction – Ingredient principles – Moulds and service –
    Basic mixtures with charted extensions

42 COLD SWEET SOUFFLÉS, MOUSSES AND FOOLS   586
    Introduction – Ingredient/production criteria – Moulds
    Holding and storage – Basic mixtures and extensions

43 MERINGUE AND MERINGUE BASED SWEETS   595
    Introduction – Ingredient principles – Types of meringue –
    Basic meringue mixtures and applications

44 HOUSE MADE ICES, SORBETS AND ICED SWEETS   605
    Introduction – Classification – Ingredients/production criteria
    – Churn frozen ice creams – Water Ices – Sorbets –
    Granites/marquises – Bombes – Parfait – Biscuit glacé – Still-
    frozen iced soufflés – Iced mousses – Cassatas – Iced coupes

45 MISCELLANEOUS SWEETS   624
    Examples of various independent sweets/puddings

46 PETITS FOURS (a basic introduction)   633
    Introduction – Petits fours sec – Petits fours glacees –
    Examples of petits fours

47 SAUCES, GLAZES/SYRUPS, FILLINGS AND MISCELLANEOUS
    PREPARATIONS   640
    Introduction – Sweet sauces – Glazes and syrups – Fillings and
    creams – Ganache – Praliné – Boiled sugar

    GLOSSARY   652

    INDEX   660

Preface

These studies are founded upon basic cookery processes and applied underlying scientific principles which aim to explain the hows and whys of culinary operations. The authors have attempted to examine these principles in relation to a wide range of foods and to show how they can be extended to produce many culinary products. Chapters 3 and 4 focus attention on certain underlying scientific aspects, which may be encountered in everyday kitchen practice.

It is envisaged that this text will be primarily of benefit to students following craft, technician and supervisory courses, which relate to catering education, and to students studying for the following qualifications:

City and Guilds of London Institute 706/1/2/3, 705 craft courses;
H.C.I.M.A. Parts A and B;
B.T.E.C./S.C.O.T.V.E.C. and N.E.B.S.S. catering courses and degree courses in hotel and catering management.

In addition the text will prove beneficial to professionals working within the hotel and catering industry and to the enterprising amateur.

R. E. Martland
D. A. Welsby

Acknowledgements

We wish to thank Michael Newton Clifford PhD, BSc, AIFST, Lecturer in Food Technology at Surrey University for his contribution to and advice on Chapters 3 and 4 and also Neville Winston Walton BA (Manc) for his guidance on French terminology.

For assistance with information concerning equipment we extend our thanks to the following companies:

Bartlett and Son Ltd
Benham and Sons Ltd
Electricity Council
Frialator International Ltd
Hobart Manufacturing Co Ltd
Litton Systems, Inc
Market Forge
Phillips Electrical Ltd
Régéthermic (UK) Ltd
Sharp Electronics (UK) Ltd
South Bend Corporation
Stotts of Oldham
Thorn Domestic Appliances (Electrical) Ltd

R.E.M
D.A.W

Introduction

Culinary work is broadly classified into three basic activities:

Larder
Kitchen / Stove ⎬ Operations
Pastry

Each of these activities is further sub-divided in accordance with the size, type, class, and work load of the catering unit. This book is composed of a series of studies related to those aspects of culinary work listed above and specific allied studies.

Modern trends in food production and service are moving away from the labour intensive systems towards more rationalized types of operation, incorporating the use of purpose designed systems, new machinery and an ever increasing range of convenience foods. However, whether a system be traditional or futuristic the classification of culinary work remains unchanged. The text is divided into FOUR main sections:

ONE   Related Studies
TWO   Larder Work
THREE   Stove Work
FOUR   Pastry Work

How to Use This Book

About the Recipe Formulations

The Concise Oxford Dictionary defines the word recipe as 'a statement of ingredients and procedures for preparing a dish', and the word formulae as 'illustrating rules and principles.' The recipe formulations used in the following studies embrace both meanings.

By using this system students and caterers become involved with the formulation of standard recipes designed to meet portion control requirements to suit particular catering operations. Furthermore the compilation of recipes from set formulae enables the student to appreciate the basic composition of many different dishes. The difference is often found to be a slight variation on a basic principle, i.e. the main ingredient used and the seasonings and flavourings change. For example:

(a) Ragoût de boeuf   — brown beef stew
(b) Boeuf bourguignonne — brown beef stew in red wine
(c) Navarin d'agneau   — brown lamb stew
(d) Goulash de veau   — paprika flavoured veal stew.

The above dishes are prepared using the same basic recipe formulations and mode of cookery, the variations being the main ingredient and flavourings used.
Advantages of using basic recipe formulations:

1. Ease of conversion into either metric or Imperial measurements.
2. Simple conversion into any given quantity.
3. Ratios are more easily understood and remembered compared with complex recipes.
4. The recipe formulations teach students to appreciate recipe balance.
5. Formulae may be changed to meet the specific cost and quality requirements of different types of catering establishments. They also help to simplify purchasing, costing and the control of commodities.

Metrication

No attempt has been made to change imperial weights and measurements into their metric equivalents. It must be noted that the amounts given relate to the ratio formulae used and are not in relation to each other. It is believed that this approach is more advantageous in the interests of accurate formulae balances and yields. Therefore it may be observed that 1 oz may equate with 25 or 30 g depending upon the product in question.

How to Use the Recipe Formulations

The recipe formulations are designed to be worked out in relation to the first and largest ingredient in each case. It is important that all ingredients in any one formula are based on the same unit of measurement e.g. lb, oz, kilogram, or gram. Where, therefore, the formula includes a combination of solids and liquids it is necessary to convert the liquid measurements into weights.

e.g. 1 pt of liquid   = 20 fluid oz
1 l of liquid   = 1,000 g

Example 1

Basic white sauce: Béchamel

Unit	Ingredient	Metric	Imperial
1	Milk	1 l = 1,000 g	1 pt = 20 oz
$\frac{1}{10}$	Butter/margarine	100 g	2 oz
$\frac{1}{10}$	Flour	100 g	2 oz
	Onion clouté		

Example 2

Cream soups (vegetable based):   Les Potages—Crèmes

Unit	Ingredient	Metric	Imperial
1	White stock	5 l = 5 kg	1 gal = 10 lb
$\frac{2}{5}$	Main vegetable (aqueous)	$\frac{2}{5} \times 5 = 2$ kg	$\frac{2}{5} \times 10 = 4$ lb
$\frac{1}{5}$	Vegetable adjunct or mirepoix	$\frac{1}{5} \times 5 = 1$ kg	$\frac{1}{5} \times 10 = 2$ lb
$\frac{1}{5}$	Béchamel	$\frac{1}{5} \times 5 = 1$ kg	$\frac{1}{5} \times 10 = 2$ lb
$\frac{1}{20}$	Butter or margarine	$\frac{1}{20} \times 5 = \frac{1}{4}$ kg (250 g)	$\frac{1}{20} \times 10 = \frac{1}{2}$ lb
$\frac{1}{20}$	Cream (optional)	$\frac{1}{20} \times 5 = \frac{1}{4}$ kg (250 g)	$\frac{1}{20} \times 10 = \frac{1}{2}$ lb
	Seasoning		
	Bouquet garni		

Example 3

Shows how the recipes are set out in the studies.

Basic White Sauce   Béchamel

Yield: 1 l (1 qt)
Cooking time: 30 min

Unit	Ingredient	Metric	Imperial
1	Milk (heated)	1 l	2 pt
$\frac{1}{10}$	Butter/margarine	100 g	4 oz
$\frac{1}{10}$	Flour	100 g	4 oz
	Onion clouté		

Method
Form a white roux using butter and . . . etc.

Examples of Sauces Derived from Béchamel: Added ingredients in relation to 1 unit i.e. ½ l/1 pt basic sauce

English term	Unit	Ingredient	Metric	Imperial	French term
Cream sauce	⅕	Fresh cream. Add to basic sauce, correct seasoning	100 ml	4 fl oz	Sauce Crème
Egg sauce	⅕	Chopped hard-boiled egg. Add ingredients to basic sauce and correct seasoning	100 g	4 oz	Sauce aux Oeufs

Notes for Guidance
All ingredients, including garnishes outlined in these studies are listed at prepared weights unless otherwise stated. For example:

(a) vegetables are washed and peeled,
(b) meat is trimmed in readiness for use.

Consequently the methods generally omit these preparatory instructions.

Metric and Imperial (British) units of Weights and Measures Commonly used in Professional Cookery and in this Text

Identification and explanation of *metric* weights and capacities.

Weights

	Name	Abbreviation used
	gram	g
	kilogram	kg

1,000 g   is equal to   1 kg/1.0 kg
500 g   is equal to   ½ kg/0.5 kg
250 g   is equal to   ¼ kg/0.25 kg

Capacities

	Name	Abbreviation used
	millilitre	ml
	decilitre	dl
	litre	l

1,000 ml	is equal to	Ⅰ l/1.0 l
500 ml	is equal to	½ l/0.5 l
250 ml	is equal to	¼ l/0.25 l
100 ml	is equal to	1 dl
10 dl	is equal to	1 l

Identification and explanation of *Imperial* weights and capacities.

Weights

	Name	Abbreviation used
	ounce	oz
	pound	lb

16 oz	is equal to	1 lb
8 oz	is equal to	½ lb
4 oz	is equal to	¼ lb

The ounce may be further divided into; ¾ oz, ½ oz, ¼ oz.

Capacities

	Name	Abbreviation used
	fluid ounce	fl oz
	gill	gill
	pint	pt
	quart	qt
	gallon	gal

1 gal	is equal to	8 pt or 4 qt or 160 fl oz		¾ pt	is equal to	15 fl oz or 3 gill
½ gal	is equal to	4 pt or 2 qt or 80 fl oz		½ pt	is equal to	10 fl oz or 2 gill
1 qt	is equal to	2 pt or 40 fl oz		¼ pt	is equal to	5 fl oz or 1 gill
1 pt	is equal to	20 fl oz				

N.B. It should be noted that the authors have purposely avoided the comparison and conversion of Imperial and metric weights and capacities. We advise students to think about and become familiar with each system independently as this approach will be more beneficial and practical.

In most cases the thin liquids used in cookery processes consist of; water, stock, wine, milk, or vinegar. When it is required to express these liquids as weights the following guides may be used:

Metric		Imperial	
1 l weighs	1,000 g or 1 kg	1 gal weighs	10 lb
½ l weighs	500 g or ½ kg	½ gal weighs	5 lb
¼ l weighs	250 g or ¼ kg	1 qt weighs	2½ lb
		1 pt weighs	1¼ lb
		½ pt weighs	10 oz
		1 gill weighs	5 oz

Convenience Products

These foods may be described as preparations from which varying degrees of labour have been removed making them more convenient and easy to use in the practical situation. The recipes in this text have not specifically included the utilization of convenience products as such foods vary in content, quality, and mode of use. Furthermore we consider that before comparisons are made regarding fresh and convenience foods it is essential that students of cookery are first able to recognize and appreciate the quality and cost of freshly produced items. Once students have developed their skills in, and understanding of professional cookery it is anticipated that they will be able to utilize convenience foods by means of culinary innovation or as major components in their own right. For example, utilizing soup powders in conjunction with freshly prepared raw materials. This may allow a reduction in raw material costs yet provide a high quality product.

Egg Sizes and their Weights

Imperial	Metric
	Size 1
Large	70 g
2 ³/₁₆ oz	Size 2
	65 g
	Size 3
Standard	60 g
	Size 4
1⁷/₈ oz	55 g
Medium	Size 5
1⁵/₈ oz	50 g
Small	Size 6
1¹/₂ oz	45 g
Extra small	Size 7

The chart illustrates the weight bands in which eggs are categorized. For example, size 1 eggs are 70 g or over; size 2 eggs weigh between 65 – 70 g; etc.

Normal Oven Temperature Guide (approximations)

Description	°C – Celsius	°F – Fahrenheit	Regulo 1 – 9
Very hot	230—260°	450—500°	8—9
Hot	205—230°	400—450°	6—7
Moderately hot	175—205°	350—400°	5
Moderate	150—175°	300—350°	3—4
Cool	120—150°	250—300°	1—2
Very cool	120° and below	250° and below	¹/₂ and below

N.B. In order to attain selected oven temperatures a pre-heating period is required which will vary according to the type of oven in use.

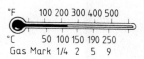

°F   100 200 300 400 500

°C   50 100 150 190 250

Gas Mark 1/4 2   5   9

Steaming Pressures

The following information may be useful when converting pressures expressed in Imperial units (lb/sq in or psi) to their metric equivalents or kg/cm².

	1 lb	= 454 g	= 0.454 kg
	1 in	= 2.54 cm	
therefore	1 sq in	= (2.54 sq cm)	= 6.45 sq cm
therefore	1 lb/sq in	= 0.454 kg/sq in	= 0.454 kg

$$= \frac{0.454 \text{ kg}}{6.45 \text{ sq cm}}$$

= 0.0704 kg/sq cm (conversion factor)

Example 1. The metric equivalent of 5 lb/sq in is calculated as follows:

5 lb/sq in   = 5 × 0.0704 kg/sq cm
               = 0.352 kg/sq cm

Example 2. The metric equivalent of 10 lb/sq in is calculated as follows:

10 lb/sq in   = 10 × 0.0704 kg/sq cm
               = 0.704 kg/sq cm

Example 3. The metric equivalent of 15 lb/sq in is calculated as follows.

15 lb/sq in   = 15 × 0.0704 kg/sq cm
               = 1.056 kg/sq cm

Note
In scientific usage kg/sq cm are expressed in kilopascals (kPa). To convert lb/sq in to kilopascals multiply by 6.9.

SECTION ONE
Related studies

1

Kitchen Attire, Equipment, and Organization

Protective Clothing

The chef's or cook's uniform has varied according to current fashion and needs. Whatever the fashion the criteria for the design and type of modern kitchen dress may be summarized as follows:

(a) to meet general and personal hygiene requirements;
(b) to act as safe and protective clothing to the wearer;
(c) to provide a uniform suitable for use in the working environment, which is comfortable, durable, and economically viable;
(d) to encourage a sense of pride, confidence, and responsibility in catering staff regarding their culinary vocation.

The kitchen uniforms illustrated show both male and female attire, pin-pointing the salient safety, hygiene and comfort factors.

General Points

Kitchen clothes of necessity are subject to frequent and thorough laundering including the starching of some items. It is expedient therefore, that caterers purchase or are provided with a plentiful supply of kitchen clothes, so that high standards of hygiene, safety, and comfort are maintained.

The following lists are a general guide to weekly requirements giving consideration to laundering and possible overtime duties.

Male

4 chef's hats, 6 chef's double breasted jackets, 6 neckerchiefs, 8 white aprons, 4 pairs of check trousers, 8 kitchen cloths (rubbers).

Female

4 overalls, 8 bib-aprons, 4 hats (net covering), 8 kitchen cloths.

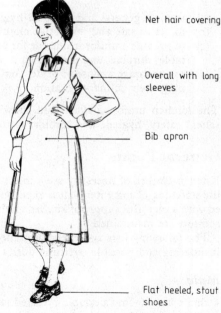

Chef's hat covers hair, height allows circulation of air

Male Uniform

Neckerchief absorbs perspiration

Double breasted jacket to give protection from heat

Long sleeves protect arms from heat and spillages

Long apron protects legs from spillages

Check trousers

Stout shoes give comfort and protection to feet

Net hair covering

Female Uniform

Overall with long sleeves

Bib apron

Flat heeled, stout shoes

N.B. The white garments reflect the heat, and act to reduce discomfort experienced when working in hot conditions. From the hygiene aspect they show stains and dirt which indicates to the wearer the need to change. Correctly dressed catering staff demonstrate a sense of professionalism that gives confidence to customers.

Footwear

Kitchen footwear should bring comfort and safety to the wearer and ease to the feet during long periods of walking and standing, as experienced by catering staff. For both sexes footwear worn in the kitchen should be essentially stout, durable, kept in good repair and be styled to protect completely the feet. Elevated heels are not suitable as they may cause instability and subsequent accidents. Likewise split shoes or worn heels are serious hazards to safety and in some industrial kitchens 'safety shoes' with reinforced toe-caps are recommended.

Fabrics and Materials used for Kitchen Uniform

Kitchen uniforms are available in pre-shrunk cotton drill or polyester/cotton and terylene/cotton mixtures. Cotton drill is best starched as part of the laundering process. The fabrics which are comprised of a mixture of man-made and natural fibres are easily laundered, do not require starching and may be drip-dried with a minimum of ironing. Recent developments include the use of disposable materials e.g. paper based chefs' hats and jackets. The hat is of the normal height and can be adjusted to fit various head sizes. Special features may include crown ventilation and a cloth head band to absorb perspiration. Such items are available for bulk purchase from suppliers.

Chef's Knives

The area of equipment least affected by technological change is that of the chef's basic knives and small equipment. Developments that have taken place have brought changes in the materials used for the manufacture of this equipment, rather than changes in design and usage. These developments have included the manufacture of high quality stainless steel knives and the introduction of non-slip, moulded plastic handles. Such changes have raised the standards of hygiene and safety. Steel knives with wooden handles are still manufactured for use in the industry but are considered less hygienic as the blades readily stain, are susceptible to rusting and unless constantly maintained suffer from metal pitting. Over a period of time wooden handles may become loose allowing food particles to lodge in the crevices, where if not removed they become a hygiene hazard.

When purchasing a set of basic knives consideration should be given to; initial purchasing price; cost of maintenance; replacement costs; discount rates; durability; ease of use and cleaning; design and safety features; guarantees; knife wallets or cases; and the variety of brands available for purchase.

Culinary operations involve a wide variety of manual skills most of which employ the use of the chef's knives. Such tasks include, chopping, slicing, dicing, boning, filleting, turning, shaping, trimming and carving, etc. These tasks have dictated the size and design of the various implements known as chef's knives. An illustrated list is provided showing the main design features and giving examples of uses for each knife.

Office Knife

This is also referred to as a vegetable, economy or paring knife.

Thin, firm, sharp blade tapering to a fine point — 9cm/3½in approx — Comfortable handle — Shallow heel

Its uses are: peeling onions; turning vegetables; turning mushrooms; segmenting fruit; eyeing tomatoes; etc.

Filleting Knife

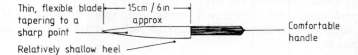

Its uses are: filleting flat and round fish; segmenting fruit. The flexible blade facilitates ease of movement, which enables the operator to remove fish fillets clear from the bone with the minimum of waste.

French Cook's Knives

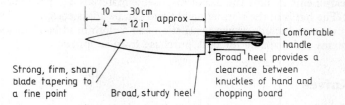

These knives could be considered as general purpose knives, as they are used for a variety of tasks, which include: the slicing, chopping, shaping, and dicing of foods. The broad heel and sharp pointed blade facilitates ease of use.

Chopping Knives (large and extra heavy)

Resembles the French cook's knife in shape and design.

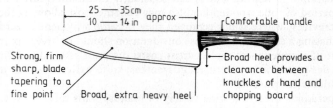

Its uses are: as for French cook's knife but the extra heavy heel makes this knife ideal for use when chopping through light bone structures, e.g. chicken frame, light chine bones.

Carving Knives

These consist of two main shapes
(1) French carving knife (tranchelard), which resembles a long version of a filleting knife.

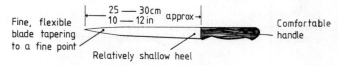

(2a) Carving knife

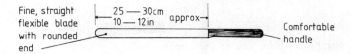

(2b) Granton (Sheffield)

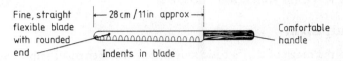

Its uses are: carving of butcher's meat, poultry and game, etc. The flexible long blade facilitates ease of movement, enabling the operator to carve evenly and economically.

Boning Knives

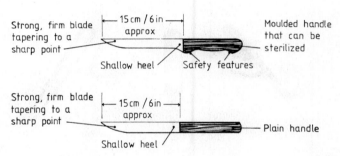

Its uses are: boning out butcher's meat, poultry, offal, and game. The firm, sharp pointed blade is designed to facilitate ease and safety when boning. Throughout boning the knife should be held 'dagger' fashion, that is with the thumb covering the rounded end of the handle. This technique, along with the design safety features prevents the operator's hand from slipping on to the sharp blade. There is a danger that the hand, which becomes moist and greasy when handling meat and fat, could easily slide down on to the blade, unless the correct technique is adopted.

Palette Knives

There are two main shapes in use.

(a) Straight handled palette knife

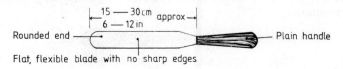

(b) Cranked handled palette knife

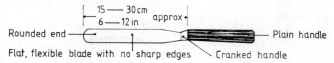

The width of blades may also vary. Its uses are: spreading and smoothing soft mixtures, e.g. purée of vegetables; shaping foods, e.g. potato galettes; lifting and turning foods during cooking, e.g. Vienna steaks, fish fillets, etc.

Small Equipment

In addition to the range of chef's basic knives, certain other small implements are commonly used. The main items are illustrated below.

Cook's Forks

Many designs exist as illustrated below. Each fork has two sharp prongs, which vary in length between 15 cm – 20 cm/6 – 8 in approximately.

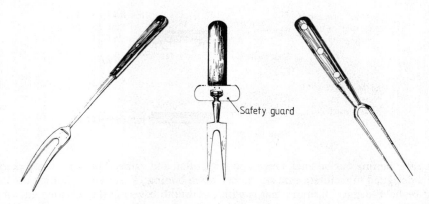

Its uses are: holding hot and cold meats in position for carving, and for placing carved portions on to service dish. It is not advisable to pierce the meat with the fork during or after cooking, as meat juices escape resulting in a loss of flavour and moisture, try to hold the meat firm with the fat or bone structure whenever possible. The fork may be of assistance when turning roast meats, etc. during cooking. In this instance the fork pierces the light bone structure, fat, or engages the trussing string to turn the meats.

Cook's Steel

This is produced from magnetized steel. The magnetism draws the knife on to the steel. The design and length of 'steel' vary, but as a guide the length may range from 25 – 30 cm (10 – 12 in) approximately.

Its use is: to maintain a sharp edge on the chef's knives. For safe practice and to avoid damage to knives, the technique of knife sharpening should be learned.

Knife Box or Wallet

In order to keep knives and other small equipment safe and in good order, some type of container is required. When a limited collection of knives is involved, the knife wallet is adequate as it is designed to hold each knife separately and safely in position. This prevents metal contact which could blunt the knive's edges. As the collection of knives and small equipment increases it is necessary to obtain a specially designed box or case.

Potato Peeler/Apple Corer

These are used for peeling and eyeing potatoes, certain vegetables and fruit. Some models have a removeable plastic handle, which once removed, enables the frame to be used for apple coring. The apple corer is used for removing core from apples particularly when apples are being cooked whole or cut into whole round slices, e.g. for apple fritters.

Lemon Decorator

There are two types in common use.

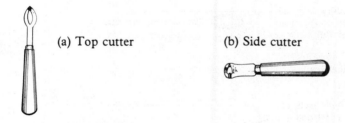

(a) Top cutter   (b) Side cutter

Both are used to decorate whole lemons by removing strips of rind from the outside skin. They may also be used to decorate vegetables in a similar manner, e.g. carrots.

Lemon Zester

This is used to remove fine zest from skin of citrus fruit, e.g. oranges and lemons.

Vegetable Scoops

These are used for cutting out rounds or oval shapes from fruits and vegetables.

(a) Round scoops (often referred to as Parisienne cutters)

(b) Oval scoops

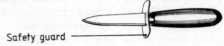

Vegetable scoops are available in various sizes.

Oyster Knife

This is used for opening fresh oysters safely.

Safety guard

Larding Needles/Pin

These are mainly used to insert strips of fat into very lean joints or cuts of meat, poultry or game.
N.B. All needles are available in various sizes

(a) French larding pin

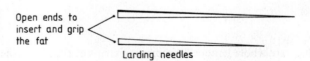

Cavity designed to accept strips of fat

French larding pin

(b) Larding needles

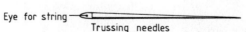

Open ends to insert and grip the fat

Larding needles

(c) Trussing needles

Eye for string

Trussing needles

Poultry Secateurs

These are used for jointing and trimming raw and cooked poultry.

Safety catch

Kitchen Scissors

These are for general use, e.g. trimming fish, removing string from foods, etc.

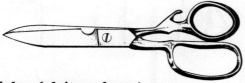

Savoy Bag and Tubes (plain and star)

These are used for piping potato dishes, gnocchi Parisienne, etc. They are available in various shapes and sizes, too numerous to outline and the bags can be made from terylene or nylon, which can be disposable. The tubes can be made from tin or nylon.

Pastry Cutting Wheel (with plain or fluted edge)

This is used for cutting ravioli paste. The wheel can be made of brass or wood.

Moulin (manually operated mill)

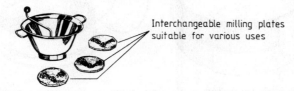

Interchangeable milling plates
suitable for various uses

The moulin is used for the preparation of fruit and vegetable purées and soups and is available in various sizes. Interchangeable milling plates suitable for various uses are shown.

Slicing Utensils

(a) Mar-For/French slicer
(b) Mandolin slicer
(c) Universal slicer

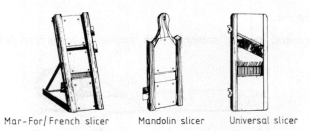

Mar-For/French slicer   Mandolin slicer   Universal slicer

All slicing utensils are designed with adjustable blades, either plain or corrugated made of steel and wood or stainless steel. They are used for slicing potatoes, and vegetables and their approximate size is 38 cm (15 in).

Conical Strainer (Chinois)

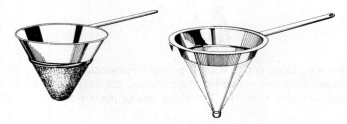

These are available in fine, medium, and coarse mesh and in various sizes. They are made of tinned steel, aluminium or stainless steel and are used for straining sauces and soups, etc.

Cook's Sieves

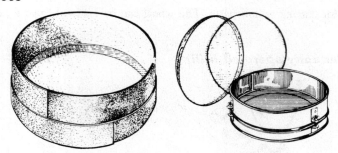

These are available with interchangeable fine, medium and coarse meshes (in wire or nylon) and in various sizes, e.g. 30 cm (12 in) diameter. The frames are usually made of wood or steel.

Grilling Tongs

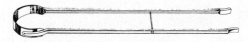

These are used to move or turn foods being grilled. Their approximate size is 50 cm (20 in) and they are usually made of heavy steel or light stainless steel.

Cooking Vessels in General Use

A visit to any major supplier of catering equipment illustrates the vast range of cooking vessels available to the caterer. The dominance of tin-lined copper vessels has long gone and, although such fine pieces of equipment may still be obtained, the range manufactured from other metals is extensive.

As with the chefs' knives many shapes and designs have evolved as a result of the manifold culinary operations in every-day kitchen work, e.g. stew pans, frying pans, sauce pans, baking trays etc.

Metals Employed

The selection of metals used in the production of cooking vessels is of prime importance and the main criteria which influence choice are as follows:

(a) degree of conductivity;

(b) toxicity—whether non-toxic when in contact with food;

(c) durability—whether the metal can withstand continual usage in an industrial kitchen;

(d) viability—able to be manufactured economically in relation to purchase price, replacement and maintenance costs, etc.;

(e) heat resistance—ability to withstand high temperatures without undue damage or danger;

(f) rust resistant whenever possible.

The metals chosen include copper, aluminium, tin, iron/steel, and the alloy stainless steel. Silver in conjunction with copper is used in the manufacture of chafing pans (pans used for cooking in the restaurant) but is too expensive for general use.

Thermal conductivities and melting points of metals used for cooking vessels

Metal/alloy	Melting point ° C approx	Coefficient of thermal conductivity $W/m^{-1}/K^{-1}$
Silver	960	418
Copper	1,083	385
Aluminium	660	238
Iron/steel	1,539	80
Tin	231	64
Stainless steel	1,425	24

This table illustrates the coefficient of thermal conductivity of the metals with silver, copper, and aluminium identified as the better conductors of heat.

Special Factors Concerning Copper Vessels

As shown above copper is a good conductor of heat and as such is ideally suited to the manufacture of cooking vessels. However, when used in general cooking operations, copper is poisonous. Furthermore when in contact with the atmosphere a toxic substance known as *verdigris* appears as a thin green film on the metal surface. By regular maintenance and cleaning this film can be removed. In order to counteract these problems manufacturers line the interior of copper cooking vessels with a coating of tin, which resists corrosion from water and the atmosphere, and which is non-toxic when in contact with food. Eventually the tin lining begins to wear thin and the copper interior becomes exposed. Re-tinning is then necessary and these requirements along with purchasing and cleaning costs make copper vessels relatively expensive.

N.B.   Copper sugar boilers are excepted from the tinning process because the high temperatures encountered cause the tin to soften and wear thin as the melting point of tin is relatively low.

Special Factors Concerning Aluminium Vessels

Aluminium is a soft metal and various gauges are used in the manufacture of cooking vessels, e.g. light, medium, and heavy gauges. However, owing to the softness of the metal, the resilience of the vessels to 'pitting' and general damage is lessened. Light gauge equipment in particular is subject to denting. After a period of time aluminium cooking vessels, when in contact with hot or boiling tap water or with certain foodstuffs, take on a dulled appearance. This is a result of a darkening effect of the natural oxide film which is always present on aluminium but which is normally colourless. The discoloration is an optical effect only and is quite harmless when in contact with food. Although this microscopic oxide film does not contaminate food it may cause discoloration, particularly when a white appearance is required, e.g. white sauces. Therefore when cooking such products in aluminium vessels care must be taken not to remove this oxide film from the sides of the saucepan. The use of a wooden spatula rather than a metal implement reduces this risk.

Certain foods exist which are unsuitable for cooking in aluminium vessels as these foods react with the metal and become discoloured, e.g. artichoke bottoms and red cabbage take on an unwanted dark appearance. In these instances other types of cooking vessels are used.

Because of its 'softness' aluminium tends to absorb and hold grease, consequently thorough cleaning, washing, and rinsing is required if greasiness is to be kept to the minimum.

Special Factors Concerning Iron/Steel Vessels

Pure iron is soft, of silver white colour and scarcely known. The metal commonly referred to as iron has an added mixture of some other substance usually carbon and varies in colour from tin white to dark grey. In general terms iron when used for the manufacture of cooking vessels takes the form of:

(a) cast iron;
(b) wrought iron;
(c) steel.

These vary marginally in carbon content and also in their properties. Iron when in contact with moisture is susceptible to rusting and consequently iron/steel cooking vessels are best employed in cooking processes that involve fat or oil rather than water. As a general rule iron/steel cooking vessels should not be washed but cleaned out with a dry clean cloth or absorbent kitchen paper. This maintains a film of grease that protects from moisture (rust) and prevents food from sticking to the vessel. For the special preparation of wrought iron omelet pans *see* p. 238.

Vitrified Cast Ironware

Recent trends include the development of cast iron vessels with coating of vitreous enamel. The enamel is fused on to the iron, protects from rust and provides a smooth cooking surface. As a result of this process these particular cast iron vessels are used for a wide variety of cooking methods that include contact with moisture, e.g. sauces and soups.

Special Factors Concerning Stainless Steel Vessels

Stainless steel is an alloy of iron, chromium, nickel and is used in the manufacture of various cooking vessels. Unlike copper (verdigris), iron (rust), or aluminium (oxide film), stainless steel does not easily tarnish or discolour as its name suggests. It is also durable and easy to clean.

These factors as well as the others previously outlined make stainless steel suitable for use in the manufacture of cooking equipment. However, stainless steel has a relatively low thermal conductivity and in order to overcome this deficiency certain vessels feature a copper or aluminium base. Vessels made entirely of stainless steel are also readily available to the caterer.

Cooking Vessels in Common Use

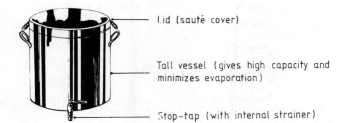

Lid (sauté cover)

Tall vessel (gives high capacity and minimizes evaporation)

Stockpot/Marmite

Stop-tap (with internal strainer)

The stockpot is usually made from tin-lined copper, aluminium or stainless steel. Its capacity is usually from 30 l (60 pt) upwards.

Stew Pans/Russes

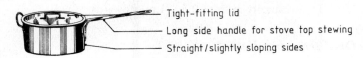

Tight-fitting lid

Long side handle for stove top stewing

Shallow Stew-pan

Straight/slightly sloping sides

N.B. Also available with short side handles for oven stewing. The stew-pan may be made from tin lined copper or aluminium.

  (a) capacity: 1.6 l (2¾ pt) upwards
  (b) diameter: 18 cm (7 in) upwards
  (c) depth: 7 cm (2¾ in) upwards.

Sugar Boiler

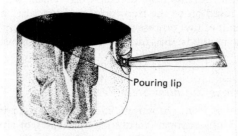

Pouring lip

This is a deep long-handled vessel made from copper. Note the pouring lip to facilitate safe pouring of liquid boiling sugar at high temperatures. It is available in various sizes, e.g. 15 cm (6 in) diameter.

General Purpose Stew-pans/Saucepans

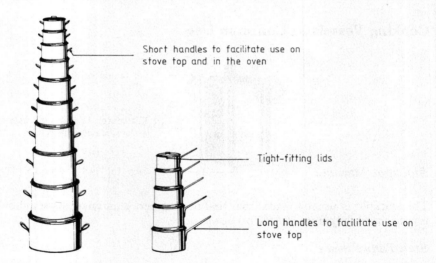

Short handles to facilitate use on stove top and in the oven

Tight-fitting lids

Long handles to facilitate use on stove top

These pans may be made from tin-lined copper, aluminium, stainless steel or vitrified iron. Their capacity is from 0.5 l (1 pt) upwards.

Oval Braising Vessel

Tight-fitting lid
Side handles

This can be made from tin-lined copper or aluminium and its capacity is from 14 l (25 pt) upwards

Bain-Marie Vessels

These are tall, slender vessels, made from tin-lined copper or aluminium with long or short side handles and tight fitting lids. They are designed to ensure maximum use of storage space in bain-marie and minimum evaporation and are available in a wide variety of sizes (capacities).

Sauteuse (French design)

This is a shallow, long handled vessel with sloping sides and a wide surface area, made of tin-lined copper. It is predominantly used in the preparation of sauces in which reductions or rapid reducing (evaporation) is required. The wide surface area ensures a speedy evaporation. It is also used for reheating vegetables in butter as the sloping sides facilitate 'tossing' of vegetables during this process and may be used for stove top stewing. It is available in various sizes, e.g. 20 cm (8 in) diameter, 7 cm ($2\frac{3}{4}$ in) deep.

Plat à Sauter/Sauté Pan

This is a shallow, long handled vessel, made of tin-lined copper or aluminium with straight sides and a wide surface area. It is ideal for use when preparing meat sautés where the food's juices are incorporated as an integral part of the finished product. It is available in various sizes, e.g. 15 cm (6 in) diameter, upwards.

Frying pans are solid based pans, made of iron, steel, aluminium, vitrified iron or stainless steel, with shallow sloping sides and a wide surface area to ensure even heat for frying foods. They are available in various sizes with long or side handles, e.g. 15 cm (6 in) base diameter, upwards.

Omelet Pan

Firm, long handle
Rounded, inner edge
Shallow sloping sides
Heavy, flat base

Omelet pans are made of heavy black wrought steel, aluminium or tin-lined copper and are available in various sizes, e.g. 15 cm (6 in) base diameter, upwards.

Pancake Pan (Crêpe Pan)

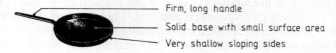

Firm, long handle
Solid base with small surface area
Very shallow sloping sides

Pancake pans are made of heavy, black wrought steel and are available in various sizes.

Roasting Tray (Plaque à Rôtir)

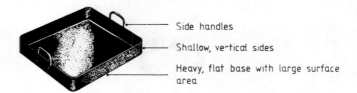

Side handles

Shallow, vertical sides

Heavy, flat base with large surface area

Roasting trays are made of heavy, black wrought steel, aluminium or tin-lined copper and are available in various sizes, e.g. 30 cm × 20 cm × 5 cm (12 in × 8 in × 2 in) approximately.

Baking Sheet (Open Ended)

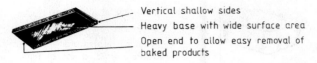

Vertical shallow sides
Heavy base with wide surface area
Open end to allow easy removal of
baked products

Baking sheets are made of heavy, black wrought steel and are available in various sizes.

Baking Sheet/Grilling Tray

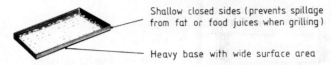

Shallow closed sides (prevents spillage
from fat or food juices when grilling)

Heavy base with wide surface area

These are made of heavy, black wrought steel, aluminium or tin-lined copper and are available in various sizes, e.g. 30 cm × 25 cm (12 in × 10 in) approximately.

Deep Frying Vessel/Friture or Friteuse

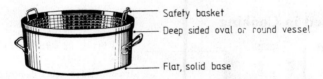

Safety basket
Deep sided oval or round vessel

Flat, solid base

These are made of heavy, black wrought steel or aluminium and are available in various sizes, e.g. approximate capacity 13 l (24 pt).

Salmon Kettle/Saumonière

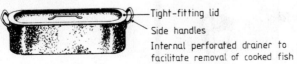

Tight-fitting lid
Side handles
Internal perforated drainer to
facilitate removal of cooked fish

This is designed specifically for cooking large, whole, round fish and is made of aluminium or tin-lined copper. It is available in various sizes, e.g. 60 cm × 20 cm × 15 cm (24 in × 8 in × 6 in) approximately.

Turbot Kettle/Turbotière

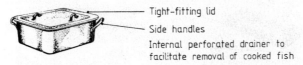

Tight-fitting lid
Side handles
Internal perforated drainer to
facilitate removal of cooked fish

This is designed specifically for cooking whole turbot and is made of aluminium or tin-lined copper. It is available in various sizes, e.g. 50 cm × 35 cm × 15 cm (19 in × 14 in × 6 in) approximately.

Trout Kettle

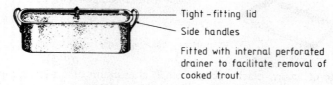

Tight-fitting lid
Side handles

Fitted with internal perforated
drainer to facilitate removal of
cooked trout

These kettles are tin-lined and used for both cooking and service in the restaurant. They are available in two sizes, e.g. 30 cm × 12 cm × 8 cm (12 in × $4\frac{1}{4}$ in × $3\frac{1}{4}$ in) approximately.

Moulds Used in Cooking

Anna mould

Tight-fitting lid with centre
handle
Straight-sided mould designed
for the cooking of anna potatoes

This is usually made of tin-lined copper. It is 15 cm (6 in) diameter and 7.5 cm (3 in) in depth (approximately).

Dariole mould

These are made of aluminium, tin-lined copper or tin plate. They are available in various sizes e.g. 5 cm depth × 5 cm diameter (2 in × 2 in) and used for a variety of purposes including sweet preparations. Other uses, e.g. baking savoury egg custard, moulding rice pilaff.

Bombe Mould

This is usually made of tin or aluminium-lined copper and is used when preparing various ices. It is 10 cm (4 in) diameter and 13 cm (5 in) in depth (approximately).

Charlotte Mould

Savarin Mould

These are made of aluminium or tin-lined copper and are used when preparing hot or cold moulded sweets. They are available in various sizes, e.g. 10 cm (4 in) and 7.5 cm (3 in) in depth, 20 cm (8 in) diameter and 5 cm (2 in) in depth respectively.

Jelly Mould

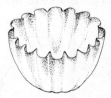

Fancy jelly moulds are available in different shapes, sizes and in various attractive designs. They are usually made of aluminium. However, the more ornate old fashioned moulds are often glass being purchased from antique/collectors shops and markets.

Other Cooking Vessels/Dishes

Sur le Plat

This is a white eared fireproof china egg dish used in the preparation of Oeuf sur le Plat. They are available in various sizes e.g. 10 cm (4 in) base diameter.

Cocotte

This is a fireproof china egg dish for Oeuf en Cocotte and is available in various sizes, e.g. 9.5 c.m. (3¾ in) diameter.

Oval Sole Dish

This dish made of French fireproof china is used for cooking and service of poached fish. It is available in various sizes, e.g. 24 cm × 13 cm (9½ in × 5¼ in) approximately.

Oval/Round Gratin Dish

This dish, made of tin-lined copper or vitrified iron is available in various sizes, e.g. 15 cm (6 in) diameter, 20 cm (8 in) oval approximately.

Oval/Round/Casseroles

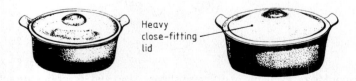

These casseroles are made of vitrified iron or ovenproof stoneware and are available in various sizes, e.g. 2.3 l (4 pt) approximately.

Soufflé Dish/Case

These are made of French fireproof china or ovenproof stoneware and are used for the preparation of hot and cold soufflés. They are available in various sizes, e.g. 20 cm (8 in) diameter approximately and have straight sides.

Pie Dish

Pie dishes can be made in aluminium, stainless steel or ovenproof stoneware. They are available in various sizes, e.g. 15 cm × 11 cm × 3 cm (6 in × 4½ in × 1¼ in) approximately.

Pudding Sleeve

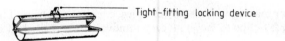

Tight-fitting locking device

This is used for cooking savoury and sweet puddings, e.g. steak and kidney pudding. Its standard length is 38 cm (15 in).

Pastry Tins

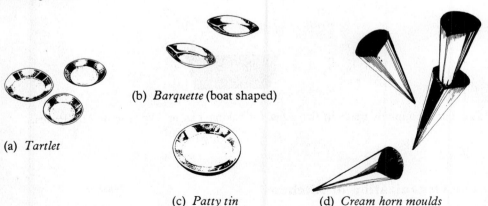

(a) *Tartlet*

(b) *Barquette* (boat shaped)

(c) *Patty tin*

(d) *Cream horn moulds*

These are used for baking pastry cases for savoury and sweet preparations, and are available in various sizes.

Brioche Tins

These are used for baking brioche and are available in various sizes, either small individual tins or larger tins, e.g. 5 cm (2 in) diameter or 20 cm (8 in) diameter approximately.

Raised Pie Mould

These are used for making various savoury pies, e.g. veal and ham. The two sides and base are held together by clips to facilitate easy removal when the baked pie has cooled.

Bread Tins

These are commonly made in two sizes, for baking 1 kg or 2 kg (1 lb or 2 lb) loaves.

The Organization of Kitchens

In order that a trade kitchen is operated efficiently, it is necessary to have a planned, controlled and co-ordinated system. The organization will vary from one establishment to another according to particular requirements, e.g. volume of trade, style of service, range and type of menus, etc. However, where traditional systems exist culinary activities are departmentalized with each section having clearly defined areas of work. The purpose of creating specialized departments is to make efficient use of labour and equipment by ensuring that the work load is evenly spread. In addition members of staff may become highly skilled by working in a specialist department.

This system of organization is generally referred to as the 'Partie system' with each partie denoting a section of kitchen work. The following plan illustrates the diverse activities, which are encountered in certain large establishments.

The Kitchen Brigade   La Brigade de Cuisine

Head Chef/Chef de Cuisine
Second or Deputy Head Chef/Sous Chef
Partie Chefs/Chefs de Partie
  Chefs responsible for each department and its work detailed as follows:

Pastry Chef/Chef Pâtissier Baker/Boulanger	} Pastry operations
Larder Chef/Chef Garde-Manger	Larder operations
Sauce Chef/Chef Saucier Fish Chef/Chef Poissonnier Roast Chef/Chef Rôtisseur Grill Chef/Chef Grillardin Vegetable Chef/Chef Entremettier Soup Chef/Chef Potager Relief Chef/Chef Tournant Assistant Chefs/Commis Chefs Apprentice/Apprenti	Kitchen/stove operations

Other personnel employed dependent upon size and nature of the establishment include:

Breakfast Chef/Chef du Petit Déjeuner
Night Chef or Duty Chef/Chef de Nuit ou Chef de Garde
Butcher/Boucher
Staff Chef/Chef Communard
Fishmonger/Poissonnier
Hors d'Oeuvre Chef/Hors d'Oeuvrier

Ancillary personnel:

Kitchen announcer (barker)/Aboyeur
  Person responsible for shouting out the customers' orders to the kitchen staff
Sculleryman (pot washer)/Plongeur
Kitchen porters
  Responsible for the general cleaning of the kitchen area
Stillroom staff
  Responsible for the preparation of certain beverages and accompaniments, e.g. tea, coffee, melba toast, breakfast toast. Afternoon teas are sometimes served from this department.
Storeman, etc.

Duties and Responsibilities of Main Kitchen Staff

Chef de Cuisine

In large traditional establishments the head chef is a member of the management team and his work is of an administrative nature. Examples include: menu planning; organization of staff and rotas; purchasing of raw materials and equipment; control of resources to achieve profit margins; etc. The exact description of a head chef's job will vary according to the size and type of establishment in which he/she is employed. In smaller units the term 'working head chef' may be used to describe the administrative and active culinary duties carried out by the head chef.

Sous Chef

The second chef deputizes for the head chef in his or her absence. In large traditional catering establishments a number of sous chefs are employed, each having clearly defined areas of authority, e.g. banquet production, speciality restaurant, floor service catering. In general, sous chefs are responsible for the daily supervision of kitchen operations.

Chefs de Partie (kitchen/stove operations)

Partie chefs may be described as technical section supervisors. They directly supervise staff, equipment and the processing of raw materials in specialized areas of food production, e.g. soups are prepared under the direction of the Potager. In addition to supervisory skills, the chef de partie must have acquired a high level of expertise in culinary skills and knowledge. This is essential as he or she is actively involved in the preparation of food for the table and the practical training of staff.

Chef Saucier

The sauce chef actively supervises the cooking and presentation for service of the following culinary products:

(a) entrées and relevés (*see* p. 77) with accompanying garnishes and sauces;
(b) certain sauces for use by other departments in the kitchen, e.g. tomato sauce to accompany egg or farinaceous dishes.

It must be noted, however that the saucier *does not* prepare:

(a) sweet sauces for pastry products;
(b) fish sauces;
(c) sauces to accompany roasts;
(d) cold sauces and dressings;

as these are prepared by the respective sections involved.

Chef Poissonnier

The fish chef cooks and presents for service the majority of hot fish products except those that are deep-fried or grilled. He/she is responsible for sauces and garnishes to accompany the dishes they produce.

Chef Rôtisseur/Chef Grillardin

Roast and grill chefs, cook and present for service the following:

(a)　roast butcher's meat, poultry, offal and game;
(b)　grilled butcher's meat, poultry, offal, game, fish and vegetables; and some fruits used as a garnish;
(c)　deep fried meats, poultry, game, offal, fish, vegetables and fruits for garnish;
(d)　preparations to be served as a savoury course at the end of a meal.

Most but not all accompanying garnishes and sauces of these products are prepared by this section.

Chef Entremettier

This chef is mainly responsible for the preparation, cooking, and presentation for service of vegetable products, except those that are deep fried or grilled. In addition this section may be responsible for farinaceous dishes, cheese and vegetable soufflés, etc.

Chef Potager

The soup chef is chiefly responsible for the preparation, cooking and presentation of hot soups and their garnishes. Cold soups are often prepared by the soup chef but are served from the larder section. In addition this section is responsible for many hot egg courses.

Chef Tournant

The relief chefs deputize for various chefs de partie on days off and during holiday periods.

Commis Chefs

Commis chefs assist the various chefs de partie with food production. They are usually graded according to their position and experience, e.g. first commis, second in command of a section.

Apprenti

Apprentices/trainee chefs are involved with learning the technical aspects of kitchen operations. They obtain knowledge from all sections of the kitchen through a controlled training scheme.

Chef de Partie (Larder operations)

Garde-Manger

The larder chef actively supervises the preparation of butcher's meat, poultry, offal, game, fish, and shell fish for use by the other sections of the kitchen, e.g. joints for roasting, fish for poaching, small cuts and large joints for entrées and relevés. In addition to such basic preparation the larder department is responsible for the provision of cold buffet, cold hors d'oeuvres and canapés, cold pies and pâtés, cooked meats and salads, cold sauces and dressings, sandwiches and many made-up preparations, e.g. cooked and raw forcemeats, etc. The following chefs, including commis and apprentices are under the direct supervision of the Chef Garde-Manger:

(a)　butcher/boucher
(b)　fishmonger/poissonnier
(c)　hors d'oeuvre chef/hors d'oeuvrier
(d)　buffet chef/chef du froid.

Chef de Partie (Pastry operations)

Chef Pâtissier

The pastry chef actively supervises the preparation, cooking and presentation of all hot and cold sweets and accompanying sauces, confectionery items and various breads. In addition this section provides the kitchen with pastry items required for savoury products, e.g. cheese straws, vol-au-vents, pastry cases, etc. According to the nature and size of the kitchen brigade the following chefs including commis and apprentices are under the direction supervision of the Chef Pâtissier:

(a) Baker/Boulanger
(b) Ice-cream Chef/Glacier

Modified Kitchen Organizations

The traditional 'Partie System' is by nature labour intensive and expensive to operate in its entirety. It is generally used where large-scale forms of traditional luxury catering exist.

Other sections of the hotel and catering industry, e.g. institutional, industrial, popular and fast food operations, etc., may employ a modified version of the partie system or operate a purpose-designed labour system to suit their own particular requirements. Terminology referring to specialist jobs may differ according to the establishment's requirements or be related to the traditional partie system. Different levels of skill will be demanded to meet the needs of various styles of catering operations, examples of which are given below.

Hospital Catering

Kitchen organization will vary in numbers and grades of staff according to the requirements of the Whitley Councils for the Health Services. The list below outlines a sample range of kitchen organization within the hospital sector indicating the nature of their respective duties.

Kitchen Superintendent or Head Cook

Both grades are mainly concerned with the general supervision of one or more kitchens. Their duties may include the following:

1. organization of the kitchen;
2. allocation of work;
3. supervision, direction and control of preparation and cooking;
4. ensuring proper standards of cleanliness;
5. ensuring the observance of safety regulations and procedures;
6. ensuring the correct and economical use of materials and equipment;
7. checking of meals issued for quantity, quality, and appearance;
8. arrangement of duty rotas;
9. discipline, training and welfare of staff;
10. requisitioning of small kitchen equipment and maintenance of inventories;
11. reporting mechanical defects and repairs;
12. control of kitchen linen and laundry;
13. indenting for kitchen supplies;

Assistant Head Cook

The nature of this post is that of a 'working' supervisor responsible to a Head Cook or Kitchen Superintendent for the direct supervision of cooks, assistant cooks and other kitchen staff dealing with the preparation, cooking, and serving of food. Other duties include assisting Head Cook or Kitchen Superintendent and deputizing for them during their 'off duty' periods.

Cook

Main duties include preparation, cooking, and despatch of all types of meals and instruction of lower grades of kitchen staff.

Assistant Cook

Assists the cook in the preparation, cooking, and service of food.

Catering Assistants

General duties in kitchens, dining rooms and associated areas; including the service of food, cleaning of premises and equipment, certain aspects of food preparation; taking cash or meal tickets; replenishing vending machines; keeping related records.

  N.B. A Senior Catering Assistant's duties relate to supervisory aspects of the Catering Assistant's work.

Kitchen Porter

Duties include: light portering and messenger tasks; operation of mechanical scrubbing machines and simple preparation of vegetables and fish, etc.

Industrial and Welfare Catering

According to size and nature of the establishment, these operations are organized similarly to Hospital catering as outlined above with different terminology used for certain jobs, e.g. Head Chef/Head Cook, Second Chef, Pastry Cook, Vegetable Cook, etc.

Popular/Fast Food Catering

These establishments require personnel with a limited range of skills. For example a popular style 'Grill Room' operation may employ a specialized Grill Chef capable of producing a limited range of grills and a proportion of convenience preparations, e.g. starters, vegetables and sweets. Similarly 'Fast Food Operations' may utilize semi-skilled staff to produce a standard range of products for the consumer.

2

Modern Kitchen Equipment

Microwave Oven

The microwave oven which is a relatively modern cooking appliance, can be described as an electronic cooking device in which food is heated by means of high frequency radio waves, known as microwaves. The microwaves are produced by a power source identified as a magnetron. This form of cooking was developed in the U.S.A. as a peaceful application of the principles used in radar during World War II.

The conventional methods of cookery employ the use of conducted, convected and radiated heat, which are briefly explained on p. 56. As can be seen these methods provide heat which penetrates food gradually from the exterior to the centre. Microwaves on the other hand do not give such heat to food, nor do they create heat within the oven cavity as experienced with conventional methods. Instead the oven is designed to beam high-frequency energy from the magnetron at the food so that the molecules of water in food are violently disturbed creating molecular friction. The friction generates heat, which converts the food's moisture into steam, heating the food throughout. Furthermore microwaves have the capacity to penetrate through certain foods instantly and produce heat wherever moisture is present. However the sealing and colouring effects associated with conventional methods are not noticeably achieved. The depth of wave penetration will depend, amongst other factors, upon the food's density but generally waves extend into food from between 2 and 3 in and beyond this depth the passage of heat relies on conduction only.

Characteristics of Microwaves

Microwaves like light rays have the following important characteristics:

(a) penetration;
(b) reflection;
(c) absorption.

Penetration

The waves are able to pass through certain substances without being absorbed. For example, glass, plastics, chinaware, scarcely absorb microwaves and allow them to pass through. Therefore food containers made from such materials do not become hot from the microwaves but they may conduct heat from the food being cooked in the oven cavity.

Reflection

Microwaves are reflected from such substances as metals, i.e. good conductors of electricity. This characteristic is used to advantage within the oven in that waves are reflected from the metallic surfaces. Consequently foods placed in the oven absorb the waves from all directions, the cooking period is fast and the need to turn foods for even cooking is eliminated. However, as a result of this reflecting characteristic, metal or metal-banded *containers* are generally unsuitable for use in microwave ovens, as waves are reflected from the container surfaces and not absorbed by the food.

Absorption

Cooking is achieved by the molecular disturbance created when the radio wave energy is absorbed by the food. As previously noted substances containing a high proportion of water easily absorb microwaves and this is true not only of food but of paper or cloth soaked with water.

Construction

A microwave oven consists of the following main components:

1. Power transformer – supplies power to the magnetron;
2. Magnetron – produces high frequency electro-magnetic waves (microwaves);
3. Waveguide – guides the microwaves from the magnetron into the oven cavity;
4. Oven cavity – a metal box in which food is placed for cooking by microwaves which enter from above;
5. Finder/window – a window in the oven door containing *very fine* perforations dimensioned to prevent any loss of microwave energy and to enable viewing of food without opening the oven door;
6. Stirrer fan/agitator – used to distribute the microwaves coming into the oven from the waveguide and to diffuse reflected energy to achieve more even cooking;
7. Stirrer motor – drives the stirrer fan;
8. Oven shelf – shelf upon which containers and food are placed for cooking.

Ovens are fitted with a built-in ventilation system to effect cooling of the magnetron and other vital components. The air may be drawn through a special dust filter that keeps the electrical and mechanical parts dust-free. Other refinements include timer controls for defrosting, cooking and reheating with automatic signalling devices. The controls may also incorporate a 'repeating feature', which enables the operator to cook a number of similar items one after the other, without having to re-set the timer. All ovens feature automatic safety devices that inactivate microwave power when the oven door is opened.

Various designs and sizes of oven are manufactured. Size is measured by output power, e.g. 1 kW, 2 kW, etc., and not by the size of the oven cavity. Oven dimensions are chosen on the basis of the frequency used and the optimum exploitation of generated energy.

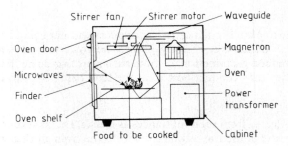

Technologists are continually improving equipment and microwave ovens are no exception. Three problems commonly associated with microwave cookery are as follows:

(a) uneven cooking or heating due to 'cold spots' (uneven wave distribution and ab-
    sorption) in the oven;
(b) inability of microwave energy to achieve significant colour changes (browning) of
    food compared with conventional cooking methods;
(c) relatively small oven capacity, which places a limit on its utility in some catering
    situations, e.g. volume catering.

To counteract these problems certain innovations and technological advances have been
implemented.

Counteracting Cold Spots

(a) *Dual magnetrons*—in order to overcome 'cold spots' manufacturers have fitted some
    ovens with *two* magnetrons, which produce more microwave energy for distribu-
    tion within the oven.
(b) *Turntable*—other manufacturers have incorporated a revolving oven shelf (turn-
    table) to ensure that foods do not experience 'cold spots' throughout the length of
    the cooking period.

Colouring Foods (browning)

(a) Techniques to effect browning of food include the development of combined units
    that incorporate a microwave oven with a separate infra-red grill, where the grill is
    used to colour the food prior to or following the period of cooking by microwaves.
(b) *Micro-browners*—another patented development is the use of micro-browners,
    which comprise specially designed ceramic containers that are able to absorb
    microwave energy. The containers are pre-heated in the microwave oven and their
    surface becomes sufficiently heated to give colour to foods placed on them, as
    would be expected by cooking on a griddle or in a shallow frying vessel. The use of
    these ceramic containers involves the turning of foods when colouring of both sides
    is required.

Micro-Aire Ovens

Micro-Aire ovens may be described as being different from but related to the conventional
microwave oven. They differ in the following ways:

(a) they combine forced-air convection and microwave energy in a single unit;

(b) they offer increased oven capacity and can be used to carry out most of the culinary operations associated with conventional and microwave cookery;
(c) they effect the browning of foods generally associated with conventional cooking methods;
(d) the oven cavity becomes heated during the cooking period;
(e) when combined systems are operated the cooking times are longer than with microwaves but are shorter when compared with conventional cooking times;
(f) both cooking methods can be used simultaneously or independently as required;
(g) traditional containers can be successfully used in the oven including those made from metals.

Combined Methods

The combined cooking is effected by the use of 'pulsed' microwaves (i.e. microwave energy is emitted intermittently at 7 second intervals throughout cooking), along with forced-air convected heat. Manufacturers claim that the oven will carry out most of the culinary operations associated with conventional and microwave units. The oven is most versatile in that it combines the speed of microwaves with the fast heat transfer of forced-air convection to cook with traditional colour, texture and flavour associated with high quality foods.

Oven Capacity

With a large potential capacity and throughput the use of the micro-aire oven is extended over a wide range of catering operations. For example, when used as the combined system it is able to cope with a 1 × 1 Gastronorm tray or six to eight separate items at the same time. Alternatively when used independently as a convection oven the insertion of a three tier rack allows for the cooking of greater numbers of portions e.g. multiportion packs (50 to 80 portions) reheated at the same time.

Examples of Cooking Times

Recent examples quoted by manufacturers include:

(a) 12 kg turkey in 55 minutes;
(b) 7 kg leg of pork in 48 minutes.

General Factors on Microwave Cooking

The speed at which food is electronically heated is determined by a number of variables and the following general observations may be of value.

Chemical Structure

Food scientists state that in general the more complex the chemical structure of food the more quickly the product will attain a high temperature. For example, 1 l of milk will reach boiling point before 1 l of water.

Shape and Form

Thinner pieces of food cook more quickly than larger and thicker portions as it is more difficult for microwaves to penetrate to the core of large, thick pieces. So cutting and slicing food into smaller/thinner portions enables the microwaves to penetrate more quickly and often instantaneously throughout the product, speeding up the heating process.

Arranging Foods

For even cooking or heating food should be distributed evenly in containers. Piling foods on to a tray in an *ad hoc* fashion may result in uneven cooking or heating.

Loss of Moisture

Food tends to release water when heated by microwaves. In order to minimize loss of moisture foods may be placed in a covered container or wrapped in plastic film.

Quantities of Food

When cooking a small quantity of food any microwave energy not absorbed by that item is wasted. This wasted energy could have been used to cook a larger quantity over a similar cooking period. In general an increase in the volume of food requires a further increase in cooking time. However if full use is made of available energy cooking times remain short and do not necessarily increase proportionately with the volume of food.

Initial Temperature of Foods

The lower the initial temperature of food before cooking or heating commences the longer the time required to complete the operation. When heating frozen items either to thaw or cook the speed of wave penetration is retarded because ice-crystals act as wave reflectors and the rise in temperature is slowed down.

State of the Food

Microwaves are able to deal with food in a raw, partly cooked or completely cooked state. The heating times will vary accordingly.

Food Containers

The materials chosen for use as containers are those that absorb little of the high frequency energy. They must be capable of withstanding high temperatures which are reached within the food during cooking, e.g. 100°C plus. The materials used must not reflect the microwaves (as is the case with metals) but allow them to pass through as light rays through a window. Cling-film wrap and roast-a-bags may be used as containers.

Summary and Safety

For recommended cooking/heating times and further detailed information consult recognized manufacturers.

It is believed that defective doors are the main source of radiation leakage from microwave ovens. Therefore, units are fitted with safety features to prevent leakage during cooking and also ensure that when the door seal is interrupted the oven will not function. However microwave ovens should be carefully checked against leakage or the possibility of exposure which could lead to microwave injury.

Forced-Air Convection Ovens

A wide range of forced-air convection ovens are manufactured, designed to meet the specific needs of a variety of catering operations. These ovens may differ in their design specifications, energy source, output potential, and utility in a similar way to conventional ovens. The principal difference between a convection oven and an ordinary (conventional) oven is the accelerated air movement within the oven cavity and the varying heat inputs applied.

According to a leading designer in this area, forced-air convection ovens may, for the sake of simplicity, be categorized as follows:

Hard Units

These are ovens that have the highest air movement speed, generally combined with the highest heat input. These units are most suitable for the reheating of bulk and individual frozen foods, but are not suitable for prime cooking or baking.

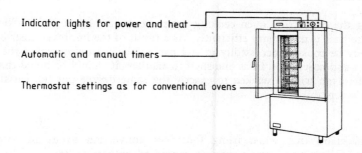

Indicator lights for power and heat

Automatic and manual timers

Thermostat settings as for conventional ovens

Medium Units

These are ovens that have a lower air movement speed, generally combined with a lower heat input. These ovens are suitable for prime cooking, some baking and if required reheating frozen foods.

Soft Units

These are ovens that have the lowest air movement speed and heat input. These ovens are suitable for some prime cooking and for baking but unsatisfactory for reheating frozen food because the time taken to reheat may constitute a health hazard.

Therefore when purchasing forced-air convection ovens, prospective buyers should consult recognized specialists who can advise on the best selection to suit the buyer's specific requirements. Some special design features which illustrate this point are listed below:

(a) bakery convection oven with steam injection facility;
(b) water injection facility, which may be used for steaming foods;
(c) counter top models for snack bar operations;
(d) roll in—roll out models where racks of food are wheeled on trolleys, direct from refrigeration or cold store, into the oven for cooking, then rolled out for service;
(e) multi-purpose units that combine a convection oven with some of the following: eye level grill; bain-marie; boiling top; griddle; or plate warmer;
(f) safety features may include; doors opening to 180°; flame failure protection devices; shelf runners to prevent food tipping on withdrawal; separate mains, control and timer switches; etc.

The Principle of Forced-Air Convection

On heating, air rises and when trapped within an oven cavity forms a convection current, which circulates within the oven. In ordinary ovens the current of heated air circulates slowly, which affects the time taken to reach the required cooking temperature. In addition variations of temperature, within the oven, occur particularly following the introduction of cooler air once the oven doors are opened.

In contrast, when employing a forced-air convection oven the circulating current of hot air is forced speedily around the oven chamber by a motorized fan or blower. This technique creates a more even and constant temperature throughout the oven because of improved heat distribution, and also shortens the time taken to pre-heat the oven. Furthermore the current of continuous moving air strips away the thin layer of moisture and cool air from the surface of foods placed into the oven, allowing heat to penetrate and cook more quickly.

When using the convection oven cooking temperatures are lower and cooking times shorter because heat is used more efficiently. As a result of the improved distribution of heat, foods may be cooked successfully in any part of the oven eliminating the need to open the doors and move food from one shelf to another. It should be noted that not all the food in the oven will be cooked to exactly the same degree but the variations experienced are acceptable.

Advantages

Manufacturers claim that when using forced-air convection ovens in correct circumstances and following adequate training certain advantages accrue:

(a) time saving—cooking and labour time;
(b) energy saving—reduction in cooking temperatures, cooking times and pre-heating times;
(c) space utilization—ovens are designed to make maximum use of production space and at the same time increase volume output;
(d) product quality and yield—foods cook more evenly giving a high quality finish with less shrinkage and therefore a higher portion yield. This is due to the shorter cooking time at lower temperatures.

Examples taken from a convection oven cooking guide

Food	Mark	Min	Shelves (Oven capacity)
Sirloin of beef 3 kg (6 lb) joints	5	115	4
Pork joints 1 kg (2½ lb)	6	55	4
Baked potatoes	7	45–60	6
Vol-au-vents	8	10	6
Rice pudding	1	60	6

Pressure Steamers

General Features

Modern pressure steamers vary in design, size, versatility, efficiency and volume output potential. Consequently models are designed to meet the needs of different types of catering operation. These models range from small back bar units designed to effect fast cooking and reheating of foods, to larger models designed to cope quickly and effectively with volume catering. Certain models feature more than one cooking compartment, providing the caterer with operational versatility so that large and small amounts of food can be steamed independently or simultaneously as demanded by the customer.

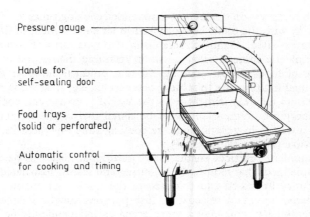

Steamer trays/pans are identified as solid/plain or perforated with either one being selected for use as required by the culinary operation in hand. As a general guide solid/plain trays are used where an amount of liquid is needed within the tray to assist cooking, or where the juice of the food being steamed is to be retained for culinary purposes, e.g. chicken essence for a sauce. Perforated trays, however, are employed when no liquid is required to assist in the cooking process, and also when foods are to be well drained. Manufacturers provide detailed charts concerning the steaming of various foods but the experienced chef will soon recognize the culinary potential of the modern pressure steamers.

Steam Supply and Pressure

All pressure steamers cook foods by using the concentrated heat of steam at varying pressures. The pressures used generally range from $0.35 - 1.05$ kg/cm^2 ($5 - 15$ psi) and are often described as:

(a)   low pressure $- 0.35$ kg/cm^2 (5 psi);
(b)   medium pressure $- 0.70$ kg/cm^2 (10 psi);
(c)   high pressure (high compression) $- 1.05$ kg/cm^2 (15 psi).

Steam may be supplied directly from a central steam supply, from an external steam generator or from a heated water-well within the steamer compartment. Other modifications to date may include such refinements as: an automatic pressure sensitive defrost cycle, which prevents the commencement of cooking until the product has reached a given temperature (ideal when cooking from a frozen or semi-frozen state); the utilization of fine needle jets within the steamer compartment, which act to project the steam directly on to foods speeding up heat penetration and cooking time. A further development is the use of superheated dry steam created when purified water is fed through tubes on to a casting which is heated to approximately 315°C (600°F). At impact the water turns to steam, rises into the compartment providing the cooking medium of heated dry steam.

Foods and Cooking Times

A wide variety of raw or pre-cooked foods may be steamed to effect cooking or reheating. Steamers according to manufacturers' specifications are able to cope effectively with many foods from a thawed or frozen condition. Cooking times commence once the correct steam pressure is reached and most models make use of automatic timers to control the selected cooking period.

When using high compression steamers recommended cooking times for listed products are remarkably swift, with the foods being cooked in an environment of dry steam from which air has been expelled. Manufacturers claim that this form of steaming prevents oxidation of vitamins and mineral salts, assists in retaining the natural colour, flavour, aroma and texture of foods during cooking. Certain products however are preferably steamed at low to medium pressure to achieve best results, e.g. steamed savoury or sweet puddings, and caterers may experiment with the use of pressure and cooking times to identify their culinary requirements. It must be stated that as the weight/load of food being steamed increases so in general does the cooking time but these increases do not appear to be extensive (see the table below).

Innovations in culinary practices enable many traditional dishes to be cooked in the steamer. For example foods that require the colouring and sealing associated with shallow frying or braising may be sealed and coloured in the traditional manner before being placed into the steamer to complete cooking. Fish portions may be steamed rather than poached and the masking/accompanying sauce prepared independently (an ideal technique for large scale banqueting).

Safety Factors

When using high compression steamers the door cannot be opened until all the pressure within the compartment has been released. When the steam is released from a conventional steamer it is wise to use the steamer door as a protective shield to safeguard oneself from hot steam that may remain within the compartment following initial steam release.

Summary

The information provided is in broad, general terms. Detailed technical information is available from manufacturers who specialize in the production and marketing of such equipment. The purchaser therefore is well advised to make full use of the advice concerning the many options now available.

Examples of recommended cooking times (approx) using a high compression steamer at 1.05 kg/cm^2 (15 psi)

Product	Load in kg (lb)	Timer setting (min)
Brussel sprouts (fresh)	2 (5)	4 – 6
Brussel sprouts (frozen)	6 (15)	11 – 13
Fish steaks (thawed)	1 (2)	3 – 6
Lobster, 1 kg (2½ lb) each (thawed)	6 (15)	11 – 12
Whole chickens, 1.5 kg (3 lb) each (thawed)	9 (18)	30

Pressureless Convection Steamer

Manufacturers of this most recent development in steaming equipment have designed a pressureless steaming unit, which equates with the efficiency and culinary utility of the modern high compression steamers previously described. It is argued that ideally food is best cooked at the lowest effective cooking temperature in order to avoid cellular damage, excess nutritional loss, over shrinkage and product discoloration. Furthermore cooking by steam in a constantly venting compartment (pressureless compartment) eliminates gases, volatiles and other undesirable by-products, which can have unfavourable effects upon the colour and flavour of foods. Therefore efficient cooking is ideal when using low temperature, constantly venting steam, but two major obstacles may remain:

(a) air;
(b) condensate.

Manufacturers state that the presence of only 0.5% of air in a steam environment can reduce the heat transfer coefficient by as much as 50%. Furthermore as air is an effective insulator its presence around food acts as a barrier to efficient heat transfer. A cooking compartment containing steam and air can only supply the temperature of the partial pressure of the steam and not of the total chamber pressure. It must however be stated that manufacturers of a high compression steamer claim to expel all air from the cooking atmosphere, therefore overcoming these problems. However physicists endorse that more heat is available for cooking in 1 lb of steam at atmospheric (zero pressure) than is available at 1 lb of steam at 15 lb of pressure. The pressureless convection steamer is designed to use the potential energy of steam at atmospheric pressure in an effective and efficient manner.

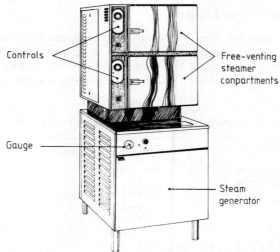

Condensate, it is claimed, is an additional barrier to efficient heat transfer because it forms around the food and insulates it against the heat energy of steam. By employing modern technology, manufacturers of the pressureless convection steamer are able to utilize the lowest practical temperature of steam i.e. 100°C (212°F) at atmospheric (zero) pressure to cook foods efficiently and retain a high level of quality control. The purified steam is generated in a boiler under pressure before being introduced into the cooking compartment directly over the food within. Because the compartment is on a constantly free-venting system no pressure build up occurs (pressureless steaming). The steam is made to act like a piston forcing out the air. Turbulent, controlled forced convection steam strips away the layer of insulative condensate from foods and cooling steam and condensate from foods is continually replaced by a fresh supply of steam from the generator.

Cooking therefore is achieved with low-temperature constantly-venting steam in a pressureless air-free environment of controlled convection, aptly described as cooking in a pressureless convection steamer. Certain models are dual purpose and may also be used as pressure steamers. Other refinements may include automatic timers with each compartment independently controlled for versatility of use. Steamer or compartment doors seal automatically when closed and may be opened safely at any time because there is no pressure within.

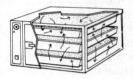 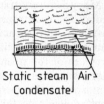

Food┘
Dynamic steam

Static steam | Air
Condensate┘

Forced convection steam—a turbulent high energy atmosphere— swirling in, around and through the food preserving moisture, nutriments and flavour.

Convection pressureless steam cooking

Conventional pressurized steam cooking

Food Cooked and Trays Used

As with high compression steamers a wide variety of foods can be cooked/reheated from raw/cooked states and from a thawed or frozen condition. Manufacturers provide guidelines concerning types of foods and cooking times involved. The types of steamer tray used are plain, solid or perforated and the same guidelines apply as for compression steamers.

Examples of approximate time settings recommended for pressureless convection steamer

Product	Timer setting (min)
Frozen jumbo asparagus spears	6
Frozen broccoli spears	2 – 3
Fresh cabbage	2 – 4
Fresh corn on the cob	6
Frozen corn on the cob	8 – 10
Frozen salmon steaks (200 g (8 oz) portions)	7
Frozen cod fillets	3
Fresh beef brisket (400 g (1 lb))	18 – 20

Summary

The information provided is of a general nature and interested caterers are advised to seek further and more detailed technical data from recognized sources.

Liquidizer

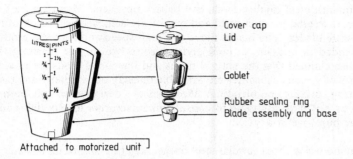

The liquidizer is a piece of kitchen machinery which uses a high speed motor to drive specially designed stainless steel blades to chop, purée, or blend foods very quickly and efficiently. Although it is not a large-scale piece of kitchen machinery its versatility and value are worth mentioning. This small machine operates at various speeds to suit the job in hand. It is particularly useful to the small volume caterer whose type of operation may not warrant investment in large-scale equipment to carry out similar work. Often the liquidizer reduces labour intensity and time taken to complete certain tasks by eliminating traditional methods, which are often laborious. In addition it may improve the overall quality of a finished product, e.g. consistency and flavour of soups, sauces, fruit juices, fruit and vegetable purées and pâtés, etc.

Examples of Culinary Uses

According to manufacturers' recommendations, this machine may be used as follows:

- (a) to purée or blend, soups, sauces, fruit juices and dressings;
- (b) to purée various pâtés and fruit preparations;
- (c) to crush ice cubes or nuts;
- (d) to mix batters, etc.

Vertical Cutter/Mixer (VCM)

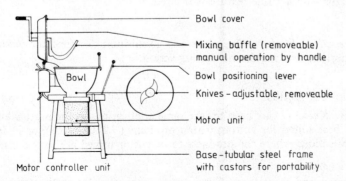

The VCM is a relatively large piece of versatile kitchen machinery which is able to cut and mix ingredients simultaneously. The machine could be described as a type of large-scale liquidizer. The high speed motor drives any one of a variety of purpose designed, interchangeable stainless steel blades that are positioned inside the bowl according to the job in hand. This machine is ideally employed in situations that require a speedy preparation of large quantities of quality foods and bakery products. Manufacturers claim that speed, volume, increased product yield and quality are achieved as a result of the cutting action of the knife blades. The blades move at a high speed and slice the products whilst they are suspended in mid-air, without giving rise to bruising or mashing. Where applicable it is also claimed that the natural juices and flavour of foods are retained. A full range of models of various capacities are available to carry out virtually any tasks that incorporate cutting, mixing, or blending. Machines are designed to suit both large and small operations but it is advisable to consult manufacturers for specialist information concerning the purchase of a VCM.

N.B.   Certain models without tubular steel frame, may be clamped on to a suitable bench or table.

Examples of Culinary Uses

According to manufacturers' recommendations these machines may be used as follows:

- (a)   prepare quantities of raw forcemeats, e.g. 12 kg (27 lb) hamburger mix in 40 sec;
- (b)   blend large volumes of soups and sauces in seconds, e.g. mayonnaise in 120 sec, soups in 30 sec;
- (c)   mix quantities of pastry and bread dough quickly, e.g. 11 kg (25 lb) bread dough in 90 sec, 11 kg (25 lb) pie pastry in 20 sec;
- (d)   cut/slice quantities of vegetables speedily, e.g. vegetables for coleslaw in 12 sec.

Knife Blades

Standard Accessories

 Shaft with Narrow Knives   is used for all cutting operations, such as sausage or hamburger mix, wieners, bologna and other meat products, vegetables for salads and coleslaw, pastry products, cake batters, cheese spreads, and making certain types of salad dressings and processing yeast doughs where a fine texture is desired.

 Knead/Mix Shaft   One-piece cast aluminium designed for mixing small quantities that require no cutting action.

Optional Extras

 Wide Knives   are used for the same applications as the narrow knives but are best suited for cutting frozen products ($-2°C$ (28°F)) or in industrial applications where the products to be cut or mixed are very dense.

 Narrow and Wide Wave Cut Knives   are used for cutting oily products; nuts, corn masa for Spanish foods, and some vegetables. Again, the wide knives are used for harder products.

Grating Shaft   is used for grating hard raw vegetables and for the mixing of dry ingredients.

Mixing Shaft   is used for blending and mixing large quantities of ingredients where no cutting action is required.

Cleaning

The machine may be cleaned using a 10 sec run with warm detergent water which is poured away and followed by hand wiping.

Bratt Pan

This piece of equipment derives its name from the German word 'Braten' which translated refers to a number of cooking methods. Bratt pans are relatively new to the U.K. but have been widely and successfully used on the continent for many years. Gas and electric models are manufactured and the cooking pan is mainly constructed of stainless steel or cast iron. Models vary in design, shape, potential utility with special features offered. The models are produced to meet various catering requirements. At present the models available are designed to meet the requirements of large volume catering but manufacturers hope to engineer a model to meet the needs of the smaller catering operation.

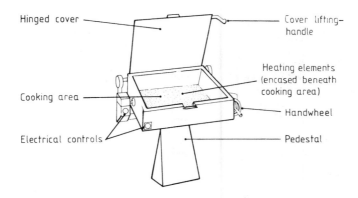

Special features may include:

(a) tilting pan with pouring lip designed to ensure safe movement of pan and also to facilitate transfer of hot foods to other receptacles;

(b) stainless steel lids (covers) hinged to open sideways and provide a working surface;

(c) operational controls sited conveniently for ease and safety of use;

(d) flame failure and thermostatic cut-out devices;

(e) automatic safety devices: to cut off heat when pan is tilted, to cut off heat if thermostat fails,

(f) non-tilt and portable models are available.

Culinary Uses

The bratt pan may be described as a multi-purpose piece of cooking equipment. Manufacturers claim that such equipment may be successfully used for: boiling; poaching; stewing; braising; shallow frying (sauté); deep frying; griddling; innovatory pot roasting; innovatory steaming; and also as a bain-marie. To have such versatility in one piece of equipment presents obvious major advantages to the catering industry. However when purchasing such equipment prospective buyers are well advised to consult recognized specialists and take advantage of the advisory services available, to ensure that the best possible model is obtained to meet the caterers own particular requirements.

Régéthermic Regenerating Oven (Cabinet)

Régéthermic ovens form part of a cook-chill food production system which was developed in France. The system operates in France as well as many other countries including the U.K. The ovens are specifically designed to regenerate rather than cook foods. They vary in design and capacity according to operational requirements and are fitted with automatic timers and simple controls to facilitate ease of use. All foods are prepared and cooked in advance by employing traditional culinary techniques. Cooked food is placed into specially designed individual or bulk containers and speedily chilled in a blast chiller. It may then be stored for up to 3 days in a refrigerator at 3°C (37°F). The aim of the system is to allow cooked food to be reconstituted at the point of consumption in such a way as to prevent it drying up or changing in appearance. The food should look and taste the same as when freshly cooked and retain as much nutritional value as possible.

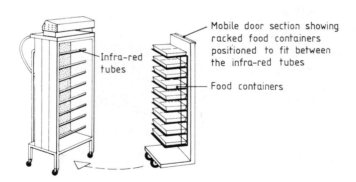

Example model of régéthermic oven (cabinet)

The Principle of Régéthermic Regeneration

The method is based on two basic concepts:

1. The use of diffused infra-red rays operating on a predetermined wave length to achieve heat penetration requirements and characteristics. The exact degree of heat for regeneration within the oven is supplied by proportionally spaced infra-

red elements, see below. The ovens are fitted with groups of infra-red tubes, which have differing heating capacities. The less powerful elements are placed near the top of the oven allowing for the heating effect of convected hot air (heat rises). This ensures a uniform distribution of heat throughout the cabinet.

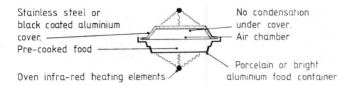

Stainless steel or black coated aluminium cover.

No condensation under cover.

Air chamber

Pre-cooked food

Oven infra-red heating elements

Porcelain or bright aluminium food container

Sectional drawing of food container

2. The simultaneous reheating of special containers and their covers. In these containers food is kept under cover in a semi-sealed atmosphere. The container is subjected to infra-red radiation, which produces gentle, continuous and uniform heat. The container then stores heat like a thermal battery and the stainless steel cover is always hotter than the food. This acts to prevent condensation, keeping the food's flavour and aroma sealed within the container. The régéthermic regenerating method uses radiated, conducted, and convected heat (*see* p. 56) in varying proportions. The air chamber containing food is heated to serving temperature (60°C–65°C (140°–149°F)).

Oven Utility

As previously stated régéthermic ovens are primarily designed to reconstitute pre-cooked, chilled foods, with an average regenerating time of 12 – 20 min. It is possible however to operate with freshly cooked foods and pre-cooked frozen foods. In the latter case regeneration time is increased.

Computerized Fryers

A recent development in deep frying equipment is the computerized fryer. Expertise, knowledge and certain manual operations normally associated with deep frying are built-in to the computerized models.

The 'fryer with a brain' may be programmed to control the following automatically:

(a) cooking times of a pre-selected range of products, to achieve the correct degree of cooking;

(b) the cooking temperatures, therefore eliminating the need for thermostats and calibration;

(c) high temperatures to ensure that the frying medium does not become too hot or reach flash point;

(d) low temperatures indicating by means of a signalling device when the oil/fat temperature drops excessively below 'set point';

(e) a shut-down effect if the fryer is not used over a pre-set period;

(f) a melt cycle to ensure safe melting of fat before the fryer automatically switches over to operating cycle;

(g) basket lifts, which operate automatically and independently to remove the products from the fryer once cooking is completed;

(h) holding timer, denoting that the holding period of the cooked product is over.

Controls are designed to be simple and offer a 'crisp' control to allow the operator to select preferred degree of crispness. The computer has a built-in test circuit to indicate that all systems are operational. Computers are programmed to cater for many standard menu items but manufacturers offer a programming service to develop a unit to suit individual needs.

Operational Information

Information is fed into the computer from a super-sensitive probe, which is immersed in the frying medium. The probe passes information about temperature and rates of temperature change created by one or more of the following variables:

(a) initial oil/fat temperature;

(b) volume of food being fried;

(c) fryer efficiency and capacity;

(d) fryer recovery rate;

(e) quantity and condition of oil/fat;

(f) product temperature and water content.

By using this information the fryer is able to compute the exact cooking times required with the end of the cooking period being indicated by an automatic signalling device. When the computer needs servicing it is easily replaced by plugging in another computer control.

General Factors

In addition to the special features outlined above, models maintain the general standards and refinements of modern fryers:

(a) compactly designed modular units;

(b) built-in filter to ensure removal of contaminants, moisture and fatty acids, therefore extending the life of the frying medium;

(c) *cool zone* that acts to keep solid particles from the heat source thus extending the life of the oil/fat and reducing the possibility of taste transfers;

(d) drain valve and oil receptacle to ensure safe and swift draining of the frying oil/fat.

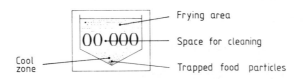

A wide range of single or multi-product models are manufactured, designed for use with gas or electric services. Potential buyers should obtain first-hand advice from manufacturers to ensure that their particular catering requirements are identified.

3

The Cooking of Food

Generally food is cooked when heat is transferred from a heat source, (e.g. stove) through to the exterior of foodstuffs by one or more of the following mechanisms:

(a) conduction
(b) convection
(c) radiation.

These processes function on the basis that where temperature differences exist heat will be transferred and directed towards areas of decreasing temperature. In order to understand how the heat transfer processes function it is helpful to know something of:

(a) the effects of heat upon food,
(b) the means by which heat is transferred through food to effect cooking.

Heat and Heat Transfer (general principles)

All foods and all bodies of matter, e.g. pots and pans consist of atoms/molecules, which are constantly in motion. When heat is applied to foods or cooking vessels this motion is greatly accelerated and friction within the foods and cooking vessels greatly increased. The friction creates heat which passes through these materials by conduction. It should be noted that in most cases heat transfer *within* foods is primarily via the conduction process, however this is *not* the case where food is mainly or exclusively liquid. In these instances heat transfer is chiefly convective and rapid when the liquid is free to move; as is the case with stock, unthickened soups and gravies, etc. Where however foods that are initially liquid become thickened and semi-solid on heating, e.g. certain starch-thickened products, then convected heat is only important at the initial cooking stage. Once the food is thickened and the movement of liquid restricted the process of heat transfer by conduction within the food increases.

Cooking with Conducted Heat

The shallow frying of fish is a good example of how the conduction process transfers heat from a hot stove to a frying pan, through to the cooking oil and on to the outer surface of the fish. Cooking is continued as heat is transferred from the exterior through to the centre of the fish by conduction. At all stages of this operation the principles associated with heat and heat transfer described in the previous section apply. These stages include the heating of the cooking vessel, the oil and fish with the latter being changed from a raw to a cooked condition by the passage of conducted heat within the fish.

Cooking with Convected Heat

Convection occurs in gases and liquids, as opposed to solids because they can move more freely. As the gas (e.g. air) or liquids (e.g. water, stock, oil) are heated their structure expands and becomes less dense. In this condition the heated areas of the gas or liquid rise to be replaced by the cooler and denser gas or liquid present. This movement forms a convection current within the air or liquid. The warmed and less dense air/liquid gradually cools by giving up heat to the foods that are being cooked. On cooling this air/liquid becomes more dense and sinks again to complete the cycle.

The *baking of pies* illustrates the use of convected hot air as a heat transfer medium. The cold air within the oven is heated becomes less dense and rises. This is replaced by cooler denser air and the convection current of hot air is set in motion. The heated air gives up heat energy to the pies where it is absorbed passing through the pies by means of conduction to effect the well-known changes associated with baked products.

Similarly convection currents occur in liquids where they are used as heat transfer mediums during such methods as boiling, poaching, stewing, braising, steaming, and deep frying. In these instances water, moisture, stock or oil are used as the convection medium, but it should be noted that the temperature of these mediums is raised by heat conducted through the cooking vessel or steam generator.

Cooking with Radiant Heat

The grilling of food is an apt illustration of how emitted heat (energy) waves are transferred rapidly through the air and directed on to the exterior surface of foods. The heat energy is absorbed at the surfaces of food where it acts to generate friction. This in turn creates heat. Cooking continues from the exterior surface of the food through to its centre as heat energy travels by means of conduction. When cooking by radiant heat the energy waves heat the foods exterior surfaces only (as their ability to penetrate further is limited) and beyond this depth cooking is accomplished by conduction.

Summary

From these notes it is evident that in most cooking operations more than one mode of heat transfer is acting simultaneously. Also where foods are cooked by these conventional methods of heat transfer, heat penetration is seen to be relatively slow, commencing at the exterior of food and gradually travelling inwards by conduction.

N.B.   For cooking with microwave energy *see* pp. 38–42.

Cooking Methods in Common Use

English term	French term	Heat transfer processes
To poach	Pocher	Conduction/convection
To boil/simmer	Bouillir/mijoter	Conduction/convection
To steam	Vapeuriser	Convection/conduction
To stew	Etuver	Conduction/convection
To braise	Braiser	Conduction/convection
To pot-roast	Poêler	Conduction/convection
To deep-fry	Frire	Conduction/convection
To shallow fry	Sauter	Conduction
To grill	Griller	Radiation/conduction
To roast (oven)	Rôtir	Convection/conduction
To roast (open-spit)		Radiation/conduction
To bake	Cuire	Convection/conduction

The Effects of Cooking on Foods

As previously stated, cooking methods involve the use of heat. These methods may differ in:

(a) how much heat or other radiant energy is applied to the food;
(b) the rate at which it is applied;
(c) the medium used for heat transfer, e.g. metal, water, fat, air;
(d) whether precautions are taken to prevent the loss of moisture or whether moisture is allowed to escape into the atmosphere.

The prime objective of cooking is to produce palatable, safe and attractive foods. However a particular food cannot necessarily be cooked by all the methods outlined in this section.

The effects described in the following sections occur during most cooking operations. The extent to which these changes occur depends upon the amount of heat energy transferred to the foods. Obviously the higher the temperature to which the food is heated and the longer the period of time for which the temperature is maintained, the greater the effects will be. As will be observed these effects will be modified by the medium employed for heat transfer, typically air (e.g. grilling, baking), water or steam (e.g. poaching, boiling, stewing) or fat (frying).

Cooking in fat creates an essentially dry environment that precludes reactions requiring water. When air is used it may be nearly dry or distinctly wet depending upon whether water is deliberately introduced (wet ovens) or derived only from the food being cooked. Cooking in water maximizes those reactions requiring the presence of water, e.g. gelling of starches and conversion of collagen in flesh foods to gelatin.

In the conventional methods of cooking there will be differences in temperature from the heat source to the centre of each item of food. The temperature differences are influenced by the nature and temperature of the heat source, the heat-conducting properties of any materials between the heat source and the food (e.g. air, cooking vessel, pastry layer, sauce, stock, oil, etc.) and their thickness. It follows that different results will be obtained when using containers of different *thermal conductivity*. For example, for best results daubes (types of stew) are generally cooked in an earthenware pot (daubière) to ensure steady even slow cooking, and certain copper-cooking vessels are often used for high speed cooking. Equally the extent of cooking-induced changes is always greater on the surface of a piece of food than at the centre; the greater the thickness of food, the greater the difference.

There are occasions when it is desirable to emphasize these differences e.g. production of a crisp brown skin on roast potatoes or French fries, the crackling on joints of pork, the semi-solid yolk and firm white of fried and soft boiled eggs. Equally there are occasions where such differences must be controlled, perhaps kept to a minimum. In principle temperature *differences* within a container can be kept to a minimum by agitation of the contents but in practice this might be undesirable where delicate foods could be broken up.

A common method to prevent differences in temperature is to use thin pieces or small portions of food which cook more quickly and more uniformly. For example, using sliced rather than whole potatoes, slicing joints of meat into steaks for grilling, frying or braising. It is possible to fry or grill entrecôte steak so that the centre is cooked and the outside browned but acceptable. It would be quite impossible to fry or grill a whole contrefilet so that the centre was cooked sufficiently without severely overcooking the outside. This problem is overcome by using a lower external temperature and a longer cooking period as used in roasting instead of frying or grilling. The same is true of sliced and whole potatoes, which may be fried, roasted or boiled.

With certain cooking methods there will be a moisture content gradient as well as a temperature gradient caused by the evaporation of moisture from an exposed surface e.g. baking and roasting, which lead to different chemical reactions at the surface compared with the centre. Water lost from the surface may be partially replaced by water moving from the interior towards the surface. This water will carry with it soluble components, particularly sugars and amino-acids, and these will be deposited at the surface as the water evaporates. Such substances are very susceptible to degrade and interact when heated, giving rise to yellow-brown or dark brown colours seen for example on the skin of roast potatoes, the crust of bread or the surface of roasted meats.

Poaching is often very brief and as it is a low temperature process its effects are mild. Frying and grilling are also brief operations that occur at much higher temperatures and are much more severe than poaching and boiling. Stewing is a long operation that permits certain changes to occur to a greater extent than during frying or grilling, and some to a lesser extent. For example, the extensive breakdown of some of the gristle is a very important feature of stewing that does not occur during frying or grilling. In contrast the fat breakdown is rather less. This marked difference occurs because stewing is a wet method, the presence of water facilitating (hydrolytic) reactions such as collagen breakdown. In contrast baking and grilling are relatively dry methods, although steam may be present during baking and foods that are grilled naturally contain water that has been at least partially sealed in the food at the beginning of the process. Cooking by immersing food in fat and oils (deep frying) is also a relatively dry process because a substantial part of the water originally present is boiled away during the frying operation.

It is important to appreciate that, from a scientific point of view, the *total time* of the cooking operation begins with the first application of heat and ends with the consumption of the food. Therefore any period of holding food in a hot condition (e.g. hot plate) prior to service or any reheating process increases the extent to which changes occur. It is quite possible that the effects of holding hot may be greater than the effects of cooking and the total effect could be an undesirable overcooking. Accordingly it can be less harmful to cook or part-cook, cool, and reheat immediately prior to service. If food is held for any length of time it is essential that a temperature is used that will prevent the growth of micro-organisms (e.g. bacteria and fungi).

The precise effects of cooking also depend upon the material being cooked. Fruits and vegetables for example differ considerably from flesh foods in structure and properties. Some of these differences are summarized in the table.

Differences in properties of foods from plant or animal origin

Foods of plant origin	Foods of animal origin
Usually *living* at the time of preparation in the kitchen	Tissues not living at this stage
Tissues have rigid cell walls	Tissues do not have distinct cell walls
Depend largely on turgor pressure* for raw texture – often served raw	Do not depend on turgor pressure for raw texture – rarely served raw
Protein content often low	Protein content often high
Starch content may be high	Starch content essentially low
Fat content usually low	Fat content variable, but usually higher

*Turgor pressure – gives raw foods of plant origin their firm and/or crisp texture before cell walls are damaged and water content is lost by preparation and cooking procedures.

The chemical and physical changes that occur during cooking operations are very complex and beyond the scope of this text but may be viewed as:

(a) physical changes in texture;
(b) chemical changes in flavour and odour;
(c) chemical changes in colour;
(d) chemical changes in nutritive value.

Since this text is not primarily concerned with nutritional aspects, the changes in nutritive value will not be discussed in detail. However everyone relies upon foods to supply the essential nutrients and it is desirable that nutrient losses should be minimized. In general the higher the temperature the longer the time of exposure to a particular temperature, the greater will be the loss. Holding cooked food hot and reheating food are particularly destructive and should only be used when unavoidable. Flavour, odour, texture and colour may also be adversely affected by these practices.

N.B.   Students interested in more detailed in-depth information concerned with the above changes should consult a comprehensive food science text (e.g. *Complete Catering Science* O. F. G. Kilgour, Heinemann) however the following notes are included to highlight some of the changes which can be seen during the preparation and cooking of foods.

Why Do We Cook Food?

There are certain dishes where some or all of the ingredients are eaten uncooked. However the majority of foods are cooked or re-heated from a cooked condition prior to service. Important reasons for cooking food are to destroy:

(a) many of the food spoilage micro-organisms;
(b) disease-producing pathogenic micro-organisms;
(c) parasites that were naturally/originally present.

Foods so treated are less susceptible to spoilage provided that there is no contamination after cooking. Accepting that the destruction of dangerous organisms is one reason for the cooking of food, the question as to how raw salads and products, such as steak tartare, can be safe, needs to be answered. Fresh fruits and vegetables are relatively unlikely to contain dangerous micro-organisms or dangerous parasites, and provided they are thoroughly washed during preparation there is little risk. Intact fruit and vegetables are living tissues and relatively resistant to attack by spoilage organisms, but the risk of spoilage rises rapidly once they are bruised or cut.

The muscles of healthy animals are normally free from dangerous micro-organisms but raw meat is more susceptible to contamination with pathogenic and spoilage organisms than raw fruits and vegetables. Accordingly raw meat for products such as steak tartare must be very fresh and handled in conditions of strict hygiene. In the absence of a cooking stage such meat would have to be visually examined for the possible presence of parasites.

A second reason for cooking food is to soften it and make it easy to chew and digest. The gelatinization of starch, the breakdown of proteins and foods' structure are significant in this respect.

A third reason for cooking food is the creation of attractive and interesting ways used to obtain the nutrients required for a healthy life.

Examples of the Effects of Cooking upon Foods

Texture Changes

When protein foods are subjected to cooking, changes in texture may occur which are referred to as setting, gelling and coagulating. Some of these changes can be observed as they occur during the cooking of meat, fish, poultry or eggs, etc. During the poaching of eggs the effect of protein breakdown (denaturation) and coagulation can be clearly seen. These effects may be speeded up by the addition of an acid (vinegar) or salt to the poaching water. The effects of denaturation and coagulation on flesh foods cause shrinkage so that the water and juices are squeezed out. These juices often form the basis of gravies and sauces which accompany the foods. Gently cooked meat on the bone will shrink less than severely cooked meat, or meat off the bone, as the extent of shrinkage depends upon the severity of the heat process, and the time length of exposure. The fact that bone does not shrink during cooking prevents the attached meat from shrinking freely.

Shrinkage of *muscle proteins** occurs at about 65°C. Meat, which is well cooked, will generally reach an internal temperature of about 80°C which is well above the shrinkage point. On the other hand meat which is cooked rare, e.g. beef will only reach an internal temperature of about 65°C and shrinkage will be less.

*Scientifically referred to as actin and myosin.

The setting/firming that occurs when cooked joints of meat are allowed to cool is associated with the cooling and setting of the fat that has dispersed throughout the meat during the cooking process.

Connective tissue proteins found in *flesh foods* as opposed to muscle proteins described above, behave differently during cooking. These proteins are commonly known as gristle (scientifically collagen, elastin and reticulin) Collagen when heated in liquid, e.g. stewed, breaks down to form water soluble gelatin. Any meat that is high in connective tissue, e.g. shin (20%) is best cooked by a slow, moist method to make it tender. Alternatively frying steak (3% connective tissue) can be cooked by a faster, dryer method and be tender. Tough stringy meat is due to a larger proportion of elastin and reticulin which do not breakdown during cooking but which can be removed from meat by careful butchery or broken up mechanically by mincing. The collagen found in *fish* is broken down much more easily than that found in meat and consequently many species of fish can be fried or grilled. It is for this reason that fish muscle easily separates (flakes) during cooking because the connective tissue, collagen has denatured to form gelatin. Fish is suited to quick methods of cookery because it contains little connective tissue.

Cooking damages the structure of *fruits* and *vegetables* and causes a rapid loss of turgor pressure (*see* p. 59). Water and water-soluble substances that were originally contained within the food structure are released and pass into air spaces between the cells. When there are extensive air spaces within the foodstuff loss of turgor pressure and replacement of air with water causes very marked changes in appearance and texture. This particular situation is illustrated by comparing cooked cabbage with raw cabbage, which when raw contains some 75% air by volume. Fruit such as apples contain some 25% air by volume but root vegetables such as carrots contain very little and accordingly there is less change in appearance and texture from this cause. The texture of vegetables and fruit is influenced by their composition as well as by cooking. Apples, pears and potatoes show marked differences in texture after cooking, reflecting their different content of several carbohydrates.

Tenderizing Methods

These apply to the preparation and cooking of flesh foods.

Before commenting on tenderizing methods applied in the preparation and cooking of flesh foods it is worth noting that the texture after cooking may vary depending on:

(a) type of animal – mammal, bird, fish, shellfish;
(b) age of animal – older muscles are tougher;
(c) location of muscle – muscles constantly in use tend to be tougher;
(d) fat content – generally the higher the fat content the juicier the texture;
(e) post-slaughter handling – incorrect handling can lead to tough flesh;
(f) cooking procedure – unsuitable cooking methods in relation to the type of flesh will lead to a tough product.

The Modification of Texture

(a) The Slaughter and Hanging of Meat

The slaughter and immediate post-slaughter handling and chilling or freezing of meat influences its quality to a considerable extent. However the caterer has no direct control during this period and must rely upon his supplier. Many caterers purchase sides of meat that are a few days old and these improve in quality if hung at chill temperatures for a period of time, e.g. lamb 3–5 days and beef 10–17 days. Game is also hung for a substantial period of time.

During this period of hanging, enzymes that are natural components of the flesh cause moderate breakdown of the tissues and produce meat of a more acceptable texture. Prolonged hanging also leads to flavour changes, particularly in game. It is most important that steps are taken during hanging to minimise microbial growth since this could lead to flavour taints or food poisoning, hence the use of chill temperatures, extreme cleanliness and sometimes ultra-violet lights in the store. Traditionally sides are hung from the Achilles tendon (in the ankle) but it is claimed that hanging from the aitch bone (in the thigh) gives more rapid tenderizing since the weight of the carcass pulls the muscle fibres apart. However, this method has less effect upon connective tissues than the traditionally enzymic method.

(b) Tenderizing Meat by Adding Enzymes

Softening (tenderization) occurs when enzymes are added to certain cuts/joints of meat for a period of time before cooking. Traditionally such enzymes are derived by introducing certain fresh fruits into the culinary product and the cooking process. Examples include meat cooked with fresh pineapple, figs, and papaya. Nowadays it is possible to purchase enzyme extracts, which can be sprinkled directly on to the meat's surface, thus avoiding the need for fresh tropical fruit and their flavouring effects.

It is important to appreciate that these added enzymes attack the meat from the outside and penetrate slowly. Further these enzymes are still active during the early stages of cooking and it is the outer layers that receive most heat and thus greater enzyme activity. Under such circumstances there is a very real risk of excessive softening (mushiness) on the outside and toughness at the centre.

An alternative approach is to inject the enzyme (typically papain derived from papaya) into the veins of the animal 30 minutes prior to slaughter. The heart and blood vessels then distribute the enzyme to all tissues of the animal (including the centre of large muscles that are to become large joints) prior to slaughter. After slaughter these enzymes operate in addition to those that were naturally present. If for some reason the animal is not slaughtered within approximately one hour of injection the enzyme is destroyed by the animals defence mechanisms and the animal suffers no harm. Carcases that have been so tenderized are available commercially. It is claimed that enzyme treatment before slaughter yields from a regular side of beef 70% of cuts suited to dry heat processing whereas without treatment only 30% of such cuts would be obtained.

Disadvantages of the treatment are over-tenderization of kidneys and tongue. It is said that the treated kidneys are well suited to uses where flavour rather than texture are required, and the tongue can be used provided the cooking process is more gentle than normal.

It is claimed that this enzyme treatment not only reduces inherent toughness but also reduces toughness induced by incorrect slaughter and post-slaughter cooling operations.

(c) Mincing

This breaks up the muscle of the connective tissue by mechanical means thus making chewing easier.

(d) Marinading

Marinades are essentially a mixture of oil and acid, which may be further flavoured by the addition of vegetables, herbs, seasoning, wine and/or spirit. Meats and fish can be marinaded in such mixtures for predetermined lengths of time to enhance flavour, in some instances effect colour changes, and generally tenderize the product. Any tenderizing effects are probably a result of alterations in acidity to a value that permits the protein to bind more water and dissolve some collagen into gelatin before cooking. These changes favour the continued conversion of collagen into gelatin during the subsequent cooking period.

(e) Pounding

Pounding is a milder form of mincing, which separates some of the fibres.

Flavour and Odour Changes

The chemistry of the flavour and odour of both raw and cooked foods is complex. Thousands of chemical compounds are known to possess specific odour and flavours and usually the smell or taste complex of any raw or cooked food contains at least 50 and possibly more than 500 such compounds, which are present in minute quantities. Changes of smell and taste that occur during cooking reflect the destruction of raw food compounds and the formation of new compounds in the cooked product. The majority of odour and flavour compounds are concentrated in the fatty components of food.

For example the fat content of meat plays an important role in contributing to juiciness after the cooking stage. During cooking the fat melts and passes through the tissues, with some passing into the drippings, also fat that is spread on the surface of meat melts and diffuses through the tissues making it more succulent. In such operations the surface temperature is sufficiently high for some fat breakdown to occur which leads to the production of characteristic odour and flavour.

Following standard recipes and procedures helps to prevent unwanted reactions since the most likely causes of unpleasant odour and flavour are:

(a) incorrect recipe balance and procedure;
(b) using inferior quality ingredients;

Incorrect cooking, e.g. overheating, localized heating due to lack of agitation or movement, can lead to overcooked, burnt, tough and bitter tasting products due to a greater than normal destruction of the ingredients present.

Starch has the ability to bind flavour and odour compounds and reduce their intensity. The harshness of overspiced products can often be corrected by adding a small quantity of starch or starch-rich ingredient.

Colour Changes

Changes in the colour of certain vegetables and fruit occur before cooking takes place and are a result of enzymic browning.

Enzymic Browning

Certain vegetables and fruits turn brown or even darker in colour when cut or damaged and exposed to air (enzymic browning). This can be minimized as follows:

(a) Adding an acid (citric acid or lemon juice)—to adjust the pH value to a level that inhibits enzymic browning.
(b) Heating—this action may however cause undesirable changes in texture and flavour.

(c) Immersion in water or coating cut surfaces with a thin film of melted butter/ oil—these procedures minimize browning because they exclude oxygen from the surfaces.

Common examples of products susceptible to enzymic browning are peeled apples, potatoes, bananas, and pears. In the case of fried mushrooms enzymic browning contributes beneficially to their colour.

The Effects of Preparation and Cooking upon Foods – Colour and Colour Changes

The colour of food influences customer acceptability. Abnormal colours (discoloration) will rarely occur unless tainted ingredients and/or incorrect procedures are used.

Plant Foods

The colouring pigment of green vegetables is chlorophyll. Unless it is partially degraded, chlorophyll is not soluble in water. Loss in colour through normal cooking methods is therefore low and usually unimportant. However on contact with acid (which may come from the vegetable itself) chlorophyll is converted to a brownish pigment which results in vegetable discoloration. Such discoloration can be prevented as follows.

Adding an Alkali to the Cooking Water   Sodium bicarbonate – N.B. excessive additions will result in the destruction of vitamin C and thiamine and soften the vegetable's texture excessively.

Cooking in an Open Vessel   As most of the acids are volatile they are removed with the steam. In these cases it is wise to renew the cooking water for each batch of cooking. This method avoids the need to use sodium bicarbonate.

Traditionally the discoloration was avoided by adding copper in the form of a coin. This is not to be recommended since copper is poisonous.

Pale Coloured Fruits and Vegetables (e.g. potato, parsnip, onion)

These contain substances, which when cooked in alkaline water, take on a yellow/cream colour. This colour change is not severe and therefore presents no problem in catering operations. If desirable the addition of a few drops of acid (lemon juice) to the cooking water avoids this colour change.

Strongly Coloured Fruits and Vegetables (e.g. carrot, tomato, red pepper, pineapple, citrus fruits and radish)

These contain carotenoid pigments, which remain fairly stable on cooking. The result is a slight reduction in the colour intensity of such products.

The Soft and Stone Fruits (e.g. strawberries, raspberries, cherries, etc.)

These contain red or purple pigments, which are water soluble. Such foods loose pigment if they are damaged then placed in cold water and also by cooking. If these pigments are treated with alkaline water they change from purple/red to blue/green, a reaction which is reversed by the addition of an acid (lemon juice). Normally the fruits themselves are sufficiently acidic and resist this change in the first instance.

Some of these fruits react with iron and other metals, e.g. tin, aluminium to produce bluish tints. Accordingly they should not be cooked in, or handled in utensils made of these metals.

A few vegetables contain red or purple pigments and should be treated similarly, the most common of these being red cabbage.

Beetroot

This contains unique pigments, which are water soluble and which show a slight colour change in alkaline water of no consequence to the caterer.

Foods of Animal Origins

The main pigments of meat and poultry are haemoglobin in the blood and myoglobin in the muscle. Meat normally contains far more myoglobin than haemoglobin since most of the blood is removed at slaughter. However, the chemical properties of haemoglobin are essentially identical to those of myoglobin and thus when blood is present or added e.g. to some stews) the changes that occur will be as described here for myoglobin.

The content of myoglobin varies, being higher in the dark muscles of meat, fish and poultry than in the pale muscles. This variation is clearly illustrated in crab, mackerel, pork and chicken. Whatever the hue, fresh meat (i.e. not frozen) should have a relatively bright surface and duller interior. If this is not so then the meat should be rejected since it has been poorly handled. However, it must be noted that protein denaturation caused by freezing leads to a duller surface colour without necessarily indicating lower quality.

The colour produced after cooking depends upon the amounts of pigment present in the raw meat and the severity of the cooking process. Mild heating converts myoglobin to *haemochrome* which is pink and typical of lightly-cooked steak. Further heating converts *haemochrome* to a grey-brown *haemichrome* which is typical of a well-cooked steak.

Green colours should never be encountered but if they are they indicate gross microbial contamination and such meat is unfit for human consumption.

Meat, fish and particularly shellfish also contain carotenoid pigments. When found in meat they impart a yellow colour to the fat. This is most frequently encountered with beef and implies that the meat is from an old animal and that it may therefore be tough. Carotenoids in fish are usually red or pink and examples include redfish, salmon, and tuna. Similar colours may also be encountered in crustacean shellfish, but this type of fish may also contain blue caroteno-protein complexes. Cooking causes the complex to break and give rise to the more typical orange-red carotenoid colour, e.g. lobster shell turns from bluey black to red/orange on cooking.

Milk, dairy products and egg yolks are coloured mainly by carotenoids and the colour intensity mainly reflects the carotenoid content of the feed the animal received. High pigmentation is not necessarily a sign of high quality.

Discoloration that may be encountered in fish and shellfish includes a rusty colour on the cut surface of white fish fillets and a black colour (black spot) on prawns and shrimps. The former is caused by incorrect bleeding of the fish after capture and the latter by incorrect handling of the prawns which permits an enzymic browning type of reaction to occur. There is little the caterer can do except reject the material and, if necessary, change supplier.

Prepared Foods

Many foods take on a yellow or brown colour as a result of cooking. Typically the reactions responsible are known as non-enzymic browning and are chemically complex. The colour-producing ingredients are typically sugars and amino acids or protein, but may be modified by other ingredients particularly acids. Often colours of this type are considered desirable, e.g. caramel, toast, roasted coffee but on occasion they may appear when not required, e.g. in white sauces, fruit juices and typically indicate over-heating. Although typical of prepared foods these reactions may occur in, for example, cooked meat, and make an important and desirable contribution to the colour particularly of the paler meats after cooking, e.g. pork and chicken.

One typical reaction in which proteins may participate is called non-enzymic or *Maillard browning*. This reaction gives the characteristic brown colouring and flavour of cooked foods, meat in particular, and although some nutritive value is lost in the process, it is offset by the increased attractiveness of the food and, therefore, its greater palatability.

4

Thickening and Binding Mechanisms

The mechanisms by which culinary products are thickened to varying degrees can be subdivided into three separate processes: starch thickening; protein coagulation; and emulsification.

Starch Thickening

Starches may be isolated from many plants, and when pure they are white, odourless, tasteless powders. Often instead of pure starches, starch-rich materials, e.g. cereals and pulses, are used as thickeners and these may be slightly coloured and have characteristic but acceptable odours and flavours. Because starch is a major component these starch-rich materials behave similarly but not identically to pure starches. Starches are commonly available from the kitchen stores in the following forms.

The nature of commodities commonly used as sources of starch

White flour	Produced from wheat. Also contains protein and fat
Cornflour	Purified maize starch
Arrowroot	A powdered root consisting almost exclusively of starch. Sometimes referred to as a fécula or fécule
Tapioca	Powdered cassava root, also a fécula and as a thickening agent very similar to arrowroot.
Fécule	Potato powder, perhaps the commonest fécula
Starchy vegetables	Potato as a fresh vegetable has a much higher moisture content and therefore lower starch content than the powder described above.
	Split peas ⎱ Starch-rich pulses also containing
	Lentils ⎰ protein and a little fat.
Farinaceous materials	Also known as cereals; include barley and rice grains. Protein and fat are also present
Special starches	Starches isolated from plants which in some cases are chemically treated to meet particular requirements. Almost pure starches. Examples include waxy maize starch, waxy rice starch, pregelatinized starches, freeze-thaw resistant starches

---

The Use of Starches and Starch-rich Materials as Thickeners

As previously stated, various starches are used as thickening agents in many culinary instances. For example starch-rich materials in the form of pulses, cereal (rice) or starchy
vegetables (potato) are used in the making and thickening of pulse and purée soups. Alternatively starch-rich materials are added to boiling liquids in the form of rice grains or
barley when producing broth-type soups. In some cases dry forms of starch granules are
added directly to boiling liquids, e.g. semolina, wheatflour or potato powder in the production of pasta, pastry, and potato mixes. However the practice of adding dry starch
granules to boiling liquids is the exception rather than the rule, and it should be noted
that in these instances starch clumping can easily occur resulting in lumpy, indigestible
products. In most cases *raw* starch granules are dispersed and separated in oil, fat or cold
liquid before they come into contact with heated liquids. Once starches are heated in a
plentiful supply of liquid certain reactions occur, which effect the release of starch
molecules from starch-rich materials and starch granules. These reactions, when controlled by the skilled cook, result in products taking on varying degrees of consistency, both
when the product is hot and when it is cooled e.g. basic béchamel has a coating consistency when hot but sets firm when cooled in readiness for storage.

The role of the skilled cook when preparing starch-thickened products is an important
one. The aim is to achieve overall product quality in terms of texture, consistency, appearance, flavour, temperature, and yield. The techniques used are many and include adequate dispersal of raw starch grains in the roux, manipulated butter or cold liquid. These
processes should ensure that each granule is free to take part in the thickening/gelatiniza-
tion process. Using the correct recipe balance and method, and thorough stirring (agitation) at all stages of preparation and cooking should prevent starch clumping and lumpiness as these techniques permit each granule to gelatinize freely. In the case of roux production further complications can arise:

(a) If the fat used contains water as is the case with meat dripping or butter, it should
     be cooled to a moderate temperature before the flour is added. Water in the fat at a
     high temperature could cause rapid, partial gelatinization and lumpiness in exactly
     the same way as insufficient liquid.
(b) If fat, whether it contains water or not is used at too high a temperature or there is a
     delay in the subsequent addition of liquid, the starch could break-down (dextrinize)
     and lose some of its thickening power.

N.B. There are some occasions where the 'browning' associated with dextrinization is
desirable. The loss of thickening power in these instances is overcome either by adding
more starch in relation to the liquid or cooking the product for longer periods. An apt example of the latter is the production of Espagnole where the longer cooking period allows
the sauce to reduce (by evaporation) to the required consistency.

In order to produce thickened products using starch-rich vegetables, cereals, or sauces it
is essential to release and/or disperse the starch available within these materials. This is
usually achieved by passing the cooked products through manual or motorized
mechanical devices: passing pulse, purée, cream and certain velouté-type soups through a
mouli, liquidizer, or vertical cutter/mixer in order to extract and or disperse the gelatinized starch.

Essentially these processes can be seen as the cook extracting gelatinized starch from a
commodity to achieve thickening (consistency) and in some cases to establish a predominant flavour.

Flavours

Starches also have the ability to bind chemical components, which are responsible for flavour. This can be seen when strong-flavoured stock is tasted before and after the addition of a starch thickener. These effects can be overcome by adding more flavour contributing agents e.g. stock concentrates, and by using well balanced formulae (recipes). The quantity of starch or starch-rich material in any recipe should be dependent upon:

- (a) the consistency aimed at in any finished product;
- (b) the influence of the starch upon a product's flavour;
- (c) the amount of starch available in the commodities used.

Consistency

Throughout the practical studies it will be seen that often different quantities of starch-rich materials in relation to similar amounts of liquid are used to achieve a like consistency. For example, when preparing purée soups from aqueous (watery) vegetables a similar consistency is achieved by using either $\frac{1}{20}$ rice to 1 unit stock, or alternatively $\frac{1}{10}$ raw potato to 1 unit stock (*see* p. 206). This illustrates that the quantities of starch-rich materials, e.g. rice or potatoes used in recipes to achieve similar consistencies may vary because the starch-rich materials themselves vary in the percentage of starch they contain. Therefore, different amounts of starch-rich materials may be used to provide similar amounts of starch in order to achieve the required consistency. The table below shows the approximate percentages of starch contained in various starch-rich commodities.

Commodity	Approximate percentage of starch
Arrowroot	90
Cornflour	90
Barley	80
Rice	80
Wheat flour (white)	78
Semolina	70
Lentils	50
Split-peas	50
Potato	17

It is worth noting that when certain types of thickened soups are produced using mainly aqueous vegetables (vegetables which are mainly comprised of water and contain little or no starch), the starch is introduced into the product by another ingredient. A good example is the addition of béchamel sauce in the production of aqueous vegetable cream soups (*see* p. 208). The table below illustrates the approximate starch content of some common aqueous vegetables.

Commodity	Approximate percentage of starch
Onion	0.5
Asparagus	0.4
Cauliflower	0.4
Carrot	nil
Cucumber	nil
Lettuce	nil
Mushroom	nil

Comments on Consistencies Achieved when Using Wheat Flour, Corn-flour, and Arrowroot as Starch Thickeners

When added to, and cooked with foods correctly, the consistencies achieved using these components will be chiefly determined by the relative proportions of starch and liquid employed. The table below is intended as an approximate guide to illustrate ratios commonly used in many traditional recipes. The starches referred to are those commonly used in daily kitchen practice but others could well be substituted. The ratios given are meant as guidelines only and not as exactitudes because the quantities required depend upon the specific properties of the different starches.

Approximate ratios of starch to liquid used to achieve varying sauce consistencies

	Basic Pouring Unit	Basic Coating Unit	Basic Binding Unit
Liquid	1	1	1
Starch	$\frac{1}{20}$	$\frac{1}{10}$	$\frac{1}{5}$

In practical sauce making the starch is commonly used in the form of a roux, a manipulated mixture, e.g. beurre manié (*see* p. 172) or as a temporary suspension, and the basic consistencies may well be adjusted (usually by adding more liquid) to suit culinary requirements.

Other Ingredients

The behaviour of starches and starch-rich ingredients is modified if other materials are present, and it makes no difference whether they are natural components of the starch-rich ingredients or a separate ingredient in the recipe.

Sugars

Sugars are available in the form of sucrose (cane or beet sugar), glucose, invert sugar, confectioner's glucose, golden syrup, etc. These ingredients may be used to sweeten starch-based products such as sauces, puddings, and fillings but these sugars also reduce the rate of gelatinization and give a softer and more liquid texture on cooling. The rate of gelatinization is reduced because the sugar 'removes' some of the water. Because of the slower gelatinization the viscosity is lower at a given degree of cooking and full cooking requires a longer period than in the absence of sugars. The magnitude of the effect is proportional to the amount of sugar added to the starch and many recipes advocate where possible the addition of sugar after gelatinization has been achieved, e.g. sugar added to sauces after they have been thickened. Although the various sugars show similar effects, they are not identical and it is not always a simple matter to change the sweetening agent in a recipe.

Acids

Acids modify the behaviour of starch-based products if present in sufficient quantity and will normally be encountered in the form of vinegars, wines, fruit juices or fruit purées. These acidic ingredients break down (hydrolyse) the large starch molecules and reduce the thickening power. This thinning effect can be overcome by using a greater amount of starch or starch-rich ingredient or by using a starch that is resistant, e.g. the starch from waxy maize or other type of modified starch. A simpler traditional way is to add the acidic component after the gelatinization stage, e.g. adding lemon juice to lemon meringue pie filling once the sauce base has gelatinized, using prepared demi-glace sauce with acids as in many derivative brown sauces. Some highly spiced oriental dishes contain starch and acidic fruit juices (typically lemon or another citrus juice). Once again the fruit juice is added towards the end of the cooking period.

Proteins

Proteins have quite marked effects upon starch-water mixtures and this is well illustrated by comparing the results of stirring cornflour (maize starch) in cold water with the result of treating wheat flour (starch 80%, proteins approximately 10%) similarly. The former (cornflour) separates out and the latter absorbs water to form a sticky elastic paste making it ideal for use with batters.

Proteins are added to starch-based formulations in many ways including egg, milk, gelatin or flesh foods. It should be noted that the incorporation of such ingredients will, by adding other materials further modify the behaviour of the starch. Usually the addition of proteins will yield some improvement in freeze-thaw stability (*see* below). Milk proteins for example help to stabilize white sauces and gelatin can be used to stabilize thick custard-based trifles. This property is associated with the ability of proteins to form three-dimensional gels and to bind water very strongly. However proteins alone are insufficient to impart freeze-thaw stability to products.

Chemically Modified Starches

When naturally occurring starches have not provided the properties required for certain catering operations food scientists have been able to obtain the desired properties by chemically modifying the natural starch. Examples include the following.

Freeze-thaw Resistant Starches

These are manufactured for use as a thickening agent in products, which are to undergo freezing and frozen storage for determined periods of time, prior to reconstitution. These starches may be used in recipes to replace natural starches or starch-rich materials and in some instances are used in conjunction with natural starches. The introduction of freeze-thaw resistant starches acts to prevent the separation of the starch from the liquid which would leave a lumpy, curdled product.

Pregelatinized or Cold-water Soluble Starches

The basis of this modification is to pre-cook the starch, to dry the product and grind it to a powder. This process can be applied to natural or modified starches and some very useful water-soluble starches are available. Perhaps the greatest use of these is in packaged instant puddings.

Syneresis (weeping)

On standing many gelatinized products release liquid and the gel structure shrinks. Commonly this phenomena is known as weeping. It can be recognized when the liquid collects around the edge of, for example, custard or a mould of gelatin products.

Protein Gelation and Coagulation

One of the most familiar but least understood changes which food proteins undergo is the change of state from a liquid to a solid. To understand this process it is necessary to know something of the nature of proteins, the causes and effects of protein breakdown (denaturation) and the associative reactions that may follow.

Denaturation (Protein Breakdown)

Proteins, which are present in plant and animal tissue, are referred to as native proteins. The application of heat and indeed other operations related to catering e.g. freezing, drying, foaming and exposure to acids also cause proteins to denature. Denaturation and the associative reactions that follow allow the proteins to take part in changes of state commonly referred to as gelling, setting, and coagulation. Many culinary products illustrate these changes, which result in their taking on a firm or relatively rigid texture. The following products illustrate these points:

(a) Baked egg custard – egg proteins coagulate during the cooking process giving the finished product a relatively rigid texture.
(b) Cooked meringues – egg white proteins are partially broken down during the whisking process and the meringues made firm by the application of gentle heat.
(c) Aspic jelly – aspic sets firm once the gelatin within it has been sufficiently heated and cooled to encourage gelation.

N.B. For the use of proteins as an emulsifier *see* p. 73 on emulsifications.

Binding Agents

Culinary binding agents seem to have been little studied from a scientific point of view. They must however be cohesive (shape-retaining) and in some cases adhesive materials (i.e. able to bind). Those in common use are based upon either cooked (gelatinized) starches, or proteins or mixtures of both. The starch-based binders often take the form of thick binding sauces, breadcrumbs, cooked potato, etc. The commonest protein-based binder is egg, heating is required to coagulate the egg proteins and produce a permanent shape-retaining effect. An extensively used starch and protein-based binder is known as a panada. Wheatflour could also be included in this category, but it should be noted that the initial binding ability is derived from the proteins (gluten) but the final shape-retaining ability is derived in part from the gelatinized starch as well as the gluten.

Emulsification (Emulsions and foams)

An emulsion represents a more or less stable association between two substances (ingredients), which would not normally mix together, e.g. oil and water, gas and solids (foams). These substances are normally immiscible. To clarify this concept examples of emulsions foams encountered in catering are listed on pp. 74–5. These can be described as being:

(a) oil-in-water emulsions, e.g. mayonnaise;
(b) water-in-oil/fat emulsions, e.g. butter;
(c) gas-in-solid/liquid foams e.g. cakes, breads, soufflés, meringues.

All emulsions (foams) consist of a *continuous phase* throughout which a *dispersed* phase is distributed. For example when producing sauce mayonnaise oil (the dispersed phase) is distributed throughout the vinegar/lemon juice (the water-based continuous phase). Alternatively when butter and margarine are produced, water (the dispersed phase) is distributed throughout the plastic-like butter fat (the continuous phase). Meringue is a good example of air (the dispersed gas phase) being distributed throughout a network of egg albumen (the continuous phase) that has been mixed with sugar. Cakes, breads, hot soufflés also illustrate the dispersion of air throughout a plastic-type network of protein (gluten), starch and perhaps fat. The examples in which a gas (air) is dispersed throughout a solid are referred to as *foams*.

Emulsion Breakdown

When an emulsion breaks it is because the once dispersed phase, e.g. oil droplets in mayonnaise, has associated to such an extent that it can no longer be contained in the continuous phase, which in this example is vinegar. Breakdown or separation is seen as the curdled appearance of mayonnaise as the oily layer separates and rises to the surface, or as a foam collapsing. In order to produce a stable emulsion it is necessary to distribute one phase throughout the other (or in practical terms one ingredient throughout the other) and to inhibit or prevent their separation. This distribution and stability is achieved by whisking/agitation and where necessary by introducing an emulsifying agent into the recipe.

The Presence of Emulsifying Agents

Emulsifying agents can be seen as molecules having two parts, one of which is soluble in oil and the other in water. These emulsifying agents act to reduce the tension between the water and the oil by forming a bridge at the junction of the oil and water phases. For example in mayonnaise production this process allows the emulsifiers to form a film around each oil droplet which prevents the oil from running together and associating.

Proteins are one of the most common emulsifying agents and are used in the form of egg yolk, milk, wheatflour, or gelatin. Their use favours the production of oil in water emulsions.

Phospholipids (fat-like substances concentrated in the yolk of egg), which include the substance known as lecithin, are potent emulsifying agents generally used in the form of egg yolks but are available as commercial extracts.

Perhaps the best known commercially available synthetic emulsifying agent is GMS – glyceryl monostearate.

Notes on Emulsion Breakdown

As previously stated emulsions break because the dispersed phase, be it oil, water, or air, associates. Some of the factors and/or conditions common to catering practices which may influence such breakdown are commented on below.

Temperature and its Effects

In an emulsion such as butter the continuous fat phase is solid at ordinary temperatures and the dispersed water droplets cannot move at all. When butter is warmed the fat melts and the water droplets become free to move more easily. Consequently they associate and the emulsion breaks. The spattering of butter in the frying pan is a result of the water droplets sinking through the melted butter oil and coming into contact with the heated base of the pan. At this point they boil violently and explode through the oil layer.

In the production of Hollandaise sauce the skill of the cook when applying heat is critical if a stable emulsion is to be produced. Overheating of the egg yolks in the early stages can cause them to coagulate and curdle. Adding the melted butter at too high a temperature could lead to the same result. If this sauce is held at too high a temperature for any length of time its consistency becomes runny, the oil droplets are then free to associate, which results in the breakdown of the emulsion. Alternatively if this particular sauce is stored at too low a temperature the butter fat solidifies and once again there is a breakdown in the emulsion. When producing mayonnaise the oil is often warmed to ensure that any semi-congealed oil caused by cool temperatures is reversed to an oily consistency. This facilitates the coating of oil droplets with emulsifying agent – egg yolk.

Chilling and freezing of some emulsions e.g. mayonnaise but not butter can lead to separation of the phases during chill storage or on thawing. Whether or not separation occurs during chill storage is largely determined by the freezing characteristics of the oil. Even a so-called pure oil consists of many oil fractions that have separate freezing points, for example pure olive oil will cloud at chill temperatures because some of the oil fractions have frozen. These easily freezable fractions may be removed by filtering (sieving) and an oil so treated is said to be winterized. Winterized oils are better suited for use in salad dressings, sauces etc. that are to be chilled or frozen.

Oils differ in their requirements for winterization. Safflower oil is stable to $-7°C$ but must be winterized for use at $-12°C$. It cannot be economically winterized for use at $-18°C$ because too great a percentage of oil solidifies at this temperature. Corn oil and soyabean oil do not require winterization for use at refrigeration temperatures. Groundnut oil is suitable for use at frozen storage temperatures because it forms a non-crystalline (amorphous) mass on freezing rather than crystalline structures. To minimize crystal formation freezing must be rapid, i.e. by blast freezer and not in a frozen storage cabinet. Freezing may damage the emulsifying agent layer on the dispersed phase, particularly in the case of proteins, which may be denatured. Frozen egg yolks therefore are less successful for mayonnaise production than are fresh egg yolks.

N.B. See pp. 188–191 for practical information concerning the preparation of Hollandaise and mayonnaise sauces.

The nature of some common emulsions and foams

Emulsion (foam)	
Milk	Oil (approximately $3\frac{1}{2}\%$) dispersed in a continuous phase of water containing proteins, sugar, acids and salts. Proteins are the main emulsifying agent. Emulsion not indefinitely stable (cream collects at the surface) unless homogenized.
Butter	Water (not exceeding 16% by law), which may contain salt, dispersed in a continuous phase of semi-solid (plastic) butter fat. Stabilized mainly by rigidity of the continuous phase.
Margarine	Essentially as butter but incorporating non-dairy fats
Dairy cream (natural)	Milk fat and air dispersed in a continuous phase of water containing proteins, acids, sugar and salts. The fat content is controlled by law; single cream 18% fat; double cream 48% fat; whipping cream 35% fat. Proteins act as emulsifiers
Non-dairy cream (synthetic)	Essentially as dairy cream but incorporating non-dairy fats.
Ice-cream	Oil and air dispersed in sugar, syrup or cornflour starch paste and ice. Air content may be 50% or more *by volume*. Fat content controlled by law and typically not less than 5%. Type of fat (dairy/non-dairy) also controlled by law. Emulsifying agent depends on type but may be milk or egg proteins or added synthetic emulsifier

Mayonnaise	Oil (not less than 25% by law and typically 70–80% by weight) and air (10% by volume) dispersed in vinegar or lemon juice and emulsified by egg-yolk proteins or lecithin
Hollandaise	Similar to the above but typically 40–50% oil by weight
Choux pastry	Oil dispersed in wheat dough containing eggs. The proteins of egg and flour function as emulsifying agents
Some sauces, gravies, soups	Oil fat dispersed in water containing salt and starch or various vegetables, meat, etc. For example the addition of a liaison to soup, sauce, white stews
Cakes and breads (including unleavened breads)	Air dispersed in a plastic network of protein, starch and perhaps fat. The air volume varies considerably and may have been whipped in, generated by yeast action or by chemical action using baking powder or baking soda and cream of tartar
Meringue	Air dispersed in a network of egg albumen (egg white protein) that has been mixed with sugar

Illustrative Kitchen-scale Science Experiments

The experiments outlined below have been chosen to illustrate some of the points made in this section. They can all be performed in a kitchen.

1   To Show the Stability of an Emulsion

Mix equal volumes of oil and water.
Whisk briskly and put aside.
Repeat using milk and 2% gelatine or liquid egg instead of water.
Compare the time required for the emulsion to break and note where appropriate the formation of a foam.

2   To Show the Effect of Synthetic Emulsifier on Emulsion Stability

Repeat experiment 1 with the addition of available synthetic emulsifiers (or a few drops of washing-up liquid). Note how effective these agents are in producing stable emulsions.

3   To Show Spattering

Heat butter or margarine gently in a saucepan.
Transfer to a glass vessel and note the separation of the dispersed aqueous phase.
Heat butter or margarine in a frying pan and cautiously note the tendency to spatter.
Repeat using fresh lard and note that this does not spatter since it does not contain water.

4   To Show Winterizing

Place samples of the available pure oils and mayonnaise in a refrigerator.
Similarly place samples in a deep freeze.
After one day's storage check for signs of cloudiness. If you now chill a sieve you will be able to remove the solid fat (a sieve at room temperature might remelt the solid fat) and thus winterize the oil.
This filtered oil on storing in the same conditions for a further day will show much less cloudiness than the original oil.

5   To Show that Different Starches Behave Differently when Heated in Water

Prepare pouring consistency sauces (1 in 20 or 5%) using e.g. cornflour (maize starch), fécule (potato starch), arrowroot, tapioca, and any chemically modified starches available.

Treat all in the same way. Note and compare the thickness of the hot gels or pastes and the nature of the gels or pastes on cooling, i.e. colour, consistency, odour, and taste.

6   To Show the Effect of other Ingredients on Starch Behaviour

(a)   Prepare pouring consistency sauces using cornflour (maize starch) in:

(i)   water;
(ii)   water containing 1% citric acid, lemon juice or vinegar;
(iii)   water containing 5% sugar;
(iv)   milk.

Critically examine the products for thickness of the hot sauce, nature of sauces on cooling, i.e. colour, consistency, odour, and taste.

(b)   Stir cornflour into cold water and allow to stand. Using the same proportions similarly treat wheat flour. Compare the appearance and consistency of these products. If a cold-water soluble pregelatinized starch is available the behaviour of this is worth comparing with cornflour and wheat flour.

7   Comparison of Freeze-thaw Stability

Prepare pouring consistency sauces using any available starches or starch-rich ingredients. Those sauces prepared in experiment 5 are ideal. Place individually into convenient containers and freeze. Leave in frozen storage for a week, then remove and allow to thaw. Examine for signs of weeping and curdling and where these changes are detected try to regenerate the sauce by the use of heat alone. If this is unsuccessful then try heating plus stirring. Decide which starches are most convenient for use in freeze-thaw recipes.

5

Entrées and Relevés

The nature of entrées and relevés are at first sight difficult to comprehend – similarities and differences exist, concerning these two courses, which require clarification.

Entrées

Generally the word entrée translated means 'enter' and when associated with traditional menu terminology refers to the first main item to appear on the menu. According to the master chef Escoffier, such items could be made up using fish, butcher's meat, poultry, offal or game. On modern menus, however, an entrée indicates a type of culinary product prepared using the above commodities excluding fish – these usually appear as the first main meat items offered on the bill of fare. Technically the term entrée refers to a type of dish that is prepared, cooked and presented in a particular manner. The characteristics of entrées are described below.

Butcher's meat, poultry, offal or game when being prepared for entrées are usually cut into portions prior to cooking. For example topside of beef cut into braising steaks or best-end of lamb into cutlets. Furthermore when producing entrées many methods of cookery are used and the completed item is dispatched from the kitchen sauced and garnished as is required to form the finished dish. The garnish may be simple or complex, the sauce served as an integral part of the dish or as a separate accompanying item.

Luncheon entrées are mainly prepared using the less expensive cuts of meat, e.g. Steak and Kidney Pie, whilst the more expensive cuts are selected for the preparation of dinner entrées e.g. Tournedos Chasseur. When an entrée is not being offered as a main course but as a preliminary course in its own right, it would not normally be accompanied by potato or vegetable dishes. Cold preparations are also served as entrées, e.g. Ham Mousse.

Examples of Entrées

<table>
<tr><td>*Déjeuner (luncheon)*</td><td>*Dîner (Dinner)*</td></tr>
<tr><td>Ragoût de Boeuf Jardinière
(beef stew with vegetables)</td><td>Tournedos Rossini
(sautéd fillet steak with Foie Gras,
truffle, and Madeira sauce)</td></tr>
<tr><td>Chop d'Agneau Champvallon
(a flavoursome lamb stew)</td><td>Côtelettes d'Agneau Réforme
(shallow-fried breaded lamb cutlets
served with Reform sauce)</td></tr>
</table>

The list of possible examples is extensive and occasions arise when dinner type entrées would be served at luncheon and vice versa according to requirements.

Relevés

In his book *The Complete Guide to the Art of Modern Cookery* Escoffier suggests that the line of demarcation between entrées and relevés was clearly defined on the old-fashioned French menus. He describes the scene of a typical French dinner at which the selection of soups and entrées would be set out on the dining table before the guests were admitted into the room, and how once the soups were served the relevés would replace the soups on the table thus relieving them. Hence the history of the name relevé. At that time relevés, as with entrées, could be produced using fish, butcher's meat, poultry, offal or game. However, on today's menu the relevé indicates a type of culinary product prepared from prime joints of butcher's meat and offal, along with good class poultry or game. Nowadays the relevé is often served as the main meat item on a dinner, banquet or à la carte menu. As a modern menu term relevé is seldom used because menus are less extensive than in the past. The word 'Viandes' (meats) is now generally used to cover a variety of meat dishes including relevés. Technically a relevé refers to a type of culinary product that is prepared, cooked and presented in a particular way. The characteristics of the relevé are outlined below and it should be noted that the main difference between dinner entrées and relevés is one of size, the latter being of greater volume. When preparing relevés only the choice joints of butcher's meat and offal are selected along with good class poultry or game. Cooking methods employed vary but usually include roasting, braising, and cooking à la poêle. The cooked meat is usually presented 'in the piece' with a sauce and garnish. The garnish may be simple or complex with the sauce being served as an integral part of the dish or as an accompaniment. Unlike entrées the meat is not cut into portions prior to cooking and it therefore requires carving for service. Carving may be carried out in the dining room at the customer's table, or alternatively in the kitchen. The relevé may be served with vegetable and potato courses but when a complex vegetable garnish is already involved these extra courses would be omitted. As for entrées, relevés may be prepared cold as well as hot, e.g. Filet de Boeuf Froid. The relevé is sometimes referred to as a 'remove' and perhaps could best be described as a large entrée.

Examples of Relevés

Filet de Boeuf Richelieu
   (poêled fillet of beef garnished with stuffed mushrooms, braised lettuce, stuffed tomatoes and small turned potatoes, served with Madiera sauce)

Selle d'Agneau Bouquetière
   (saddle of lamb roasted, garnished with neat bouquets of various vegetables, served with roast gravy)
Canard Braisé a l'Orange
   (braised duck with orange sauce, garnished with orange segments and blanched zest)
The list of examples is extensive.

N.B.   When a traditional kitchen brigade is employed hot entrées and relevés are the responsibility of the Saucier and cold preparations the Chef Garde-Manger.

SECTION TWO
Larder work

6

Cold Sauces – Dressings and Dips

Introduction

Cold sauces and dressings are used frequently throughout culinary work. They are extensively used during the preparation and service of specific larder products, namely salads and hors d'oeuvre as outlined in Chapter 7.

Their function is to add *flavour, moistness* and, at times, *cohesion* to numerous culinary preparations. As a result, the use of sauces and dressings in such products creates a variety of *flavours, textures* and *colours* to please and stimulate the prospective diner.

Notes of Mayonnaise-based Sauces/Dressings

Although mayonnaise is a relatively stable emulsion, conditions may arise which will cause the already prepared mayonnaise to 'break' or separate into an unacceptable product of curdled appearance. To prevent such an occurrence basic guidelines need to be adhered to:

(a) Store and 'hold' mayonnaise in *cool* conditions (overly warm or very cold conditions may result in separation).
(b) Unless mayonnaise has been prepared using 'winterised oil' (*see* p. 74), it *must not* be stored frozen as this will cause the emulsion to break down.
(c) Store in suitable sealed containers to reduce skinning and tainting from other strong flavoured products.

Notes on Oil-based Dressings

Oil-based dressings, typically vinaigrette, etc. are essentially *temporary emulsions* a physical state created by agitation. On standing, however, the oil and vinegar/water separate with the oil phase rising to the surface. Such dressings therefore need to be re-emulsified just before application. This is achieved by agitation, e.g. whisking or shaking and the dressing then applied to the respective salads.

Oil-based dressings are best held/stored at near room temperature (N.R.T.), if they are kept chilled or refrigerated the oil begins to congeal which spoils the appearance and the normally free-running nature of the dressing which is essential when tossing or dressing salads. The guidelines below should ensure success when making, holding and applying vinaigrette type products:

(a) For production choose good quality ingredients, namely oil, vinegar, fresh herbs and flavourings.
(b) Prepare and mix dressings well in advance allowing the flavours to fully blend.
(c) Hold/store prepared dressings at N.R.T. for best results.
(d) Always re-emulsify the dressings (by agitation or whisking) just before use to ensure the dressing is thoroughly blended together.
(e) Ensure the ingredients being flavoured/moistened have been properly prepared (e.g. drained/dried) before the dressing is applied.
(f) Do not use excessive amounts of dressing but allow the dressing to lightly 'clothe' the ingredients. The 'tossing' technique is an ideal way of achieving this requirement.
(g) When dressing green leaf salads apply the dressing 'just on or at the point of service' for best results.

Notes on Fresh Cream-based Dressings

Fresh cream-based dressings need the same care and attention as any fresh cream product regarding safe, hygienic holding/storage procedures. The product is best stored/held in covered containers on refrigeration (1–4°C/34–40°F) until required for use. Cream-based dressings are generally prepared with fresh whipping cream and whisked to a light consistency for light coating/moistening purposes (*see* p. 84 and below for typical examples).

Natural Yoghurt and Dressings

Natural yoghurt is commonly used as part of salad dressings/sauces. It may be used exclusively as the basic ingredient but more often it is used to lighten and modify mayonnaise or cream-based dressings/sauces previously described. Its introduction often provides a lighter product of a more piquant flavour as well as reducing the overall fat content. Such dressings/sauces are held/stored as for mayonnaise and cream-based products.

Dips

Dips are invariably extensions of basic dressings/sauces or may be made to a specific recipe (*see* p. 88–90). Dips are a welcome and tasty accompaniment generally offered with crudites (*see* p. 107), or at-the-bar snippets available in many catering establishments. All dips should be handled/stored as for mayonnaise or cream-based dressings/sauces and they are mainly served in small earthenware/china dishes or similar receptacles.

Cream: Yoghurt-based Dressings
SOUR CREAM DRESSING   Crème Acidule

Yield: 250 ml (½ pt)

Unit	Ingredient	Metric	Imperial
1	Fresh (whipping) cream	200 ml	8 fl oz
¼	Lemon juice or white vinegar	50 ml	2 fl oz
	Salt and cayenne pepper to taste		

Method

Place all ingredients into a mixing bowl and whisk to a dressing of light consistency. Season to taste, cover and store chilled for use.

Examples of Dressings Derived from Sour Cream Dressing: Added Ingredients in Relation to 1 Unit 200 ml (8 fl oz) Fresh Cream

Name	Ingredient	Method
Curried cream dressing	Curry paste	Blend in to taste
Horse-radish cream dressing	Horse-radish sauce	Blend in to taste
Mustard cream dressing	Dijon or English mustard Pinch caster sugar	Blend in to taste
Yoghurt cream dressing	Natural yoghurt Pinch caster sugar	Blend in to taste

N.B.   Sour cream dressing and subsequent derivatives may be modified by replacing a proportion of the fresh cream with natural yoghurt.

Cold Emulsified Sauces and Dressings
MAYONNAISE SAUCE   Sauce Mayonnaise
Yield: 600 ml (1¼ pt)

Unit	Ingredient	Metric	Imperial
1	Oil 4 egg yolks Vinegar (tablespoon) Squeeze of lemon juice Pinch of English mustard Pinch salt/cayenne pepper	500 ml	1 pt

Method

Thoroughly whisk together egg yolks, half of the vinegar, mustard, salt and cayenne pepper. Add the oil gradually; whisking thoroughly and continuously until a stable emulsion is formed. Whisk in lemon juice and correct seasoning. Extra vinegar may be added to adjust flavour as required.

N.B.   For technical points to consider when preparing mayonnaise, *see* pages 191, 192.

Examples of Sauces Derived from Mayonnaise: Added Ingredients to 1 Unit ½ (1 pt)

Unit	Ingredient	Metric	Imperial	Name	Uses
⅕	Tomato ketchup	100 ml	4 fl oz	Cocktail	Sea food
¹⁄₁₀	Double cream (lightly			sauce	cocktail
	beaten)	50 ml	2 fl oz		
	Worcester sauce (to				
	flavour)				
Combine with mayonnaise. Adjust consistency					
				Sauce	Cold fish
				Andalouse	dishes
As for Cocktail Sauce, add ¹⁄₁₀ (50 g/2 oz) of finely diced pimento					
½	Aspic (melted and cool)	250 ml	½ pt	Mayonnaise	Coating and
				Colée	binding
					cold foods
Combine aspic with mayonnaise, use prior to setting					
⅕	Gherkins	100 g	4 oz	Sauce	Deep fried
¹⁄₁₀	Capers	50 g	2 oz	Tartare	fish
	Fine herbs (pinch)				
	Chop ingredients finely and combine with				
	mayonnaise				
	Adjust consistency				
	As for sauce tartare but			Sauce	Deep fried
	lightly flavoured with			Rémoulade	fish
	anchovy essence				
⅕	Spinach purée	100 g	4 oz	Sauce Vert	Cold fish
	Fine herbs (pinch)				dishes
	Small bunch watercress				
	Chop together herbs and watercress leaves,				
	mix with spinach purée and pass				
	through a fine sieve				
	Combine with mayonnaise and season to				
	taste				

Examples of Dressings Derived from Mayonnaise: Added Ingredients to 1 Unit ½ l (1 pt) Mayonnaise

Unit	Ingredient	Metric	Imperial	French term
	Added flavourings:			Escoffier
	Lemon juice			dressing
	Worcester sauce			
	Chili sauce			
	Paprika			
	Chopped chives			
	Combine with mayonnaise to taste,			
	adjust consistency			

Unit	Ingredient	Metric	Imperial	French term
	Fine herbs Combine finely chopped herbs with mayonnaise, adjust consistency			Fine herbs dressing
1/10	Tomato ketchup	50 ml	2 fl oz	Thousand
1/10	Green pepper	50 g	2 oz	Isles
1/10	Red pepper	50 g	2 oz	dressing
	Mild chili sauce (to flavour) Finely dice peppers, combine with mayonnaise, add chili sauce to taste Adjust consistency			
1/2	Natural yoghurt Combine with mayonnaise	250 ml	1/2 pt	Yoghurt dressing

Oil-based Dressing
VINAIGRETTE DRESSING

Vinaigrette

Yield: 1/2 (1 pt)

Unit	Ingredient	Metric	Imperial
1	Salad oil	375 ml	15 fl oz
1/3	Selected vinegar	125 ml	5 fl oz
	Salt, mill pepper		

Method

Mix together vinegar, salt and mill pepper. Add oil and whisk briskly to form an emulsion. Use as required.

N.B.   Always re-whisk before use.

Examples of Dressings Derived from Vinaigrette: Added Ingredients to 1 Unit ½ 1 (1 pt) Vinaigrette

Unit	Ingredient	Metric	Imperial	Name
1/40	Diluted English mustard to flavour Combine with vinaigrette	15 g	1/2	English dressing
	As for English dressing, add caster sugar to taste			Americaine dressing
1/20	Dijon mustard to flavour Combine with vinaigrette	30 g	1 oz	French dressing

Unit	Ingredient	Metric	Imperial	
	Chopped garlic Combine with vinaigrette to taste			Garlic dressing
$\frac{1}{20}$	German mustard to flavour Combine with vinaigrette	30 g	1 oz	German dressing
	As for vinaigrette but use lemon juice in place of vinegar			Lemon dressing
	As for lemon dressing but use sesame oil instead of salad oil, flavour with chopped garlic			Sesame and garlic dressing
$\frac{1}{5}$	Roquefort cheese Pass cheese through a fine sieve, gradually add vinaigrette whisking continuously	100 g	4 oz	Roquefort dressing
	As for vinaigrette but use walnut oil instead of salad oil			Walnut oil dressing

Dips: Soured Cream-based
SOURED CREAM DIP

Yield: 250 ml ($\frac{1}{2}$ pt)

Unit	Ingredient	Metric	Imperial
1	Soured cream	200 ml	8 fl oz
$\frac{1}{4}$	Natural yoghurt	50 ml	2 fl oz
Flavourings and seasonings	Tobasco Worcester sauce Salt and cayenne		

Method

Mix yoghurt, flavourings and seasonings in a mixing bowl. Gradually beat in the soured cream to form a dipping consistency. Correct the seasoning. Cover and store chilled until required.

Examples of Dips Derived from Sour Cream Dip: Added Ingredients in Relation to 250 ml (½ pt) Soured Cream

Name/yield	Unit	Ingredient	Metric	Imperial
Blue cheese dip 150 g (6 oz)	½	Blue vein cheese (crumbled) Mix in well with the basic soured cream dip	125 g	5 oz
Cream cheese and onion dip 200 g (8 oz)	1	Cream cheese Spring onions (cut into small rings to flavour and garnish) Beat the cream cheese to a soft consistency. Mix into the soured cream dip along with the onions	250 g	10 oz
Watercress and walnut dip	½	Walnuts (finely chopped) Small bunch of watercress (finely chopped) Combine above ingredients with the sour cream dip	125 g	5 oz

N.B.   Many of the sauce/dressings outlined on pp. 86–7 can also be used as dips.

Dips: Avocado-based
AVOCADO DIP

Yield: 250 ml (½ pt)

Unit	Ingredient	Metric	Imperial
1	Avocado flesh (very ripe)	200 g	8 oz
¼	Mayonnaise (thick)	50 ml	2 fl oz
	Garlic cloves (2) crushed		
	Squeeze lemon juice		
	Salt and milled black pepper		

Method

Rub ripe avocado and garlic through a coarse sieve into a bowl. Season with salt/milled black pepper and flavour with lemon juice to taste. Blend in thick mayonnaise to form a thick-creamy dip. Cover and store chilled until required.

GUACAMOLE

Yield: 250 ml (½ pt)

Unit	Ingredient	Metric	Imperial
1	Avocado flesh (very ripe)	200 g	8 oz
¼	Tomato concassé	50 g	2 oz
¹⁄₁₆	Onion (finely diced)	12.5 g	1 oz
Flavourings	Garlic cloves (2 finely chopped)		
and	Lemon juice (2 tablespoons)		
seasonings	Chopped chives (1 tablespoon)		
	Tabasco (dash only)		
	Salt and milled black pepper		

Method

Slice the very ripe avocado/tomato flesh and place into a bowl with oil, lemon juice, seasoning and tabasco. Mash the contents (or rub through a coarse sieve) to form a soft mixture. Add garlic, onion, chives and mix well. Correct the seasoning, cover and store chilled until required.

7

Salads

Salads (or salades – French term) could be defined as preparations generally made up of cold ingredients. They may be simple or complex by nature and be cohered and flavoured using salad dressings, sauces, herbs and seasonings.

Quality salads, it is said, are a delight; inferior salads an abomination. The secrets of a perfect salad of whatever composition involve the selection of quality materials, correct blending methods and service procedures. A well prepared salad should always look cool, inviting, refreshing and attractive. The rules associated with salad making are outlined below:

Rules for Salad Making

1. Ingredients used should be of a first-class quality, in fresh condition and, when appropriate, seasonal.
2. Roots and coarse ribs should be removed along with withered or discoloured sections as part of normal preparation.
3. Washed ingredients should not be allowed to soak in water (unless necessary) but quickly washed, drained and dried. Over-storage in water could cause changes in texture/flavour and, in some cases, loss of water soluble nutrients (vitamins and minerals). However, ingredients must be washed thoroughly to remove any grit, dirt or insects. Sometimes certain ingredients are stored in a shallow tray of iced water to help maintain their crispness (e.g. fresh watercress).
4. Withered ingredients should be discarded as they impair appearance, flavour and texture.
5. Generally, lettuce leaves should be torn with the fingers and not cut/shredded with a knife, the latter can cause excessive bruising and some discolouration.
6. Generally, salads are best prepared just prior to service or as near to service time as is practically possible with fresh green salads usually prepared to order. All materials should be stored in a cool place, preferably in a sealed plastic-type container to retain flavour, colour and texture of the foods.
7. Dressings are best applied to tossed green/mixed salads at the last moment or on request by the customer. In the case of certain salads, the sauces/dressings may be applied at an earlier stage if a period of masceration is needed – e.g. coleslaw.

However, if the dressings are applied too far in advance, the salad appearance and texture can be impaired; for example, lettuce will wilt and become discoloured whilst other ingredients may lose moisture leading to salads having a watery appearance and softened texture.

8. Unless a recipe dictates otherwise, specific ingredients can be blanched and their strong flavours modified to prevent their dominating the taste of a salad. Typical examples include raw garlic, onion and peppers.

9. To wash drain/dry certain salad materials, particularly greens, a salad basket/clean cloths or modern salad preparation machine may be used. The ingredients are gently washed, drained and dried without any excessive bruising taking place. Salad dressings, especially oil-based, adhere more readily to well drained/dried food materials. As a rule salad materials should be cleaned/washed in *cold* water.

10. When salad materials *are* to be cut using a knife – e.g. chiffonnade of lettuce or sorrel, stainless steel knives are ideal as their steel counterparts will cause bruising and discolouration to many salad ingredients.

Preparing the Salads

Where a large traditional kitchen brigade operates, a member of the larder department under the direction of the Chef Garde-Manger is responsible for the preparation of all cold salads.

Salad Classification

Two categories of salad exist:

1. Plain, simple or single.
2. Mixed, compound, composite or complex.

1. Plain, Simple or Single Salads

These salads consist of two types:

(a) *Green salads* typically made up of green leaf ingredients.
(b) *Vegetable salads* comprise essentially of one main vegetable-type ingredient which dominates the overall flavour.

2. Mixed, Compound, Composite or Complex Salads

This group of salads are prepared from a combination of many ingredients which are cohered and flavoured using selected dressings and sauces. By character, these salads are more complex than the simple salads previously outlined. In many cases, their composition surrounds a base commodity to which other ingredients are added.

Special Characteristics of Compound Salads

1. The food materials used are often cut into selected shapes – julienne, macédoine, paysanne, jardinière, thus providing a variety of shapes and designs.
2. Compound salads are dressed dome-shaped in crystal glass bowls, wooden salad bowls or flatter shaped 'saladiers' which allow room for border garnishing often associated with this type of product.

The place of salads on the menu and contemporary trends

To state categorically where salads are or should be served on the menu is difficult as both types of salads are used in many different ways. The list below provides some indication of how salads may be featured on menus.

(a) As a side salad to accompany cold meats, grills/roasts/frys of butcher's meats, poultry, game, fish and shellfish.
(b) As part of an *hors d'oeuvre varié* selection.
(c) As a *single hors d'oeuvre* starter.
(d) As part of a salad range offered alongside *cold buffet items*.
(e) As part of a salad range offered alongside a *hot carvery*.
(f) As a refresher of the palate between courses.
(g) A recent development within the realms of the 'new cuisine' is the emergence of the combination of hot and cold ingredients as a type of salad starter or single hors d'oeuvre. Examples include *roasted pigeon with tossed mixed salad* or sautéd scallops with artichoke bottoms and tossed mixed salad.

Summary

Because salads are an excellent source of health giving nutrients (essentially vitamins/ minerals) and also roughage, they are a constant feature on the modern menu. They meet the needs of informed consumers who demand health giving foods for a fitter life. Furthermore, salad ingredients provide the creative cook with an extensive range of colourful and tasty ingredients with which to please and delight the prospective diner.

SIMPLE SALADS   Salades Simples

Examples of Simple Salads: Ingredients for 4 Portions. Amounts in Relation to the Main Ingredient

Name	Unit	Ingredient	Metric	Imperial
Salade d'Asperges (Asparagus salad)	1 ¼	Cooked asparagus Lemon dressing Trim stems, arrange asparagus neatly in a service dish, coat with lemon dressing. Season to taste	300 g 75 ml	12 oz 3 fl oz
Salade de Betterave (Beetroot salad)	1 ¼ ⅛	Cooked beetroot Vinaigrette Onion brunoise Cut beetroot into desired shape (bâtons, dice), mix with remainder of ingredients. Arrange neatly in a service dish. Season to taste	200 g 50 ml 25 g	8 oz 2 fl oz 1 oz
Salade de Céleri-rave (Celeriac salad)	1 ¼	Celeriac Mustard cream dressing Wash and peel celeriac, cut into julienne. Combine with dressing and season to taste. Arrange neatly in a service dish	200 g 50 ml	8 oz 2 fl oz

Name	*Unit*	*Ingredient*	*Metric*	*Imperial*
Salade de Champignons (Mushroom salad)	1	Button mushrooms	200 g	8 oz
	¼	Lemon dressing	50 ml	2 fl oz
		Chopped parsley		
		Wash mushrooms thoroughly, drain well. Slice thinly and mix with remainder of ingredients. Season to taste. Arrange neatly in a service dish		
Salade de Concombres (Cucumber salad)	1	Cucumber	200 g	8 oz
	¼	Vinaigrette	50 ml	2 fl oz
		Wash and peel cucumber, slice thinly and arrange in a service dish, coat with vinaigrette, season to taste		
Salade d'Endive Belge (Belgium endive salad)	1	Belgium Endive	200 g	8 oz
	¼	Vinaigrette	50 ml	2 fl oz
		Wash endive thoroughly, drain well. Arrange leaves in a service dish, coat with vinaigrette, season to taste		
Salade d'Endive (Curly chicory salad)	1	Curly chicory	200 g	8 oz
	¼	Vinaigrette	50 ml	2 fl oz
		Wash chicory thoroughly, drain well. Arrange leaves in a service dish, coat with vinaigrette. Season to taste		
Salade de Haricot Vert (Green bean salad)	1	Cooked green beans	300 g	12 oz
	¼	Vinaigrette	75 ml	3 fl oz
		Fine herbs (chopped)		
		Arrange beans in a service dish, coat with vinaigrette and sprinkle with fine herbs. Season to taste		
Salade de Pomme de Terre (Potato salad)	1	Cooked potato	300 g	12 oz
	¼	Mayonnaise	75 ml	3 fl oz
	⅙	Vinaigrette	50 ml	2 fl oz
	⅙	Chopped onions or chives	50 g	2 oz
		Chopped parsley		
		Cut potatoes into dice, combine with vinaigrette, chopped onion or chives and leave to stand for approximately 30 minutes. Combine with mayonnaise and season to taste. Arrange in a service dish, sprinkle with chopped parsley		

Name	Unit	Ingredient	Metric	Imperial
Salade de Tomate	1	Skinned tomatoes	300 g	12 oz
(Tomato salad)	¼	Vinaigrette or garlic dressing	75 ml	3 fl oz
	⅙	Chopped onion	50 g	2 fl oz
		Chopped parsley		
		Slice tomatoes and arrange neatly in a service dish, add chopped onion and coat with dressing. Season to taste, sprinkle with chopped parsley		

N.B.   Other simple salads may be prepared using single salad items. The dressings used may be varied and served separately according to individual taste.

Common examples of these salads are:

Lettuce Salad	Salade de Laitue
Heart of Lettuce Salad	Salade de Coeur de Laitue
Sorrel Salad	Salade d'Oseille
Cos Lettuce Salad	Salade de Romaine

Compound Salads
Fruit-based Compound Salads

Salades Composées

EXOTIC SALAD

Salade Exotique

Yield: 4 portions

Unit	Ingredient	Metric	Imperial
1	Melon balls (ripe)	200 g	8 oz
¼	Pineapple (fresh: diced)	50 g	2 oz
¼	Avocado (ripe: prepared sliced)	50 g	2 oz
¼	Prawns (fresh: peeled)	50 g	2 oz
	2 Oranges (peeled: segmented)		
	4 Small crisp lettuce leaves		
	4 Prawns (in shell)		
	1 Tablespoon lemon juice		
	Curried cream dressing (mild) *see* p. 85★		

★ Sufficient curried cream dressing to flavour, moisten and lightly cohere.

Method

Place all prepared fruits into a salad bowl, add lemon juice and blend well with the contents. Now mix in the fresh prawns and cohere with the mild curried cream dressing. Dress the salad mixture on small crisp lettuce leaves, decorate with prawns in shell and serve fresh.

JAPONAISE SALAD   Salade Japonaise

Yield: 4 portions

Unit	Ingredient	Metric	Imperial
1	Tomato concassé	200 g	8 oz
1	Pineapple (fresh: medium diced)	200 g	8 oz
	2 Lettuce hearts		
	Lemon juice (fresh 2 tablespoons)		
Seasonings	Orange juice (fresh 2 tablespoons)		
and	Caster sugar (1 level teaspoon)		
flavourings	Salt and milled pepper		
	Acidulated cream*		

* Sufficient to lightly moisten and flavour.

Method

Break lettuce hearts into leaves, wash and drain well. Marinade tomato concassé with 1 tablespoon lemon juice, caster sugar and seasoning. Macerate pineapple with the remaining lemon and orange juices. Carefully combine tomato and pineapple preparations. Dress the salad on the lettuce leaves and moisten with acidulated cream on service.

WALDORF SALAD   Salade Waldorf

Yield: 4 portions

Unit	Ingredient	Metric	Imperial
1	Celeriac (peeled: diced)*	200 g	8 oz
1	Russet apples (prepared: diced)	200 g	8 oz
	8 Walnut halves		
	4 Lettuce leaves (prepared: crisp)		
	2 Tablespoons lemon juice		
	Mayonnaise to flavour and cohere**		

* If celeriac is not available replace with celery.
** Sufficient mayonnaise to flavour and cohere the ingredients.

Method

Place prepared celeriac/apple into a salad bowl and flavour with lemon juice. Add the mayonnaise and thoroughly blend-in to cohere the contents. Dress on lettuce leaves, decorate with walnuts and serve fresh.

FLORIDA SALAD

Salade Florida

Yield: 4 portions

Ingredients	Method
4 Oranges (peeled: segmented) 2 Lettuce hearts (prepared: quartered) Orange zest (julienne: blanched) Acidulated cream to moisten*	Loosely break lettuce hearts and arrange onto service dish Dress with oranges, moisten with acidulated cream, garnish with julienne of blanched orange zest and serve fresh

* Sufficient acidulated cream to lightly moisten and flavour.

MIMOSA SALAD

Salade Mimosa

Yield: 4 portions

Ingredients	Method
2 Oranges (peeled: segmented) 1 Banana (peeled: sliced) Small bunch grapes (peeled: pipped) 2 Lettuce hearts (quartered: washed, drained) Squeeze lemon juice Fresh cream to moisten*	Place orange segments, sliced banana, prepared grapes into a bowl. Moisten the fruit mixture with lemon juice, fresh cream and carefully blend together. Arrange in presentation dish and surround with quarters of lettuce heart. Serve fresh

* Sufficient to lightly cohere and moisten the ingredients.

Leaf-based compound salads
MIXED GREEN SALAD

Salade Verte

Yield: 4 portions

Unit	Ingredient	Metric	Imperial
1	Green salad leaves (prepared crisp, e.g. round, cos, iceberg lettuce, curled chicory, Belgium endive and watercress)*	200 g	8 oz
Flavourings	Vinaigrette/French or herb dressing to moisten and flavour Clove of garlic (lightly crushed)		

* Any combination of green salad leaves are used to produce an interesting salad. Larger lettuce leaves are carefully torn to even sizes.

Method

Rub the inside surface of a salad bowl (preferably wooden) with the crushed garlic clove to introduce the garlic oil. *On service* place the salad leaves (excepting watercress) into the bowl and moisten with dressing. Using a salad spoon and fork gently toss the leaves and lightly pass through the dressing. Present for service garnished with dressed watercress leaves (i.e. watercress leaves lightly coated with vinaigrette).

Examples of Salads Derived from Mixed Green Salad: Added Ingredients to 1 Unit, i.e. 200 g (8 oz) Mixed Green Salad

Name	Unit	Ingredient	Metric	Imperial
French salad	½	Tomatoes (sliced)	100 g	4 oz
	¼	Cucumber (sliced)	50 g	2 oz
Salade Française	¼	Cooked beetroot (sliced)	50 g	2 oz
		2 Eggs (hard-boiled and quartered)		
		As for mixed green salad but use lettuce only moistened and flavoured with French dressing. Present garnished with dressed tomato, cucumber, beetroot and quartered hard-boiled egg		
Mixed salad	½	Tomatoes (sliced)	100 g	4 oz
Salade panachée	¼	Cucumber (sliced)	50 g	2 oz
	¼	Cooked beetroot	50 g	2 oz
	¼	Peppers (sliced)	50 g	2 oz
		4 Radishes (sliced)		
		As for mixed green salad. Decorate with the above ingredients previously moistened/flavoured with vinaigrette		
		N.B. Other suitable vegetable salad ingredients can be used in this salad		

N.B.   For the above salads dressing may be offered separately.

Meat/Fish Based Compound Salads

MEAT SALAD   Salade de Viandes

Yield: 4 portions

Unit	Ingredient	Metric	Imperial
1	Cooked meats (diced or strips)*	200 g	8 oz
½	Tomato concassé	100 g	4 oz
¼	Fine French beans (whole cooked al denté)	50 g	2 oz
¼	Button mushrooms (raw and sliced)	50 g	2 oz
⅛	Gherkins (strips or slices)	25 g	1 oz
Flavourings and seasonings	Fine herbs		
	Garlic dressing to moisten and flavour		
	Salt and milled black pepper		

* A variety of assorted cooked meats can be used, e.g. chicken, beef, ham, tongue, duck, turkey, etc.

Method

Place prepared meats, vegetables, gherkins, chopped herbs in a salad bowl and season. Add sufficient garlic dressing to moisten and flavour. Dress in presentation dish and serve fresh.

SEAFOOD SALAD

Salade de Fruits de Mer

Yield: 4 portions

Unit	Ingredient	Metric	Imperial
1	Cooked white fish (prepared: flaked)*	100 g	4 oz
1	Cooked salmon (prepared: flaked)	100 g	4 oz
½	Prawns	50 g	2 oz
½	Cooked scallops (sliced)	50 g	2 oz
½	Cooked scampi (sliced)	50 g	2 oz
½	White crab meat (flaked)	50 g	2 oz
½	Cucumber (peeled, diced)	50 g	2 oz
	4 Crisp lettuce/sorrel leaves (shredded)		
Flavourings and seasonings	Lemon dressing to moisten and flavour Salt and milled black pepper to taste		

* Halibut, turbot or white fish of a similar firm texture are ideal.

Method

Combine together fish, shellfish, cucumber and shredded lettuce carefully. Moisten/flavour with lemon dressing and season to taste. Dress in presentation dish and serve fresh.

Farinaceous-based Compound Salads

PASTA SALAD

Salade de Pâtes

Yield: 200 g (8 oz)

Unit	Ingredient	Metric	Imperial
1	Cooked pasta shapes (e.g. shells, wheels)*	100 g	4 oz
½	Tomates concassées	50 g	2 oz
½	Mushrooms (button/whole/blanched)	50 g	2 oz
Flavouring and seasonings	Herb dressing to moisten and flavour Salt and milled black pepper		

* Small cooked pasta shapes are ideal for this salad. A combination can be used.

Method

Combine all ingredients carefully and season to taste. Dress in presentation dish and serve.

Extensions/Variations of Pasta Salad: Added Ingredients in Relation to 1 Unit, i.e. 100 g (4 oz) Cooked Pasta

Name	Unit	Ingredient	Metric	Imperial
Pasta and meat salad	¼	Cooked ham (cut in strips)	25 g	1 oz
Salade de pâtes et viandes	¼	Salami (cut in strips) Combine with pasta salad	25 g	1 oz

Name	Unit	Ingredient		Metric	Imperial
Pasta and Shellfish salad	¼	Cooked mussels (fresh)		25 g	1 oz
	¼	Shelled prawns		25 g	1 oz
Salad de pâtes et fruits de Mer		Combine with pasta salad			

RICE SALAD   Salade de Riz

Yield: 200 g (8 oz)

Unit	Ingredient	Metric	Imperial
1	Rice (long-grain/cooked)★	100 g	4 oz
½	Cooked ham/salami (diced)	50 g	2 oz
¼	Peppers (prepared: diced)	25 g	1 oz
¼	Tomato concassé	25 g	1 oz
¼	Cooked sweetcorn	25 g	1 oz
Flavouring and seasonings	Vinaigrette to moisten and flavour Salt and milled black pepper		

★ Plain boiled or cold pilaff ideal for the base for rice salad.

Method

Combine all ingredients carefully and season to taste. Dress in presentation dish and serve.

Extensions/Variations of Rice Salad: Added Ingredients in Relation to 1 Unit, i.e. 100 g (4 oz) Cooked Rice

Name	Unit	Ingredient	Metric	Imperial
Mixed rice salad	½	Hazelnuts	50 g	2 oz
Salad de riz mélangé	¼	Sultanas	25 g	1 oz
	¼	Pineapple (diced)	25 g	1 oz
		Combine ingredients with basic rice salad		
Rice and bean salad	½	Red kidney beans (cooked)	50 g	2 oz
Salad de riz et haricots	¼	Flageolet beans (cooked)	25 g	1 oz
trois	¼	Lima beans (cooked)	25 g	1 oz
		Combine ingredients with basic rice salad		

Vegetable-based Compound Salads
PEPPER SALAD   Salade de Poivrons

Yield: 4 portions

Unit	Ingredient	Metric	Imperial
1	Raw capsicums (red, yellow, green: prepared)	200 g	8 oz
	Cut into julienne		
½	Tomatoes (skinned and de-seeded, cut into strips)	100 g	4 oz
¼	Onion rings (small and blanched)	50 g	2 oz
Flavourings and	2 Garlic cloves (finely chopped)		
seasonings	Lemon dressing to moisten		
	Salt and milled black pepper		

Method

Place peppers, tomatoes, onion rings and garlic into a bowl. Moisten with lemon dressing and season to taste. Chill and macerate for 30 minutes. Dress in presentation dish and serve fresh.

SCOTTISH STYLED CELERIAC SALAD   Salade de Celeri-rave Écossaise

Yield: 4 portions

Unit	Ingredient	Metric	Imperial
1	Celeriac (prepared julienne and blanched)	200 g	8 oz
½	Smoked salmon (cut into fine strips)	100 g	4 oz
½	Artichoke bottoms (cooked, cold, sliced)	100 g	4 oz
Flavourings and	Garlic dressing to moisten		
seasonings	Squeeze lemon juice		
	Salt and milled black pepper		

Method

Place celeriac, smoked salmon, artichoke bottoms into a bowl. Moisten with lemon juice, garlic dressing and season to taste. Chill and macerate for approximately 30 minutes. Dress in presentation dish and serve fresh.

VEGETABLE SALAD   Salade de Légumes or Salade Russe

Yield: 4 portions

Unit	Ingredient	Metric	Imperial
1	Carrots ⎰ Cut into macédoine, bâtons or julienne,	100 g	4 oz
½	Turnips ⎱ cooked refreshed to al denté	50 g	2 oz
½	Green peas ⎰ Cooked, refreshed to al denté	50 g	2 oz
½	French beans ⎱	50 g	2 oz
½	Sweetcorn (kernels)	50 g	2 oz
Flavourings and	Vinaigrette (1 tablespoon)		
seasonings	Mayonnaise (thick)★		
	Salt and milled black pepper		

★ Sufficient mayonnaise to bind and flavour, approximately 125 ml (¼ pt).

Method

Place all vegetables (cooked) into a salad bowl and mix well. Flavour with vinaigrette, season and cohere with mayonnaise. Dress in presentation dish and serve fresh.

POTATO AND WATERCRESS SALAD   Salade Cressonnière

Yield: 4 portions

Unit	Ingredient	Metric	Imperial
1	Potatoes (small: cooked)*	400 g	1 lb
⅛	White wine (medium)	50 ml	2 fl oz
	Watercress (2 bunches)		
	Hard boiled eggs (1 sliced)		
Flavourings and	Vinaigrette to moisten		
seasonings	Chopped parsley: chervil		
	Salt and milled black pepper		

* May be boiled in their skins, allowed to cool then peeled; or peeled, boiled and allowed to cool.

Method

Cut the potatoes into thin slices whilst still *warm*. Wash and pick the watercress leaves. Place potatoes, watercress leaves, parsley, chervil, salt and pepper into presentation dish and combine carefully to form a pyramid. Add wine and vinaigrette to moisten. Decorate with slices of hard boiled egg. Serve immediately.

MIXED POTATO SALAD   Salade de Pommes de Terre Melangé

Yield: 4 portions

Unit	Ingredient	Metric	Imperial
1	Potatoes (small: cooked)*	200 g	8 oz
½	Celery (small slices)	100 g	4 oz
½	Dessert apples (peeled: diced)	100 g	4 oz
Flavourings and	Yoghurt dressing (*see* p. 87) to		
seasonings	moisten		
	Chives, tarragon, chervil parsley		
	(all chopped)		
	Squeeze lemon juice		
	Salt and cayenne pepper		

* May be boiled and allowed to cool in their skins, or peeled, boiled and cooled.

Method

Cut the potatoes into 1 cm (½ in) dice and place into a bowl. Add celery, diced dessert apple, chopped herbs, salt and cayenne. Flavour with lemon juice and cohere contents thoroughly but carefully with the yoghurt dressing (mayonnaise-based). Correct seasoning, dress in presentation dish and serve fresh.

NIÇOISE SALAD
Salade Niçoise

Yield: 4 portions

Unit	Ingredient	Metric	Imperial
1	French beans (cold, cooked al denté	200 g	8 oz
½	Tomatoes (skinned, de-seeded and quartered)	100 g	4 oz
½	Potatoes (cooked: diced)*	100 g	4 oz
¼	Tuna fish (tinned: flaked)	50 g	2 oz
Flavourings and seasonings	Garlic dressing to moisten Anchovy fillets (drained) Capers (drained) Stoned olives Salt and milled black pepper		

* May be boiled in their skins, allowed to cool then peeled, or peeled, boiled and allowed to cool.

Method

Place French beans, potatoes, tomatoes, tuna fish, salt, pepper into a salad bowl and mix together carefully. Now moisten and flavour with garlic dressing. Dress in presentation dish, decorate with anchovy fillets, stoned olives, capers and serve fresh.

COLESLAW

Yield: 4 portions

Unit	Ingredient	Metric	Imperial
1	White cabbage	200 g	8 oz
¼	Carrot (grated large cut)	50 g	2 oz
⅛	Onion (shredded)	25 g	1 oz
Flavourings and seasonings	White vinegar (1 tablespoon) Pinch caster sugar Thick mayonnaise to bind* Salt and milled black pepper		

* Sufficient mayonnaise to bind and flavour, approximately 125 ml (¼ pt). Yoghurt dressing (*see* p. 87) can be used as an alternative to mayonnaise.

Method

Quarter the cabbage and remove the centre stalk. Wash, drain and cut the cabbage into fine shreds. Place shredded cabbage, shredded onion and grated carrot into a salad bowl. Moisten with vinegar, add caster sugar, seasoning and mix together well. Add sufficient thick mayonnaise to bind and flavour. Dress in presentation dish and serve fresh.

Hot (Warm) Salads

SALAD OF MUSHROOMS   Salade des Champignons

Yield: 4 portions

Unit	Ingredient	Metric	Imperial
1	Lettuce leaves (prepared/crisp)	400 g	1 lb
½	Mushrooms (prepared sliced)*	200 g	8 oz
	2 Tablespoons cooking oil		
Flavourings and	Clove garlic (prepared/chopped)		
seasonings	Fine herbs (fresh/chopped)		
	Sour cream dressing to flavour/ garnish		
	Salt and milled black pepper		

* A variety of cultivated and edible wild mushrooms can be used.

Method

Shred the fresh crisp lettuce and put aside. Heat cooking oil in shallow fry-pan, add lettuce and toss for a few moments only to warm and slightly soften. Remove, drain over fry-pan and place onto service dish/dishes.

Add mushrooms and garlic to the hot fry-pan, season with salt/pepper, add fine herbs and toss for a few minutes until lightly cooked. Place hot ingredients onto the warm lettuce, decorate with a thread of sour cream dressing and serve immediately.

N.B.   This salad must be prepared, cooked and served to order for best results.

SALAD OF CHICKEN LIVERS   Salade aux Foies de Volaille

Yield: 4 portions

Unit	Ingredient	Metric	Imperial
1	Salad leaves (small prepared crisp)*	400 g	1 lb
½	Chicken livers (prepared)	200 g	8 oz
⅛	Lean bacon (lardons/blanched)	50 g	2 oz
	2 Tablespoons cooking oil		
	2 Tablespoons wine vinegar		
Flavourings and	1 Clove garlic (prepared chopped)		
seasonings	Vinaigrette to moisten and flavour		
	Salt and milled black pepper		

* A variety can be used, e.g. lettuce, raddichio, endive, etc.

Method

Lightly moisten and flavour the combined salad leaves with vinaigrette and place onto presentation dish/dishes. Put aside.

Remove any gall bladder and stained parts from chicken livers, halve and lightly season with salt and milled black pepper. Heat cooking oil in sauté pan, add garlic, blanched lardons, chicken livers and cook briskly for a short time until sealed brown and just cooked (livers soft inside).

Remove hot ingredients from the pan (use perforated spoon to drain) and place onto the dressed salad leaves. Deglaze the pan with wine vinegar and pour over the salad to moisten and flavour. Serve immediately.

N.B.   This salad must be prepared, cooked and served to order for best results.

8

Cold Hors D'Oeuvre

Hors d'oeuvre can be grouped as *hot* or *cold* varieties. Generally the cold selections feature on menus more frequently than their hot counterparts. The purpose of hors d'oeuvre on the menu is to stimulate the diner's appetite during the early stages of the meal. Foods prepared for service as hors d'oeuvres are characterised by their size (small portions), appearance (attractive) and taste (often piquant and/or spicy flavour). They are eaten in proportionately small quantities and used as appetisers to stimulate the flow of gastric juices.

They appear as starter courses on the bill of fare and/or as preliminary items before the meal begins, e.g. cocktail canapés served with pre-meal drinks. Cold hors d'oeuvre preparations are the responsibility of the 'chef d'oeuvrier', a member of the chef garde-manger's larder team.

N.B. A recent development within 'nouvelle cuisine' is the combination of hot and cold ingredients as hors d'oeuvre items, namely hot salads. Typical examples include:

(a) Slices of underdone roasted pigeon breast served hot, garnished by mixed green salad with French dressing.
(b) Sautéd langoustine/sliced artichoke bottoms garnished with mixed green salad and raddicchio dressed with vinaigrette.

Other examples of hot salads are featured on p. 104.

Cold Hors d'Oeuvre Classification

The classifications used for cold hors d'oeuvres are at first sight difficult to comprehend but, in essence, their descriptions become self-explanatory:

1. *Single* hors d'oeuvre comprise essentially of one main item per portion which is served individually in a plain form with a garnish, dressing and/or accompaniment. Single hors d'oeuvre generally take the form of essentially one food item such as smoked salmon or chilled melon, however compound items can appear on menus as single hors d'oeuvre choices, e.g. Salade Niçoise.
2. *Varied* dressed hors d'oeuvres comprise essentially of a wide selection of hors d'oeuvre which may include both *simple* and *compound* items including salads (see Chapter 7) which make up the choice of hors d'oeuvre varié.

3. *Cocktail canapés* are special hors d'oeuvre which form a small meal before the main meal, i.e. preliminary tasters which are generally served with pre-meal drinks. Accordingly, with their style and presentation they may be referred to as hors d'oeuvre moscovite, zakouski or hors d'oeuvre à la russe. Generally they surround a centre-piece of some type usually determined by the canapés being produced (*see* below for details). Often they are served as part of a finger buffet selection.

4. *Crudités* comprise a selection of raw vegetables cut into small portions served with well flavoured savoury dips. Examples include raw cucumber, carrots, cauliflower, celery, celeriac, mushrooms, fennel, capsicums, etc., with garlic, avocado and/or cheese dip, etc. (*see* pp. 88–90).

Typical Characteristics of Cold Hors D'Oeuvre Selections

Appearance – varied shapes/dimensions, dainty and neat, colourful, simply garnished, cleanly finished, balanced display and layout for presentation. Appropriately served with the applicable centre-pieces and accompaniments.

Flavour – varied flavours of spicy, piquant and delicate natures designed to stimulate the flow of the gastric juices.

Texture – contrasting by way of the mixed commodities and production procedures adopted in the selection and preparation of the hors d'oeuvres.

N.B.   Hors d'oeuvre of all varieties provide an interesting way of utilising cooked or left-over foods alongside raw commodities.

Service of Hors d'Oeuvre

All varieties may be served on both luncheon and dinner menus. Certain hors d'oeuvre are preferably suited to luncheon and dinner respectively due to economic factors and the pertinent menu planning criteria.

Service Styles Used

(a) *Plated* – in simple or varied form. Other dishes than plates are used for the presentation of hors d'oeuvre items, e.g. seafood shells, specifically designed dishes from which the food is eaten.

(b) *Tray or trolley* – generally used for a selection of varied items, i.e. hors d'oeuvre varié. The tray and trolley can be specifically designed for the presentation of hors d'oeuvre, or made up from ravier dishes.

(c) *Silver/flats* – usually employed for the service of good quality single hors d'oeuvre, e.g. saumon fumé and cocktail canapés.

Cocktail Canapés/Finger Hors d'Oeuvre

These items consist of tiny portions produced essentially from savoury foods which are attractively presented upon various shaped bases made-up from breads, biscuits and pastry cases, etc. They are attractively decorated and generally lightly coated with aspic (although sometimes they are left plain). The reasons for applying the aspic:

(i) To produce an *attractive* appearance, i.e. clear gloss and shine.

(ii) To maintain a *fresh* product appearance by reducing the effects of moisture loss, shrinkage and product discolouration during service.

(iii) To enhance the overall flavour by sealing-in the food's natural juices and flavours.

Bases Used

The bases used can always be described as being tiny or petite. They are prepared in many shapes, e.g. rounds, triangles, squares, oblongs, diamonds, etc., to provide contrasting design. Similar principles of production apply as with hors d'oeuvre in that a wide variety of foods, flavours, colours, textures and shapes are employed in order to provide well-balanced selections for service to the customer. The list below provides examples of the bases (cases) used for the production of canapés.

Bread – plain buttered breads, toasted/fried breads, e.g. croûtes.
Biscuits – savoury.
Choux pastry cases – carolines (small c-shaped eclairs), duchesses (tiny eclairs), petite choux buns.
Pastry bases – short/puff pastries into bouchées, cannelons, etc.
Barquettes – *croustades* – *tartlettes* – are shaped patty tin moulds which are lined with a selected pastry, baked blind and later filled with selected ingredients. The barquettes are boat-shaped, whereas the other two are round.
Cassolettes – prepared by deep frying batter, moulded on the outside of a ladle bowl (preferably using an iron ladle).

Special Types

Canapés à la russe/Russian style

Decorated aspic-coated small canapés on various bases, presented on a silver flat covered with a cloth serviette or dish paper. A hedgehog impaled with morsels of cold food on cocktail sticks (e.g. grapefruit hedgehog) used as a centrepiece.

Hors d'oeuvre Moscovite

A classic type of finger hors d'oeuvre presented on a flat mirrored with aspic and surrounding a centrepiece of 'set Russian salad bordered with chopped aspic jelly'. The surrounding finger hors d'oeuvre are small, neat and appetising and may be coated with chaud-froid sauce and aspic glaze, or plainly with clear aspic.

Typically hors d'oeuvre Moscovite are produced using the following type of products:

(a) Stuffed eggs
(b) Stuffed tomatoes
(c) Salmon/ham cornets
(d) Savoury bouchées
(e) Savoury barquettes/tartelettes
(f) Savoury cannelons (puff pastry horns)
(g) Savoury choux pastry items, namely duchesses and carolines.

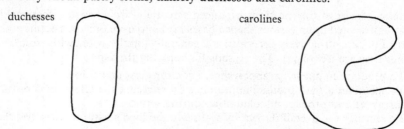

duchesses   carolines

Hot Hors d'Oeuvre

Over the years, the hot variety of hors d'oeuvre or hot starter courses have increased in popularity. They can be served as a single item or in a varied presentation, whichever, the basic rules applying to taste, colour, shape, texture, variety and presentation apply with these hot products. As with cold canapés, hot hors d'oeuvre can be offered as a preliminary appetizer with drinks before a meal commences, as a menu course, or in the form of a hot finger buffet. Typical examples of cooked items used as hot hors d'oeuvre include small portions of scampi-goujonettes-fritots – savoury croquettes/beignets-bouchées-bacon rolls-meat balls-canapés accompanied with selected sauces, garnishes and dips. Popular hot vegetable starters such as globe artichokes, asparagus and corn on the cob could also be included in the list.

Traditionally, many of the entrées used in *modern* cookery as main items were presented as small hot hors d'oeuvre but this practice is seldom used with modern functions.

Notes on Hors d'Oeuvre Varié Presentation

Choosing items for inclusion as part of the hors d'oeuvre varié selection requires careful planning if the total choice offered is to provide an interesting, attractive, appetising, economic and well-balanced product. Although hors d'oeuvre varié provides the chef with an ideal means of utilising left-over cold food, the temptation to over-employ such foods, irrespective of planning guidelines, must be resisted.

Guidelines/Hors D'Oeuvre Varié Selections/Preparations

The characteristics relating to appearance, texture, flavour, quality and quantities outlined on p. 107 can be attained by using the guidelines below:

Colour (variety/harmony)	Use basic food commodities of differing colours.
	Use varied dressings/sauces of dissimilar appearance.
	Use food garnishing materials of contrasting colours.
	Arrange the individual products to provide a mixed harmonious colour scheme.
Texture contrasts	Use varied base commodities of differing textures.
	Use different dressings/sauces of contrasting consistencies.
	Use food garnishing materials of differing textures.
	Use cooked and raw commodities to provide contrast.
Flavour (variety/contrasts)	Use a wide variety of base commodities for mixed flavours.
	Use a number of dressings/sauces of distinctly piquant and varied flavours.
	Use different seasonings/spices of distinctly varying flavours.
Quantity shape/form	Prepare the ingredients small, dainty, uniform and neat.
	Use varied shapes and forms (cuts and shapes).
	Offer only small portions of each hors d'oeuvre.

Arrange the individual hors d'oeuvre for display in such a way as to provide colour, variety, harmony with contrasting shapes and forms.

Overall balance and garnish

Garnish the total hors d'oeuvre presentation *after* the *whole* selection has been arranged. *Do not* garnish each individual hors d'oeuvre in isolation but garnish the whole picture.

Use plain/simple garnishing techniques/materials for a neat clean finish. *Do not* over-elaborate.

It is inadvisable to use lettuce bases or shredded lettuce border decoration and the like, but rather allow each product its own individual impact (lettuce and the like wilt very quickly, adversely affecting appearance and texture).

FRUIT COCKTAILS   Cocktail des Fruits

These cocktails may be prepared using a selected fruit or various combinations of fruit. The fruit juice is always saved and added to the completed dish. It is usual to serve fruit cocktails ready portioned in either coupes or glasses. To add interest, various liquors may be added, e.g. Port, Crème de Menthe, etc. These cocktails should be served chilled.

Preparation of Fruits

Orange and Grapefruit

Cut top and bottom off the fruit, place onto a chopping board. Using a sharp, stainless steel knife remove skin/pith and cut between membranes to remove individual segments; squeeze remaining skin and membrane to extract juice.

Melon (ripe)

Halve the melon and remove the seeds. Cut flesh into neat dice or gouge out melon balls using a round vegetable scoop (*see* p. 18).

Other Fruits

Remove outside skin and centre core or stone, when necessary. Cut fruit into neat dice or slices.

FRUIT COCKTAILS   Cocktail des Fruits

Yield: 4 portions

Ingredients	Preparation
Selected fruit and juice (see chart below) Selected liquor (optional/to flavour)	As indicated above

Method

Cut fruit into segments or dice, arrange neatly in service coupe or glass. Sprinkle with fruit juice and selected liquor if required. Decorate with a maraschino cherry. Serve ice cold.
  N.B.   It is usual to serve sugar separately.

Examples of Fruit Cocktails for 4 Portions. Oranges and Grapefruit Amounts Indicate Quantity of Individual Fruits, not Weights. Fruit Should be Segmented or Diced as Indicated Above

Menu term	Ingredients	Preparation
Florida cocktail	2 Oranges	Segmented
Cocktail Florida	2 Grapefruits	
	4 Maraschino cherries to decorate	Left whole
Grapefruit cocktail	4 Grapefruits	Segmented
Cocktail de pamplemousse	4 Maraschino cherries to decorate	Left whole
Orange cocktail	4 Oranges	Segmented
Cocktail d'orange	4 Maraschino cherries to decorate	Left whole
Mixed fruit cocktail	2 Oranges	Segmented
Cocktail des fruits melangé	1 Grapefruit	
	Pineapple (150 g/6 oz) prepared	Diced
	Other fruits may be used	
Exotic fruit cocktail	1 Grapefruit	Segmented
Cocktail des fruits exotique	1 Orange	
	1 Kiwi Fruit	Peeled/sliced
	Mango (100 g/4 oz) prepared	Diced
	Melon (100 g/4 oz) prepared	Diced/scooped balls
	Kirsch to flavour	
Melon cocktail	Melon (400 g/1 lb) prepared	Diced/scooped balls
Cocktail de melon	4 Maraschino cherries to decorate	Left whole
Melon cocktail with crème de menthe	Melon (400 g/1 lb) prepared	Scooped balls/diced
Cocktail de melon au crème de menthe	Creme de Menthe to flavour	
Melon cocktail with mandarine napoleon	Melon (400 g/1 lb) prepared	Scooped balls/diced
Cocktail de melon au mandarine napoleon	Mandarine napoleon to flavour	
Melon cocktail with port	Melon (400 g/1 lb) prepared	Scooped balls/diced
Cocktail de melon au porto	Port to flavour	

Menu term	*Ingredients*	*Preparation*
Melon and prawn cocktail	Melon (400 g/1 lb) prepared	Scooped balls/diced
Cocktail de melon aux crevettes roses	Prawns (100 g/4 oz) peeled	Seasoned
	Cocktail sauce (100 ml/4 fl oz)	
	Combine melon and prawns with sauce. Serve in coupes or glasses. May be decorated with an individual prawn	

Fruit Juices

Fruit juices are often served on the menu as a first course. They may be purchased ready prepared or prepared fresh to order. The juice is extracted by hand or with an electrical juice extractor, it is served chilled in glasses without further sweetenings or flavourings. Typical examples are orange, grapefruit, grape and pineapple juices.

Tomato Juice   Jus de Tomates

Skin tomatoes (*see* p. 166), rub through a fine sieve, season with salt, mill pepper, Worcester sauce and a drop of tabasco. Serve chilled.

Vegetable Juices

These are becoming increasingly popular. The peeled vegetables are diced, liquidised and then rubbed through a fine sieve. These preparations are seasoned prior to service and served chilled. Typical examples are carrot juice, tomato and watercress juice, and vegetable juice combinations.

Grapefruit Halves   Demi Pamplemousse

Yield: Half a grapefruit per portion

Cut the fruit in half between top and base, remove pips and then the centre core. With a sharp, stainless steel knife cut around each segment to loosen it from its dividing membrane.

Chilled Grapefruit Halves   Demi Pamplemousse Frappé

Place prepared grapefruit halves in a coupe and decorate centre of fruit with a Maraschino cherry. Serve chilled and offer caster sugar separately.

Grapefruit Halves Grilled with Rum   Demi Pamplemousse Grillé au Rhum

Sprinkle prepared grapefruit halves with brown sugar and grill under salamander until light brown. Pour on rum (25 ml/1 fl oz) and serve hot.

Melon

Many varieties of melon are available, e.g. Charentais, Honeydew, Cantaloupe, etc. Availability and market price will often determine the variety used, as will consumer requirements.

Chilled Melon   Melon Frappé

Methods of service:

1. Wedges

Halve melon lengthways and remove seeds. Cut each half into wedges according to size required. Free the melon flesh from skin, cut flesh into even sized pieces and reform wedge. Decorate with a cocktail stick garnished with an orange slice representing a sail (melon boats). Alternatively, melon may be completely removed from skin and arranged for service. Serve chilled.

2. Melon Halves on Ice

Use medium size melons, cut in half, as applicable, and remove seeds. When served in this style, melon may be flavoured with a suitable liquor, e.g. Port, Crème de Menthe, etc. In these cases the liquor is poured into the half chilled melon prior to service and the product served on a bed of crushed ice.

3. Whole Melon

Proceed as for half melons, but use a smaller fruit, serve whole with top loosened to remove seeds and then replaced for service.

Melon with Parma Ham   Melon et Jambon de Parme

Take two wedges of chilled honeydew melon and remove the flesh from the skin. Place fruit on a service dish and accompany with very thin slices of Parma ham.

Alternatively, the melon may be wrapped in the Parma ham or sliced and placed on top of the thinly sliced plated ham.

VEGETABLES WITH VINAIGRETTE
(using cooked vegetables)   Légumes Vinaigrette

Yield: 4 portions

Unit	Ingredient	Metric	Imperial
1	Selected cooked vegetables/cold (cooked al denté/see chart below)	400 g	1 lb
¼	Vinaigrette	100 ml	4 fl oz
	Salt and pepper		

Method

Trim cooked vegetables as applicable and arrange neatly in suitable service dish.
Service 1: Season and lightly moisten vegetables with dressing.
Service 2: Serve vinaigrette and seasoning separately for customer preference.

Examples of Vegetables with Vinaigrette: Using the Above Formula

Name	Main vegetable	Preparation
Artichoke with Vinaigrette Artichauts Vinaigrette	4 Globe artichokes (small)	Once cooked, refresh and drain. Trim outer leaves. Carefully remove soft central purple leaves and put aside. Remove the inner fibrous choke and discard. Invert the soft purple leaves and replace into the artichoke to decorate the opening at the top. Service style 2
Asparagus with Vinaigrette Asperges Vinaigrette	Fresh asparagus	Once cooked, refresh and drain. Trim if required.

AVOCADO PEAR   Poire d'Avocat

Yield: 4 portions (2 avocado pears)

Unit	Ingredient	Metric	Imperial
	Avocado pears (ripe – see yield above)		
1	Selected filling	100 g	4 oz
½	Selected sauce	50 ml	2 fl oz
	Salt and pepper		

Method

Cut avocado pears in half from top to base, carefully remove the stone. Place avocado in service dish. Combine filling with sauce and season to taste. Place mixture in centre of avocado halves, serve as required.

N.B.   Avocado pears are best cut as required in order to prevent the flesh discolouring.

Examples of Avocardo Dishes Using the Above Formula.

Amounts for 4 portions

English term	Unit	Ingredient	Metric	Imperial	French term
Avocado with crab	1 ½	White crab meat Cocktail sauce (p. 86)	100 g 50 ml	4 oz 2 fl oz	Avocat au crabe
Avocado with prawns	1 ½	Prawns Cocktail sauce (p. 86)	100 g 50 ml	4 oz 2 fl oz	Avocat aux crevettes
Avocado vinaigrette	1	Vinaigrette dressing (p. 87) Vinaigrette dressing may be served separately	100 ml	4 fl oz	Avocat vinaigrette

N.B.   Other fillings and sauces may be used according to requirements.

EGG MAYONNAISE   Oeuf Mayonnaise

Yield: 4 portions

Ingredients	Preparation
4 Hard boiled eggs	Shelled/cold
Mayonnaise (150 ml/6 fl oz)	
4 Lettuce leaves	Washed, drained, dried
4 Anchovy fillets	Cut into strips
8 Capers	Drained
Salt and pepper	

Method

Shell hard boiled eggs and halve lengthwise. Place on service dish, season and coat with mayonnaise. Decorate with thin strips of anchovy fillets and capers arranged trellis fashion. Place lettuce leaves around the service dish to garnish.

Egg Mayonnaise with Prawns   Oeufs Mayonnaise aux Crevettes

As for egg mayonnaise, but omit anchovy fillets and capers. Decorate with 100 g (4 oz) shelled prawns.

Egg Mayonnaise with Smoked Salmon   Oeufs Mayonnaise au Saumon Fumé

As for egg mayonnaise, but omit anchovy fillets and capers. Decorate with 50 g (2 oz) smoked salmon cut into thin strips.

Stuffed Eggs   Oeufs Dur Farci

Yield: 4 portions

Ingredients	Preparation
4 Hard boiled eggs	Shelled/cold
Mayonnaise (50 ml/2 fl oz)	
Butter (25 g/1 oz)	Softened (pommade)
4 Lettuce leaves	Washed, drained, dried
Salt and pepper	

Method

Shell hard boiled eggs and halve lengthwise. Remove the egg yolk, sieve, combine with mayonnaise and butter to form a paste of piping consistency. Season to taste. Pipe back into the egg white using a piping bag and small star tube. Place eggs on service dish and surround with lettuce leaves.

  N.B. Stuffed eggs may be garnished with prawns, julienne of smoked salmon, etc. according to taste.

Stuffed Eggs with Tuna   Oeufs Dur Farci au Thon

Proceed as for stuffed eggs but combine 50 g (2 oz) of tuna purée with sieved egg yolk and mayonnaise mixture.

Curry-Flavoured Stuffed Eggs   Oeufs Dur Farci au Currie

Proceed as for stuffed eggs but flavour sieved egg and mayonnaise mixture with curry paste to taste.

Vegetables in the Greek Style   Légumes à la Grecque
Vegetables in the Portuguese Style   Légumes à la Portugaise

The terms 'à la Grecque' and 'à la Portugaise' when applied to vegetable hors d'oeuvres indicates that the vegetables have been cooked in a particular liquor. After completion of cooking the vegetables are allowed to cool in their respective liquors in order to absorb their flavours.

Preparation of cooking liquor à la Grecque
Yield: ½ (1 pt)
Cooking time: 10 minutes

Unit	Ingredient	Metric	Imperial
1	Water	½	1 pt
⅕	Oil	1 dl	4 fl oz
⅒	Lemon juice	50 ml	2 fl oz
	10 Corriander seeds		
	10 Peppercorns		
	Sprig parsley		
	Pinch thyme		
	Bay leaf		
	Salt to taste		

Method

Simmer all the ingredients together for 10 minutes, use as required. Do not strain.

Cooking vegetables à la Grecque:

Cover prepared vegetables with cooking liquor and simmer gently until cooked (al denté). Allow to cool, serve in cooking liquor.

Preparation of cooking liquor à la Portugaise
Yield: ½ (1 pt)
Cooking time: 5 minutes

Unit	Ingredient	Metric	Imperial
1	Tomato concassé (p. 164)	400 g	1 lb
¼	White wine	100 ml	4 fl oz
⅛	Oil	50 ml	2 fl oz
⅛	Onion brunoise	50 g	2 oz
1/16	Tomato purée	25 g	1 oz

Unit	Ingredient	Metric	Imperial
1	Clove crushed garlic Sprig thyme Bay leaf Salt and mill pepper		

Method

Sweat the onion and garlic in the oil until cooked. Add remainder of the ingredients and simmer for 4–5 minutes, season to taste and use as required. Do not strain.

Cooking vegetables à la Portugaise:

Cover prepared vegetables with cooking liquor and simmer gently until cooked (al denté). Allow to cool, serve in cooking liquor.

Examples of Vegetables Cooked à la Grecque and à la Portugaise

Vegetable	Preparation	Menu term
Artichoke bottoms	Prepare artichoke (p. 271), cut into quarters	Fonds d'artichauts à la grecque Fonds d'artichauts à la portugaise
Cauliflower	Cut into florets, blanch and refresh	Choufleur à la grecque Choufleur à la portugaise
Celeriac	Cut into batons, blanch and refresh	Célèri-rave à la grecque Célèri-rave à la portugaise
Celery	Cut into batons, blanch and refresh	Céleri à la grecque Céleri à la portugaise
Fennel	Blanch and refresh, cut into quarters	Fenouil à la grecque Fenouil à la portugaise
Leek	Blanch and refresh, cut into required shape, e.g. cylinders, strips	Poireaux à la grecque Poireaux à la portugaise
Button mushrooms	Trim stalks and peel, if necessary	Champignons à la grecque Champignons à la portugaise
Button onions	Blanch and refresh	Oignons Bouton à la grecque Oignons Bouton à la portugaise

Gulls Eggs — Oeufs de Mouette

Small brown speckled eggs that are usually purchased hard boiled and in their shells. They are served on a bed of mustard and cress arranged to represent a bird's nest. It is usual to serve 3 or 4 eggs per portion.

When purchased raw, gulls eggs should be boiled for 5–6 minutes before use.

Quails Eggs   Oeufs de Caille

Proceed as for gulls eggs but serve 5–6 per portion. Quails eggs are also commercially available hard boiled, shelled and pickled.

Seafood Mayonnaise   Mayonnaise de Fruits de Mer

Yield: 4 portions

Unit	Ingredient	Metric	Imperial
1	Selected cooked sea food/cold (see chart below for details)	400 g	1 lb
½	Basic mayonnaise	200 ml	8 fl oz
Garnish and flavourings	4 Crisp lettuce leaves (small/prepared) 2 Hard boiled eggs/shelled 2 Skinned fresh tomatoes ¼ Cucumber/peeled (half diced/half sliced) Lemon dressing (p. 88) Picked parsley or dill Salt and milled pepper		

Method

Combine flaked fish (minus skin/bone), chopped hard boiled egg (1 egg only), diced
cucumber together and season. Flavour/lightly moisten with lemon dressing and add
sufficient mayonnaise to cohere. Dress 4 portions on crisp lettuce leaves, garnish with
sliced cucumber, quartered hard boiled egg, quartered tomatoes, and finish with picked
parsley or dill. Keep refrigerated and present for service as required.

Examples of Seafood Mayonnaise: Using the Above Formula

Name	Main seafood ingredients	French term
Salmon mayonnaise	Cooked cold flaked salmon (bone/skin free)	Mayonnaise de saumon
Tuna fish mayonnaise	Cooked cold flaked tuna fish (bone/skin free)	Mayonnaise de thon
Seafood mayonnaise	Cooked cold mixed flaked fish (bone/skin free), e.g. salmon/halibut/turbot	Mayonnaise de fruits de mer
Lobster mayonnaise	Cooked cold shelled lobster-meat cut into collops	Mayonnaise de homard

SHELLFISH WITH MAYONNAISE   Crustaceans Nature à la Mayonnaise

Portion size by number of shellfish served

Ingredients	Directions
Selected shellfish	Cooked and cold/shelled
Mayonnaise	Sufficient to accompany portions served
Lemon wedges	To accompany
Picked parsley	To garnish
Salt/pepper	To accompany

Method

Arrange prepared shellfish (see chart below) decoratively on the service platter/dish garnished with lemon wedge and picked parsley. Present for service with an accompaniment of sauce mayonnaise, salt/pepper mill and finger bowl.

Examples of Shellfish with Mayonnaise: Using the Above Formula

Name	Main shellfish ingredients	French term
King prawns with mayonnaise	Cold cooked shelled jumbo prawns or Cold cooled shelled Dublin Bay prawns	Langoustine Nature à la mayonnaise
Crayfish with mayonnaise	Cold cooked shelled crayfish	Ecrevisse Nature à la mayonnaise

SHELLFISH COCKTAILS   Cocktail de Crustaceans

Yield: 4 portions

Unit	Ingredient	Metric	Imperial
1	Selected cooked shellfish/cold (see chart below for details)	200 g	8 oz
½	Cocktail sauce Prepared crisp lettuce/shredded or torn Squeeze lemon juice Selected garnish (see chart) Salt and milled pepper	100 ml	4 fl oz

Method

Flavour shellfish lightly with salt, pepper and a squeeze of lemon juice. Place small amounts of shredded/torn lettuce in the base of cocktail glasses or other suitable service dishes. Combine shellfish with the cocktail sauce. Divide the shellfish mixture equally into the service dishes, garnish and serve.

Examples of Shellfish Cocktails: Prepared Using the Above Formula

Name	Main ingredient	Typical garnish	French term
Prawn cocktail	Shelled cooked prawns	Small lemon twist or wedge/ unshucked prawn on edge of service dish	Cocktail de crevettes roses
Shrimp cocktail	Shelled cooked shrimps	Small lemon twist or wedge/ unshucked shrimp on edge of service dish	Cocktail de crevettes
Crab cocktail	Prepared cooked white crab-meat (prepared/flaked)	Small lemon twist or wedge on edge of service dish/prepared white crab-meat/pinch chopped parsley	Cocktail de crabe
Lobster cocktail	Prepared cooked sliced lobster tail	Small lemon twist or wedge on edge of service dish/lobster claw meat(whole)/lobster coral	Cocktail de homard
Mixed seafood cocktail	Prepared cooked shelled selected shellfish	Small lemon twist or wedge on edge of service dish/sieved egg yolk/white/chopped parsley	Cocktail de fruits de mer

N.B.   The garnishes can be varied and include other suitable ingredients, e.g. cucumber caviar, but whatever, the presentation should be simple providing a neat, attractive appearance.

SOUSED FISH
Poisson Mariné

Yield: 4 portions (4–8 fish fillets)
Cooking time: 20 minutes approx.
Cooking temperature: 205°C (400°F)

Unit	Ingredient	Metric	Imperial
	Selected fish fillets (see chart below for details)		
1	Vinegar/water: equal quantities	125 ml	5 fl oz
⅕	Button onions/prepared sliced and blanched★	25 g	1 oz
⅕	Small carrots/prepared sliced and blanched★	25 g	1 oz
Flavourings and seasonings	Bay leaf Sprig thyme Pinch pickling spice Salt and milled black pepper Chopped or picked parsley to garnish		

★ Blanching: plunge the vegetables for a few minutes in boiling water, refresh cold/drain.

Method

Season the prepared fish fillets with salt and milled black pepper. As appropriate (see chart) roll fillets with skin outside and secure with a cocktail stick (optional). Place close together in an oven-proof dish, sprinkle over the pickling spice, blanched carrots/onion rings, bay leaf and thyme. Pour on the vinegar/water liquid and cover with lightly oiled cartouche. Place in a moderate oven until just cooked. Once cooked remove from the oven and put aside to cool. Remove cartouche. Serve cold in liquor garnished with chopped or picked parsley.

Examples of Soused Fish: Prepared Using the Above Formula

Name	Quantity	Main fresh fish ingredient	French term
Soused herring	4	Herring fillets (skin retained/rolled)	Hareng dieppoise
Soused mackerel	4	Mackerel fillets (skin retained/rolled)	Maquereau à la dieppoise
Soused sardines	8	Fresh sardine fillets (skin retained/*not* rolled)	Sardines à la dieppoise
Soused smelts	8	Fresh smelt fillets (skin retained/*not* rolled)	Éperlans à la dieppoise

N.B.   When fillets are large, they are best rolled for sousing and service, e.g. herring and mackerel fillets. The fillets of smaller fish, however, typically fresh sardines/smelts may be soused flat. In these cases, the cooking time will be shortened.

POTTED FISH/SHELLFISH

Yield: 4 portions

Unit	Ingredient	Metric	Imperial
1	Selected cooked fish/shellfish (see chart below for details)	200 g	8 oz
1	Butter	200 g	8 oz
Flavourings and seasonings	Squeeze lemon juice Pinch of mace Pinch of nutmeg Salt and milled pepper		

Method

Melt the butter over a low heat, pour into a basin and skim away froth. Place selected fish in sauteuse over low heat and moisten with melted butter-oil taking care not to add the sediment. Flavour with lemon juice, spices, seasonings and toss briskly until hot (1 or 2 minutes). Fill the cold small pots with the mixture, press to pack lightly and, if necessary, top-up with more clarified butter to complete. Allow to cool, refrigerate to set firm. For service turn out and serve plainly garnished with an accompaniment of buttered brown bread.

Examples of Potted Fish/Shellfish: Prepared Using the Above Formula

Name	Main cooked fish ingredient/directions
Potted prawns	Fresh prawns/cooked and shelled
Potted shrimps	Fresh shrimps/cooked and shelled
Potted scallops	Fresh scallops/shelled, cooked and diced small
Potted salmon	Fresh cooked salmon/free of bone, skin and flaked

DRESSED CRAB

Ingredients	Mise-en-place: Instructions
Fresh crab	Cooked and cold/scrubbed and rinsed clean
Breadcrumbs	White fresh/pre-soaked in milk and squeezed out
Vinaigrette	Small amount only as moistening/flavouring agent
Mayonnaise	Small amount only to moisten and flavour
Egg	Hard boiled/white and yolk sieved separately/for garnish
Parsley	Fresh/finely chopped for garnish
Anchovy fillets	Drained and trimmed into strips for garnish
Stuffed olives	Sliced for garnish
Lemon juice	Squeeze for flavouring
Worcester sauce	Dash for flavouring
Salt and pepper	Seasoning to taste

Method

Preparing the crab

Twist off legs and claws from the crab and put aside. Place onto its back, tail end nearside. Ease the body (crab purse), to which the legs were originally attached, free from the shell by pushing up with both thumbs simultaneously, keeping the main shell intact. Remove and discard the sac and gills (dead men's fingers) from the shell. Scrape out the soft brown crab-meat from the shell and put aside. Remove pincers from the claws, crack and remove all white crabmeat. Put aside. Dissect the body (purse) and remove any white/dark crab-meat (use a fork or fine pointed knife to remove meat from the honeycombed body sections). Put aside respectively. Clean the inside of the main shell and break/trim to the natural line by gentle pressure. Dry the shell and brush the exterior lightly with oil to give a sheen.

Dressing the crab

Flake all the white meat and clear off any shell and bone structure, put into a clean bowl, flavour/moisten with vinaigrette and season. Rub all dark meat through a fine sieve, flavour with lemon juice, Worcester sauce, mix with soaked breadcrumbs and mayonnaise to form a paste (approx. half breadcrumbs to meat) and season.

To dress the crab, fill the centre of the shell with the dark meat and mould-in with a palette knife. Fill both end cavities with the prepared white meat generously. Garnish the natural dividing lines between the white and dark meats with parallel lines of chopped egg yolk/white and parsley. Decorate with strips of anchovy fillet and slices of stuffed olive. Keep refrigerated and present for service as required.

N.B.   The white meat may be placed onto small crisp lettuce leaves within the shell.

Bought-in Proprietary Products

An extensive variety of products can be bought-in ready processed. Generally they require minimum preparation/garnish to prepare them for service. Many such commodities are available under world famous brands, are of excellent quality and served frequently in high class catering establishments. Buying-in proprietary quality products reduces specific overhead costs, whilst also maintaining a high standard product for the consumer. Typical examples include the following:

Fish-Based Products

Name	Description/preparation	Portion size/ weight	Service/accompaniment
Bismark herrings	Raw salted herring (boned) sliced onions pickled in a spiced white vinegar-based liquor. Store refrigerated	1 herring per portion	Serve plainly garnished with picked parsley
Rollmops	As for Bismark herrings but rolled tail to head, cylindrical and pickled. Store refrigerated	1 rollmop per portion	Serve plainly garnished with picked parsley
Real caviar	Caviar is roe (eggs) taken from fish of the Sturgeon family. It is extracted on catching the fresh fish, prepared and packed salted in containers	15 g ($\frac{1}{2}$ oz) per portion	Often served in small ornamented pots on a bed of crushed ice or ice socle
	Main types: Beluga, Ocietrova, Sevruga *Purchased:* Fresh – pressed or pasteurised *Pressed caviar* Produced using damaged eggs which are salted then pressed. Store refrigerated		*Accompaniments:* (i) Hot toast with butter (ii) Blinis: hot buckwheat pancakes served flat with butter N.B. At the same time a standard garnish of chopped parsley, chopped onion, chopped egg yolk and chopped egg white may be offered in side dishes

Name	Description/preparation	Portion size weight	Service/accompaniment
Lumpfish roe (black or orange/red colour)	The roe of lumpfish is similar in appearance to real caviar, but *not* in quality and taste. Two colours are available, namely *black* or *orange/red*. Lumpfish roe is sometimes known as *mock caviar*	15 g (½ oz) per portion	Served as for caviar
Smoked eel Anguille fumée	Typical smoked versions include common and conger eels *Preparation* Cut the eel into sections, loosen and remove entire skin and put aside. Fillet eel flesh from the bone. Re-form the flesh (minus the bone) and cover with the skin to retain moisture	100 g (4 oz)	Serve plainly garnished with lemon, tomato and lettuce. Accompany with horseradish cream, thin slices of brown bread and butter
Smoked mackerel Maquereau fumé	Available whole or as fillets *Preparation/whole fish* For whole mackerel, remove fin bones, loosen the skin but leave attached as a covering to retain moisture. Brush skin lightly with a little oil *Preparation/fillets* Trim away hard edges and any fin bones, retain skin and brush flesh lightly with a little oil	200 g (8 oz) (on the bone) per portion or as individual fillets (usually *one* per portion)	As for smoked eel
Smoked trout Truite fumée	Trout available smoked whole (usually Rainbow trout) *Preparation* As for whole mackerel	150 g (6 oz) (on the bone) per portion	As for smoked mackerel
Smoked salmon Saumon fumé	Large fillets (sides) are smoked. Scotch considered the best quality due to the presence of fat between the flesh/muscles which provides a moist and succulent product. Other less expensive brands are drier *Preparation* Thinly trim away the exterior hard dry surface from the flesh side including the hard edges (a result of the smoking/curling process). Remove all the bones and carve the flesh on the slant into very thin slices, working from tail to head	35 g/50 g (1½/2 oz) per portion	Garnish with trimmed lemon wedge and serve with an accompaniment of thin slices of brown bread and butter

Meat/Offal-based Products

Name	Description/preparation	Portion size weight	Service/accompaniment
Foie gras	Terrine prepared from specially fattened goose livers and garnished with truffle. The most famous is from Strasbourg; it is considered a delicacy and is very expensive	15 g/25 g ($\frac{1}{2}$ oz/1 oz) 1 slice per portion	Chopped aspic jelly and picked watercress
Raw hams Jambon cru	Raw hams may be purchased on or off the bone. In either case, the hard crusted exterior is carefully removed and the ham sliced very thinly. An electric meat slicer is often used *Main types* Bayonne (French). Cured, smoked and dried Parma (Italian). Cured and dried Westphalian (German). Cured, smoked and dried	50 g (2 oz) 2 or 3 thin slices, according to size per portion	May be served with melon (p. 113)
Various sausages Saucisse varié	Numerous types of sausage are commercially available, their recipes and methods of preparation are closely guarded by the various manufacturers *Preparation* When an outer skin is evident, it is removed and the sausage is thinly sliced for service *Some examples:* Mortadella – Pork and garlic sausage, often with pistachio nuts Bierwurst – Pork and beef sausage, spiced and usually smoked Garlic sausage – Pork flavoured with garlic Liverwurst – Liver sausage Bologna – Smoked pork and beef sausage	50 g (2 oz) per portion	Overlap slices on a service dish, garnish with picked parsley A selection of assorted sausages is often served as an hors d'oeuvre
Salami	A type of sausage prepared from raw meats (pork and beef). They may be smoked and cured prior to air drying. Many varieties are commercially available *Preparation* Remove the outer protective skin, slice thinly	50 g (2 oz) per portion	Overlap slices on a service dish, garnish with picked parsley

Name	Description/preparation	Portion size weight	Service/accompaniment
Salami contd.	*Some examples:* Danish, French pepper, German, Hungarian, Milano (Italian)		
Smoked turkey Dindonneau fumé	The turkey is marinated and then par-boiled prior to smoking. It is sliced thinly for service and it is usual to serve a mixture of leg and breast meat per portion	75 g (3 oz) per portion	Arrange neatly on a service dish. Garnish with picked watercress

9
Sandwiches

Sandwiches are reputedly named after John Montague, The Earl of Sandwich. Folklore has it that he was a compulsive gambler who ate his meals sandwiched between pieces of bread in order not to leave the gambling table. This story cannot be confirmed, but may well have some elements of truth.

In many modern catering units, sandwiches are prominently featured on menus. Numerous hot and cold varieties are commonly available and eaten as snacks, packed meals, afternoon teas, picnics, etc.

In the larger hotels, sandwiches are prepared by the larder section, but in the smaller establishments they are prepared by various kitchen staff. Sandwiches are also frequently featured on the menus of public houses, snack and sandwich bars.

Comments on the Preparation of Cold Sandwiches

1. Breads may vary according to the type of sandwich being prepared, e.g. white, brown, French stick, bridge rolls, etc. Due to healthier eating trends, wholemeal bread is often featured and becoming increasingly popular.
2. When preparing sandwiches with fish fillings, brown bread is generally used.
3. Whenever possible, sandwiches are best prepared to order. However, when catering for large numbers this is not always practicable: in these instances sandwiches may be kept fresh by covering with a damp cloth, and removing crusts just prior to service.
4. Butter should be creamed before use in order to ensure that it is soft for even spreading. Sometimes flavoured butters are used, e.g. mustard butter.
5. The fillings for sandwiches may be a single item or a combination of foods. In most instances these fillings should be seasoned and in some cases flavoured according to taste, e.g. mustard with meats, lemon juice with smoked salmon.
6. When salads and other uncooked foods are to be featured they *must* be fresh, carefully trimmed and, when applicable, washed, drained and dried before use.
7. When preparing sandwiches for children, a variety of different fillings may be used. These may include bovril, grated chocolate, honey, banana, etc. It is also common to cut the sandwiches into different shapes using various cutters, e.g. crinkle cutters, teddy bear cutters, etc. This practice may well be considered wasteful on other

occasions, but at children's parties it will serve to create interest amongst the children as well as stimulating their appetites.

8. It is often necessary to wrap sandwiches for picnics, packed lunches, etc. Wrappings used should serve to keep sandwiches fresh and in a hygienic condition, as well as ensuring that they retain their original shape without crushing or squashing. Examples of wrappings in common use are greaseproof paper or bags, cling film, tin foil and purpose designed sandwich boxes. Purpose designed sandwich boxes generally have a transparent covering on one side. Transparent wrappings are ideal for display at self-service counters, ensuring that the customer can see and select the sandwich of his or her choice.

Types of Sandwiches – Cold Varieties

Conventional and Buffet Sandwiches

These usually consist of various foods sandwiched between slices of buttered white or brown bread, according to the type of filling.

Conventional sandwiches are most commonly cut into two triangles with the crusts left intact or removed according to the establishment's practice, and the customer's requirements. They may be garnished with lettuce, watercress, mustard and cress, tomatoes and cucumber, etc.

Buffet sandwiches always have the crusts removed and are cut into small neat shapes, e.g. triangles, fingers or squares. They may be garnished with lettuce, watercress, tomatoes, etc.

Bridge rolls may also be used for buffets in which case they are halved, buttered, with a filling placed neatly on each half.

Afternoon Tea Sandwiches

These are eaten as a light meal in the afternoon, usually accompanied with bread and butter, scones, various jams and small afternoon tea cakes. They consist of various fillings sandwiched between two slices of buttered white or brown bread. The crusts are always removed and the sandwiches cut into small neat shapes, e.g. triangles, fingers or squares, often garnished with mustard and cress. These sandwiches are quite light by nature as they constitute part of a light afternoon meal.

Continental Sandwiches

Usually eaten as a snack, these sandwiches are often substantial in size and may be cut into pieces to facilitate eating. They consist of a piece of French stick cut into half lengthwise, buttered and filled with a single food, e.g. cheese, or more commonly a combination of foods, e.g. various meats, salad and mayonnaise, cheese and pickle, etc.

Open or Scandinavian Sandwiches

Various breads are used as a base for these sandwiches onto which selected foods are placed. As these sandwiches are left open, it is essential that they have an attractive appearance – a combination of foods are often used for one sandwich, e.g. rolled ham slices, lettuce, tomato and mayonnaise dressing, etc.

Examples of Cold Sandwiches

Conventional and Buffet Sandwiches

Breads used	Typical fillings	Service and garnish

Sandwich bread
  white
  brown
	Sliced cooked meats
	Various sausages and salami
	Potted meats and fish
	Tinned fish: tuna, sardines, etc.
	Various cooked fish: prawns, crab,
	  salmon, etc.
	Smoked salmon
	Various cheeses
		Conventional sandwiches:
		  cut prepared sandwich into two
		  triangles, leave crusts intact or remove
		  as required. Arrange neatly on a
		  service dish with a dish paper
		Buffet sandwiches:
		  Remove crusts, cut into small neat
		  triangles, fingers or squares. Arrange
		  neatly on a service dish with a dish
		  paper
		Garnish: lettuce, tomatoes, mustard and
		  cress, radishes, cucumber, etc.

Afternoon Tea Sandwiches

Breads used	Typical fillings	Service and garnish

Sandwich bread
  white
  brown
	Potted meats and fish
	Meat and fish pastes
	Various cheeses
	Boiled eggs with mayonnaise and
	  cress
	Sliced tomato
	Sliced cucumber
	Fresh or smoked salmon
		Remove crusts from prepared
		  sandwiches and cut into small neat
		  triangles, fingers or squares
		Arrange neatly on a service dish with a
		  dish paper.
		Garnish with mustard and cress

Continental Sandwiches

Breads used	Typical fillings	Service and garnish

French sticks	Sliced cooked meats
	Various sausage and salami
	Tinned fish: tuna, sardines, etc.
	Various cooked fish/shellfish
	Smoked fish/meats
	Various cheeses
	Salad combinations
		Cut bread into half lengthwise, butter
		  and fill as required
		Served whole or cut into large pieces
		Place on a service dish with a dish
		  paper. May be garnished with
		  watercress

Open or Scandinavian Sandwiches

Breads used	Typical fillings	Service and garnish

Sandwich bread
    white
    brown
Wholemeal
Rye
Pumpernickle
Bread rolls
French sticks
	As for Continental sandwiches
	    with the addition of:
	Pickled and soused fish
	Dressed with:
	Thick mayonnaise
	Soured cream
	Natural yoghurt
	Mustards, etc.
		Arrange filling neatly onto slices of
		    bread ensuring that foods selected
		    look attractive and complement each
		    other. Place on a service dish with a
		    dish paper
		Owing to the attractive appearance of
		    these sandwiches no further garnish is
		    required

Hot Sandwich Varieties

General Comments

Hot sandwiches have been listed on the menu for many years, but never has there been such a wide selection of types and flavours as available on contemporary menus and in take-away catering outlets. Old faithfuls such as bacon, sausage, cheese, hot roast meat and turned egg remain popular in both plain and toasted forms. Generally these are produced using conventional equipment, namely salamanders and automatic toasters. The humble hot dog and burger with their varieties of dressings and garnishes are 'old stagers' in the league of hot sandwiches. Other well established hot sandwiches outlined in this section are featured on menus world-wide; club and bookmaker sandwiches and the French sandwich versions of croque monsieur and croque madame are typical.

Toasting Contact Grill/Griddle

The modern toasting contact-grills which colour, cook, seal and cut the prospective sandwich simultaneously are largely responsible for the plethora of tasty fillings available on snack menus under 'toasted sandwich varieties'. Such machines, whilst successfully employed in producing old favourites, e.g. ham and cheese, also allow for the introduction of more moist and less traditional fillings which are sealed in the sandwich during the cooking process (a design feature is responsible for the sealing action). Examples include savoury mince, curried and other spiced, moist fillings. Sandwiches which are to be cooked using the specifically designed contact-grills/griddles are buttered externally to facilitate cooking and colouring as the action is more akin to griddling than conventional grilling.

Garnish and Side-Dishes

Hot sandwiches are generally offered as a snack-type meal often made more substantial by the garnish and accompanying side dishes. Club-sandwich with frites and salad being a typical example. The varied guises of the burger are well known with many outlets featuring the beefburger as their principal base product.

Hot Pitta Breads

Pitta breads, *flat leavened bread* are an ideal medium for the preparation of unusual but very substantial hot snack sandwiches. After heating, each pitta bread is cut/split along one edge to form a pouch-like bag into which respective hot fillings with garnish/dressings are placed. These products are available as both take-away or on-site snacks (*see* p. 133 for examples).

Examples of Hot Sandwiches
CLUB SANDWICHES (Standard)

Yield: 1 portion

Ingredients	Mise-en-place/preparation
Hot fresh toast	3 slices/buttered/trimmed of crusts
Lettuce leaves/fresh	Wash, drain, dry and hold for garnish
Tomato/firm/fresh	Slice and hold for garnish
Mayonnaise/thick	For dressing
Cold cooked chicken	2 slices per sandwich
Grilled back bacon/hot	2 rashers per sandwich
Salt/pepper	For seasoning
Cocktail sticks	For service
Dish-papers	For service

Method

Arrange lettuce/tomato slices onto two slices of hot buttered toast, season with salt/pepper and dress each with some thick mayonnaise. Top one with the sliced cooked chicken, the other with the hot bacon and stack one on top of the other (dry toast-side down). Enclose the top with the remaining toast (plain-side up) to form a triple layered sandwich with two distinct fillings.

Service style 1: cut diagonally into quarters, secure each quarter with a cocktail stick and arrange for service on platter with dish-paper.

Service style 2: leave sandwich square/oblong, secure each corner with a cocktail stick and serve as above with knife and fork.

Club Sandwich Variations

Name	Variation
Club Sandwich Royal	As for 'standard club' but include a garnish of sliced hard-boiled egg in each filling
Princess Club Sandwich	As for 'standard club' but replace cooked chicken with cooked turkey. Include also a slice of Swiss cheese

N.B.   Innovations on the 'standard club sandwich' are easily prepared using other fillings, e.g. cooked ham/tongue, hot minute steak, etc.

BOOKMAKER SANDWICH: 1 (Steak sandwich)

Yield: 1 portion

Ingredients	Mise-en-place/preparation
Plain bread/fresh	2 slices/crusts retained/lightly buttered
Rump steak/raw	1 (6 oz/150 g approx.) prepared
English mustard	To flavour
Salt/pepper	To season

Method

Season/grill or shallow-fry the steak to the required degree and flavour with mustard. Sandwich between 2 slices of bread and place between two plates or boards under pressure until cooled (this releases some of the steak juice which is soaked up on the bread). Cut in half (crusts retained) and serve as appropriate.

BOOKMAKER SANDWICH: 2 (Hot toast steak sandwich)

Yield: 1 portion

Ingredients	Mise-en-place/preparation
Hot fresh toast	2 slices/buttered/crusts retained
Minute steak	Prepared raw
Salt/pepper	To season
English mustard	To flavour
Sprig parsley	For garnish
Dish-paper	For service

Method

Season steak, grill/shallow fry underdone then flavour with mustard. Sandwich between 2 slices of hot buttered toast and press between two plates/boards. Cut in half or sections. Present on a service platter with dish-paper garnished with parsley sprig.

CROQUE MONSIEUR (Sandwich version)

Yield: 1 portion

Ingredients	Mise-en-place/preparation
Plain bread	2 slices/trimmed of crusts
Gruyère cheese	2 thin slices (approx. size/shape of bread)
Cooked ham	1 thin slice (approx. size/shape of bread)
Clarified butter	Sufficient for shallow frying function
Dish-paper	For service

Method

Sandwich the ham between the two slices of cheese then enclose between the two slices of plain, trimmed bread. Shallow fry steadily in clarified butter on both sides until golden brown and hot. Present for service.

Service style 1: cut in half to form two rectangles, secure each with a cocktail stick and arrange for service on platter with dish-paper.

Service style 2: leave sandwich whole and serve as above with knife and fork.

Croque Madame (Sandwich version)

As for Croque Monsieur but place a shallow-fried egg on top of the flat surface (see service style 2) to complete.

HOT PITTA BREADS

Yield: 1 portion

Ingredients	Mise-en-place/preparation
Hot pitta bread/large*	Heat 1 and split to form a pouch
Lettuce leaves/fresh	Wash/drain/dry for garnish
Tomato/firm/fresh	Slice for garnish
Cucumber/fresh	Slice for garnish
Mayonnaise/thick	For dressing
Selected mustard	For flavour, e.g. Dijon, herb, etc.
Selected filling	See chart below
Salt/pepper	For seasoning
Paper napkins	For service

* On heating quickly, the flat pitta bread puffs up (steam generation inside pitta bread) and can be readily split and opened along *one* edge to form a pouch. The breads may be in a fresh or frozen condition prior to heating as they quickly defrost. Suggested methods (i) *by microwave* (ii) *under salamander*. Other methods can be used, e.g. hot cabinet.

Method

Fill the hot split pitta bread with main filling, garnish with lettuce, tomato, cucumber and lightly season. Dress and flavour with mayonnaise and selected mustard. Present for service in a paper napkin.

Suggested main fillings:

Hot roast carved meats	Beef, lamb, turkey, pork, etc.
Hot grilled/shallow fried meats	Sausage (split), bacon, minute steak, meat escalopes, kebabs, spiced variations, etc.
Hot grilled fish	Seafood kebabs (removed from skewer)
Vegetarian-based	Stir-fried vegetable combinations flavoured with soya sauce

N.B.   Obviously suitable combinations can be used, e.g. sausage and bacon. The cook can create many other interesting fillings, and the garnishing ingredients varied.

10

Cold Pies

Cold pies have been a regular feature on English menus for many years. They are often purchased from manufacturers ready prepared, e.g. pork pies, gala pies, poultry pies, etc. Such mass produced pies are generally of a high quality, with many established brand names in the market place. Home-made pies are often considered superior in flavour and appearance, as the creative chef is free to vary fillings and seasonings to suit establishment and customer requirements.

As well as being featured on traditional menus, pies are also included in picnic hampers, packed lunches and pub food selections. In addition, many buffets would not be considered complete without their inclusion.

Categorisation of Cold Pies

In the main, cold pies are grouped into two categories:

1. Pies that are prepared in a pie dish or basin and covered with a puff pastry crust prior to baking, referred to as layered pies.
2. Those that are completely enclosed in pastry prior to baking, often called *raised* pies, generally prepared manually or by machine. In the latter case the process is partially or fully automatic, whilst the former is a process of manual skill.

The raised pie pastry cases are produced by one of *two* distinct methods, namely by *inversion around the exterior of a mould*, typically around a wooden pie block, or *inversion within a mould*, typically a tin pie mould which is lined with the selected pastry. In both cases a hollow inverted pastry case is produced to receive respective fillings.

Raised pie moulds are available in many different shapes and sizes; they may be individual, large rectangular moulds or of a more ornamental nature. The particular mould chosen is often determined by the method of production and/or the intended use of the pie, e.g. individual moulds for picnics and packed lunches, rectangular moulds when slices of pie are required and ornamental moulds for buffet presentation.

The fillings for both these varieties of pies are often similar and are generally raw prior to baking. They may consist of various meats, poultry, game, flavoured with herbs, onions and seasonings, etc. The moistening agent is usually aspic, although a well flavoured stock is frequently used in conjunction with gelatine.

Service of Cold Pies

Layered cold pies are generally presented for service in the cooking vessel (pie dish) surrounded with a paper pie collar and a portion removed or loosened from the dish to facilitate service.

Alternatively, raised pies are removed from the mould if applicable, and served whole/portioned, as required. In these instances the pies are placed onto a wooden board or service dish with the minimum of garnish.

Smaller raised pies may be served whole or ready sliced. The portions may be presented on individual service dishes or on large flats plainly garnished, e.g. with fresh watercress. When cold pies are presented for buffet display, they are generally presented on flats and garnished with salad materials.

Production Factors/Layered and Raised Pies

(a) Baking:

Generally the larger the pie the slower the baking required if the filling and pastry are both to be cooked to the required degree/quality. However, to prevent sagging/bulging it is advisable to initially bake/set the pies at a high temperature for the first 15–20 minutes and continue baking to completion at a lower temperature. This technique is particularly important for large pies.

When high volume batches of large pies are baked, they are well spaced allowing the heat to fully circulate and penetrate each pie.

(b) Seasoning, flavourings:

Pie seasonings are varied to meet regional and market requirements. Typical examples include the use of standard seasonings (salt and pepper) and spiced seasonings (salt, pepper, nutmeg, mace, cayenne, etc.). Additional flavour variations may include the introduction of herbs in dried or fresh form.

(c) Stocks and aspics:

Used as moistening, flavouring and jellying agents (on cooling the liquid sets in the pie). Generally a combination of well flavoured stock and aspic is used to ensure setting. For specific pies, aspics can be flavoured with liquor, e.g. port flavoured aspic with game pies.

(d) Steam vents:

Vents are necessary to allow the steam generated during baking to escape, thus preventing the upper pie crust from bulging and lifting. The stock/aspic jelly is poured into the cooked pie through the vent when the pie has cooled down.

Production Factors/Specific to Cold Raised Pies

The pastry most commonly used is of the hot/boiled water varieties, *see* pp. 490–1 for recipes. The benefit of this type of pastry is its malleability which facilitates moulding and raising.

The flour used in the recipes is of *medium* strength which provides good colour, stability and an acceptable eating quality. The ideal shortening agent used for these pastries is lard.

Moulding the pastry case:

Generally, care should be taken to maintain an even thickness of pastry from base to sides to top. However, in the case of the *wooden block method*, the pie case may be slightly thicker around the sides near the base than at the top, with the taper being very gradual. During production, the block is periodically rolled (dusted lightly) in a little flour to prevent sticking.

Once moulded, the shells are best left in a cool place for a few hours (prior to filling) to rest and firm-up, this practice reduces the sagging effect which can occur during the baking process. Likewise when using tin pie moulds they should be well 'proven' and lightly greased prior to use. It is essential to maintain the condition of such moulds as 'rusting' can easily develop. Furthermore, great care should be exercised when lining and raising the pastry within the mould to ensure no air-spaces or holes develop.

Faulty lining will cause the pastry to crack during cooking allowing juices to leak onto the tin. As a result, sticking and de-moulding difficulties arise.

Filling the pastry case:

To enable the pies to stand and set on baking, the prepared meat filling should be carefully inserted and adequately fill the raw pastry case. Care at this stage prevents the formation of air-spaces between the pastry walls and meat. At the same time, care must also be taken not to *overfill* the case or exert excessive pressure when filling, as this generally results in swelling or bulging of the pastry walls during the cooking process.

COLD ENGLISH LAYERED PIES
(Baked in pie dishes with a puff pastry crust)

Yield: 8–12   Setting temperature: 200°C (400°F)
Baking time: 1½–2 hours   Baking temperature: 150°C (300°F)

Unit	Ingredient	Metric	Imperial
1	Selected raw meat (see chart below)	480 g	1 lb
1	Boneless gammon/ham (raw, trimmed of fat/rind, cut into thin slices)	480 g	1 lb
½	Streaky bacon/raw (rindless lining rashers)	240 g	8 oz
½	Puff pastry	240 g	8 oz
¼	Onion (finely chopped)	120 g	4 oz
	Chopped parsley		
	Salt and pepper		
	Aspic jelly/white gelatinous veal stock/cold*		

* Sufficient veal stock to moisten pie filling during cooking and aspic jelly to fill the pie when cold.

Method

To prepare the filling, line a 1½ pt (750 ml) pie dish with thin rindless/boneless bacon rashers allowing 6 cm (2½ in) of each slice to over-hang the sides of the dish. Now fill with alternating layers of selected meat (see chart below) and cut ham sprinkling each layer with chopped parsley and onion. Fold the ends of the lining bacon over to totally enclose the filling. Form a hole through the centre of the filling and pour in the cold free-running veal stock to moisten.

Moisten pie dish rim and surround with a ribbon of puff pastry, lightly water-wash then cover with a sheet of rolled out puff pastry (3 mm/⅛ in thick) carefully, trim/seal/crimp edges, decorate with puff pastry leaves and egg-wash for baking.

Now form a vent in the centre of the pastry to allow vapour to escape during baking. Allow to rest for 30 minutes prior to baking (reduces pastry shrinkage on cooking).

Place on tray into a hot oven 200°C (400°F) to set and colour the pastry to a pale brown. Reduce the oven temperature to 150°C (300°F) and continue baking to complete. (It may be necessary to cover pastry with foil at some stage of baking to prevent over-browning.) On completion, remove pie from oven and put aside to cool. Once cool, pour sufficient melted aspic jelly through the vent (use a funnel) to fill the pie. Clean the edges of the dish and place on refrigeration to set. For service loosen one portion and present the whole pie in its dish surrounded with a paper pie-collar.

Name	Selected meat	Preparation
Cold veal and ham pie	Raw veal cushion	Cut veal into escalopes, bat-out thinly, season with salt and pepper
Cold chicken and ham pie	Boneless raw chicken (skinned legs/breasts)	Remove skin and excess sinew, cut into neat even pieces, bat-out thinly, season with salt and pepper
Cold chicken, ham and herb pie	As for above	As above, but sprinkle chicken flesh with suitable fresh chopped herbs (e.g. parsley, chervil) before assembly
Cold turkey and ham pie	Raw skinned turkey breast	Cut skinned raw turkey breast into escalopes, bat-out thinly, season with salt and pepper

RAISED PIES (Cold)

Yield: 8 portions
Baking time: 2 hours

Setting temperature: 200°C (400°F)
Baking temperature: 150°C (300°F)

Unit	Ingredient	Metric	Imperial
1	Selected raw meat (bone/skin remove – see chart below)	800 g	2 lb
½	Hot-water pastry/boiled (pp. 490–1)	400 g	1 lb
¼	Cold water	200 ml	8 fl oz
	Seasoning (p. 135)		
	Jellying stock/white*		
	Egg wash		

* Proportions of seasoning used: ½ oz (10 g) per 1 lb (400 g) raw meat. When using salt bacon/ham along with non-cured meat the seasoning is reduced accordingly. Rich white gelatinous stock is produced using the bones and trimmings from the chosen meat, e.g. pork/veal, for jellying purposes.

Method

Thoroughly mix the coarsely minced or diced meat/s with the cold water until the water is fully incorporated into the meat. Add and mix-in the seasoning. (To test for seasoning, cook a little of the mixture and taste, adjust if required.) Store the meat mixture on refrigeration (or over ice) until required. Take approximately three quarters of the hot pastry and hand raise around a block (traditionally wooden) or inside selected pie moulds/tins and form the pie case to the required dimensions (once moulded the cases are held in a cold place allowing them to rest and firm-up prior to filling).

When set, fill the pie cases evenly with the prepared raw meat. Roll out the remaining pastry (slightly larger than the surface dimensions) for the lid, moisten the top edges of the pastry case and cover/seal with the pastry-lid. Seal and crimp the top edge to provide a neat finish. Decorate the surface with pastry leaves and cut a small vent in the centre (to allow vapour release during baking, and for the addition of gelatinous stock on cooling). Brush with egg-wash as appropriate (a weaker egg-wash solution may be used initially to prevent over-colouring in the early stages of baking) and place in a pre-heated oven at the setting temperature for approximately *20 minutes* (allow space between pies to ensure even and thorough cooking). Reduce the baking temperature and continue until cooked (if necessary cover the pies with foil to prevent over-browning).

Once cooked, cool and de-mould. Using a funnel, jelly the pies by pouring the free running cool stock through the vent and into the pie. Store chilled on refrigeration allowing the jelly to set.

Typical Hand Raised Pies Using Above Formula:

Name	Main meats/directions	Jellying stock
Pork pie	75% raw lean pork to 25% raw pork fat coarsely minced	Gelatinous white pork stock/aspic jelly
Veal and ham pie	50% raw lean veal to 50% raw gammon or raw ham cut into small cubes	Gelatinous white veal stock/aspic jelly
Veal, ham and egg pie	As above, but insert *shelled hard-boiled* eggs continuously along centre of filling lengthways	Gelatinous white veal stock/aspic jelly
Gala pie	As for veal, ham and egg pie, but use pork pie filling (see above) and include hard boiled egg as above	Gelatinous white pork stock/aspic jelly
Venison pie	75% venison to 25% belly pork. All meats fully trimmed of bone, skin, sinew then cubed N.B. *Omit* spiced seasoning and replace with salt/milled black pepper, chopped/ground mixed herbs*	Gelatinous game stock/aspic jelly

N.B.   Other game may be used as appropriate.

* Chopped/ground herbs may be added to all pies typically sage/thyme/bay/parsley, as required.

11

Terrines – Pâtés – Galantines

Terrine, pâté and galantine are frequently offered on traditional menus as single hors d'oeuvre, or as part of a cold buffet selection (decorated galantines are often featured on the cold buffet table). All three are similar in composition and in the way they are produced; however, the subtle differences which differentiate each one from the other need to be explained.

Classification of Terrines, Pâtés and galantines

Generally these products are produced from raw or semi-raw ingredients which are prepared into a form of forcemeat mixture. The mixture may be coarse or fine textured and the product produced in the form of a terrine or traditional pâté, the latter referred to nowadays as pâté en croûte (a term used to clarify any misunderstanding of traditional and contemporary culinary jargon, see notes below).

Terrine describes a product which is cooked, cooled and served cold in a *terrine vessel*. Generally the forcemeat preparation is enclosed in thin sheets of pork barding fat or streaky bacon used to line the terrine vessel and fully envelop the respective forcemeat filling. Once cooked, the product is allowed to cool under a light weight, then stored on refrigeration for use. Traditionally the terrines were of earthenware construction (terre – earth) but other materials are now used for their manufacture.

Pâté 'correctly' applied describes an essentially raw forcemeat mixture which is enclosed and baked in a pastry case/mould, allowed to cool, filled with aspic jelly, stored on refrigeration to set, sliced and served cold. In contemporary cuisine, however, the term 'pâté' is applied as a misnomer to many terrine-styled products, e.g. pâté maison. In order to differentiate and clarify matters, the term 'pâté en croûte' is often used to describe classical pâtés, e.g. pâté en croûte de gibier.

Galantine denotes a raw forcemeat preparation of boneless/skinless/sinewless poultry, namely chicken, turkey or duck. The forcemeat is enclosed in its own entire raw skin, wrapped and secured in a clean cloth, simmered to cook in the appropriate white stock, then allowed to cool in the stock under a light weight until cold. The drained cold galantine is often decorated for cold buffet display and service.

Comments on the Preparation of Pâtés, Terrines and Galantines

Types of Pastry Used

The pastry most commonly used is pâté à pâté, a type of short pastry prepared by using medium strength flour. The shortening agent may be lard, margarine or butter, but most often is a combination of lard and butter/margarine. The flour and shortening agent are rubbed together until the fat is evenly distributed and then sufficient cold water/beaten egg added to form a firm malleable dough. This recipe combination will form a pastry of good colour, stability and an acceptable eating quality, the lard ensuring a pastry that is easy to work and crisp to eat on cooking.

Pork Back Fat

Pork fat, in one form or another, is an essential ingredient in many pâtés and terrines. The best type comes from the back of the pig and is called 'bardes au lard', this fat is firm and easily cut into thin slices or various shapes. Pork back fat does not disintegrate during cooking and is, therefore, well suited to pâté/terrine production.

When pork fat is combined with forcemeats it adds essential flavour and ensures that the finished product is moist and of a light texture. Cut into thin sheets, it is used to line moulds and terrines in which various forcemeats are enclosed. Lean pieces of meat are used to garnish the centre of pâtés/terrines and when wrapped in pork fat they remain moist during cooking. Long strips or squares of back fat are also used as a garnish within the forcemeat mixture.

Testing for Seasoning

Raw forcemeats need to be tested for seasoning before they are used and cooked in any product. A simple method is to cook and taste a tiny portion of the raw mixture and adjust accordingly.

Pâté Moulds/Terrines

Pâté moulds are available in many different shapes and sizes: they may be plain rectangular in shape or of a more ornamental nature. In general they are made of tin and should be well 'proven' and lightly greased prior to use.

A terrine is essentially a dish in which meat, game, fish and now vegetable products are cooked. Traditionally they were made from glazed pottery, earthenware or porcelain, but recent trends have included the development of cast iron vessels with a coating of vitreous enamel, these becoming increasingly popular as they are attractive in appearance and highly durable. Many different shapes are available but the oval or rectangular terrines are probably the most popular.

Testing for Cooking

To ensure pâtés/terrines are adequately cooked, a needle is placed into the centre of the mixture for a few seconds, when removed the needle should be clean with no uncooked mixture adhering to it. The needle will also be hot to the touch indicating the temperature at the centre of the product, and that cooking is complete.

Cooling of Terrines and Galantines

After completion of cooking, terrines should be cooled under a light weight. This produces a close textured filling which is both moist and readily cut into portions without breaking. Once cooked, the terrine is removed from the bain marie and a wooden board placed onto the top of the cooked forcemeat (sometimes with additional weights as required) until cold. Galantines on the other hand are cooled under a light weight whilst in their cooking liquor ensuring that they keep moist, close textured, well flavoured as well as having a flattened surface for decoration purposes.

Service of Pâté, Terrines and Galantines

Terrines may be presented in their cooking vessel with a portion loosened or removed from the dish to facilitate service. Alternatively, the product may be turned out from the terrine, sliced into portions then garnished with croûtes of aspic jelly and picked watercress. When a more attractive presentation is required, the top surface of the terrine can be decorated. In this case, the top layer of bardes au lard is removed, the terrine decorated and finished with a light coating of aspic.

Pâtés and galantines may be presented whole to be portioned in the dining room or cut into individual portions and served garnished with aspic croûtes and picked watercress.

Traditionally, pâtés, terrines and galantines are served as a first course or alternatively as part of a cold buffet.

Contemporary Trends

As well as being featured on traditional menus, pâtés and terrines are often included in picnic hampers, packed lunches and as pub food selections.

HOUSE TERRINE
Terrine Maison

Yield: 400 g (1 lb)
Cooking time: 1 hour
Oven temperature: 175°C (350°F)

Unit	Ingredients	Metric	Imperial
1	Chicken livers (trimmed)	200 g	8 oz
½	Lean pork/cut into pieces	100 g	4 oz
½	Larding bacon/unsmoked (thinly sliced)	100 g	4 oz
¼	Fat pork/cut into pieces	50 g	2 oz
¼	Fat bacon/unsmoked/cut into pieces	50 g	2 oz
¼	Onion/prepared chopped	50 g	2 oz
¼	Butter	50 g	2 oz
Flavourings and seasonings	1 Medium clove garlic/chopped		
	1 Glass Brandy		
	1 Glass Sherry/medium		
	Pinch thyme, bay leaf powder, marjoram		
	Pinch nutmeg, mace, allspice		
	Salt and pepper to taste		

Method

Melt butter in a sauté pan over a low to medium heat. Add onions/chopped garlic and sweat under cover to soften without colour. Remove lid, add lean/fat pork, fat bacon and cook until meats seal without any significant browning. Add herbs, spices, seasoning and livers to seal (keep livers under-cooked). Remove ingredients from the heat, mince and rub through a fine sieve or liquidise to a smooth mixture.

Blend-in the brandy/sherry and season to taste. Carefully line the selected terrine with larding bacon allowing extra length over the sides for folding over to fully enclose the mixture. Fill the lined terrine generously with the mixture and enclose in larding bacon. Cover the terrine with a lid then cook in bain marie for approximately 1 hour. Once cooked, remove from the oven and pierce with a needle to test for adequate cooking (when withdrawn the needle will be clean and hot if the mixture is adequately cooked at the centre). Cool under light pressure to close the texture (place light weight directly onto the surface until cold and set). Store chilled in readiness for service.

Service

Serve in small portions with an accompaniment of hot fingers of toast.

DUCK TERRINE   Terrine de Canard

Yield: 8 portions
Cooking time: 1–1¼ hours
Cooking temperature: 175°C (350°F)

Unit	Ingredients	Metric	Imperial
	Medium duck		
1	Lean pork/cut into pieces	200 g	8 oz
⅔	Belly pork/cut into pieces	150 g	6 oz
⅔	Pork back fat/thinly sliced	150 g	6 oz
½	Onion/chopped	100 g	4 oz
¼	Whole egg	50 g	2 oz
¼	Butter	50 g	2 oz
Flavourings and	1 Orange/zest and juice		
seasonings	1 Medium clove garlic/chopped		
	1 Glass Brandy		
	1 Glass orange curaçao		
	Pinch thyme, bay, marjoram		
	Pinch nutmeg, allspice		
	Salt and mill pepper to taste		

Method

Bone the duck, removing any skin and sinew. Place the duck breasts in a shallow container and marinade for approximately 2 hours in the orange juice, brandy and orange curaçao. Remove duck breasts from marinade and wrap in thin slices of pork back fat, keep the marinade to flavour duck forcemeat. Line the selected terrine with remainder of thinly sliced pork back fat, allowing extra length over the sides to fully enclose the filling.

Preparation of forcemeat

Melt the butter in a saucepan over a low to medium heat, add onions and sweat under cover to soften without colour, allow to cool. Dice remaining raw duck flesh and duck liver then combine with cooked onions, belly pork and lean pork, pass twice through a fine mincer. Place mixture in a bowl over ice and beat thoroughly, add the egg and continue beating, slowly adding the liquors from the marinade, orange zest, chopped herbs, nutmeg and allspice. Season forcemeat with salt and milled pepper to taste.

Half fill the lined terrine with forcemeat, add the duck breasts, one behind the other along the length of the terrine, cover with the remaining forcemeat, then fold over the pork back fat to fully enclose. Cover the terrine with a lid and cook in a bain marie for $1\frac{1}{4}$ to $1\frac{1}{2}$ hours. Once cooked, remove from oven and pierce with a needle to test for adequate cooking (when withdrawn the needle will be clean if the terrine is adequately cooked at the centre). Cool under light pressure to close the texture (place a light weight directly across the surface until cold and set). Store chilled in readiness for use.

Service

Serve in small portions with an accompaniment of hot fingers of toast.

When the terrine is to be portioned in the dining room, the top surface may be decorated. In this case, remove top layer of pork fat, decorate terrine with slices or segments of orange and coat with aspic.

N.B. When a more decorative terrine is required the forcemeat may be flavoured and garnished with diced truffle and shelled pistachio nuts prior to cooking.

VARIOUS PÂTÉS

Pâtés en Croûte Varié

Yield: 8 portions
Cooking time: $1–1\frac{1}{2}$ hours

Setting temperature: 220°C (425°F)
Baking temperature: 170°C (325°F)

Unit	Ingredients	Metric	Imperial
1	Selected main meat/raw (see chart below)	400 g	1 lb
$\frac{1}{2}$	Pork and veal/lean, raw	200 g	8 oz
$\frac{1}{2}$	Pork fat/raw	200 g	8 oz
$\frac{1}{4}$	Pork back fat/raw (cut into long thick strips)	100 g	4 oz
$\frac{1}{4}$	Cooked lean ham/tongue (cut into long thick strips)	100 g	4 oz
$\frac{1}{8}$	Whole eggs/beaten	50 ml	2 fl oz
$\frac{1}{8}$	Double cream/half whipped	50 ml	2 fl oz
$\frac{1}{8}$	Farce à gratin★	50 g	2 oz
$\frac{1}{8}$	Cognac	50 ml	2 fl oz

Two cloves chopped garlic/thin strips black truffle/shelled pistachio nuts.
To flavour: mixed herbs/allspice/nutmeg/salt/cayenne and milled pepper.
Bardes au lard: sufficient thin sheets of pork back fat to line pastry mould and enclose filling.
Selected pastry: sufficient to fully line mould and enclose the filling (see method for choice of pastry, namely pâte à paté, hot water pastry or rough puff (see Chapter 30).
Gelantinous stock: sufficient appropriate stock/aspic for jellying purposes.

★ Selected liver, e.g. chicken/game sweated with a little chopped shallot, bacon scraps in butter until lightly sealed, flavoured with brandy, liquidised to a fine purée and seasoned to taste.

Method

Meat strips for marinade: cut approximately *one third* weight of combined main prime meat, lean pork and veal (200 g/½ lb in total) into long thick strips. Combine with prepared strips of pork back fat, strips of cooked ham/tongue, truffle strips, pistachio nuts, moisten with the cognac to marinade and put aside.

Main raw forcemeat:

Pass remaining main meat, veal, pork, pork fat twice through fine mincer and place into a mixing bowl.

Working over ice thoroughly incorporate beaten egg, cognac drained from the marinade, farce à gratin, chopped garlic, herbs, spices and seasoning. To complete gradually and thoroughly beat in the fresh double cream to form a smooth firm mixture. Shallow fry a morsel of the mixture to test the seasoning, correct accordingly and put aside.

Pâté en croûte No. 1: (raised in a hinged pâté mould using pâté à pâté hot water pastry.

Roll out/cut pastry to the required dimensions to suit the mould by 6 mm (¼ in) thick including sufficient for pastry top and decoration. Put pastry for top and decoration aside. Carefully line greased hinged mould completely with the remaining pastry leaving a small overlap around the top edges (1 cm/½ in) and form the raised pastry mould. Now line the inside of the pastry mould completely with the thin sheets of 'bardes au lard', leaving sufficient overhang to completely envelope the forcemeat filling. At this point, spread approximately *one third of the prepared forcemeat* evenly across the base of the mould.

Arrange *one half* of the marinaded meat/fat/truffle strips and pistachio nuts neatly length-ways along the forcemeat pressing them down gently to surround with forcemeat. Repeat this layering process with remaining forcemeat and garnishing foods, finishing with a final layer of forcemeat (three in all). Fold the fat lining and dough over at the edges allowing the pork fat to fully enclose the filling. Brush folded pastry edges with egg-wash. Cut out two or three steam vents in the pastry lid and surround with pastry circles, cover the pâté with the tailor-made pastry lid, press down and seal to clear the top edges of the mould. Crimp around the top edges of the pastry, decorate with pastry shapes as required and brush with a light egg-wash solution to avoid over-browning. Place foil chimneys in the steam vents to prevent juices overflowing onto the pastry crust during baking. Rest the pâté for 30 minutes on refrigeration prior to baking.

Baking process:

Bake in a pre-heated oven for 15–20 minutes at 220°C (425°F) to set, reduce to 170°C (325°F) and continue for approximately 1 hour longer to complete baking. Remove from the oven, test for adequate cooking* (see chart below), if cooked allow to cool or continue as needed. Once cooked/cooled unhinge and remove the mould, jelly the pâté through the vents using appropriate stock/aspic and place on refrigeration to set.

Pâté en croûte No. 2 (wrapped and baked in pastry: rough puff)

Roll out pastry/dough to the required dimensions (approximately 3 mm/⅛ in thick) to fully envelop the forcemeat mixture. Arrange sufficient sheets of thin barding fat (over the *first third of the pastry*) to completely envelope the forcemeat mixture. Arrange the forcemeat as for pâté en croûte no. 1 and overlap/enclose with the barding fat. Now roll forward in the pastry, egg-wash the underside front edge and completely roll over to form a tightly sealed cylindrical shape. Place onto a greased baking sheet with the seal underneath. Trim off excess pastry, form steam vents and decorate as above. Egg-wash, rest, bake, jelly and set on refrigeration as for no. 1 above.

* Cooking test: Insert thin skewer/needle into centre of hot pâté through to the base. Allow a few seconds, withdraw. If needle is free of mixture and hot the pâté is cooked.

Pâtés en Croûte Prepared Using the Above Formula

Name	Selected main meat/stock preparation	French term
Game pâté	Selected game/free of bone, skin, sinew, etc. Game stock	Pâté de gibier
Duck pâté	Duck meat/free of bone, skin, sinew, etc. Duck stock	Pâté de ganard
Chicken pâté	Chicken meat/free of bone, skin, sinew, etc. Chicken stock	Pâté de volaille/poulet
Rabbit pâté	Rabbit meat/free of bone, skin, sinew, etc. Rabbit stock	Pâté de lapin

N.B.   Other pâtés en croûte may be prepared using the formula given above, e.g. turkey, ham, veal and pork, venison, etc.

CHICKEN GALANTINE   Galantine de Volaille/Poulet

Yield: 8 portions
Cooking time: $1\frac{1}{4}$–$1\frac{1}{2}$ hours

Unit	Ingredients	Metric	Imperial
	1 Medium Chicken		
1	Lean pork/diced	200 g	8 oz
1	Lean veal/diced	200 g	8 oz
$\frac{1}{2}$	Pork back fat	100 g	4 oz
$\frac{1}{2}$	Cooked ham	100 g	4 oz
$\frac{1}{2}$	Cooked tongue	100 g	4 oz
$\frac{1}{2}$	Double cream	100 ml	4 fl oz
$\frac{1}{4}$	Egg	50 g	2 oz
$\frac{1}{4}$	Truffle/small dice	50 g	2 oz
$\frac{1}{8}$	Pistachio nuts/shelled	25 g	1 oz
Seasonings and flavourings	1 Glass Brandy Pinch nutmeg, cayenne Salt and pepper to taste Chicken stock/white*		

* Sufficient white stock to cover galantine during cooking

Method

Singe the chicken and remove any loose feathers, cut off the winglets. Cut along the back of the chicken with a small sharp knife and carefully remove the skin taking care not to puncture it. Clear the skin of any excess fat and then soak in cold water for 30 minutes (this whitens and loosens the skin), remove skin from water and dry thoroughly. Arrange the skin neatly onto a clean damp white cloth or tea towel with the inside of the skin uppermost. Cut flesh from chicken and remove all sinew/bones, etc. Cut chicken breasts, pork back fat, cooked ham and cooked tongue into long strips ¼ in thick, place in a shallow container with shelled pistachio nuts and diced truffle; pour over the brandy and allow to marinade for 1 hour. Drain off the brandy and keep to flavour the forcemeat.

Forcemeat:

Mix together the boned-out trimmed chicken meat, diced pork, diced veal and pass through a fine mincer several times. Add egg, season to taste with cayenne, salt, pepper, nutmeg and beat together. Slowly add the brandy and cream, mixing thoroughly to form a smooth mixture. Place a layer of forcemeat along the centre of the chicken skin, neatly arrange half the strips of ham, tongue, chicken breast and pork fat on the forcemeat. Sprinkle with pistachio nuts and diced truffle. Repeat this process and finish with a layer of forcemeat. Wrap the chicken skin around the forcemeat and carefully roll up in the cloth to form a large sausage shape, tie ends to secure.

Place the galantine in white chicken stock, bring to the boil and then simmer gently for 1¼ to 1½ hours until cooked. Remove galantine from stock, unwrap and then tie in cloth ensuring ends are tightly secured. Place back in stock and cool under a light weight to ensure a closed even texture and a flat top surface for decoration. When cold remove from cloth, trim the ends and decorate for service.

Decoration of galantine

Place galantine onto a cooling wire, mask with white chicken chaud froid sauce, decorate as required and lightly coat with aspic jelly. Place on a service dish and garnish with croûtons of aspic jelly.

12

Cold Buffet: Rudimentary Concepts

Formerly the classic-styled cold buffet presentation was either reserved for very special important occasions, or offered as a regular feature on the grand menus of luxurious establishments. Typical of the latter were the ocean-going pre/post war passenger liners and famous shore-based luxury establishments renowned for the opulence of their cold buffet displays. Likewise, reputable outside catering firms would frequently produce magnificent cold buffet pieces in their central kitchens for transportation, display and service at selected venues.

Contemporary trends indicate a growing and continuing popularity of the cold buffet across wide sectors of the industry. The classic-styled form described above remain, but many hotels, restaurants, public houses, outside caterers and the like regularly provide modest small-scale cold buffet selections all the year round. The prominence of the *carvery and salad bar* in modern units is an indication of these developments. Furthermore, the caterers' obligation and commitment towards providing health giving foods will establish the cold buffet as a regular choice on menus.

Sales Aspects

From a sales viewpoint, the cold buffet offers many important advantages. Attractive food displays, for example, stimulate impulse sales. Customer participation in partial or self-service reduces the cost of labour whilst involving the service staff directly with customers.

Buffet service can be organized to cope with large volumes of trade at speed or paced leisurely, and the replenishment of the buffet table readily controlled. Furthermore, at the end of service unsold foods can be sensibly and safely utilized. Therefore, the cold buffet enables the caterer to provide a 'value for money product' for a realistic profit.

Buffet Layout/Service

The layout of buffet tables varies according to the type of buffet, number of customers, selection of food stuffs, etc. In most cases, however, the buffet is assembled on large rectangular tables which may be slightly elevated in the centre to set off the main dishes or centre-piece. Whatever the case, it is essential to organize the food stuffs in such a manner as to ensure that customers move along the buffet table with the minimum congestion. This may be achieved by following simple guidelines outlined below.

Operational Layout for Medium Sized Cold Buffet, Two Service Points

		Service personnel			
Desserts	Salads	Main buffet dishes		Salads	Desserts
Cheeses	Dressings	Meats	Meats	Dressings	Cheeses
Biscuits, bread	Sauces	Fish	Fish	Sauces	Biscuits, bread
Accompaniments	Accompaniments	Poultry	Poultry	Accompaniments	Accompaniments
		Game, pies, etc.	Game, pies, etc.		

Crockery, service cutlery

Customer flow

The number of service points may vary accordingly with the size of buffet, number of customers and room dimension. It may be necessary, particularly in the case of large functions, to locate several similar buffet tables around the dining room to facilitate efficient service.

Hygiene Factors

Safe hygienic practices are essential throughout preparation, production, display, service and clearing of the cold buffet. Strict controls must be established and monitored throughout. Modern day chilled display units, transparent food coverings, food handlers' gloves, etc. assist the caterer in the provision of safe food for public consumption. Where the buffet table is not purpose designed, i.e. not refrigerated, then the holding of food on refrigeration and the timing of the lay-up display, service and clearing are critical. Cold buffets, therefore, must be presented in an attractive, fresh and safe condition.

Types of Cold Buffet

Cold buffets vary considerably in terms of their opulence, variety, style, layout, presentation for service, materials cost and selling price. However, as a method of producing and selling food, the cold buffet is universally featured across a wide range of catering outlets, from the modest to the grand. Often the occasion determines the type and scale of food display. Typical are the more economic finger buffets which adequately meet the needs of the small informal soirée, and the stylish grand classical array suited to the more important formal public function.

1. Classic Cold Buffet

This style of cold buffet presentation is generally reserved for the formal important function, generally catering for large numbers of invited guests. However, the style is frequently used for the small but important occasion. The classic cold buffet is characterised by its obvious magnificence and splendour, its wide selection of expensive foods which are decorated and garnished to a high standard of craftsmanship. Buffet centre-pieces are the norm, including the non-edible varieties such as splendid carvings in ice, fat and the like. Chaudfroid sauces, aspics, glazes being the traditional materials used by the buffet chef are abundantly featured. Such buffets are very substantial by nature offering generous selections of cold starters, main items with salads, sweets, cheeses and beautiful arrays of fresh fruits in the basket, 'la corbeille des fruits'. As far as the foods used are concerned only choice commodities are prepared, prime joints/cuts of butcher's meats, high quality poultry and game, seasonal whole fish and shellfish and first-class salad materials/vegetables/fruits are typical. The buffet is generally presented whole or partially carved as required for service; whatever the classic cold buffet can only be described as a splendid and grand display of cold foods.

2. Smörgasbord: A Scandinavian Buffet

This type of food presentation is an integral part of Scandinavian culture. The Smörgasbord buffet is very much a daily event in the national life of Scandinavian citizens and its popularity has long since spread to other countries, including the U.K. Overall the buffet composition traditionally includes a wide selection of both *cold and hot* food varieties, the hallmarks of which are *product variety* and *simplicity of presentation*.

As Smörgasbord is a daily event, and one which may last over many hours, simplicity of presentation is essential, and the elaborate decorative/garnishing work associated with the classic cold buffet previously outlined is considered impractical. However, although plainly and simply garnished, the buffet is a most attractive and appetising food display.

Service Procedures

The style is generally self-service. First, the customer selects at random from the hors d'oeuvre whatever is desirable, along with breads, cheeses, butter, etc. Following this, and using another clean plate, selections are chosen from the cold main items. The customer can refill repeatedly as dictated by appetite and time. Next, another clean but hot plate with which to sample the range of hot food items provided. Once again, repeated refills are the order of the day before going on to the light sweets and desserts. The general rule throughout the courses is to return as often as you like and sample as much as you like. Obviously, sensible gourmets of the Smörgasbord sample selections of small quantities eating at their leisure.

As a rule, exempting drinks, the total Smörgasbord is offered at an inclusive price to the customer, a genuine value for money feast. The replenishment of the buffet table is critical to any Smörgasbord and the back-up kitchen services must be organized accordingly.

The Smörgasbord table is generally long in shape with a hot foods display and elevation features. These design characteristics and the planned buffet layout allow for a smooth customer traffic flow and a minimum of hold-ups/bottle necks during the service period.

3. The Finger Buffet Style

Finger buffets aptly describe the type of foods displayed. Generally the food items are relatively small enough to manage without the customary cutlery (sometimes just a mouthful, e.g. cocktail canapés). As a rule, this form of buffet caters for the low budget occasion, but this is not always so. Perhaps two main types of finger buffet display are commonly featured, namely 'the Cocktail Buffet' essentially comprised of a wide selection of cocktail canapés (*see* pp. 107–8), or a more 'General Finger Buffet' made up of a wide selection of plainly garnished foods. The typical cocktail buffet, a favourite for the cocktail party, is usually presented on trays which are displayed on a buffet table or circulated by the service staff. In either case no cutlery is required and often no plates either. For the more substantial and/or up-market finger styled buffet some cutlery/crockery may be desirable. For example, plastic clip-on wine glass (paris goblet) holders which fit securely on to plates are now available and well suited to the informal finger buffet occasions allowing customers ease of movement and service.

Finger Buffet Composition: typical products

Cocktail canapés
Sausage rolls
Savoury bouchées
Savoury cannelons
Cheese straws
Savoury croissants
Savoury éclairs/choux buns, etc.
Savoury barquettes/tartelettes
Savoury croquettes
Pizza portions
Quiche portions
Savoury fritters
Croque monsieur (slices)

Crudités with dips
Open/closed sandwiches
Scotch egg portions
Cooked chicken portions plain/spiced
Cooked frogs legs plain/spiced
Deep-fried goujons/scampi
Kebabs (small)
Fondant fancies
Small cake varieties
Sweet eclairs/choux buns
Fruit/sweet tartelettes
Sweet fritters (beignets)
etc.

4. Modern Cold Buffet Trends

Many popular contemporary catering outlets offer some form of *modified* cold buffet display as a standard daily feature, with certain units specialising entirely in this form of food presentation. Traditional and popular restaurants, hotel butteries, carveries and public houses are typical. Outside contract caterers have always used the cold buffet as an ideal off-site form of providing safe food, and will no doubt continue with this trend. Significantly major equipment suppliers now provide many attractive refrigerated cold buffet display units which can be fixed/mobile to suit almost any circumstance. Such a flexible provision will encourage the continued growth of the 'buffet froid'.

Cold Buffet Garnish and Decorations

When garnishing and decorating any form of cold buffet from the classic to the finger-buffet style fundamental working principles apply. The concepts of *shape, form, design, colour, temperature, impact* and *balance* are critical if the chef is to be successful in this important area of food presentation and sales.

Non-classical decoration and garnish embraces the essentially plain/simple forms of presentation *without* the use of aspics, chaudfroid sauces and the like. In addition to the points listed above, a few guidelines specific to these types of plain decoration are given:

1. For freshness of food decoration and garnishing materials $\longrightarrow$ Purchase/prepare/hold (as applicable) $\longrightarrow$ Correctly by procedure at appropriate time at the correct temperature

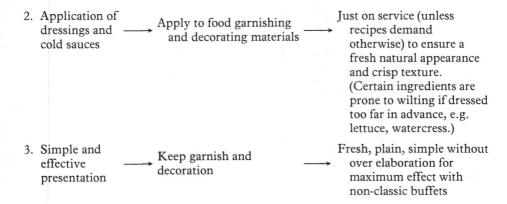

2. Application of dressings and cold sauces ⟶ Apply to food garnishing and decorating materials ⟶ Just on service (unless recipes demand otherwise) to ensure a fresh natural appearance and crisp texture. (Certain ingredients are prone to wilting if dressed too far in advance, e.g. lettuce, watercress.)

3. Simple and effective presentation ⟶ Keep garnish and decoration ⟶ Fresh, plain, simple without over elaboration for maximum effect with non-classic buffets

Classic Cold Buffets Garnish and Decoration

Typical examples of food materials used for decorating and garnishing purposes are outlined below on pp. 153–4 and the important distinction as to what is considered as *decoration* and what is *garnish* for classic cold buffet presentation needs to be clarified.

Decoration: decorative food materials are not pre-portioned for service with buffet items but applied directly on to buffet pieces as edible decoration only. Obviously portions of such food decoration are eaten once the buffet pieces are carved or individually portioned for service, but it is pot-luck as to which morsel of decoration finds its way on to the customer's plate; decorated joints of butcher's meats/hams decorated whole fish such as salmon typify the use of edible decoration. Decorative items such as fat and ice carvings, pulled and blown sugar displays, pastillage, etc. are also categorised as non-served/non-edible decoration.

Garnish: food garnishes on the other hand are items produced separately to the main buffet items, but which form part of the whole display without being directly attached to buffet pieces. Typical are stuffed eggs, stuffed tomatoes, small moulds of cold mousse, filled pastry cases, e.g. barquettes, small moulds of food in aspic or mayonnaise colée, etc. Furthermore, such items are evident in appropriate/sufficient portions to accompany the carved/served main items.

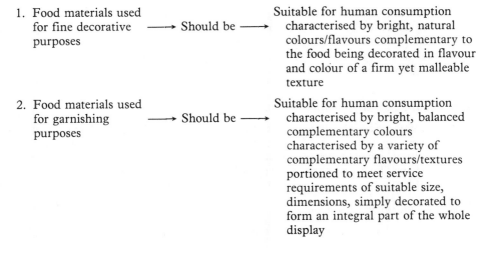

1. Food materials used for fine decorative purposes ⟶ Should be ⟶ Suitable for human consumption characterised by bright, natural colours/flavours complementary to the food being decorated in flavour and colour of a firm yet malleable texture

2. Food materials used for garnishing purposes ⟶ Should be ⟶ Suitable for human consumption characterised by bright, balanced complementary colours characterised by a variety of complementary flavours/textures portioned to meet service requirements of suitable size, dimensions, simply decorated to form an integral part of the whole display

Decoration of Classical Cold Buffet Pieces

Food decorated for buffets may vary from small individual portions, e.g. breast of chicken to large joints of meat or whole fish, e.g. whole salmon. It is essential, however, that the decoration employed be *pleasing to the eye* and *complementary* in *appearance/taste* to the food item. In general the food commodities employed for decorative purposes are placed directly on to the buffet piece or used to enhance the appearance of the serving dish. Such foods must be *fresh, brightly coloured, edible* and should not dominate the flavour of the finished product.

Some chefs are gifted with a natural talent for decorative work, producing buffet items of outstanding artistic merit, drawing pictures with foodstuffs as an artist uses paints on canvas. However, in most cases, decorative work is time-consuming and dependent upon efficient planning, advanced preparation and the use of a variety of simple but painstaking techniques.

Planning and design

1 The type of design used should be planned in advance, this may be *floral, symmetrical* or of a *free hand design*. Whichever is employed, diagrams, templates, stencils, photographs, etc. showing layout and colour patterns are advisable and will help to ensure varied design and prevent repitition.

Aspic cutters/templates

2. Cutters are an essential part of the larder chef's equipment. They are available in various shapes and sizes, the most common being petal, halfmoon, star, triangle, diamond, tear-drop, etc. These shapes can be used to construct flowers, simple borders, as well as symmetrical patterns. Mosaic is a popular design utilising two or three different colours shaped with a triangular or diamond cutter. When larger shapes are required, a paper template may be prepared from a freehand drawing or tracing and food cut to shape following the lines of the prepared template.

Dipping the foods in aspic

3. Food stuffs used to compile various decorations should be dipped in aspic prior to being placed on to the buffet items. This will ensure that the decoration retains its fresh appearance and adheres correctly to the buffet product. On completion, it is usual to mask the decorated buffet piece/s lightly with a coating of the appropriate aspic jelly to provide a fresh transparent appearance.

Handling the decorative materials

4. Food items used for decoration are often difficult to handle. Cocktail sticks and small tweezers are useful tools when transferring and siting the decorative food materials. In addition, small shapes can easily become dry, quickly losing their fresh appearance and shape. To prevent this occurrence they are held fresh in aspic ready for use.

Socle: food platform/plinth

5. Socles are sometimes used to give height to foods when placed on service dishes.

They elevate and show-off decorated items to advantage, with the main item standing above the garnish and service dish.

Socles are made from various bases (potato, rice, semolina, etc.) the most common being semolina. This is prepared by whisking semolina into boiling water to form a thick smooth gelatinised mixture. The preparation is then poured into the required moulds, allowed to cool and set before turning out for use. Socles may be coated with chaudfroid sauce, decorated and then masked with aspic before being used as a platform for the decorated buffet piece/s.

The centrepiece

6. Cold buffet layout is often designed around an individual main centrepiece or a number of centrepieces. Such pieces may be considered edible and for consumption, e.g. decorated salmon, beef ribs, ham and the like, or alternatively as non-edible displays such as fat/ice carvings, pulled/blown sugar or pastillage models. Whatever, the centrepiece/s are intended to impress the customer and stimulate interest in buffet display.

Decorated skewers (hâtelettes)

7. The silver skewers used for buffet presentations are usually 15–20 cm (6–8 in) long and often have elaborately designed handles (e.g. crown, sword, fleur de lys, small fish or shellfish). They may be used to accompany joints of meat, poultry, game, whole fish and shellfish, etc. in which instances they are decorated according to requirements. Suitable items of food should complement the completed dish and may include tomatoes, either whole or crowns, small lettuce hearts, peppers, various vegetables, small fruits etc. These foods are placed on to the skewer which is then impaled into the buffet item strategically so as not to interfere with initial carving or portioning.

Examples of Foods Typically Used to Garnish Cold Buffet Items

Food material	Examples of presentation style
Artichoke bottoms (cooked)	Whole or stuffed
Asparagus tips (cooked)	Arrange into small bouquets
Cucumber	Sliced thinly or cut to resemble castles or crowns which may be stuffed
Fruits	Various fruits cut into slices, wedges, halved or left whole, may be stuffed
Hard boiled eggs (hens, quails, gulls)	Sliced, quartered, halved or stuffed
Lemons and oranges	Sliced, quartered, segments, baskets and stuffed
Mushrooms	Whole, turned and stuffed
Radishes	Sliced, whole or cut to resemble flowers
Tomatoes (skinned)	Sliced, quartered, crowns, whole and stuffed
Pastry cases (bouchées, barquettes, tartlets, etc.)	Various shapes of pastry cases filled as required, e.g. savoury mousse
Vegetables	Various vegetables blanched, refreshed, drained and neatly trimmed. Arrange into small bunches or bouquets. May be used to stuff other foods, e.g. pastry cases, artichoke bottoms, etc.

Examples of Foods Typically Used for Decorating Cold Buffet Items

Food material	Basic preparation
Green:	
Cucumber peel	Peel cucumber skin, taking care to ensure strips are long and intact. Blanch, refresh and drain well before use. Cucumber skin can be used raw but tends to curl on standing
Leak	Blanch the stem, refresh and drain well. Cut in half lengthwise and separate leaves ready for use
Tarragon leaves	Carefully remove from stem, plunge into boiling water for 5 seconds, refresh and drain well before use
Watercress leaves	As for tarragon leaves
Red:	
Carrot	Peel carrot, then plunge into boiling salted water until cooked 'al denté'. Refresh and drain well. Slice thinly or cut into thin strips with a potato peeler ready for use
Radishes	Slice thinly and use as required. Radishes may also be cut to resemble flowers or crowns
Red pepper	Cut in half and remove seeds. Blanch, refresh and drain well before use
Tomatoes	Skin: carefully cut from raw tomato and use as required, e.g. shape to resemble a rose
	Flesh: skin tomato, cut in half, remove seeds and juice. Cut flesh as required
White:	
Egg white	Separate the egg whites carefully, place them in a buttered dariole mould and cook in a bain-marie until set. Cool, then remove from mould, cut to shape as required
Turnip	Proceed as for carrot
Black:	
Garnishing paste	A proprietary preparation that is purchased in tins. Cut thinly and use as required
Truffle	A black fungus that is usually imported from France in small tins. Cut thinly and use as required

N.B. The lists of decorative/garnishing commodities above are meant only as a basic guide for the practitioner. The experienced buffet chef will utilise a wide range of food materials when practising the art of cold buffet presentation.

Sauces Chaud-Froid

Literally translated, chaud-froid denotes hot-cold which aptly describes the preparation/production of chaud-froid sauce varieties. Chaud-froid sauces are specifically utilised for decorative/flavouring purposes when producing cold buffets in the classic style. Traditionally, the sauce varieties are produced from starch (roux) thickened basic sauces which are further modified/enriched by the addition of aspic jelly, and in most, but not all cases, fresh cream. The basic sauces commonly used include velouté and demi-glace varieties with bechamel used to a lesser extent.

Characteristics

Colour varieties: creamy white, rich bronze/brown, pale delicate green or pink.
Appearance: correct colour, refined, smooth textured fresh appearance with a high gloss impact.
Consistency: when hot/cool a light/medium velvety coating consistency which when cold develops into a setting/holding texture.
Flavour: correct fine flavour of chicken, veal, fish, duck, game etc. some of which can be enhanced with wines, spirits, fortified wines, etc. All correctly seasoned.

CHAUDFROID SAUCE Sauce Chaudfroid

Yield: 1 (approx. 1 qt)
Cooking time: 30 min.

Unit	Ingredient		Metric	Imperial
1	Selected sauce	see chart below	1	2 pt
¾	Selected aspic		750 ml	1½ pt
¼	Fresh cream		250 ml	½ pt
	Seasoning: salt			
	white pepper			

Method

Bring the selected sauce to the boil, add aspic, reboil and reduce by a third to form a smooth glossy sauce of coating consistency. Add the cream, reboil and season to taste. Pass through a fine chinois and tammy (optional), allow to cool stirring occasionally to prevent a skin forming. Use as required.

N.B. Chaudfroid sauce should be used when cool and before it has reached setting point, this ensures that foods are coated evenly and smoothly in readiness for decoration.

Examples of Chaudfroid Sauces Using the Above Formula

Name	Ingredient	French term
White chaudfroid sauce	Chicken velouté Basic aspic	Sauce chaudfroid blanc
Pink chaudfroid sauce	Sauce aurore Basic aspic	Sauce chaudfroid aurore
Green chaudfroid sauce	Chicken velouté Basic aspic	Sauce chaudfroid vert

Proceed as for chaudfroid sauce but add ¼ unit (250 g/10 oz) of spinach puree flavoured with fine herbs, reboil before passing through a fine chinois and tammy (essential).

Brown chaudfroid sauce	Demi glace Basic aspic	Sauce chaudfroid brun

Proceed as for chaudfroid sauce but replace the cream with ⅛ unit (125 ml/5 fl oz) of madeira or port wine.

Name	Ingredient	French term
Fish chaudfroid sauce	Fish velouté Fish aspic	Sauce chaudfroid de poisson

Savoury Aspic Jelly

Savoury aspic is a basic requirement when decorating specific types of cold canapé and cold buffet pieces in the classical style. The principal functions of aspic in relation to larger products are:

1. To impart flavour without predominating   ⟶   In cold savoury mousse varieties
In chaudfroid sauces

2. To impart setting/gloss properties under suitable conditions   ⟶   In sauces chaudfroid/mayonnaise colée
In specific menu items, e.g. oeufs mollet en gelée
In aspic moulds (prawns in aspic)

3. To provide a clear transparent coating on attractively decorated cold foods   ⟶   Large decorative cold buffet pieces
Cocktail canapés
Individual portions of cold food for display

4. To extend the freshness and appearance of cold foods on display   ⟶   Decorated cold buffet pieces
Cold buffet garnishing foods
Hors d'oeuvre moscovite

Aspics, therefore, are employed to impart flavour, introduce setting properties, provide clear, transparent, gloss-like characteristics to foodstuffs and extend their fresh/attractive appearance during the service/display period.

BASIC ASPIC JELLY   Gelée d'Aspic Ordinaire

Yield: 1/1 qt
Cooking time: $1\frac{1}{2}$ hours

Unit	Ingredient	Metric	Imperial
1	Cold veal stock (white)	1	2 pt
$\frac{1}{4}$	Beef shin (minced)	250 g	10 oz
$\frac{1}{5}$	Mirepoix (small dice)	200 g	8 oz
$\frac{1}{5}$	Dry white wine	200 ml	8 fl oz
$\frac{1}{20}$	Egg white	50 g	2 oz
$\frac{1}{20}$	Leaf gelatine	50 g	2 oz
	Bouquet garni		
	Salt and pepper		

Method

Soak gelatine in cold water until soft. Thoroughly mix all ingredients in cooking vessel, add softened gelatine and allow to stand for approximately 30 minutes prior to cooking. Commence cooking by bringing slowly to simmering point, stirring occasionally. Once boiling point is reached, allow to simmer gently for $1\frac{1}{2}$ hours without any further stirring or undue agitation. On completion of cooking strain carefully through a wet muslin, degrease and correct seasoning using salt only (pepper tends to make the aspic cloudy). Cool, then refrigerate ready for use.

N.B. The type of stock used is determined by the flavour of aspic required. In addition browned game, poultry carcasses, etc. may be added to appropriate aspics to enhance the flavour, e.g. Gelée de Volaille, as above using chicken stock; Gelée de Gibier, as above using game stock.

FISH ASPIC JELLY

Gelée de Poisson

Yield: 1/1 qt
Cooking time: 1 hour

Unit	Ingredient	Metric	Imperial
1	Cold fish stock	1	2 pt
1/4	Fillets of whiting (minced)	250 g	10 oz
1/5	Dry white wine	200 ml	8 fl oz
1/10	Onion (small dice)	100 g	4 oz
1/10	Leek (small dice)	100 g	4 oz
1/20	Celery (small dice)	50 g	2 oz
1/20	Egg white	50 g	2 oz
1/20	Leaf gelatine	50 g	2 oz
	Seasonings: pinch thyme		
	bay leaf		
	parsley stalk		
	salt and pepper		

Method

Soak gelatine in cold water until soft. Thoroughly mix all ingredients in cooking vessel, add softened gelatine. Commence cooking by bringing slowly to simmering point, stirring occasionally. Once boiling point is reached, allow to simmer gently for 1 hour without any further stirring or undue agitation. On completion of cooking, strain carefully through a wet muslin, degrease and correct seasoning using salt only (pepper tends to make the aspic cloudy). Cool then refrigerate ready for use.

Kitchen: stove work

13

Basics of Culinary Practice

Mise-en-place translated means 'put in place', in kitchen terms it refers to organized advanced preparation of basic materials in both a raw and cooked state. Such mise-en-place enables the kitchen staff to cook and present food for service with the minimum of difficulty and in good time.

Organized working methods, partnered by knowledge, skill and innate talent are the chef's roadway to successful cookery. Whether the culinary delight be simple or exotic, well planned mise-en-place is essential if a smooth operation is to be achieved.

Basic mise-en-place for stove work is divided into the following groups:

1. basic flavourings in common use;
2. basic garnishes and other common preparations;
3. basic stocks essences and glazes. Thickening and binding agents;
4. basic sauces,—foundation and non-derivative types.

Basic Flavourings and their Uses

Flavourings are used to enhance the taste of a variety of savoury preparations. During the production of food for the table there are a number of basic flavourings that are frequently employed. They may be added in good measure, or in small amounts, according to the strength of the flavouring desired in the completed dish. A flavouring, therefore, may play a major role in the taste of a product or be used to savour delicately. For example:

(a) thyme is used to predominate when preparing thyme and parsley stuffing, but is used more delicately in stews and soups as part of the bouquet garni.
(b) garlic is used to predominate when preparing garlic flavoured butter, but used more delicately as a flavouring in French onion soup. Flavourings are infused, extracted or added just prior to service.

Flavourings in Common use

Bouquet Garni (an infused flavouring)

Consists of a variety of selected herbs and vegetables, neatly secured in a leek leaf or piece of muslin. The flavouring is used delicately, as over use would result in the bouquet garni predominating.

1 sprig of thyme
1 bay leaf
1 small piece of celery
few parsley stalks, few crushed peppercorns

Other herbs may be used to complement a particular flavour, e.g. basil with tomato, rosemary with lamb. The bouquet can be purchased commercially in made-up sachets.

Onion Cloué (piqué) — an infused flavouring

A peeled onion into which a selected number of cloves are pressed, one of which impales a bay leaf to the onion.

1 medium onion
4 cloves
1 bay leaf

Also referred to as a studded onion.

MIREPOIX (AN EXTRACTED FLAVOUR)

Mirepoix in a culinary sense indicates the use of a basic preparation of roughly cut vegetables, sometimes with pieces of streaky bacon, and a pinch of aromates.

Unit	Ingredient	Metric (g)	Imperial (oz)
1	Onion	400	16
1	Carrot	400	16
$\frac{1}{2}$	Celery	200	8
$\frac{1}{4}$	Streaky bacon ⎱ optional	100	4
	Aromates ⎰		

Method and Uses

Roughly cut the prepared vegetables to the selected size. *A fine cut* is used when a speedy extraction of flavour is required, e.g. in sauce reductions, this ensures maximum extraction of flavour in the shortest possible time. *A medium cut* is employed when a lengthy 'sweating' process is used in the initial cooking stage, e.g. soups and stews. This larger size reduces the risk of over-cooking (burning). The full extraction of flavour is completed by the end of the cooking period. *A large cut* is often used when the mirepoix is employed as a base upon which pieces of meat are braised or pot-roasted. The large cut reduces the risk of the vegetables burning and full extraction of flavour is achieved by the end of the cooking time.

fine cut — brunoise
medium cut — 1 cm ($\frac{1}{2}$ in) approximately.
large cut — size determined by size of cooking vessel

White Mirepoix or Vegetable Adjunct (an extracted flavour)

Used and prepared as for mirepoix but omitting one or more of the ingredients, e.g. carrot would be omitted where a white colour is required in a finished product, e.g. cream of cauliflower soup. During the preparation of curry sauce, onion is used as a vegetable flavouring.

Scorched Mirepoix/Vegetable Adjunct

Vegetables browned on a hot griddle plate.

Preserved Garlic (an added flavour)

Crush the cloves of garlic with the flat side of a chopping knife and remove the outer skin. Sprinkle the crushed cloves liberally with salt and chop this mixture finely. Put into a suitable container and cover the preserved garlic with edible oil for storage. The oil acts as a seal and reduces the risk of discoloration. Garlic is chopped in salt

(a) to facilitate ease of chopping;
(b) to absorb the 'oil' from the garlic released during chopping;
(c) to act as a preservative.

Due to the high concentration of salt in this preparation, care must be exercised when seasoning foods to which preserved garlic has been added. Correctly stored, the prepared garlic will keep in good condition for a long period. It may be used to enhance the flavour of selected soups, stews, sauces, entrées, etc.

Garlic Pellets (an added flavour)

Finely chop or mince fat bacon and combine with chopped parsley. Add a hint of freshly chopped or preserved garlic and shape into small pellets. Used to flavour minestrone.

DUXELLE (AN ADDED FLAVOUR)

A savoury mixture used for stuffings, fillings and sauces.
Yield: 400 g (1 lb)
Cooking time: 5 min

Unit	Ingredient	Metric (g)	Imperial (oz)
1	Mushroom trimmings (brunoise)	400	16
$1/_2$	Onion brunoise	200	8
$1/_8$	Butter/oil	50	2
	Chopped parsley		
	Hint of garlic		
	Pinch of nutmeg		
	Salt and pepper		

To Prepare as a Stuffing

Add $1/_4$ unit (100 g [4 oz]) fresh breadcrumbs to the basic cooked duxelle and sufficient tomatoed demi-glace to develop a suitable texture.

Method

Place the onions and mushrooms into the melted butter and oil, sweat over a gentle heat without colouring. Season the ingredients during the cooking process. Once the ingredients are cooked, remove from the heat, add the parsley, seasonings, herbs and spices.
   Use immediately or place into a covered container to cool, store in refrigerator.

Tomato Concassé (an added flavour)

Yield: 400 g (1 lb) tomatoes
gives 200 g (8 oz) concassé approximately

Method

Remove 'eye' from tomatoes.
Place into a perforated basket and plunge into boiling water for 5 – 10 seconds, withdraw and plunge immediately into cold water. This blanching and refreshing process prevents the tomatoes from over cooking and at the same time allows the skins to be removed with ease. Cut the skinned tomatoes in half, remove seeds and juice and keep for use. Roughly chop the remaining tomato flesh to form concassé.
Use as an added flavour, garnish or filling.

TOMATES CONCASSÊES (AN ADDED COOKED FLAVOURING)

Yield: 400 g (1 lb)
Cooking time: 3 – 5 min

Unit	Ingredient	Metric (g)	Imperial (oz)
1	Tomato concassé	400	16
$\frac{1}{8}$	Onion brunoise	50	2
$\frac{1}{16}$	Butter/oil	25	1
	Hint of garlic		
	Pinch of salt		
	Pepper and sugar		

Method

Sweat the onions in butter/oil without colouring. Add remaining ingredients and continue to sweat for a few seconds. Remove from the heat, use immediately, or place into a container to cool, cover and store in a refrigerator.
Use as a savoury filling or garnish.

Basic Garnishes and Other Common Preparations

Decorative garnishes are frequently added to food preparations immediately prior to service. They enhance the appearance of the finished products making them more interesting and appetising. Indeed in many instances it is the garnish which enables a basic preparation to appear on a menu under a number of different guises, for example,

(a) Consommé *Célestine* (small julienne of savoury pancake)
    Consommé *Brunoise* (cooked brunoise of spring vegetables)
(b) Poulet Sauté *Bonne Femme* (bacon lardons, button onions, cocotte potatoes)
    Poulet Sauté *Doria* (cooked shaped cucumber)
(c) Contrefilet de Boeuf Rôti *à l'Anglaise* (Yorkshire pudding, horseradish sauce, roast gravy and watercress)
    Contrefilet de Boeuf *Bouquetière* (cooked vegetables presented as small bouquets)

In order to effect an efficient service, and present a high quality product it is necessary to have garnishes prepared in advance, without their flavour or appearance having been adversely affected. Garnishes are prepared from a variety of foods. Some are used in a raw state, e.g. fresh watercress, whereas others are par-cooked and refreshed in readiness for speedy reheating at service time, e.g. vegetables for bouquets. Whatever the nature of the garnish advanced preparation is essential.

Points for Consideration when Garnishing Foods

(a) Attractively presented food acts as a sales incentive by stimulating the diner's appetite (e.g. food display in a self-service unit).
(b) The size and arrangement of the garnish needs to be in proportion to the size of the culinary product that it is to decorate.
(c) Garnishes need to be seasoned independently.
(d) Garnishes need to be arranged to facilitate ease of service and also to ensure adequate portioning.

Garnishes, Cuts or Shapes in Common Use

Green vegetables

(French beans, cauliflower bouquets, garden peas) Usually par-boiled, refreshed (*see* p. 267) and stored in readiness for reheating as required.

'Turned' vegetables

(Turnips, carrot, cucumber—*Légumes tourné*) Portions of raw vegetables 'turned' i.e. cut into barrel shape using an office knife. Usually simmered, refreshed, then reheated as required.

Shaped vegetables

Classical cuts.
A variety of vegetables may be prepared in the following shapes:

Brunoise   Vegetables cut to a very fine dice. The name is attributed to the Brunoy district of France renowned for the growing of fine spring vegetables.

Macédoine   Vegetables cut into small cubes—$\frac{1}{2}$ cm ($\frac{1}{4}$ in). The name is said to be derived from Macedonia, a country formed by small states which were conquered by Alexander the Great.

Julienne   Vegetables cut into very thin strips—2–3 cm ($1-1\frac{1}{2}$ in long). The name is said to be associated with the eighteenth century French chef, Jean Julienne who bequeathed his fortune to the poor of Paris.

Jardinière   Vegetables cut to a 'baton' shape approx $2\frac{1}{2}$ cm × $\frac{1}{2}$ cm × $\frac{1}{2}$ cm (1 in × $\frac{1}{4}$ in × $\frac{1}{4}$ in). Jardiner translates as 'gardener' associating this garnish with garden vegetables

Paysanne   Vegetables cut into small thin triangles, circles and squares. Paysanne means 'peasant style' and originally indicated roughly cut vegetables, the above shapes have been refined from these origins.

N.B.   The sizes mentioned are meant only as a guide and may be varied as required.

Potato Garnishes in Common Use

Straw potatoes — Pommes pailles
Matchstick potatoes — Pommes allumettes ⎫
Game chips (crisps) — Pommes chips ⎬ see p. 303
Game chips (perforated) — Pommes gaufrettes ⎭
Turned potatoes — Pommes tourné shaped as for turned vegetables, usually cooked just prior to service. The method of cookery will vary according to requirements.

Skinned Tomatoes

Remove eye from tomato then plunge into boiling water for approximately 5 – 10 seconds, plunge immediately into cold water to prevent further cooking. Remove skins, drain off water and store in refrigerator for use.

Button Onions (Oignons Bouton)

May be cooked with or without colour and used for garnishing purposes.

With Colour (browned—glacés à brun)   Sauté the raw onions in cooking oil/butter, add a pinch of sugar to facilitate browning (i.e. sugar caramelises). Lightly season and cook to a golden brown. When browned cover with lid to complete cooking, use immediately.

The browned onions can be par-cooked, cooled and stored for use at a later stage. They are reheated by tossing in heated oil/butter.

Without Colour (kept white—glacés à blanc)   Par-cook in sufficient seasoned acidulated water (squeeze of lemon), allow to cool in liquor and store in refrigerator for use at a later stage. Complete cooking and preparation for service by:

(i)   Re-heating in the liquor.
(ii) Straining, then reheating by tossing onions in heated butter/margarine without colour.

N.B.   May be cooked 'à blanc' (*see* p. 268)

Par-cooked Mushrooms

Place the mushrooms into sufficient simmering acidulated water (squeeze of lemon) and a knob of butter. Cook to 'just done', and store in cooking liquor. The resultant liquor may be used in other culinary preparations e.g. sauces. The par-cooked mushrooms may be reheated with or without colour in melted butter.

Artichoke Bottoms (Fonds d'artichauts)

To prepare, hold the globe artichoke at the stalk end and peel away all the leaves until the base and fibrous matter are visible. Using a stainless steel knife remove the stalk, rub the base with a squeeze of lemon juice to prevent discoloration, trim to shape.

The fibrous matter is more easily removed once the base is cooked. Simmer the base in a 'blanc' (*see* p. 268) to 'just done', allow to cool, remove the fibrous matter with a stainless steel spoon. The artichoke bottoms can be used immediately or stored for a short while in the cooking liquor. The fonds can be reheated by tossing in melted butter (sliced or whole).

Lemon Garnishes

Using a stainless steel knife

Wedges   Trim the pointed ends of the lemon and leave a covering of pith to facilitate handling. Cut the lemon in half lengthways and then each half into wedges. Remove pips and pith to ensure that juice can be easily extracted.

N.B.   A stainless knife is used in preference to steel because it does not stain when in contact with the acid of lemon.

The skin of the lemon may be decorated with a 'channel cutter' before being cut into wedges. Used with deep fried fish, etc.

Rounds/fillets   Trim the pointed ends of the lemon until the fruit is visible. Using a stainless steel knife remove the outer skin and pith completely. Slice the skinned lemon into rounds and remove pips. Rounds are often dipped into chopped parsley or lightly dipped into paprika in order to add colour to the garnish. Remove fillets by cutting between pith segmentation and the fruit.
They are used to garnish shallow fried fish, cooked escalopes of veal/pork, etc.

N.B.   A stainless steel knife avoids staining of knives and foods.

Chopped Parsley

Wash the parsley before removing the leaves from the stalks. Dry well by squeezing out the excess moisture and complete the drying in a clean cloth. Remove stalks, squeeze the parsley leaves into a tight ball and chop finely.

Bouquets of Parsley or Watercress (small bunches)

Wash and store in a shallow trough of iced water until required for use. The iced water acts to keep the bouquets as crisp and fresh looking as possible.

Bread Garnishes and Preparations

Stale bread is used for the following preparations (staleness ensures ease of cutting).

Shapes   Croûtons or sippets — small to medium dice of bread
Croûtes/croûtons   — usually cut round or heart shaped.

Browned Breadcrumbs (White breadcrumbs cooked to a golden brown colour.)

All the above are shallow fried in oil or clarified butter/margarine to a golden brown colour, crisp texture, drained well and placed on absorbent kitchen paper to remove excess grease.

Flûtes   Toasted slices cut from thin French sticks.

N.B.   The above garnishes are used to decorate or accompany soups, entrées, roasts, etc.

Lardons of Bacon

Usually streaky bacon cut into bâton shapes, blanched for a few minutes in boiling water, strained and finished by colouring quickly in a sauté or frying pan. The lardons are often stored after blanching and later reheated for service.

Used as a garnish with various entrées.

Other Basic Preparations

Browned Flour

A preparation used in the making of a brown roux. The browned flour speeds up the browning process and develops a characteristic flavour of its own. Ideally suited for the production of Espagnole.

To brown, spread the plain flour evenly on to a suitably sized baking tray and place in a moderate oven to colour golden brown. During the browning process it is necessary to agitate the flour from time to time. This ensures even browning. Once the flour is sufficiently browned, sift through a cane sieve and store in a dry container in readiness for use.

Breadcrumbs and Raspings

Stale white bread minus the crusts is passed through a machine or a cane sieve to produce fresh white breadcrumbs. For raspings the whole loaf including the crusts is dried then passed through a fine mincer.

Clarified Butter

Heat the butter slowly until the whey has completely evaporated and the fat is separated from the milk solids. Pour off the butter fat into a container and store for use. Used chiefly as a cooking medium.

The reason for clarifying butter is to remove the possibility of the butter burning during cooking and spoiling the food. It is the milk solids that easily burn.

Dripping (rendered fat)

An economic means of utilizing fat trimmings.
Mince the trimming and place into a friture with a little water (this prevents the fat from sticking to the friture and burning in the early stages of cooking). Render over a slow heat until the fat is fully extracted and the water content has evaporated. This is indicated when fat ceases to bubble.

Strain clear fat into clean friture or pour into containers for storage. Store in cold room. Used as a frying medium.

N.B. First class dripping is produced from beef fat only. Second class is produced from a variety of animal fats.

Basic Stocks, Essences and Glazes

Fonds de Cuisine (foundations of the kitchen)

Stock forms the essential basis for many culinary products including soups, sauces, gravies and main courses. Stock, therefore, is a premier basic culinary requirement, adding flavour and body to various dishes.

Stock liquor is a base of water into which flavour from selected bones and vegetables is extracted by a gentle boiling process. Other flavours are infused into the stock from such basic flavourings as a bouquet garni and onion clouté. Once the cooking time is complete the resultant strained liquor is termed stock.

Guidelines for Stock Production

(a) Choose fresh ingredients to ensure a longer life for the stock and to avoid unpleasant flavours, a result of using tainted ingredients.

(b) Scrape the bones to remove fat. This reduces the grease content of the stock.

(c) Chop the bones to facilitate full extraction of flavour.

(d) At the onset of the cooking process place the ingredients into cold rather than hot water, boiling water seals in, rather than extracts the flavour in the early stages.

(e) Use clean equipment to prevent food spoilage from harmful bacteria and dirt.

(f) On boiling, skim, degrease and simmer the stock. These practices prevent the stock from clouding, becoming greasy and losing volume due to rapid boiling and excessive evaporation.

(g) It is wise to leave the stock without seasoning. The stock will be utilized in the preparation of culinary products which will be seasoned at a later stage.

(h) Convenience stocks are of a highly seasoned nature and care must be employed when seasoning products with which they are used.

(i) Once the stock is cooked and full extraction of flavour achieved, strain into a clean stock pot. It is a mistake to leave bones and vegetables in the pot as they will begin to break up, re-absorb some of the stock flavour, cause obstruction and result in a cloudy stock.

Means of Preventing Stock from Souring

(a) Prepare regular quantities of fresh stock to cater for kitchen requirements, usually on a weekly basis.

(b) Store stock by cooling quickly for refrigeration. Reheat amounts as required.

(c) Reduce to concentrated form, i.e. stock glaze and store in a covered container 'on refrigeration'.

(d) Keep stock at boiling point and use as required.

ORDINARY BROWN WHITE STOCK

Fond Brun/Blanc Ordinaire

Yield: 5 l (1 gal)
Cooking time: see chart below

Unit	Ingredient	Metric	Imperial
1	Cold water	5 l	1 gal
$\frac{1}{2}$	Selected bones (trimmed and chopped)	2.5 kg	5 lb
$\frac{1}{10}$	Mirepoix (left whole)	500 g	1 lb
	for white stocks and sliced for brown to increase surfaces available for browning		
	Flavourings: bouquet garni mushroom and tomato trimmings		

N.B. For white stocks only the bones/meat content are blanched before use to remove scum.

Method for Brown Stocks

Place the chopped bones into a roasting tray and brown in a moderately hot oven. Brown the sliced mirepoix by scorching the vegetables on a hot griddle plate, take care not to over brown the mirepoix or bones otherwise a bitter flavour may result.

Once browned, place the bones and mirepoix into a clean stock pot, cover the contents with the water, place on the heat and bring the contents slowly to the boil. On boiling skim and degrease the stock, add bouquet garni and any trimmings, simmer gently.

Throughout the cooking process remove scum and grease as they rise to the surface. At the same time clean the inside of the pot from any scum sediment sticking to the upper sides, using a clean, damp cloth. After full extraction strain the stock for use.

Method for White Stocks

The same method as above omitting the browning process. As already mentioned it is unnecessary to slice the mirepoix. Appropriate bones/meat are blanched prior to use.

Stocks prepared using the above formula

English	French	Selected bones	Cooking time (hr)
Beef stock	Fond de Boeuf	Beef	6—8
Veal stock	Fond de Veau	Veal	6—8
Mutton stock	Fond de Moûton	Mutton/lamb	4
Game stock*	Fond de Gibier	Stewing game and selected game bones	4
Chicken stock	Fond de Volaille	Boiling fowl, chicken carcasses, necks and giblets	2—4

* Game stock is prepared using brown method only.

The above stocks may be prepared as brown or white. For example brown beef stock (fond brun de boeuf) or white beef stock (fond blanc de boeuf).

ESTOUFFADE (an enriched brown stock)

Yield: 5 l (1 gal)
Cooking time: until meat is cooked

Unit	Ingredient	Metric	Imperial
1	Beef/veal stock (brown)	5 l	1 gal
½	Beef/veal shin	2.5 kg	5 lb

Method

Place the meat into a hot oven to seal and colour to a golden brown, place into a stock pot, cover with the stock, bring slowly to the boil, skim and degrease. Simmer the contents until the meat is cooked. Strain the estouffade for use. The cooked meat may be further utilized in a variety of made-up dishes.

Store as for stocks (*see* p. 169)

FISH STOCK   **Fumet de Poisson**

Yield: 5 l (1 gal)
Cooking time: 20 – 30 min from simmering point

Unit	Ingredient	Metric	Imperial
1	Cold water	5 l	1 gal
$\frac{1}{2}$	White fish bones and trimmings (chopped)	2.5 kg	5 lb
$\frac{1}{20}$	Sliced onions	250 g	8 oz
$\frac{1}{20}$	Butter	250 g	8 oz
	Flavourings:		
	parsley stalks		
	few milled peppercorns		
	bay leaf		
	squeeze of lemon juice		

N.B.   Use bones, flesh, trimmings of fresh white fish typically sole turbot, whiting. Wash in fresh cold running water before use.

Method

Sweat the onions and chopped fish bones in melted butter for a few minutes over gentle heat. Do not allow the ingredients to take on colour. Add peppercorns, lemon juice, and water, bring contents slowly to the boil and skim the stock. At this stage introduce the remaining ingredients and simmer the stock for a further 20 minutes. Strain immediately and use as required. Over cooking of the fish bones may result in a bitter stock.

Essences and Glazes

Stock essence is the result of stock reduced by half to a more concentrated form. A stock glaze (glace de fond) describes the essence further reduced to a gelatinous consistency. The liquid glaze is poured into containers, allowed to cool, then stored in a refrigerator. On cooling the glaze sets firm.

Essences and glazes are used to strengthen the flavour of culinary products, e.g. stocks, sauces, stews, etc.

Stock Glazes

Chicken glaze (*Glace de Volaille*)
Meat glaze (*Glace de Viande*)
Fish glaze (*Glace de Poisson*)

General Comments

Kitchens working along traditional lines continue to make use of freshly prepared stocks, in the main two general stocks are prepared from a variety of selected bones, e.g. white and brown stock for general use. In addition to those two main stocks other stocks of a specific flavour are produced for use in particular culinary preparations, e.g. fish, veal, chicken, game, and mutton stocks.

Convenience preparations may be used as a substitute for traditional stocks. They may also be added to freshly prepared stock to strengthen flavour.

Practical Applications of Thickening and Binding Agents

As previously stated starch is employed as a thickening and binding agent in a number of culinary products. Many items are thickened to varying degrees of consistency and common examples include; soups, sauces, gravies, stews and braises, etc. When using fat/oil as the medium to disperse starch for use as a thickener the most common methods are as follows.

Roux

A mixture of melted fat or oil and flour which is cooked to achieve varying degrees of colour.

Beurre Manié (manipulated butter)

Butter and flour mixed together to form a soft paste.

Roux

An example of roux proportions is given.

Unit	Ingredient	Metric (g)	Imperial (oz)
1	Flour	50	2
1	Fat or oil	50	2

White Roux   Roux Blanc

Melt the fat over gentle heat, add the flour and mix well. Cook gently for a few minutes without allowing the roux to take on any apparent change of colour. Use for white sauces, soups, white stews, and white braised preparations, etc.

Blond or Fawn Roux   Roux Blond

As above but cooked for a longer period without allowing the roux to undergo any significant change in colour. Used in the preparation of sauces and soups, etc.

Brown Roux   Roux Brun

As above, but continue to cook over gentle heat until the roux takes on a rich brown colour. Take care not to burn the roux as this will create a bitter flavour in the final product. N. B. *Browned flour* (p. 168) can be used for this preparation and it has the advantage of colouring more quickly. This reduces the risk of burning by shortening the cooking time. Used in the preparation of Espagnole (basic brown sauce).

N.B.   Generally butter or margarine are used for the preparation of white and blond roux; oil, dripping or lard for brown roux.

Beurre Manié (manipulated butter)

Mix together equal quantities of butter and flour to form a soft paste. Add small amounts to boiling liquids stirring or whisking to achieve the required consistency.

N.B.   In order to ensure that starch-thickened products do not have a 'raw' starch flavour it is necessary to simmer/boil the products for a period of time.

Temporary Suspensions

When using a cold liquid medium to disperse starch for use as a thickening agent, the selected starch e.g. cornflour, arrowroot or modified, is mixed thoroughly in sufficient liquid before being used.

Panadas (binding agents)   Panade

As previously stated in Chapter 4 binding agents are based on either cooked starches or proteins, or mixtures of both. The principal panadas are listed below. They play a prominent part in the *larder preparations* of various products, which are despatched to the kitchen for cooking. Their main function in recipes is to act as a binding/shape-retaining/extending commodity.

Types of Panada

Bread, flour, frangipane, potato, and rice panadas. Thick basic sauces are also used as binding agents and sometimes referred to as sauce panadas.

Liaisons

Liaisons Oeuf et Crème

This is a liaison of egg yolks and fresh cream. The quantities of egg yolks and cream vary in accordance with the recipe in which the liaison is to be used. Whatever the amounts the cream and yolks are thoroughly mixed together for use. They are added to the product just prior to service and care must be taken not to boil the product once the liaison has been added otherwise it will curdle.

Liaison au Sang

This is a more obscure thickening using blood. This liaison is used in the thickening of certain speciality items, such as game stew, jugged hare, and coq au vin. In these instances the blood is collected from the evisceration and cleaning process of game and poultry. It is then whisked together with cold water in a ratio of approximately 1 part blood to $\frac{1}{4}$ part water. As with the egg and cream liaison it is added just prior to service and removed from the direct heat to prevent boiling and curdling.

Basic Sauces — foundation and non-derivative types

When a full kitchen brigade is employed a great number of sauces are the responsibility of the Chef Saucier. He/she is a prominent member of the brigade whose work requires a vast amount of culinary expertise and artistic flair. Sauces are also prepared by other members of the brigade as part of their general responsibilities. Fish sauces for example are the responsibility of the Chef Poissonier, and sauces to accompany most meats would be prepared by the Chef Rôtisseur. In smaller brigades the preparation of sauces may be carried out by other members of the kitchen staff.

In some instances sauces date back over a century and many owe their identity to a particular continent, country, region or person. Examples of these associations are illustrated in the following list:

(a) Sweet and sour sauces of the Orient;
(b) Chilli sauces from Latin America;

(c) Curry sauces from India;
(d) Espagnole sauce from Spain;
(e) Tomato sauce from Italy (Salsa Pomodori);
(f) Béchamel sauce from France.

The functions of sauces in culinary work are to:

1. introduce harmony and contrast to culinary products;
2. add to the nutritive value of the food, often cheaply;
3. create more interesting ways of enjoying food;
4. add contrast in taste, texture and colour;
5. aid digestion, complement and counteract foods which they accompany, e.g. sharp flavoured sauces with fatty foods—apple sauce with roast pork.

Sauces may be classified as follows:

(a) basic foundation sauces and their derivatives;
(b) non-derivative sauces.

Basic Sauces

Basic foundation sauces are those from which many derivative sauces are produced.

Sauce Béchamel

A white coloured savoury sauce made from infused milk and a white roux (*see* p. 172).

Sauce Veloutée

A blond coloured savoury sauce made from white stock and a blond roux (*see* p. 172).

Espagnole

A brown sauce made from brown stock and a brown roux (*see* p. 172).

Demi-Glace or Half-Glaze

A refined Espagnole sauce.

N.B.   The above sauces are all starch thickened.

Basic Emulsified Foundation Sauces

Sauce Hollandaise

This sauce is an emulsification of egg yolk, melted butter and a vinegar reduction.

Sauce Béarnaise

This is an emulsification of egg yolks, melted butter, and an aromatic vinegar reduction.

Sauce Mayonnaise

This sauce is an emulsification of egg yolk, edible oil and flavoured vinegar (larder preparation).

Non-derivative/Independent Sauces and Gravies

Foreign

Jus Lié	Thickened gravy
Sauce Kari	Curry sauce
Sauce Tomate	Tomato sauce
Sauce Portugaise	Portuguese sauce
Sauce Provençale	
Sauce Bigarade	Orange flavoured sauce
Sweet and Sour Sauce	
Sauce Homard	Lobster sauce
Sauce Smitane	Sour cream sauce
Sauce Bolognaise	Savoury meat sauce.

N.B.   For roast gravies (jus rôti) *see* p. 389.

English

Apple sauce	Sauce Pommes
Bread sauce	Sauce Pain
Cranberry sauce	Sauce Airelles Coussinette
Cumberland sauce	
Mint sauce	Sauce Menthe

Butter Sauces

Hot butter sauces	
Hard butter sauces	Beurre Composé

Independent à la Carte Sauces

Many sauces used in à la carte work, are either derivatives of the foundation sauces or are independently prepared in their own right, e.g. Sauce Provençale. In addition, other sauces for à la carte purposes are often prepared using cream, butter, wine, spirit, liqueur, refined/reduced stocks in various combinations and often without starch for thickening. In these cases cream/butter acts to lié sauces.

General Faults in Sauce Production

The aim in sauce production is to prepare sauces of correct consistency, colour, texture and gloss, coupled with a distinct flavour pertaining to the particular sauce.
This ideal is not always achieved. Some of the more common faults are listed below.

Lumpiness

This may be caused by the following:

(a)   roux too dry when liquid is added. The dry roux is a result of using incorrect roux balance, i.e. insufficient fat to flour;

(b)   adding the liquid too quickly to the roux and not stirring continuously to the boil. A smooth textured sauce is achieved by adding the liquid slowly to the roux and mixing thoroughly and continuously to boiling point;

(c) insufficient mixing of a temporary starch suspension before stirring into a boiling liquid, e.g. thickening of Jus Lié with arrowroot starch. Unless the suspension is sufficiently blending with cold liquid, dry starch granules will form lumps once added to the boiling liquid.

(d) allowing a skin to form which later could be stirred into the sauce before its completion. The skin is formed when the surface of the sauce comes into contact with air. This skin formation is prevented by covering the completed sauce with one of the following:

    (i)   a film of melted butter;
    (ii) a greased paper (cartouche);
    (iii) a lid covering

(e) by allowing sauce to congeal on the sides of the cooking vessel which later could be stirred into sauce. This is prevented by clearing the sauce from the pan sides once sauce is completed or by re-straining the sauce.

Poor Gloss

This is caused by insufficient cooking of the sauce or using a sauce which has not been passed, tammied or liquidized. A tammied sauce is one that has been passed through a lightly moistened fine cloth. High gloss is achieved by preparing the sauce correctly and aided by the addition of butter just prior to service; technically this process is termed 'monter au beurre' (mounting with butter).

Incorrect Consistency

This is a result of incorrect formula balance. Over or under cooking of the sauce results in too thick a sauce due to excessive evaporation or too thin a sauce due to insufficient cooking around boiling point. Around boiling point the starch molecules effect full thickening (see p. 62).

Greasiness

This is caused by incorrect formula balance, i.e. too much fat in roux or failure to skim off surface grease as it rises. The use of greasy stock may cause this fault.

Poor Colour

Poor colour is a result of incorrect cooking of the roux in the early stages, using dirty cooking vessels or unsuitable utensils, e.g. using a metal whisk when preparing a white sauce in an aluminium saucepan. The sauce turns grey when the metal whisk comes into contact with the sides of the saucepan, removing the grey film from the aluminium, which then discolours the sauce.

Raw Starch Flavour

This is a result of insufficient cooking of the starch. Starch needs to reach boiling point, and be simmered for a further period to avoid raw starch flavour.

Bitter Flavour

This is caused by over browning or burning of the roux.

N.B.   For faults in emulsified sauces (see p. 190).

Starch Thickened Foundation Sauces

BASIC WHITE SAUCE (made from milk and a white roux)   Béchamel

Yield: 1 l (1 qt)
Cooking time: 30 min

Unit	Ingredient	Metric	Imperial
1	Milk (heated)	1 l	2 pt
$\frac{1}{10}$	Butter/margarine	100 g	4 oz
$\frac{1}{10}$	Flour (plain)	100 g	4 oz
	Onion clouté		

Method

Form a white roux using butter and flour. Gradually add the heated milk to the roux stirring thoroughly and continuously to the boil. Add onion clouté and simmer gently for approximately 30 minutes. Remove onion clouté, strain sauce through fine chinois. Cover to prevent skin formation (*see* p. 176). Place in bain-marie to keep hot, use as required. The prepared sauce may be cooled, refrigerated, then reheated and finished as required at a later stage.

This sauce can be used as a thickening agent in cream soups, or extended into suitable derivative sauces as shown in following table.

Examples of sauces derived from sauce béchamel: (Added ingredients in relation to 1 unit $\frac{1}{2}$ l (1 pt) basic sauce)

English term	Unit	Ingredient	Metric	Imperial	French term	Examples of uses
Anchovy sauce		Flavour with anchovy essence to taste			Sauce aux Anchois	Poached, boiled, grilled fish
Cheese sauce	$\frac{1}{10}$ $\frac{1}{20}$	Grated Cheddar cheese Egg yolk when being glazed or gratinated Add ingredients to basic sauce (do not re-boil after yolk has been added). Correct seasoning	50 g 25 g	2 oz 1 oz	Sauce Mornay	Poached/ boiled eggs and fish. Boiled vegetables, cooked pasta
Cream sauce	$\frac{1}{5}$	Fresh cream Add to basic sauce. Correct seasoning	100 ml	4 fl.oz	Sauce Crème	Poached/ boiled fish and eggs. Boiled vegetables

English term	Unit	Ingredient	Metric	Imperial	French term	Examples of uses
Egg sauce	¹/₅	Chopped hard boiled egg	100 g	4 oz	Sauce aux Oeufs	Poached/ boiled fish
		Add ingredients to basic sauce. Correct seasoning				
Mustard sauce		Sufficient diluted English mustard to flavour. Correct seasoning			Sauce Moutarde	Grilled herrings and mackerel
Onion sauce	¹/₅	Onion brunoise sweated without colour, add to basic sauce. Correct seasoning	100 g	4 oz	Sauce aux Oignons	Boiled eggs, roast mutton
Refined onion sauce		As above passed through fine chinois			Sauce Soubise	Roast mutton, roast veal, poached/ boiled eggs
Parsley sauce		Sufficient chopped parsley to garnish and flavour. Correct seasoning			Sauce Persil	Poached/ boiled fish, vegetables, and ham

N.B.   All the above sauces are seasoned with salt and pepper to taste, and adjusted for consistency to suit requirements.

BASIC BLOND SAUCE
(made from white stock and a blond roux)   Sauce Veloutée or Velouté

Yield: 1 l/1 qt
Cooking time: 45 min

Unit	Ingredient	Metric	Imperial
1	White stock (chicken, veal, fish, mutton)	1 l	2 pt
¹/₁₀	Butter/margarine	100 g	4 oz
¹/₁₀	Flour	100 g	4 oz
	Bouquet garni and mushroom trimmings		

Method

Form a blond roux using butter and flour. Gradually add the stock to the roux stirring thoroughly and continuously to the boil. Add remaining ingredients and simmer gently for 45 minutes. Strain through a fine chinois. Cover to prevent skin formation (*see* p. 176).

Place in bain-marie to keep hot, use as required. The prepared sauce may be cooled and refrigerated, then reheated and finished as required.

This sauce can be used as a thickening agent in velouté soups or extended into suitable derivative sauces as shown in following chart.

N.B. The name of the velouté is determined by the flavour of the stock used, i.e.

Stock	English	French
Chicken	Chicken Velouté	Velouté de Volaille
Fish	Fish Velouté	Velouté de Poisson
Mutton	Mutton Velouté	Velouté de Mouton
Veal	Veal Velouté	Velouté de Veau

N.B. All the following sauces are seasoned with salt and pepper to taste and adjusted for consistency to suit requirements. The following sauces, other than caper sauce, are often served with poached chicken preparations, vegetable and egg courses.

Examples of Sauces Derived from Chicken/Veal Velouté

English term	Unit	Ingredient	Metric	Imperial	French term
		Added ingredients in relation to 1 unit ½ l (1 pt) basic sauce			
Supreme sauce	$1/_5$	Cream	100 ml	4 oz	Sauce Suprême
	$1/_{20}$	Butter	25 g	1 oz	
		Squeeze of lemon juice			
		Combine ingredients with basic sauce, season to taste			
		Added ingredient in relation to 1 unit ½ l (1 pt) of supreme sauce—Sauce Suprême			
Tomatoed supreme sauce	$1/_5$	Tomato sauce	100 ml	4 fl.oz	Sauce Aurore
		Combine with supreme sauce to flavour and colour. Season to taste			
Curry flavoured supreme sauce	$1/_{10}$	Onion brunoise	50 g	2 oz	Sauce Indienne
	$1/_{10}$	Apple diced	50 g	2 oz	
	$1/_{10}$	Coconut milk (*see* p. 103)	50 ml	2 fl.oz	
	$1/_{20}$	Butter	25 g	1 oz	
	$1/_{40}$	Curry powder/paste	12.5 g	$1/_2$ oz	
		Sweat onions and apple in butter without colour. Add curry powder/paste and sweat a further few minutes. Add coconut milk and supreme sauce. Simmer for 20 minutes, correct seasoning, pass through fine strainer or liquidize and use as required			

English term	Unit	Ingredient	Metric	Imperial	French term
		Added ingredients in relation to 1 unit ½ l (1 pt) – Sauce Suprême			
Paprika sauce	$\frac{1}{5}$	White wine (dry)	100 ml	4 fl.oz	Sauce Hongroise
	$\frac{1}{20}$	Onion brunoise	25 g	1 oz	
	$\frac{1}{20}$	Butter	25 g	1 oz	
	$\frac{1}{40}$	Paprika	12.5 g	½ oz	
		Sweat onion in butter without colour. Add paprika, swill out with wine, reduce by a half. Add supreme sauce, correct seasoning, and simmer for 20 minutes. Pass through fine strainer or liquidize for use			
Mushroom sauce	$\frac{1}{5}$	Button mushrooms (sliced)	100 g	4 oz	Sauce Champignon (blanc)
	$\frac{1}{20}$	Butter	25 g	1 oz	
		Sweat mushrooms in butter without colour, add supreme sauce, correct seasoning and use as required			
German sauce	$\frac{1}{10}$	Egg yolks (mix with a few drops of cold water)	50 g	2 oz	Sauce Allemande
		Combine yolks with supreme sauce, correct seasoning, *do not reboil*			
Poulette sauce	$\frac{1}{10}$	Egg yolks (mix with few drops cold water)	50 g	2 oz	Sauce Poulette
	$\frac{1}{10}$	Mushroom essence Chopped parsley	50 ml	2 fl.oz	
		Combine ingredients with supreme sauce, correct seasoning, do not reboil			

Ivory sauce/Sauce Ivoire (Albufera). Add 1 fl oz (25 ml) meat glaze (glace de viande) to taste to the Sauce Suprême.

Examples of Sauces Derived from Velouté de Mouton: Added ingredients in relation to 1 unit ½ l (1 pt) basic sauce

	Unit	Ingredient	Metric	Imperial	
Caper Sauce	$\frac{1}{10}$	Cream	50 ml	2 fl.oz	Sauce aux Câpres
	$\frac{1}{10}$	Whole capers	50 g	2 oz	
		Add ingredients to basic sauce, season to taste adjust consistency			
		Serve with boiled mutton			

Examples of Sauces Derived from Velouté de Poisson: Added ingredients in relation to 1 unit ½ l (1 pt)

English term	Unit	Ingredient	Metric	Imperial	French term
Cheese sauce for fish	$\frac{1}{10}$ $\frac{1}{10}$ $\frac{1}{20}$	Grated Cheddar cheese Cream Egg yolk when being glazed or gratinated	50 g 50 ml 25g	2 oz 2 fl.oz 1 oz	Sauce Mornay de Poisson
		Add ingredients to basic sauce, season to taste (do not reboil after adding egg yolk)			
Mushroom sauce for fish	$\frac{1}{5}$ $\frac{1}{10}$	Sliced mushrooms (sweated without colour) Cream Squeeze lemon juice	100 g 50 ml	4 oz 2 fl.oz	Sauce Champignon de Poisson
		Add ingredients to basic sauce, season to taste			
Shrimp or prawn sauce	$\frac{1}{10}$ $\frac{1}{10}$	Picked prawns/shrimps Cream Cayenne pepper	50 g 50 ml	2 oz 2 fl.oz	Sauce aux Crevettes/ Crevettes Roses
		Add ingredients to basic sauce, season to taste			
White wine sauce	$\frac{1}{5}$ $\frac{1}{10}$	Dry white wine Cream Squeeze of lemon juice	100 ml 50 ml	4 fl.oz 2 fl.oz	Sauce Vin Blanc
		Reduce white wine by half add basic sauce, cream and lemon juice. Season to taste			
Bercy sauce	$\frac{1}{20}$	Shallots (brunoise) As for white wine sauce with shallots added to wine reduction. Finish with chopped parsley	25 g	1 oz	Sauce Bercy
Granville sauce	$\frac{1}{10}$ $\frac{1}{10}$	Button mushrooms (sliced and sweated) Picked shrimps	50 g 50 g	2 oz 2 oz	Sauce Granville
		As for white wine sauce with the addition of the above ingredients. Garnish with finely chopped truffle			

Thermidor sauce	As for white wine sauce with addition of			Sauce Thermidor
	$^1/_{10}$ Grated Cheddar cheese	50 g	2 oz	
	$^1/_{10}$ Cream	50 g	2 oz	
	$^1/_{20}$ Egg yolk when being glazed or gratinated	25 g	1 oz	
	English mustard (diluted)			

Lightly flavour with diluted English mustard. (Do not reboil after egg yolk has been added.) Season to taste

Paprika sauce	$^1/_5$	White wine (dry)	100 ml	4 fl.oz	Sauce Hongroise
	$^1/_{10}$	Onion brunoise	50 g	2 oz	
	$^1/_{10}$	Butter	50 g	2 oz	
	$^1/_{40}$	Paprika (flavour to taste)	12.5 g	$^1/_2$ oz	

Sweat onion in butter without colour, add wine and reduce. Add paprika, basic sauce, simmer for 10 – 15 minutes, season to taste, pass through a fine chinois or liquidize

N.B. The above sauces are served with fish/shellfish dishes and various fish preparations. They are seasoned to taste with salt and pepper and adjusted for consistency to suit requirements.

Whenever any of the above sauces are to be used for a glazed dish, egg yolks or a sabayon should be added to the sauce just prior to glazing. The proportions are 1/10 (50 g [2 oz]) egg yolk/sabayon to 1 unit ($^1/_2$ l [1 pt]) completed sauce. Once egg has been added do not reboil otherwise the sauce will separate.

Sabayon

Mix yolks of egg with a few drops of water and whisk over bain-marie to ribbon stage. Use to enrich sauces and assist when a glazed appearance is required.

BASIC BROWN SAUCE (Spanish origin)   Espagnole

Yield: $^1/_2$ l (1 pt) (approximately)
Cooking time 4 – 6 hr
Cooking temp: 120 – 150°C (250 – 300°F)

Unit	Ingredient	Metric	Imperial
1	Brown stock	1 l	2 pt
$^1/_5$	Mirepoix (large and scorched)	200 g	8 oz
$^1/_{20}$	Flour (white or browned *see* p. 78)	50 g	2 oz
$^1/_{20}$	Dripping	50 g	2 oz
$^1/_{40}$	Tomato purée	25 g	1 oz
	Bouquet Garni, mushroom and tomato trimmings		

Method

Form a brown roux with the flour and dripping, allow to cool, add tomato purée and mix in thoroughly. Gradually add the stock, stirring thoroughly and continuously to the boil, skim and degrease, add scorched mirepoix, trimmings and bouquet garni.
Cover with greased cartouche and a tight fitting lid, cook gently:

(a) in the oven;
(b) on the stove top.

On completion of cooking strain through a fine chinois, in readiness for extension into demi-glace.

HALF-GLAZE   Demi-Glace (a refined Espagnole)

Yield: 1 l (1 qt)
Cooking time: 2–3 hr approximately or until sauce is sufficiently reduced

Unit	Ingredient	Metric (l)	Imperial (qt)
1	Espagnole	1	1
1	Estouffade/brown stock	1	1

Method

Combine the above preparations and reduce by half to form a smooth glossy sauce of pouring consistency. Strain through a fine chinois and tammy (optional). Cover to prevent skin formation (*see* p. 176), place in a bain-marie to keep hot, use as required.
The prepared sauce may be cooled and refrigerated then reheated, and finished as required.

Examples of Sauces Derived from Sauce Demi-Glace: Added ingredients to 1 unit demi-glace (½ l (1 pt))

English term	Unit	Ingredient	Metric	Imperial	French term	Examples of uses
Bercy sauce	⅕	White wine (dry)	100 ml	4 fl.oz	Sauce	Grilled
	1/10	Shallots (brunoise)	50 g	2 oz	Bercy	meats
		Milled peppercorns/				
		Pinch of salt				
		Chopped parsley				
		Beef marrow				
		(poached and diced)				
		Form a reduction with wine, shallots, peppercorns, add demi-glace and simmer 10 minutes. Correct seasoning. Garnish with parsley and marrow				

English term	Unit	Ingredient	Metric	Imperial	French term	Examples of uses
Bordelaise sauce	1/5 1/10	Red wine Shallots (brunoise) Milled peppercorns/ Pinch of salt Pinch of thyme Bay leaf Beef marrow (poached)	100 ml 50 g	4 fl.oz 2 oz	Sauce Bordelaise	Grilled and sautéed meats
		Form a reduction with wine, shallots, peppercorns and aromats. Add basic sauce, simmer 20 minutes, pass through fine chinois. Correct seasoning, garnish with slices of beef marrow				
Burgundy sauce	1/5 1/10	Burgundy wine (red) Shallots (brunoise) Milled peppercorns/ Pinch of salt Pinch of thyme Bay leaf	100 ml 50 g	4 fl.oz 2 oz	Sauce Bourguig- nonne	Sautéed meats, poultry
		Form a reduction with shallots, wine, aromats and seasonings, add basic sauce, simmer 20 minutes, strain through fine chinois, correct season- ing and consistency				
Chateau- briand sauce	1/5 1/10	White wine (dry) Shallots (brunoise) Pinch of thyme Tarragon Milled pepper Chopped parsley Bay leaf Squeeze of lemon juice	100 ml 50 g	4 fl.oz 2 oz	Sauce Chateau- briand or Sauce Crapau- dine	Grilled meats, poultry
		Form reduction with wine, shallots, bay leaf, seasoning and thyme. Add basic sauce, simmer 10 minutes, pass through fine chinois, add lemon juice, parsley and tarragon, correct seasoning				

Chasseur sauce	$\frac{1}{5}$	White wine (dry)	100 ml	4 fl.oz	Sauce	Sautéed
	$\frac{1}{5}$	Sliced button mushrooms	100 g	4 oz	Chasseur	meats,
	$\frac{1}{10}$	Shallots (brunoise)	50 g	2 oz		poultry
	$\frac{1}{10}$	Tomato concassé	50 g	2 oz		
	$\frac{1}{10}$	Butter	50 g	2 oz		

Chopped parsley and tarragon
   to garnish

Sweat shallots and mushrooms in
   butter without colour, add wine and
   form a reduction. Add basic sauce
   and simmer for 10 minutes.
   Add chopped tarragon, tomato concassé and parsley. Correct seasoning

Devilled sauce	$\frac{1}{5}$	White wine (dry)	100 ml	4 fl.oz	Sauce	Grilled
	$\frac{1}{10}$	Shallots (brunoise)	50 g	2 oz	Diable	meats,
						poultry

Milled peppercorns
Pinch of cayenne pepper
Chopped parsley

Form a reduction, with wine, shallots,
   and peppercorns. Add basic sauce,
   simmer 10 minutes and strain
   through fine chinois. Add parsley,
   cayenne pepper to garnish and
   flavour. Correct seasoning

Italian sauce	$\frac{1}{5}$	Mushroom (brunoise)	100 g	4 oz	Sauce	Meat and
	$\frac{1}{10}$	Shallots (brunoise)	50 g	2 oz	Italienne	poultry
	$\frac{1}{10}$	Cooked ham (brunoise)	50 g	2 oz		
	$\frac{1}{10}$	Butter/oil	50 g	2 oz		

Flavoured with hint of garlic and
   pinch of fine herbs.

Form a duxelle (*see* p. 73) with
   shallots, mushrooms, butter and
   garlic. Add ham, basic sauce and
   flavourings. Simmer 10 minutes.
   Correct seasoning

Brown onion sauce	$\frac{2}{5}$	Onion (shredded)	200 g	8 oz	Sauce	Liver, made-
	$\frac{1}{10}$	Butter	50 g	2 oz	Lyonnaise	up dishes
	$\frac{1}{10}$	Wine vinegar	50 ml	2 fl.oz		

Sweat onions in butter to light colour,
   swill out (deglaze) with vinegar to
   form a reduction. Add basic sauce
   and simmer for 10 minutes. Season
   to taste

English term	Unit	Ingredient	Metric	Imperial	French term	Examples of uses
Madeira sauce	$^1/_{10}$	Madeira Add to basic sauce just prior to service. Season to taste	50 ml	2 fl.oz	Sauce Madère	Sautéed meats, cooked ham, meat fillings
Périgueux sauce		Garnish Madeira sauce with brunoise of truffle Truffle essence may be added to flavour. Season to taste			Sauce Périgueux	Sautéed meats
Wine merchants sauce	$^1/_5$ $^1/_{10}$	Red wine (claret) Shallots (brunoise) Squeeze of lemon juice Form a reduction with wine and shallots. Add basic sauce and simmer for 10 minutes. Flavour with lemon juice	100 ml 50 g	4 fl oz 2 oz	Sauce Marchand de Vin	Grilled, sautéed meats
Piquant sauce	$^1/_5$ $^1/_{10}$	Shallots ⎫ Capers ⎬ brunoise Gherkins ⎭ Wine vinegar Pinch of fine herbs Form a reduction with all ingredients, add demi-glace sauce and simmer for 10 minutes. Correct seasoning	100 g 50 ml	4 oz 2 fl oz	Sauce Piquante	Grilled meats, made-up dishes
Pepper sauce	$^1/_5$ $^1/_{10}$ $^1/_{10}$ $^1/_{10}$	Mirepoix (brunoise) Red wine Vinegar (wine) Oil/butter Pinch of thyme Bay leaf Few milled peppercorns Sweat mirepoix in butter to light colour. Swill out (deglaze) with wine/vinegar, add aromats, peppercorns and form a reduction. Add demi-glace, simmer 20 minutes, correct seasoning. Strain through fine chinois	100 g 50 ml 50 ml 50 g	4 oz 2 fl oz 2 fl oz 2 oz	Sauce Poivrade	Grilled, sautéed meats/ game

Port wine sauce	$^1/_{10}$	Port wine	50 ml	2 fl oz	Sauce Porto	Meats, game
		Add wine to demi-glace just prior to service. Correct seasoning and serve				
Réform sauce		Add the following to Sauce Poivrade			Sauce Réform	Sautéed lamb cutlets
	$^1/_5$	Julienne of cooked { Ham Tongue Mushroom Egg white Beetroot Gherkin	100 g	4 oz		
	$^1/_{10}$	Port wine	50 ml	2 fl oz		
	$^1/_{20}$	Redcurrant jelly	25 g	1 oz		
Tomatoed demi-glace	$^1/_2$	Tomato sauce	250 ml	10 fl oz	Demi-glace Tomate	Sautéed meat, poultry
		Add to basic demi-glace				
Tarragon sauce	$^1/_5$	White wine (dry) Chopped tarragon	100 ml	4 fl oz	Sauce Estragon	Sautéed, grilled meats, poultry
		Form a reduction with above, add basic sauce, simmer 10 minutes. Season to taste				
Sherry sauce	$^1/_{10}$	Sherry	50 ml	2 fl oz	Sauce Xérès	Sautéed, grilled meats, offal
		Add to basic sauce just prior to service. Season to taste				
Brown mushroom sauce	$^1/_5$	Button mushrooms (sliced, sweated)	100 g	4 oz	Sauce Champignon Brun	Grilled, sautéed meats
		Add to sherry sauce. Season to taste				
Robert sauce	$^1/_5$ $^1/_{10}$ $^1/_{10}$	White wine (dry) Onion (brunoise) Butter Diluted English mustard to flavour	100 ml 50 g 50 g	4 fl oz 2 oz 2 oz	Sauce Robert	Grilled meats, fish
		Sweat onions in butter without colour. Form a reduction with wine, add basic sauce, flavour with mustard. Season to taste				
Charcutière sauce		As for Sauce Robert, garnished with 1/20 unit (25 g/1 oz) julienne of gherkins			Sauce Charcutière	Grilled pork

Notes on Above Sauces

(a) Where the method indicates the use of a *reduction*, this implies that the liquid, e.g. wine/vinegar, is reduced by a half.

(b) All the sauces are seasoned with salt and pepper to taste and adjusted for consistency to suit requirements.

(c) In order to improve the flavour, gloss and consistency of a sauce the relevant 'Glace de Fond' e.g. chicken, fish, meat, etc., and knobs of butter, i.e. monter au beurre (*see* p. 176), may be added. Reducing the sauce will improve its flavour and gloss. It will also act to thicken the sauce by the process of evaporation.

Emulsified Foundation Sauces

HOLLANDAISE SAUCE   Sauce Hollandaise

Yield: ½ l (1 pt)

Unit	Ingredient	Metric	Imperial
1	Melted butter (unsalted)	400 g	1 lb
¹/₄	Egg yolks	100 g	4 oz
¹/₁₆	Vinegar/lemon juice	25 ml	1 fl oz
	1 Tablespoon of cold water		
	Few milled peppercorns		
	Pinch of cayenne		
	Pinch of salt to season		

Method

Form a reduction with vinegar/lemon and peppercorns in a sauteuse, reduce completely. Swill out with cold water, allow to cool. Place egg yolks and strained reduction into a mixing bowl and whisk to ribbon stage over a bain-marie.

Gradually whisk in the melted butter until an emulsion is formed (sauce thickens and becomes stable).

Add salt and cayenne pepper to season.

A squeeze of lemon juice may be added if a more piquant flavour is required.

Pass through a tammy (*see* p. 176) and keep warm.

This sauce can be served with poached fish and vegetables.

Examples of Sauces Derived from Sauce Hollandaise: Added Ingredients to 1 unit ½ l (1 pt) Hollandaise sauce

Unit	Ingredient	Metric	Imperial	French term	Examples of uses
¹/₁₀	Whipped cream	50 ml	2 fl oz	Sauce Divine	Poached fish
¹/₁₀	Sherry (reduce by half)	50 ml	2 fl oz		
	Fold into basic sauce				

Unit	Ingredient	Metric	Imperial	French term	Examples of uses
	Lightly flavoured with the juice and grated zest of blood oranges			Sauce Maltaise	Boiled asparagus
$^1/_{10}$	Whipped cream	50 ml	2 fl oz	Sauce Mousseline	Poached fish vegetables
	Fold into basic sauce				
$^1/_{10}$	Beurre noisette (*see* p. 200)	50 g	2 oz	Sauce Noisette	Boiled vegetables and grilled meats
	Cool and stir into basic sauce				

BÉARNAISE SAUCE

Sauce Béarnaise

Yield: $^1/_2$ l (1 pt)

Unit	Ingredient	Metric	Imperial
1	Melted butter (unsalted)	400 g	1 lb
$^1/_4$	Egg yolks	100 g	4 oz
$^1/_{16}$	Shallots (brunoise)	25 g	1 oz
$^1/_{16}$	Tarragon vinegar/lemon juice	25 ml	1 fl oz
	1 Tablespoon of cold water		
	Milled peppercorns Tarragon stalks Chopped chervil and tarragon Pinch of cayenne Salt to season		

Method

Form a reduction with vinegar/lemon juice, peppercorns and tarragon stalks in a sauteuse, reduce completely. Swill out with the cold water, and allow to cool. Place the egg yolks and strained reduction into a mixing bowl and mix to ribbon stage over a bain-marie. Gradually mix in the melted butter until the emulsion is formed (sauce thickens and becomes stable). Add salt and cayenne pepper to season. Pass through tammy, add chopped tarragon and chervil. A squeeze of lemon juice may be added if a more piquant flavour is required. Keep warm for service.

This sauce can be served with grilled meats and fish.

Examples of Sauces Derived from Sauce Béarnaise: Added ingredients to 1 unit ½ l (1 pt) Sauce Béarnaise

Unit	Ingredient	Metric	Imperial	French term	Examples of uses
¹/₁₀	Tomato purée	50 g	2 oz	Sauce Choron	Grilled steaks
	Blend purée with béarnaise sauce				
	Flavour delicately with warm meat glaze			Sauce Foyot/ Valoise	Eggs and sweetbreads

Technical Points to Consider when Preparing Warm Emulsified Sauces

Fault

Scrambled appearance of sauce due to coagulation, shrinking and hardening of egg protein at around 55°C (158°F) so care must be taken to:

(a) ensure that egg yolks do not become too hot when whisking to ribbon stage over the bain-marie;
(b) prevent the melted butter overheating before adding to the eggs;
(c) prevent the sauce from overheating before service.

Fault

Curdled sauce which may be a result of one, or more of the following:

(a) insufficient agitation (manual or mechanical) during mixing;
(b) too much mechanical agitation which breaks down the protective layer of emulsifying agent;
(c) adding melted butter too quickly to the egg yolks;
(d) using incorrect formula balance;
(e) using egg yolks which lack sufficient emulsifying agent, e.g. stale yolks.

Therefore care must be taken to:

(a) ensure the melted butter is not added too quickly to the egg yolks;
(b) whisk briskly when adding the melted butter;
(c) prepare sauce just before service;
(d) ensure fresh eggs are used.

Correcting a Curdled Sauce

(a) Place a small amount of boiling water into a clean mixing bowl. Gradually whisk the curdled mixture on to the water.
(b) Place fresh egg yolks into clean mixing bowl. Gradually whisk the curdled mixture on to the yolks over a bain-marie.

Cold Emulsified Sauces

MAYONNAISE SAUCE   Sauce Mayonnaise

Yield: 600 ml (1¼ pt)

Unit	Ingredient	Metric	Imperial
1	Oil 4 Egg yolk Vinegar (tablespoon) Squeeze of lemon juice Pinch of English mustard Pinch salt/cayenne pepper	500 ml	1 pt

Method

Thoroughly whisk together egg yolk, half of the vinegar, mustard, salt and cayenne pepper. Add the oil gradually; whisking thoroughly and continuously until a stable emulsion is formed. Whisk in lemon juice and correct seasoning. Extra vinegar may be added to adjust flavour as required.

Examples of Sauces Derived from Mayonnaise: Added ingredients to 1 unit ½ l (1 pt) mayonnaise

Unit	Ingredient	Metric	Imperial	French term	Uses
⅕ ⅒	Gherkins Capers Fines herbes (pinch) Chop ingredients finely and combine with mayonnaise. Adjust consistency	100 g 50 g	4 oz 2 oz	Sauce Tartare	Deep fried fish
	As for sauce Tartare but lightly flavoured with anchovy essence			Sauce Rémoulade	Deep fried fish

N.B.   Other derivatives are prepared from this sauce for use in the larder.

Technical Points to Consider when Preparing Mayonnaise

Fault

Unstable emulsion caused:

(a) when the ingredients have been at too low a temperature, thus preventing the emulsifying agents from coating the oil droplets successfully. (Oil congeals at low temperatures.)

(b) by using stale egg yolks which consequently provide insufficient emulsifying agent
(c) by inadequate whisking when adding oil to the egg yolks, thus preventing even distribution of oil into egg.
(d) by adding oil too quickly in the initial stages of preparation. This prevents a thorough mixing of yolks and oil resulting in the sauce separating.
(e) by using incorrect formula balance, therefore providing insufficient emulsifying agent in relation to oil.

Correcting Unstable Mayonnaise

Mix the unstable emulsion on to fresh egg yolks or on to a few drops of boiling water. Use a clean bowl and proceed as for making mayonnaise.

Alternatively incorporate broken mayonnaise into prepared stable mayonnaise.

Foreign Non-Derivative Sauces

THICKENED GRAVY   Jus Lié

Yield: $\frac{1}{2}$ l (1 pt)
Cooking time 2 to 3 hours

Unit	Ingredient	Metric	Imperial
1	Stock chicken/veal	1 l	2 pt
$\frac{1}{2}$	Chopped bones chicken/veal	500 g	1 lb
$\frac{1}{5}$	Mirepoix (medium)	200 g	8 oz
$\frac{1}{40}$	Tomato purée	25 g	1 oz
*	Arrowroot	25 g	1 oz
	Mushroom and tomato trimmings		
	Bouquet garni		
	Seasoning		

* Sufficient arrowroot to lightly lié (thicken) the sauce.

Method

Brown the bones and mirepoix in a hot oven then place into a suitable cooking vessel. Add tomato purée and cover with the stock. Bring to the boil, skim, add trimmings, bouquet garni and seasoning. Cover with a lid and simmer until extraction of flavour is complete. Strain off the stock, blend arrowroot with a little cold water and stir into the boiling stock to form a thickened gravy. Pass through a fine chinois, tammy, correct consistency and season to taste.

This can be used as a sauce accompaniment to meat dishes.

CURRY SAUCE   Sauce Kari/Cari

Yield: ½ l (1 pt)
Cooking time: 45 min to 1 hr

Unit	Ingredient	Metric	Imperial
1	Stock (white or brown)	500 ml	1 pt
$\frac{1}{5}$	Onion (brunoise)	100 g	4 oz
$\frac{1}{10}$	Apple (diced)	50 g	2 oz
$\frac{1}{10}$	Margarine	50 g	2 oz
$\frac{1}{20}$	Flour	25 g	1 oz
$\frac{1}{20}$	Curry powder	25 g	1 oz
$\frac{1}{40}$	Tomato purée	12.5 g	½ oz
	Added flavourings		
$\frac{1}{20}$	Coconut milk*	25 ml	1 fl oz
$\frac{1}{20}$	Diced chutney	25 g	1 oz
	Seasoning/garlic purée to taste		

* Coconut milk is dessicated coconut, soaked in milk for 30 minutes and then strained.

Method

Sweat onions in margarine without colour. Add curry powder and apples and cook gently for a few minutes. Add flour to form a roux, cool slightly, add tomato purée. Mix in the stock stirring thoroughly and continuously to the boil, skim and simmer for 30 minutes. Add garlic, coconut milk and chutney, simmer a further 10 minutes. Season to taste.
 This sauce can be served with vegetables, eggs, meats, fish, poultry etc.

TOMATO SAUCE   Sauce Tomate

Yield: 1 l (1 qt)
Cooking time: 2 hr

Unit	Ingredient	Metric	Imperial
1	White stock	1 l	2 pt
$\frac{1}{5}$	Mirepoix - medium	200 g	8 oz
$\frac{1}{10}$	Tomato purée	100 g	4 oz
$\frac{1}{20}$	Margarine	50 g	2 oz
$\frac{1}{20}$	Flour	50 g	2 oz
	Flavourings:		
	bacon scraps		
	tomato trimmings		
	bouquet garni		
	garlic clove, crushed		
	basil, clove		
	seasoning		

Method

Sweat mirepoix and bacon scraps in fat without colour. Add flour to form a blond roux, cool slightly, add tomato purée. Gradually add stock stirring thoroughly and continuously to the boil. Skim, add remaining flavourings, simmer to complete cooking. Strain through fine chinois, correct seasoning and consistency.

This sauce can be served with fish, pasta and meat dishes, etc.

PORTUGUESE SAUCE   Sauce Portugaise

Yield: $\frac{1}{2}$ l (1 pt) (approx.)
Cooking time: 15 – 20 min

Unit	Ingredient	Metric	Imperial
1	Tomato sauce	250 ml	10 fl oz
$\frac{4}{5}$	Tomato concassé	200 g	8 oz
$\frac{2}{5}$	White wine (dry)	100 ml	4 fl oz
$\frac{1}{5}$	Shallots (brunoise)	50 g	2 oz
$\frac{1}{10}$	Oil/butter	25 g	1 oz
	2 Cloves garlic, chopped		
	Pinch of basil		
	Chopped parsley		
	Milled peppercorns		
	Pinch salt		

Method

Sweat shallots in oil without colour, deglaze with wine, add garlic, basil, parsley and seasoning.
Reduce by half, add tomato sauce and tomato concassé.
Simmer for approximately 5 minutes, correct seasoning and consistency and use as required.
DO NOT STRAIN
This sauce can be used for fish, poultry and pasta preparations.

Sauce Provençale

Yield: $\frac{1}{2}$ l (1 pt)
Cooking time: 5 – 10 min

Unit	Ingredient	Metric	Imperial
1	Tomato concassé (*see* p. 164) (tinned tomatoes often used)	500 g	1$\frac{1}{4}$ lb
$\frac{1}{10}$	White wine	50 ml	2 fl oz
$\frac{1}{10}$	Shallots (brunoise)	50 g	2 oz
$\frac{1}{20}$	Oil/butter	25 g	1 oz
	Flavourings:		
	4 cloves garlic, chopped		
	pinch of fine herbs and basil		
	Seasoning to taste		

Method

Sweat shallots and garlic in butter/oil without colour, deglaze with wine, and reduce by a half. Add tomato concassé, herbs and seasoning to taste. Simmer for a few minutes.
This sauce can be used with fish, poultry, pasta etc.

ORANGE SAUCE
Sauce Bigarade

Yield: ½ l (1 pt)
Cooking time: 30 to 45 min

Unit	Ingredient	Metric	Imperial
1	Thickened duck's gravy or Jus lié	500 ml	1 pt
⅕	Orange juice	100 ml	4 fl oz
¹⁄₂₀	Lemon juice	25 ml	1 fl oz
	Blanched julienne of orange and lemon zest to garnish. Season to taste		

Method

Combine Jus lié with orange/lemon juice and reduce by a quarter. Strain through fine chinois and tammy. Add garnish and season to taste.
N.B. A pinch of sugar may be added if the sauce is too sharp in flavour. A glass of curaçao may be added to enhance the flavour.
This sauce is served with braised and poêled ducklings.

SWEET AND SOUR SAUCE

Yield: ½ l (1 pt)
Cooking time: 30 min

Unit	Ingredient	Metric	Imperial
1	Jus lié	500 ml	1 pt
¹⁄₁₀	Onion brunoise	50 g	2 oz
¹⁄₁₀	Red or green pepper (brunoise)	50 g	2 oz
¹⁄₁₀	Butter	50 g	2 oz
¹⁄₁₀	Sugar (soft brown)	50 g	2 oz
¹⁄₁₀	Vinegar	50 ml	2 fl oz
¹⁄₂₀	Carrot (grated)	25 g	1 oz
¹⁄₂₀	Lemon juice	25 ml	1 fl oz
¹⁄₄₀	Tomato purée	12.5 g	½ oz
	Flavourings: grated ginger root dash of soy sauce grated orange zest garlic purée, all added to taste. Seasoning		

Method

Sweat onion, peppers, carrot in butter without colour for a few minutes, add sugar and lightly caramelize. Add vinegar and lemon juice, reduce by half. Add tomato purée and jus lié, mix well bring to the boil and skim. Add flavourings and seasonings then simmer to complete cooking. Cover with lid to prevent excess evaporation. Adjust seasoning and use as required. Acidity or sweetness may be adjusted according to taste.

This sauce can be used with pork, chicken, kebabs, etc.

LOBSTER SAUCE   Sauce Homard (Americaine)

Yield: 1 l (1 qt)
Cooking time: $1 - 1\frac{1}{4}$ hr

Unit	Ingredient	Metric	Imperial
	1 hen lobster (live)		
1	Fish stock	1 l	2 pts
$\frac{1}{10}$	White wine	100 ml	4 fl oz
$\frac{1}{10}$	Tomato concassé	100 g	4 oz
$\frac{1}{10}$	Mirepoix (brunoise)	100 g	4 oz
$\frac{1}{20}$	Flour	50 g	2 oz
$\frac{1}{20}$	Butter	50 g	2 oz
$\frac{1}{20}$	Brandy	50 ml	2 fl oz
$\frac{1}{20}$	Tomato purée	50 g	2 oz
	Hint of garlic		
	Bouquet garni		
	Pinch of salt and pepper		

Preparation of Live Lobster

Place live lobster on to chopping board, pierce head with point of knife and split head lengthways (leave tail whole). Separate tail from head and cut tail into thick slices. Remove claws and crack claw shell with back of a heavy chopping knife. Remove cream of lobster from head and any coral and set aside ready for use. Discard sack from the head.

Preparation of Sauce

Heat butter in cooking vessel, add lobster shell/flesh, and cook until shell turns red. Add mirepoix, garlic and continue cooking for a few minutes and add flour to form roux. Add tomato purée, moisten with white wine and fish stock stirring thoroughly and slowly to the boil. Skim, add bouquet garni, tomato concassé and seasoning. Cover with a lid and simmer until lobster is cooked. Remove from heat and separate lobster from cooking liquor. Pick lobster meat from the shells and cool to store for future use. Replace shells into cooking liquor, add cream and coral of lobster and continue cooking to extract full flavour. Strain sauce through chinois, correct consistency and seasoning, add brandy and use as required.

This sauce can be used with fish, shellfish and egg preparations.

SOUR CREAM SAUCE

Sauce Smitane

Yield: $\frac{1}{4}$ l ($\frac{1}{2}$ pt approx.)
Cooking time: 5 – 8 min

Unit	Ingredient	Metric	Imperial
1	Sour cream (double)	500 ml	1 pt
$\frac{1}{10}$	Onion brunoise	50 g	2 oz
$\frac{1}{20}$	Butter	25 g	1 oz
	Squeeze of lemon juice		
	Pinch of cayenne pepper		
	Seasoning		

Method

Sweat onions in butter to light brown colour, add cream, lemon juice and reduce to required consistency. Season to taste.

This sauce can be served with bitoks, pojarskis, etc.

SAVOURY MEAT SAUCE

Sauce Bolognaise

Yield: 4 portions
Cooking time 1 – 1$\frac{1}{2}$ hr

Unit	Ingredient	Metric	Imperial
1	Demi-glace	500 ml	1 pt
1	Lean minced beef	500 g	1$\frac{1}{4}$ lb
$\frac{1}{5}$	Red wine	100 ml	4 fl oz
$\frac{1}{5}$	Onion brunoise	100 g	4 oz
$\frac{1}{5}$	Tomato concassé	100 g	4 oz
$\frac{1}{10}$	Oil	50 ml	2 fl oz
$\frac{1}{20}$	Tomato purée	25 g	1 oz
	Seasoning		
	Garlic purée to taste		

Method

Sweat onions in oil to light brown, add meat, seal, colour brown. Add tomato purée, wine and reduce. Add sauce to cover meat, bring to boil, skim and season, simmer until the meat is cooked (cover with lid to prevent excessive evaporation), stir occasionally to prevent meat adhering to bottom of saucepan. Add tomato concassé, and garlic. Correct seasoning and consistency, use as required.

This sauce can be used with pasta preparations.

APPLE SAUCE   Sauce Pommes

Yield: $\frac{1}{4}$ l ($\frac{1}{2}$ pt approx.)
Cooking time: 10 min

Unit	Ingredient	Metric	Imperial
1	Cooking apples (sliced)	400 g	16 oz
$\frac{1}{8}$	Margarine	50 g	2 oz
	Sugar to taste	50 g	2 oz
	Squeeze of lemon juice to taste		

Method

Sweat apples in margarine, without colour, cook to purée. Add sugar and lemon juice to taste.

N.B. To produce a smooth textured sauce pass through sieve or liquidizer.

This sauce can be used as an accompaniment with roast pork, duckling, goose, etc.

BREAD SAUCE   Sauce Pain

Yield: $\frac{1}{4}$ l ($\frac{1}{2}$ pt approx)
Cooking time: 30 min

Unit	Ingredient	Metric	Imperial
1	Milk	250 ml	10 fl oz
$\frac{1}{10}$	White breadcrumbs	25 g	1 oz
$\frac{1}{10}$	Butter	25 g	1 oz
	Studded onion (clouté)		
	Seasoning		
	Pinch of nutmeg		

Method

Simmer onion clouté with milk for approximately 15 minutes. Remove clouté and add breadcrumbs to milk, mix thoroughly. Simmer 'for a few minutes, season, adjust consistency and finish with a knob of butter.

This sauce accompanies roast poultry and game.

CRANBERRY SAUCE   Sauce Airelles Cousinettes

Yield: $\frac{1}{4}$ l ($\frac{1}{2}$ pt approx.)
Cooking time 15 min

Unit	Ingredient	Metric (g)	Imperial (oz)
1	Cranberries	300	12
$\frac{1}{8}$	Sugar	37.5	$1\frac{1}{2}$
	Squeeze of lemon juice		

Method

Place all ingredients in a stainless steel or copper cooking vessel and simmer to a purée. Pass through sieve/liquidizer when smooth sauce is required.

This sauce is used as an accompaniment to roast turkey.

CUMBERLAND SAUCE

Yield: $\frac{1}{2}$ l (1 pt)
Cooking time 15 min

Unit	Ingredient	Metric	Imperial
1	Redcurrant jelly	500 ml	1 pt
$\frac{1}{5}$	Port wine	100 ml	4 fl oz
$\frac{1}{5}$	Orange juice	100 ml	4 fl oz
$\frac{1}{10}$	Lemon juice	50 ml	2 fl oz
$\frac{1}{20}$	Blanched chopped shallots	25 g	1 oz
	Seasonings—pinches of:		
	Salt		
	Cayenne pepper		
	English mustard		
	Ginger to taste		
	Garnish of blanched		
	julienne of orange zest		

Method

Melt jelly over heat, add wine, fruit juices, shallots and seasonings. Bring to boiling point, strain, correct seasoning and add garnish. Remove from heat and allow to cool.

This sauce is classically served cold to accompany cold meats, e.g. game, duck, ham. May also be served hot with baked or grilled ham, in which case sauce may require further thickening with arrowroot.

Mint Sauce   Sauce Menthe

Pick, wash and chop mint leaves with a little sugar. Place into china bowl and moisten with malt vinegar. Sweeten with sugar to taste.
N.B.   Sugar acts to absorb moisture from mint leaves and to facilitate chopping. Vinegar may be slightly diluted with water.

This sauce is served with roast lamb.

Hot Butter Sauces

Hot butter sauces are often used with vegetables, fish, meat, offal, and poultry dishes. They can be served to complete a dish or as a accompaniment e.g. Poisson Meunière (*see* p. 329) beurre meunière to complete, buerre fondu to accompany asparagus, etc.

Sauce	Unit	Ingredient (4 portions)	Metric	Imperial	Method (degree of cooking)
Beurre Fondu (melted butter)	1	Butter Squeeze of lemon juice	100 g	4 oz	Melt butter, pour off oil leaving the whey, flavour oil with lemon juice
Beurre Noisette (brown butter)	1	Butter Squeeze of lemon juice	100 g	4 oz	Add butter to pre-heated frying pan and cook until golden brown. Remove from heat, add lemon juice. Stir to use
Beurre Meunière	1	Butter Squeeze of lemon juice Chopped parsley	100 g	4 oz	As for Beurre Noisette, garnish with chopped parsley
Beurre Noir (black butter)	1	Butter Flavour with few drops vinegar Squeeze of lemon juice Chopped parsley	100 g	4 oz	Add butter to pre-heated frying pan and cook to brown. Remove from heat, add lemon juice, vinegar, garnish chopped parsley. Stir to use
Beurre Noir aux Câpres (black butter with capers)		As for Beurre Noir, plus whole capers to garnish			As for Beurre Noir, garnish with capers

The above sauces are usually prepared as required, but may be prepared in advance and kept hot in the bain-marie. The flavouring and colour of butter sauces is achieved by the varying degrees to which the butter solids are cooked.

Hard Butter Sauces—Beurre Composé

These preparations are used to accompany a variety of grilled meat or fish dishes and as such add interest and flavour to various products. They are easily prepared in advance and stored refrigerated in readiness for use.

HARD BUTTER SAUCES   Beurre Composé

Unit	Ingredient	Metric	Imperial
1	Butter	200 g	8 oz
*	Main flavouring (prepared)		
	Squeeze of lemon juice		
	Seasoning		

* *See* chart below

Method

Cream butter until soft, combine with flavouring and seasoning to taste. Roll in dampened greaseproof paper to cylindrical shape, approximately 2½ cm (1 in) wide. Store refrigerated.

To use cut into slices ½ cm (¼ in) thick and:

(a) place in sauceboat of iced water (keeps butter solid in hot atmosphere), e.g. to accompany grilled fish, or;
(b) place on to hot food for service, e.g. grilled steak or;
(c) in the preparation of a culinary product, e.g. snails in garlic butter or;
(d) add to sauces to enhance their flavour.

Added ingredients in relation to 1 unit butter i.e. 200 g (8 oz)

Name	Unit	Ingredient	Metric	Imperial	Additional directions
Beurre d'Anchois (anchovy butter)		Anchovies pounded with butter of anchovy essence to taste* Pinch of cayenne pepper			Combine ingredients together with the butter
Beurre d'Ail (garlic butter)		Garlic (chopped) Parsley (chopped) Pinch of pepper			Finely chop the garlic, parsley and combine with the butter
Beurre aux Crevettes (shrimp butter)	½	Picked shrimps Pinch of cayenne pepper Chopped parsley	100 g	4 oz	Pound shrimps with sufficient of the butter to form a paste. Pass through fine cane sieve, add cayenne and chopped parsley

* Rinse anchovies, dry well, pound with butter, rub through sieve and combine with other ingredients.

Name	Unit	Ingredient	Metric	Imperial	Additional directions
Beurre aux Fines Herbes (herb butter)		Fine herbs to flavour (chervil, chives, parsley, tarragon) Pinch of pepper			Finely chop the fresh herbs, mix all ingredients with the butter
Beurre d'Homard (lobster butter)	$\frac{1}{8}$	Cooked spawn and coral of lobster Pinch of cayenne pepper	25 g	1 oz	Pound coral and spawn with sufficient of the butter to form a paste. Pass through fine cane sieve. Mix all ingredients with the butter
Beurre Maître d'Hôtel (parsley Butter)		Chopped parsley to flavour Squeeze of lemon juice Pinch of pepper			Combine all ingredients with the butter
Beurre Moutarde (mustard butter)		Dry English mustard to flavour Pinch of pepper			Sift mustard into butter and mix well

CHEESE STRAWS   Paillettes au Fromage

Yield: 4 portions
Cooking time: 10 min
Cooking temp: 205°C (400°F)

Unit	Ingredient	Metric (g)	Imperial (oz)
1	Puff pastry	100	4
$\frac{1}{2}$	Parmesan cheese (grated)	50	2
	Cayenne pepper (pinch)		
	Pinch of salt		

Method

Roll out puff pastry into rectangular shape 3 mm ($\frac{1}{8}$ in) thick. Lightly egg wash and sprinkle evenly with cheese, pinch of cayenne and salt. Cut into lengths of 6 mm ($\frac{1}{4}$ in) wide. Twist to curl and place firmly on to lightly greased baking sheet. Rest before baking then cook in the oven until crisp and golden brown. Remove from oven and whilst still hot cut into 10 cm (4 in) lengths ensuring that the ends are neatly trimmed. Allow to cool and store for use.

SAVOURY EGG CUSTARD   Royale

Yield: 4 portions
Cooking time: 30 – 40 min
Cooking temp: 150°C (300°F)

Unit	Ingredient	Metric	Imperial
1	Whole egg	50 g	2 oz
1	White stock	50 ml	2 fl oz
	Seasoning, salt and pepper		

Method

Whisk together egg and stock, season to taste. Pour mixture through a fine chinois into a buttered mould. Place the mould into a bain-marie and cook in the oven until completely set. Allow to cool, carefully turn out of mould and cut into diamonds, circles, squares, etc. Store moistened with stock or consommé.

N.B.   Royale is most commonly used to garnish consommé. It may be coloured and flavoured prior to cooking as required, e.g.

Green royale — colour and flavour with purée of spinach;
Red royale — colour and flavour with tomato purée.
For choux pastry *see* p. 488.

14

Soups: Les Potages

Soups are a common feature offered on many types of menu in a wide variety of catering establishments. Such units range from fast food operations to the more traditionally based luxury catering systems.

Where a large 'Brigade de Cuisine' is employed the 'Chef Potager' is responsible for the preparation of soups and their garnishes.

The function of soup on the menu is to stimulate the customer's appetite rather than act as a complete meal. For this reason many soups are of a light and delicate nature. Hot soups are a welcome feature on winter menus, conversely cold soups are ideal in the summertime.

Soups may be classified in the following manner: *thickened* and *unthickened*.

Thickened Varieties

1. *Purée soups* — a type of soup thickened either by the main ingredient or a starch-based additive.
2. *Cream soups* — passed soups that have béchamel sauce as their main thickening agent.
3. *Velouté soups* — passed soups that have a velouté sauce or blond roux as their main thickening agent.
4. *Brown soups* — passed soups produced from flavoured brown stock thickened by a brown roux.
5. *Bisques* — passed shellfish soups that are traditionally thickened with starch in the form of rice, but may be thickened by the roux method.

Unthickened Varieties

6. *Broths* — unstrained soups prepared from a stock base flavoured and garnished by vegetables, meats, fish and cereals.
7. *Consommés* — Refined, clear soups prepared from a rich stock base.

Unclassified Varieties

Speciality soups that cannot be listed with the above types because of their unique mode of preparation.

Soups and the Menu

It is recommended that the more substantial types of soup be served at luncheon and those of a more delicate nature for dinner.
Luncheon — purées, creams, broths and brown soups;
Dinner — consommés, creams, veloutés and bisques.

Preparing and Cooking Soups

It is recommended that during the cooking of soups (except consommés) the cooking vessel be covered with a lid to avoid excessive evaporation (*see* p. 217 for consommé).

Vegetable trimmings are ideally suited for economic soup production e.g. mushroom stalks and peelings, celery tops, etc.

In the production of cream- and velouté-based soups it is taken for granted that basic béchamel and velouté sauces would be en place (hot or cold) for use.

Thickened Soups

1. Purées

This type of soup is produced from one of the following:

(a) Vegetables containing a high percentage of starch e.g. — pulse vegetables.
(b) Aqueous Vegetables i.e. watery vegetables e.g. celery, leaks onions etc.

Purée soups produced from *starchy vegetables* need no other thickening agent as starch based vegetables act as self-thickeners.

Alternatively, purée soups produced from aqueous vegetables need the assistance of a starchy food to effect cohesion. The ingredients most commonly used for this purpose are rice or potatoes.

(a) PURÉE SOUP

Potage Purée
(for pulse vegetables)

Yield: 4 portions
Cooking time. $1 - 1\frac{1}{2}$ hr (approximately)

Unit	Ingredient	Metric	Imperial
1	White stock	1 l	2 pt
$\frac{1}{5}$	Pulse vegetable (main)	200 g	8 oz
$\frac{1}{10}$	Mirepoix (large including bacon)	100 g	4 oz
	Bouquet garni		
	Salt and pepper		

Method

Place stock, pulse vegetable and mirepoix in saucepan. Bring to the boil, skin and simmer. Add bouquet garni, cover with lid and continue cooking until pulse falls. Remove bouquet garni and bacon. Pass through soup machine and then through medium conical strainer. Reboil, correct consistency and seasoning, garnish as required. Serve accompanied with soup croûtons (*see* p. 167)

Extensions of Soups Using Above Formula: Garnish in relation to 1 unit stock i.e. 1 l (2 pt)

English term- main ingredient	Unit	Ingredient for garnish	Metric	Imperial	French term
Purée of haricot bean soup		Chopped parsley			Potage Soissonnaise
Purée of red bean soup	$\frac{1}{20}$	Finish with: dry red wine	50 ml	2 fl oz	Potage Condé
Purée of lentil soup		Chopped parsley			Potage de Lentilles
Purée of lentil soup	$\frac{1}{20}$	Diced cooked bacon Pinch of chopped chervil	50 g	2 oz	Potage Conti
Purée of lentil soup	$\frac{1}{40}$ $\frac{1}{40}$	Boiled rice Butter	25 g 25 g	1 oz 1 oz	Potage Esaü
Purée of green split pea soup					Potage St Germain
Purée of yellow split pea soup		Chopped parsley			Potage Égyptienne

N.B. For best results dried pulses should be soaked overnight in cold water, but they must be weighed *prior to soaking* to obtain correct consistency.

(b) PURÉE SOUP

Potage Purée
(for aqueous vegetables)

Yield: 4 portions
Cooking time: 1 hr (approximately)

Unit	Ingredient	Metric	Imperial
1	White stock	800 ml	$1\frac{1}{2}$ pt
$\frac{2}{5}$	Main vegetable (sliced)	320 g	12 oz
$\frac{1}{10}$	Mirepoix or vegetable adjunct	80 g	3 oz
$\frac{1}{10}$	Potato (sliced) or	80 g	3 oz
$\frac{1}{20}$	Patna rice	40 g	$1\frac{1}{2}$ oz
$\frac{1}{20}$	Margarine or butter Bouquet garni Salt and pepper	40 g	$1\frac{1}{2}$ oz

Method

Melt fat in saucepan, add main vegetable and mirepoix, sweat without colour and season lightly. Add the stock, bring to the boil, skim, add potato *or* rice, bouquet garni and continue to simmer until all the vegetables are cooked. Cover with lid to prevent excess evaporation.

Remove bouquet garni, liquidize or pass the soup through machine and then through a medium conical strainer. Reboil, correct seasoning and consistency, garnish as required. Accompany with soup croûtons.

Examples of Soups Using Above Formula

English term—main ingredient	*Garnish for 4 portions*	*French term*
Purée of carrot soup	Chopped parsley	Purée de Carottes
Purée of cauliflower soup	Small cauliflower sprigs (cooked) 50 g (2 oz) and chopped parsley	Purée Dubarry
Purée of celery soup	Chopped parsley	Purée de Céleri
Purée of Jerusalem artichoke soup	Chopped parsley	Purée Palestine
Purée of leek soup	Chopped parsley	Purée de Poireaux
Purée of onion soup	Chopped parsley	Purée d'Oignon
Purée of potato soup*	Chopped parsley	Purée Parmentier
Purée of pumpkin soup	Chopped parsley	Purée de Potiron
Purée of swede soup	Chopped parsley	Purée de Rutabaga
Purée of sprout soup		Purée Flamande
Purée of turnip soup		Purée Navet
Purée of vegetable soup (combined aqueous vegetables)		Purée de Légumes
Purée of watercress soup	As for potato soup, but cooked with a bunch of watercress — garnished with blanched watercress leaves	Purée Cressonnière

N.B. Either thickening agent may be used when preparing the above soups with the exception of *purée of potato soup**. In this case the amount of main vegetable i.e. 320 g (12 oz) of potato is sufficient to both flavour and thicken this soup. Extra vegetable adjunct can therefore be added to improve the flavour in the amount of 80 g (3 oz). Generally, when using vegetables with a delicate flavour, as the main ingredient, best results are achieved by thickening with rice.

2. *Creams*   Crèmes

With only a few exceptions, the principal thickening element used in the production of cream soup is that of sauce béchamel. The predominant flavour of the soup is determined by the recipe balance.

The class of vegetables best suited to cream soup production are the aqueous type. Starchy vegetables, in general act as self-thickeners and need no other thickening element.

It is worth mentioning at this stage that there are many soups appearing on the menu as creams, which are basically velouté or purée soups to which cream has been added prior to service. The word 'cream' in these instances refers to the addition of cream rather than the underlying principle of cream soup production.

USING AQUEOUS VEGETABLES

Yield: 4 portions
Cooking time: 1 hr (approximately)

Unit	Ingredient	Metric	Imperial
1	White stock	800 ml	$1\frac{1}{2}$ pt
$\frac{2}{5}$	Main vegetable (sliced)	320 g	12 oz
$\frac{1}{5}$	Mirepoix or vegetable adjunct (sliced)	160 g	6 oz
$\frac{1}{5}$	Béchamel (*see* p. 177)	160 ml	6 fl oz
$\frac{1}{20}$	Butter or margarine	40 g	$1\frac{1}{2}$ oz
$\frac{1}{20}$	Cream (optional)	40 ml	$1\frac{1}{2}$ fl oz
	Bouquet garni		
	Salt and pepper		

Method

Melt fat in saucepan, add all vegetables, season lightly and sweat without colour. Add stock, bring to boil, skim. Add bouquet garni, simmer until all vegetables are cooked (cover with lid).

Remove bouquet garni, add béchamel sauce, mix well and reboil. Liquidize or pass through soup machine and then through fine chinois. Reboil, correct seasoning and consistency, garnish as required.

N.B.   If cream is used, add on service. Cream soups are often served accompanied with soup croûtons (*see* p. 167). N.B.B. This soup can be thickened by *replacing* béchamel with $\frac{1}{40}$ (20 g/$\frac{3}{4}$ oz) flour to form a white roux with sweated vegetables .

Extensions of Soups Using Above Formula: Garnish in relation to 1 unit stock i.e. 800 ml ($1\frac{1}{2}$ pt)

English term-main ingredient	Unit	Ingredient	Metric (g)	Imperial (oz)	French term
Cream of asparagus soup		4 Cooked asparagus tips			Crème d'Asperges/ Argenteuil
Cream of carrot soup		Chopped parsley			Crème de Carottes
Cream of carrot soup	$\frac{1}{20}$	As above plus: boiled rice	40	$1\frac{1}{2}$	Crème Crécy
Cream of cauliflower soup	$\frac{1}{20}$	Small cooked sprigs of cauliflower	40	$1\frac{1}{2}$	Crème de Chou-fleur / Dubarry
Cream of celery soup	$\frac{1}{20}$	Cooked julienne of celery	40	$1\frac{1}{2}$	Crème de Céleri
Cream of cucumber soup	$\frac{1}{20}$	Small cucumber balls	40	$1\frac{1}{2}$	Crème Concombre/ Doria
Cream of leek soup					Crème Poireaux
Cream of lettuce soup		Shredded lettuce lightly sweated			Crème de Laitue/ Judic

English term—main ingredient	Unit	Ingredient	Metric (g)	Imperial (oz)	French term
Cream of mushroom soup (¹/₅ main unit may be used 160 g (6 oz)	¹/₂₀	Julienne of cooked mushrooms	40	1¹/₂	Crème de Champignons
Cream of onion soup					Crème d'Oignon
Cream of spinach soup					Crème d'Épinards/Florentine
Cream of sweetcorn soup	¹/₂₀	Cooked corn kernels	40	1¹/₂	Crème de Maïs/Washington
Cream of vegetable soup					Crème de Légumes
Cream of watercress soup [¹/₅ main unit may be used 160 g (6 oz)]		Blanched watercress leaves			Crème Cressonnière

N.B. Other aqueous vegetable soups may be prepared using the basic recipe. The above soups may be garnished with chopped parsley as required.

3. *Velouté Soups*   Veloutés

The French word velouté translated into English means velvety. This describes the finished texture and appearance of the soup. The principal thickening element is a blond roux or a velouté sauce, which may be flavoured using different stock bases according to requirements. When preparing meat, poultry, or fish veloutés the predominant flavour is determined by the stock used. Alternatively when producing aqueous vegetable velouté soups the flavour of the main vegetable predominates.

In order to achieve the velvety finish required, a liaison of egg yolks and cream is added just before service. Once this has been added the soup must not be allowed to reboil otherwise it will take on a curdled appearance, a result of egg yolk coagulation.

VELOUTÉ (for meat, poultry, fish soups)

Yield: 4 portions
Cooking time: 1 hr approximately

Unit	Ingredient	Metric	Imperial
1	Selected white stock	1 l	2 pt
¹/₁₀	Vegetable adjunct sliced (optional)	100 g	4 oz
¹/₂₀	Flour	50 g	2 oz
¹/₂₀	Butter	50 g	2 oz
¹/₂₀	Cream ⎫ liaison	50 ml	2 fl oz
¹/₂₀	Egg yolk ⎭	50 g	2 oz
	Bouquet garni		
	Salt and pepper to season		

N.B. When a vegetable adjunct is used care must be taken to use vegetables that will enhance rather than impair the colour of the finished soup, e.g. omit carrots when a 'white' appearance is required.

Method

Melt fat in saucepan, add the adjunct, lightly season and sweat without colour. Add the flour to form a blond roux. Gradually pour in the stock, bring to the boil, stirring continuously, skim, add bouquet garni, simmer until cooked (cover with lid).

Once cooked remove bouquet garni, liquidize or pass through a soup machine, then through fine chinois. Reboil, correct seasoning and consistency, remove from heat and add liaison just before service (do not reboil).

Extensions of Velouté Soups Using Above Formula: Garnish in relation to 1 unit stock i.e. 1 l (2 pt)

Menu term	Main stock	Unit	Ingredient	Metric (g)	Imperial (oz)
Velouté de Volaille (chicken velouté)	Chicken	$^1/_{20}$	Julienne of cooked chicken	50	2
Velouté de Poisson (fish velouté)	Fish		Chopped parsley		
Velouté Dieppoise (mussel velouté)	Fish and mussel cooking liquor	$^1/_{20}$ $^1/_{20}$	Budded mussels Shrimps/prawns Chopped parsley	50 50	2 2
Velouté aux Huîtres (oyster velouté)	Fish and oyster cooking liquor		8 poached oysters Chopped parsley		

N.B. Many velouté soups may be prepared using the above recipe. By adding a more complex garnish to the basic soup the name of the soup changes, e.g. Velouté Germinal—chicken velouté flavoured with tarragon, garnished with asparagus tips and chervil.

Velouté Agnès Sorel

Using basic recipe prepare a chicken velouté replacing vegetable adjunct with unit [200 g (8 oz)] mushroom brunoise. Garnish completed soup with:

$^1/_{40}$ unit Julienne of cooked tongue   25 g (1 oz);
$^1/_{40}$ unit Julienne of cooked chicken   25 g (1 oz);
$^1/_{40}$ unit Julienne of cooked mushrooms   25 g (1 oz).

VEGETABLE VELOUTÉS

Veloutés des Légumes
(using a main flavouring of aqueous vegetables)

Yield: 4 portions
Cooking time: 1 hr (approximately)

Unit	Ingredient	Metric	Imperial
1	White stock	800 ml	1½ pt
²⁄₅	Main vegetable (sliced)	320 g	12 oz
¹⁄₅	Vegetable adjunct (sliced)	160 g	6 oz
¹⁄₅	Chicken velouté (*see* p. 178)	160 ml	6 fl oz
¹⁄₁₀	Cream ⎫ mix to form liaison Egg yolk ⎬	80 ml	3 fl oz
¹⁄₂₀	Butter or margarine	40 g	1½ oz
	Bouquet garni		
	Salt and pepper		

Method

Melt fat in saucepan, add all vegetables, season lightly and sweat without colour. Add stock, bring to the boil and skim. Add bouquet garni and simmer until all vegetables are cooked (cover with lid).

Remove bouquet garni, add velouté, reboil, mixing well. Liquidize or pass through soup machine and then through fine chinois. Reboil, correct seasoning and consistency.

Add liaison just prior to service. *DO NOT REBOIL* soup once liaison has been added, otherwise soup will curdle. N.B. This soup can be thickened by *replacing* chicken velouté with ¹⁄₄₀ (20 g/³⁄₄ oz) flour to form a blond roux with sweated vegetables.

Extensions of Aqueous Vegetable Velouté Soups using Above Formula: Garnish in relation to 1 unit stock i.e. 800 ml (1½ pt)

English term- main ingredient	Unit	Ingredient	Metric	Imperial	French term
Asparagus velouté soup soup		8 cooked asparagus tips			Velouté d'Asperges
Cucumber velouté soup	¹⁄₂₀ ⎰	Cucumber balls Boiled rice	40 g	1½ oz	Velouté Doria
Mushroom velouté soup [(¹⁄₅ main unit may be used 160 g (6 oz)]	¹⁄₂₀	Julienne of cooked mushroom	40 g	1½ oz	Velouté de Champignons
Watercress velouté soup [¹⁄₅ main unit may be used 160 g (6 oz)]		Blanched watercress leaves			Velouté Cressonnière

N.B. Other aqueous vegetable velouté soups may be prepared using the basic recipe. The above soups may be garnished with chopped parsley as required.

General Note   Many soups which are prepared by the velouté methods appear on menus as 'creams'. Generally in these instances the egg yolk is omitted.

4. *Thickened Brown Soups*   Potages Brun Lié

Soups prepared from a base of brown stock, flavoured with a mirepoix, selected meat and thickened with a brown roux.
This type of soup is traditionally served for luncheon or at suppertime.

THICKENED BROWN SOUP   Potage Brun Lié

Yield: 4 portions
Cooking time: 2 to 3 hr according to meat used, *see* below

Unit	Ingredient	Metric	Imperial
1	Brown stock	1 l	2 pt
$1/5$	Selected meat (medium cut)	200 g	8 oz
$1/5$	Mirepoix (medium cut)	200 g	8 oz
$1/20$	Dripping	50 g	2 oz
$1/20$	Flour	50 g	2 oz
$1/40$	Tomato purée	25 g	1 oz
	Bouquet garni		
	Salt and pepper		

Method

Melt fat in cooking vessel, add meat and vegetables, lightly season, cook to brown colour.
    Add flour and cook gently to form a brown roux. Cool, add tomato purée, brown stock, stir to boil, skim, add bouquet garni and simmer until meat is cooked. Cover with lid to minimize evaporation.
    Remove meat and bouquet garni then pass the soup through a fine strainer. Adjust seasoning and consistency.
    Dice the cooked meat, add to soup and reheat for service.
    N.B.   Browned flour, (*see* p. 168) may be used when forming the roux.
    Due to the long cooking process it is necessary to add extra stock to replace stock lost by evaporation over the long cooking periods.

Examples of Soups Prepared Using Above Formula

English term	Main meat	Flavouring at service	Cooking time approximate (hr)	French term
Kidney soup	Ox-kidney		$2^1/_2$	Soupe aux Rognons
Oxtail soup	Oxtail (tail ends only	Dry sherry (glass)	3	Queue de Boeuf Lié
Game soup	Assorted game	Port (glass)	$2^1/_2$	Soupe de Gibier

English term	Main meat	Flavouring at service	Cooking time approximate (hr)	French term
Hare soup	Hare	Port (glass)	2½	Soupe de Lièvre
Pheasant soup	Pheasant	Port (glass)	2½	Potage Faisan
Mock turtle soup	Calves head. N.B. Add *Turtle herbs* 20 minutes before completion of soup	Dry sherry (glass)	2½	Potage Fausse Tortue

5. *Shellfish Soups*   Bisques

Bisques may be defined as thickened, passed, classical seafood soups prepared from a base of fish stock flavoured with selected shellfish and mirepoix. They are enhanced with wine, brandy and thickened with starch usually in the form of rice. Due to the delicacy of their flavour and the high cost of production bisques are best suited to service at dinner.

SHELLFISH SOUP   Bisque

Yield: 4 portions
Cooking time: 45 min – 1 hr

Unit	Ingredient	Metric	Imperial
1	Fish stock	1 l	2 pt
²/₅	Shellfish (live where possible *see* p. 356)	400 g	1 lb
¹/₁₀	Mirepoix (brunoise)	100 g	4 oz
¹/₁₀	Dry white wine	100 ml	4 fl oz
¹/₂₀	Brandy	50 ml	2 fl oz
¹/₂₀	Cream	50 ml	2 fl oz
¹/₂₀	Butter	50 g	2 oz
¹/₂₀ ★	Rice/white	50 g	2 oz
¹/₄₀	Tomato purée Bouquet garni Seasoning	25 g	1 oz

★ Simmer rice in ¹/₄ / ¹/₂ pt of the fish stock until cooked soft and put aside.

Method

Sweat prepared shellfish (*see* p. 214) and mirepoix in melted butter until shellfish adopts a cooked colour, e.g. lobster turns red. Add white wine and reduce, flame with brandy and lightly season. Moisten with remaining fish stock, add tomato purée, bring to boil, skim, add bouquet garni and simmer for 20 minutes. Remove shellfish from the liquor and separate fish meat from shell. Set shellfish meat aside for garnish and other uses. Crush remaining shell and replace into the cooking liquor. Reboil for a further 10 minutes then pass liquor into a saucepan.

Incorporate the cooked rice preparation (*see* ★) above, liquidize and pass through a chinois to form a thickened soup.

Reboil, adjust seasoning and consistency, add cream and garnish with brandy flavoured diced shellfish meat.

N.B.   When shellfish is unduly expensive it is possible to obtain an acceptable flavour by preparing the soup with the shells of certain shellfish along with rich fish stock, e.g. crushed lobster or crab shells.

Examples of Bisques Prepared Using Above Formula: Garnish in relation to 1 unit i.e. 1 l (2 pt) stock

Menu term	Main shellfish and preparation	Unit	Ingredient	Metric (g)	Imperial (oz)
Bisque de Crabe (crab bisque)	Crab claws (cracked)	$\frac{1}{20}$	White crab meat	50	2
Bisque de Homard (Lobster bisque)	Lobster, split (sack removed from head), claws cracked, remainder cut into pieces	$\frac{1}{20}$	Diced, cooked lobster meat flavoured with brandy.	50	2
Bisque de Crevettes (prawn or shrimp bisque)	Whole prawns or shrimps	$\frac{1}{20}$	Cooked prawns or shrimps	50	2

Unthickened Soups

Broths   Bouillons—Potages

Broth is comprised of savoury stock liquor, flavoured and garnished with a combination of vegetables, vegetables and meat, or vegetables and seafood.

In most cases broth contains a cereal ingredient, usually rice or barley. The flavour is enhanced by herbs, seasonings and occasionally spices. Often broth has the appearance of a thickened soup, a result of the starch content extracted from the cereal ingredient during cooking. However, because the soup remains unpassed, full thickening is not effected.

Broths are sub-divided into three types according to the method of preparation:

(a) when the vegetables are added directly to a stock base which contains a meat ingredient, e.g. stewing mutton as for mutton broth;

(b) when the vegetables are sweated in fat without colour in the initial stages of preparation just prior to the addition of stock;

(c) fish flavoured broths e.g. chowders.

UN-SWEATED BROTH TYPE

Yield: 4 portions
Cooking time: $1\frac{1}{2} - 2$ hr

Unit	Ingredient	Metric	Imperial
1	White stock	1 l	2 pt
$\frac{1}{5}$	Meat content (raw)	200 g	8 oz
$\frac{1}{5}$	Vegetable content (fine dice) carrot – celery – leek – onion – swede – turnip	200 g	8 oz
$\frac{1}{40}$	Barley	25 g	1 oz
	Bouquet garni		
	Chopped parsley		
	Seasoning		

Method

Blanch and refresh meat to remove scum. Replace meat in cooking vessel and cover with the stock. Bring to the boil, skim, add bouquet garni, barley and seasoning. Simmer until meat and barley are almost cooked.

Add the prepared vegetables and continue to simmer until vegetables are cooked. Remove meat content and bouquet garni. Cut meat into small pieces and replace in the broth. Correct seasoning and consistency for service. Garnish with chopped parsley.

N.B. For large-scale production vegetables could be coarsely minced or passed through bowl cutter before cooking.

Examples of Soups Using Above Formula

English term	Meat content	Garnish	French term
Beef broth	Stewing beef	Chopped parsley	Bouillon de Boeuf
Chicken broth	Boiling fowl	Chopped parsley	Bouillon de Volaille
Game broth	Assorted stewing game	Chopped parsley	Bouillon de Gibier
Scotch mutton broth	Stewing mutton	Chopped parsley	Potage Éccossais

SWEATED BROTH TYPE

Yield: 4 portions
Cooking time: 45 min – 1 hr

Unit	Ingredient	Metric	Imperial
1	White chicken stock	1 l	2 pt
$\frac{2}{5}$	Main vegetable (cut into selected shape *see* below)	400 g	1 lb
$\frac{1}{20}$	Garnishing vegetables (when required)	50 g	2 oz
$\frac{1}{40}$	Butter/margarine	25 g	1 oz
	Bouquet garni		
	Seasoning		

Method

Sweat main vegetables in fat content without colour, lightly season. Add the stock, bring to boil, skim, add bouquet garni and simmer until vegetables are almost cooked. Add additional garnish, complete cooking. Correct seasoning and consistency for service.

Extensions of Broths Using Above Formula: Garnish in relation to 1 unit i.e. 1 l (2 pt) stock

Menu term	Main vegetables	Unit	Garnish	Metric	Imperial
Potage Bonne Femme (leek and potato soup)	Equal quantities of leek and potato cut into paysanne.	$^1/_{20}$	Cream Chopped parsley	50 ml	2 fl oz
Cocky-Leeky soup	Julienne of leek	$^1/_{20}$ $^1/_{40}$	Julienne cooked chicken Julienne cooked prunes Chopped parsley	50 g 25 g	2 oz 1 oz
Potage Paysanne	Paysanne of: carrot, leek, onion, potato, swede, turnip, green cabbage, celery	$^1/_{40}$ $^1/_{40}$	Green peas Diced French beans Chopped parsley	25 g 25 g	1 oz 1 oz
Minestroni (minestrone)	As for Potage Paysanne	$^1/_{40}$ $^1/_{40}$	Tomato concassé Raw spaghetti Tomato purée (to colour) 8 Garlic pellets (see p. 73) Grated parmesan cheese to accompany	25 g 25 g	1 oz 1 oz

SHELLFISH BROTH   Chowder

Yield: 4 portions
Cooking time: 30 min

Unit	Ingredient	Metric	Imperial
1	Fish stock	1 l	2 pt
$^1/_5$	Budded shellfish (plus the cooking liquor)	200 g	8 oz
$^1/_5$	Vegetable adjunct (paysanne of leek and potato)	200 g	8 oz
$^1/_{10}$	Belly pork (blanched and diced)	100 g	4 oz
$^1/_{10}$	Tomato concassé	100 g	4 oz
$^1/_{10}$	Cream	100 ml	4 fl oz
$^1/_{40}$	Butter/margarine Bouquet garni Chopped parsley Salt and pepper	25 g	1 oz

Method

Sweat pork and vegetable adjunct in the butter without colour until soft, lightly season. Add stock, shellfish and liquor, bring to boil, skim, add bouquet garni and simmer until vegetables are cooked.

Add tomato concassé, correct seasoning, finish with cream and garnish with chopped parsley.

N.B. On service *crushed water biscuits or fresh breadcrumbs* may be added to soup to act as a thickener. Alternatively chowders may be thickened with beurre manié.

Examples of Soups Prepared Using Above Formula

English term	Main shellfish	Garnish
Clam chowder	Clams	Chopped parsley
Mussel chowder	Mussels	Chopped parsley
Oyster chowder	Oysters	Chopped parsley
Scallop chowder	Scallops	Chopped parsley
Seafood chowder	Assorted shellfish	Chopped parsley

Clear Soups   Consommés

Consommés are refined clear soups prepared from good quality stocks which are flavoured and clarified by a combination of ingredients.

Clarification Process

During cooking the protein content, derived mainly from the egg white and minced beef, coagulates, flocculates and rises to the surface of the consommé. This action results in a clarified liquid being produced. Once cooking is complete the clear liquid lies beneath the mass of coagulated protein and other ingredients.

Points For Consideration

(a) In order to allow the egg white to disperse thoroughly, mix all the ingredients and allow to stand for a period prior to cooking.

(b) Use fat-free stock in order to prevent excess fat causing a greasy product.

(c) Once the consommé has been brought to the boil it is important to ensure that it simmers gently, without stirring for the remainder of the cooking period as rapid boiling or stirring will result in a clouded consommé. For the same reason do not cover the soup with a lid as this would disturb and inhibit the formation of congealed protein.

(d) A tall, deep, thick bottomed cooking vessel is ideally suited for consommé production, this type of vessel is designed to prevent excessive evaporation during cooking and helps to maintain an even temperature throughout.

(e) When most of the grease has been skimmed away from the completed consommé, any remaining grease is removed by passing pieces of absorbent paper across the surface of the consommé.

(f) The desired colour of consommé is amber.

BASIC CONSOMMÉ   Consommé Ordinaire

Yield: 4 portions
Cooking time: 1½ hr

Unit	Ingredient	Metric	Imperial
1	Cold stock (white or brown)	1 l	2 pt
⅕	Beef shin (minced)	200 g	8 oz
⅕	Mirepoix (scorched *see* recipe 1)	200 g	8 oz
¹/₂₀	Egg white	50 g	2 oz
	Bouquet garni		
	Salt and pepper		

N.B.   The type of stock used is determined by the flavour required in the consommé. In addition browned game, poultry carcasses, etc. may be added to appropriate consommés to enhance the flavour.

Method

Thoroughly mix all ingredients in cooking vessel and allow to stand approximately 30 minutes prior to cooking.

Commence cooking by bringing slowly to simmering point, stirring occasionally. Once boiling point is reached allow to simmer gently without any further stirring or undue agitation.

On completion strain carefully through wet muslin, degrease and correct seasoning. Reheat and garnish for service.

Examples of Consommés Prepared Using Above Formula
Garnish in relation to 1 unit i.e. 1 (2 pt)

Menu Term	Unit	Ingredient	Metric	Imperial
Consommé en Tasse (consommé served in a cup)				
Consommé Brunoise (consommé with vegetables)	¹/₂₀	Cooked brunoise of vegetables: carrot turnip leek celery	50 g	2 oz
Consommé Célestine (consommé with savoury pancake)	¹/₄₀	Julienne of savoury pancake	25 g	1 oz
Consommé Julienne (consommé with vegetables)	¹/₂₀	Cooked julienne of vegetables: carrot turnip leek celery	50 g	2 oz

Menu Term	Unit	Ingredient	Metric	Imperial
Consommé Madrilène (consommé with celery and tomato	$^1/_5$	Celery (add to consommé throughout cooking period)	200 g	8 oz
	$^1/_{20}$	Tomato purée (add to consommé throughout cooking period)	50 g	
		Garnish:		
	$^1/_{20}$	tomato concassé	50 g	2 oz
	$^1/_{40}$	small celery batons (cooked)	24 g	1 oz
	$^1/_{40}$	diced pimento (cooked)	25 g	1 oz
		shredded sorrel (sweated in butter)		
	$^1/_{40}$	vermicelli (cooked)	25 g	1 oz
Consommé Alphabétique (consommé with shaped pasta)	$^1/_{40}$	Cooked alphabet pasta	25 g	1 oz
Consommé Vermicelle (consommé with vermicelli)	$^1/_{40}$	Cooked vermicelli pasta	25 g	1 oz
Consommé au Porto (consommé with port wine)	$^1/_{20}$	Port wine	50 ml	2 fl oz
Consommé au Xérès (consommé with sherry)	$^1/_{20}$	Sherry	50 ml	2 fl oz
Consommé Tortue (consommé with turtle flavour)		1 sachet of turtle herbs		
	$^1/_{20}$	*Diced cooked turtle meat	50 g	2 oz
	$^1/_{20}$	Sherry	50 ml	2 fl oz
		Add turtle herbs to prepared consommé and infuse for 20 minutes before removing sachet.		
Consommé Royale (consommé with savoury egg custard)	$^1/_{20}$	Cooked egg custard (savoury *see* p. 203)	50 g	2 oz

* When using dried turtle meat it must be soaked for at least 24 hr and then boiled for 6 – 8 hr in water until tender.

Jellied Consommé   Consommé en Gelée

In summertime consommés are often served cold in a light jellied form. If necessary the gelatinization may be assisted by the addition of $^1/_{40}$ unit gelatine in relation to the completed amount of consommé. Consommé au Porto en Gelée (*see* above) or Consommé Madrilène en Gelée (*see* above but omit vermicelli garnish).

Miscellaneous Soups

A selection of common soups, which cannot be strictly grouped under the former classifications, due to the method of preparation adopted.

FRENCH ONION SOUP

Soupe à l'oignon Française

Yield: 4 portions
Cooking time: 30 – 45 min

Unit	Ingredient	Metric	Imperial
1	Brown stock	1 l	2 pt
1/2	Onions (shredded)	500 g	20 oz
1/20	Margarine/butter	50 g	2 oz
	Chopped garlic (1 to 2 cloves)		
	Salt and pepper		
1/40*	Flour (when thickened soup is required)	25 g	1 oz
	Toasted flûtes (p. 167)		
	Grated cheese for garnish		

*N.B.   This soup may be served thin or slightly thickened. In the latter case the flour forms a roux with the browned onions.

Method

Fry onions in melted fat until lightly browned. Season lightly, add stock, bring to the boil and skim. Simmer until onions are cooked, add garlic and correct seasoning. Serve in earthenware soup dish. Garnish with cheese-flavoured gratinated flûtes (p. 167).

MULLIGATAWNY

Yield: 4 portions
Cooking time: 1 hr

Unit	Ingredient	Metric	Imperial
1	Chicken stock	1 l	2 pt
1/10	Onion (chopped)	100 g	4 oz
1/20	Apple (chopped)	50 g	2 oz
1/20	Butter/margarine	50 g	2 oz
1/20	Flour	50 g	2 oz
1/40	Curry powder	25 g	1 oz
1/40	Tomato purée	25 g	1 oz
1/40	Chutney (chopped)	25 g	1 oz
1/40	Cooked patna rice	25 g	1 oz
	Chopped garlic/2 cloves		
	Salt and pepper		

Method

Sweat onions and apples in melted fat until soft, lightly season, add curry powder and cook gently for a few minutes, add flour to form a roux.

Cool, add tomato purée and gradually add stock stir to boil, skim and add remaining ingredients. Simmer until cooked. Liquidize or pass through soup machine and then through medium chinois. Re-boil, correct seasoning/consistency and lightly garnish with cooked patna rice.

N.B. Soup may be finished with cream on service.

TOMATO SOUP
Potage de Tomates

Yield: 4 portions
Cooking time: 1½ hr

Unit	Ingredient	Metric	Imperial
1	White stock	1 l	2 pt
⅕	Mirepoix (medium cut – include bacon scraps)	200 g	8 oz
¹/₁₀	Tomato purée	100 g	4 oz
¹/₂₀	Butter/margarine	50 g	2 oz
¹/₂₀	Flour	50 g	2 oz
	Bouquet garni (to include basil, clove, crushed garlic)		
	Salt and pepper		

Method

Sweat mirepoix in melted fat without colour and lightly season. Add flour to form a blond roux. Cool and then add tomato purée. Add stock, gradually stirring to the boil, skim add bouquet garni and simmer until soup is cooked. Cover with lid.

Pass through medium chinois, adjust seasoning and consistency, reboil and serve accompanied with soup croûtons.

The flavour of tomato soup may be made more piquant (sharp) by the addition of 'a gastric'. A gastric is a mixture of vinegar and sugar (usually half sugar to vinegar) and is used in small quantities.

N.B. Tomato soup is usually prepared from tomato purée rather than fresh tomatoes mainly in the interests of economy and culinary method. The soup has been classified miscellaneous as a result of this mode of preparation.

Extensions of Tomato Soup Prepared Using Above Formula: Garnish in relation to 1 unit i.e. 1 l (2 pt) stock

Menu term	Unit	Ingredient	Metric	Imperial
Crème de Tomates (cream of tomato soup)	¹/₁₀	Cream	100 ml	4 fl oz
		Chopped parsley		
Crème Portugaise	¹/₁₀	Cream	100 ml	4 fl oz
	¹/₂₀	Boiled patna rice	50 g	2 oz

CRÈME SOLFÉRINO

Yield: 4 portions
Cooking time: 10 – 15 min

Unit	Ingredient	Metric	Imperial
1	Cream of tomato soup	500 ml	1 pt
1	Purée Parmentier (*see* p. 118)	500 ml	1 pt
$^1/_{10}$	Small potato and carrot balls (cooked)	50 g	2 oz
	Chopped parsley		
	Seasoning		

Method

Combine tomato and potato soups in a saucepan, bring to boil and correct seasoning and consistency. Garnish with pre-cooked potato and carrot balls and decorate with chopped parsley for service.

FISH SOUP (MODERN STYLE)   Soupe de Poissons Moderne

Traditionally this soup is prepared from a variety of Mediterranean fish which, because of their small size and boney structure, are unsuitable for many culinary operations. The traditional method requires that the cooked soup is pressed through a sieve in order to remove the fish flesh from the bones and obtain maximum flavour. The ingredients and method shown below is a modification which simplifies the process by using filleted fish so that the soup can be liquidized.

Yield: 4 portions
Cooking time: 30 – 45 min

Unit	Ingredient	Metric	Imperial
1	Fish stock	1 l	2 pt
$^2/_5$	Small rock fish filleted (cut in pieces)	400 g	1 lb
$^1/_{10}$	Dry white wine (optional)	100 ml	4 fl oz
$^1/_{10}$	Potato (roughly diced)	100 g	4 oz
$^1/_{20}$	Tomato purée	50 g	2 oz
$^1/_{20}$	Vegetable adjunct (onion roughly chopped	50 g	2 oz
$^1/_{20}$	Gruyère cheese (grated)	50 g	2 oz
$^1/_{40}$	Oil	25 ml	1 fl oz
	Bouquet garni		
	Freshly chopped parsley		
	2 cloves of garlic (finely chopped)		
	Pinch of saffron		
	Freshly ground black pepper		
	Salt to season		
	4 croûtes of French bread (toasted)		
	Garlic dressing/Rouille*		

*Garlic Dressing	Egg yolk	50 g (2 oz)	Seasoning	to taste
or	Chopped garlic	2 cloves	Lemon juice	squeeze
Rouille	Saffron	pinch	Oil	100 ml (4 fl oz)

Method (garlic dressing/rouille)

Whisk together egg yolk, garlic, saffron, seasoning and lemon juice. Whisk the oil in gradually, as in the making of mayonnaise, to form an emulsified garlic dressing.

Method (soup production and service)

Heat oil in the saucepan, add adjunct, chopped garlic and sweat gently until the vegetables are softened. Add fish and tomato purée and continue gentle cooking for 2 minutes. Stir in the wine, fish stock, bring to the boil and skim. Add potato, bouquet garni, saffron and seasoning. Simmer gently for approximately 30 – 45 minutes. Remove Bouquet garni, liquidize the soup and pour into clean saucepan. Reheat, correct seasoning and consistency.

Spread toasted croûtes with garlic dressing and sprinkle with grated gruyère cheese. To serve ladle soup into dishes, garnish with croûtes and chopped parsley.

Bouillabaisse

A type of soup/stew (*see* pp. 354–5).

RUSSIAN BORTSCH   Bortsch à la Russe

Yield: 4 portions
Cooking time: 30 min

Unit	Ingredient	Metric	Imperial
1	Duck consommé (made from rich duck stock)	1 l	2 pt
$\frac{1}{5}$	Julienne of: leek, celery, carrot, onion, cabbage	200 g	8 oz
$\frac{1}{10}$*	Beetroot juice	100 ml	4 fl oz
	Julienne of:		
$\frac{1}{20}$	cooked beef	50 g	2 oz
$\frac{1}{20}$	cooked breast of duck	50 g	2 oz
$\frac{1}{40}$	cooked beetroot	25 g	1 oz
$\frac{1}{40}$	Butter	25 g	1 oz
	Seasoning		

*To prepare beetroot juice grate some raw beetroot, wrap in muslin and squeeze to extract the juice.

Method

Sweat vegetables in butter without colour, add duck consommé, bring to boil, skim and simmer until vegetables are cooked. Add beetroot juice, reboil and correct seasoning. Garnish with julienne of cooked beef, duck and beetroot, degrease and serve.

Bortsch Accompaniments

(a) Sauceboat of cold beetroot juice;
(b) sauceboat of soured cream;
(c) sauceboat of tiny duck patties (small choux or puff pastry cases filled with duck forcemeat).

POTAGE GERMINY

Yield: 4 portions
Cooking time: 15–20 min

Unit	Ingredient	Metric	Imperial
1	White chicken stock	800 ml	1½ pt
⅕	Cream (double) ⎱ liaison	160 ml	6 fl oz
⅒	Egg yolks ⎰	80 g	3 oz
1/20	Butter	40 g	1½ oz
1/40	Sorrel (julienne)	20 g	¾ oz
	Seasoning		

Method

Sweat sorrel in half of the butter without colour, add stock and simmer briskly for 10 minutes to extract flavour. Remove from heat, stir in liaison of yolks and cream to effect a light thickening, do not allow to reboil otherwise egg yolks will curdle and spoil the appearance of the soup. Blend in remaining butter, correct seasoning and serve with an accompaniment of cheese straws (p. 202).

CREAM OF GREEN PEA SOUP (USING FRESH/FROZEN PEAS)
Crème St Germain

Yield: 4 portions
Cooking time: 45 min–1 hour

Unit	Ingredient	Metric	Imperial
1*	White stock	500 ml	1 pt
⅘	Shelled peas	400 g	1 lb
⅕	Cream	100 ml	4 fl oz
⅒	Diced onion	50 g	2 oz
⅒	Butter	50 g	2 oz
	Sprig of mint		
	Pinch of sugar		
	Seasoning		
	Soup croûtons (*see* p. 167)		

*Extra stock may be required to adjust consistency.

Method

Sweat onions in butter without colour, add peas, sugar, mint, stock and seasoning cover with a lid and simmer until peas are tender. Liquidize or pass through soup machine and medium conical strainer. Adjust consistency, blend in cream, correct seasoning and serve with soup croûtons.

Extensions of Crème St Germain Using Above Formula: Garnish in relation to 1 unit i.e. 500 ml (1 pt) stock

Menu term	Unit	Ingredient	Metric (g)	Imperial (oz)
Crème Lamballe/Cream of pea soup with tapioca	$1/20$	Cooked tapioca	25	1
Crème Longchamp/Cream of pea soup with vermicelli and sorrel	$1/20$ $1/40$	Cooked vermicelli Sorrel (julienne-sweated)	25 12.5	1 $1/2$
Crème St Cloud/Cream of pea soup with lettuce and chervil	$1/20$	Julienne of lettuce and chervil (sweated)	25	1

GAZPACHO (A COLD SPANISH SOUP)

Yield: 4 portions

Unit	Ingredient	Metric	Imperial
1	Tomato juice	500 ml	1 pt
$1/4$	Iced water	125 ml	5 fl oz
$1/4$	Tomato concassé	125 g	5 oz
$1/4$	Peeled cucumber (small dice)	125 g	5 oz
$1/4$	Green pepper ⎫ brunoise	125 g	5 oz
$1/10$	Onion ⎭	50 g	2 oz
$1/20$	Mayonnaise	25 ml	1 fl oz
$1/20$	Wine vinegar	25 ml	1 fl oz
	Flavourings: clove of chopped garlic dash of Worcester sauce dash of Tobasco sauce squeeze of lemon juice seasoning		

Method

Combine all ingredients other than cucumber and season to taste. Allow to stand for 2 hours in a cool place. Correct seasoning, add cucumber and serve chilled.

N.B. This soup may be prepared by the Chef Garde-Manger.

VICHYSSOISE (COLD LEEK AND POTATO SOUP)

Yield: 4 portions
Cooking time: 1 hr

Unit	Ingredient	Metric	Imperial
1	Chicken stock	800 ml	1½ pt
²/₅	White of leek ⎫ sliced	320 g	12 oz
¹/₅	Potato ⎭	160 g	6 oz
¹/₁₀	Cream	80 ml	3 fl oz
¹/₂₀	Butter	40 g	1½ oz
	Bouquet garni		
	Chopped chives (garnish)		
	Seasoning		

Method

Sweat leeks and potato in butter without colour and lightly season. Add stock bring to the boil, skim, add bouquet garni, cover with lid and simmer until vegetables are cooked. Remove bouquet garni, liquidize or pass through a soup machine and through a fine conical strainer. Correct seasoning, stir over ice until cold, add cream, garnish with chives and serve chilled.

PETITE MARMITE

Yield: 4 portions
Cooking time: 45 min

Unit	Ingredient	Metric	Imperial
1	Beef consommé	1 l	2 pt
¹/₅	Carrot and turnip (small, turned)	200 g	8 oz
¹/₅	Julienne of: leek, cabbage, celery	200 g	8 oz
¹/₁₀*	Blanched beef and chicken dice	100 g	4 oz
	4 Slices of beef marrow		
	Toasted flûtes		
	Chopped parsley		
	Seasoning		

*Meat content is blanched to remove congealed blood particles and scum which would impair the appearance of the soup.

Method

Add the blanched beef and chicken dice to the consommé, bring to the boil and skim. Simmer until the meat is almost cooked, add carrot and turnip and simmer for 5 minutes, add remaining julienne of vegetables. Continue simmering until meat and vegetables are cooked, correct seasoning and add marrow just before service. Serve in small earthenware marmite pots accompanied with toasted flûtes of bread and grated parmesan cheese.

Extensions of Petite Marmite Using Above Formula: Garnish in relation to 1 unit i.e. 1 l (2 pt) stock

Menu term	Unit	Ingredient	Metric (g)	Imperial (oz)
Petite Marmite Béarnaise	$\frac{1}{40}$	Boiled patna rice	25	1
	$\frac{1}{40}$	Julienne of cooked potato	25	1
Croûte au Pot		As for Petite Marmite omitting beef and chicken dice		

15

Egg Cookery and Extensions

Throughout culinary work eggs are employed in a number of ways. Examples of their general use may be listed as follows:

(a) to aerate — soufflés, batters;
(b) to bind — potato dishes, stuffings;
(c) to coat — coating foods with breadcrumbs;
(d) to enrich and thicken — sauces, soups, and white stews;
(e) to emulsify — hollandaise, béarnaise, mayonnaise sauces;
(f) to glaze and colour — used as egg wash on goods for baking and browning under the salamander.

In addition egg dishes appear on the traditional menu as a course in their own right and are often chosen as a preliminary item prior to the main dish. However, they may also be selected as a main course item, e.g. omelets, curried eggs.

Egg dishes are ideal for use in the more modern type of fast-food operation, e.g. hotel buttery, bistro, snack bar, motorway operation, etc. In these circumstances they may be served as a meal 24 hours a day and in most instances are cooked to order.

When a traditional kitchen brigade is employed, all cold egg dishes are the responsibility of the Chef Garde-Manger (Larder Chef), hot egg dishes for luncheon and dinner the responsibility of the Chef Entremettier (Vegetable Chef), and egg dishes for breakfast prepared by the Breakfast Chef. The allocation of these duties may vary from one establishment to another according to the size and nature of the brigade.

Eggs   Les Oeufs

Egg dishes may be classified according to the method of cookery used. They are as follows:

Method I: Poached Eggs   Oeufs Pochés

Prepare a shallow pan or tray containing lightly acidulated (vinegar), seasoned (salt) water. Bring to simmering point, break in eggs and poach gently until white sets firm and yolks remain soft.

Remove eggs with perforated spoon and drain well, use immediately or 'refresh' and-store in iced water for later use. *To re-heat* plunge into simmering seasoned water for approximately 30 seconds to 1 minute.

Method II: Poached en Bain-Marie   Oeufs Moulés

Half fill cooking vessel with water to form bain-marie. Bring to boiling point, prepare egg moulds with seasoning (salt and pepper) and knob of butter to flavour and prevent eggs from sticking to moulds.

Break eggs one at a time into individual moulds, cover with lid and cook gently en bain-marie until white sets firm and yolk remains soft (approximately 3–5 minutes). Turn out from moulds and serve.

Lid to cover

Lightly seasoned buttered moulds

Steam vents

Half-filled with water

Examples of Dishes Prepared Using Oeufs Pochés: Ingredients for 4 Portions Using 4 Poached Eggs (1 per portion)

English term	Unit	Ingredient	Metric	Imperial	French term
Egg with asparagus served in pastry cases	1	Cream sauce 8 Asparagus spears (cooked) 4 small savoury pastry cases	250 ml	10 fl oz	Oeuf Poché Argenteuil
		Trim 4 small asparagus tips for garnish. Finely chop remaining asparagus and cohere with a little of the sauce. Heat the mixture and place in base of pastry case. Sit hot eggs into cases, napper with sauce, garnish with hot asparagus tips and serve			
Egg with muffins, tongue and hollandaise sauce	1 $^2/_5$	Hollandaise sauce Sliced cooked tongue 4 croûtes toasted (muffins buttered) 4 slices truffle for garnish	250 ml 100 g	10 fl oz 4 oz	Oeuf Poché Bénédictine
		Place heated tongue on to croûtes of muffin. Sit heated egg on to tongue and napper with sauce, garnish with truffle			

English term	Unit	Ingredient	Metric	Imperial	French term
Egg with rice and curry sauce	1 $^1/_5$	Curry sauce Patna rice (boiled)	250 ml 50 g	10 fl oz 2 oz	Oeuf Poché Bombay or Indienne
		Put a bed of hot rice into buttered egg dish. Sit heated egg on to rice and napper with sauce and serve			
Egg in cheese sauce	1 $^1/_5$	Mornay Sauce Grated cheese	250 ml 50 g	10 fl oz 2 oz	Oeuf Poché Mornay
		Place heated eggs in buttered and sauced egg dish. Coat with sauce, sprinkle with grated cheese and gratinate for service. N.B. May be presented in pastry cases			
Egg in cheese sauce with spinach	$^2/_5$	Cooked leaf spinach	100 g	4 oz	Oeuf Poché Florentine
		Prepare as for Oeuf Poché Mornay but placing eggs on a bed of heated spinach			
Egg in pastry case with cooked chicken	1 $^2/_5$	Supreme sauce Diced cooked chicken 4 small savoury pastry cases	250 ml 100 g	10 fl oz 4 oz	Oeuf Poché à la Reine
		Cohere chicken with a little sauce. Heat the mixture and place in base of pastry cases. Sit heated eggs on to bed of chicken, napper with sauce and serve			
Egg in pastry case with cooked sweetcorn		As for Oeuf Poché à la Reine but replace chicken with sweetcorn			Oeuf Poché Washington

Boiled Eggs   Oeufs Bouillis

Eggs are boiled to varying degrees according to requirements and may be served with or without shell.

Method

Place eggs into metal basket and plunge into simmering water, reboil and simmer for required time. Commence timing once water has reboiled.
The stages of boiling are:

(1) *Soft boiled (in shell)*   *Oeuf à la Coque*   *Boiling Time (3 – 4 min)*

Served in shell, timed to the customer's personal requirements.

(2) *Soft boiled and shelled*   *Oeuf Mollet*   *Boiling Time (5 min)*

On completion of boiling 'refresh' in cold water, remove shells carefully and reheat in boiling water ($\frac{1}{2}$ min) as required. Prepare and garnished as for poached eggs (*see* above).

(3) *Hard boiled*   *Oeuf Dur*   *Boiling Time (8 – 10 min)*

Served with or without shell. Often refreshed and shelled immediately in readiness for use.

Examples of Dishes Prepared Using Oeufs Durs (Hard Boiled Eggs): Ingredients for 4 portions using 4 hard boiled eggs (1 per portion)

English term	Unit	Ingredient	Metric	Imperial	French term
Egg with rice and curry sauce	1 $\frac{2}{5}$	Curry sauce Patna rice (boiled)	250 ml 100 g	10 fl oz 4 oz	Oeuf Dur Bombay or Indienne
		Place a bed of hot rice into buttered egg dish. Sit halved or quartered egg on to rice, napper with sauce and serve			
Egg in white onion sauce	1	White onion sauce Chopped parsley	250 ml	10 fl oz	Oeuf à la Tripe
		Place halved or quartered eggs into buttered sauce egg dish. Napper with sauce and garnish with parsley and serve			
Stuffed egg in cheese sauce	1 $\frac{2}{5}$ $\frac{1}{5}$	Cheese sauce Duxelle Grated cheese	250 ml 100 g 50 g	10 fl oz 4 oz 2 oz	Oeuf Chimay
		Halve eggs lengthways, remove yolk and sieve finely. Mix sieved yolk with duxelle and cohere with a little sauce. Replace mixture into egg white cavity to form a mound. Place in buttered sauced egg dish, napper with sauce, sprinkle with cheese. Bake in hot oven till golden brown 205°C (400°F)			
Stuffed egg with aurore sauce		Prepare as for Oeuf Chimay, but substitute cheese sauce with Sauce Aurore. N.B. Béchamel coloured and flavoured with tomato purée may be used			Oeuf Aurore

Egg in Cocotte

Indicates egg cooked in a small glazed earthenware dish (cocotte), garnished in various ways. When served as a preliminary course one egg per person is the accepted portion. These dishes are served for luncheon or dinner and are presented in and eaten from the cocotte dish in which they are cooked. All these items are cooked to order.

Oeuf en Cocotte

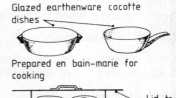

Glazed earthenware cocotte dishes

Prepared en bain-marie for cooking

Lid to cover.

Whole egg   Garnish   Water

Method

Butter and season cocotte dishes, break in eggs one at a time. Place cocottes in prepared bain-marie (only sufficient water to half cover cocotte). Cover with lid and cook on stove top until white of egg is set but yolk remains soft. Once cooked pour away the condensation that has formed on egg surface. Serve immediately.

N.B. When a garnish is employed it is usually placed in the base of the cocotte before the egg is put in position. Upon completion of cooking the eggs may be finished with a cordon of sauce or cream and decorated with parsley.

Examples of Dishes Prepared Using Oeuf En Cocotte: Ingredients for 4 portions using 4 eggs (1 per portion)

English term	Unit	Ingredient	Metric	Imperial	French term
Egg garnished with mushroom and cooked mutton	1	Jus lié	100 ml	4 fl oz	Oeuf en Cocotte Bergère
	½	Minced mutton (cooked)	50 g	2 oz	
	½	Chopped mushroom (cooked)	50 g	2 oz	
Cohere mushrooms and mutton with a little sauce and place in base of cocotte before adding eggs to cook. Once cooked finish with a cordon of sauce					
Egg garnished with poached beef marrow and bordelaise sauce	1	Bordelaise sauce	100 ml	4 fl oz	Oeuf en Cocotte Bordelaise
		8 thin slices of poached beef marrow			
Garnish base of each cocotte with one slice of marrow before adding eggs to cook. Once cooked finish with a cordon of sauce and a slice of marrow					
Egg with cream	1	Double cream	100 ml	4 fl oz	Oeuf en Cocotte à la Crème
Once egg is cooked finish with a cordon of cream					

English term	Unit	Ingredient	Metric	Imperial	French term
Egg with thickened veal gravy	1	Jus lié	100 ml	4 fl oz	Oeuf en Cocotte Jus Lié
		Once egg is cooked finish with cordon of sauce			
Egg garnished with foie gras and Périgueux sauce	1	Périgueux sauce	100 ml	4 fl oz	Oeuf en Cocotte Périgourdine
		4 Thin slices of foie gras			
		Garnish base of each cocotte with one slice of foie gras before adding eggs to cook. Once cooked finish with a cordon of sauce			
Egg garnished with asparagus and Périgueux sauce	1	Périgueux sauce	100 ml	4 fl oz	Oeuf en Cocotte Petit-Duc
		8 Asparagus spears heated			
		Trim 4 small asparagus tips for garnish. Chop remaining asparagus and place in base of each cocotte before adding eggs to cook. Once cooked garnish with asparagus tips and cordon of sauce			
Egg garnished with tomatoes	1 $\frac{1}{2}$	Tomato sauce Tomatoes concassées	100 ml 50 g	4 fl oz 2 oz	Oeuf en Cocotte Portugaise
		Garnish base of each cocotte with tomato before adding eggs to cook. Once cooked finish with a cordon of sauce			
Egg garnished with creamed chicken	1 $\frac{1}{2}$	Double cream Minced cooked chicken	100 ml 50 g	4 fl oz 2 oz	Oeuf en Cocotte à la Reine
		Cohere chicken with half cream and place in the base of each cocotte before adding eggs to cook. Once cooked finish with a cordon of cream			
Egg garnished with onions and soubise sauce	1 $\frac{1}{2}$	Soubise sauce Sliced onion (sweat without colour)	100 ml 50 g	4 fl oz 2 oz	Oeuf en Cocotte Soubise
		Cohere onion with a little sauce and place in the base of each cocotte before adding eggs to cook. Once cooked finish with a cordon of sauce			

Egg Baked in China Plate (dish)   Oeuf Sur le Plat

China plate:
Sur le Plat dish

Indicates an egg baked in a buttered ovenproof china dish which may be garnished in a variety of ways. When served as a preliminary course one egg per person is the accepted portion. These dishes may be served at lunch or dinner and are presented in and eaten from the dish in which they are cooked. All these dishes are cooked to order.

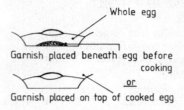

Whole egg

Garnish placed beneath egg before
cooking

_or_

Garnish placed on top of cooked egg

Method

Butter and season sur le plat dish, place on stove top to heat. Break in eggs one at a time and cook until white begins to set. Place in moderately hot oven to complete cooking. This is complete when white is set firm and yolk remains soft. Serve immediately.

N.B.   When a garnish is employed it may be placed in the base of the dish before egg is added or used to garnish once egg is cooked. These dishes are often finished with a cordon of sauce or cream and decorated with parsley.

Examples of Dishes Prepared Using Oeuf Sur Le Plat: Ingredients for 4 portions using 4 eggs (1 per portion)

English term	Unit	Ingredient	Metric	Imperial	French term
Egg with grilled ham and tomato sauce	1	Tomato sauce	100 ml	4 fl oz	Oeuf Sur le Plat Américaine
		4 Thin slices grilled ham			
		Garnish base of dish with ham before adding egg to cook. Once cooked finish with a cordon of tomato sauce			
Egg with grilled chipolata sausage and tomato sauce	1	Tomato sauce	100 ml	4 fl oz	Oeuf Sur le Plat Bercy
		8 Grilled cocktail chipolata sausages			
		Once egg is cooked garnish with sausage and finish with a cordon of tomato sauce			

English term	Unit	Ingredient	Metric	Imperial	French term
Egg with cream	1	Double cream	100 ml	4 fl oz	Oeuf Sur le Plat à la Crème
		Once egg is cooked finish with cordon of double cream			
Egg with chicken livers, mushrooms, and Madeira sauce	1	Madeira sauce	100 ml	4 fl oz	Oeuf sur le Plat Chasseur
	½	Chicken livers (diced, sautéed)	50 g	2 oz	
	½	Mushrooms (diced, sautéed)	50 g	2 oz	
		Once egg is cooked garnish with mushrooms and chicken livers cohered with sauce			
Egg garnished with shrimps and shrimp sauce	1	Shrimp sauce (p. 181)	100 ml	4 fl oz	Oeuf sur le Plat aux Crevettes Grises
	½	Picked shrimps (heated)	50 g	2 oz	
		Once egg is cooked garnish with shrimps and finish with cordon of sauce			
Egg with grilled bacon		4 Slices of grilled bacon			Oeuf sur le Plat au Lard
		Garnish base of dish with bacon before adding egg to cook			
Egg with grilled bacon, gruyère cheese and cream	1	Double cream	100 ml	4 fl oz	Oeuf sur le Plat Lorraine
	½	Gruyère cheese (grated)	50 g	2 oz	
		4 Slices of grilled bacon			
		Garnish base of dish with bacon and cheese before adding egg to cook. Once cooked finish with cordon of cream			
Egg with spinach and cheese sauce	1	Cheese sauce	200 ml	8 fl oz	Oeuf sur le Plat Florentine
	½	Leaf spinach (cooked)	100 g	4 oz	
	¼	Grated cheese	50 g	2 oz	
		Garnish base of dish with spinach before adding egg to cook. Once cooked napper with sauce, sprinkle with cheese and gratinate under salamander			

Shallow Fried Eggs   Oeufs Frits

Indicates eggs gently cooked with oil/bacon fat/lard in a shallow frying vessel until white is firm while yolk remains soft. These eggs may be cooked to customer requirements e.g. well cooked yolk. Fried eggs are served at breakfast and are also served in fast food operations as snack meals 24 hours a day. In addition they are used as a garnish when preparing certain entrées, e.g. Escalope de Veau Holstein and Vienna Steaks.

Method

Cover the base of a shallow cooking vessel with clean frying oil or selected fat. Heat gently, break in eggs one at a time and fry steadily until the white sets firm and yolk remains soft. During frying baste eggs frequently with fat/oil to ensure even cooking. Remove with egg slice, drain well and serve.

N.B.   Ensure at the onset that the cooking fat/oil is not too hot, otherwise egg white will over-cook, become crisp, brown and indigestible.

Turned Egg

As above but fried on both sides until well cooked.

Deep Fried Egg   Oeuf Frit à la Française

Egg which is deep fried in oil, shaped during cooking by enveloping the yolk with the white. Chiefly used as a garnish, e.g. Poulet Sauté Marengo.

Method

Half fill omelette pan with oil and heat to frying temperature. Break in the egg, then using an oiled wooden spatula manipulate the white around the yolk as the egg begins to set. Continue cooking to light brown colour. Using perforated spoon remove cooked egg, drain well and serve.

SCRAMBLED EGGS   Oeufs Brouillés

Indicates seasoned, beaten eggs cooked in butter until eggs coagulate to become firm and fluffy in texture. Scrambled eggs may be served for breakfast, garnished and served as a course at luncheon, dinner or as a snack meal in fast food establishments.

Yield: 4 portions
Cooking time: 5 – 10 min approx.
(will take longer with larger quantities)

Unit	Ingredient	Metric	Imperial
1	Beaten whole egg	400 g	1 lb
$1/_8$	Milk	50 ml	2 fl oz
$1/_8$	Butter	50 g	2 oz
	Seasoning: salt and white pepper to taste		

Method

Mix eggs, milk and seasoning together.
Melt butter over gentle heat in saucepan, add eggs and mix thoroughly with wooden

spoon until eggs lightly set (coagulate). Correct seasoning and serve immediately. N.B.

(a) May be enriched before service with a little cream.

(b) When using aluminium pan do not mix with metal whisk during cooking otherwise eggs will discolour.

(c) Large quantities are best cooked en bain-marie as they take a longer time to cook and the chance of burning is reduced by this method.

Examples of Dishes Prepared Using Oeufs Brouillés: Ingredients for 4 portions using 8 eggs (2 per portion)

English term	Unit	Ingredient	Metric	Imperial	French term
Scrambled eggs with ham, mushrooms, and asparagus	1 ½	Cooked diced ham Cooked diced mushrooms 4 Asparagus tips (heated)	100 g 50 g	4 oz 2 oz	Oeufs Brouillés Archiduchesse
		Heat ham, mushrooms in a little butter, combine carefully with scrambled egg. Place in selected service dish, garnish with asparagus and serve			
Scrambled eggs with mushrooms	1	Cooked sliced mushrooms	100 g	4 oz	Oeufs Brouillés aux Champignons
		Combine hot mushrooms with scrambled egg and serve			
Scrambled eggs with diced fried croûtons	1	Diced croûtons (shallow fried)	100 g	4 oz	Oeufs Brouillés aux Croûtons
		Surround scrambled egg with croûtons and serve As above finished with chopped parsley			Oeufs Brouillés Grand' Mère
Scrambled eggs with chicken livers and Madeira sauce	1 1	Madeira sauce Chicken liver (diced, sautéed in butter)	100 ml 100 g	4 fl oz 4 oz	Oeufs Brouillés aux Foies de Volaille
		Cohere chicken livers with half sauce. Place in centre of scrambled egg, finish with cordon of sauce			
Scrambled eggs with tomatoes	1	Tomato concassé	100 g	4 oz	Oeufs Brouillés Portugaise
		Heat tomato in a little butter and combine with scrambled egg			

All garnishes are seasoned to taste.

Omelets   Les Omelettes

To the layman the making of an omelet appears to be a simple operation, however if a satisfactory product is to be achieved a great deal of skill is required.

Omelets are served for breakfast, luncheon, dinner and frequently as a meal in fast food establishments. In general 2 – 3 eggs are used per omelet according to portion control requirements and sizes of eggs used. Omelets are generally served in one of two ways either flat or folded (cigar shaped).

The garnish or flavouring may be added in a variety of ways:

(a) combined with egg before cooking;
(b) placed into centre of omelet before it is folded;
(c) placed on top of omelet, in a cavity after folding is complete.

General Points Concerning Omelet Preparation

Omelet Pans

These are made from heavy gauge wrought iron or steel. When the pans are new or sticking they need to be *'proved'* before use. This is achieved by filling the pan with plenty of salt and heating them on the stove top or in a moderate oven for 2 to 3 hours. The salt is then removed and the pan wiped clear with a clean dry cloth. At this stage the pan is half filled with cooking oil and steadily heated on the stove top for a further period until the pan is smooth, black and shiny in appearance. Once in general use the omelet pans should on no account be washed but instead wiped clean with a dry cloth after use. If the pan is washed it will lose its non-stick characteristic, will need re-proving and may also rust from contact with the water. Always store omelet pans clean and brushed with a film of oil to prevent bacterial infection and rusting.

Degree of Cooking Omelets

The texture of the completed omelet should be soft, with a firm exterior and a moist centre, this is termed *baveuse*. Ideally the exterior of the completed omelet should have just begun to colour. However, the texture and colour of an omelet may vary according to customer requirement and also when a glazed finish is required. Omelets are generally cooked to order.

Service of Omelet

For service omelets are placed on lightly buttered flats, then brushed gently with melted butter. This gives the omelet a shiny appearance.

General Mise-en-place for Omelet Production

1. Collect eggs required.
2. Small bowl and fork for mixing eggs.
3. Seasonings, fillings, flavourings and garnishes.
4. Jug of cooking oil and knobs of butter.
5. Prepared heated omelet pan half filled with oil.
6. Service dishes.
7. Clean dry cloth for wiping pan clean after use.
8. Melted butter and brush to butter service dishes and cooked omelet.

Plain Omelet   Omelette Nature

Yield: 2 – 3 eggs = 1 portion
Cooking time: approximately 1 min

Method

Break eggs into bowl, season and beat with a fork, mix thoroughly to disperse white and yolk evenly. This ensures an omelet of even colour and texture. Remove oil from heated omelet pan, place pan directly over heat, add knob of butter and allow to melt.

   Pour in the eggs, shake pan briskly whilst gently stirring with the fork to distribute egg evenly around base of the pan.

Once egg begins to set, remove pan from heat, loosen around edge with fork, tilt pan downwards slightly, fold nearside of omelet to centre, tap pan handle briskly to move omelet to far edge of pan. Fold far side of omelet to centre to form cigar (oval) shape, seal quickly with fork and turn out on to buttered service dish. Brush surface with melted butter and serve.

Flat Omelet

Add garnish to egg before making the omelet, turn out without folding, coloured side uppermost. N.B. Seal non-presentation side under salamander before turning out. Alternatively the omelet can be toss/turned in pan to seal/colour.

Stuffed and Folded Omelet

Place filling in centre of omelet before folding.

Folded and Stuffed Omelet

Slit turned out omelet along centre of top surface, place in the filling.

Folded Omelet

Add garnish to egg before cooking.

Examples of Omelet Extensions: Ingredients for 4 portions of filling (2/3 eggs per omelet)

English term	Unit	Ingredient	Metric	Imperial	French term
Flat Omelets					
Spanish omelet	1	Diced pimento (cooked)	100 g	4 oz	Omelette Espagnole
	1	Tomato concassé	100 g	4 oz	
	1	Diced onion (sweated without colour	100 g	4 oz	
		4 Anchovy fillets } 4 Stoned olives } garnish for decoration			
		Hint of chopped garlic			
		Chopped parsley			
		Combine all ingredients with egg omitting garnish. Cook and serve flat. Garnish with olive wrapped in anchovy fillet			

English term	Unit	Ingredient	Metric	Imperial	French term
Omelet farmer's style	1	Finely diced cooked ham Chopped parsley	100 g	4 oz	Omelette Fermière
		Combine ingredients with egg, cook and serve flat			
Omelet peasant style	1	Finely diced potato (cooked)	100 g	4 oz	Omelette Paysanne
	1	Diced cooked bacon Chopped fine herbs and sorrel	100 g	4 oz	
		Combine ingredients with egg, cook and serve flat			
Potato omelet	1	Diced sautéed potatoes Chopped parsley	100 g	4 oz	Omelette Parmentier
		Combine ingredients with egg, cook and serve flat			

Stuffed Omelets (folded)

The omelets listed below are stuffed according to service style.

Turkish omelet	1	Diced cooked chicken livers cohered in Madeira sauce	100 g	4 oz	Omelette à la Turque
		Cordon of Madeira sauce to garnish			
Shrimp omelet	1	Picked shrimps cohered with shrimp sauce	100 g	4 oz	Omelette aux Crevettes Grises
	1	Mornay sauce	250 ml	10 fl oz	Omelette Arnold Bennett (modern version)
	2/5	Cooked smoked haddock flaked and cohered with double cream	100 g	4 oz	
	1/5	Grated cheese	50 g	2 oz	
		Stuff omelet with haddock, turn out on to service dish, napper with sauce, sprinkle with grated cheese and gratinate to serve			

English term	Unit	Ingredient	Metric	Imperial	French term
Ingredients as for modern version, *see* p. 240, but cook/serve flat. Place salpicon of haddock on to presentation side, coat lightly with a little of the cheese sauce, sprinkle with grated cheese and gratinate.					Omelette Arnold Bennett (traditional version)
Tomato omelet	1	Tomates concassées	100 g	4 oz	Omelette aux Tomates/
		Cordon of tomato sauce garnish			Portugaise

Folded Omelets

For the omelets below the garnish is mixed with eggs prior to cooking.

English term	Unit	Ingredient	Metric	Imperial	French term
Mushroom omelet	1	Sliced mushrooms sweated in butter	100 g	4 oz	Omelette aux Champignons
Herb omelet		Fine herbs to garnish and flavour			Omelette Fines Herbes
Cheese omelet	1	Grated cheese	100 g	4 oz	Omelette au Fromage
Ham omelet	1	Finely diced cooked ham	100 g	4 oz	Omelette au Jambon
Ham and potato omelet	1	Finely diced potato	50 g	2 oz	Omelette Limousine
	1	Finely diced ham	50 g	2 oz	
		Toss garnish in butter until cooked, combine with eggs			
Bacon and cheese omelet	1	Small diced fried bacon	50 g	2 oz	Omelette Lorraine
	1	Gruyère cheese (grated)	50 g	2 oz	
		Chopped chives			

Savoury Souffle Omelet

Separate yolks/whites (2–3 eggs per portion), add pinch salt to whites and whisk to a peak. Fold yolks, whites, selected filling together and season to taste. Proceed as for normal omelets but without undue stirring/shaking and allow the omelet to set at the base. Now place under salamander to seal/soufflé at the surface. Serve *flat or folded* as required. May be cooked in the oven.

Typical flavourings: plain, cheese, herb and garlic or combination of these, etc.

16
Farinaceous Cookery and Extensions

The word farinaceous is derived from 'farine' meaning flour, and is used to classify culinary products prepared from rice, pasta and various types of gnocchis (small dumplings)

Where a traditional kitchen brigade is employed, farinaceous preparations are usually the responsibility of the 'Chef Entremettier' (Vegetable Chef), this responsibility may vary according to the nature and size of the brigade.

Farinaceous products may be served for luncheon or dinner and appear in a variety of guises:

(a) as a menu course e.g. spaghetti bolognaise;
(b) as an accompaniment e.g. boiled rice and curries;
(c) as a garnish e.g. gnocchi with goulash;
(d) as a substitute for vegetables e.g. braised rice to replace potatoes.

Farinaceous dishes are ideal for use in modern units as explained for egg dishes (p. 139). They may be classified as follows:

1. Rice   – Riz
2. Gnocchi – Noques
3. Pasta   – Pâtes alimentaires

Rice Products

The types of rice commonly used in the kitchen are broadly classified as 'long grain (patna, piedmont) and 'short' grain (carolina), the latter being used for rice-based sweet preparations.

All the products in this study are prepared using long-grained rice which on cooking remains intact, dry and fluffy without the grains sticking together.

Points for Consideration when Cooking Rice

(a) When boiling rice, use plenty of lightly seasoned water to allow the rice grains freedom of movement during cooking. An approximate guide is 10 units water to 1 unit rice.

(b) At the commencement of boiling, the rice should be stirred to prevent clogging or sticking. Once the grains are cooked care must be taken, when stirring, not to damage the softened grains, as this would spoil the appearance of the finished product. Likewise in the cooking of pilaff and risotto a double pronged cook's fork is used for stirring, after the initial cooking period.

(c) The appearance and texture of cooked rice should be fluffy and firm. Overcooked rice becomes soggy, taking on an unpleasant watery texture and flavour.

(d) When Piedmont rice is not available for risotto other long-grained varieties are used.

(e) The main differences between a pilaff and a risotto are:

    (1) the mode of cookery used, pilaff is braised in the oven, risotto is stewed on the stove top;

    (2) less stock is used when cooking a pilaff, and as a result the stock is fully absorbed into the rice giving a drier appearance than that of the more moist risotto.

(f) The stock proportions used in both the pilaff and risotto may vary according to the absorption rates of rice and the length and speed of the cooking period.

PLAIN BOILED RICE   Riz Nature

Yield: 200 g or 8 oz = 4 portions
Cooking time: 15 – 20 min

Unit	Ingredient	Metric	Imperial
1	Rice patna	200 g	8 oz
	Salt to taste		
*	Water (boiling)	2 l	4 pt

* 10 units *water* to 1 unit *rice* approximately 10:1.

Method

Season boiling water, add rice grains, stir to the boil, reduce heat and simmer until just cooked (*al dente*). Once the rice is cooked place the vessel under slow running cold water to cool rice and remove excess starch. This is indicated when water clears. Drain well in colander. At this point the grains should separate readily.

Spread grains on to lightly greased shallow trays, cover with a clean cloth and place in slow oven/hot cupboard to dry and reheat. Stir occasionally with fork to prevent sticking. Use as required.

Fried Rice

Quickly shallow fry dried boiled rice in a film of cooking oil, margarine or butter. The rice is fried without colour and seasoned to taste. A garnish may be added to improve appearance and flavour, e.g. cooked pimentoes, cooked sliced mushrooms, saffron, etc.

STEWED SAVOURY RICE (ITALIAN STYLE)   Rizotto

Yield: 200 g or 8 oz = 4 portions
Cooking time: 20 – 30 min

Unit	Ingredient	Metric	Imperial
1	Rice (piedmont/patna)	200 g	8 oz
1/4	Onion (brunoise)	50 g	2 oz
1/8	Butter/margarine	25 g	1 oz
	Seasoning to taste		
	Bouquet garni		
*	White stock (heated usually chicken)	600 ml	1 1/4 pt

* 3 units *stock* to 1 unit *rice* approximately 3:1.

Method

Sweat onions in butter without colour, add rice, mix well. Add stock, stir to the boil, add bouquet garni and seasoning. Cover with lid and simmer gently on stove top until rice is cooked. Stir occasionally to prevent rice from sticking to bottom of cooking vessel. Using a fork stir in a knob of butter and any further seasoning. Remove bouquet garni and serve as required.

BRAISED SAVOURY RICE (INDIAN STYLE)   Pilaff/Pilaw/Pilau

Yield: 200 g or 8 oz of rice = 4 portions
Cooking time: 15 – 20 min
Cooking temperature: 205°C (400°F)

Unit	Ingredient	Metric	Imperial
1	Rice patna	200 g	8 oz
1/4	Onion brunoise	50 g	2 oz
1/8	Butter/margarine	25 g	1 oz
	Seasoning to taste		
	Bouquet garni		
*	Heated white stock (usually chicken)	400 ml	16 fl oz

* 2 units *stock* to 1 *unit* rice approximately 2:1.

Method

Sweat onions in butter without colour, add rice and mix well. Add stock, stir to the boil, add bouquet garni and seasoning. Cover with greased cartouche and lid. Braise in oven until rice is cooked and all stock has been absorbed. Stir occasionally with a fork to keep rice grains separated. Once cooked stir in knob of butter and any further seasoning. Remove bouquet garni and use as required.

Examples of Rice Dishes Using Basic Risotto/Pilaff: Added ingredients in relation to 1 unit i.e. 200 g (8 oz) rice

English Term Risotto/Pilaff	Unit	Ingredient	Metric (g)	Imperial (oz)	French Term Rizotto/Pilaff
Chicken	1	Diced cooked chicken	200	8	à Volaille
Ham	1	Diced cooked ham	200	8	au Jambon
Liver	1	Sautéed chicken livers	200	8	au Foie de Volaille
Mushroom	1	Sliced cooked mushrooms	200	8	aux Champignons
Prawn	1	Cooked prawns (other shellfish may be used)	200	8	aux Crevettes Roses
		Garnish:			Créole
	$^1/_2$	sliced cooked mushrooms	100	4	
	$^1/_4$	diced cooked pimento	50	2	
	$^1/_4$	tomato concassé	50	2	
Piedmont style		As for Créole, flavoured:			Piémontaise
	$^1/_4$	grated parmesan cheese diced truffle	50	2	
Italian style		Flavoured:			Italienne
	$^1/_4$	grated parmesan cheese	50	2	
Milan style		Flavoured and garnished:			Milanaise
	$^1/_2$	sliced cooked mushrooms	100	4	
	$^1/_4$	tomato concassé	50	2	
	$^1/_4$	grated parmesan cheese	50	2	
		N.B. Use saffron flavoured/coloured stock			

Other combinations may be prepared as required. The quantities indicated may be halved when the rice dish is served as a garnish.

Alternatively, when serving pilaff/risotto products the meat is prepared separately, often in a sauce and acts to accompany the rice. An example would be chicken in white sauce served with risotto/pilaff.

PAELLA (SPANISH STEWED RICE)

Yield: 200 g or 8 oz rice = 4 portions
Cooking time: 20 – 30 min

Unit	Ingredient	Metric	Imperial
1	Rice (long grain)	200 g	8 oz
1	Chicken (raw pieces off/on bone)	200 g	8 oz
$\frac{1}{2}$	Prawns (picked)	100 g	4 oz
$\frac{1}{2}$	Mussels (budded leave in half shell and retain liquor)	100 g	4 oz
$\frac{1}{4}$	Garlic sausage (sliced)	50 g	2 oz
$\frac{1}{4}$	Onion (chopped)	50 g	2 oz
$\frac{1}{4}$	Tomato concassé	50 g	2 oz
$\frac{1}{4}$	Pimento (diced)	50 g	2 oz
$\frac{1}{4}$	Green peas (cooked)	50 g	2 oz
$\frac{1}{8}$	Cooking oil	25 ml	1 fl oz
	Seasoning		
	Garlic chopped/2 cloves		
	Bouquet garni		
*	White stock (chicken) flavoured and coloured with saffron		

* 3 units *stock* to 1 *unit* rice approximately i.e. 3:1 = 600 ml (24 fl oz)

Method

Sweat onions, pimento, chicken in oil to light brown colour. Add rice and mix well. Add stock, stir to the boil, add bouquet garni, seasoning and garlic. Cover with lid and simmer gently until rice is half cooked. Using a fork mix in remaining ingredients to include mussel liquor. Complete cooking and correct seasoning.

Notes

The word *paella* refers to a two-handled shallow iron pan in which the dish is cooked and served. The ingredients for paella will vary according to region of origin.

Gnocchi (Tiny Dumplings)   Noques

Gnocchi products are in the main of Italian peasant origin and are prepared using a starch base of flour, potatoes, semolina or maize flour.
The types of gnocchi are:

(a) *Gnocchi Parisienne* — Paris style made from a base of choux pastry;
(b) *Gnocchi Romaine* — Roman style made from a base of semolina with milk as the liquid;
(c) *Gnocchi Piémontaise* — Piedmont style made from a base of potatoes;
(d) *Polenta* — Made from a base of maize flour with water as the liquid.

N.B.   All gnocchis are served with an accompaniment of grated parmesan.

CHOUX PASTRY FOR SAVOURY PREPARATIONS   Pâte à Choux

Cooking time: 15 – 20 min

Unit	Ingredient	Metric	Imperial
1	Water	125 ml	5 fl oz
⅕	Flour (strong)	100 g	4 oz
⅖	Butter/margarine	50 g	2 oz
	Salt to season		
★	Whole egg		

★ Sufficient to produce a soft stable piping mixture approximately 3 eggs.

Method

Combine water and butter, bring to the boil, add sifted flour, stir continuously and thoroughly to the boil. Continue cooking until mixture cleans the sides of the saucepan and is of a smooth texture. This ensures adequate cooking of starch. Cool slightly then beat the eggs in gradually until a smooth pipeable mixture is achieved. Use as required.

N.B.   All the egg may not be required as this will vary according to the strength of the flour.

ROMAN STYLE DUMPLINGS   Gnocchi Romaine
(cheese flavoured)

Yield: 4 portions
Cooking time: 5 – 10 mins
Cooking temperature: 205°C (400°F)

Unit	Ingredient	Metric	Imperial
1	Milk	500 ml	1 pt
¼	Semolina	120 g	5 oz
1/20	Butter	25 g	1 oz
1/20	Grated parmesan cheese	25 g	1 oz
1/20	Egg yolk	25 g	1 oz
	Seasoning		
	Pinch of nutmeg		
	Hint of garlic		
	Parmesan to gratinate		

Method

Butter a shallow tray and line with greased greaseproof paper, put aside. Combine milk, garlic, nutmeg and seasoning, pour into saucepan and bring to the boil. Sprinkle semolina into milk and whisk briskly to boiling point. Using a wooden spatula continue mixing to achieve a smooth consistency. Beat in butter, egg yolk, cheese and mix well. Spread the hot mixture evenly into the prepared tray approximately 2 cm (³⁄₄ in) deep. Allow to cool, refrigerate to set firm.

Turn out mixture on to board, remove paper. Cut into required shapes, e.g. discs or crescents. Place into buttered gratin dish, sprinkle with parmesan and a little melted butter. Place into hot oven for 5 – 10 minutes, until golden brown and gratinate under salamander if required.

N.B. Gnocchi Romaine may be served with a cordon of tomato sauce, or may be lightly masked with mornay sauce prior to being baked in the oven.

PARIS STYLE DUMPLINGS IN MORNAY SAUCE   Gnocchi Parisienne

Yield: 4 portions
Cooking time: 15 min

Unit	Ingredient	Metric	Imperial
1	Mornay sauce	250 ml	10 fl oz
★⁴/₅	Choux pastry (savoury)	200 g	8 oz
	Nutmeg to taste		
	Grated parmesan to gratinate		

*N.B. Indicates amount of egg used when making choux pastry.

Method

Using 1 cm plain tube and bag, pipe small dumplings into plenty of simmering seasoned water (use a sharp wet knife to cut dumplings away from the tube). Poach gently for 8 – 10 minutes until the dumplings have increased in volume and have taken on a lighter colour. Strain dumplings and place in buttered gratin dishes. Flavour sauce with a pinch of nutmeg and napper (coat) dumplings. Sprinkle with parmesan cheese and gratinate to golden brown for service.

POTATO DUMPLINGS   Gnocchi Piémontaise

Yield: 4 portions
Cooking time: 10 – 15 min

Unit	Ingredient	Metric (g)	Imperial (oz)
1★	Mashed potatoes	200	8
¹/₄	Plain flour	50	2
¹/₈	Whole egg (beaten)	25	1
¹/₈	Butter	25	1
¹/₈	Grated parmesan cheese	25	1
	Seasoning		
	Pinch of nutmeg		
	Hint of garlic		
	Parmesan and melted butter to gratinate		

* Mashed potato is weighed at cooked weight.

Method

Dry the potato over heat and place into a mixing bowl. Add egg, butter, parmesan, nutmeg, garlic, seasoning, and combine with flour to form a stable mixture. Allow to cool and set. Divide into 16 portions and shape into tiny dumplings. Mould on to a floured tray and depress lightly with a fork.

To Cook   Place into plenty of seasoned simmering water and poach for 5 minutes until the dumplings float. Drain well and place in buttered gratin dishes. Sprinkle with parmesan and a little melted butter, gratinate golden brown.

N.B.   Gnocchi piémontaise may be finished with a cordon of tomato sauce, or may be lightly masked with mornay sauce prior to being gratinated.

CORN MEAL DUMPLINGS   Polenta

Yield: 4 portions
Cooking time: 3 – 5 min

Unit	Ingredient	Metric	Imperial
1	Water	500 ml	1 pt
$\frac{1}{4}$	Corn meal (or semolina)	125 g	5 oz
$\frac{1}{10}$	Oil	50 ml	2 fl oz
	Seasoning		
	Pinch of nutmeg		
	Hint of garlic		

Method

Butter a shallow tray and line with greased greaseproof paper, put aside. Combine water, garlic, nutmeg and seasoning, pour into saucepan and bring to the boil. Sprinkle corn meal into water and whisk briskly to boiling point. Using a wooden spatula continue mixing to achieve a smooth consistency. Spread the hot mixture evenly into the prepared tray approximately 2 cm ($\frac{3}{4}$ in) deep. Allow to cool, refrigerate to set firm. Turn out the mixture on to a board, remove paper. Cut into required shapes (discs, crescents) and sauté in oil and a little garlic until golden brown.

Place into buttered gratin dish, sprinkle with parmesan cheese and gratinate. Finish with beurre noisette.

Pasta Products   Pâtes Alimentaires

These are prepared from dried commercial preparations or freshly made pasta dough.

The commercial products are made from stiff dough which is forced through machines from which the dough emerges in a variety of designs and shapes. The pastas are then dried before packing for sale.

Common examples of pasta include:

Dry	*Fresh*
Spaghetti	Ravioli
Macaroni	Canneloni
Lasagne	Lasagne
Noodles	Noodles
Vermicelli	

Numerous varieties of pasta are available many of which may be prepared from a fresh dough or bought commercially as a dried preparation. These pastas may vary in flavour and colour, e.g. plain, egg, spinach and tomato.

Points for consideration when boiling pasta

1. Plunge pasta into plenty of seasoned boiling water to ensure even cooking and prevent the pasta from clogging together. Add few tablespoons cooking oil to the water.
2. In the initial stages of boiling, stir the pasta to separate and prevent clogging.
3. Cook pasta to '*al dente*' stage (firm and with a bite) 12 – 15 minutes.
   Over cooking will cause pasta to become soggy and unappetising.
4. Once cooked, drain pasta well in colander and use immediately or 'refresh' carefully and store in iced water ready for use. The iced water keeps pasta fresh and also prevents clogging during storage.
5. When placing filling into pasta it is piped with a plain tube or put into place with a spoon.
6. It is traditional to accompany pasta products with grated parmesan cheese.
7. When using dry pasta allow 50 g (2 oz) per portion.

(a) Basic Pasta Doughs (fresh made)

NOODLE DOUGH   Pâte à Nouilles

Yield: 4 portions

Unit	Ingredient	Metric	Imperial
1	Strong flour	200 g	8 oz
$\frac{5}{8}$	Whole egg (beaten)	125 g	5 oz
$\frac{1}{8}$	Oil	25 ml	1 fl oz
	Pinch of salt to taste		

Method

Sift flour and salt and form a well. Pour oil and egg into well, combine with flour to form a smooth and developed dough. Cover with damp cloth and rest in a cool place for at least 30 minutes before use.

To make Noodles   Roll pastry into 36 cm (18 in) wide thin sheet, dust with semolina or strong flour. Roll each sheet into a cylindrical shape and cut immediately into 3 mm ($\frac{1}{8}$ in) widths. Unroll strips immediately and partly allow to dry on floured trays. Use as required.

RAVIOLI PASTE   Pâte à Ravioli

Yield: 4 portions

Unit	Ingredient	Metric	Imperial
1	Strong flour	120 g	4 oz
$\frac{1}{2}$	Water	60 ml	2 fl oz
$\frac{1}{8}$	Oil	15 ml	$\frac{1}{2}$ fl oz
	Pinch of salt to taste		

Method

Sift flour and salt and form a well. Pour oil and water into well, combine with flour, form a smooth and developed dough. Cover with damp cloth, rest in a cool place for at least 30 minutes before use.

(b) Basic Savoury Stuffings for Pasta Products

SPINACH STUFFING   Farce à la Florentine

Yield: 4 portions
Cooking time: 10 min

Unit	Ingredient	Metric (g)	Imperial (oz)
1	Spinach (cooked purée)	200	8
$\frac{1}{4}$	Onion brunoise	50	2
$\frac{1}{8}$	Egg yolk	25	1
$\frac{1}{8}$	Butter	25	1
	Pinch of nutmeg		
	Hint of chopped garlic		
	Seasoning to taste		

Method

Sweat onions without colour in butter, add spinach and dry thoroughly over heat (drive off moisture by evaporation). Add remaining ingredients, mix thoroughly, season to taste.

ITALIAN STUFFING   Farce Italienne

Yield: 4 portions
Cooking time: 10 min

Unit	Ingredient	Metric (g)	Imperial (oz)
1	Spinach (cooked, purée)	100	4
1	Beef (cooked, minced)	100	4
$1/_4$	Brains (cooked)	25	1
$1/_4$	Onion brunoise	25	1
$1/_4$	Egg yolk	25	1
$1/_4$	Butter	25	1
	Pinch of nutmeg		
	Hint of chopped garlic		
	Seasoning to taste		

Method

Sweat onion without colour in butter, add spinach and dry thoroughly over heat (drive off moisture by evaporation). Add remaining ingredients, mix thoroughly, season to taste.

RAVIOLI OR CANNELONI

Yield: 4 portions
Cooking time: 20 – 25 min

Unit	Ingredient	Metric	Imperial
1	Selected sauce	250 ml	10 fl oz
$4/_5$	Selected stuffing	200 g	8 oz
$4/_5$★	Ravioli paste	200 g	8 oz
	Grated parmesan and melted butter to gratinate		

N.B.   ★Indicates amount of flour used when making ravioli paste.

Method for Ravioli

Roll out ravioli paste into a large paper-thin rectangle. Dust with strong flour or semolina during rolling. Lightly mark pastry into two halves using back of knife. Do not cut.

Space small mounds of selected filling across and down half of the rolled out paste. Water wash the clear half.

Carefully fold the second half of pastry on top of the filled half, pressing down firmly around fillings to seal. Avoid air pockets.

Using a ravioli cutter or knife cut pasta into squares along the sealed lines.

Separate ravioli squares and place on greaseproof paper for cooking. Simmer gently in boiling water to '*al dente*' stage. Drain well in colander, place in buttered gratin dish, napper with sauce, sprinkle with grated parmesan and bake in hot oven (5 – 10 min) to colour golden brown. Serve immediately.

N.B. This dish may be gratinated under salamander.

Method for Canneloni

Roll out the ravioli paste into a large paper-thin square. Dust with strong flour or semolina during rolling. Cut into 8 cm or 3 in squares. Cook gently in boiling salted water to '*al dente*' stage. Refresh in cold water and drain well in colander. This facilitates handling. Spread drained pasta squares on to clean cloth to dry.

Place portion of filling across bottom third of square and roll up neatly into cylindrical shape. Place in buttered gratin dish, napper with sauce, sprinkle with grated parmesan and bake in hot oven (5 – 10 min) to colour golden brown. Serve immediately.

Examples of Dishes Prepared Using Ravioli

Name of dish	Stuffing used	Sauce used
Ravioli/Canneloni Florentine	Florentine stuffing	Mornay
Ravioli/Canneloni Italienne	Italian stuffing	Tomate or Jus lié
Ravioli/Canneloni au Gratin	Either stuffing	Mornay

Other preparations may be created using suitable stuffings to include fish stuffings, e.g. lobster, crab, etc.

LASAGNE

Yield: 4 portions
Complete cooking time: 45 min

Unit	Ingredient	Metric	Imperial
1	Mornay sauce (thin)	400 ml	16 fl oz
1*	Bolognaise sauce	400 g	1 lb
½†	Ravioli paste	200 g	8 oz
	Grated parmesan and melted butter to gratinate		

N.B.   *Indicates amount of meat used when preparing bolognaise sauce
       † Indicates amount of flour used when making ravioli paste.

Method

Roll out ravioli paste in large thin rectangle 20 cm (8 in) wide. Cut rectangle in strips 20 cm × 6 cm (8 in × 2½ in). Cook gently in boiling salted water to '*al dente*' stage. Refresh in cold water and drain well in colander. This facilitates handling. Place on clean cloth to dry.

Butter a gratin dish and napper base with a layer of bolognaise sauce. Follow with a thin layer of mornay sauce and a layer of pasta. Repeat this process until all pasta is used and complete with a final layer of pasta masked with a thin coat of mornay sauce. Sprinkle with grated parmesan and melted butter. Bake in hot oven for 20 – 30 minutes until hot and golden brown. Serve immediately.

BOILING, REFRESHING AND REHEATING PASTA — SPAGHETTI, NOODLES, MACARONI ETC.

Yield: 4 portions
Boiling time: fresh pasta, 7 – 12 min
Boiling time: dry pasta, 12 – 15 min
Reheating time: 3 – 5 min

Unit	Ingredient	Metric (g)	Imperial (oz)
1	Selected pasta (cooked)	200	8
⅛	Butter/oil	50	2
	Seasoning		

Method

Boiling   Plunge pasta into plenty of lightly salted boiling water. Simmer until cooked to '*al dente*'. Drain and use immediately or refresh in cold water, drain well in colander and store in iced water ready for reheating.

Reheating   Drain pasta well in colander. Heat butter/oil in sauté pan, add pasta, seasoning and toss continuously until thoroughly heated. Garnish as required, see below.

Alternatively, reheat in a chauffant, *see* p. 654, or via microwave.

Pasta Extensions Using Above Formula: Added ingredients in relation to 1 unit, i.e. 200 g (8 oz) pasta

Name of dish	Unit	Ingredient	Metric	Imperial
au Beurre (with butter)		As in formula using butter only		
Italienne (Italian style)	¼	Cream	50 ml	2 fl oz
	⅛	Grated parmesan cheese	25 g	1 oz
		Hint of garlic		
		Flavour with parmesan and garlic, cohere with cream		
Napolitaine (Naples style)		As for Italienne with:		
	1	tomato sauce	200 ml	8 fl oz
	½	tomato concassé	100 g	4 oz
		Add to pasta when reheating		
Milanaise (Milan style)		As for Napolitaine with:		
	½	Cooked julienne { ham tongue mushroom	100 g	4 oz
		Julienne of truffle to garnish		
		Add to pasta when reheating		
Bolognaise (with meat sauce)		As for Italienne with: Sauce Bolognaise (*see* p. 197)		
Niçoise (Nice style)		As for Italienne with:		
	½	tomates concassées	100 g	4 oz
		Add when reheating pasta.		
au Gratin (gratinated with cheese)		As for Italienne with:		
	1	Mornay sauce	200 ml	8 fl oz
	⅛	Grated parmesan cheese	25 g	1 oz
	⅛	Melted butter	25 g	1 oz
		Combine sauce with pasta Italienne. Place into buttered gratin dishes, sprinkle with parmesan and melted butter. Gratinate in hot oven 230°C/450°F until golden brown.		
aux Moules (with mussels)		As for au Beurre with:		
	1	budded mussels with liquor	200 g	8 oz
	¼	cream	50 ml	2 fl oz
		hint of chopped garlic		
		chopped parsley		
		Add mussels, cream and garlic when reheating pasta. Garnish with chopped parsley		

N.B.   All the above are seasoned with salt and pepper to taste.

Spetzli (Alsatian cookery)

This pasta appears as short, thin strips, which on cooking remain intact with a soft texture. Spetzli or Spätzle (German) is best bought commercially in a dried form for cooking. It is cooked as on p. 254 and best used immediately after cooking.

Spetzli is used as a garnish or accompaniment with main course items (e.g. pork and veal sautés) or specifically to garnish a goulash in replacement of Gnocchi Parisienne. It can also be used in its own right as a pasta course and integrated with selected flavours and garnish.

SPETZLI (SPÄTZLE)

Yield: 4 portions
Cooking time: 5 min

Unit	Ingredient	Metric	Imperial
1	Flour (cake)	200 g	8 oz
$5/_8$	Whole egg	125 g	5 oz
$1/_2$	Milk	100 ml	4 fl oz
	Salt to taste		
	Pinch of nutmeg		

Method

Sift flour, salt, nutmeg together and form a well. Whisk milk and eggs together and pour into well. Combine ingredients to form a slack mixture. Pass mixture through coarse colander and gently simmering seasoned water and simmer until cooked.

Drain well and use immediately or refresh and store for use.

Spetzli Provençale

Toss drained Spetzli quickly in melted butter, season with a pinch of salt, pepper and a hint of garlic. Place into gratin dish, sprinkle with chopped parsley and serve.

17

The Principle and Practice of Boiling

To Boil	Bouillir
To Simmer	Mijoter

Strictly speaking there are only a few occasions when food is actually boiled for long periods of time. In most instances food is simmered rather than boiled. Normally, rapid boiling takes place at around 100°C (212°F) whereas simmering requires a slightly lower temperature. Simmering is identified when the surface of the liquid is barely agitated as a result of the convection current set in motion during cooking.

On many, but not all occasions, simmering is preferred to rapid boiling because:

(a) evaporation loss and shrinkage are minimized;
(b) the texture and colour of products are not unduly impaired.

The liquids most commonly used as mediums for boiling are: water, stock, milk, and court-bouillon which usually remain unthickened during cooking. An exception is when a thickened 'blanc' *see* p. 268 is used for boiling certain vegetables, e.g. artichoke bottoms.

Boiling is begun in one of two ways:

1. By placing food into cold liquid which is gradually brought to boiling point. This method is adopted when the primary purpose is to:

   (a) extract the flavour from the product, e.g. stocks;
   (b) gradually soften hard fibrous materials, e.g. carrots and parsnips;
   (c) prevent damage to items which would lose their shape if plunged into boiling liquid, e.g. whole fish.

2. By plunging food directly into boiling liquid. This method is adopted when it is necessary to:

   (d) seal in the food's flavour, e.g. small cuts of fish, leg of mutton;
   (e) set the protein and colour of foods, e.g. green vegetables;
   (f) reduce the overall cooking time, e.g. boiled eggs, green vegetables.

Notes Concerning Boiling

The technique of boiling may be used for the cooking of a wide variety of commodities including animal protein, vegetables, farinaceous products and eggs. When a traditional kitchen brigade is employed the following Chefs de Partie are involved with the preparation and cooking of boiled products:

Chef Saucier   — butcher's meats, offal, poultry. etc.
Chef Poissonnier   — fish preparations
Chef Entremettier   — vegetables to include potatoes
Chef Garde-manger   — involved with initial preparation of meats and fish prior to
                      cooking.

Selected Cooking Vessels

The size and shape of cooking vessels will be determined by the volume of food being cooked. Steam jacket boilers of various sizes are often used for commercial boiling when large quantities are involved. On most occasions boiling vessels are covered with a lid, which helps to retain heat and speed-up the cooking process.

Preparing and Boiling Vegetables

Many vegetables contain water-soluble vitamins and minerals which are easily lost during preparation and cooking. It is therefore expedient to prepare, wash and cook vegetables quickly, and at no time allow them to soak for long periods in cold water.

Speedy cooking is also essential if vegetables are to remain crisp, nutritious, flavoursome and colourful. Over-cooking of vegetables results in:

(a) loss of flavour;
(b) poor colour;
(c) watery textures;
(d) low nutritive value.

Boiling Meats

It is important to ensure that meats are adequately covered with water/stock during boiling. When the resultant liquor is to be prepared as a sauce the stock level must not be excessive otherwise the cooking liquor will lack strength and flavour.

Skimming and Degreasing (for meat, etc.)

In order to ensure that the cooking liquor remains clear and grease-free it is necessary to skim away scum and grease as they rise to the surface.

Boiling of Butcher's Meat and Poultry

Although all meat can be cooked by boiling, it is not a satisfactory method of cooking tender cuts as it is difficult to retain the flavour of meat cooked in this way. Preserved meats, offal, and poultry however, are ideally suited to the boiling technique as they are often of a tougher structure. Certain meats need to be soaked in cold water prior to cooking to remove the excess salt, e.g. gammons and pickled beef. The time for soaking will vary according to the saltiness of the meat.
This saltiness will be determined by the following:

(a) the weight, thickness, fattiness, and texture of the meat in question;
(b) the strength of the brine used and the length of time the meat has been pickled in the solution.

It is therefore difficult to determine an exact soaking time for the cuts of meat before boiling, but they are usually soaked overnight. When boiling uncured meats or poultry initial soaking is eliminated. On some occasions the resultant cooking liquor is served as part of the dish in an unthickened or thickened form, e.g. boiled beef and carrots moistened with the liquor, or boiled leg of mutton served with caper sauce made from the cooking liquor.

Selection and Preparation of Meats for Boiling

Meat	Preparation
Beef joints	
Silverside, brisket, thin flank, topside, plate, Ox-tongue	Where necessary trim excess fat and sinew, roll and tie if required, e.g. brisket, thin flank. If joints have been pickled in brine, soak overnight in cold water before cooking
Bacon joints	*Gammon/shoulder*
Whole gammon, shoulder joints, hock, middle, corner of gammon. Collar, fore hock of shoulder	Left whole or boned, rolled and secured with string. Soak overnight in cold water before cooking. May be dissected into smaller cuts
Ham*	Left whole, trim end of knuckle bone, remove any mould. Soak overnight in cold water before cooking
Mutton Joints	
Leg of mutton	Remove pelvic bone, trim end of leg bone, leave whole for use. If necessary secure chump end of leg with string

* Ham is the hind leg of a porker pig that has been cut from the side of pork (banjo shaped) and is then cured in a number of ways according to the region/country of origin, e.g. York ham, Parma ham. This should not be confused with gammon, which is the hind leg from a side of bacon.

BOILED MEATS   Viandes Bouillies

Yield: 4 portions 600 g (1¼ lbs) meat off the bone
        1 kg (2 lb) meat on the bone
Cooking times: beef/mutton 25 min per 400 g (1 lb) and 25 min over
               Gammon/ham/tongue 20 min per 400 g (1 lb) and 20 min over

Unit	Ingredient	Metric (g)	Imperial (oz)
1	Selected meat	600	20
²/₅	Mirepoix (left whole)	240	8
	Bouquet garni		
	Seasoning (not required for pickled meats)		
*	Water		

* Sufficient water to cover adequately meat being boiled.

Method I: for Pickled Meats

Place meat in cooking vessel, cover with cold water, bring to the boil, skim add vegetables and bouquet garni. Cover with lid and simmer gently until meat is tender. Use as required.

Method II: for Fresh Meats

As above but commence cooking in boiling water.

Service   After carving moisten meat with cooking liquor and decorate with garnish for service.

Examples of Dishes Prepared Using Above Formula—garnish, in relation to 1 unit 600 g (1¼ lb) meat

English term-main ingredient	Unit	Ingredient	Metric	Imperial	French term
Boiled pickled beef English style	²/₅	Turned carrots 4 Whole onions (small) *8 Suet dumplings	240 g	8 oz	Boeuf Bouilli à l'Anglaise
		Cook garnish in cooking liquor			
Boiled beef French style	⁴/₅	Cabbage (quartered and tied)	480 g	16 oz	Boeuf Bouilli à la Française
	²/₅	Celery ⎱ tied in neat	240 g	8 oz	
	²/₅	Leek ⎰ bundles	240 g	8 oz	
	¹/₅	Turned carrots	120 g	4 oz	
	¹/₅	Turned turnips	120 g	4 oz	
		Cook garnish in cooking liquor			
Boiled ham or gammon with parsley sauce	¹/₂	Parsley sauce	300 ml	10 fl oz	Jambon Bouilli à Sauce Persil
		Serve sauce separately in a sauceboat			
Boiled leg of mutton with caper sauce	¹/₂	Caper sauce	300 ml	10 fl oz	Gigot de Mouton Sauce aux Câpres
		Prepare sauce from cooking liquor and serve separately in a sauceboat			
Boiled ox-tongue English style		As for boiled beef English style			Langue de Boeuf Bouillie à l'Anglaise
Boiled ox-tongue with Madeira sauce	¹/₂	Madeira sauce	300 ml	10 fl oz	Langue de Boeuf Bouillie à sauce Madère
		Serve sauce separately in a sauceboat			
Boiled ox-tongue with spinach and Madeira sauce	¹/₂ ²/₅	Madeira sauce Cooked leaf spinach	300 ml 240 g	10 fl oz 8 oz	Langue de Boeuf Bouillie Florentine
		Dress sliced tongue on bed of cooked leaf spinach, serve sauce separately in a sauceboat			

N.B.   Other suitable garnishes may be served with boiled meat.

* For 8 suet dumplings (4 portions) use 100 g (4 oz) flour when making suet pastry.

Calf's Head   Tête de Veau

Preparation Prior to Cooking

Remove any hairs from the head. To remove flesh from bone make an incision down centre of head to the nostrils. Keeping close to the bone carefully ease away flesh from bone and remove tongue from jaw. Wash the flesh and tongue and place into acidulated water until required. Saw across crown of head and carefully remove brains. Soak the brains in gently running cold water, remove membrane and wash away any blood. Blanch and refresh tongue and flesh to set protein and remove any scum. Trim the tongue and cut the flesh into 5 cm (2 in) squares.

Sauce Vinaigrette for Calf's Head

Garnish $\frac{1}{4}$ l ($\frac{1}{2}$ pt) vinaigrette with onion brunoise, chopped capers and chopped parsley.

CALF'S HEAD WITH VINAIGRETTE SAUCE   Tête de Veau Vinaigrette

Yield: 4 portions
Cooking time:
For tongue and flesh $2\frac{1}{2}$ hr
For brains 5 – 10 min

Unit	Ingredient	Metric	Imperial
	1 Calf's head (brains, tongue and flesh)		
1	Blanc (*see* p. 268)	4 l	1 gal
$\frac{1}{8}$	Court-bouillon (*see* es pp. 264–5	$\frac{1}{2}$ l	1 pt
$\frac{1}{10}$	Mirepoix (left whole)	400 g	1 lb
$\frac{1}{20}$	Vinaigrette sauce	200 ml	8 fl oz
	Salt and pepper to taste		
	Bouquet garni and picked parsley		

Method

Place tongue, flesh, mirepoix and bouquet garni into simmering blanc. Skim, lightly season and cover with greased cartouche and continue simmering until tongue and flesh are cooked. Gently simmer brains in court-bouillon until cooked. Remove tongue, flesh and brains from cooking liquors. Skin the tongue.

Service   Place cooked meat from calf's head into serving dish with slices of tongue and brains. Moisten lightly with cooking liquor and accompany with sauce vinaigrette.

BOILED PIGS' TROTTERS   Pieds de Porc Bouillis

Yield: 4 portions
Cooking time: 2½ hr

Unit	Ingredient	Metric (g)	Imperial (oz)
	4 Pig's feet (singed and trimmed)		
1	Mirepoix (left whole)	200	8
	Bouquet garni		
	Seasoning		
	Squeeze of lemon juice		
★	Water		

★ Sufficient to cover pig's feet during boiling.

Method

Blanch and refresh pig's feet to remove scum. Place in clean cooking vessel, with vegetables, seasoning and squeeze of lemon juice. Cover with water, bring to the boil, skim, add bouquet garni, cover with a lid and simmer until tender. Serve whole or remove bone if required, accompanied with a suitable sauce, e.g. Sauce Poulette, Vinaigrette, etc.

Boiled Chicken   Poulet Bouilli/Poché

On the menu, boiled chicken dishes are often referred to as being poached, they are in fact simmered very gently and as such closely relate to the poaching method of cookery.

Yield: 4 portions 1 medium chicken
Cooking times: chicken 1 – 1½ hr
              boiling fowl 2 – 3 hr

Unit	Ingredient	Metric (g)	Imperial (lb)
	1 Whole trussed chicken or fowl		
1	Mirepoix (left whole)	400	1
	Seasoning		
	Bouquet garni		
★	Water or white chicken stock		

★ Sufficient liquid to cover adequately chicken being boiled.

Method

Place the chicken in cooking vessel, cover with cold water or stock, bring to the boil, skim, add vegetables and bouquet garni. Cover with lid and simmer gently until chicken is tender. Remove chicken from stock and allow to stand and set. Remove skin, joint or carve into required portions. Prepare Sauce Suprême (*see* p. 179) from cooking liquor. Keep sauce ready for use. See chart below.

Extensions of Dishes Using Above Formula: Sauce and Garnish for 4 portions

English term	Unit	Ingredient	Metric	Imperial	French term
Boiled chicken with rice and supreme sauce	1 $^2/_5$	Sauce Suprême Rice pilaff	500 ml 200 g	1 pt 8 oz	Poulet Poché au Riz Sauce Suprême
		Dress chicken portions on a bed of rice, napper with sauce and serve			
Boiled chicken with rice and asparagus sauce	1 $^2/_5$ $^1/_5$	Sauce Suprême Rice pilaff Purée asparagus 12 Asparagus tips	500 ml 200 g 100 g	1 pt 8 oz 4 oz	Poulet Poché Argenteuil
		Add asparagus purée to Sauce Suprême. Arrange chicken portions on bed of rice, napper with sauce and garnish with asparagus tips			
Boiled chicken with rice and mushroom sauce	1 $^2/_5$ $^1/_5$	White mushroom sauce (*see* p. 180) Rice pilaff Button mushrooms (glacés à blanc)	500 ml 200 g 100 g	1 pt 8 oz 4 oz	Poulet Poché au Riz Sauce Champignons
		Dress chicken portions on a bed of rice, napper with sauce and garnish with mushrooms			
Boiled chicken with rice and paprika sauce	1 $^2/_5$ $^1/_5$	Sauce Hongroise Rice pilaff Tomato concassé	500 ml 200 g 100 g	1 pt 8 oz 4 oz	Poulet Poché Hongroise
		Garnish rice with tomato concassé. Arrange chicken portions on to bed of rice and napper with sauce			
Boiled chicken with rice and curry-flavoured sauce	1 $^2/_5$ $^1/_5$	Sauce Indienne (*see* p. 179) Rice pilaff Mushrooms ⎫ Tongue ⎬ Julienne Truffle ⎭	500 ml 200 g 100 g	1 pt 8 oz 4 oz	Poulet Poché à la Stanley
		Dress chicken portions on bed of rice, sprinkle with julienne garnish and napper with sauce for service			

N.B. Amount shown for pilaff in recipe indicates amount of rice used to prepare pilaff.

Service   As an alternative to serving the chicken on a bed of rice, it may be presented surrounded by rice pyramids which have been shaped in buttered dariole moulds and turned out for service.

Boiled Fish   Poisson Bouilli

When boiling fish either whole or in portions, great care is required to ensure that the fish keeps its shape and texture throughout cooking. Fish flesh is composed of muscle, divided into flakes, which vary in size according to the type of fish. The composition of fish protein is similar to meat except there is far less connective tissue present. Therefore, the fish muscle is not held together as firmly as in meat protein.

The connective tissue in fish is collagen, which when heated in moist conditions changes into gelatine causing the flakes to separate easily on cooking (*see* p. 161). For this reason fish usually cooks more quickly than meat and is more tender, but great care is needed during cooking to prevent it from breaking up on service.

The liquids commonly used for boiling fish are termed court-bouillons, which vary according to the type of fish being cooked. When boiling whole fish it is recommended that the fish is placed into COLD bouillon and brought slowly to the boil to simmer gently. This enables the fish to retain its shape and prevents the skin from splitting. Alternatively small cuts of fish (usually on the bone) are immersed in simmering court-bouillon to cook. This sets the fish protein and speeds up the cooking time. In all cases the fish is cooked until tender, indicated when flesh begins to leave the bone and the flakes to separate.

Menu Term for Boiled Fish

On the menu, boiled fish dishes are often referred to as 'poached'. They are in fact simmered very gently and as such are closely related to the poaching method of cookery.

Court-Bouillons

These fall into two main categories:

(a) for oily fish, e.g. salmon, trout, mackerel, salmon trout, etc;
(b) for white fish, e.g. halibut, turbot, cod, brill etc.

N.B.   Court-bouillons may also be used for cooking some meat dishes e.g. calf's brains. A combination of milk and water may be used when cooking white fish for invalids.

COURT—BOUILLON (FOR OILY FISH)

Yield: 1 l (2 qt) approx.
Cooking time: 30 min

Unit	Ingredient	Metric	Imperial
1	Water	$1\frac{1}{2}$ l	3 pt
$\frac{1}{10}$	Vinegar	150 ml	6 oz
$\frac{1}{20}$	Carrots (sliced)	75 g	3 oz
$\frac{1}{20}$	Onion (sliced)	75 g	3 oz
	6 crushed peppercorns		
	Parsley stalks		
	Bouquet garni		
	Salt to season		

Method

Combine all ingredients, bring to the boil, skim and simmer for 30 minutes. Strain through a muslin in readiness for use.

COURT—BOUILLON (FOR WHITE FISH)

Yield: 1 l (2 qt) approx.

Unit	Ingredient	Metric	Imperial
1	Water	1 l	2 pt
$^1/_{20}$	Lemon juice (1 large lemon)	50 ml	2 fl oz
	Salt to season		
	Parsley stalks		

Method

Combine all ingredients together in readiness for use.

BOILED FISH   Poisson Bouilli/Poché

Yield: 4 portions
Cooking time: Small cuts 5 – 10 mins. Whole fish according to size.

Unit	Ingredient	Metric (g)	Imperial (lb)
*	Selected court-bouillon		
1	Selected fish (whole piece, or cuts on the bone, e.g. Darne, Tronçon)	800	2
	Seasoning		

* Sufficient court-bouillion to cover fish during cooking.

Method 1: For Whole or Large Pieces of Fish

Lightly season the prepared fish and allow to stand for 10 minutes to absorb the seasoning. Place in cooking vessel and cover with selected cold court-bouillon. Bring slowly to the boil and allow to simmer gently until fish is cooked. Drain well, remove skin and serve lightly moistened with the cooking liquor. Whole or large pieces of fish are usually trimmed and portioned in the restaurant for service.

Method 2: For Small Cuts of Fish on the Bone

Lightly season the prepared cuts of fish and allow to stand for 10 minutes to absorb the seasoning. Bring selected court-bouillon to boiling point, place the fish portions into the bouillon and simmer gently until cooked. Drain well, remove skin and centre bone of darnes. For flat fish cuts leave bone intact to prevent fish portion from breaking up unless its removal would not impair appearance of fish on presentation.

When fish is to be served cold remove from heat just prior to completion of cooking and allow to cool in the court bouillon. This allows the flavours in the bouillon to impregnate the fish.

N.B. All hot boiled fish dishes are served with a garnish of plain boiled shaped potatoes, sprig of parsley, lemon wedge and an accompanying sauce/liquor after which the dish is named. Turbot poché hollandaise/Saumon poché hollandaise are common examples.

Examples of Accompanying Sauces for Selected White or Oily Fish

à Sauce Hollandaise	— Sauceboat of hollandaise sauce
à Sauce Mousseline	— Sauceboat of mousseline sauce
au Beurre	— Sauceboat of melted butter
au Court-Bouillon	— Moistened with cooking liquor, garnished with button onions and decorated carrot rondels (cooked in the bouillon)

For Selected White Fish Only

à Sauce Anchois	— Sauceboat of anchovy sauce
à Sauce Crème	— Sauceboat of cream sauce
à Sauce aux Oeufs	— Sauceboat of egg sauce
à Sauce Persil	— Sauceboat of parsley sauce
à Sauce Crevettes Grises/Roses	— Sauceboat of shrimp or prawn sauce

Miscellaneous Boiled Fish Dishes

Skate with Black Butter   Raie au Beurre Noir

Simmer fish in court-bouillon (for white fish), until cooked, drain and place on to service dish. Lightly cover with black butter [100 g (4 oz)] for four portions. Garnish with capers and chopped parsley. N.B. If cooked with skin on, remove before flavouring with black butter.

BLUE TROUT   Truite au Bleu

Yield: 4 portions 4 live trout 150 g (6 oz) each
Cooking time: 5 – 10 min

Unit	Ingredient	Metric	Imperial
	4 Selected live trout		
1	Prepared bouillon (for oily fish *see* p. 264)	1 l	2 pt
$1/_{10}$	Button onions (sliced into rings)	100 g	4 oz
$1/_{10}$	Carrot (grooved and thinly sliced)	100 g	4 oz
$1/_{10}$	Malt vinegar (to colour trout)	100 ml	4 fl oz
$1/_{10}$	Turned boiled potatoes	100 g	4 oz
	Sprigs of parsley to garnish		

Method: Preparation of Trout

Stun trout, slit belly to remove gut, membrane and blood, remove gills and wash inside the trout with cold running water. Pour vinegar over trout and turn continuously until blue.

Cooking of Trout   Bring bouillon with vegetable garnish to the boil and simmer for 3 – 4 minutes to soften vegetables. Add trout and simmer gently for 5 minutes. Serve moistened with cooking liquor, garnish with onion and carrot slices, shaped boiled potatoes, wedge of lemon and sprigs of parsley. Accompany with sauce hollandaise or melted butter.

N.B.   This dish is cooked and served to order and may be presented in the room in a small copper fish kettle in which the fish has been cooked. In this case the garnish of potatoes, lemon and parsley are served separately with the sauce. When cooked the shape of the fish is distorted and its skin broken. The head and skin are removed for service.

Boiling Live Shellfish (in the shell)   Although live shellfish may be boiled in court-bouillon (*see* p. 265) they are more commonly cooked by plunging into plenty of boiling salted water, simmered for a specified time, drained and allowed to cool for use.

Boiling Times for Live Shellfish (Crustaceans)

Name	French	Cooking times from boiling point (min) (approx)
Crab	Crabe	15 – 25
Crayfish	Écrevisse	8 – 10
Crawfish	Langouste	20 – 25
Lobster	Homard	20 – 25
Prawns	Crevettes Roses	5 – 8
Scampi	Langoustine	8 – 10
Shrimps	Crevettes Grises	5 – 8

Boiled shellfish are served both cold and hot. The hot shellfish dishes are often prepared from pre-boiled items which have been allowed to cool.

Boiling of Vegetables

In general vegetables are boiled in seasoned water with the exception of those that are boiled in a 'blanc' preparation (*see* p. 268), or acidulated water i.e. (water and squeeze of lemon juice), in order to keep them white.

As a rule, vegetables grown above the ground and frozen vegetables are plunged into boiling water at the commencement of cooking and boiled briskly until cooked. Those grown beneath the ground are placed into cold water, brought to boiling point, and simmered more gently.

Vegetables Grown Above the Ground or Frozen Vegetables

Cooking commences in boiling water which acts to:

(a) speed up the cooking time;
(b) set the natural colour of the vegetable;
(c) eliminate the enzymic action which destroys vitamin C (the enzymic action is eliminated by high temperatures);
(d) keep vegetables crisp and of fresh appearance.

Most green vegetables lose their appetizing colour if left too long in a hot cupboard and this deterioration is a problem when cooking for large numbers. A technique used in the trade to minimize this effect is the process of *blanching and refreshing* when the vegetables are cooked to *al dente* or just done, cooled immediately in cold water and drained. Later the vegetables can be quickly re-heated for service in a number of ways. This process prevents overcooking and maintains the fresh colour and crisp texture of the vegetables. After being well drained, blanched and refreshed, vegetables may be stored chilled in readiness for use. When this technique is not adopted staggered cooking times should be used.

Vegetables Grown Beneath the Ground

Cooking starts in cold water which is heated to boiling/simmering point. This acts to:

(a) extract the starch from certain root vegetables, e.g. potatoes;
(b) tenderize the fibrous structure of certain vegetables to aid digestion and palatability, e.g. turnips;
(c) prevent vegetables from breaking up during cooking, e.g. potatoes and swedes.

Boiled Vegetables   Légumes Bouillis

Method 1

(For vegetables that are plunged into boiling salted water) –
   Yield: 400 g (1 lb) prepared vegetables = 4 portions.
   Plunge vegetables into boiling salted water. Boil until tender. Drain well and serve as required.

Method 2

(For vegetables that are plunged into boiling seasoned acidulated water) –
   As for above but flavour water with lemon juice in order to keep vegetables white.

Method 3

(For vegetables that commence cooking in cold water) –
   Cover vegetables with cold water, season, bring to boil simmer gently until tender. Drain well and serve as required.

Method 4

(For vegetables cooked in a blanc – 'à blanc') –

PREPARATION OF BLANC   Blanc

Unit	Ingredient	Metric	Imperial
1	Water	1 l	2 pt
$\frac{1}{40}$	Flour	25 g	1 oz
	Squeeze of lemon juice		
	Salt to season		

Combine ingredients, stir to boil, strain and use. Plunge vegetables into boiling blanc, simmer until cooked, drain and serve as required.

N.B. For boiling times and service of vegetables see respective charts.

1 Vegetables That are Plunged into Boiling Salted Water: Cooking times from boiling point

English	French	Preparation for Boiling	Cooking times (approx.) (min)	Examples of methods of Presentation
Asparagus	Asperges	Scrape stems lightly towards the base, tie into even bundles and trim the bases	12-20	au Beurre, au Beurre Fondu, Amandine, Hollandaise, Nature, Purée
Broad beans	Fèves	Pod the beans	15-20	au Beurre, à la Crème, à Sauce Persil, Nature
Brussel sprouts	Choux de Bruxelles	Remove decaying leaves, make a small incision at the base of each sprout, wash well in cold water	5-10	au Beurre, Milanaise, Nature, Polonaise
Broccoli	Brocolis	Remove outer leaves, trim base of stem, wash well	10-15	au Beurre, Amandine Hollandaise, Milanaise, Mornay, Nature, Polanaise
Cabbage Cabbage (spring)	Chou Chou de Printemps	Trim away decaying leaves, quarter to remove stalks, wash well	10-15	au Beurre, Nature
Chicory	Endive	Wash leaves very thoroughly	20-25	au Beurre, à la Crème Mornay, Nature, Purée
Cauliflower	Choufleur	Remove green leaves, trim base and hollow out the stem at the base. Wash well	12-15	au Beurre, Amandine aux Fines Herbes Hollandaise, Milanaise, Mornay, Nature, Polonaise
Cucumber	Concombre	Remove outer peel, cut into 3 cm (1½ in) cylinders and then into neat wedges. (may be turned)	5-10	au Beurre, à la Crème, Glacé, Milanaise, Nature, Persillé
Curly kale	Chou Frisé	Remove course stalks, wash well	15-20	au Beurre, Nature
French beans	Haricots Verts (Fins)	Top and tail, wash well	8-10	au Beurre, à la Crème, Nature, Tourangelle
Ladies' fingers or gumbo	Okra	Wash well. Do not remove stem	10-15	au Beurre, Hollandaise, Nature

English	French	Preparation for Boiling	Cooking times (approx.) (min)	Examples of methods of Presentation
Leeks	Poireaux	Discard damaged outer leaves, trim tops (retain for soups, etc.) Lightly trim the root, half split lengthways, leaving root intact wash well. Tie into neat bundles for cooking	15–20	au Beurre, à la Crème Mornay, Nature
Marrow (baby)	Courgette	Peel, trim stalk, wash well. Leave whole or slice or shape	8–10	au Beurre, à la Creme, aux Fines Herbes, Mornay, Nature, Persillée
Marrow	Courge	Remove outer skin, cut in half lengthways, remove seeds with a spoon, cut into 5 cm (2 in) squares, wash well	8–10	
Peas (garden)	Petits Pois	Pod the peas	15–20	au Beurre, à la Menthe, Nature, Purée
Young peas in the pod	Mange Tout (eat all)	Top and tail, leave peas in pod	8–10	au Beurre, Glacés Hollandaise, Nature
Pumpkin	Potiron	As for marrow	20–30	As for marrow
Runner beans		Top and tail, remove strings of the beans from sides. Wash well and slice into strips	10–15	au Beurre, Nature
Sea kale	Chou de Mer or Chou Marin	Trim away damaged stalks and roots, wash well, tie in bundles	20–25	au Beurre, à la Crème, Hollandaise, Nature
Leaf spinach	Épinards en Branches	Remove leaves from stems and wash well	8–10	au Beurre, à la Crème, Mornay, Nature, Purée
Sweetcorn (on the cob)	Maïs	Remove outer green leaves and fibres, wash well, trim ends	10–15	au Beurre Fondu, Nature
Sweetcorn (off the cob)	Maïs	Prepare as above, when cooked remove kernels with a spoon	10–15	au Beurre, à la Crème, Nature

See pp. 273–4 for methods of presentation.

2 Vegetables that are Plunged into Boiling, Seasoned, Acidulated Water Cooking Times from Boiling Point

English	French	Preparation	Cooking times (min)	Examples of methods of presentation
Artichokes (globe)	Artichauts	Cut across the top removing quarter of leaves. Trim points of leaves, remove stem at the base. Place slice of lemon on base and secure with string. Place into water with base uppermost. When cooked, remove string, lemon, heart and choke	40–45	au Beurre Fondu, Hollandaise
Artichokes (Jerusalem)	Topinambours	Wash well, peel and place in acidulated water before cooking	20–25	au Beurre, à la Crème, aux Fines Herbes, Nature, Persillés, Purée
Celeriac	Céleri-rave	Wash and peel, cut to required shape (cubes, strips, etc.) Place into acidulated water before cooking	25–30	au Beurre, à la Crème, aux Fines Herbes, Nature

See pp. 273–4 for methods of presentation.

3 Vegetables that Commence Cooking in Cold Water

English	French	Preparation for Boiling	Cooking time from boiling point (min)	Examples of methods of presentation
Beetroot	Betterave	Trim off tops and wash well	60–120	au Beurre, à la Crème, Nature
Carrots	Carottes	Top and tail, peel, wash well, cut into selected shape (wedges, slices, turned, cubed)	10–25	au Beurre, à la Crème, Glacées, Persillées, Purée Vichy
Kohlrabi	Chou-rave	Remove leaves from bulb and trim roots. Wash well in cold water and remove thick peel. Leave whole, slice, dice or cut to shape according to requirements	30–60	au Beurre, à la Crème, Nature, Persillés

Onions	Oignons	Peel, trim root leaving intact	20–30	à la Crème, Nature
Parsnips	Panais	Wash, peel and re-wash, cut into wedges lengthways. Remove fibrous root from the centre if tough	20–30	au Beurre, à la Crème, Nature, Persillés, Purée
Swedes	Rutabaga	Wash, trim ends and remove thick peel. Slice or cut to desired shape (cubes, bâtons or turned)	15–20	au Beurre, Nature, Persillés, Purée
Turnips	Navets	As for swedes	25–30	au Beurre, Nature, Persillés, Purée

See pp. 273–4 for methods of presentation.

4 Vegetables Cooked in a Blanc 'à Blanc' Cooking Times from Boiling Point

English	French	Preparation	Cooking times (min)	Examples of methods of presentation
Artichoke bottoms	Fonds d' Artichauts	Cut away stalk from base, using a stainless steel knife, rub base lightly with lemon juice. Pluck away all the leaves until artichoke bottom is clear of leaves, place in acidulated water in readiness for cooking. Choke remains during cooking and is removed by using a stainless steel spoon. Leave whole, quarter or slice for service.	20–25	au Beurre, à la Crème, aux Fines Herbes, Hollandaise, Mornay, Nature, Persillés
Fennel	Fenouil	Trim stalks and root, wash well, cook whole or in quarters according to size of fennel	60–90	au Beurre, à la Crème, aux Fines Herbes, Milanaise, Mornay, Nature, Persillés, Poulette
Salsify (Oyster plant)	Salsifi	Wash well, peel, section into 5 cm (2 in) cylinders. Place in acidulated water ready for cooking	40–45	au Beurre, à la Crème, aux Fines Herbes, Nature, Persillés, Poulette, Tourangelle

See pp. 273–4 for methods of presentation.

Boiled Pulse Vegetables

Yield: 250 g (10 oz) of dried vegetable = 4 portions

Method

Soak vegetables overnight in cold water. Drain and wash thoroughly. Cover with cold water and season. Bring gradually to the boil and simmer gently until tender. Drain well and serve as required.

Cooking times from boiling point.

English	French	Cooking time (hr)	Presentation style
Butter beans		$1\frac{1}{2}-2$	Nature, à la Menthe, au Beurre
Haricot beans	Haricots Blancs	$1\frac{1}{2}-2$	Nature, Bretonne, au Beurre
Kidney beans (green)	Haricots Flageolets	$1\frac{1}{2}-2$	Nature, au Beurre
Kidney beans (red)	Haricots Rouges	$1\frac{1}{2}-2$	Nature, au Beurre
Lentils	Lentilles	$1\frac{1}{2}-2$	Purée, Purée à la Crème
Marrowfat peas		$\frac{3}{4}-1$	Nature, au Beurre, à la Menthe. These peas may be cooked until they 'fall' and thicken the cooking liquor

See below for methods of presentation.

Common Modes of Vegetable Presentation

au Beurre	Brush with melted butter
au Beurre Fondu	Accompany with sauceboat of melted butter
à la Crème	Lightly napper or cohere vegetable with cream sauce or fresh cream
à la Menthe	Add fresh mint leaves during cooking to flavour. Garnish with blanched mint leaves
Amandine	Sauté some almonds in a little butter, sprinkle over vegetables. Garnish with chopped parsley
aux Fines Herbes	Brush with butter and sprinkle with fine herbs
Bretonne	Cohere with tomato sauce to complete cooking
Glacés/ées (f)	Boil in minimum of water with knob of butter, pinch of sugar. At end of cooking period reduce liquor to give vegetables glossy appearance
Hollandaise	Accompany with sauceboat of Hollandaise sauce or lightly mask vegetable for presentation
Maltaise	Accompany with sauceboat of Maltese sauce
Milanaise	Sprinkle with parmesan cheese, gratinate and finish with Beurre Noisette
Mornay/au Gratin	Coat with cheese sauce, sprinkle with cheese and gratinate

Nature	Serve plain boiled
Persillées/és (m)	Brush with melted butter and sprinkle liberally with chopped parsley
au Sauce Persil	Cohere with parsley sauce
Polonaise	Sprinkle with sieved hard boiled egg, chopped parsley, fried breadcrumbs and beurre noisette to finish
Poulette	Cohere with poulette sauce (*see* p. 180)
Purée	*See* method (below)
Tourangelle	Cohere with cream sauce flavoured with garlic
Vichy	Cook as for glacé using Vichy Water (French mineral water)

Other Boiled Vegetable Dishes

Yield: 400 g (1 lb) total weight for 4 portions

Bouquietière	A selection of vegetables served in bouquets: artichoke bottoms, cauliflower, shaped carrots, shaped turnips, French beans, etc., serve au beurre. Cauliflower is coated with hollandaise sauce when used in this garnish
Jardinière	Bâtons of carrots and turnip, garden peas and French beans, serve au beurre
Macédoine	As above but cut carrots and turnips into small cubes, serve au beurre
Primeurs	As for Bouquetière but using new/spring vegetables, serve au beurre
Haricots Panaches	Selection of beans mixed together e.g. French beans, kidney beans, broad beans, etc., serve 'au beurre'
Petits Pois Flamande	Combine selected quantity of garden peas with half as many shaped carrots (bâtons or cubes)

Vegetable Purées   Purées de Légumes

Method

Pass boiled, drained vegetables through a medium sieve or mouli. Place into a saucepan and dry out excess moisture over heat. Correct seasoning and finish with knob of butter and cream if required. Serve dome-shaped in a vegetable dish. Decorate using palette knife. (Often used as a garnish.)

BOILED POTATOES   Pommes de Terre Bouillies

Yield: 400 g (1 lb) prepared potatoes = 4 portions
Cooking time: 20 min from boiling point, approximately.

Method

Old Potatoes   Cut potatoes to even size or required shape (to ensure even cooking), place in cooking vessel, cover with cold water, season, bring to boil and simmer until tender. Drain and use as required.

New Potatoes   Lightly scrape or scrub potatoes clean. Cook as above but commence in boiling salted water.

When scrubbed and not scraped or peeled, remove peel after cooking.

Examples of Dishes Prepared from Plain Boiled Old Potatoes: Added Ingredients and Preparation to 1 unit i.e. 400 g (1 lb) boiled potatoes

English term	Preparation	French term
Plain boiled potatoes	Boiled cut or turned potatoes served plain	Pommes Nature
Parsley potatoes	As for Pommes Nature, brush with melted butter, garnish liberally with freshly chopped parsley	Pommes Persillées
	Boiled potatoes (large noisette shape). Finish as for Pommes Persillées	Pommes Quelin
Boiled in jackets	Small to medium sized potatoes boiled whole in their jackets (skins). Served plain	Pommes en Robe de Chambre

English term	Unit	Ingredient	Metric	Imperial	French term
Potatoes with cream	$\frac{1}{8}$	Cream (fresh)	50 ml	2 oz	Pommes à la Crème
	$\frac{1}{16}$	Butter	25 g	1 oz	
		Milk (to barely cover potatoes)			
		Peel potatoes that have been boiled in their jackets, slice into $\frac{1}{2}$ cm ($\frac{1}{4}$ in) rondels, barely cover with milk and cream, add butter and seasoning. Reboil, simmer for 3 – 4 minutes and serve			
		As for Pommes à la Crème, sprinkle with chopped parsley			Pommes Maître d'Hôtel
Snow potatoes		Pass boiled potatoes through a masher into service dish. Serve immediately			Pommes à la Neige
Mashed potatoes	$\frac{1}{8}$	Boiled milk	50 ml	2 fl oz	Pommes Purée
	$\frac{1}{16}$	Butter	25 g	1 oz	
		Pass boiled potatoes through masher return to clean pan, add milk and butter over heat. Season to taste. Serve as required, e.g. dome shaped			
Mashed potatoes with a cordon of cream	$\frac{1}{8}$	Fresh cream	50 ml	2 fl oz	Pommes Purée à la Crème
		As for Pommes Purée but finished with a cordon of cream			

English term	Unit	Ingredient	Metric	Imperial	French term
Creamed potatoes	1/8	Fresh Cream	50 ml	2 fl oz	Pommes Mousseline
		As for Pommes Purée, combine with cream			
Mashed potatoes with cheese	1/8	Grated cheese	50 g	2 oz	Pommes Purée au Gratin
		As for Pommes Purée sprinkle with grated cheese and gratinate			
Mashed potatoes with ham, pimentoes and parsley	1/8	Finely chopped cooked ham	50 g	2 oz	Pommes Biarritz
	1/16	Finely diced pimento Chopped parsley	25 g	1 oz	
		Combine ingredients with Pommes Purée, serve as required			

Examples of Dishes Prepared from Plain Boiled New Potatoes

English term	Presentation for service	French term
Plain boiled new potatoes	Serve plain boiled	Pommes Nouvelles
Minted new potatoes	During boiling add bunch of mint to flavour. Brush with butter and garnish with blanched mint leaves	Pommes Nouvelles à la Menthe
New potatoes with parsley	Plain boil new potatoes, brush with butter and sprinkle liberally with chopped parsley	Pommes Nouvelles Persillées
New potatoes boiled in their jackets	Cook in jackets (skins), serve plain boiled	Pommes en Robe de Chambre

18

The Principle and Practice of Poaching

To Poach

Pocher

Poaching may be defined as cooking in a minimum amount of liquid, which ideally should never be allowed to boil, but rather maintain a temperature of almost simmering intensity, i.e. just below boiling point.

Foods suitable for poaching vary, as does the length of cooking time, the latter being determined by the type and structure of the product. Examples of foods commonly cooked by this method include fish, poultry, fruits, eggs, and certain offal.

Poaching Fish

Fish may be poached in various poaching liquors. The choice of the poaching medium is determined by the dish being prepared, the type of fish, its size and texture.

Examples of poaching liquors in common use with fish include wine, milk, fish stock or a combination of such liquors. Throughout the cooking process the poaching liquor remains unthickened and only partly covers the fish. The resultant liquor is usually used to form a coating sauce which completes the dish. Many fish dishes that appear on the menu as poached are in fact boiled and are explained and outlined in Chapter 17 concerning boiling.

Poaching Chicken

This usually involves the poaching of chicken breasts, i.e. suprêmes with white chicken stock used as the poaching liquor. At times the stock may be flavoured with wine. As with fish certain chicken dishes appear on the menu as poached but are in fact boiled, these are also explained in Chapter 17.

Quenelles

N.B.   Finer forcemeats of chicken, veal, and fish are also poached and presented in the same manner as for classical poached fish and suprêmes of chicken (*see* recipes 86 and 84 respectively).

In general when poaching any of the above products the poaching liquor is cool at the commencement of the process, being heated gradually to the temperature required. If the products were placed into hot stock or liquor there would be a possibility of some distortion or breaking up, particularly in the case of fish.

Poached Offal

The offal most commonly poached is brains (sheeps' or calves') and the poaching liquor used is a type of court bouillon flavoured with lemon juice.

For explanation of poached eggs and fruits see Chapters 15 and 36 respectively.

Points for Consideration

Short Poaching

This study is concerned with 'short poaching', a term used to describe the poaching of small, tender cuts of fish, poultry, meat and offal. Due to the size and structure of the foods being poached the cooking time is short, enabling the chef to cook and present items quickly for service.

Foods poached by this method require speedy and gentle poaching, which is best achieved by *oven poaching*. Alternatively many dishes that appear on the menu as poached are in fact boiled. In these cases the cooking time involved is usually longer, requiring a gentle simmering action on the stove top. this ensures that the food is thoroughly cooked. These types of dishes are explained in Chapter 17.

Covering Foods for Poaching

During the process many foods are only part covered with liquid and therefore a paper and/or lid covering is required. This ensures that even heat is maintained within the cooking vessel and that steam generated is retained to ensure complete cooking of the food in the shortest possible time. Over-cooking results in excessive shrinkage and dry, unpalatable foods.

Draining Poached Items

Once cooked, poached items need to be well drained otherwise the undrained liquor mixes with the resultant masking sauce spoiling both appearance and consistency. Draining is assisted by placing poached items on to a clean cloth or absorbent paper before completing the dish for service.

Service

Before arranging food for service, the service dish is lightly sauced to prevent items adhering to the base of the dish. This facilitates ease of service. When presenting a glazed/gratinated items the service dish may be decorated with a border of duchess potato. In addition to improving appearance, the border prevents sauce spilling over on to the rim of service dish. Speed of operation and organized methods are essential if a good class product is to be achieved.

When a traditional kitchen brigade is employed the preparation of foods for poaching would be the responsibility of the Chef Garde-manger. The poaching of foods outlined in this study would be the responsibility of:

Chef Poissonnier — Fish products and fish sauces
Chef Saucier   — Entrées

Chicken and Offal

Volaille et Abats

POACHED BREAST OF CHICKEN

Suprême de Volaille Poché

Yield: 4 portions
Cooking time: 12 – 15 min
Cooking temperature: 175°C (350°F)

Unit	Ingredient	Metric (ml)	Imperial (pt)
1	4 Suprêmes of chicken (prepared) Selected sauce (*see* chart) Squeeze of lemon juice Seasoning	500	1
*	White chicken stock (cold)		

* Sufficient just to cover chicken portions during cooking.

Method

Lightly season chicken suprêmes and place into buttered cooking vessel. Add squeeze of lemon juice and just cover with chicken stock. Bring steadily to boiling point, cover with buttered cartouche and place in oven or stove top to poach until cooked. Remove suprêmes from stock and drain well. Lightly sauce the base of service dish, neatly arrange suprêmes on to the dish, napper with sauce, garnish and complete as required for service.

   N.B.   Cooking liquor may be reduced to a glace de volaille and added to selected sauce to enhance the flavour.

Examples of Dishes Prepared Using Above Formula: Selected Sauce and Garnish for 4 Portions in Relation to Formula

English term	Unit	Ingredient	Metric	Imperial	French term
Poached chicken breasts with spinach and cheese	1 $1/_5$ $1/_5$	Supreme sauce Grated cheddar cheese Cooked leaf spinach Parmesan to gratinate	500 ml 100 g 100 g	1 pt 4 oz 4 oz	Suprême de Volaille Poché Florentine

Combine grated Cheddar cheese with sauce. Lightly sauce base of service dish, lay in bed of spinach and place in poached suprêmes. Napper with sauce, sprinkle with parmesan and gratinate

English term	Unit	Ingredient	Metric (g)	Imperial (oz)	French term
Poached chicken breasts with mushroom sauce	1	White mushroom sauce (Velouté based) 8 Mushroom heads (à blanc) Chopped parsley	500 ml	1 pt	Suprême de Volaille Poché aux Sauce Champignons
		Garnish poached chicken with mushrooms, napper with sauce and decorate delicately with chopped parsley			
Poached chicken breasts with supreme sauce and vegetables	1 ⅕	Supreme sauce Cooked julienne of vegetables (carrot – celery – leek – mushroom)	500 ml 100 g	1 pt 4 oz	Suprême de Volaille Poché Polignac
		Add garnished to sauce and napper for service			
Poached chicken breasts with asparagus	1	Supreme sauce 12 Asparagus tips (cooked) 4 slices of truffle 4 Heart shaped croûtons (fried)	500 ml	1 pt	Suprême de Volaille Poché Princesse
		Napper poached suprêmes with sauce, garnish with asparagus, slices of truffle and croûtons			

POACHED CALVES'/LAMBS' BRAINS
Cervelles de Veau/d'Agneau Pochées

Yield: 4 portions
Cooking time: 15 – 20 min
Cooking temperature: 175°C (350°F)

Unit	Ingredient
	4 Brains (remove membrane and wash gently to remove blood
*	Court-bouillon (*see* p. 268)

* Sufficient bouillon just to cover brains during poaching.

Method

Place brains in cooking vessel, add court-bouillon barely to cover. Bring slowly to the boil cover with greased cartouche and lid. Place in oven to poach until cooked. Once cooked remove brains, drain well, serve with sauce and garnish as required (*see* below).

Examples of Poached Brain Dishes Using Above Formula: Sauce and Garnish for 4 portions

English term	Unit	Ingredient	Metric (g)	Imperial (oz)	French term
Poached brains with nutbrown butter	1	Beurre noisette Chopped parsley	100	4	Cervelles Pochées au Beurre Noisette
		Pour butter over poached brains, sprinkle with chopped parsley and serve			
Poached brains with black butter and capers	1 ¼	Beurre noir Capers Chopped parsley	100 25	4 1	Cervelles Pochées au Beurre Noir
		Add capers to beurre noir and pour over poached brains. Sprinkle with chopped parsely and serve			

Poached Fish   Poisson Poché

Poaching is employed in the cooking of a wide variety of fish and shellfish, some are left whole whilst others are prepared into smaller cuts.

The items most commonly used are as follows.

Whole Fish/Shellfish

English term	French term	Yield for 4 portions
Dover sole	Sole Douvres	4 × 300 g (12 oz)
Oysters	Huîtres	16 to 24
Scallops	Coquilles St. Jacques	400 g (1 lb) shelled weight
Scampi	Langoustine	400 g (1 lb) shelled weight

Fish Cuts in Common Use for Short Poaching in the Oven

English term	French term	Yield for 4 portions	Explanation & Illustration
Fillet	le Filet	4–8 according to size and requirements	A cut of flat fish free from bone

Supreme	le Suprême	4 × 125 g (5 oz) portions	A cut on the slant taken from large fish fillets

	le Délice	4 – 8 according to size and requirements	Small fillets of fish neatly folded

	la Paupiette	4 – 8 according to size and requirements	Small fillets of fish rolled into cylindrical shape. Paupiettes are often filled with a fish stuffing before rolling

Fish Commonly Prepared into Small Cuts for Poaching

English term	French term	Type of cut
Brill	Barbue	Suprêmes
Cod	Cabillaud	Suprêmes
Dover sole	Sole Douvres	Filet-délice- paupiettes
Frogs' legs	Cuisse de Grenouilles	Left whole
Haddock	Aigrefin	Suprêmes
Hake	Colin	Suprêmes
Halibut	Flétan	Suprêmes
Lemon sole	Sole Limande	Filets-délice-paupiettes
Plaice	Plie	Filet-délice-paupiettes
Salmon	Saumon	Suprêmes
Salmon trout	Truite Saumonée	Suprêmes
Turbot/young turbot	Turbot/Turbotin	Suprêmes

N.B.   For explanation of cuts *see* above.

Classical Poached Fish Dishes Using Small Cuts of Fish and Whole Dover Sole

Yield: 4 portions
Cooking time: 5 – 10 min
Cooking temperature: 205°C (400°F)

Unit	Ingredient	Metric	Imperial
	Selected fish portions (*see* pp. 281–2)		
1	Cream (double)	200 ml	8 fl oz
½	White wine (dry)	100 ml	4 fl oz
¼	Butter	50 g	2 oz
¹⁄₁₆	Shallots/onion brunoise	12.5 g	¹⁄₂ oz
	Squeeze of lemon juice		
	Fish stock★		
	Fish velonté (light consistency)†		

★*Fish stock* — sufficient to adjust consistency of sauce and ²⁄₃ cover fish for poaching.
†The amount of velouté used will vary accordingly with volume/consistency of sauce required.

Method

Lightly butter base of poaching vessel, sprinkle with shallots. Lay fish portions neatly on to bed of shallots, lightly season and flavour with squeeze of lemon juice. Pour on wine and stock to part cover fish portions. Cover with buttered cartouche and poach in hot oven until fish is just cooked. Once cooked pour cooking liquor into sauteuse and reduce quickly to form a glace de poisson. Add cream, bring to the boil, reduce to light coating consistency, add required velouté, adjust seasoning/consistency and if appropriate pass through chinois. Use as required.

Service

1. *Not glazed:* Lightly sauce the base of service dish, neatly arrange well-drained fish on to dish, napper with sauce, garnish as required and serve.
2. *Glazed:* Enrich sauce with egg yolk or sabayon (do not reboil). Lightly sauce base of service dish, neatly arrange well-drained fish on to dish, napper with sauce, glaze under hot salamander and serve.
3. *Gratinated:* Proceed as for glazed fish but sprinkle with grated parmesan cheese before gratinating under hot salamander. Garnish as required and serve.

N.B.   When using whole dover sole, on completion of poaching remove side bones. Gently ease upper fillets away from backbone and snip main part of backbone to remove. Reshape fish ready for service.

When adding egg yolk or sabayon to the sauces which are to be glazed or gratinated use ¹⁄₁₀ unit egg yolk to 1 unit sauce (e.g. 25 g [1 oz] egg yolk to 250 ml [¹⁄₂ pt] sauce).

Alternative Method of Preparing Sauce for Classical Poached Fish Dishes

Where a richer sauce is required the velouté content is replaced with additional double cream. Cream is reduced to coating consistency. This method is particularly suited where a speedy à la carte service is required. Obviously the cost of the dish is substantially increased. N.B. The cream (usually double) is reduced to a coating consistency.

Examples of Dishes Prepared Using Above Formula: Added Ingredients and Garnish for 4 Portions in Relation to Above Formula

English term	Unit	Ingredient	Metric (g)	Imperial (oz)	French term
1 Poached Fish Dishes — not glazed					
Fish in white wine sauce		8 fleurons Garnish completed dish with fleurons			Poisson Vin Blanc
	$\frac{1}{5}$	Julienne of cooked mushrooms and truffle 8 fleurons Combine mushrooms and truffle with the sauce before coating the fish Garnish with fleurons	50	2	Poisson Polignac
	$\frac{1}{5}$	Julienne of cooked vegetables and truffle (carrot, leek, celery) Combine above with sauce before coating the fish	50	2	Poisson Suchet
Poached fish Granville style	$\frac{1}{5}$	Sliced cooked mushrooms Picked shrimps Finely chopped truffle Combine above with sauce before coating the fish	50	2	Poisson Granville
Poached fish Dieppe style	$\frac{1}{5}$ $\frac{1}{10}$ $\frac{1}{10}$	Budded mussels Picked shrimps Cooked button mushrooms (à blanc) Chopped parsley Garnish completed dish with above	50 25 25	2 1 1	Poisson Dieppoise
	$\frac{2}{5}$	Tomato concassé Chopped parsley Prior to poaching add tomato to fish. Finish sauce with chopped parsley before coating the fish	100	4	Poisson Dugléré

English term	Unit	Ingredient	Metric (g)	Imperial (oz)	French term

2 Poached Fish Dishes — glazed

		Chopped parsley Garnish sauce with parsley before coating fish for glazing			Poisson Bercy
	$\frac{1}{5}$	Sliced mushrooms	50	2	Poisson Bonne Femme
		Chopped parsley Place sliced mushrooms on to fish prior to poaching. Finish sauce with chopped parsley before glazing			
	$\frac{1}{5}$ $\frac{1}{5}$	Tomato concassé Sliced mushrooms Chopped parsley Place mushrooms and tomatoes on to fish prior to poaching. Finish sauce with chopped parsley before glazing	50 50	2 2	Poisson Bréval/ d'Antin
	$\frac{1}{5}$ $\frac{1}{10}$	Sliced mushrooms Picked shrimps Place mushrooms and shrimps on to fish prior to poaching. Coat with sauce for glazing	50 25	2 1	Poisson Saint-Valéry
	$\frac{2}{5}$	Muscat grapes (green) (skinned de-pipped and chilled) Place chilled grapes on to cooked fish portions prior to masking with sauce for glazing	100	4	Poisson Véronique

3 Poached Fish Dishes — glazed or gratinated

Poached fish in cheese sauce	$\frac{1}{5}$	Grated cheddar cheese Add cheese to sauce before coating to glaze or gratinate	50	2	Poisson Mornay
	$\frac{2}{5}$ $\frac{1}{5}$	Duxelle Grated cheddar cheese 8 slices truffle Place poached fish on a bed of duxelle. Add cheese to sauce, mask fish and gratinate or glaze. Garnish with slices of truffle	100 50	4 2	Poisson Cubat

English term	Unit	Ingredient	Metric (g)	Imperial (oz)	French term
	$^2/_5$	Cooked leaf spinach	100	4	Poisson Florentine
	$^1/_5$	Grated Cheddar cheese	50	2	
		Place poached fish on a bed of spinach. Add cheese to sauce, mask fish and glaze or gratinate			
	$^1/_5$	Grated Cheddar cheese	50	2	Poisson Walewska
		8 Slices of cooked lobster tail			
		8 slices of truffle			
		Add cheese to sauce, decorate cooked fish with slices of lobster. Mask with sauce, glaze or gratinate			

POACHED SHELLFISH DISHES, using Scallops (Coquilles St Jacques), Oysters (Huîtres), Scampi (Longoustines) and Frogs Legs (Cuisses de Grenouilles)

Yield: 4 portions
Cooking time: 5 – 10 min
Cooking temperature: 205°C (400°F)

Unit	Ingredient	Metric	Imperial
1	Selected shellfish (free from shell)	400 g	1 lb
1	Selected sauce (*see* chart)	400 ml	16 fl oz
	Squeeze of lemon juice		
	Seasoning		
★	Fish stock		

★ Sufficient stock to barely cover shellfish during poaching.

Method

Place shellfish in cooking vessel, season and flavour with lemon juice. Barely cover with stock, bring to boiling point, cover with buttered cartouche and place in a hot oven to poach until just done. Drain shellfish well, lightly sauce base of service dish, neatly arrange shellfish on to dish, napper with sauce and glaze or gratinate as for poached fish (*see* p. 283).

Examples of Poached Shellfish Dishes Prepared Using Above Formula

English term	Selected sauce and garnish	Metric	Imperial	French term
In white wine sauce with parsley	Bercy sauce (fish based) (p. 181) Glazed for service			Bercy
In white wine sauce with truffle	Sauce vin blanc Garnish of chopped truffle Glazed for service			Parisienne
In cheese sauce	Fish mornay sauce Parmesan cheese to gratinate for service			Mornay
With spinach and cheese sauce	Fish mornay sauce Cooked leaf spinach	100 g	4 oz	Florentine
	Place poached shellfish on a bed of spinach mask with sauce and gratinate or glaze			

N.B.   Other suitable sauces and garnishes may be used for the above dishes.

POACHED SMOKED FISH
(Smoked cod, haddock)

Yield: 4 portions
Cooking time: 10 – 12 min
Cooking temperature: 205° (400°F)

Unit	Ingredient	Metric (g)	Imperial (oz)
1	Selected smoked fish (cut into portions)	500	20
$1/10$	Butter	50	2
	Pepper to season		
★	Milk		

★ Sufficient milk to cover the fish during cooking.

Method

Lay portions of fish (skin down) in a buttered cooking vessel. Lightly season with pepper and cover with milk and a knob of butter. Cover with a greased cartouche and place in the oven until cooked. Once cooked remove from oven, drain fish portions and remove any bone. Arrange fish on to service dish, moisten with a little cooking liquor and serve.

N.B.   Alternatively smoked fish may be cooked by simmering on stove-top in milk or milk and water.

HADDOCK MONTE CARLO

Yield: 4 portions
Cooking time: 15 min
Cooking temperature: 205°C (400°F)

Unit	Ingredient	Metric	Imperial
1	Smoked haddock (cut into portions)	500 g	$1\frac{1}{4}$ lb
$\frac{1}{5}$	Tomato concassé (heated)	100 g	4 oz
$\frac{1}{10}$	Cream	50 ml	2 fl oz
$\frac{1}{10}$	Butter	50 g	2 oz
	4 Poached eggs		
*	Beurre manié		
†	Milk		
	Pepper to season		

* Sufficient to thicken lightly cooking liquor.
† Sufficient milk to cover the fish during cooking.

Method

Cook as for poached smoked fish. Once cooked remove from oven, drain fish portions, remove any bone and place in service dish, keep hot. Lightly thicken the cooking liquor with beurre manié and enrich with cream. Crown each fish portion with a poached egg, napper with sauce and surround each egg with hot tomato concassé to garnish. Serve immediately.

19
The Principle and Practice of Steaming

To Steam Vapeur

Commercial steaming involves cooking with water vapour (steam), under varying degrees of pressure. The minimum pressure generally used in trade operations is around 0.35 kg/cm² (5 psi). The boiling point of water at normal atmospheric pressure is 100°C (212°F), a temperature that will not increase no matter how long boiling continues. If however atmospheric pressure is increased the boiling temperature may be raised. This is the underlying principle of steaming under pressure.

During steaming heat is transferred from the water vapour to the food, which acts to cook and tenderize the products concerned. Many foods may be cooked successfully by this method, e.g. vegetables, fish, butcher's meat, offal, poultry, and various puddings. The steaming process reduces the risk of overcooking protein. Therefore, steamed products are easily digested and thus suitable for service to invalids. In addition there is less loss of the soluble nutrients from foods than with the other moist methods of cookery.

When a traditional kitchen brigade is employed the following Chefs de Partie may be involved with the preparation and cooking of steamed products:

Chef Garde-Manger — involved with initial preparation of meats and fish prior to cooking
Chef Saucier — butcher's meat, poultry, etc.
Chef Pâtissier — preparation of suet pastry and sweet puddings for steaming
Chef Poissonnier — fish products
Chef Entremettier — vegetables to include potatoes.

Points for Consideration

Safety

Where a water-well is an integral part of a steamer it is essential to check for sufficient water prior to igniting. If this routine safety measure is ignored the steamer is liable to be seriously damaged.

Once foods are placed in the steamer ensure that the doors are sealed firmly to achieve correct pressure within. Before opening the doors release steam pressure as indicated by manufacturer's recommendations. On opening, use the door as a shield from escaping steam. When steaming puddings always cover with greased greaseproof paper and a pudding cloth to protect foods from condensed steam.

Where high pressure steamers are used check the cooking times as recommended by the manufacturer. Ensure that steamers are cleaned thoroughly after use and maintained frequently according to manufacturer's recommendations.

Steaming of Butcher's Meat, Offal, and Poultry

Pieces of meat, offal, and poultry that are suitable for boiling may also be steamed. When steaming at low pressure the cooking times for meats are similar to boiling times per equal unit of weight. Where pressure is increased cooking times are reduced.

Steamed meats may lack some of the colour and flavour associated with other methods of cooking but this may be counteracted by serving them with flavoursome sauces and colourful garnishes.

Steaming is ideally suited to bulk catering and for meat products where significant amounts of stock are *not* required.

Preparation of Meats for Steaming

Lightly season meat and secure with string as required:

(a) when no stock is required place meat on perforated steamer tray;
(b) when stock is required place the meat in a deep steaming vessel.

Set meat to steam until cooked.
Steamed meats may be served and garnished similarly to boiled meats (*see* Chapter 17).

Steaming of Fish

Whole fish and smaller cuts of fish may be cooked by this method. Steaming of small cuts may be adopted when cooking for large numbers, e.g. banqueting. This method facilitates ease of preparation and cooking without undue loss of colour or flavour. Where a sauce is required it would be prepared independently. Cooking times similar to boiled/poached fish unless they are reduced by high pressure steaming.

Preparation of Fish for Steaming

Lightly season and flavour with lemon juice and steam as for meats. Steamed fish may be served and garnished similarly to boiled and poached fish dishes (*see* Chapters 17 and 18).

Steaming of Vegetables to Include Potatoes

Vegetables suitable for boiling may also be steamed although when steaming at low pressure green vegetables tend to lose their fresh green appearance. As for meats and fish, steaming is an ideal method for cooking vegetables and potatoes when catering for large numbers. Preparation and cooking times are similar to those for boiled vegetables unless they are reduced by high pressure steaming.

Preparation of Vegetables and Potatoes for Steaming

Lightly season vegetables and place into perforated steamer tray. Set to steam until cooked. Steamed vegetables and potatoes may be prepared and served similarly to their boiled counterparts.

Steaming of Eggs

Where large numbers of hard boiled eggs are required they may be steamed in their shell then treated as for boiled eggs. At low pressure, steaming time is approximately 15 minutes.

STEAMED BEEFSTEAK PUDDING

Yield: 4 portions
Cooking time: 3 – 4 hr

Unit	Ingredient	Metric (g)	Imperial (oz)
1	Stewing beef diced $[1\,^1\!/_2$ cm $(^3\!/_4$ in)]	500	20
$^1\!/_5$	Onion brunoise	100	4
*	Brown stock		
	Seasoned flour		
	Salt and pepper to taste		
	Chopped parsley (optional)		
	Few drops of Worcester sauce		
†	Suet pastry		

* Sufficient stock barely to cover meat.
† Sufficient for 4 portions approximately 150 g (6 oz) flour prepared into suet pastry (*see* recipe 30).

Method

Roll out two-thirds of suet pastry and line greased pudding basin. Lightly season the meat and roll through seasoned flour. Combine meat with onion, parsley and Worcester sauce. Place filling into lined basin, moisten with stock and roll out remaining pastry to form sealed lid. Cover with greased greaseproof paper and pudding cloth. Set to steam until cooked. Once cooked, clean the basin, surround with clean serviette and present for service.

Extensions of Basic Formula: Added Ingredients to 1 Unit – 500 g (1¼ lb) of Meat

Name of dish	Unit	Ingredient	Metric (g)	Imperial (oz)
Steak and mushroom pudding	$^1\!/_{10}$	Sliced mushrooms Add to filling	50	2

Name of dish	Unit	Ingredient	Metric (g)	Imperial (oz)
Steak and kidney pudding	$\frac{1}{5}$	Diced ox-kidney	100	4
		Add to filling		
Steak, kidney and oyster pudding	As for steak and kidney with the addition of oysters to filling 2 oysters per portion			
Steak, kidney and mushroom pudding	$\frac{1}{5}$	Diced ox-kidney	100	4
	$\frac{1}{10}$	Sliced mushrooms	50	2
		Add to filling		

N.B.   For steak puddings using cooked fillings *see* Chapter 26 on combined methods.

20

The Principle and Practice of Frying

There are two methods of frying:

(a) deep frying
(b) shallow frying

In both cases foods are cooked in heated fat or oil, either by submerging the food completely (deep frying) or by cooking in the minimum of oil/fat (shallow frying). All manner of foods may be cooked by these methods, e.g. animal protein, vegetables, fruits, etc.

To Fry (Deep) Frire

Deep frying is cooking in selected oil or clarified fat in a friture. The cooking medium selected must be capable of being heated to high temperatures without burning. Temperatures will vary according to the food being fried and are determined by the extent of cooking and colouring required. Frying temperatures may vary from 160 – 195°C (320 – 380°F) approximately. As a guide fat/oil is ready for use when it is quite still and gives off a faint bluish haze. Examples of frying mediums in common use are as follows: cotton seed oil, palm, vegetable oil, and first class dripping.

How Food is Cooked by the Deep-Frying Process

During the process food is immersed in the heated frying medium. The exterior of the product may or may not be protected with a coating (e.g. batter, flour, breadcrumbs), but whatever the case the high temperature seals the exterior of the food. At this stage the moisture content within the food takes in heat, steam is then created which in turn acts as a cooking medium.

When deep frying *battered products,* they are best placed directly into a friture without a frying basket. Battered products tend to adhere to the baskets making them difficult to handle when removing from the friture on cooking. During frying many foods require turning to ensure even cooking, e.g. fish, meats, beignets, etc. When starting to fry it may be necessary to agitate foods gently to prevent their sticking together, e.g. battered foods, potato dishes.

Draining Foods for Service

On completion of frying the products should be drained well before service to remove excess grease. This may be achieved by:

(a) draining the food well over the fryer;
(b) placing cooked articles on to absorbent paper;
(c) always serving deep-fried foods on dish papers to absorb any remaining grease.

Care of Friture

After *each* fry the fat is cleaned with a fine mesh strainer to remove fried scraps and particles *before* continuing the next fry. After an extensive frying period the fat is drained from the friture and strained. The friture is cleaned and the strained fat/oil carefully replaced.

Items Required for Deep-Frying Operation

Frying baskets and fine-mesh sieves
Trays for scraps, fat drips, blanched and cooked foods
Cloth for cleaning hands
Seasonings
Foods to be fried
Protective coatings (flour, batter).

Operational Layout

Food ⟶ Coating ⟶ Friture ⟶ Drip and scraps trays ⟶ Food trays
(*Utensils to hand as required*)

Notes Concerning Deep Frying

Where a traditional kitchen brigade is employed all deep frying other than for pastry goods, is the responsibility of the Chef Rôtisseur.

Cooking Times

As indicated in the charts, this will vary according to size, structure, and nature of the product being fried and the temperature used.

Preparation for Frying

When using the various coatings for frying it is essential to cover the food completely and at the same time ensure a light even coating. This is achieved by:

(a) passing foods lightly through seasoned flour and shaking off excess flour before coating with batter;
(b) panéing food lightly and shaking off excess crumbs before patting the food into shape. Ensure the crumbs used for coating are finely sieved (not coarse) and re-sieved when required.
(c) where batter is used, test that the consistency for coating is correct (not too heavy) and that on coating only a light covering is applied.

N.B.   Do not allow foods that have been coated in flour to stand for any length of time prior to cooking. The flour absorbs moisture from the food, becomes sticky and results in the food being difficult to handle. If fried in this condition the quality of the end-product would be impaired. This may be corrected by washing away sticky exterior, drying the article and re-flouring just before cooking.

Safety Factors

Deep frying can be a hazardous operation unless carried out with the utmost care and skill. It must be noted that *smoking fat is burning fat,* and if left unattended may reach flash point and burst into flames.

Care must be taken in the preparation of foods for deep frying:

(a) Wet foods need to be 'well drained' before frying otherwise the excess water boils when in contact with the hot fat often causing some of the fat to spill over the sides of the friture. This may result in serious accidents to staff and premises, e.g. burns and fire.

(b) Overloading the friture with food will displace the oil causing it to overflow – as a result accidents may occur. This is prevented by ensuring that the level of the frying medium in the friture does not exceed two thirds full (often indicated by a safety marker), and that the amount of food to be fried is not excessive at any one time. *NOTE*: In the event of a fat fire, extinguish with a foam extinguisher. *DO NOT USE WATER* as this causes further danger by spreading the fire.

(c) Whenever possible use a frying basket to ensure safe handling of food.

(d) *Organizational factors.* It is important that food and equipment are at hand and organized if a safe efficient system is to operate.

(e) When placing food into the fryer, dip items gently away from the body to prevent fat splashing, which could result in skin burns.

Protective Coatings for Deep-Fried Foods

Due to the high temperatures used when deep frying it is often necessary to surround foods with a protective coating prior to cooking. Such coatings are used to:

(a) prevent the surface of foods from being burnt or overcooked, which would make them indigestible;

(b) prevent moisture escaping from foods and spoiling the frying medium;

(c) to protect food from oil which would otherwise be absorbed by the food resulting in a greasy product;

(d) to seal in the food's moisture, which on heating turns to steam and cooks the food;

(e) offer variety in flavour, colour, and texture to the finished product.

<table>
<tr><td>

FRYING IN BATTER
YEAST BATTER

Yield: 1 l (2 pt) approx.

</td><td>

Frit
Pâte à Frire

</td></tr>
</table>

Unit	Ingredient	Metric	Imperial
1	Water (tepid)	500 ml	1 pt
$^4/_5$	Flour	400 g	1 lb
$^1/_{40}$	Yeast	12.5 g	$^1/_2$ oz
	Pinch of salt		

Method

Sift flour and salt into basin and form a well. Cream yeast in water thoroughly and pour into the well. Gradually beat in the flour to form a smooth batter. Cover with a damp cloth and allow to ferment in warm place for approximately 45 minutes to 1 hour.

Before use beat thoroughly and adjust to light coating consistency.

EGG BATTER   Pâte à Frire

Yield: 1 l (2 pt) approx.

Unit	Ingredient	Metric	Imperial
1	Water	500 ml	1 pt
$\frac{4}{5}$	Flour	400 g	1 lb
$\frac{1}{5}$	Whole egg	100 g	4 oz
$\frac{1}{40}$	Baking powder	12.5 g	$\frac{1}{2}$ oz
	Pinch of salt		

Method

Sift flour, baking powder and salt into basin and form a well. Whisk water and egg together thoroughly and pour into well. Gradually beat in the flour to form a smooth batter. Allow batter to stand in cool place to rest the gluten and enable the starch to effect full thickening. Before use adjust to light coating consistency.

N.B.   Before coating with batter items are passed lightly through seasoned flour to form a dry surface which enables the batter to adhere to the food. If the batter is allowed to rest in a warm area the baking powder would begin to work thus reducing its ability to aerate successfully when used at a later stage.

ENGLISH STYLE   à l'Anglaise (pané)

Coated in seasoned flour, egg wash and breadcrumbs.
Prepare food, pass through seasoned flour, egg-wash (eggs beaten with a little milk) and breadcrumbs. Lightly pat food to remove any excess crumbs. Re-shape items where required.

FRENCH STYLE   à la Française

Coated with milk and seasoned flour.
Prepare food, pass through milk and seasoned flour, shake well to remove excess flour and fry immediately.

N.B.   On no account allow foods coated in flour to stand for any length of time prior to cooking. This results in the flour absorbing moisture from the food and becoming soggy, which consequently spoils the appearance of the finished article.

ORLY STYLE   à l'Orly

Applied only to fish. Fish is lightly marinated, passed through seasoned flour and batter for deep frying, and served with tomato sauce, lemon and parsley (*see* p. 300).

Deep-Fried Chicken/Pork/Veal (raw)

Yield: 4 portions take: (a) One medium chicken (cut for sauté) or (b) 4 chicken suprêmes as required or (c) 500 g (1¼ lb) raw chicken/pork off bone cut into 2½ cm (1 in) chunks or (d) 8 chicken drumsticks (e) 4 × 150 g (6 oz) escalopes of veal.

Name of dish	Preparation and cooking	Frying temperature °C (°F)	Frying time (min)
Deep-fried chicken southern style	Season chicken, cut for sauté, pass through seasoned flour and frying batter. Deep fry until cooked and golden brown. Serve garnished with: 4 slices of grilled bacon 4 pineapple fritters 4 corn cakes 250 ml (½ pt) tomato sauce	175 – 190 (350 – 375)	8 – 10
Pilon de Volaille Frit (deep-fried chicken drumsticks)	Season drumsticks, pané, deep fry and serve garnished with deep fried parsley, dress with cutlet frills.	175 – 190 (350 – 375)	8 – 10
Suprême de Volaille Kiev (supreme of chicken Kiev)	Stuff the chicken supremes with garlic butter (*see* p. 201), season and pané. Deep fry until cooked and golden brown, serve garnished with deep fried parsley and dress with cutlet frills	175 – 190 (350 – 375)	8 – 10
Suprême de Volaille Cordon Bleu (supreme of chicken cordon bleu)	As for Kiev but replace garlic butter with: 4 thin slices of cooked ham 100 g (4 oz) grated gruyère cheese	175 – 190 (350 – 375)	8 – 10
Fritots de Volaille/Pork★ (deep-fried chicken/ pork (off bone)	Season chunks of chicken, pass through seasoned flour and frying batter. Deep fry until cooked and golden brown. Garnish with deep fried parsley. May be accompanied with sweet and sour sauce and rice pilaff	175 – 190 (350 – 375)	5 – 8

★ Marinade the pieces of meat in a light mixture of lemon juice, oil, chopped garlic, chopped fresh herbs and seasoning for a few hours or overnight.

Name of dish	Preparation and cooking	Frying temperature °C (°F)	Frying time (min)
Wiener Schnitzel (deep-fried veal escalopes)	Season and pané veal. Deep fry until cooked and golden brown. Serve garnished with deep fried parsley and lemon wedge or rondel	175 – 190 (350 – 375)	5 – 6

N.B.   Drain deep-fried products well and place on dish papers to absorb any excess grease.

DEEP-FRIED FISH   Poisson Frit

Deep frying is employed for cooking a wide variety of fish and shellfish, some are prepared and left whole and others prepared into smaller cuts. The whole fish/shellfish and cuts most commonly deep fried are listed below.

Whole Fish (prepared for cooking)

English term	French term	Yield 4 portions
Smelts	Éperlans	16 smelts
Dover sole	Sole Douvres	4 × 300 g (12 oz) approx.
Whiting	Merlan	4 × 200 g (8 oz) approx.
Whitebait	Blanchailles	400 g (1 lb)
Sprats	Melettes	8 – 12 sprats

Shellfish

English term	French term	Yield 4 portions
Oysters	Huîtres	16 – 24 oysters
Scallops	Coquilles Saint Jacques	400 g (1 lb) shelled weight
Scampi	Langoustine	400 g (1 lb) shelled weight

Fish That are Commonly Prepared into Small Cuts for Deep Frying (see overleaf)

English term	French term	Common cuts for deep frying (see overleaf)
Cod	Cabillaud	Filet-Suprême-Goujon
Dover sole	Sole Douvres	Filet-en Tresse-Goujon/ettes
Haddock	Aigrefin	Filet-Suprême-Goujon
Hake	Colin	Filet-Suprême-Goujon
Lemon sole	Sole Limande	Filet-en Tresse-Goujon/ettes
Monk		Goujon/ettes
Plaice	Plie	Filet-en Tresse-Goujon/ettes
Whiting	Merlan	Filet

Fish Cuts in Common use for Deep Frying

English term	French term	Yield 4 portions	Explanation and illustration
Fillet	le Filet	4 – 8 fillets according to size and requirements	A cut of fish free from the bone, taken from flat fish (4 fillets), round fish (2 fillets)
Supreme	le Suprême	4 × 125 g (5 oz) pieces	A cut (on the slant) taken from large fish fillets
Plaited	en Tresse	4 – 8 fillets according to size and requirements	Plaited fillets of fish (using small fillets only)
Thin strips	les Goujons	500 g (1¼ lb) cut into strips	Fillets cut into thin strips approximately 6 cm (2½ in) long by ½ cm (¼ in) thick
Tiny thin strips	les Goujonettes	500 g (1¼ lb) cut into strips	Fillets cut into very small thin strips as for goujons but cut smaller

Styles of Deep Frying

Name of dish	Preparation and cooking	Suggested accompanying sauce	Frying temperature °C (°F)	Frying time (min)
Poisson Frit à l'Anglaise (fried fish English style)	Pané prepared fish, deep fry until cooked and golden brown. Garnish with lemon wedge and deep fried picked parsley	Tartare sauce Sauce Tartare	175 – 190 (350 – 375)	3 – 6
Poisson Frit à la Française (fried fish French style)	Pass prepared fish through milk and seasoned flour, deep fry until cooked and golden brown. Garnish as above	Tartare/Rémoulade sauces Sauce Rémoulade	175 – 190 (350 – 375)	3 – 6
Poisson à l'Orly (fried fish Orly style)	Marinate prepared fish for 15 – 30 minutes in oil, lemon juice and chopped parsley. pass through seasoned flour and batter. Deep fry until cooked and golden brown. Garnish as above.	Tomato Sauce Sauce Tomates	175 – 190 (350 – 375)	3 – 6
Sole Douvres Colbert (Dover sole Colbert)	Take whole prepared soles (minus skin, eyes, fins, gut). Cut down the backbone on one side of the fish. Commence filleting to within 3 cm (1 in) of the sides, leave fillets attached. Fold fillets towards the sides. Snip the backbone in three places, pané and deep fry steadily until cooked. Remove backbone and garnish cavity with the parsley butter and wedge of lemon. N.B. White skin is often retained	Parsley butter/Beurre Maître d'Hôtel	175 – 190 (350 – 375)	6 – 10
Merlan en Colère (deep-fried curled whiting)	Take whole prepared whiting (minus skin, eyes guts and gills). Place tail in mouth to secure, pané, deep fry until cooked and golden brown. Serve garnished with fried picked parsley and wedge of lemon	Tartare/Rémoulade Sauces	175 – 190 (350 – 375)	6 – 10

Name of dish	Preparation and cooking	Suggested accompanying sauce	Frying temperature °C (°F)	Frying time (min)
Blanchailles Diable (devilled white-bait*)	Pass whitebait through milk and seasoned flour. Place on to cane sieve and shake well to remove excess flour and to separate fish. Deep fry until crisp and golden brown. Drain and lightly sprinkle with salt and cayenne pepper. Garnish with lemon wedges and deep fried picked parsley		190 (375)	1–2
Blanchailles Frites (fried whitebait)	As above omitting cayenne pepper.			1–2
Fritto Misto Mare (Italian) (fried sea-food mixture)	A selection of fish/shell fish, prepared for frying, passed through *milk and seasoned flour* or *seasoned flour and batter*. Deep fry until crisp and golden brown, garnish with lemon wedges and deep-fried picked parsley, drain well and serve	Tartare/Rémoulade	175–190 (350–375)	3–6

* When handling whitebait in a hot atmosphere it is necessary to keep it in iced water to prevent the fish from decomposing and breaking up. The cold temperature keeps the whitebaits natural oil congealed and retards growth of micro-organisms.

Deep-Fried Vegetables   Légumes Frits

Using Raw Vegetables
Yield: 4 portions 300 g (12 oz) prepared weight

Name of dish	Preparation and cooking	Frying temperature C° (°F)	Frying time (min)
Aubergine Frite à la Française (deep-fried egg plant)	Trim ends of egg plant, decorate with channel cutter or peel away skin. Cut into ½ cm (¼ in) slices, pass through milk and seasoned flour, deep fry until golden brown and crisp. Drain, sprinkle lightly with salt and serve	190 (375)	2–3

Courgettes Frites à la Française (deep-fried baby marrows)	Trim ends, cut into ½ cm (¼ in) slices on the slant or lengthways. Continue as for egg plant	190 (375)	2–3
Oignons Frits à la Française (deep-fried onion rings)	Trim and peel onions, thinly slice into rings and separate. Omit small rings. Continue as for egg plant	190 (375)	2–3
Champignons Frits (deep fried mushrooms)	Select medium sized mushrooms, wash well, trim stalk and (peel if necessary) Pass through seasoned flour, lightly batter and deep fry until crisp and golden brown. Drain well, sprinkle with salt and serve	190 (375)	2–3

N.B.   Drain deep-fried products well and present on dish papers to absorb any excess grease.

Using Par-Cooked Vegetables (Par-boiled, Refreshed and Drained)
Yield: 4 portions 300 g (12 oz) prepared weight

Name of dish	Preparation and cooking	Frying temperature °C (°F)	Frying time (min)
Beignets de Chou-fleur (cauliflower fritters)	Cut cauliflower into neat fleurettes, pass through seasoned flour and lightly batter. Deep fry until cooked and golden brown. Drain well, sprinkle lightly with salt and serve	175–190 (350–375)	3–5
Beignets de Panais (parsnip fritters)	Pass parsnip fingers through seasoned flour and lightly batter. Continue as for cauliflower	175–190 (350–375)	3–5

Deep-Fried Potatoes   Pommes de Terre Frites

Using prepared raw potatoes
Yield: 4 portions 400 g (1 lb) prepared weight

Name of dish	Preparation and cooking	Frying temperature °C (°F)	Frying time (min)
Pommes Chips (crisps)	Cut into very thin slices on a mandolin. Cover with cold water and stand for 30 minutes to remove excess starch, change water after 15 minutes. Too much starch causes crisps to stick together during cooking. Drain well, deep fry until golden brown and crisp. Agitate potatoes during frying to keep separated. Drain well, lightly sprinkle with salt and serve.	190 (375)	3–4

Name of dish	Preparation and cooking	Frying temperature °C (°F)	Frying time (min)
Pommes Gauffrettes (perforated crisps)	Cut into very thin perforated slices on a mandolin. Proceed as for crisps	190 (375)	3–4
Pommes Pailles (straw potatoes)	Cut into fine julienne on a mandolin or with a knife. Proceed as for crisps	190 (375)	1–2
Pommes Allumettes (matchstick potatoes)	Cut into large julienne. Proceed as for crisps	190 (375)	2–3
Pommes Mignonnette (potato bâtons)	Cut into small neat bâtons. Proceed as for crisps	190 (375)	3–4
Pommes Frites (chipped potatoes)	Cut potatoes into large bâtons by machine or manually	165–190 (330–375)	5–10
	Blanch in friture 165°C (330°F) without colour and until chips begin to soften. Drain and place on trays until required. To complete cooking submerge in hot friture 190°C (375°F) until crisp and golden brown. Drain, sprinkle lightly with salt and serve		
Pommes Pont Neuf (thick chipped potatoes)	Cut potatoes as for chipped potatoes but approximately twice as thick. Proceed as for chipped potatoes	165–190 (330–375)	10–15
Pommes Bataille (potato cubes)	Cut potatoes in 1 cm (½ in) dice. Proceed as for chipped potatoes	165–190 (330–375)	5–8

Drain deep-fried products well on dish papers to remove any excess grease

Deep-Fried Soufflé Potatoes   Pommes Soufflées

Trim potatoes into cylindrical shape. Cut into ¼ cm (⅛ in) slices and place in cold water to stand. Drain well and place into moderately hot fat [approximately 175°C (350°F)], agitate carefully throughout to prolong frying period, prevent colouring and lightly aerate in initial frying. When potatoes begin to souffle, remove from friture and place into second friture at a high temperature (190°C (375°F)) until potatoes soufflé completely are golden brown and crisp. Sprinkle lightly with salt and serve.

CHOUX PASTRY BASED FRITTERS

Beignets Soufflés

Yield: 4 portions
Frying time: 5 – 8 min
Frying temperature: 175 – 190°C (350 – 375°F)

Unit	Ingredient	Metric (g)	Imperial (oz)
1	*Choux pastry	100	4
1	Main flavouring Seasoning	100	4

* Indicates amount of egg used when making choux pastry.

Method

Combine ingredients and season to taste. Shape into ovals using dessert spoons, place on to lightly oiled paper. Place into friture and fry steadily until fritters soufflé, become crisp and golden brown. Drain well, lightly sprinkle with salt and serve.

Examples of Dishes Prepared Using above Formula

English term	Main ingredient and garnish	French term
Cheese fritters	Grated cheese (Cheddar/parmesan)	Beignets au Fromage
Crab fritters	White crab meat, garnish with lemon wedges	Beignets de Crabe

N.B.   Drain deep-fried products well and present on dish papers to absorb any excess grease.

DEEP-FRIED FRUITS (used to garnish meats)

Beignets de Fruits

Banana Fritters

Beignets de Banane

Yield: 4 portions 2 small bananas
Cooking time: 2 – 3 min
Frying temperature: 175 – 190°C (350 – 375°F)

Method

Peel bananas just before cooking (if peeled and left to stand for any length of time fruit turns black due to enzymic browning, *see* p. 64). Pané, or pass through milk and flour or flour and batter. Deep fry until cooked and golden brown, drain well and serve as required.

To Fry (Shallow)

Sauter

The French term used to describe foods that are shallow fried is sauter. Literally translated 'sauter' means to jump or leap, which seems far removed from the preparation and cooking of foods. There are times, however, when items being shallow fried are 'tossed' and give the appearance of leaping or jumping.

Shallow Fried in Butter   Sauté au Beurre

Denotes foods cooked or reheated by shallow frying in butter.

Meunière

A French term used to denote shallow-fried fish, which is garnished in a particular manner (*see* p. 329).

Technique of Shallow Frying

Shallow frying can be simply defined as cooking in heated oil or selected fat. The initial starting temperature of the melted fat or oil needs to be high in order to seal and cook the food quickly. Placing food into a cool frying medium would cause the food to absorb the fat/oil and consequently adversely affect the quality of the finished product. Various oils and fats attain smoking point at different temperatures, e.g. olive oil 250°C (480°F) and butter 140°C (280°F) approximately.

Shallow frying is carried out in frying or sauté pans according to the dish being cooked. Foods are cooked in the minimum of oil, on both sides with the presentation side being cooked first. This ensures ease of handling for presentation. On many occasions the meat juices form a sediment in the cooking vessel and are deglazed with wine to form part of an accompanying sauce. The types of food suitable for this process are small pieces of tender meat, made-up dishes, fish, vegetables and fruits. The tougher cuts of meat are unsuitable for shallow frying.

Ensure that the cooking medium is at a sufficiently high temperature to seal and colour the food. At too low a temperature the fat/oil is absorbed by the food making it greasy and unpalatable. Also at a low temperature food is not adequately coloured or sealed and as a result the finished product may be of inferior quality.

When initial colouring and sealing of the food has been effected the cooking temperature is lowered to allow the food to cook through evenly. Continual cooking at a high temperature will result in overcooked, burnt, indigestible products.

When plain frying for large quantities it is necessary to change the frying medium and clean the pan before re-use. This is required because food particles burn and spoil the appearance of other fried foods. Care must be taken when handling certain foods during shallow frying because of their delicate structure, e.g. fish. Shallow-fried foods are lightly drained prior to service. When shallow frying those items that deteriorate on standing, e.g. steaks, and which also require an accompanying sauce/garnish, it is advisable to have the sauce and garnish prepared in advance of cooking.

Notes Concerning Shallow Frying

Where a traditional kitchen brigade is employed shallow frying is the shared responsibility of the following Chefs de Partie.
    Chef Saucier   — Meat, poultry, game and offal entrées.
    Chef Poissonier   — Fish dishes.
    Chef Entremettier — Vegetable and potato dishes.
    Breakfast Cook   — Shallow fried breakfast dishes.

Cooking Times

These are indicated in the formulae and will vary according to the size, structure, and nature of the product being cooked.

Preparation for Shallow Frying

Season raw foods prior to cooking to ensure flavour. Do not allow foods which have been coated in flour to stand for any length of time prior to cooking (for reason *see* p. 294).

POULTRY   Volaille

Shallow-Fried Chicken   Sautés de Poulet

In readiness for shallow frying (sauter) chicken is usually prepared in one of three ways.

1   Using Whole Chicken Cut into Joints (using medium/large chicken)

	English term	French term
	Winglets	Ailerons
	Wing	Aile
	Breast	Blanc ou poitrine
	Drumstick	Pilon de cuisse
	Thigh	Gras de cuisse

N.B.   The carcase/winglets are generally used for stock-making. Traditionally the trimmed carcase pieces were cooked with sautés to provide flavour and although not served were used as a platform for presentation of chicken.

2 For Smaller Chicken Cut into Two Legs—Two Breasts

	English term	French term
	Breast	Suprême de volaille
	Leg	Cuisse de volaille

3 Using Chicken Breasts (Two per Chicken)

	English term	French term
	Breast	Suprême de volaille

SHALLOW-FRIED CHICKEN   Poulet Sauté

Yield: 4 portions
Chicken cut for sauté
Cooking time: 15 – 25 min

Method 1: Brown Sautés

Lightly season chicken pieces and shallow fry in a film of oil or clarified butter. Commence by cooking the leg joints, after a few minutes add breast and wing cuts. Sauté steadily until evenly browned, tender and cooked through. Remove chicken from sauté pan and keep hot. Drain off excess oil/fat leaving a thin film with which to prepare sauce. Form the sauce (*see* below) replace chicken into sauce and simmer to complete cooking. Portion chicken into service dish, cover with sauce, garnish as required and serve.

Method 2: White Sautés

Proceed as for Method 1 but use butter as the frying medium and cook chicken with the minimum of colour.

Name	Unit	Ingredient	Metric	Imperial	Method of sauté
Poulet Sauté	1	Chicken velouté	250 ml	10 fl oz	White
Archiduc	3/5	Cream	150 ml	6 fl oz	
	1/5	Onion (brunoise)	50 g	2 oz	
	1/5	Brandy	50 ml	2 fl oz	
	1/10	Madeira	25 ml	1 fl oz	
		Squeeze of lemon juice			
		Seasoning			
		Garnish—4 slices truffle			

Name	Unit	Ingredient	Metric	Imperial	Method of sauté

Sweat onions in sauté pan without colour, deglaze
with brandy and Madeira, add velouté and cream
to form a sauce. Flavour with lemon juice and
season to taste. Garnish completed dish

Name	Unit	Ingredient	Metric	Imperial	Method of sauté
Poulet Sauté Bercy	1	Demi-glace	400 ml	16 fl oz	Brown
	1/4	White wine (dry)	100 ml	4 fl oz	
	1/8	Shallots	50 g	2 oz	
		Milled peppercorns/salt			
		Garnish:			
	1/4	mushrooms (sliced sweated)	100 g	4 oz	
	1/4	chipolatas (grilled)	100 g	4 oz	

Sweat shallots without colour in sauté pan, deglaze
with wine and form a reduction. Add demi-glace,
correct seasoning. Garnish completed dish with
mushrooms and chipolatas

Name	Unit	Ingredient	Metric	Imperial	Method of sauté
Poulet Sauté Bonne Femme	1	Demi-glace	400 ml	16 fl oz	Brown
	1/4	White wine	100 ml	4 fl oz	
		Milled peppercorns/salt			
		Garnish:			
	1/4	button onions (glacés à brun)	100 g	4 oz	
	1/4	lardons of bacon (blanched and sautéd)	100 g	4 oz	
	1/4	cocotte potatoes (see p. 334)	100 g	4 oz	

Deglaze sauté pan with wine, reduce, add demi-glace.
Correct seasoning. Garnish completed dish

Name	Unit	Ingredient	Metric	Imperial	Method of sauté
Poulet Sauté Bourguignonne	1	Demi-glace	400 ml	16 fl oz	Brown
	1/4	Burgundy wine (red)	100 ml	4 fl oz	
	1/8	Shallots (brunoise)	50 g	2 oz	
		Milled peppercorns/salt			
		Pinch thyme and bay leaf			
		Garnish with:			
	1/4	button onions (glacés à brun)	100 g	4 oz	
	1/4	button mushrooms (glacés à brun)	100 g	4 oz	
	1/4	lardons of bacon (blanched and sautéd)	100 g	4 oz	
		4 heart-shaped croutons decorated with parsley			

Form a reduction in sauté pan with shallots, wine,
herbs, pepper. Add demi-glace, correct seasoning.
Garnish completed dish

Name	Unit	Ingredient	Metric	Imperial	Method of sauté
Poulet Sauté Champeaux	1	Demi-glace	400 ml	16 fl oz	Brown
	¹/₄	White wine (dry)	100 m!	4 fl oz	
		Seasoning			
		Garnish:			
	¹/₄	button onions (glacés à brun)	100 g	4 oz	
	¹/₄	cocotte potatoes (*see* p. 334)	100 g	4 oz	

Deglaze sauté pan with wine, reduce, add demiglace, correct seasoning. Garnish completed dish

Name	Unit	Ingredient	Metric	Imperial	Method of sauté
Poulet Sauté Chasseur	1	Demi-glace	400 ml	16 fl oz	Brown
	¹/₄	White wine (dry)	100 ml	4 fl oz	
	¹/₄	Button mushrooms (sliced)	100 g	4 oz	
	¹/₄	Tomato concassé	100 g	4 oz	
	¹/₈	Shallots (brunoise)	50 g	2 oz	
		Chopped parsley/tarragon/seasoning			

Sweat shallots and mushrooms, in sauté pan, deglaze with wine, reduce, add demi-glace, tarragon, parsley and tomato concassé. Simmer for 10 minutes

Name	Unit	Ingredient	Metric	Imperial	Method of sauté
Poulet Sauté Duroc		As for Chasseur garnished with cocotte potatoes			Brown

Name	Unit	Ingredient	Metric	Imperial	Method of sauté
Poulet Sauté Hongroise	1	Hongroise sauce (*see* p. 180)	400 ml	16 fl oz	White
	¹/₄	Tomato concassé	100 g	4 oz	
	¹/₄	Cream	100 g	4 oz	
	¹/₄	Onion (brunoise)	100 g	4 oz	
		Pinch of paprika			
		Chopped parsley			
		Seasoning			

Sweat onions in sauté pan without colour, flavour lightly with paprika. Swill out with cream, add hongroise sauce and tomato concassé, correct seasoning. Garnish complete dish with chopped parsley.
N.B. Usually served with braised rice

Name	Unit	Ingredient	Metric	Imperial	Method of sauté
Poulet Sauté Portugaise	1	Tomato sauce	250 ml	10 fl oz	Brown
	⁴/₅	Tomato concassé	200 g	8 oz	
	²/₅	White wine (dry)	100 ml	4 fl oz	
	¹/₅	Shallots (brunoise)	50 g	2 oz	
		Chopped garlic (hint)			
		Pinch of basil			
		Pinch of chopped parsley			
		Milled peppercorns/salt to taste			

Sweat shallots in sauté pan without colour, deglaze with wine, add garlic, basil, parsley and seasoning. Reduce by half, add tomato sauce and tomato concassé. Simmer for 2–3 minutes, correct seasoning.

Poulet Sauté	1	Tomato concassé	400 g	1 lb	Brown
Provençale	⅛	White wine (dry)	50 ml	2 fl oz	
	⅛	Shallot (brunoise)	50 g	2 oz	
		Pinch of salt/milled peppercorns			
		Chopped garlic (hint)			
		Pinch of fine herbs and basil			
		Sweat shallots and garlic without colour in sauté pan, deglaze with wine and reduce by half. Add tomato concassé, herbs, season to taste. Simmer for a few minutes			

N.B. The above sauces are adjusted to correct consistency.

SHALLOW-FRIED CHICKEN BREASTS   Suprêmes de Volaille Sautés

Yield: 4 portions 4 suprêmes (*see* p. 307)
Cooking time: 10 – 15 min

Method 1: Brown Sautés Using Panéd Chicken Suprêmes

Shallow fry prepared chicken (presentation side first), in a film of oil/clarified butter until cooked and golden brown on both sides. Remove chicken from sauté pan, garnish (*see* below) lightly moisten with beurre noisette and a cordon of sauce jus lié. Dress with cutlet frills.

Method 2: White Sautés Using Lightly Floured and Seasoned Suprêmes of Chicken

Shallow fry chicken in clarified butter (presentation side first) with the minimum of colour. When cooked remove suprêmes from sauté pan and keep hot. Drain off excess butter from pan leaving a thin film with which to prepare a sauce. Form the sauce (*see* below) napper, garnish as required and serve.

Examples of Chicken Sautés using Suprêmes: Preparation of Sauce and Garnish for Four Portions

Name	Unit	Ingredient	Metric	Imperial	Method of sauté
Suprême de Volaille Sauté Archiduc		As for 'Poulet Sauté Archiduc' (*see* p. 218) using chicken suprêmes			White
Suprême de Volaille Sauté à la Crème	1	Cream (double)	300 ml	10 fl oz	White
	⅕	Sherry	60 ml	2 fl oz	
		Pinch of cayenne			
		Pinch of salt			
		Deglaze sauté pan with sherry, reduce, add cream and simmer to required consistency. Season with salt and cayenne pepper			

Name	Unit	Ingredient	Metric	Imperial	Method of sauté
Suprême de Volaille Sauté à la Crème aux Champignons	1 ²/₅ ¹/₅	Cream (double) Mushrooms white (sliced) Sherry Squeeze of lemon juice Pinch of salt/cayenne pepper	300 ml 120 g 60 ml	10 fl oz 4 oz 2 fl oz	White

Sweat mushrooms in sauté pan without colour, deglaze with sherry and lemon juice and reduce. Add cream and simmer to required consistency, season with salt and cayenne pepper

Suprême de Volaille Sauté Doria	1	Cucumber (turned and cooked in butter)	100 g	4 oz	Brown panéd

Garnish with cucumber

Suprême de Volaille Sauté Hongroise		As for Poulet Sauté Hongroise (*see* p. 180)			White

Suprême de Volaille Sauté Maréchale		12 Cooked asparagus tips 4 Truffle slices			Brown panéd

Garnish with above

Suprême de Volaille Sauté Maryland		4 Small corn cakes (*see* p. 463) ⎫ shallow fried 4 Small bananas (remove top half ⎬ in butter of skin) ⎭ 4 Grilled bacon rolls 4 Grilled tomatoes			Brown panéd

Horseradish sauce (hot or cold)

Garnish with above, serve horseradish sauce separately.

Suprême de Volaille Sauté Sandeman	1 ²/₅ ¹/₅ ¹/₁₀	Cream (double) Sweet peppers (julienne) Sherry Whisky Pinch of salt and pepper	300 ml 120 g 60 ml 30 ml	10 fl oz 4 oz 2 fl oz 1 fl oz	White

Sweat peppers in sauté pan without colour, deglaze with sherry and whisky, and reduce. Add cream and simmer to required consistency. Correct seasoning

Beef Sautés   Sautés de Boeuf

Small cuts of beef commonly used for sauté.

English term	French term	Yield 4 portions	Explanation and illustration
			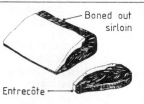
Sirloin steak	Entrecôte	4 × 200 g (8 oz)	Steaks cut from the boned out sirloin (contrefilet)
Minute steak	Entrecôte à la Minute	4 × 150 g (6 oz)	Sirloin steaks batted out thinly
			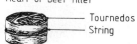
	Tournedos	4 × 150 g (6 oz)	Small round steaks cut from middle of the fillet of beef secured with string

Tail of beef fillet cut into strips or slices	Émincé de Filet Mignon de Boeuf	500 g (1¼ lb)	Filet Mignon de Boeuf

BEEF SAUTÉS

Sautés de Boeuf

(Using cuts shown above)
Yield: *see* chart above
Cooking time: According to requirements

Method

Season selected beef cuts and shallow fry on both sides in clarified butter/oil, to meet customers' requirements. Remove steaks from sauté pan and place aside for service. Drain off excess grease from sauté pan, form the sauce (*see* chart), napper and garnish for service.
   N.B.   All tournedos are placed on croûtes of fried bread for service. Bread absorbs juices from the steak.

Examples of Beef Sautés: Preparation of Sauce an Garnish for 4 Portions

Name	Unit	Ingredient	Metric	Imperial	Examples of cuts used
au Beurre Noisette	1	Beurre noisette	100 g	4 oz	Entrecôte/ Entrecôte à la Minute
aux Champignons	1 ¹/₁₀	Sauce Champignon (à brun) Sherry Chopped parsley	300 ml 30 ml	10 fl oz 1 fl oz	Entrecôte/ Entrecôte à la Minute/ Tournedos
		Deglaze sauté pan with sherry, add sauce champignon and garnish completed dish with chopped parsley			
au Poivre à la Créme	1 ¹/₁₀	Cream (double) Brandy Crushed peppercorns	300 ml 30 ml	10 fl oz 1 fl oz	Entrecôte
		Press peppercorns into the raw meat, lightly season with salt. Cook as for sauté. *Sauce:* Deglaze sauté pan with brandy, add cream and simmer to required consistency. Season to taste.			
Bordelaise	1 ¹/₁₀	Sauce Bordelaise Red wine 8 Slices of poached beef marrow Chopped parsley	300 ml 30 ml	10 fl oz 1 fl oz	Entrecôte/ Tournedos
		Deglaze sauté pan with wine, add sauce. Napper steaks with sauce and garnish with marrow and parsley			

Name	Unit	Ingredient	Metric	Imperial	Examples of cuts used
Chasseur	1	Sauce Chasseur	300 ml	10 fl oz	Entrecôte/
	$\frac{1}{10}$	White wine (dry)	30 ml	1 fl oz	Tournedos/
					Émincé de
		Deglaze sauté pan with wine and add sauce			Filet Mignon
à l'Estragon	1	Sauce Estragon	300 ml	10 fl oz	Entrecôte
	$\frac{1}{10}$	White wine (dry)	30 ml	1 fl oz	Tournedos
		Blanched tarragon leaves			
		Deglaze sauté pan with wine and add sauce. Napper steaks with sauce and garnish with tarragon leaves			
Fleuriste	1	Demi-glace	300 ml	10 fl oz	Tournedos
	$\frac{1}{5}$	White wine (dry)	60 ml	2 fl oz	
		4 Tomatoes filled with Jardinière garnish Seasoning			
		Deglaze sauté pan with wine add demi-glace, correct consistency and seasoning. Napper tournedos and surround with cooked tomato garnish			
Hongroise	1	Sauce Hongroise (*see* p. 180)	300 ml	10 fl oz	Émincé de
	$\frac{1}{10}$	White wine (dry)	30 ml	1 fl oz	Filet Mignon
		Pinch of paprika			
		Season meat with paprika and cook as for sauté. Deglaze sauté pan with wine and add the sauce			
Marchand de Vin	1	Sauce Marchand de Vin	300 ml	10 fl oz	Entrecôte/
	$\frac{1}{10}$	Red wine	30 ml	1 fl oz	Entrecôte à la Minute
		Deglaze sauté pan with wine and add the sauce			
Périgordine	1	Sauce Madère	300 ml	10 fl oz	Tournedos
	$\frac{1}{10}$	Madeira	30 ml	1 fl oz	
		4 slices of truffle			
		Deglaze sauté pan with madeira and add the sauce. Napper steaks with sauce, garnish with truffle			
Rossini		As for Périgordine with the addition of 4 slices of sautéed foie gras to garnish steaks			Tournedos

Name	Unit	Ingredient	Metric	Imperial	Examples of cuts used
Strogonoff	1	Cream (double)	300 ml	10 fl oz	Émincé de
	$1/_5$	Mushrooms (sliced)	60 g	2 oz	Filet Mignon
	$1/_5$	Tomato concassé	60 g	2 oz	
	$1/_5$	Onion (brunoise)	60 g	2 oz	
	$1/_{10}$	White wine (dry)	30 ml	1 fl oz	
		Squeeze of lemon juice			
		Pinch of tarragon			
		Chopped parsley			
		Seasoning			

Sweat onions and mushrooms without colour, Deglaze with wine and lemon juice, add cream and simmer to required consistency. Add herbs, tomato concassé and season to taste

Lamb Sautés   Sautés d'Agneau

Small cuts of lamb commonly used for sauté.

English term	French term	Yield 4 portions	Explanation and illustration

Prepared best-end of lamb

Cutlet

| Lamb cutlets | Côtelettes d'Agneau | 8 prepared cutlets | Cutlets cut from best-end of lamb |

Loin with noisettes cut off on slant, lightly batted out and trimmed

Wedge-shaped noisette

| Lamb noisettes (nut) | Noisette d' Agneau | 8 prepared noisettes | Noisettes cut from boned out loin of lamb |

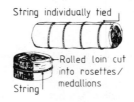

Lamb Rosettes/ Médaillons	Rosettes/ Médaillons d'Agneau	8 prepared rosettes/ médaillons	Rosettes cut from boned out loin of lamb tied into a cylinder

Fillet of lamb cut into slices	Émincé de Filet Mignon d'Agneau	500 g (1¼ lb)	Filet mignon taken from saddle of lamb May be left whole for certain dishes

LAMB SAUTÉS   Sautés d'Agneau
(Using cuts shown above)

Yield: *see* chart
Cooking time: 4 – 10 min
(according to customers' requirements)

Method 1: Prepared pané

Shallow fry prepared lamb on both sides in clarified butter/oil to meet customers' require-ments. Remove from sauté pan garnish, lightly moisten with beurre noisette. Dress cutlets with frills.

Method 2: Left Plain

Season lamb, shallow fry on both sides in clarified butter/oil to meet customers' require-ments. Remove from sauté pan and place aside for service. Drain excess grease from sauté pan, form the sauce (see chart), napper and garnish for service.

N.B. Noisettes/rosettes are placed on croûtes of fried bread for service – the bread absorbs juices from the lamb.

Examples of Lamb Sautés: Preparation of Sauce and Garnish for 4 Portions

Name	Unit	Ingredient	Metric	Imperial	Examples of cuts used	Method of preparation for sauté
à l'Anglaise	1	Beurre noisette	100 g	4 oz	Côtelettes	Pané
Chasseur		As for Sauté of Beef Chasseur (p. 314)			Émincé de Filet Mignon	Plain
Clamart	1 ¹/₁₀	Sauce Madère Madeira 4 Artichoke bottoms filled with cooked peas or peas purée (*see* p. 274) Deglaze sauté pan with Madeira and add sauce. Napper lamb and surround with cooked artichoke bottoms	300 ml 30 ml	10 fl oz 1 fl oz	Noisettes/ Rosettes	Plain
Fleuriste		As for Sauté of Beef Fleuriste (p. 314)			Noisettes/ Rosettes	Plain
Hongroise		As for Sauté of Beef Hongroise (p. 314)			Émincé de Filet Mignon	Plain
Maréchale		As for Suprême de Volaille Sauté Maréchale (p. 311)			Côtelettes	Pané
Masséna	1	Sauce Béarnaise 4 Artichoke bottoms (cooked *see* p. 166) 8 slices poached marrow Fill artichoke bottoms with bearnaise sauce to garnish cooked noisettes. Place a slice of marrow on each noisette	300 ml	10 fl oz	Noisettes/ Rosettes	Plain
Niçoise	1 ²/₅ ²/₅ ²/₅ ¹/₅	Jus lié Tomato concassé French beans (reheated in butter) Cocotte potatoes White wine (dry) Deglaze sauté pan with white wine, add sauce correct seasoning. Napper lamb and garnish: place tomato on top of each rosette and surround with potatoes and French beans	300 ml 120 g 120 g 120 g 60 ml	10 fl oz 4 oz 4 oz 4 oz 2 fl oz	Rosettes/ Noisettes	Plain

Name	Unit	Ingredient	Metric	Imperial	Examples of cuts used	Method of sauté
Réform	1	Sauce Réform	250 ml	10 fl oz	Côtelettes	Pané
		Pané cutlets with the addition of finely chopped ham and parsley in the crumbs. Cook as for method 1, serve sauce Réform separately				

Veal and Pork Sautés   Sautés de Veau/Porc

Small cuts of veal and pork commonly used for sauté

English term	French term	Yield 4 portions	Explanation and illustration

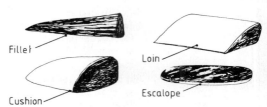

Rib-bone ends

Back bone removed (chined) and rib-ends trimmed for cutlets (see pork cutlet)

Cutlet

Veal/pork cutlets	Côte de Veau/Porc	4 × 150 g (6 oz) cutlets	Cutlets taken from best-end of veal/pork

Fillet

Loin

Cushion

Escalope

Veal/pork escalopes	Escalope de Veau/Porc	4 × 150 g (6 oz) escalopes	Batted out slices of veal/pork taken from fillet or cushion of veal and fillet or boned-out pork loin

Studded with fat

Veal grenadins	Grenadin de Veau	8 × 75 g (3 oz) grenadins	Thick escalopes from fillet or cushion of veal which are studded (piquéd with strips of bacon/pork fat)

Studded with fat / truffle
String to keep in shape

| Veal médaillons | Médaillon de Veau | 4 × 150 g (6 oz) médaillons | Médaillons are round cuts (small tournedos) taken from fillet or cushion of veal, shaped like tournedos and secured with string. May be studded with fat or truffle. |

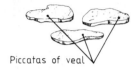

Piccatas of veal

| Veal piccata | Piccata de Veau | 12 × 50 g (2 oz) piccatas | Tiny escalopes taken from fillet of veal |

VEAL AND PORK SAUTÉS   Sautés de Veau/Porc
(Using cuts shown above)

Yield: 4 portions (*see* chart)
Cooking time: 3 – 10 min (according to cuts used)

Method 1: Prepared Pané

Shallow fry prepared cuts in a film of oil/clarified butter until cooked and golden brown on both sides. Remove veal/pork cuts from sauté pan, garnish (*see* chart) moisten with beurre noisette and a cordon of sauce Jus lié.

  N.B.   Cutlets are dressed with frills.

Method 2: Prepared in Seasoned Flour

Shallow fry on both sides in a film of clarified butter, cook to light brown colour. When cooked remove veal/pork from sauté pan and keep hot. Drain off excess butter from pan, leaving a thin film with which to prepare a sauce. Form sauce (*see* chart), napper garnish as required and serve.

Examples of Veal/Pork Sautés: Preparation of Sauce and Garnish for 4 Portions

Name	Unit	Ingredient	Metric	Imperial	Examples of cuts used	Method of preparation for sauté
à l'Anglaise	1	Beurre noisette	100 g	4 oz	Escalopes/ Côtes	Pané

Name	Unit	Ingredient	Metric	Imperial	Examples of cuts used	Method of preparation for sauté
à la Crème		As for Suprême de Volaille à la Crème (p. 310)			Escalopes/ granadins/ médaillons/ piccatas	Floured
à la Crème aux Champ-ignons		As for Suprême de Volaille à la Crème aux Champignons (p. 311)			Escalopes/ grenadins/ medaillons/ piccatas	Floured
au Madère	1 $^1/_{10}$	Sauce Madère Madeira	300 ml 30 ml	10 fl oz 1 fl oz	As above	Floured
		Deglaze sauté pan with Madeira and add sauce				
aux Champignons		As for Beef Sauté aux Champignon *see* p. 313			As above	Floured
Cordon Bleu		4 Slices of cooked ham 4 Slices of gruyère cheese 4 Rondels of peeled lemon			Escalopes	Pané
		Place ham and cheese in one half of raw escalope, fold over to seal, bat edges, pané and cook as for method one. Garnish with lemon				
Holstein		4 Shallow fried eggs 8 Slices of anchovy fillet 4 Rondels of peeled lemon			Escalopes	Pané
		Garnish cooked escalopes by placing eggs on top. Finish with criss-cross of anchovy and lemon slices				
Italienne		Garnish with Spaghetti Italienne (*see* p. 255)			Côtes/ escalopes	Pané
Maréchale		As for Suprême de Volaille Sauté Maréchale (*see* p. 311)			Côtes/ escalopes	Pané

Name	Unit	Ingredient	Metric	Imperial	Examples of cuts used	Method of preparation for sauté
au Marsala	1 1 ¹/₄	Strong veal stock Marsala (dry) Butter Seasoning	100 ml 100 ml 25 g	4 fl oz 4 fl oz 1 oz	Grenadin/ piccata	Floured
		Deglaze sauté pan with Marsala and veal stock, boil briskly and reduce until sauce takes on a glazing consistency. Add butter, season to taste.				
Milanaise		Garnish with Spaghetti Milanaise (*see* p. 255)			Côtes/ escalopes	Pané
Napolitaine		Garnish with Spaghetti Napolitaine see p. 255)			Côtes/ escalopes	Pané
Viennoise		4 Stuffed olives 4 Anchovy fillets 4 Rondels of peeled lemon 1 Hard boiled egg (sieve white and yolk separately) Chopped parsley			Escalopes	Pané
		Place lemons on to cooked escalopes, wrap olives in anchovy fillets and place on to lemon. Decorate escalope with sieved egg and chopped parsley.				

Venison Sautées   Sautées de Venaison

Small cuts of venison commonly used for sauté

English term	French term	Yield 4 portions	Explanation and illustration
			Noisettes ——————
Venison noisettes	Noisettes de Venaison	8 × 75 g (3 oz) noisettes	*Noisettes* are cut slantways from boned out loin of venison, lightly bat out to shape

| Venison cutlets | Côtelettes de Venaison | 8 × 75 g (3 oz) cutlets | Long saddle of venison with best-end |

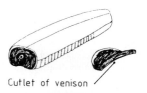

Cutlet of venison

Cutlets taken from best-end of venison, and lightly batted to shape

VENISON SAUTÉES (Using cuts shown above)

Sautées de Venaison

Yield: 4 portions (*see* chart)
Cooking time: 8 – 10 min

Preparation for Cooking

Marinade cuts of venison in red wine for 24 hours before use.

Method

Season cuts of venison with salt and mill pepper. Shallow fry in a film of oil/clarified butter to saignant (underdone). Remove meat from sauté pan, keep hot, pour away excess grease and congealed blood, prepare sauce (see chart), napper and garnish as required. Dress cutlets with frills.

N.B. If sautéed venison is overcooked it becomes dry and tough.

Examples of Venison Sautées: Preparation of Sauces and Garnish for 4 Portions

Name	Unit	Ingredient	Metric	Imperial
au Porto	1	Sauce Porto	300 ml	10 fl oz
	1/10	Port	30 ml	1 fl oz
		Deglaze sauté pan with port and add sauce. Bring to boil and napper venison		
aux Cerises	1	Sauce Poivrade	300 ml	10 fl oz
	1	Poached stoned red cherries	300 g	10 oz
	1/10	Red wine	30 ml	1 fl oz
		Deglaze sauté pan with wine and add sauce. Add cherries, bring to the boil and napper venison		
Chasseur		As for Sauté of Beef Chasseur (*see* p. 314)		
Smitane	1	Sauce Smitane	300 ml	10 fl oz
		Napper venison with sauce		

SHALLOW-FRIED OFFAL   Sautés d'Abats

Shallow Fried Liver   Foie Sauté

Yield: 4 portions
Cooking time: 3 – 5 min
400 g (1 lb) calves, lambs', pigs' liver – skin liver remove tubes and gristle. Cut slantways
into thin slices.

Method

Pass liver through seasoned flour and shallow fry quickly in oil on both sides until sealed
and just cooked. Present for service with accompanying sauce and garnish (*see* chart).

Sauce and Garnish for 4 Portions

English term	French term	Unit	Ingredient	Metric	Imperial
Fried liver with onion sauce	Foie de Veau/ d'Agneau Sauté Lyonnaise	1	Sauce Lyonnaise	300 ml	10 fl oz
			Lightly napper liver with a little sauce and serve remainder in sauceboat		
Fried liver with bacon	Foie de Veau/ d'Agneau Sauté au Lard	1 1	Beurre noisette Sauce Jus lié 8 Thin rashers of grilled bacon	100 g 100 ml	4 oz 4 fl oz
			Garnish cooked liver with bacon, surround with a cordon of Jus lié and napper with beurre noisette		

SHALLOW-FRIED KIDNEYS   Rognons Sautés

Yield: 4 portions
8 Lambs kidneys – cut in half lengthways, remove skin and centre gristle.
Cooking time: 5 – 8 min

Method

Season kidneys and shallow fry in a film of oil or clarified butter until sealed and just
cooked. Remove from sauté pan and keep hot. Drain off excess fat and congealed blood,
leaving a thin film of oil/butter with which to prepare a sauce. Form sauce (*see* chart),
napper kidneys, garnish as required and serve.
   N.B.   The following dishes may be served with a rice pilaff.

Preparation of Sauce and Garnish for 4 Portions

Name	Unit	Ingredient	Metric	Imperial
Rognons Sautés Chasseur		Prepare sauce and finish as for Sauté de Boeuf Chasseur (*see* p. 314).		
Rognons Sautés au Madère	1	Sauce Madère	300 ml	10 fl oz
	$^1/_{10}$	Madeira	30 ml	1 fl oz
		Deglaze pan with Madeira and add sauce. Bring to boil and napper kidneys		
Rognons Sautés Turbigo		As for Rognon Sauté au Madère garnished:		
	1	Button mushrooms (glacés à brun)	100 g	4 oz
		8 small chipolatas		
		4 heart-shaped croûtes		
		Chopped parsley		

SHALLOW-FRIED CHICKEN LIVERS IN MADEIRA SAUCE
Foie de Volaille Sauté à Sauce Madère

Yield: 4 portions
Cooking time: 4 – 6 min

Unit	Ingredient	Metric	Imperial
1	Chicken livers	400 g	1 lb
$^5/_8$	Sauce Madère	250 ml	10 fl oz
$^1/_8$	Madeira	50 ml	2 fl oz
$^1/_8$	Butter	50 g	2 oz
	Seasoning		

Method

Trim livers by removing gall bladders and stained liver. Cut in half, lightly season and sauté very quickly in hot butter until sealed and cooked. Remove livers into serving dish and keep hot. Remove excess grease from sauté pan, deglaze with Madeira, add sauce, correct seasoning and strain over liver to serve.

N.B.   Usually served with an accompaniment of braised rice.

SHALLOW-FRIED CALVES SWEETBREADS   Ris de Veau Sautés

Yield: 4 portions 600 g (1 $^1/_4$ lb)
Cooking time: 5 – 8 min

Preparation of Sweetbreads Prior to Shallow Frying

Using white braised sweetbreads (p. 370) drain from unthickened cooking liquor), allow to cool and press gently between trays until set. Pressing ensures close texture and ease of handling. Slice into *thick* escalopes and prepare for shallow frying.

Method 1: Prepared Pané

Shallow fry in a film of oil/clarified butter until cooked and golden brown on both sides. Place in service dish and garnish (*see* chart). Serve moistened with beurre noisette and a cordon of Sauce Jus lié.

Method 2: Prepared in Seasoned Flour

Shallow fry on both sides in a film of clarified butter, cook to light brown. Remove from sauté pan and keep hot. Drain off excess butter from pan leaving a thin film with which to prepare sauce if required (*see* chart). Form the sauce, napper sweetbreads, garnish as required and serve.

Examples of Ris De Veau Sautés: Preparation of Sauce and Garnish for 4 Portions

Name	Unit	Ingredient	Metric	Imperial	Method of preparation for sauté
Escalope de Ris de Veau à l'Anglaise	1	Beurre noisette	100 g	4 oz	Pané
Escalope de Ris de Veau aux Champignons	1 ²/₅ ¹/₁₀	Cream (double) Mushrooms (sliced) Brandy Squeeze of lemon juice Chopped parsley Seasoning	300 ml 120 g 30 ml	10 fl oz 4 oz 1 oz	Floured
		Sweat mushrooms in sauté pan without colour, deglaze with brandy and lemon juice. Add cream and simmer to coating consistency. Correct seasoning. Napper sweetbreads and garnish with chopped parsley			
Escalope de Ris de Veau Florentine	1 ⁴/₅ ¹/₅	Sauce Mornay Cooked leaf spinach Grated cheese	300 ml 240 g 60 g	10 fl oz 8 oz 2 oz	Floured
		Place cooked escalopes on spinach in buttered serving dish. Napper with mornay sauce, sprinkle with grated cheese, gratinate and serve			
Escalope de Ris de Veau Maréchale		12 Cooked asparagus tips 4 Slices truffle			Pané
		Garnish sweetbreads with above			

Shallow-Fried Miscellaneous Dishes

BASIC RAW FORCEMEAT FOR BITOKS (beef, veal or pork)

Bitoks

Yield: 4 portions
Cooking time: 8 – 10 min

Unit	Ingredient	Metric (g)	Imperial (oz)
1	Selected raw meat (lean, finely minced)	360	12
$1/4$	White breadcrumbs (soaked in milk)	90	3
$1/4$	Onion brunoise (sweated in butter)	90	3
$1/8$	Whole egg (beaten)	45	$1^1/2$
	Seasoning		
	Chopped parsley		
	Oil (for shallow frying)		

Method

Squeeze breadcrumbs to remove milk. Re-mince meat with breadcrumbs then add onion, parsley, seasoning and mix thoroughly, binding with the egg. Refrigerate to set. Fry a small portion to test for seasoning. Correct seasoning if required. Divide the mixture into eight portions and shape each into a medallion on a lightly floured board. Shallow fry steadily in oil on both sides until cooked and browned.

Drain, and present with a suitable sauce and garnish, *see* below. The sauce may be used to napper the bitoks or served in a sauceboat as an accompaniment.

Examples of Dishes Prepared Using the Above Formula

Menu term	Main ingredient	Garnish	Sauce
Bitok de Boeuf (hamburger steak)	Beef	French fried onions	Piquante
Vienna Steak	Beef	Shallow fried egg	Lyonnaise
Bitok de Porc (pork Bitok)	Pork	Chopped parsley	Smitane/Chasseur/ Hongroise
Bitok de Veau (veal Bitok)	Veal	Chopped parsley	As for pork

N.B.   Other suitable garnishes and sauces may be used for Bitoks.

BASIC RAW FORCEMEAT FOR POJARSKI (for veal or chicken)

Côtelette de Veau/Volaille Pojarski

Yield: 4 portions
Cooking time: 8 – 10 min

Unit	Ingredient	Metric	Imperial
1	Chicken or veal (lean and finely minced)	360 g	12 oz
¼	White breadcrumbs (lightly soaked in milk)	90 g	3 oz
⅛	Double cream	45 ml	1½ fl oz
⅛	Melted butter	45 g	1½ oz
	Squeeze of lemon juice		
	Pinch of nutmeg		
	Chopped parsley		
	Seasoning		

Method

Squeeze breadcrumbs to remove any excess milk. Combine minced meat with soaked breadcrumbs and pass through fine mincer to ensure even distribution. Add seasoning, nutmeg, and parsley. Place mixture in refrigerator or into a mixing bowl over ice to chill. Gradually work in the cream and melted butter and flavour with lemon juice. Mix until stiff. Fry off a small portion to test for seasoning and correct if necessary. Divide mixture into four equal portions and mould into cutlet shapes. Pané and shallow fry on both sides until cooked and golden brown. Drain well and present for service moistened with beurre noisette and accompanied by a selected sauce.

Examples of Dishes Prepared Using the Above Formula

Menu term	Main ingredient	Selected sauce
Côtelette de Veau Pojarski (veal Pojarski)	Lean veal (raw)	Chasseur/Smitane/Réform
Côtelette de Volaille Pojarski (chicken Pojarski)	Lean chicken (raw)	Chasseur/Smitane/Réform

N.B. Pojarskis may be served and garnished as for panéed veal escalopes/chicken suprêmes (*see* pp. 319 and 310 respectively).

Shallow-Fried Fish

Poisson Meunière

Shallow frying is employed for cooking a wide variety of fish and shellfish. Certain small fish are left whole whereas others are prepared into smaller cuts. The whole fish, shellfish and cuts most commonly used for shallow frying are listed below.

Whole Fish (prepared for cooking)

English term	French term	Yield 4 portions
Dover sole	Sole Douvres	4 × 300 g/12 oz
Herring	Hareng	4 × 200 g/8 oz
Mackerel	Maquereau	4 × 200 g/8 oz
Trout	Truite	4 × 200 g/8 oz
Whiting	Merlan	4 × 200 g/8 oz
Shellfish		
Scallops	Coquilles St. Jacques	400 g/1 lb shelled wt
Scampi	Langoustine	400 g/1 lb shelled wt

Fish Commonly Prepared in Small Cuts for Shallow Frying

English term	French term	Common cuts (see pp.210 and 239)
Cod	Cabillaud	Filet – Darne – Suprême
Brill	Barbue	Suprême – Tronçon
Dover Sole	Sole Douvres	Filet – Goujons
Haddock	Aigrefin	Filet – Suprême – Darne
Hake	Colin	Filet – Suprême – Darne
Halibut	Flétan	Suprême – Tronçon
Lemon sole	Sole Limande	Filet – Goujons
Monk		Goujons
Plaice	Plie	Filet – Goujons
Red Mullet	Rouget	Filet
Salmon	Saumon	Suprême – Darne
Salmon Trout	Truite Saumonée	Suprême
Skate	Raie	Wing
Turbot	Turbot	Suprême – Tronçon

Fish Cuts in Common Use for Shallow Frying

Filet
Suprême } de Poisson – as for deep frying (*see* p. 299).
Goujons

English term	French term	Yield 4 portions	Explanation and illustration
Steak of round fish	Darne	4 × 150 g (6 oz)	A cut of round fish on the bone

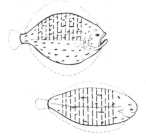

Steak of flat fish	Tronçon	4 × 150 g (6 oz)	A cut of flat fish on the bone

(a) Cut in half lengthways then into tronçons

(b) Cut across completely

SHALLOW-FRIED FISH (using cuts shown above)

Poisson Meunière

Yield: 4 portions (*see* chart)
Cooking time: 3 – 10 min
according to cut used

Unit	Ingredient	Metric (g)	Imperial (oz)
	Selected fish (*see* chart above)		
1	Butter	100	4
¹/₂	Seasoned flour	50	2
¹/₂	Oil/clarified butter	50	2
	Garnish of 4 lemon slices/segments (without skin)		
	Chopped parsley		
	Squeeze of lemon juice		

Method

Pass fish through seasoned flour and shallow fry on both sides in oil (presentation side first) until cooked and golden brown. Remove fish to service dish, garnish with lemon. Prepare 'beurre meunière' (*see* p. 200) with butter and lemon juice, pour over fish and garnish with chopped parsley.

N.B.   Fish may be shallow fried in clarified butter and garnished with lemon wedge and sprig of parsley in place of beurre meunière. In these instances the term meunière would not be appropriate on the menu and the term doré could be used, e.g. Filet de Sole Doré (gilded sole).

Extensions of Fish Meunière: Garnish for 4 Portions

Menu term	Unit	Ingredient	Metric (g)	Imperial (oz)
Poisson Amandine	1	Flaked almonds	100	4
		Bake almonds brown, sprinkle over fish and finish à la meunière		
Poisson Belle Meunière		4 Mushroom heads 4 Slices of tomato 4 Soft roes		
		Shallow fry garnish and place on fish, finish à la meunière		
Poisson Bretonne à la Meunière	1 1	Picked shrimps Sliced mushrooms	50 50	2 2
		Shallow fry garnish, sprinkle over fish and finish à la meunière		
Poisson Cléopâtre à la Meunière	1 1	Picked shrimps Capers 4 Soft roes	50 50	2 2
		Shallow fry garnish and place on fish, finish à la meunière		
Poisson Doria	1	Shaped cucumber	100	4
		Cook cucumber in butter, garnish fish and finish à la meunière		
Poisson Grenobloise	1	Capers	50	2
		Sprinkle capers over fish and finish à la meunière		

N.B.   Generally with the exception of Poisson Grenobloise the above meunière preparations are garnished with lemon slices (without skin). Grenobloise is garnished with lemon segments (without skin).

Poisson Murat	1 1	Cooked artichoke bottoms (*see* p. 166) Potatoes (dice)	100 100	4 4
		Sauté potatoes until cooked and golden brown, slice artichoke and toss quickly with potatoes, sprinkle over fish and finish à la meunière		
		For goujons garnish and fish may be tossed in in butter together		

SHALLOW FRIED SCAMPI/SCALLOPS WITH TOMATOES AND GARLIC

Scampi/Coquilles St. Jacques
Sautée Provençale

Yield: 4 portions
Cooking time: 5 – 8 min

Unit	Ingredient	Metric	Imperial
1	Scampi/scallops (shelled)	400 g	1 lb
3/4	Tomato concassé	300 g	12 oz
1/8	White wine (dry)	50 ml	2 fl oz
1/8	Shallots (brunoise)	50 g	2 oz
1/8	Seasoned flour	50 g	2 oz
1/8	Oil/butter	50 g	2 oz
	Hint of garlic		
	Pinch of fine herbs and basil		
	Pinch of salt/milled pepper		

Method

Sweat shallots in oil for a few minutes without colour, pass scampi through seasoned flour and add to shallots cook to light brown. Add garlic, déglacé with white wine reduce by half, add tomato concassé, herbs and simmer for 2 – 3 minutes. Correct seasoning and serve accompanied with rice pilaff.

SCAMPI NEWBURG

Langoustine Newburg

Yield: 4 portions
Cooking time: 5 – 8 min

Unit	Ingredient	Metric	Imperial
1	Scampi (shelled)	400 g	1 lb
3/4	Cream (double)	300 ml	12 fl oz
1/8	Butter	50 g	2 oz
1/8	Madeira	50 ml	2 fl oz
1/8	Egg yolk		
1/16	Brandy	25 ml	1 fl oz
	Seasoning		
	Rice pilaff for 4 portions (p. 244)		

Method

Mix egg yolk with a little of the cream to form a liaison and put aside.
Season scampi and gently sauté in heated butter until cooked. Flame with brandy, add Madeira and reduce by half. Pour on the cream, bring to boil and simmer briskly to coating consistency. Correct seasoning, remove from heat, stir in liaison and do not reboil. Serve with an accompaniment of rice pilaff. Garnish scampi with slices of truffle which have been flavoured in brandy.

SCAMPI THERMIDOR

Langoustine Thermidor

Yield: 4 portions
Cooking time: 5–8 min

Unit	Ingredient	Metric	Imperial
1	Scampi (shelled)	400 g	1 lb
¾	Sauce thermidor (*see* p. 182)	300 ml	12 fl oz
⅛	Butter	50 g	2 oz
	Seasoning		
	Parmesan to gratinate		
	4 Slices truffle		

Method

Season scampi and gently sauté in heated butter until cooked. Lightly sauce service dish, add cooked scampi, napper with sauce, sprinkle with parmesan cheese and gratinate. Garnish with slices of truffle.

Shallow-Fried Vegetables/Potatoes

Légumes/Pommes de Terre Sautés/ées

Vegetable and potato preparations in this study are shallow fried from raw. Other dishes that are pre-cooked then completed by shallow frying are outlined in Chapter 27 under combined methods.

SHALLOW FRIED EGG PLANT/ BABY MARROW WITH TOMATO AND GARLIC

Aubergine/Courgette Sautée Provençale

Yield: 4 portions
Cooking time: 10–15 min

Unit	Ingredient	Metric (g)	Imperial (oz)
1	Aubergine or courgette (peeled and sliced)	400	16
½	Tomato concassé	200	8
¼	Onion (shredded)	100	4
⅛	Oil/butter	50	2
	Hint of chopped garlic		
	Pinch of fine herbs and basil		
	Pinch of salt/milled peppercorns		

Method

Sweat onion in oil without colour, add aubergine or courgettes. Add garlic, herbs and seasoning, cover with lid and sweat for 10 min. Add tomato concasse; correct seasoning, simmer for 1 – 2 minutes and serve.

SHALLOW-FRIED MUSHROOMS   Champignons Sautés

Yield: 4 portions
Cooking time: 3 – 5 min

Unit	Ingredient	Metric (g)	Imperial (oz)
1	Mushrooms (trimmed and washed)	400	16
1/8	Butter	50	2
	Chopped parsley		
	Pinch of salt/milled peppercorns		

Method

Place mushrooms in heated butter, lightly season and shallow fry until cooked and light brown. Drain well and serve sprinkled with chopped parsley.

Shallow-Fried Onions   Oignons Sautés

Peel and shred onions and proceed as for Champignons Sautés. Usually used as an accompaniment with hamburgers, sausages, liver, etc.

Shallow-Fried Button Onions   Oignons Bouton Sautés

Peel onions and continue as for Champignons Sautés. (Pinch of sugar may be added to effect browning.)

SHALLOW-FRIED POTATOES   Pommes de Terre Sautées

Yield: 4 portions
(using raw potatoes)
Cooking time: 15 – 20 min (according to shape of potato used)

Unit	Ingredient	Metric (g)	Imperial (oz)
1	Potatoes (peeled and cut to required shape)	400	16
1/8	Oil/butter	50	2
	Seasoning		
	Chopped parsley		

Method

Cut potatoes into required shape (*see* chart below). Sauté in oil/butter until cooked and golden brown. Drain off fat, lightly season and serve sprinkled with chopped parsley.

Potato Dishes Prepared using Sauté Method of Cookery

Name	Shape of potato cut and garnish
Pommes Sautées à Cru	Slice potatoes into even rondels
Pommes Sautées Columbine	Slice potatoes into even rondels add julienne of pimento during cooking
Pommes Parmentier	Cut potatoes into 1 cm ($\frac{1}{2}$ in) cubes
Pommes Sablées	As for Parmentier but sprinkle with breadcrumbs near end of cooking
Pommes Cocotte	Turn potatoes into small barrels
Pommes Noisette	Scoop potatoes into balls using a parisienne cutter
Pommes Parisienne	As for Pommes Noisette but roll in melted meat glaze for service

21

The Principles and Practice of Stewing and Braising

To Stew   Étuver

The French verb 'étuver' literally translated means 'to cook in its own juice'. In culinary terms stewing can best be defined as slowly cooking food in its own juices with the aid of a minimum amount of moistening agent in the form of stock, wine, beer, sauce, butter, etc. During cooking the liquid is flavoured by extractives from the stewed food, the result is a highly-flavoured liquor or sauce which forms an integral part of the stew. Throughout this process, which is generally a lengthy one, evaporation is kept to a minimum by covering the stewing vessel with a tight-fitting lid and by simmering the stew on the stove top or in an oven (oven stewing).

Condensation, which continually forms on the inside of the lid, acts as a self-basting process keeping the food moist. If the rate of evaporation is not kept to a minimum the stew will become dry and could burn. Therefore it may be necessary to add additional liquid as needed throughout the cooking period.

Once cooked the liquid and food are usually served together to form the complete dish.

Tougher cuts of meat may be made tender and palatable by this method (*see* Chapter 3 p. 58 concerning foods selected for stewing). Foods for stewing are cut into small pieces or cuts before cooking and may comprise of meats, fish, vegetables and fruit.

Notes concerning Stewing and Braising

The techniques of stewing or braising may be employed when cooking animal protein, vegetables or fruit. When a traditional kitchen brigade is employed the following Chefs de Partie are usually concerned with the preparation and cooking of braises and stews:

Chef Saucier   — butcher's meats, offal, poultry and game dishes
Chef Poissonnier   — fish dishes
Chef Entremettier   — vegetable dishes including potatoes
Chef Garde-Manger   — involved with initial preparation of
                        meats and fish prior to cooking

Breakfast Cook or
  Chef Pâtissier   — fruit dishes for breakfast.

Suitable Meats for Stewing and Braising

Item	Stewing Cuts	Braising cuts and joints
Lamb	Middle neck, breast, shoulder, chump	Shoulder (whole), chump, tongue, heart, sweetbreads
Beef	Shin, topside, silverside, thin and thick flank, chuck, sticking piece, plate, leg of mutton cut, ox kidney tripe	Topside, thick flank, middle rib, chuck, leg of mutton, ox liver, ox heart, ox tongue
Pork	Shoulder belly, spare rib	Shoulder
Veal	Neck, shoulder, breast, knuckle, kidney	Neck, shoulder, best end, saddle, leg cuts, sweetbreads, tongues
Poultry	Chicken	Duck, turkey winglets
Game	feathered game, furred game — rabbit, hare, venison, (neck, shoulder, breast)	Rabbit, hare, wild duck, feathered game, e.g. pheasant

Cooking times

These are indicated in the recipes and will vary according to the size, structure and nature of food being cooked.

Preparation

All the initial preparation of meats and fish would be carried out in the larder, under the direction of the Chef Garde-Manger. Certain joints for braising may be larded and/or marinaded prior to cooking (*see* p. 360) to ensure adequate portions.

Selecting the vessel

The size and shape of the cooking vessel will be determined by the volume of the food being cooked and whether cooking is carried out on the stove top or in the oven. The size of vessel used will also affect the amount of stock employed in the recipe and the degree of adjustment required to correct the consistency of the finished sauce.

Stock

The flavour and colour of stock used will be determined by the type of meat being cooked and the colour required in the finished dish, e.g. brown beef stew using brown beef stock.

Achieving Correct Colour And Flavour

When a *brown colour* is required the meat and vegetables are sealed and browned in oil/dripping at a high temperature to ensure correct colour and sealing of the meat. Colouring is also achieved by browning the roux (when employed) and by using brown stock. If a *white coloured* product is required less heat is applied to seal gently and without browning. The most suitable cooking mediums for this process are butter and margarine. Where a roux is employed it is cooked to the blond stage before being moistened with stock to effect a white colour. In some instances meats used for white stews are blanched and refreshed as a means of sealing the meat and also extracting the scum, which would otherwise discolour the resultant sauce.

Care during cooking

Throughout cooking, items need to be checked periodically to ensure that stock levels are maintained and that the food is not adhering to the base of the cooking vessel as this could result in a burnt stew. Over cooking results in unpalatable meat which breaks up, becomes stringy in texture and difficult to handle.

Adjusting the sauce

On completion of cooking the flavoursome liquor is adjusted for consistency. This is achieved by one of the following:
  (a) reducing the sauce;
  (b) whisking in beurre manié, arrowroot or cornflour, and reboiling to cook the starch and effect thickening;
  (c) adding demi-glace, jus lié or velouté sauce as required by the dish in question.

Stewing

Meat stews

Stewing meat is an economical method of cooking as it allows the use of the less expensive cuts of meat.
Generally meat stews can be categorised as follows:

Brown stews

The articles being cooked are browned, which results in the stew taking on a bronze colour.
    Examples of brown stews are:
Brown beef stew – Ragoût de Boeuf
Brown lamb stew – Navarin d'Agneau

White Stews

The article being stewed is kept white at the beginning of and throughout the cooking process.
    Examples of white stews:
White lamb stew – Blanquette d' Agneau
White chicken stew – Fricassée de Volaille

Miscellaneous Stews

This refers to stews that cannot be strictly classified as above.
Examples of such stews are:
Spiced stews – curries, goulashes, Chile Con Carne, Osso Bucco
Poultry and game stews - Coq au Vin, Salmis, Civet
Unthickened stews – Lancashire Hot Pot, Chop d'Agneau Champvallon, Irish Stew.

BROWN STEW   Ragoût Brun

Yield: 4 portions
Cooking time: 1½—2 hrs
Cooking temperature:
Moderate oven 150° C (300° F)

Unit	Ingredient	Metric (g)	Imperial (oz)
1	Stewing meat (prepared large dice)	600	20
⅕	Mirepoix (medium) or Onion (finely diced) — According to requirements *see* chart	120	4
¹⁄₂₀	Flour	30	1
¹⁄₂₀	Oil or dripping	30	1
¹⁄₄₀	Tomato purée	15	½
	Bouquet garni		
	Seasoning		
	Hint of garlic		
★	Brown stock/liquid		

★ Sufficient stock to cover meat during cooking and also form a lightly thickened sauce with the roux. An *approximate guide* is EQUAL QUANTITIES OF STOCK TO MEAT i.e. 1:1.

Method

Lightly season meat with salt and pepper and seal quickly in heated oil/dripping to colour light brown. Add mirepoix or onion and continue cooking to golden brown. Add flour and singe brown. Add tomato purée, stir in stock, bring to boil and skim. Add bouquet garni and additional flavourings.

Cover with tight-fitting lid, stew gently on stove top or in moderate oven, check periodically until meat is cooked. Once cooked remove meat into a clean vessel, correct consistency and seasoning of sauce, reboil and strain through fine chinois on to the meat. Garnish as required and serve.

Examples of Brown Stews Prepared from Above Formula:

Main ingredient and Garnish (in relation to 1-unit 600 g (1¼ lb) selected meat)

English term	Unit	Ingredient	Metric (g)	Imperial (oz)	French term
Lamb Stews Brown lamb stew		Stewing lamb (use mirepoix for formula)			Navarin d'Agneau
		As above garnished with:			Navarin d'Agneau:
	²/₅	{ glazed turned carrots, turnips and { button onions à brun	240	8	Printanier
Brown lamb stews with vegetables	²/₅	{ glazed paysanne { of vegetables	240	8	Paysanne
	²/₅	{ glazed julienne { of vegetables	240	8	Julienne
	²/₅	{ glazed jardinière { of vegetables	240	8	Jardinière
Brown lamb stew	¹/₅	Glazed turned carrots	120	4	Navarin d'Agneau
Bourgeoise	¹/₅	Glazed button onions à brun	120	4	Bourgeoise
	¹/₁₀	Lardons of bacon	60	2	
Brown Beef stews Brown beef stew		Stewing beef (use mirepoix for recipe)			Ragoût de Boeuf
Brown beef stew with vegetables		As for lamb stew, *see* chart above			
Brown beef stew Bourgeoise		As for lamb stew, *see* chart above			Ragoût de Boeuf Bourgeoise
Brown beef stew with dumplings		Garnish with 8 suet dumplings (*see* p. 510)			Ragoût de Boeuf à L'Anglaise
Brown beef stew in red wine		Replace half of the stock with red wine			Ragoût de Boeuf au Vin Rouge

English term	Unit	Ingredient	Metric (g)	Imperial (oz)	French term
Beef Burgundy style	$\frac{1}{5}$ $\frac{1}{5}$ $\frac{1}{10}$	As for Vin Rouge garnish with: glazed button onions à brun glazed button mushrooms à brun lardons of bacon 4 heart-shaped croûtons	120 120 60	4 4 2	Boeuf Bourguig- nonne
Savoury beef mince		Minced stewing beef (use onion in formula) N.B. Leave unstrained May be garnished with: Fried heart-shaped croûtons and a border of duchess potatoes			Hachis de Boeuf
Brown Veal Stews Brown veal stew		Stewing veal (use mirepoix in recipe)			Ragoût de Veau
Brown veal stew with vegetables		As for lamb stew, *see* chart above			
Brown veal stew with white wine		Replace quarter of the stock with white wine			Ragoût de Veau au Vin Blanc
Veal Marengo style	$\frac{1}{5}$ $\frac{1}{5}$ $\frac{1}{5}$	As for Ragoût de Veau au Vin Blanc but garnish with: glazed button onions à brun glazed button mushrooms à brun tomato concassé Add to the completed stew just prior to service and garnish with 4 heart-shaped croûtons and chopped parsley	120 120 120	4 4 4	Ragoût de Veau Marengo

Other Brown Stews Prepared Using Above Formula

Brown rabbit stew		Stewing rabbit (ready jointed) use mirepoix in recipe. Garnish as for lamb			Ragoût de Lapin
Stewed ox-kidney		Ox-kidney (use mirepoix in recipe)			Ragoût de Rognon de Boeuf

White Stew   Ragoût Blanc

Blanquette

This indicates a thickened white stew usually made from veal, lamb or rabbit. The meat is stewed in flavoured white stock from which a velouté sauce is produced at the end of cooking period. This forms part of the complete dish.

Fricassée

This indicates a thickened white stew usually made from veal, poultry or rabbit. The meat is stewed in a thickened sauce throughout the cooking period with the sauce forming part of the complete dish.

   N.B. Both the above preparations are enriched with a liaison of egg yolk and cream just prior to service.

White Stew   Blanquette

Yield: 4 portions
Cooking time: 1-1½ hrs
For *rabbit* take 1 small rabbit

Unit	Ingredient	Metric	Imperial
1	Stewing meat (prepared large dice or jointed)	600 g	1¼ lb
⅕	Mirepoix (left whole)	120 g	4 oz
¹/₁₀	Cream ⎫ liaison	60 ml	2 fl oz
¹/₁₀	Egg yolk ⎭	60 g	2 oz
¹/₂₀	Butter	30 g	1 oz
¹/₂₀	Flour	30 g	1 oz
	Bouquet garni		
	Seasoning and squeeze of lemon juice		
★	White stock		

★ N.B. Sufficient stock to cover meat during cooking, an *approximate guide* is EQUAL QUANTITIES OF STOCK TO MEAT i.e. 1:1

Method

Blanch and refresh meat to remove scum which would otherwise discolour sauce and spoil appearance of finished blanquette.
Season meat, place in saucepan with mirepoix, cover with stock, bring to boil, skim, add bouquet garni, seasoning and cover with tight-fitting lid. Stew gently on top of stove and check periodically until meat is tender. Once meat is cooked strain off the cooking liquor.

Prepare a blond roux with butter and flour, add stock to form a velouté, correct seasoning and consistency. Add lemon juice, re-heat the meat in the sauce, remove from heat, add liaison, garnish and serve as required.

N.B. Once liaison is added do not reboil otherwise egg will curdle in sauce.

White Stew   Fricassée

Yield: 4 portions
Cooking time: 1-1½ hr
Cooking temperature: moderate oven 150° C (300° F)
Poultry — 1 medium chicken
Game — 1 small rabbit

Unit	Ingredient	Metric	Imperial
1	Stewing meat (prepared large dice or jointed)	600 g	1¼ lb
$\frac{1}{10}$	Onion brunoise	60 g	2 oz
$\frac{1}{10}$	Cream ⎫ liaison	60 ml	2 fl oz
$\frac{1}{10}$	Egg yolk ⎬	60 g	2 oz
$\frac{1}{20}$	Butter	30 g	1 oz
$\frac{1}{20}$	Flour	30 g	1 oz
	Bouquet garni		
	Seasoning and squeeze of lemon juice		
	Mushroom trimmings		
★	White stock		

★ N.B. Sufficient stock to cover meat during cooking and also to form a lightly thickened sauce with the roux. An *approximate guide* is EQUAL QUANTITIES OF STOCK TO MEAT i.e. 1:1.

Method

Season meat with salt and pepper, melt butter in sauté pan, add meat and onion, cover with lid and sweat gently without colour to seal. Add flour to form a blond roux, moisten with stock, bring to boil, skim, add bouquet garni, mushroom trimmings and seasoning.

Cover with tight-fitting lid and stew gently on stove top or in a moderate oven. Check periodically until meat is cooked. Once cooked, remove meat and place into clean vessel. Reduce sauce to pouring consistency, correct seasoning, add lemon juice, pass through fine chinois. Re-heat meat with sauce, remove from heat, add liaison, garnish and serve as required.

N.B. Once liaison is added do not reboil otherwise egg will curdle in the sauce.

Examples of Blanquettes and Fricassées Using Above Formula

English term	Main ingredient	French term
Blanquettes		
White lamb stew	Stewing lamb	Blanquette d'Agneau
White pork stew	Stewing pork	Blanquette de Porc
White veal stew	Stewing veal	Blanquette de Veau
White rabbit stew	Rabbit (jointed and trimmed)	Blanquette de Lapin
Fricassées		
White chicken stew	Chicken (cut for sauté)	Fricassée de Volaille
White pork stew	Stewing pork	Fricassée de Porc
White veal stew	Stewing veal	Fricassée de Veau
White rabbit stew	Rabbit (jointed and trimmed)	Fricassée de Lapin

Examples of Garnishes Used for Blanquettes and Fricassées

	Unit	Ingredient	Metric (g)	Imperial (oz)	
Ancient style	$^1/_5$	Glazed button onions à blanc	120	4	à l'Ancienne
	$^1/_5$	Glazed button mushrooms à blanc 4 Heart-shaped croûtons	120	4	
With asparagus		Garnish: 12 asparagus tips			Argenteuil
Finely chopped spring vegetables	$^2/_5$	Garnish: brunoise of vegetables sweated in butter without colour and mixed throughout sauce prior to service	240	8	Brunoise
Mother's style	$^2/_5$	Garnish: julienne of vegetable prepared and served as for brunoise	240	8	Bonne Maman
With mushrooms	$^2/_5$	Garnish: button mushrooms glazed without colour	240	8	aux Champignons

| With cucumber | $^2/_5$ | Garnish: cucumber (turned and poached) | 240 | 8 | Doria |

All the above dishes are usually garnished with freshly chopped parsley and shallow fried heart-shaped croûtons.

Miscellaneous Stews

(a) Spiced Stews

MEAT CURRY   Kari de Viande

Yield: 4 portions
Cooking time: 1 – 2 hr
Cooking temperature: moderate oven 150°C (300°F)

Unit	Ingredient	Metric	Imperial
1	Stewing meat (prepared large dice)	600 g	1 $^1/_4$ lb
$^1/_5$	Onion (finely diced)	120 g	4 oz
$^1/_{10}$	Dripping or margarine	60 g	2 oz
$^1/_{20}$	Curry powder	30 g	1 oz
$^1/_{20}$	Flour	30 g	1 oz
$^1/_{40}$	Tomato purée	15 g	$^1/_2$ oz
★	Stock		
	Salt to season		
Flavourings			
$^1/_{10}$ †	Coconut milk	60 ml	2 fl oz
$^1/_{10}$	Diced apple	60 g	2 oz
$^1/_{20}$	Diced chutney	30 g	1 oz

★ Sufficient stock to cover meat during cooking and also form a lightly thickened sauce with the roux. An approximate guide is *equal* quantities of *stock to meat*.
† Coconut milk — soak desiccated coconut in milk for 20 – 30 minutes, squeeze out for use.

Method

Season the meat lightly with salt and roll in a little of the curry powder. Melt fat in cooking vessel, add meat and onions and seal quickly. Add remaining curry powder and cook slowly for a few minutes. Add flour and colour to light brown, cool slightly, add tomato purée then moisten with stock.

Bring to boil, skim, add seasoning, cover with tight-fitting lid and stew gently on stove top or in moderate oven, check periodically until meat is almost cooked. At this stage add flavourings, continue cooking until meat is tender. Correct consistency and seasoning, serve with an accompaniment of plain boiled rice.

N.B.   Varying quantities of curry powder may be added according to the type of powder used and *hotness* of curry required.

Examples of Curries Prepared Using Above Formula

English term	Main ingredient	French term
Beef curry	Stewing beef	Kari de Boeuf
Lamb curry	Stewing lamb	Kari d'Agneau
Mutton curry	Stewing mutton	Kari de Mouton
Veal curry	Stewing veal	Kari de Veau
Chicken curry*	Chicken portions	Karide Poulet

* Use raw portions on/off the bone.

In addition to rice it is usual to serve various accompaniments with the curry. These are presented attractively in small ravier dishes. They may include the following:

Deep fried or grilled popadums
Grilled bombay duck
Diced mango chutney
Browned coconut
Fried sultanas
Nuts

Diced apple/sliced banana in acidulated cream
Sliced fresh mango
Diced papaw
Fried plantain
Diced pineapple
Sliced tomato

HUNGARIAN GOULASH   Goulache Hongroise

Yield: 4 portions
Cooking time: $1\frac{1}{2} - 2$ hr
Cooking temperature: Moderate oven 150°C (300°F)

Unit	Ingredient	Metric (g)	Imperial (oz)
1	Stewing meat (prepared large dice)	600	20
$\frac{1}{5}$	Onion (finely diced)	120	4
$\frac{1}{20}$	Dripping	30	1
$\frac{1}{20}$	Paprika	30	1
$\frac{1}{20}$	Flour	30	1
$\frac{1}{40}$	Tomato purée	15	$\frac{1}{2}$
	Salt to season		
*	Stock		
	Garnish of:		
	8 small turned potatoes (blanched)		
	12 gnocchi parisienne (plain boiled)		
	chopped parsley		

* Sufficient stock to cover meat during cooking and form a lightly thickened sauce. An *approximate guide* is EQUAL QUANTITIES OF STOCK TO MEAT i.e. 1:1.

Method

Season meat lightly and roll in a little paprika. Melt fat in cooking vessel, add meat and onions to seal quickly. Add remaining paprika and cook slowly for a few minutes. Add flour, colour light brown, cool slightly, add tomato purée then moisten with stock. Bring to the boil, skim, add seasoning, cover with tight-fitting lid and stew gently on stove top or in moderate oven, check periodically until meat is almost cooked. At this stage add blanched potatoes and continue cooking until meat is tender and potatoes are cooked.

Correct consistency and seasoning, garnish with plain boiled gnocchi and parsley for service.

Examples of Goulash Using Above Formula

English term	Main ingredient	French term
Beef goulash	Stewing beef	Goulache de Boeuf Hongroise
Lamb goulash	Stewing lamb	Goulache d'Agneau Hongroise
Mutton goulash	Stewing mutton	Goulache de Mouton Hongroise
Pork goulash	Stewing pork	Goulache de Porc Hongroise
Veal goulash	Stewing veal	Goulache de Veau Hongroise

STEWED BEEF MEXICAN STYLE   Chili Con Carne

Yield: 4 portions
Cooking time: $1\frac{1}{2} - 2$ hr
Cooking temperature: moderate oven 150°C (300°F)

Unit	Ingredient	Metric	Imperial
1	Coarse mince/small dice of lean beef	500 g	$1\frac{1}{4}$ lb
$\frac{1}{5}$	Dried red kidney beans* (soaked overnight)	100 g	4 oz
$\frac{1}{5}$	Onions (diced)	100 g	4 oz
$\frac{1}{5}$	Tomato concassé	100 g	4 oz
$\frac{1}{20}$	Oil	25 ml	1 fl oz
$\frac{1}{40}$	Tomato purée	12.5 g	$\frac{1}{2}$ oz
†	2 Chili peppers (finely chopped)		
	Salt to taste		
‡	Stock		

* Increase to $\frac{2}{5}$ unit when using processed beans.
† Only small amounts used approximately $1 - 2$ chilis per 500 g ($1\frac{1}{4}$ lb) meat.
‡ Sufficient stock to cover meat. Approximately equal quantity of stock to meat.

Method

Sweat onions and chilis in oil for a few minutes, add meat to seal and colour, season lightly. Add tomato purée, soaked beans, tomato concassé and sufficient stock just to cover meat. Cover with tight-fitting lid and stew gently on stove top or in moderate oven. Check periodically until meat and beans are cooked. Correct seasoning and serve.

N.B.   Chili con carne is often served with plain boiled rice or pilaff. If using processed beans they will be added for the last 30 minutes of cooking time.

STEWED KNUCKLE OF VEAL MILAN STYLE   Osso-Bucco Milanaise

Yield: 4 portions
Cooking time: $2-2\frac{1}{2}$ hr
Cooking temperature: 150°C (300°F)

Unit	Ingredient	Metric	Imperial
1	Veal knuckle (cut into pieces on bone)	1 kg	$2\frac{1}{2}$ lb
$\frac{1}{5}$	Mirepoix (brunoise)	200 g	8 oz
$\frac{1}{5}$	Tomato concassé	200 g	8 oz
$\frac{1}{5}$	Dry white wine	200 ml	8 fl oz
$\frac{1}{20}$	Oil	50 ml	2 fl oz
$\frac{1}{40}$	Flour	25 g	1 oz
$\frac{1}{40}$	Tomato purée	25 g	1 oz
	Salt and pepper		
	Hint of chopped garlic		
	Squeeze of lemon juice		
	Chopped parsley – basil – thyme – bay leaf		
*	Stock (white chicken or veal)		

* Sufficient to cover meat during cooking and form a lightly thickened sauce.

Method

Season veal and pass through the flour. Seal quickly in heated oil to colour light brown, add mirepoix, cover with lid and sweat gently for a few minutes, add tomato purée and wine. Add stock, bring to boil, skim, add seasoning, garlic and herbs. Cover with tight-fitting lid and stew gently in moderate oven until meat is tender.

Add tomato concassé, squeeze of lemon juice, correct seasoning, simmer for 2–3 minutes, garnish with chopped parsley and serve accompanied by Rizotto Milanaise (*see* p. 245).

(b) Poultry and Game Stews

CHICKEN IN RED WINE   Coq au Vin

Yield: 4 portions
Cooking time: 45 min–1 hr
Cooking temperature: 150°C (300°F)

Take a medium-sized chicken and cut for sauté.

Unit	Ingredient	Metric	Imperial
	One chicken (cut for sauté)		
1	Red wine	500 ml	1 pt
1/5	Chicken stock	100 ml	4 fl oz
1/10	Oil	50 ml	2 fl oz
1/20	Butter ⎱ beurre manié	25 g	1 oz
1/20	Flour ⎰	25 g	1 oz
1/40	Meat glaze	12.5 g	1/2 oz
	Bouquet garni		
	Seasoning/hint of chopped garlic		
	Garnish of:		
1/5	button onions	100 g	4 oz
1/5	button mushrooms	100 g	4 oz
1/5	blanched lardons of bacon	100 g	4 oz
	4 fried heart-shaped croûtons		
	Chopped parsley		

Method

Season chicken, seal and colour quickly in oil. Remove chicken and place in stewing vessel with bouquet garni and garlic. Sauté onions, mushrooms and lardons in chicken residue until lightly browned, put aside. Swill out (deglaze) sauté pan with red wine and stock, bring to boil, season and pour on to chicken. Cover with tight-fitting lid and stew in the oven until chicken is tender. Remove chicken and place into a clean cocotte or serving dish. Garnish with onions, mushrooms and lardons. Reduce cooking liquor by a third, add chicken glaze and thicken to required consistency using beurre manié, correct seasoning. Strain sauce on to chicken, replace in oven to re-heat thoroughly. Serve in cocotte garnished with croûtons and chopped parsley.

N.B.   Fried croûtons may be spread with a purée of the cooked liver of the chicken. Traditionally this dish is prepared using a freshly killed bird, its blood being used to thicken the sauce. In this instance the sauce must not reboil otherwise it will curdle.

FEATHERED GAME STEW   Salmis de Gibier

Yield: 4 portions
Cooking time: 45 min – 1 hr
For 4 portions: 1 medium pheasant or   Faisan
        2 wild ducks or   Canard Sauvage
        2 grouse   Grouse
The above game birds are roasted underdone *see* p. 389 skinned and jointed into portions. Carcass retained for use in sauce.

Unit	Ingredient	Metric	Imperial
1	Demi-glace	500 ml	1 pt
$1/2$	Red wine	250 ml	10 fl oz
$1/10$	Onion brunoise	50 g	2 oz
$1/10$	Butter	50 g	2 oz
$1/20$	Brandy	25 ml	1 fl oz
	Seasoning		
	salt and crushed peppercorns,		
	bay leaf		
	Garnish of		
$1/5$	glazed button mushrooms		
	à brun	100 g	4 oz
	4 heart shaped croûtons		
	Chopped parsley		

Method

Chop the carcass and trimmings then sauté in butter with shallots, peppercorns and bay leaf until brown. Flame with brandy, déglacé with red wine and reduce by a half. Add demi-glace, simmer and reduce to extract game flavour from bones until sauce reaches required consistency, season to taste. Place jointed game in buttered cocotte, strain sauce through a fine chinois on to the game. Cover with a lid and reheat in hot oven. Serve garnished with mushrooms, heart shaped croûtons and chopped parsley.

Furred Game Stews   Civet de Gibier

For this type of game stew the raw meat is first of all placed in a red wine marinade and stored in a refrigerator for a minimum of eight hours. The marinade impregnates the meat during this period.

RED WINE MARINADE

Yield: 4 portions

Unit	Ingredient	Metric	Imperial
1	Red wine	500 ml	1 pt
$1/5$	Mirepoix (medium dice)	100 g	4 oz
$1/10$	Oil	50 ml	2 fl oz
	Seasoning		
	salt, crushed peppercorns		
	Hint of crushed garlic		
	Bouquet garni		

Method

Combine all ingredients together and place in bowl ready for use.

PREPARATION OF CIVET

Yield: 4 portions
Cooking time: $2\frac{1}{2} - 3\frac{1}{2}$ hr
Cooking temperature: 150°C (300°F)

For 4 portions — small hare (skinned)   Civet de Lièvre
                800 g (2 lb) venison   Civet de Venaison

The above game is jointed or cut into pieces and placed in the marinade, retain blood to thicken the sauce.

Unit	Ingredient	Metric	Imperial
	Game and marinade		
1	Game stock	500 ml	1 pt
$\frac{1}{20}$	Flour	25 g	1 oz
$\frac{1}{20}$	Dripping	25 g	1 oz
$\frac{1}{20}$	Tomato purée	25 g	1 oz
	Seasoning		
	Retained blood (mixed with a little cold water)		

Method

Remove game and vegetables from marinade and fry in the dripping to seal and colour. Add flour and singe in hot oven, add tomato purée, moisten with liquor from marinade, add sufficient stock to cover the meat. Bring to the boil, skim cover with tight fitting lid and stew in a moderate oven. Check periodically until meat is cooked adjusting consistency if required. Remove meat from sauce, place in service dish and keep hot. Reboil the sauce remove from heat, add blood to thicken. Correct seasoning, strain sauce over the hare. Garnish as required and serve.

N.B.   Once blood liaison is added do not reboil or sauce will curdle.

Examples of Dishes Using Above Recipe: Garnish—in Relation to 1 Unit Game Stock i.e. $\frac{1}{2}$ l (1 pt)

English term	Unit	Ingredient	Metric (g)	Imperial (oz)	French term
English style jugged hare		8 Forcemeat balls deep-fried: chop game liver and mix with a little sausage meat, roll in balls, pané and deep fry			Civet de Lièvre à l'Anglaise

English term	Unit	Ingredient	Metric g	Imperial oz	French term
Burgundy style jugged hare	$\frac{1}{5}$	Glazed button mushrooms à brun	100	4	Civet de Lièvre Bourguignonne
	$\frac{1}{5}$	Glazed button onions à brun	100	4	
	$\frac{1}{10}$	Cooked lardons of bacon 4 Heart-shaped croûtons	50	2	

N.B.   All civets are served with an accompaniment of red-currant jelly.

(c)   Unthickened Stews

LANCASHIRE HOT-POT

Yield: 4 portions
Cooking time: $2 - 2\frac{1}{2}$ hr
Cooking temperature: 150°C (300°F)

Unit	Ingredient	Metric	Imperial
1	Middle neck lamb cutlets	600 g	$1\frac{1}{4}$ lb
1	Potatoes (peeled and sliced into thin rounds)	600 g	$1\frac{1}{4}$ lb
1	Onions (shredded)	600 g	$1\frac{1}{4}$ lb
$\frac{1}{20}$	Dripping	30 g	1 oz
	Seasoning of salt and pepper		
	Chopped parsley		
⋆	White stock		

⋆ Amount of stock will vary according to size of cooking vessel used.

Method

Lightly season the meat, potatoes, and onions. Fry meat in dripping to colour and seal on both sides. Place a layer of potatoes and onion on the base of an earthenware dish, follow with some of the fried meat. Repeat layering process and finish with a neat layer of overlapping potatoes.

Pour in sufficient stock to come just beneath surface of top layer of potatoes. Brush surface with melted dripping. Place in moderate oven until cooked and golden brown. Clean sides of dish, sprinkle with chopped parsley and serve. Accompany with pickled red cabbage.

LAMB CHOP CHAMPVALLON   Chop d'Agneau Champvallon

Yield: 4 portions
Cooking time: 2 hr
Cooking temperature: Moderate oven 150°C (300°F)

Unit	Ingredient	Metric (g)	Imperial (oz)
	4 chump chops (1 per portion)		
1	Potatoes (peeled and sliced into thin rounds)	500	20
$2/_5$	Onions (shredded)	200	8
$2/_5$	Tomatoes (skinned and sliced)	200	8
$1/_{20}$	Dripping	25	1
	Bay leaf, pinch of thyme		
	Seasoning of salt and pepper		
	Hint of garlic and chopped parsley		
★	White stock		

* Amount of stock will vary according to size of cooking vessel used.

Method

Lightly season meat, potatoes and onions. Fry meat in dripping to colour and seal on both sides. Place a layer of onions and potatoes on the base of an earthenware dish, follow with the chops. Cover chops with the tomatoes, onions, garlic, bay leaf, and thyme. Finish with a neat layer of overlapping potatoes.

Pour in sufficient stock to come just beneath surface of top layer of potatoes. Brush surface with melted dripping and place in a moderate oven until cooked and golden brown. Clean sides of dish, sprinkle with chopped parsley and serve.

IRISH STEW

Yield: 4 portions
Cooking time: 1½ hr

Unit	Ingredient	Metric (g)	Imperial (oz)
1	Stewing lamb (large dice)	500	20
1	Potatoes (turned - keep trimmings)	500	20
$1/_4$	Celery (sliced)	125	5
$1/_4$	Onion (sliced)	125	5
$1/_4$	Leek (sliced)	125	5
$1/_4$	Button onions (to garnish)	125	5
	Bouquet garni		
	Seasoning of salt and pepper		
	Chopped parsley		
★	White stock		

* Amount of stock will vary according to size of cooking vessel used.

Method

Blanch, refresh and drain the lamb to remove scum (scum would impair the appearance of finished stew). Place in a stew pan with onions, leeks, celery, bouquet garni and barely cover with white stock. Bring to the boil and simmer for three-quarters of the stewing time. Add turned potatoes, potato trimmings and button onions, continue cooking until meat and vegetables are cooked. Correct seasoning, garnish with chopped parsley.

STEWED TRIPE AND ONIONS

Yield: 4 portions
Cooking time: 2 hr

Unit	Ingredient		Metric (g)	Imperial (oz)
1	White tripe (large trimmed pieces)		600	20
$1/2$	Onions shredded		300	10
$1/20$	Butter or margarine	white roux	30	1
$1/20$	Flour		30	1
★	Milk			
	Seasoning of salt and pepper			

★ Sufficient milk to cover tripe. This will vary according to size and shape of cooking vessel.

Method

Blanch and refresh tripe to remove scum which would impair appearance of finished dish. Place tripe, onions, seasoning in stew pan and cover with milk. Bring to boil and stew gently until tripe is tender. Prepare a white roux with fat and flour, form a white sauce of coating consistency using the cooking liquor. Cook sauce for 10 minutes to ensure starch is cooked. Mix the sauce with the strained tripe and onion, reboil, correct seasoning and serve.

Stewed Fish   Matelote de Poisson

Matelote is the French culinary term for a fish stew. Strictly speaking matelotes are prepared from freshwater fish and in some instances are served as fish soups.

EEL STEW   Matelote d'Anguille

Yield: 4 portions
Cooking time: 30 min

Unit	Ingredient	Metric	Imperial
1	Freshwater eels (prepared skinned and jointed)	500 g	1¼ lb
³/₅	Red or white (dry) wine	300 ml	12 fl oz
¹/₅	Onion (brunoise)	100 g	4 oz
¹/₅	Cream	100 ml	4 fl oz
¹/₁₀	Butter	50 g	2 oz
¹/₂₀	Flour	25 g	1 oz
	Bouquet garni		
	Hint of garlic		
	Chopped parsley		
	Salt and pepper		
	Garnish with		
¹/₅	glazed button onions à blanc	100 g	4 oz
¹/₅	glazed button mushrooms à blanc	100 g	4 oz
	French bread		

Method

Sweat onion brunoise in half the butter without colour, add eels and continue to sweat and seal. Add bouquet garni, garlic, chopped parsley, seasoning and moisten with wine. Bring to boil, skim, cover with tight-fitting lid and stew until eels are tender. Place strained eel in serving dish and keep hot.

Prepare beurre manié with remaining butter and flour, thicken cooking liquor to pouring consistency, add cream, correct seasoning and strain over eels. Garnish with button onions, mushrooms and chopped parsley and serve accompanied with slices of French bread.

N.B.   Other fish stews (matelotes) may be similarly prepared using other types of fish and shellfish.

French Fish Soup/Stew   Bouillabaisse

Strictly defined, bouillabaisse is a type of fish soup prepared by the stewing method. Many varieties of this dish are found in the Mediterranean region where they are served as a soup or stew, but the most popular is that from Marseilles. The recipe below produces a generally acceptable culinary adaptation and one that is untypically prepared using skinned/filleted fish for ease of serving and eating.

Bouillabaisse

Yield: 4 portions
Cooking time: 30 min
For 4 portions use a combination of the following prepared fish:

whiting, red mullet, conger eel, John Dory, squid (cut into sections free from skin and bone), crayfish and mussels (both in shell)

Unit	Ingredient	Metric	Imperial
1	Selected fish	500 g	1¼ lb
$\frac{1}{5}$	White wine (dry)	100 ml	4 fl oz
$\frac{1}{5}$	Onion (shredded)	100 g	4 oz
$\frac{1}{5}$	Leek (julienne)	100 g	4 oz
$\frac{1}{5}$	Tomato concassé	100 g	4 oz
$\frac{1}{10}$	Olive oil	50 ml	2 fl oz
	Bay leaf		
	Pinch of fennel		
	Hint of garlic		
	Pinch of saffron		
	Chopped parsley		
	Salt and milled pepper		
*	Fish stock		
	Garnish of French bread		

* Sufficient stock to cover fish for cooking. This will vary according to whether the bouillabaisse is to be served as a soup or stew.

Method

Sweat onions and leeks in oil without colour. Add all fish (other than shellfish), bay leaf, garlic, fennel, parsley and seasoning. Cover with lid and sweat for a few minutes to extract flavours. Moisten with wine and sufficient stock to just cover the fish. Bring to the boil, skim, add shellfish then saffron to flavour and colour. Cover with tight-fitting lid and stew gently until cooked. Adjust seasoning and serve with an accompaniment of sliced French bread.

N.B. French bread may be flavoured with cut garlic and served with bouillabaisse. Slices of French bread may be piqued with garlic strips and then toasted or baked to a golden colour.

LOBSTER AMERICAINE   Homard Américaine

Yield: 4 portions
Cooking time: 20 – 30 min

Unit	Ingredient	Metric	Imperial
	2 Hen lobsters (live)		
1	Fish stock	250 ml	½ pt
$\frac{3}{5}$	White wine	150 ml	6 fl oz
$\frac{2}{5}$	Tomato concassé	100 g	4 oz
$\frac{2}{5}$	Mirepoix brunoise	100 g	4 oz
$\frac{1}{5}$	Oil	50 ml	2 fl oz
$\frac{1}{5}$	Butter	50 g	2 oz
$\frac{1}{5}$	Brandy	50 ml	2 fl oz
$\frac{1}{20}$	Tomato purée	12.5 g	½ oz
	Chopped parsley		
	Hint of garlic		
	Squeeze of lemon juice		

Preparation of Live Lobster

Place live lobster on chopping board, pierce head with point of knife and split head lengthways (leave tail whole). Separate tail from head and cut tail into thick tronçons. Remove claws and crack claw shell with back of heavy chopping knife. Remove liver (cream of lobster) from head and any coral, mix with butter ready for use. Discard sack from head. Retain carapace (head) and tail-fan shell for decoration.

Cooking of Lobster

Heat oil in cooking vessel, add lobster and cook until shell turns red. Add mirepoix brunoise, garlic and sweat to soften. Flame with brandy, add wine, fish stock, tomato purée, tomato concassé, squeeze of lemon juice and seasoning. Bring to boil, skim, cover with lid and stew gently for 15 minutes. Remove from heat, separate lobster from cooking liquor. Remove lobster meat from shell and place into a buttered service dish (keep hot). Reboil cooking liquor and add prepared butter mixture to thicken sauce. Adjust seasoning and pass through a coarse chinois on to lobster meat. Decorate with head and tail-fan of lobster shell, sprinkle with chopped parsley and serve accompanied with rice pilaff.

N.B.   Rice and lobster are usually served separately in timbales.

LOBSTER NEWBURG (using live lobster)   Homard Newburg à Cru

Yield: 4 portions
Cooking time: 20 min

Unit	Ingredient	Metric	Imperial
	2 Hen lobsters (live)		
1	Fish stock	250 ml	½ pt
1	Cream (double)	250 ml	½ pt
⅕	Marsala	50 ml	2 fl oz
⅕	Butter	50 g	2 oz
⅒	Brandy	25 ml	1 fl oz
⅒	Oil	25 ml	1 fl oz
	Salt and pepper to taste		

Preparation of Live Lobster

As for Homard Américaine (*see* above) including preparation of butter. A little flour may be added to butter mixture to aid thickening.

Cooking of Lobster

Heat oil in cooking vessel add lobster and cook until it turns red. Flame with brandy, add marsala and reduce by a half. Add cream, fish stock and seasoning. Bring to the boil, skim, cover with lid and stew gently for 15 minutes. Remove from heat and separate lobster from cooking liquor. Remove lobster meat from shell and place into a buttered service dish (keep hot). Reboil cooking liquor, add prepared butter mixture to thicken sauce. Adjust seasoning and pass through chinois on to the lobster meat. Decorate with head and tail of lobster shell for service. Serve accompanied with rice pilaff.

N.B.   Hen lobsters are selected for the above dishes because of their coral, which acts to flavour and colour the sauce.

STEWED MUSSELS IN WHITE WINE
Moules Marinière

Yield: 4 portions
Cooking time: 10 – 12 min

Unit	Ingredient		Metric	Imperial
1	Mussels (in shell, washed and scraped)		1 kg	2½ lb
⅕	Fish stock		200 ml	8 fl oz
¹⁄₁₀	Dry white wine		100 ml	4 fl oz
¹⁄₂₀	Onion (brunoise)		50 g	2 oz
	Squeeze of lemon juice			
	Salt and cayenne pepper			
	Chopped parsley			
★	Beurre manié			

★ Sufficient beurre manié lightly to lié the sauce.

Method
Place mussels into a sauteuse with onions, wine, stock, lemon juice, and seasoning. Cover with lid and bring to boiling point, stew for a few minutes to cook mussels and open the shells. Remove mussels from cooking liquor, discard the top shells of opened mussels. Loosen mussels from bottom shell remove any beard, replace mussels into shells and arrange in serving dish (keep hot). Decant the cooking liquor into clean sauteuse leaving behind sediment and sand. Bring to boil, lightly lié with beurre manié, add chopped parsley, correct seasoning and pour onto the mussels for service.

Extensions of Moules Marinière: Added Ingredients in Relation to 1 Unit i.e. 1 kg (2½ lb) Mussels

English term	Unit	Ingredient	Metric	Imperial	French term
Mussels in cream sauce	¹⁄₁₀	Fresh cream (double) Finish sauce with cream	100 ml	4 fl oz	Moules à la Crème
Mussels in poulette sauce	¹⁄₁₀	Fresh cream (double)	100 ml	4 fl oz	Moules à la Poulette
	¹⁄₂₀	Egg yolk	50 g	2 oz	
		Omit beurre manié and thicken cooking liquor with liaison of yolks and cream. *DO NOT REBOIL*			

Vegetable Stews   Légumes Étuvés

A number of vegetables are cooked by the stewing method and are usually served as an accompaniment with a main course item. They are also ideal as a course for vegetarians.

STEWED PEAS   Petits Pois Etuvés

Yield: 4 portions
Cooking time: 30 min (for frozen vegetables reduce by half)

Unit	Ingredient	Metric (g)	Imperial (oz)
1	Shelled peas	200	8
1/2	Button onions (prepared)	100	4
1/4	Lettuce (prepared)	50	2
	Beurre manié to lié		
	Pinch of sugar		
	Salt to taste		

Method

Place peas, onions, and lettuce in pan, barely cover with boiling water, season with sugar and salt. Cover with tight-fitting lid and stew gently until the vegetables are cooked. Lightly thicken with beurre manié, correct seasoning and serve.

Extensions Using Above Formula: Added Ingredients in relation to 200 g (8 oz) shelled peas

English term	Unit	Ingredient	Metric (g)	Imperial (oz)	French term
Peas French style		As for Étuvés			Petit Pois à la Française
Peas housewife style	1/2	As above with cooked lardons of bacon	100	4	Petit Pois Bonne Femme
Peas peasant style	1/2	As for Étuvés with paysanne of vegetables	100	4	Petit Pois Paysanne

MARROW
PUMPKIN

Courge Provençale
Potiron Provençale

Yield: 4 portions
Cooking time: 30 – 45 min

Unit	Ingredient	Metric	Imperial
1	Marrow/pumpkin (large dice)	400 g	1 lb
$\frac{1}{2}$	Tomato concassé	200 g	8 oz
$\frac{1}{4}$	Onion (shredded)	100 g	4 oz
$\frac{1}{8}$	Oil	50 ml	2 fl oz
	Hint of garlic		
	Pinch of basil		
	Bay leaf		
	Salt and milled pepper		
	Chopped parsley to garnish		

Method

Sweat onion and garlic in oil without colour for a few minutes. Add marrow, continue sweating, and add tomato, herbs and seasoning. Cover with a tight-fitting lid and stew gently until the vegetables are cooked. Correct seasoning, garnish with parsley and serve.

Ratatouille

Yield: 4 portions
Cooking time: 45 min
Cooking temperature: (moderate oven) 150°C (300°F)

Unit	Ingredient	Metric	Imperial
1	Courgette ⎱ peeled and sliced	200 g	8 oz
1	Aubergine ⎰	200 g	8 oz
1	Tomatoes (skinned and quartered)	200 g	8 oz
$\frac{1}{2}$	Green pepper ⎱ cut into rough julienne	100 g	4 oz
$\frac{1}{2}$	Red pepper ⎰	100 g	4 oz
$\frac{1}{2}$	Onion dice	100 g	4 oz
$\frac{1}{4}$	Oil	50 ml	2 fl oz
	Hint of garlic		
	Salt and milled pepper		
	Chopped parsley		

N.B.   Skinned and quartered tomatoes may be replaced by tomato concassé.

Method

Sweat onion, peppers and garlic in oil without colour. Add courgettes, aubergines, and seasoning. Cover with a tight-fitting lid and stew gently on stove top or in oven. When half cooked add tomatoes and continue cooking until vegetables are tender. Garnish with chopped parsley and serve.

To Braise   Braiser

The technique of braising may be described as a long, slow, moist process by which various foods are cooked in the oven, under cover in the minimum of liquor. As with stewing the highly-flavoured liq.1or or sauce becomes an integral part of the complete product. This technique may involve a combination of cooking liquors (stock, wine, sauce or beer), and cooking methods. In most cases oven braising is preceded by one of the following:

(a) *Shallow frying and sweating* – the initial method used to colour and seal in the flavour of the meat prior to its being braised in the oven. Often utilized for small cuts of butcher's meat and offal.

(b) *Flash roasting* (p. 389) – used for large pieces of butcher's meat, poultry, game and offal, for the reasons outlined in (a).

(c) *Blanching and refreshing in boiling water* – the method used to ensure the colour of the vegetables is retained and their structure made pliable for shaping. Certain offal are also blanched and refreshed before braising commences, enabling the scum to be removed and also setting the meat firm to ensure ease of handling. Cured meats selected for braising are usually blanched and boiled for a longer period, in order to remove excess saltiness and soften hardened protein (one of the results of curing). The permutation of cooking methods will depend upon the foods being braised.

The Braising of Butcher's Meat, Poultry, Offal and Game

The braising of meats may be broadly categorized as follows.

Brown Braising

(a) Using small cuts of meat and offal where the food is portioned prior to braising, e.g. braised steaks; or

(b) Where meat and poultry are braised 'in the piece' then carved into portions once cooking is complete, e.g. braised topside.

White braising

The method is as shown above but keeping braised items white in colour (omit red meats).

Ancilliary Larder Preparations of Meats, etc. for Braising

To Lard or Piqué Meat

When the meat for braising is inserted with strips of pork or bacon fat enabling it to remain moist during cooking whilst at the same time reducing excess shrinkage.

Marinating the Meat

The meat is allowed to stand in a marinade (*see* p. 349) prior to cooking. The marinade enhances colour, flavour and is used as an integral part of the cooking liquor during braising.

Brown Braising

Using Small Cuts of Butcher's Meat and Poultry

The following preparations are similar to many brown stews. They are, however, traditionally cooked in the oven (oven stewing) and appear on the menu as braised items, e.g. braised steaks.

BROWN BRAISED MEATS/POULTRY (SMALL CUTS)

Viande Braisée/Volaille Braisée à Brun

Yield: 4 portions
Cooking time: $1\frac{1}{2} - 2$ hr
Cooking temperature: 150°C (300°F)

Unit	Ingredient	Metric (g)	Imperial (oz)
1	Braising meat (*see* chart below)	600	20
$\frac{1}{5}$	Mirepoix (medium)	120	4
$\frac{1}{20}$	Flour	30	1
$\frac{1}{20}$	Oil or dripping	30	1
$\frac{1}{40}$	Tomato purée	15	$\frac{1}{2}$
	Bouquet garni		
	Seasoning		
★	Brown stock/liquid		

★ Sufficient stock to cover meat during cooking and also form a lightly thickened sauce. An *approximate guide* is EQUAL QUANTITIES OF STOCK TO MEAT i.e. 1:1. This will vary according to size and shape of cooking vessel.

Method

Lightly season meat with salt and pepper, seal quickly in heated oil/dripping until brown. Remove meat from cooking vessel and place into braising pan. Sweat vegetables in remaining oil until brown. Add the flour and form a brown roux. Add tomato purée, stir in stock, bring to the boil and skim, add bouquet garni and seasoning. Pour sauce over meat and cover with lid. Braise steadily in a moderate oven, check periodically until meat is cooked. Once cooked remove meat into a clean vessel, correct seasoning and consistency of sauce. Reboil and strain sauce through fine chinois on to the meat. Garnish as required and serve.

Examples of Meats Braised using Above Formula

English term	Main ingredient	French term
Braised steaks	Beef steaks (braising)	Biftecks Braisés
Braised lamb chops	Lamb chops (braising)	Chops d'Agneau Braisés
Braised veal chops	Veal cutlets (braising)	Chops de Veau Braisés

English term	Main ingredient	French term
Braised beef or veal olives	Prepared olives: Prepare escalopes of beef or veal and fill with forcemeat stuffing (*see* p. 388) roll into cylinders, and secure with string. Use as required. Remove string for service service	Paupiettes de Boeuf/Veau Braisés
Braised chicken ballotines	Prepared ballotines: Bone out chicken legs leaving skin and flesh intact. Fill with forcemeat stuffing (*see* p. 388) secure with string and use. Remove string for service	Ballotines de Volaille Braisés

Garnishes for Above Braised Meats: Garnish — in Relation to 1 Unit i.e. 600 g (1¼ lb) Braising Meat

English term	Unit	Garnish	Metric (g)	Imperial (oz)	French term
Spring vegetables	$\frac{1}{5}$	Glazed turned carrots	120	4	Printanier
	$\frac{1}{5}$	Glazed button onions à brun	120	4	
	$\frac{1}{5}$	Glazed turned turnips	120	4	
Peasant style	$\frac{2}{5}$	Cooked paysanne of vegetables	240	8	Paysanne
Gardener's style	$\frac{2}{5}$	Cooked jardinière of vegetables	240	8	Jardinière
	$\frac{1}{5}$	Glazed turned carrots	120	4	Bourgeoise
	$\frac{1}{5}$	Glazed button onions à brun	120	4	
	$\frac{1}{10}$	Lardons of bacon	60	2	
In red wine		Replace half stock with red wine			au Vin Rouge

BEEF BRAISED IN BEER   Carbonnade de Boeuf

Yield: 4 portions
Cooking time: 1½ – 2 hr
Cooking temperature: 150°C (300°F)

Unit	Ingredient	Metric	Imperial
1	Lean braising beef (cut/ batted-out into small escalopes)	600 g	1¼ lb
½	Onions (shredded)	300 g	10 oz
½	Brown ale	300 ml	10 fl oz
1/20	Flour	30 g	1 oz
1/20	Oil or dripping	30 g	1 oz
	Seasoning		
	Hint of garlic		
	Chopped parsley		
★	Brown stock		

★ Sufficient to cover meat during cooking.

Method

Pass meat through seasoned flour, seal and brown quickly in oil or dripping. Remove meat from pan and put aside. Sweat onions in remaining fat until light brown. Layer onions and meat alternately in a casserole and lightly season each layer. Sprinkle with garlic and pour on the beer, top up just to cover with stock. Cover with lid and braise steadily in a moderate oven until meat is cooked. Once cooked, degrease, adjust seasoning, garnish with chopped parsley, serve.

Cooking 'en Daube'

Cooking 'En Daube' is akin to braising/oven stewing with the selected meat being cooked in a daubière (earthenware cooking vessel) which is covered with a tight-fitting lid. Prior to cooking, the meat is 'larded', lightly seasoned, flavoured with fine herbs and chopped garlic. It is then placed in a marinade for 4 hours before cooking.

Daube de Boeuf/Mouton

Yield: 4 portions
Cooking time: 2½ – 3 hr
Cooking temperature: 150°C (300°F)

Unit	Ingredient	Metric	Imperial
1	Meat (beef topside/leg of mutton – large cubes)	600 g	1¼ lb
1	Red wine	600 ml	1 pt
¼	Bacon (cut into large lardons and blanch)	150 g	5 oz
¼	Mirepoix	150 g	5 oz
1/20	Brandy	30 ml	1 fl oz
1/20	Oil	30 ml	1 fl oz
1/40	Tomato purée	15 g	½ oz
	Chopped fine herbs and garlic		
	Bouquet garni		
	Seasoning		
★	Stock (brown)		

★ Stock may be required in addition to wine to ensure meat is covered for cooking.

Method

Lard the cubes of meat with bacon fat, lightly season and roll in chopped garlic and fine herbs. Place in daubière with bouquet garni, lardons, mirepoix, tomato purée, oil, brandy and cover with red wine to marinade. Allow to stand for approximately 4 hours. Add stock just to cover meat (if required), cover with a light-fitting lid and set to cook in hot oven 230°C (450°F) until liquor comes to boiling point. Reduce heat to 150°C (300°F) and continue cooking until meat is tender. Degrease, correct seasoning and serve in cleaned cooking vessel.

Brown Braises of Offal

BRAISED OX-TAIL   Queue de Boeuf Braisée

Yield: 4 portions
Cooking time: 3 – 4 hr
Cooking temperature: 150°C (300°F)

Unit	Ingredient	Metric	Imperial
1	Ox-tail (sectioned)	1 kg	2$\frac{1}{2}$ lb
$\frac{1}{5}$	Mirepoix (medium)	200 g	8 oz
$\frac{1}{40}$	Flour	25 g	1 oz
$\frac{1}{40}$	Dripping	25 g	1 oz
$\frac{1}{40}$	Tomato purée	25 g	1 oz
	Seasoning		
	Bouquet garni		
★	Brown stock		

★ Sufficient stock to cover meat during cooking.

Method

Lightly season ox-tail with salt and pepper, seal quickly in dripping until light brown, add mirepoix continue cooking until brown. Add the flour and singe. Cool slightly, add the tomato purée, moisten with stock, bring to boil, skim. Add bouquet garni, seasoning, cover with a lid and braise in the oven until tender. Stir periodically to ensure even cooking. Once cooked remove ox-tail into clean vessel, correct consistency and seasoning of sauce, strain over meat, garnish as required and serve.

Garnishes: Printanier, Jardinière, Paysanne, etc. as for braised cuts of meat (*see* p. 362)

BRAISED LAMBS' HEARTS   Coeur d'Agneau Braisé

Yield: 4 portions
4 lambs' hearts
Cooking time: 2 – 2$\frac{1}{2}$ hr
Cooking temperature: 150°C (300°F)

Unit	Ingredient	Metric (g)	Imperial (oz)
	4 Lambs' hearts (trimmed)		
1	Mirepoix (medium)	120	4
1/4	Flour	30	1
1/4	Dripping	30	1
1/8	Tomato purée	15	1/2
	Bouquet garni		
	Seasoning of salt and pepper		
	Chopped parsley		
★	Brown stock		

★ Sufficient stock to cover hearts during cooking and form a lightly thickened sauce.

Method

Lightly season hearts with salt and pepper, seal quickly in dripping until light brown. Add mirepoix and continue cooking until brown. Add flour and singe, cool slightly, add tomato purée, moisten with stock, bring to boil and skim. Add bouquet garni, seasoning, cover with lid and braise in the oven until tender. Check periodically to adjust consistency. Once cooked place hearts into clean vessel, correct consistency and seasoning of sauce, strain over meat, garnish with chopped parsley and serve.

Garnishes: Printanier, Jardinière, Paysanne, etc. as for braised cuts of meat (*see* p. 362)

N.B. The hearts may be filled with stuffing (*see* p. 362) before braising. E.g. Coeur d'Agneau Braisé Farci.

BRAISED LIVER AND ONIONS   Foie de Boeuf Braisé Lyonnaise

Yield: 4 portions
Cooking time: 1 1/2 – 2 hr
Cooking temperature: 150°C (300°F)

Unit	Ingredient	Metric (g)	Imperial (oz)
1	Ox-liver (portioned)	400	16
1/2	Onions (shredded)	200	8
1/8	Dripping	50	2
1/16	Flour	25	1
★	Brown stock	25	1
	Seasoning of salt and pepper		
	Extra seasoned flour		

★ Sufficient stock to cover meat during cooking and also form a lightly thickened sauce.

Method

Pass meat through the seasoned flour, seal and brown quickly in dripping. Remove liver and place in braising vessel. Sweat onions in remaining fat until golden brown, add flour to form a roux. Moisten with stock and bring to boil to form sauce. Skim, season and pour over the liver. Cover with a lid and braise in the oven until tender. Stir periodically to ensure even cooking. Once cooked degrease, correct seasoning, consistency and served unstrained.

BRAISED LAMBS' TONGUES   Langues d'Agneau Braisées

Yield: 8 lambs' tongues
Cooking time: 2 hr
Cooking temperature: 150°C (300°F)

Unit	Ingredient	Metric	Imperial
	8 Lambs' tongues (blanched and refreshed)		
1	Brown stock	600 ml	1 pt
$1/5$	Mirepoix (medium)	120 g	4 oz
$1/20$	Flour	30 g	1 oz
$1/20$	Dripping	30 g	1 oz
$1/40$	Tomato purée	15 g	$1/2$ oz
	Bouquet garni		
	Salt and pepper		
	Chopped parsley		

Method

Cover blanched tongues with brown stock, bring to boil, skim, cover with lid and stew gently for one hour. Remove tongues and refresh in cold water, skin, trim and drain. Sweat mirepoix in dripping to brown, add flour to form a brown roux. Cool slightly, add tomato purée and moisten with cooking liquor and extra stock to form lightly thickened sauce. Place tongues in braising dish with bouquet garni, cover with sauce, season and braise under cover until meat is tender. Once cooked place tongues in clean vessel, correct consistency and seasoning of sauce, strain over meat and serve garnished with chopped parsley.

Braised Lambs' Tongues Florentine   Langues d'Agneau Braisées Florentine

As above served on a bed of cooked leaf spinach.

BRAISED SWEETBREADS (Brown)   Ris Braisés à Brun

Yield: 4 portions
Cooking time: 1 – 1½ hr
Cooking temperature: 150°C (300°F)

Unit	Ingredient	Metric (g)	Imperial (oz)
1	Sweetbreads (pre-soaked in running water to remove blood)	600	20
$\frac{1}{5}$	Mirepoix medium	120	4
$\frac{1}{20}$	Butter/margarine	30	1
	Arrowroot to thicken		
	Bouquet garni – chopped parsley		
	Salt and pepper		
★	Brown stock		

★ Sufficient stock barely to cover sweetbreads during cooking.

Method

Blanch and refresh sweetbreads, skin and remove ducts. Sweat mirepoix in butter to light brown, add sweetbreads, season, moisten with stock barely to cover. Bring to boil, skim, add bouquet garni. Cover with a greased cartouche and tight-fitting lid, braise in oven until tender. Once cooked remove sweetbreads and put aside. Reduce cooking liquor, lié with arrowroot, correct seasoning and strain sauce over sweetbreads. Serve garnished with chopped parsley.

(b) Braising in the Piece (Joints of Butcher's Meat, Poultry, and Offal)

As for small braising the meat is cooked in stock, wine or sauce or a combination of these liquors with added flavourings of vegetables and herbs. During braising, the meat is basted with the cooking liquor to effect a glazed appearance. Once cooked the meat is carved into portions and served with the thickened cooking liquor and the garnish.

Cooking times vary according to the type of meat being braised. As previously explained some meats are larded and marinaded in readiness for braising.

BROWN BRAISED MEATS (Joints)   Pièce de Viande Braisée à brun

Yield: 4 – 6 portions
Cooking time: $2 - 2\frac{1}{2}$ hr
Cooking temperature: 150°C (300°F)

Unit	Ingredient	Metric	Imperial
1	Braising meat (prepared)	1 kg	$2\frac{1}{2}$ lb
$\frac{1}{5}$	Mirepoix (large cut)	200 g	8 oz
$\frac{1}{20}$	Dripping or oil	50 g	2 oz
$\frac{1}{40}$	Tomato purée	25 g	1 oz
	Bouquet garni		
	Arrowroot to thicken		
	Salt and pepper		
	Chopped parsley		
★	Brown stock/wine		

★ Sufficient stock/wine to cover two-thirds of the meat during braising.

Method

Heat dripping in braising vessel, add mirepoix and seasoned meat then seal and colour in a very hot oven. Cover with stock two-thirds of the meat bring to boil, skim and degrease. Add tomato purée, bouquet garni, and seasoning. Braise steadily under cover until meat is almost cooked, basting periodically to effect a glaze. At this stage remove meat and lightly thicken liquor to pouring consistency using arrowroot. Correct seasoning. Strain sauce over meat and continue cooking until meat is tender. Serve as required.

Service

1. Allow meat to set for a period and carve into portions. Napper with sauce, garnish and serve.
2. Present meat whole, lightly napper with sauce, garnish and serve with a sauceboat of braising sauce. Carve the meat at the table.

N.B.   Alternatively the sauce may be prepared by reducing the braising stock and adding demi-glace/jus lié sauce to thicken.

Examples of Braised Dishes Using Above Formula: Added Ingredients in Relation to 1 Unit i.e. 1 kg (2½ lb) Braising Beef

English term	Unit	Ingredient	Metric (g)	Imperial (oz)	French term
Braised beef		Plain braised beef			Pièce de Boeuf Braisé
Braised beef in red wine		Braised marinaded beef (*see* p. 349) (use wine, herbs and vegetables from marinade when braising to replace mirepoix and some of the stock)			Pièce de Boeuf Braisé au Vin Rouge
Braised beef Bourgeoise		As for Vin Rouge garnished with:			Pièce de Boeuf Braisé Bourgeoise
	¹/₁₀	turned glazed carrots	100	4	
	¹/₁₀	glazed button onions à brun	100	4	
	¹/₂₀	lardons of bacon (cooked)	50	2	
Braised beef in the fashion	¹/₅	As for Bourgeoise: add Calf's foot during cooking then dice to garnish	200	8	Pièce de Boeuf Braisé à la Mode
Braised beef burgundy style		As for Vin Rouge garnished with:			Pièce de Boeuf Braisé Bourguignonne
	¹/₁₀	glazed button onions à brun	100	4	
	¹/₁₀	glazed button mush-rooms à brun	100	4	
	¹/₂₀	lardons of bacon (cooked) 4 shaped croûtons	50	2	

English term	Unit	Ingredient	Metric (g)	Imperial (oz)	French term
Using veal as main meat					
Braised cushion of veal		Plain braised cushion of veal			Noix de Veau Braisée
Braised cushion of veal bourgeoise	$^1/_{10}$ $^1/_{10}$ $^1/_{20}$	Garnish: glazed turned carrots glazed button onions à brun lardons bacon (cooked)	100 100 50	4 4 2	Noix de Veau Braisée Bourgeoise
Braised cushion of veal with spinach	$^1/_5$	Garnish: cooked leaf spinach	100	4	Noix de Veau Braisée Florentine
Braised stuffed shoulder of veal		Veal shoulder stuffed with lemon, parsley and thyme stuffing (*see* p. 387) then plain braised			L'Epaule de Veau Farcie Braisée
Braised stuffed breast of veal		As for above using breast of veal			Poitrine de Veau Farcie Braisée

N.B. Many other garnishes may be used.

Braised Offal (Large pieces)

Braised Ox-Heart   Coeur de Boeuf Braisé

As for p. 367 using ox-heart.

Braised Ox-tongue   Langue de Boeuf Braisée

Preparation for Braising

Place tongue in cold water and bring to boil, skim and simmer for one hour. Refresh and remove skin and gristle. Proceed as for the brown braised meats recipe using tongue as main meat. Garnish as for Braised Cushion of Veal (*see* above).

Braised Poultry

BRAISED DUCK WITH ORANGE   Canard Braisé à l'Orange

Yield: 4 portions
Use 1 medium duck
Cooking time: 2 hr
Cooking temperature: 150°C (300°F)

Unit	Ingredient	Metric	Imperial
	1 Medium duck		
1	Demi-glace	600 ml	1 pt
$\frac{1}{4}$	Brown stock	150 ml	5 fl oz
$\frac{1}{4}$	Fresh orange juice	150 ml	5 fl oz
$\frac{1}{20}$	Fresh lemon juice	30 ml	1 fl oz
$\frac{1}{20}$	Butter	30 g	1 oz
	Bouquet garni		
	Seasoning		
	Orange segments and blanched julienne of zest to garnish		

Method

Place seasoned duck in braising pan and brown in a hot oven. Drain off excess grease, add sauce, stock and bouquet garni, braise under cover in a moderate oven basting frequently until tender. Remove duck from sauce, put aside. Degrease the sauce and reduce to coating consistency. Pass through fine chinois, add orange and lemon juice, correct seasoning and consistency. Add zest of orange, remove sauce from heat and whisk in the butter. Napper duck with sauce and garnish with orange segments. This dish is usually carved at the table and is served accompanied with extra sauce.

N.B.   The flavour of this sauce may be enhanced by the addition of a measure of an orange liqueur, e.g. Curaçao.

White Braising

(a)   Using Small Cuts

The item most commonly used for small white braising is sweetbreads. The main purpose throughout cooking is to keep the food white and present the finished product in a white sauce produced from the cooking liquor.

BRAISED SWEETBREADS (WHITE)   Ris Braisés à Blanc

Yield: 4 portions
Cooking time: $1 - 1\frac{1}{2}$ hr
Cooking temperature: 150°C (300°F)

Unit	Ingredient	Metric (g)	Imperial (oz)
1	Sweetbreads (pre-soaked in running water to remove blood)	600	20
$\frac{1}{5}$	Mirepoix medium	120	4
$\frac{1}{20}$	Butter	30	1

Arrowroot to thicken
Bouquet garni
Chopped parsley
Squeeze of lemon juice
Salt and pepper
* White stock (veal where
    possible)

---

* Sufficient stock barely to cover sweetbreads during cooking.

Method

Blanch and refresh sweetbreads, skin and remove ducts. Sweat mirepoix in butter without colour, add sweetbreads, season, moisten with stock barely to cover. Bring to boil, skim, add bouquet garni. Cover with greased cartouche and tight-fitting lid, braise in oven until tender.

Once cooked remove sweetbreads and put aside. Reduce cooking liquor, lightly lié with arrowroot, correct seasoning, add lemon juice and strain sauce over sweetbreads. Serve garnished with chopped parsley.

White Braising

(b) Using Large Cuts

The meat most commonly used for large white braises is veal.

BRAISED VEAL (WHITE)   Pièce de Veau Braisé à Blanc

Yield: 4 – 6 portions
Cooking time: 1½ – 2 hr
Cooking temperature: 150°C (300°F)

Unit	Ingredient	Metric	Imperial
1	Braising veal (cushion)	1 kg	2½ lb
⅕	Mirepoix (large cut)	200 g	8 oz
¹⁄₂₀	Butter	50 g	2 oz
	Bouquet garni		
	Arrowroot to thicken		
	Salt and pepper		
	Chopped parsley		
*	White veal stock		
	Squeeze of lemon juice		

* Sufficient stock to cover two-thirds of the meat during braising.

Method

Sweat lightly seasoned veal and mirepoix in butter without colour. Cover two-thirds of the meat with stock, bring to boil, skim, add bouquet and seasoning. Cover with greased cartouche and tight-fitting lid, braise steadily in oven until meat is tender, basting periodically to effect a glaze. Remove veal from liquor and put aside, lightly lié sauce to pouring consistency using arrowroot, correct seasoning and strain.

Service

1. Allow meat to set for a period and carve into portions. Napper with sauce, garnish and serve.
2. Present meat whole, lightly napper with sauce, garnish and serve with a sauceboat of braising sauce.
   Carve the veal at the table.

N.B.   Alternatively the sauce may be prepared by reducing the braising liquor and adding (i) veal velouté/cream, (ii) sauce suprême, (iii) butter pieces only, i.e. monter de beure, (iv) double cream to well-reduced liquor.

Garnishes Commonly Used with White Braises: Added Ingredients in Relation to 1 Unit i.e. 1 kg (2½ lb) Braising Veal

Name of garnish	Unit	Ingredient	Metric	Imperial
à la Crème	$^1/_{10}$	Finish sauce with cream	100 ml	4 fl oz
à l'Ancienne	$^1/_{10}$ $^1/_{10}$	As above garnish with: glazed button onions à blanc glazed button mushrooms à blanc 4 heart-shaped croûtons	100 g 100 g	4 oz 4 oz
aux Champignons	$^1/_5$	As for à la Crème garnish: glazed button mushrooms à blanc	200 g	8 oz
Bonne Maman	$^1/_5$	Garnish: glazed julienne of vegetables à blanc	200 g	8 oz
Demidoff	$^1/_5$	Garnish glazed paysanne of vegetables à blanc julienne of truffle	200 g	8 oz

Braised Fish   Poisson Braisé

Braising is generally associated with stuffed whole fish and in some cases the smaller cuts of round and flat fish on the bone. Due to the structure of fish (*see* p. 61) the cooking times are less than for meats. The method of braising fish is as follows.

Yield: 4 portions
4 small whole fish
4 cuts on the bone [150 g (6 oz) each)]
Piece of large fish on bone [600 g (1¼ lb)]
Cooking time: dependant on size of fish
Cooking temperature: 150°C (300°F)

Unit	Ingredient	Metric	Imperial
	Selected fish (*see* yield)		
1	Mirepoix (brunoise)	150 g	5 oz
1	Wine (red or dry white)	150 ml	5 fl oz
⅕	Butter	30 g	1 oz
	Bouquet garni		
	Salt and pepper		
	Beurre manié for thickening		
*	Fish stock		

* Sufficient to cover two-thirds of the fish during braising.

Method

Place mirepoix, and fish into buttered braising vessel, add wine and stock to cover two-thirds of the fish. Bring to boil, skim, add bouquet garni, cover with buttered cartouche and braise in oven basting frequently until fish is cooked. Remove fish put aside to drain. Strain cooking liquor reduce and thicken lightly with beurre manié. Napper fish with sauce, sprinkle with chopped parsley and serve.

Service   Whole pieces of fish may be carved at the table.

   N.B.   Various garnishes may be served with braised fish, in which case the dishes would take on the name of the garnish e.g. Poisson Braisé Julienne—garnished with cooked julienne of vegetables; Poisson Braisé Doria—garnished with glazed, turned, cucumber.

The Braising of Vegetables

Prior to cooking in the oven most vegetables selected for braising are blanched in boiling water and refreshed. This initial process helps to retain the colour of the vegetables and make their structure more pliable for shaping.

Once refreshed and shaped the vegetable portions are placed on to a fine mirepoix in a lightly buttered braising vessel. Stock is then added to half cover the vegetables and they are then braised slowly under cover until cooked. The resultant liquor is often served with the vegetables in the form of a strained thickened sauce.

This method of cookery is particularly suited to the more fibrous vegetables i.e. celery, onions, leeks, cabbage, etc.

Selection and Preparation of Vegetables for Braising

Vegetable	Preparation
Celery	Trim root, remove celery tops to leave hearts (tops to be used for soup, stews, etc.), remove any decaying stalks. Cut in half lengthways and wash thoroughly. Blanch for 10 minutes and refresh, drain ready for use
Cabbage	Remove coarse outer leaves and four large green leaves (trim). Quarter cabbage and remove centre stalk, wash well. Blanch the four large green leaves and quarters for 5 minutes approximately, refresh and drain. Season cabbage, wrap quarters in green leaves, shape into firm balls and squeeze in clean cloth to shape and remove excess moisture
Stuffed cabbage	As above but stuff with sausage meat
Endive (Belgium)	Discard damaged outer leaves, wash thoroughly, leave whole for braising, blanch for 10 minutes, refresh and drain. Shape as required.
Leek	Discard damaged outer leaves, trim tops (retain for soups, stews, etc.) Lightly trim root, half split lengthways leaving root intact, wash well, blanch for 5 minutes, refresh and drain
Lettuce	Lightly trim base, discard damaged outer leaves, wash thoroughly keeping whole. Blanch for 5 minutes, refresh and drain. Squeeze well to remove moisture, shape into cigar shape, leave whole or cut in half lengthways. Neatly fold in point of lettuce to form an even shape.
Onions	Lightly trim root and remove onion skins, blanch for 10 minutes refresh and drain for use. N.B. Select medium onions
Stuffed peppers	Wash, cut across top removing stalk. This opens a cavity ready for stuffing. Shake peppers to remove seeds. Stuff with rice pilaff ready for use
Fennel	Trim tops, stems and base, wash well, blanch for 10 minutes and refresh for use

BRAISED VEGETABLES

Légumes Braisés

Yield: 4 portions
Cooking times: 1 – 2½ hr
Cooking temperature: 150°C (300°F)

Unit	Ingredient	Metric (g)	Imperial (oz)
1	Four selected vegetable portions (prepared *see* chart)	400	16
¼	Mirepoix (fine cut)	100	4
¹⁄₁₆	Butter or margarine	25	1
	Salt and pepper		
★	White stock		
	Arrowroot, jus lié or demi-glace where thickening is required		

★ Sufficient stock to half cover vegetable during braising.

Method

Sweat mirepoix with butter in braising vessel without colour. Place selected vegetable on to mirepoix, season and half cover with stock. Cover with buttered cartouche and lid. Braise in the oven until tender. Once cooked remove vegetables to drain well. Prepare thickened sauce if required.

Preparation of Sauce When Required

1. Reduce cooking liquor by a half, lié with arrowroot, correct seasoning strain and coat vegetables.
2. Reduce cooking liquor to a glaze add demi-glace or jus lié correct seasoning and strain to coat vegetables.

Examples of Dishes Prepared Using Above Formula

English term	Sauce and garnish	French term
Braised celery in juice	Coat lightly with thickened stock	Céleri Braisé au Jus
Braised celery in cheese sauce	Napper with mornay sauce sprinkle with grated cheese and gratinate	Céleri Braisé Mornay
Braised celery with parmesan cheese	Napper with demi-glace, sprinkle with grated parmesan and gratinate	Céleri Braisé au Parmesan
Braised celery with poached beef marrow	As for 'Céleri Braisé au Jus' then garnished with slices of poached beef marrow and chopped parsley	Céleri Braisé à la Moelle

Braised Belgium endive ⎫		Chicorée Braisée
Braised leeks	⎬ All may be sauced and garnished as for	Poireaux Braisés
Braised onions	celery	Oignons Braisés
Braised fennel ⎭		Fenouil Braisé
Braised cabbage ⎫	Lightly coat with thickened stock	Chou Braisé
Braised stuffed cabbage ⎭		Chou Farci Braisé
Braised lettuce in juice	Lightly coat with thickened stock. When used as a garnish the lettuce is usually placed on to heart-shaped croutons to absorb excess moisture	Laitues Braisées au Jus
Stuffed braised peppers	Garnish with chopped parsley	Piments Farcis Braisés

BRAISED CHESTNUTS   Marrons Braisés

Yield: 4 portions
Cooking time: 30 – 45 min
Cooking temperature: 150°C (300°F)

To Shell Chestnuts

1. Slit the shell of chestnut on both sides. Plunge into boiling water and simmer for 5 minutes. Remove shells and inner skins.
2. Slit shells and oven bake until shell splits open. Remove shells and inner skins.

Unit	Ingredient	Metric (g)	Imperial (oz)
1	Shelled chestnuts	400	16
$1/_8$	Celery stalks	50	2
$1/_{16}$	Butter	25	1
	Salt and pepper		
	Chopped parsley		
*	Brown stock (veal or chicken)		

* Sufficient stock to half cover chestnuts during braising.

Method

Sweat chestnuts and celery in butter without colour, lightly season, half cover with stock. Cover with buttered cartouche and a lid. Braise in oven until chestnuts are tender. Once cooked remove chestnuts and put aside to drain. Strain cooking liquor and reduce to a glaze. Toss chestnuts in glaze and serve garnished with chopped parsley.

BRAISED RED CABBAGE FLEMISH STYLE   Chou-Rouge Flamande

Yield: 4 portions
Cooking time: 3 hr
Cooking temperature. 150°C (300°F)

Preparation of Cabbage   Discard damaged outer leaves, quarter, remove stalk, wash well.

Unit	Ingredient	Metric	Imperial
1	Red cabbage (prepared and shredded)	400 g	1 lb
1/4	Apples (peeled and sliced)	100 ml	4 fl oz
1/8	Wine vinegar	50 ml	2 fl oz
1/16	Butter or margarine	25 g	1 oz
1/16	Sugar	25 g	1 oz
	Salt and pepper		

Method

Butter a braising dish add cabbage, vinegar, sugar and seasoning, cover with buttered cartouche and tight-fitting lid. Braise in oven, stirring periodically until three-quarters cooked. Add apples and continue cooking until tender. Correct seasoning and serve.

   N.B.   Certain cooking vessels are unsuitable for this product because the foods present react with the metal impairing the colour of the cooked cabbage. *See* p. 65.

BRAISED SAUERKRAUT (Pickled White Cabbage)   Choucroute Braisée

Yield: 4 portions
Cooking time: 3 hr
Cooking temperature: 150°C (300°F)

Unit	Ingredient	Metric (g)	Imperial (oz)
1	Sauerkraut	400	16
1/4	Carrot (left whole)	100	4
1/4	Onion clouté	100	4
1/16	Butter or margarine	25	1
	Few juniper berries in muslin		
	Bouquet garni		
	Salt and pepper		
*	White stock		

* Sufficient barely to cover sauerkraut during cooking.

Method

Butter braising vessel, add all ingredients, barely cover with stock. Cover with buttered cartouche and a tight-fitting lid. Braise in oven, stirring periodically until sauerkraut is cooked. Remove onion, bouquet garni, juniper berries and carrots. Correct seasoning and serve garnished with sliced carrot.

SAUERKRAUT WITH GARNISH   Choucroute Garniture

As above formula plus:

Unit	Ingredient	Metric (g)	Imperial (oz)
$\frac{1}{2}$	Piece of blanched streaky bacon	200	8
$\frac{1}{2}$	Frankfurters (4 – 8)	200	8

Method

Add bacon piece to sauerkraut at commencement of cooking period. When almost cooked add frankfurters to heat through.

Service   Place sliced bacon, carrot and whole frankfurters on a bed of sauerkraut to garnish.

Potato Dishes Cooked Using the Braising Principle

Although these do not appear on the menu as braised potato dishes the method of cookery adopted is akin to the braising technique. Many of these dishes are cooked and served in a casserole.

POTATOES   Pommes de Terre

BERRICHONNE POTATOES   Pommes Berrichonne

Yield: 4 portions
Cooking time: 1 hr
Cooking temperature: 175°C (350°F)

Unit	Ingredient	Metric (g)	Imperial (oz)
1	Potatoes [diced 1½ cm (½ in) or small turned]	400	16
$\frac{1}{4}$	Streaky bacon (blanched lardons)	100	4
$\frac{1}{4}$	Onion (medium diced)	100	4
	Salt and pepper		
	Hint of garlic		
	Chopped parsley		
	Melted butter		
*	White stock		

* Sufficient stock to half cover potatoes.

Method

Place onions, potatoes and bacon in casserole, add garlic and season lightly. Half cover with hot stock, brush with melted butter and braise in the oven until potatoes are cooked and golden brown. At this stage most of the stock will have been absorbed by the potatoes. Serve, brushed with melted butter and sprinkled with chopped parsley.

POTATOES BRITTANY STYLE
Pommes Bretonne

As for Pommes Berrichonne (diced) but replace bacon with tomato concassé.

HUNGARIAN POTATOES
Pommes Hongroise

As for Pommes Bretonne flavoured with paprika.

POTATOES WITH BACON AND ONIONS
Pommes au Lard

As for Pommes Berrichonne but replace diced onions with button onions.

SAVOURY POTATOES
Pommes Boulangère

Yield: 4 portions
Cooking time: 1½ hr
Cooking temperature: 175°C (350°F)

Unit	Ingredient	Metric (g)	Imperial (oz)
1	Potatoes [sliced into 2 mm (⅛ in) rounds]	400	16
½	Onions shredded	200	8
	Salt and pepper		
	Melted butter		
	Chopped parsley		
*	White stock		

* Sufficient stock almost to cover the potatoes.

Method

Mix two-thirds of potatoes with onion, lightly season and place in casserole. Neatly lay remaining potatoes overlapping on top of filled casserole. Add hot stock almost to cover the potatoes and brush surface with melted butter. Braise in the oven until potatoes are cooked to golden brown and the stock absorbed by the potatoes. Serve brushed with melted butter and sprinkled with chopped parsley.

POTATOES WITH BACON AND CHEESE
Pommes Savoyarde

As for Pommes Boulangère with the addition of:

Unit	Ingredient	Metric (g)	Imperial (oz)
¼	Streaky bacon (blanched lardons)	100	4
¼	Gruyère cheese (grated)	100	4
	Chopped garlic		

Method

Mix bacon, garlic and cheese with two-thirds potatoes and all the onions. Continue as for Pommes Boulangère. Sprinkle a little cheese on top layer of potatoes before cooking.

DAUPHINOISE POTATOES   Pommes Dauphinoise

Yield: 4 portions
Cooking time: 45 min – 1 hr
Cooking temperature: 175°C (350°F)

Unit	Ingredient	Metric (g)	Imperial (oz)
1	Potatoes (thinly sliced, net weight)	400	16
¼	Gruyère cheese (grated)	100	4
	Salt and pepper		
	Hint of chopped garlic		
	Melted butter		
	Chopped parsley		
*	Milk (boiled)		

* Sufficient boiled milk to half cover potatoes. Some recipes advocate fresh cream as a replacement for milk.

Method

Mix half of grated cheese with potatoes, garlic and seasoning. Lightly grease casserole with melted butter, fill with potato mixture, sprinkle with remaining cheese and half cover with boiled milk.

Braise in the oven until potatoes are cooked golden brown and the milk has been absorbed by the potatoes. Serve brushed with melted butter and sprinkled with chopped parsley.

DELMONICO POTATOES   Pommes Delmonico

Yield: 4 portions
Cooking time: 1 hr
Cooking temperature: 175°C (350°F)

Unit	Ingredient	Metric (g)	Imperial (oz)
1	Potatoes [diced 1½ cm (½ in) net wt]	400	16
⅛	White breadcrumbs	50	2
	Salt and pepper		
	Pinch of nutmeg		
	Melted butter		
*	Milk (boiled)		

* Sufficient boiled milk to almost cover potatoes on cooking.

Method

Season potatoes, place in casserole and sprinkle with nutmeg. Barely cover with boiled milk and braise in oven until potatoes are almost cooked. Sprinkle liberally with bread-crumbs and melted butter, continue cooking in hot oven until potatoes are cooked and gratinated. Serve as required.

FONDANT POTATOES
Pommes Fondant

Yield: 4 portions
Cooking time: 45 min – 1 hr
Cooking temperature: 175°C (350°F)

Unit	Ingredient	Metric (g)	Imperial (oz)
1	Potatoes (large turned net wt)	400	16
$1/_8$	Butter (melted)	50	2
	Salt and pepper		
★	White stock		

★ Sufficient stock to half cover potatoes on cooking.

Method

Place potatoes in braising vessel, lightly season, half cover with stock and brush with melted butter. Braise in moderate oven until potatoes are cooked to a light brown colour and have absorbed the stock. Brush with melted butter and serve.

CRETAN POTATOES
Pommes Cretan

As for Pommes Fondant but flavour stock with thyme.

CHAMPIGNOL POTATOES
Pommes Champignol

As for Pommes Fondant but sprinkle cooked fondant with grated cheese and gratinate.

22

The Principle and Practice of Roasting

To Roast   Rôtir

Modern roasting may be defined as a method of cooking with dry convected heat in an oven cavity. The dryness of the atmosphere within the oven is modified by the presence of steam. The steam is generated by the action of heat upon the moisture content within the food. Traditional roasting is carried out over an open fire on a rotating spit and the moisture is driven off in the open atmosphere. Modern roasting spits powered by electricity and gas are available for domestic and industrial use.

Foods commonly roasted include prime joints of butcher's meats, poultry, game and certain vegetables. Joints of meat chosen for roasting are designated as first or second class roasting joints, the former being the prime cuts of butcher's meat. To ensure a successful roast product the joints should contain a proportion of surface and intra-muscular fats, which act to keep the lean meat moist and prevent undue shrinkage during cooking.

Initially, on roasting meats are subjected to a high temperature, which seals in the juices by coagulating the surface protein (albumen). Once this is achieved the cooking temperature is reduced to allow even steady cooking. Not all the meat juices are retained, and those that escape into the roasting tray are employed in the formulation of accompanying gravies.

Notes for Guidance

Where a traditional kitchen brigade is employed the following members are involved with the preparation for, and the cooking of, roast products:

Chef Garde-Manger	— basic preparation of meats for roasting
Chef Entremettier	— basic preparation and roasting of vegetables
Chef Rôtisseur	— roasting of butcher's meat, poultry and game.

1. Preparation of Meats for Roasting

Seasoning and Flavouring

Prior to cooking, meats are lightly seasoned with salt and pepper and flavoured with herbs if required. Certain items for roasting may also be filled with a selected stuffing. These procedures enhance the flavour of the finished product.

Larding and Barding

These techniques (inserting or covering meat with pork fat) are used when items selected for roasting need extra fat. This acts to provide moisture throughout roasting preventing the meat from drying out and shrinking excessively.

Use of Trivets

A trivet raises the items being roasted out of the fat, which lies in the base of the cooking vessel. As a result any frying of meat surfaces is prevented. Trivets may be formed with raw bones, but are also commercially available in the form of metal racks.

2. Care in Cooking

Basting

This is a technical term used to denote the action of moistening meat with melted fat and cooking juices during roasting. This process is carried out at regular intervals by *spooning* the melted fat and juices over the meat.

Turning Items During Roasting

When oven-roasting without a spit, large joints of butcher's meat, poultry and game require turning at intervals, to ensure even cooking and colouring.

3. Testing for Cooking

See chart for roasting times and degrees of cooking (*see* p. 386). As a general guide meat is:

(a) underdone (rare) when juices run red and bloody;
(b) rare to medium when juices run pink;
(c) just done when juices run clear.

In order to exude meat juices, press the surface of the joint firmly.

Butcher's Meat, Poultry, and Game Commonly Selected for Roasting

English term	French term	Basic preparation in brief	First or second class roast
Beef joints			
Sirloin (on bone)	Aloyau de Boeuf	Chine, trim and season	First
Strip loin (off bone)	Contrefilet de Boeuf	Trim and season	First
Ribs ⎫ Wing			First
on ⎬ Fore	Côte de Boeuf	Chine trim and season	First
bone ⎭ Middle			Second
Fillet heart	Coeur de Filet de Boeuf	Trim, lard and season	First

English term	French term	Basic preparation in brief	First or second class roast
Lamb joints			
Leg	Gigot d'Agneau	Trim knuckle and aitchbone secure with string and season. Aitchbone may be removed after cooking	First
Shoulder	Épaule d'Agneau	Trim knuckle and season, or bone out stuff, roll and secure with string	Second
Best-end	Carré d'Agneau	Skin, chine, trim and score. Trim ends of cutlet bone and season	First
Breast	Poitrine d'Agneau	Skin, bone out, stuff roll, season and secure with string	Second
Long saddle	Selle d'Agneau	Skin, trim, score, secure flaps with string and season (kidneys removed).	First
Short saddle	Selle d'Agneau	Remove chump and continue as above	First
Loin	Longe d'Agneau	Bone, roll, season and secure with string (May be stuffed)	First
Crown	Curonne d'Agneau	Prepare best-ends of lamb shape into crown and sew with string to secure	First
Pork joints			
Leg	Cuissot de Porc	Remove aitchbone, and trotter, score rind and rub with salt	First
Loin (may include chine bone)	Longe de Porc	Trim and loosen meat from chine bone, but leave intact. Score rind and rub with salt	First
Shoulder	Épaule de Porc	Bone out shoulder (may be stuffed), score rind, rub with salt and secure with string	Second
Spare rib	Échine de Porc	Trim, score rind, rub with salt and secure with string	Second
Veal joints			
Leg (small)	Cuissot de Veau	Remove aitchbone, trim knuckle, lard, season and secure with string	First
Loin	Longe de Veau	Trim and loosen meat from chine bone but leave intact, season (may be boned, stuffed and rolled)	First
Best-end	Carré de Veau	Chine and trim. Scrape end of cutlet bones and season	First
Breast	Poitrine de Veau	Bone, trim, stuff, roll, season and secure with string	Second
		N.B. All veal joints, due to lack of fat content are best barded or larded to provide moisture during roasting. Otherwise meat will cook dry and shrink excessively	

English term	*French term*	*Seasons*	*Basic preparation in brief*	*First or second class roast*
Poultry				
Chicken (baby)	Poussin		Clean, singe and trim, Remove wishbone, stuff if required, season and truss for roasting	First
(small)	Poulet de Grain			
(medium)	Poulet Reine			
(large)	Poularde			
Capon	Chapon		As for chicken	First
Duck	Canard			
Duckling	Caneton			
Goose	Oie			First
Gosling	Oison			
Turkey	Dinde		As for chicken but remove heavy sinews from legs	First
Turkey (young)	Dindonneau			
Game				
Feathered				
Pheasant	Faisan	Oct. – Jan.	Clean, singe, trim and remove wishbone. Season, truss and bard	First
Partridge	Perdreau	Sept. – Jan.	As for pheasant	First
Grouse	Grouse	Aug. – Dec.	As for pheasant	First
Quail	Caille	All year	As for pheasant	First
Guinea fowl	Pintade	All year	As for pheasant	First
Wild duck	Canard Sauvage	Sept. – Feb.	As for pheasant but omit barding	First
Teal	Sarcelle	Sept. – Feb.	As for wild duck	First
Snipe	Bécassine	Aug. – Jan.	Partially draw by removing gall bladder, gizzard and intestines. Trim, season, bard then truss with beak	First
Woodcock	Bécasse	Oct. – Jan.	As for snipe	First
Plover	Pluvier	Sept. – Dec.	As for snipe but trussed with string	First
Furred				
Saddle of hare	Râble de Lièvre	Aug. – March	Trim, remove sinew, lard and season	First
Saddle of venison	Selle de Venaison	June – Jan.	As for saddle of hare	First
Haunch of venison	Hanche de Venaison	June – Jan.	As for saddle of hare	First

A Guide to Roasting Times

Meat	Approximate times	Degree of cooking
Beef	15 min per ½ kg (1 lb) and 15 min over	Underdone
	20 min per ½ kg (1 lb) and 20 min over	Rare to medium
Lamb/mutton	20 min per ½ kg (1 lb) and 20 min over	Just done
Pork	25 min per ½ kg (1 lb) and 25 min over	Well done
Veal	25 min per ½ kg (1 lb) and 25 min over	Just done
Chickens	15 min per ½ kg (1 lb) and 15 min over	Just done
Ducks/Goose	20 min per ½ kg (1 lb) and 20 min over	Well cooked
Goose	20 min per ½ kg (1 lb) and 20 min over	Well cooked
Turkey	20 min per ½ kg (1 lb)	Just done
Pheasant	30 min to 50 min per pheasant	Just done
Partridge	15 min to 25 min per partridge	Just done
Grouse	20 min to 25 min per grouse	Rare to medium
Quail	8 min to 10 min per quail	Just done
Guinea fowl	30 min to 50 min per fowl	Just done
Wild duck	20 min to 25 min per duck	Underdone
Teal	15 min to 20 min per teal	Underdone
Snipe	10 min to 15 min per snipe	Just done
Woodcock	15 min to 20 min per woodcock	Just done
Plover	15 min to 20 min per plover	Just done
Hare Saddle	15 min to 25 min per saddle	Rare to medium
Venison	15 min per ½ kg (1 lb) and 15 min over	Underdone

Preparation of Stuffings and Accompaniments for Roasts

Stuffing   Farce

Prepared stuffings are used in a variety of ways in culinary operations:

- (a) to stuff and flavour joints, cuts of butcher's meat, poultry and game prior to cooking, e.g. loins of lamb, boned, stuffed and rolled prior to roasting, beef olives rolled and stuffed prior to cooking;
- (b) prepared and cooked separately and served to accompany roast meats and stews, e.g. roast pork with sage and onion stuffing, deep fried forcemeat balls with Jugged Hare;
- (c) to act as a stuffing for vegetables, e.g. tomatoes filled with duxelle stuffing.

SAGE AND ONION STUFFING   Farce de Sauge et Oignon

Yield: 4 portions
Cooking time: 20 min (when cooked separately in oven)
Cooking temperature: 150°C (300°F)

Unit	Ingredient	Metric (g)	Imperial (oz)
1	White breadcrumbs	100	4
1	Onion (brunoise)	100	4
¹/₂	Dripping or margarine	50	2
	Sage to flavour		
	Pinch chopped parsley		
	Seasoning		
★	Stock or beaten egg		

Methods

Sweat onions in fat without colour, lightly season during cooking. Add breadcrumbs, sage and parsley to form stuffing and adjust seasoning.

Method 1   *When preparing* and cooking the stuffing as a separate item moisten with a little stock, place into greased cooking vessel, cover with cartouche and bake in moderate oven.

Method 2   *When using* to stuff a cut or joint before cooking bind stuffing with beaten egg prior to use. Egg protein coagulates during cooking, sets the stuffing preventing it from breaking up during carving.

LEMON, PARSLEY AND THYME STUFFING

Farce de Persil et Thym au Citron

Yield: 4 portions
Cooking time: 20 min (when cooked separately in oven)
Cooking temperature: 150°C (300°F)

Unit	Ingredient	Metric	Imperial
1	Breadcrumbs	100 g	4 oz
¹/₂	Suet (finely chopped)	50 g	2 oz
¹/₄	Lemon juice and grated zest	25 ml	1 fl oz
	Thyme ⎫		
	Parsley (chopped) ⎬ to taste		
	Seasoning ⎭		
★	Stock or beaten egg		

Method

Combine breadcrumbs, suet, lemon juice and herbs to form stuffing. Adjust seasoning and proceed as for sage and onion stuffing.

SAUSAGEMEAT STUFFING (FORCEMEAT)

Yield: 4 portions

Unit	Ingredient	Metric (g)	Imperial (oz)
1	Sausagemeat (pork)	100	4
$\frac{1}{2}$	Breadcrumbs	50	2
$\frac{1}{2}$	Suet (finely chopped)	50	2
$\frac{1}{4}$	Beaten egg	25	1
	Mixed herbs to taste		
	Seasoning		

Methods

Combine all ingredients thoroughly to form stuffing.

Method 1   Generally used to stuff poultry before roasting and some vegetables for braising.

Method 2   In addition may be rolled into forcemeat balls, panéed an deep fried to accompany certain game stews.

CHESTNUT STUFFING   Farce de Marrons
(For roast turkey)

Yield: 4 portions
Cooking time: 45 min (when cooking as a separate item in oven)
Cooking temperature: 150°C (300°F)

Unit	Ingredient	Metric (g)	Imperial (oz)
1	Sausagemeat stuffing	100	4
$\frac{1}{2}$	Braised chestnuts		
	(*see* p. 376),	50	2
	coarsely chopped		

Methods

Combine ingredients thoroughly to form stuffing.

Method 1   When cooking separately, place in greased cooking vessel, cover with cartouche and bake, or roll into cylindrical shape, wrap in foil and steam. When cooked slice into portions.

Method 2   Use raw to stuff the crop of turkey before roasting.

YORKSHIRE PUDDING

Yield: 4 portions
Cooking time: individual 15 – 20 min, tray 20 – 30 min
Cooking temperature: 205°C (400°F)

Unit	Ingredient	Metric	Imperial
1	Milk or milk and water	250 ml	10 fl oz
$^2/_5$	Flour	100 g	4 oz
$^1/_5$	Whole egg*	50 g	2 oz
$^1/_{10}$	Dripping/lard	25 g	1 oz
	Salt to taste		

* The amount of egg may be doubled for improved lift.

Method

Sift flour and salt into mixing bowl and form a well. Lightly beat egg and half of the milk together, then pour into well. Commence formation of batter by beating flour and liquid together. Gradually add remaining liquid, whisking thoroughly to form a smooth batter. Allow to stand and rest before use.

Divide dripping into pudding moulds or tray and heat thoroughly in the oven. Remove from oven, fill with batter mixture and bake until risen and cooked. Serve immediately.

Method

Oven Roasting   Place prepared butcher's meat, poultry or game on to trivet in a roasting tray. Brush with melted fat, place in hot oven to seal exterior of meat [approximately 10 – 15 min at 205°C (400°F)]. Reduce temperature to moderate heat [150°C (300°F)] and continue roasting until cooked to required degree. Throughout roasting baste item frequently in order to keep the meat moist and add flavour. Once cooked remove meat from oven and allow to set for carving approximately 20 – 30 min.
N.B.   When roasting large joints of meat, poultry or game it will be necessary to turn the item from time to time to ensure even cooking.

Flash Roasting   A term used to describe speedy roasting at a high temperature. This method is particularly suitable for roasting small items of game and for certain beef cuts required underdone, e.g. contrefilets and fillets of beef.

Roast Gravy   Jus Rôti

Take roasting tray containing fat and roast meat sediment. Pour off excess fat leaving behind sediment. Heat sediment on stove top to colour brown, then deglaze with selected brown stock to form roast gravy. Season to taste, strain through fine chinois, degrease and serve as required.

Thickened Roast Gravy   Jus Rôti Lié

As for roast gravy but lightly thickened by the addition of moistened arrowroot.

Experimental Roasting

In today's cost-conscious environment, caterers are continually having to evaluate production methods in order to improve their efficiency and profitability. The techniques employed range from the use of modern technology in the form of plant, equipment, and systems, to the more simple cooking aids such as roasting bags, tin foil, and thermo pins, etc. Continual experiments are conducted in order to determine the most efficient ways of roasting meats with regard to savings in time, energy and labour, whilst at the same time improving the quality and yield of the product. Where comparisons have been made with traditional oven roasting it has been ascertained that roasting in foil or bags reduces the cooking time, results in a higher portion yield and eliminates the need for basting (therefore saving labour time).

Traditional Accompaniments with Roast Butcher's Meat, Poultry, and Game

English term	French term	Traditional garnish
Roast beef	Boeuf Rôti à l'Anglaise	Yorkshire pudding, roast gravy, horse-radish sauce, watercress
Roast lamb	Agneau Rôti	Roast gravy, mint sauce, watercress
Roast mutton	Mouton Rôti	White onion sauce, roast gravy, redcurrant jelly, watercress
Roast pork	Porc Rôti	Roast gravy, sage and onion stuffing, apple sauce, watercress
Roast veal	Veau Rôti	Thickened roast gravy, lemon, parsley and thyme stuffing, watercress
Roast chicken (English style)	Poulet Rôti à l'Anglaise	Roast gravy, bread sauce, grilled bacon, game chips, watercress
Roast chicken with stuffing	Poulet Rôti Farci	Roast gravy, parsley and thyme stuffing, watercress
Roast chicken with stuffing (English style)	Poulet Roti Farci à l'Anglaise	Roast gravy, bread sauce, parsley and thyme stuffing, grilled bacon, game chips, watercress
Roast duck/duckling	Canard/Caneton Rôti	Roast gravy, sage and onion stuffing, apple sauce, watercress
Roast gosling/ goose (f)	Oison Rôti/Oie Rôtie	As for duck
Roast turkey (young m)	Dindonneau Rôti ⎫	Roast gravy, bread sauce, chestnut stuffing, grilled chipolatas, grilled bacon, cranberry sauce, watercress
Roast turkey (f)	Dinde Rôtie ⎬	
Roast guinea-fowl	Pintade Rôtie à l'Anglaise	As for Poulet Rôti à l'Anglaise

Roast

Pheasant	Faisan Rôti ⎫	Roast gravy, brown breadcrumbs, game chips,
Partridge	Perdreau Rôti	bread sauce, watercress, grilled bacon
Grouse	Grouse Rôtie	(optional).
Quail	Caille Rôtie ⎬	N.B. The roasted game is presented on a fried
Woodcock	Bécasse Rôtie	croûton of appropriate size spread with game
Snipe	Bécassine Rôtie	farce. Alternatively shallow-fried heart-shaped
Plover	Pluvier Rôti ⎭	croûtes spread with game farce may be offered

Roast

Wild duck	Canard Sauvage Rôti	Roast gravy, watercress, orange salad
Teal	Sarcelle Rôtie	
Roast saddle of hare	Râble de Lièvre Rôti	Roast gravy, forcemeat balls, redcurrant jelly, watercress
Roast venison	Venaison Rôtie	Roast gravy, redcurrant jelly, watercress. N.B. Sauce Poivrade is often served

N.B.   When required, certain items for roasting may be flavoured with selected fresh herbs prior to cooking or served with an accompanying garnish other than the traditional English accompaniment. *See* below.

English term	French term	Garnish and explanation
Roast lamb with rosemary	Agneau Rôti au Romarin	Rub exterior of meat liberally with rosemary before roasting
Roast lamb with garlic and rosemary	Agneau Rôti à l'Ail et Romarin.	Piqué joint with strips of garlic before roasting Rub well with rosemary
Roast chicken with tarragon	Poulet Rôti à l'Estragon	Rub exterior of chicken liberally with tarragon before roasting
Roast lamb with Boulangère potatoes	Agneau Rôti à la Boulangère	Complete roasting by placing joint on top of cooked boulangère potatoes. Serve lamb and potatoes together
Roast fillet of beef with Dubarry garnish	Coeur de Filet de Boeuf Rôti Dubarry	Serve garnished with fleurettes of cauliflower mornay and château potatoes

N.B.   All the above are served with roast gravy (unthickened). Other suitable garnishes may be employed in a similar fashion. In many instances roasts are accompanied by side salads e.g. roast beef with green salad.

Carving of Roast Meats, Poultry, and Game

Carving requires a high level of competence and skill to ensure that roasted meats are attractively presented to the customer in correct portions. For the best results roasted meats are allowed to stand and set after cooking to facilitate carving and to gain maximum portion yield.

In general, meats should be carved across the grain to ensure a short-fibred, tender cut of meat. If the meat is carved with the grain these fibres remain long and stringy, which results in the meat being tougher and less palatable. Throughout carving the selected knife needs to be kept sharp to ensure ease of operation. Carving may be carried out in the kitchen or at the customer's table according to the mode of service and the establishment's style.

When carving feathered game or poultry it is usual to serve a combination of leg and breast meat per portion, however, smaller items may be served whole or jointed according to their size. For instance:

(a) small ducklings divided into two;
(b) small chickens portioned into two legs, and two breasts;
(c) baby chickens and quail, served whole;
(d) medium-sized chicken or pheasant jointed into 4 portions as shown in carving diagrams (*see* overleaf).

Lamb/Agneau

Leg/Gigot

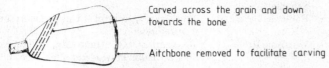

Carved across the grain and down towards the bone

Aitchbone removed to facilitate carving

Shoulder/Épaule

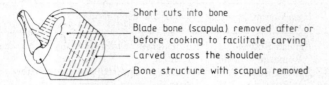

Short cuts into bone

Blade bone (scapula) removed after or before cooking to facilitate carving

Carved across the shoulder

Bone structure with scapula removed

Saddle/Selle

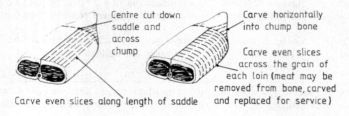

Centre cut down saddle and across chump

Carve horizontally into chump bone

Carve even slices across the grain of each loin (meat may be removed from bone, carved and replaced for service)

Carve even slices along length of saddle

Best End/Carré

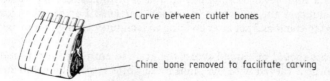

Carve between cutlet bones

Chine bone removed to facilitate carving

Pork/Porc

Leg/Cuissot (also for gammon)

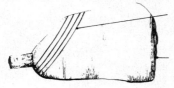

Carved across the grain and
down towards the bone

Aitchbone removed to facilitate
carving

Beef/Boeuf

Rib of Beef/Côte de Boeuf

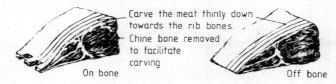

Carve the meat thinly down
towards the rib bones.

Chine bone removed
to facilitate
carving

On bone   Off bone

Poultry/Volaille (also for some feathered game)

Chicken/Poulet — Carved (jointed) into 4 portions

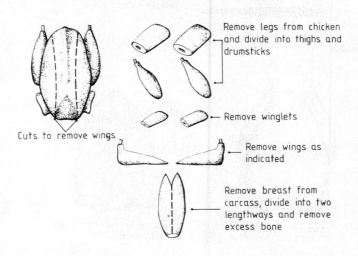

Remove legs from chicken
and divide into thighs and
drumsticks

Remove winglets

Remove wings as
indicated

Cuts to remove wings

Remove breast from
carcass, divide into two
lengthways and remove
excess bone

Duck/Canard — Carved (jointed) into 4 portions

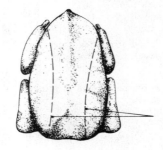

Cuts to remove wings

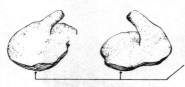

Remove legs from duck and divide into two as required. It is possible to remove all bone from legs after roasting before carving each into pieces (two)

Remove wings as indicated

Remove breast from carcass, divide into two lengthways and remove excess bone

Turkey/Dinde

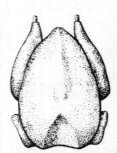

Neck cavity which may be filled with a stuffing

Remove legs from turkey and carve into portions free from bone

Carve breast into even, thin slices

ROAST VEGETABLES
Légumes Rôtis

Few vegetables are cooked by this method the most common being potatoes and parsnips.
Yield: 4 portions
Cooking time: *see* chart
Cooking temperature: 205°C (400°F)

Unit	Ingredient	Metric (g)	Imperial (oz)
1	Main item (prepared – *see* chart below)	400	16
1/8	Dripping or oil	50	2
	Seasoning		

Method

Heat dripping or oil in a roasting tray on stove top, add well-drained vegetables, lightly season and agitate roasting tray to coat vegetables with the fat and prevent them from sticking to the cooking vessel.

Place in oven and roast until golden brown and cooked. During roasting baste and turn vegetables to ensure even cooking and to prevent them from adhering to the tray. Once cooked, remove from oven, drain well and serve.

Examples of Roast Vegetables

English term	French term	Preparation	Approximate cooking time (min)
Roast potatoes	Pommes Rôties	Peel potatoes and cut to even size	45
Château potatoes	Pommes Château	Peel potatoes and turn to even shape	45
Roast parsnips	Panais Rôtis	Peel and trim, cut into wedges lengthways. Remove fibrous core from centre if tough	30

23

The Principle and Practice of Pot-Roasting

To Pot-Roast   Poêler

Cooking à la Poêle may be defined as cooking on a bed of aromatic herbs with vegetables in a covered casserole or container, using butter for basting. Only the choice tender joints of butcher's meat, game, and poultry are suitable for this method as little or no moisture is employed during cooking to aid tenderization. Pot-roasting acts to retain the natural juices and flavour of the food being cooked. Upon completion of cooking the juices are utilized in the preparation of an accompanying sauce.

Notes for Guidance

Certain foods, e.g. chicken are poêled and served in a casserole or cocotte dish. In these instances they are designated 'en cocotte' on the menu, e.g. Poulet en Cocotte. Many relevés and entrées (*see* p. 77) are cooked by this method.

When a traditional kitchen brigade is employed the following Chefs de Partie are involved with pot-roasted products:

Chef Garde-Manger   —   involved with initial preparation of meats prior to cooking
Chef Saucier   —   relevés and entrées.

Poêle is considered to be a mode of cookery ideally suited for use with premier joints of butcher's meat, poultry, and game. Pot-roasting must not be confused with the domestic-style casserole, which is in essence a type of oven-stew or braise more suited to the tougher cuts of meats. Prior to cooking 'à la Poêle', certain prime joints containing little fat are larded and/or barded with pork fat, which keeps the meat moist and minimizes shrinkage during cooking.

Cooking Vessels

Cooking à la Poêle may be carried out in oven-proof earthenware dishes (cocottes) or in deep metal poêle pots. Cocottes are commonly used with poultry and for some feathered game.

Basting

Throughout cooking the food is enclosed with a tight-fitting lid, which provides a self-basting process, a result of condensation within the vessel. In addition the product is basted in the normal way. When colouring is required the lid is removed near the end of the cooking period.

Service

Whilst the sauce is being prepared the cooked meat is allowed to stand and set to facilitate carving. On service the joint may be presented whole for carving at the table or be carved in the kitchen. For illustrated carving techniques *see* Chapter 22.

Poêled products may be served 'en cocotte' or on a service flat according to requirements.

Examples of Joints Suitable for Poêle

Selected meat	Preparation for Poêle	Portion Yield	Cooking time (approximately)
Poultry and game			
1 Medium chicken		4	$1 - 1\frac{1}{4}$ hr
1 Large duck	Cleaned and trussed.	4	2 hr
2 Small ducklings		4	$1\frac{1}{2}$ hr
2 Small pheasant	Barded	4	$1 - 1\frac{1}{4}$ hr
2 Saddles of hare	Trim away sinew, piqué with pork fat then place in red wine marinade	4	25 – 30 min
Beef			
Fillet 800 g (2 lb)	Trim away sinew, lard with pork fat	4 – 6	20 – 30 min
Strip sirloin 800 g (2 lb)	Trim away sinew and excess fat	4 – 6	25 – 30 min
Lamb			
Saddle $3\frac{1}{2}$ kg (7 lb)	Trimmed and secured with string (left on bone)	8 – 10	$2 - 2\frac{1}{2}$ hr
Loin 800 g (2 lb)	Boned and rolled (may be stuffed before rolling). Secure with string	4	1 hr
Veal			
Cushion 800 g (2 lb)	Trim, lard with pork fat and secure with string	4	$1 - 1\frac{1}{2}$ hr

N.B.   Other premier joints may be cooked by the poêle method.

POT ROAST

Poêler

Yield: 4 portions (*see* chart above)
Cooking time: *see* chart above for individual cooking times.
Cooking temperature: 175°C (350°F)

Unit	Ingredient	Metric	Imperial
	Selected meat (*see* chart above)		
1	Demi-glace or jus lié	500 ml	1 pt
²/₅	Mirepoix (medium cut to include aromates)	200 g	8 oz
¹/₁₀	Butter	50 g	2 oz
	Seasoning		
	Garnish		
	Wine/spirit or other liquid { See charts below		

Method

Brush base of cooking vessel lightly with butter, add mirepoix and aromates. Lightly season selected joint and place on to mirepoix. Brush joint liberally with remaining butter, cover with lid and pot roast in pre-heated oven, basting frequently. Once cooked remove joint from cooking vessel and put aside to set in readiness for service.

Deglaze with selected wine/spirit, reduce over heat, add jus-lié or demi-glace and continue to reduce to correct consistency. If cooking has been carried out in earthenware cocotte dish prepare sauce in a sauteuse to avoid damaging the cocotte. Pass sauce through fine chinois, degrease and adjust seasoning.

Service (chicken ducks, and feathered game)   Remove string and cut into portions, place in cocotte, coat with sauce, garnish as required and serve.

Service (ducks, saddle of hare, and butcher's meat)   Remove string from joints, carve into portions, arrange neatly on sauced service flat, surround with garnish, lightly napper with a little sauce. Serve accompanied with extra sauce.

N.B.   Alternatively the above preparations may be left whole and carved at the table.

Extensions of Above Formula Using Chicken: Selected Garnish Wine—Spirit in Relation to 1 Unit—½ l (1 pt) Sauce

French term	Unit	Ingredient	Metric	Imperial
Poulet en Cocotte Bonne Femme	$1/_5$	Cocotte potatoes	100 g	4 oz
	$1/_5$	Button onions (glacés à brun)	100 g	4 oz
	$1/_5$	Lardons (cooked)	100 g	4 oz
		Chopped parsley		
Poulet en Cocotte Champeaux	$1/_5$	Cocotte potatoes	100 g	4 oz
	$1/_5$	Button onions (glacés à brun)	100 g	4 oz
	$1/_{10}$	Dry white wine	50 ml	2 fl oz
		Chopped parsley		
Poulet en Cocotte aux Chipolata	$1/_5$	Cooked chipolatas	100 g	4 oz
	$1/_5$	Button onions (glacés à brun)	100 g	4 oz
	$1/_5$	Braised chestnuts	100 g	4 oz
	$1/_{10}$	Lardons (cooked)	50 g	2 oz
	$1/_{10}$	Dry white wine	50 ml	2 fl oz
		Chopped parsley		
Poulet en Cocotte Fermière	$2/_5$	Cooked paysanne of vegetables	200 g	8 oz
		Chopped parsley		
Poulet en Cocotte à la Paysanne	$1/_5$	Cooked paysanne of vegetables	100 g	4 oz
	$1/_5$	Cocotte potatoes	100 g	4 oz
	$1/_{10}$	Lardons (cooked)	50 g	2 oz
	$1/_{10}$	Dry white wine	50 g	2 oz
		Chopped parsley		
Poulet en Cocotte Grand 'Mère	$1/_5$	Fried croûtons (bâton shaped)	100 g	4 oz
	$1/_5$	Quartered mushrooms (sautéed)	100 g	4 oz
		Chopped parsley		

Extensions of Above Formula Using Ducks or Ducklings: Selected Garnish — Wine/Spirit in Relation to 1 Unit — ½ l (1 pt) Sauce

French term	Unit	Ingredient	Metric	Imperial
Canard/Caneton Poêle aux Cerises	$2/_5$	Stoned cherries	200 g	8 oz
	$1/_{10}$	Madeira	50 ml	2 fl oz
Canard/Caneton Poêle à l'Orange	$2/_5$	Orange segments	200 g	8 oz
	$1/_5$	Orange juice	100 ml	4 fl oz
	$1/_{10}$	Lemon juice	50 ml	2 fl oz
	$1/_{20}$	Orange curacao	25 ml	1 fl oz
		Blanched julienne of orange zest to garnish		

Extensions of Above Formula Using Game: Selected Garnish — Wine/Spirit in Relation to 1 Unit — ½ l (1 pt) Sauce

French term	Unit	Ingredient	Metric	Imperial
Faisan en Cocotte	$1/_5$	Button onions (glacés à brun)	100 g	4 oz
	$1/_5$	Quartered mushrooms (sautéed)	100 g	4 oz
	$1/_{10}$	Madeira	50 g	2 oz
		Chopped parsley		
Râble de Lièvre	$2/_5$	Button mushrooms (sautéed)	200 g	8 oz
Poêle Saint-Hubert	$1/_{10}$	Red wine	50 ml	2 fl oz
	$1/_{20}$	Vinegar	25 ml	1 fl oz
		Few crushed peppercorns		
		Chopped parsley		

Extensions of Above Formula Using Butcher's Meat: Selected Garnish — Wine/Spirit in Relation to 1 Unit — ½ l (1 pt) Sauce

French term	Unit	Ingredient	Metric	Imperial
Filet de Boeuf	$1/_{10}$	Madeira	50 ml	2 fl oz
Richelieu		8 Stuffed mushrooms		
		4 Portions braised lettuce on croûtes		
		4 Stuffed tomatoes		
		8 Small pommes château		
		Chopped parsley		
Contrefilet de Boeuf	$2/_5$	Cooked French beans	200 g	8 oz
Niçoise	$1/_{10}$	Madeira	50 ml	2 fl oz
		8 Small cooked tomatoes		
		8 Small pommes château		
Selle d'Agneau à la	$1/_{10}$	Madeira	50 ml	2 fl oz
Dubarry		8 Cauliflower fleurettes au gratin		
		8 Small pommes château		
Longe d'Agneau	$1/_{10}$	Madeira	50 ml	2 fl oz
Clamart		4 Cooked artichoke bottoms filled with		
		purée of green peas		
		8 Small pommes château		
Noix de Veau	$1/_5$	Button mushrooms (glacés à brun)	100 g	4 oz
Mercédès	$1/_{10}$	Madeira	50 ml	2 fl oz
		4 Cooked tomatoes		
		4 Portions braised lettuce on croûtes		
		8 Small pommes croquettes		

N.B.   Many other garnishes may be served with preparations cooked à la poêle.

24

The Principle and Practice of Baking

To Bake   Cuire

Baking may be defined as cooking in the oven with convected dry heat without any significant amount of fat or liquid. During baking the natural moisture within foods is heated and produces an amount of steam, which in turn modifies the dry convected heat.

The action of convected hot air strips away the thin layer of moisture and cool air from the surface of foods being baked. This in turn allows heat to penetrate and cook the food. Modern forced air convection ovens (*see* p. 42) are fitted with a fan or blower designed to speed up the current of convected air and maintain an even temperature throughout. This results in cold air and moisture being removed from foods more quickly, allowing the heat to penetrate and cook foods more speedily. When using conventional ovens attention must be given to the varying degrees of heat within the oven cavity, a result of a slower convection current. This is illustrated by observing that the top of the oven is usually hotter than the bottom section, e.g. top and bottom heat.

A wide variety of foods may be baked including fish, butcher's meat, poultry, offal, game, vegetables including potatoes.

Points for Consideration

Where a traditional kitchen brigade is employed the following Chefs de Partie will be involved:

Chef Poissonnier — baked fish products
Chef Saucier   — baked meat, poultry and game products, e.g. entrées and
                     relevés

Chef Entremettier — vegetable and potato products including vegetable and
cheese soufflés
Chef Pâtissier — dough and pastry bases
Chef Garde-Manger — basic preparation of meats, fish, poultry and game, etc.

Preparation of Utensils

Care must be taken to ensure baking trays and other cooking vessels are clean and adequately greased to meet cooking requirements: otherwise foods may become soiled and
stick to cooking trays or vessels.

Oven Temperatures

Ensure that the oven is pre-heated to the required temperature otherwise cooking times
will be increased and the quality of finished products impaired.

Pastry

When covering pies with pastry do not stretch the paste otherwise it will shrink during
cooking and slide into the pie dish. When trimming the pastry to fit the dish use a knife at
an angle away from the dish to allow for shrinkage during cooking. Before baking pastry
products allow resting time so that the pastry can relax, this prevents excessive shrinkage
and tough pastry.

Service

Dry baked products or those presented for service in the cooking vessel are served on dish
papers or serviettes to facilitate ease of service and to enhance appearance.

N.B. For 'Pies' and products that involve baking in addition to another method of
cookery see chapters concerning 'Combined Methods'.

Baked Butcher's Meat, Poultry, and Game

Although baking is considered to be a dry method of cookery, there are certain products
which of necessity are baked with a significant amount of moisture. Baked pies are
examples which illustrate this point. The extra moisture, usually in the form of stock, is
essential if the filling is to be thoroughly cooked without becoming too dry.

BAKED PIES

Steak Pie

Yield: 4 portions
Cooking time: 2 – 2½ hr
Setting temperature: 205°C (400°F)
Cooking temperature: 150°C (300°F)

Unit	Ingredient	Metric (g)	Imperial (oz)
1	Stewing beef (1½ cm (¾ in) dice)	500	20
⅕	Onion brunoise	100	4
	Seasoned flour		
	Pinch of salt and pepper to taste		
	Chopped parsley (optional)		
⋆	Puff pastry		
†	Brown stock		

⋆ Sufficient for *4 portions* approximately *200 g (8 oz)* at prepared weight.
† Sufficient stock barely to cover meat, approximately ½ unit stock to meat.

Method

Preparation   Lightly season meat and roll through seasoned flour. Mix onions, parsley with the meat, and place filling in the pie dish, add stock to moisten. Roll out puff pastry 3 mm (⅛ in) thick, moisten edge of pie dish and line with strip of pastry. Moisten pastry edge and cover with remaining pastry, taking care not to stretch the pastry otherwise it will shrink and slide into pie dish during baking. Seal well, trim and decorate with pastry trimmings as required. Rest before baking allowing pastry to relax (avoids excess shrinkage during baking). Eggwash for baking.

Baking   Set pie to bake in a hot oven until pastry becomes firm and light brown in colour. At this stage reduce oven temperature to 150°C (300°F) and continue baking until meat is cooked. Once cooked, clean edges of pie dish and surround with pie collar for service.

N.B.   Once pastry is adequately coloured to golden brown, cover with a piece of damp greaseproof paper to prevent overcolouring and excessive cooking of pastry.

Due to the long cooking process it may be necessary to remoisten the paper from time to time.

Extensions of Basic Formula: Added Ingredients to 1 Unit — 500 g (1¼ lb) meat

Name of dish	Unit	Ingredient	Metric (g)	Imperial (oz)
Steak and mushroom pie	⅒	Sliced mushrooms Add to filling	50	2
Steak and kidney pie	⅕	Diced ox-kidney Add to filling	100	4
Steak, kidney and mushroom pie	⅕ ⅒	Diced ox-kidney Sliced mushrooms Add to filling	100 50	4 2

POULTRY AND GAME PIES (boneless)

Yield: 4 portions
= 1 medium chicken cut for sauté
= 1 medium rabbit jointed
= 2 pigeons halved minus carcass
Cooking time: $1\frac{1}{2}-2$ hr
Setting temperature: 205°C (400°F)
Cooking temperature: 150°C (300°F)

Unit	Ingredient	Metric (g)	Imperial (oz)
1	Selected poultry or game (*see* chart below)	500	20
$\frac{1}{5}$	Sliced mushrooms	100	4
$\frac{1}{10}$	Lardons of bacon/blanched	50	2
$\frac{1}{10}$	Onion brunoise	50	2
	Flour/plain		
	Pinch of salt and pepper		
	Chopped parsley/1 clove chopped garlic		
*	Puff pastry		
†	White stock		

* Sufficient for *4 portions* approximately 200 g (8 oz).
† Sufficient stock barley to cover meat.

Method

Remove skin, fat, sinew/bone from meat and cut into thick ($\frac{1}{2}$ in/2 cm) strips. Season meat, roll lightly through seasoned flour. Place in pie dish with bacon, garlic, onions, mushrooms, parsley and stock to moisten. Roll out puff pastry 3 mm ($\frac{1}{8}$ in) thick, moisten edge of pie dish and line with strips of pastry. Moisten this edge and cover with remaining pastry taking care not to stretch the pastry. Seal well, trim and decorate with pastry trimmings as required. Rest and egg-wash before baking.

Baking   Set pie to bake in a hot oven until pastry becomes firm and light brown in colour, at this stage reduce oven temperature to 150°C (300°F) and continue baking until meat is cooked. Once cooked, clean edge of pie dish and surround with pie collar for service.

Examples of Pies Prepared using Above Formula

Name of dish	Main ingredient	
Chicken pie	Medium chicken	– use breast/leg meat
Pigeon pie	Pigeons	– use breast meat only
Rabbit pie	Medium rabbit	– use back, leg and shoulder meat

HOT VEAL AND HAM PIE

Yield: 4 portions
Cooking time: 1½ – 2 hr
Setting temperature: 205°C (400°F)
Cooking temperature: 150°C (300°F)

Unit	Ingredient	Metric (g)	Imperial (oz)
1	Stewing veal [2½ cm (1 in dice)]	400	16
¼	Gammon [2½ cm (1 in dice)]	100	4
¼	Onion brunoise	100	4
⅛	Sliced mushrooms	50	2
	Seasoned flour		
	Pinch of salt/pepper		
	Chopped parsley		
	Squeeze of lemon juice		
★	Puff pastry		
†	White stock		

★ Sufficient pastry for 4 portions approximately 200 g (8 oz) prepared weight.
† Sufficient stock barely to cover meat.

Method

Lightly season veal, combine with gammon, roll through seasoned flour and place in pie dish. Sprinkle with mushrooms, onion and parsley, moisten with stock and lemon juice. Cover with pastry and bake as for chicken pie.

FILLET OF BEEF IN PUFF PASTRY (en Croûte)

Filet de Boeuf Wellington

Yield: 4 portions
Cooking time: 20 – 30 min
Cooking temperature: 205°C (400°F)

Unit	Ingredient	Metric (g)	Imperial (oz)
1	Beef fillet (cut from centre—left whole)	600	20
⅕	Duxelle	120	4
⅒	Pâté de foie gras	60	2
	Oil		
	Salt and pepper		
	Madeira sauce to accompany		
★	Puff pastry		

★ Sufficient pastry to cover fillet approximately 250 g (10 oz), prepared weight.

Method

Lightly season fillet and seal quickly in a film of oil in hot oven or on stove top. Allow to cool. Combine foie gras and duxelle and spread over top of the fillet. Roll out puff pastry into oblong shape 3 mm ($\frac{1}{8}$ in) thick. Wrap fillet neatly in pastry with the seal underneath the fillet. Decorate with pastry trimmings and allow to rest.

Brush with egg-wash and bake in hot oven until golden brown and cooked. The fillet should be medium rare on carving. Serve accompanied with Madeira sauce and carve at the table.

CORNISH PASTIES

Yield: 4 portions
Cooking time. 20 – 30 min
Cooking temperature: 175° (350°F)

Unit	Ingredient	Metric (g)	Imperial (oz)
1*	Short pastry	200	8
$\frac{3}{4}$	Stewing lamb or beef (finely diced)	150	6
$\frac{1}{2}$	Potato (finely diced)	100	4
$\frac{1}{4}$	Onion brunoise	50	2
	Salt and pepper		
	Chopped parsley		

* *Weight* indicates amount of flour used to prepare short pastry.

Method

Combine meat, potato, onion, chopped parsley and seasoning to form filling. Roll out pastry 3 mm ($\frac{1}{8}$ in) thick and cut out into 14 cm ($5\frac{1}{2}$ in) rounds. Moisten edges with water and place filling in centre. Draw two opposite edges of pastry together and seal well to enclose filling. Egg-wash and bake until golden brown and cooked. Serve plain or with a suitable sauce, e.g. jus lié.

TOAD IN THE HOLE

Yield: 4 portions
Cooking time: 20 – 30 min
Cooking temperature: 205°C (400°F)

Unit	Ingredient	Metric	Imperial
1	Pork/beef sausage	400 g	1 lb
$\frac{5}{8}$*	Yorkshire pudding batter	250 ml	10 fl oz
$\frac{1}{8}$	Dripping	50 g	2 oz

* Refers to the amount of liquid used to prepare the batter.

Method

Place dripping and sausage in a tray and set in hot oven for few minutes. Remove from oven and pour the batter on to the sausages. Replace in oven and bake until batter is cooked and golden brown. Serve accompanied with jus lié.

Baked Fish   Poisson (Cuire au Four)

This method of cookery is best suited for use with fillets of fish, small whole round fish, and certain smaller cuts. In some instances the fish is filled with a selected stuffing prior to baking e.g. lemon, parsley, and thyme stuffing *see* p. 387.

Once baked, the product may be served in its own juices or accompanied with a suitable sauce and garnish.

Fish Commonly Used for Baking

English term	French term	Cuts commonly used	Yield for 4 portions
Cod	Cabillaud	Darnes	4 × 150 g (6 oz)
Haddock	Aigrefin	Darnes	4 × 150 g (6 oz)
Hake	Colin	Darnes	4 × 150 g (6 oz)
Herring	Hareng	Whole and stuffed (*see* p. 299)	4 × 200 g (8 oz)
Mackerel	Maquereau	Whole and stuffed (*see* p. 299)	4 × 200 g (8 oz)
Red mullet	Rouget	Whole and stuffed (*see* p. 299)	4 × 200 g (8 oz)
Trout	Truite	Whole and stuffed (*see* p. 299)	4 × 200 g (8 oz)
Pike	Brochet	Small fillets or suprêmes	4 × 150 g (6 oz)

N.B. If baking 'fish in the piece' use 500 g (1¼ lb) fish at prepared weight. For whole fish to be stuffed, backbone is removed prior to stuffing and cooking.

BAKED FISH   Poisson au Four

Yield: 4 portions
Cooking time: 10 – 15 min
Cooking temperature: 175° (350°F)

Unit	Ingredient	Metric (g)	Imperial (oz)
1	Selected fish (*see* chart) Melted butter Squeeze of lemon juice Seasoning 4 lemon wedges/sprigs parsley	50	2

Method

Brush base of cooking vessel with butter. Rub fish with lemon juice and lightly season. Place fish into cooking vessel, brush with melted butter, cover with buttered cartouche and bake until cooked. Serve moistened with cooking liquor, garnish with lemon wedges and bouquets of parsley. May be accompanied with a suitable sauce, e.g. baked herrings with mustard sauce. N.B. After cooking, centre bone and outer skin are removed from darnes for service. Where darnes are stuffed, centre bone is removed before cooking and stuffing placed in the cavity.

Examples of Dishes Prepared Using Above Formula

English term	Suggested accompanying sauce for 4 portions	Metric	Imperial	French term
Baked fish steaks	Beurre Fondu	100 g	4 oz	Darne de Poisson au Four
Baked stuffed fish steaks	Sauce Tomate	250 ml	10 fl oz	Darne de Poisson Farcie au Four
Baked stuffed herrings/mackerel	Sauce Moutarde	250 ml	10 fl oz	Hareng/Maquereau Farci au Four
Baked stuffed red mullet	Sauce Portugaise/Provençale	250 ml	10 fl oz	Rouget Farci au Four
Baked stuffed trout	Beurre Maître d'Hôtel	50 g	2 oz	Truite Farcie au Four

N.B. Other suitable sauces may be served with baked fish.

Baked Fillet of Pike English Style   Filet/Suprême de Brochet à l'Anglaise

Method

Rub fish with lemon juice and lightly season, pass through seasoned flour, melted butter and white breadcrumbs. Proceed as for baked fish.

Baked Vegetables   Légumes au Four

The vegetables commonly cooked by this method are often filled with a stuffing prior to baking. Few are served plain baked. The main exceptions being tomatoes and potatoes.

Preparation of Vegetables for Baking

English term	French term	Preparation for baking	Yield for 4 portions	Cooking time (min)
Baked stuffed baby marrow	Courgettes Farcies au Four	Top and tail marrow, wash blanch 3–5 min and refresh. Cut in half lengthways, remove seeds, lightly season and fill with duxelle stuffing	400 g (1 lb)	15–20
Baked stuffed cucumber	Concombre Farci au Four	Peel cucumber, cut into 8 cm (3 in) lengths and proceed as for baby marrow	400 g (1 lb)	5–10
Baked stuffed mushrooms	Champignons Farcis au Four	Select large open flap mushrooms, remove stalks, peel and wash. Lightly season and fill with duxelle stuffing	12 mushrooms	5

English term	French term	Preparation for baking	Yield for 4 portions	Cooking time (min)
Baked tomatoes	Tomates au Four	Skin tomatoes, lightly season	8 medium tomatoes	5
Baked stuffed tomatoes	Tomates Farcies au Gratin	Skin tomatoes, remove top third of tomato, scoop out seeds, lightly season, fill with duxelle and sprinkle with breadcrumbs	8 medium tomatoes	5
Baked stuffed tomatoes Portuguese style	Tomates Farcies Portugaise	As for stuffed tomatoes but filled with pilaff	8 medium tomatoes	5
Tomatoes Provençale style	Tomates Provençale	Skin tomatoes, cut into half, lightly season. Sprinkle with mixture of white breadcrumbs, chopped parsley, garlic and few drops of oil	8 medium tomatoes	5
Stuffed tomatoes Italian style	Tomates Farcies Italienne	As for stuffed tomatoes but filled with risotto	8 medium tomatoes	5

N.B. When using duxelle, pilaff, or rissotto for stuffing vegetables the amounts may vary, but as a guide use 100 g (4 oz) per 4 portions.

Method of Baking Vegetables

Baking temperature: 205°C (400°F)
Place prepared vegetables on lightly oiled baking sheet. Brush with melted butter and bake quickly in hot oven to cook. Serve garnished with bouquet of picked parsley.

BAKED POTATOES   Pommes au Four

Yield: 4 portions
take 4 large potatoes
Cooking time: 1½ hr
Cooking temperature: 175°C (350°F)

Method

Scrub potatoes well in cold water. Lay evenly on bed of salt on a baking tray, prick with a fork to prevent splitting (the salt bed acts to absorb moisture from potatoes and to flavour). Bake in the oven until potatoes are cooked. Lift potatoes from salt bed and remove any salt adhering to potato skin. To serve plain baked, criss-cross top of potato with sharp office knife, squeeze the potato open and fill cavity with butter. Garnish with bouquet of parsley and serve.

Extensions of Baked Potatoes: Added Ingredients and Method for 4 Portions Using 4 Large Baked Potatoes

French term	Unit	Ingredient	Metric	Imperial
Pommes Gratinées	1	Grated cheese	100 g	4 oz
	½	Butter	50 g	2 oz
		Seasoning		
		Cut potatoes in half, scoop out centre, mash with butter and seasoning. Refill potato cases, sprinkle with cheese, re-bake in oven until golden brown		
Pommes Ménagère		As for pommes gratinées with the addition of Cooked ham brunoise	100 g	4 oz
		Combine with mashed potato before refilling potato case		
Pommes Arlie		As for pommes gratinées with addition of	50 ml	2 fl oz
	½	Cream		
		Chopped chives		
		Combine cream and chives with mashed potato before refilling potato cases		
Pommes Surprise	1	Cream	100 ml	4 fl oz
	½	Butter	50 g	2 oz
		Seasoning		
		Make a small aperture in the potato skin and remove potato. Pass through potato machine, combine with cream, butter and seasoning. Pipe back in potato skin and place in oven to reheat and seal aperture, serve as required		
Pommes Macaire	1	Butter	50 g	2 oz
		Seasoning		
		Scoop out potato from skins, mash and combine with butter and seasoning. Fill heated, buttered anna mould with the potato mixture and press lightly. Place in hot oven to re-bake to golden brown (approximately 10–15 min). Turn out brush with melted butter and serve as required		
Pommes Robert		As for macaire with the addition of		
	1	Egg yolk	50 g	2 oz
		Chopped chives		
		Combine ingredients with mashed potato before re-baking in mould		

Pommes Byron	As for macaire but finished with			
	1	Grated cheese	50 g	2 oz
	1	Cream	50 ml	2 oz

Hollow centre of turned out Pommes
Macaire, fill with cheese and cream then
gratinate in hot oven for service

ANNA POTATOES   Pommes Anna

Yield: 4 portions (to fill small mould of 15 cm (6 in) diameter)
Cooking time: 30–45 min
Cooking temperature: 205°C (400°F)

Unit	Ingredient	Metric (g)	Imperial (oz)
1*	Potatoes (trimmed to cylindrical shape)	600	20
$1/_5$	Butter (melted)	120	4
	Salt and pepper		

* In order to obtain this amount of prepared potatoes trimmed to shape, it is necessary to commence with approximately 800 g (2 lb) at unpeeled weight.

Method

Slice potatoes 1 mm ($1/_{16}$ in) rounds (approximately). Do not store potatoes in water as the starch content is required to enable potatoes to adhere together during cooking. Heat buttered anna mould on stove top, pull to side of stove and overlap potato rounds to form a base at bottom of the mould. Lightly season and brush with melted butter, continue this process until mould is full. Place filled mould over heat until potatoes become loose at base of mould, press lightly, cover with lid and bake in oven until cooked. When cooked ensure potatoes are loose in mould, turn out for service.

N.B.   During cooking it is necessary to press potatoes to ensure they stick together. Optionally, sides of anna mould may be lined with potatoes when layering.

Extensions of Anna Potatoes: Added Ingredients with Method in Relation to 1 Unit 600 g (1¼ lb) Potatoes

French term	Unit	Ingredient	Metric (g)	Imperial (oz)
Pommes Voisin/ Ambassadeur	$1/_5$	Grated cheese	120	4
		Proceed as for pommes anna but sprinkle grated cheese between potato layers		
Pommes Darphin		Proceed as for pommes anna but cut potatoes into julienne		
Pommes Nana		Proceed as for pommes darphin but cook in copper dariole moulds		

Other Baked Products

Pizzas

In recent years these products along with others have become popularized as a result of the development of speciality restaurants, e.g. Pizza Houses, Bistros, Hamburger restaurants, etc., and the changing tastes of well-travelled customers. Another factor contributing to their popularity is the constant need for caterers to maintain a supply of reasonably priced products and keep within cost limits.

PIZZA

Yield: 4 × 20 cm (8 in) pizzas
Bulk fermentation time (B.F.T.): 1 hr
Baking time: 15 – 20 min
Baking temperature: 205°C (400°F)

Pizza Dough

Unit	Ingredient	Metric	Imperial
1	Strong flour	400 g	1 lb
⁵/₈	Water [27°C (80°F)]	250 ml	10 fl oz
¹/₁₆	Lard	25 g	1 oz
¹/₁₆	Yeast	25 g	1 oz
	Good pinch of salt		

Method

Sift flour and salt together, rub in the fat content and form a well. Combine all yeast with three-quarters of the water and pour into the well. Mix ingredients together to commence formation of dough adding remaining water as required. Knead thoroughly to form smooth elastic well developed dough. Cover with damp cloth and stand in warm place for the required B.F.T. period. Knock back (knead) gently, divide into four pieces and roll out into 4 × 20 cm (8 in) rounds, dock★ well. Place on to lightly greased baking sheets, arrange selected pizza filling on top of dough (*see* below) and prove for 10 – 15 minutes until dough begins to rise. Bake in pre-heated oven until cooked. Remove from baking sheet and serve immediately.

★ Docking – a technique used to pierce pastry or bread in order to inhibit normal rising.

BASIC PIZZA FILLING

Yield: sufficient for 1 × 20 cm (8 in) pizza

Unit	Ingredient	Metric (g)	Imperial (oz)
†1	Tomatoes concassées (see p. 164)	200	8
½	Selected cheese (thin slices)	100	4
	Pinch of basil – marjoram – oregano		
	Salt and pepper		

† Tinned tomatoes may be used in this preparation.

Method

Spread surface of rolled out raw dough with layer of tomatoes, sprinkle with seasoning and herbs. Arrange cheese slices to cover surface, finish with additional ingredients as required (see chart below), and bake.

Added Ingredients in Relation to Basic Pizza Filling

Name	Unit	Ingredient	Metric (g)	Imperial (oz)
Pizza Napolitana		8 Anchovy fillets		
		8 Black olives (stoned)		
Pizza with Parma ham		4 Slices of Parma ham		
Pizza with mushrooms	1	Mushrooms (sliced and sweated)	200	8
Pizza Mare (pizza with seafood)	1	Scampi / Mussels (budded) / Prawns	200	8
Pizza with spiced sausage	½	Selected sliced continental sausage	100	4

Pizzas often take their name from the region of origin or the main flavouring being used. Other suitable pizzas may be prepared to requirements of customers and culinary flair of the chef.

Savoury Flans   Quiches

The term Quiche denotes an open flan, which is filled and garnished with a savoury filling.

BASIC PREPARATION OF QUICHES

Yield: 4 portions
Cooking time: 20 – 30 min
Cooking temperature: 175°C (350°F)

Unit	Ingredient	Metric	Imperial
1	Milk	200 ml	8 fl oz
$\frac{1}{2}$	Whole egg	100 g	4 oz
	Salt and pepper		
	Chopped parsley/garlic		
	Selected filling (see chart)		
*	Short pastry		

* Sufficient pastry to line 15 cm (6 in) flan ring, using approximately 150 g (6 oz) of flour.

Method

Roll out pastry to 3 mm ($\frac{1}{8}$ in) thick and line greased flan ring.
Neatly arrange selected filling in base of flan case, sprinkle with chopped parsley and flavour with garlic. Beat eggs, milk, and seasoning together and pour into flan case, garnish top if required and bake until cooked. Once baked remove flan ring and serve as required. May be served hot or cold.

Savoury Flan Fillings: Added Ingredients in Relation to 1 Unit 200 ml (8 fl oz) Milk

Name	Unit	Ingredient	Metric (g)	Imperial (oz)
Quiche aux Oignons (onion flan)	1	Onions (sliced and sweated)	200	8
Quiche au Fromage avec Oignons (cheese and onion flan)	As for onion flan with addition of: $\frac{1}{2}$	Grated cheese	100	4
Quiche Lorraine (cheese and bacon flan)	$\frac{1}{2}$	Lean bacon slices	100	4
	$\frac{1}{2}$	Grated cheese	100	4
		Hint of chopped garlic		
Quiche Forestière (Savoury flan)	$\frac{1}{2}$	Lean bacon slices	100	4
	$\frac{1}{4}$	Onions (sliced and sweated)	50	2
	$\frac{1}{4}$	Mushrooms (sliced and sweated)	50	2
	$\frac{1}{4}$	Grated cheese	50	2
Quiche Fruits de Mer (Seafood flan)	$\frac{1}{2}$	White crab meat	100	4
	$\frac{1}{4}$	Prawns	50	2
	$\frac{1}{4}$	Mussels (budded)	50	2

Other fillings may be used according to taste. These products may be prepared in individual moulds, e.g. barquettes or tartlet moulds.

Baked Soufflés (Savoury)

The making of soufflés is a simple operation, which has been surrounded by unnecessary mystique. If the formula and methods outlined below are followed carefully, little difficulty should be encountered in achieving good results.

Soufflés are prepared to order, and served immediately on completion of cooking. If they are left to stand they gradually fall losing their initial volume and texture. They are usually served as a preliminary or savoury course.

Points for Consideration

Care must be taken to:

(a) prepare a smooth, thick sauce as a base for the soufflé. This is enriched by the addition of the egg yolks;

(b) beat the egg whites until stiff but not dry, this facilitates folding in;

(c) mix approximately a quarter of the beaten whites with the basic mixture (panada) in order to soften the consistency before the remaining whites are folded in. This ensures a more even distribution of the whites resulting in a good lift;

(d) pre-heat the oven to the required temperature before baking. If the oven is too cold the soufflé will not cook or rise sufficiently, if too hot the soufflé will over-bake on the exterior leaving the interior under-cooked.

(e) test whether a soufflé is cooked through by inserting a knife into the centre, which should come out 'clean'.

CHEESE SOUFFLÉ   Soufflé au Fromage

Yield: 4 portions
Cooking time: 35 – 45 min
Cooking temperature: 175°C (350°F)

Unit	Ingredient	Metric	Imperial
1	Milk	200 ml	8 fl oz
¾	Whole egg/separated (3 eggs)	150 g	6 oz
½	Grated cheese	100 g	4 oz
¼	Butter (melted)	50 g	2 oz
⅛	Egg white (1 white)	25 g	1 oz
⅛	Flour	25 g	1 oz
	Pinch of salt		
	Pinch of cayenne pepper		

N.B.   When preparing soufflé use a combination of cheese namely: 75g/3 oz cheddar with 25 g 1 oz parmesan.

Method

Brush soufflé mould liberally with some of the melted butter. Form a white roux with remaining butterflour, add milk and form a thick white sauce. Pull aside and blend-in cheese, yolks, garlic, cayenne, salt to season, transfer to mixing bowl and cool slightly. Beat egg whites until stiff and add a quarter of the whites to the basic mixture. Fold in the remaining whites gently until they are evenly distributed through the mixture. Three-quarters fill the prepared soufflé mould, place on to a baking sheet and bake in the pre-heated oven until risen, cooked, and golden-brown. Serve immediately.

N.B.   Cooking may be commenced by placing the soufflé mixture, in its dish, into a stove-top bain marie. Once the souffle has begun to rise it is removed from the water on to a baking sheet in order to complete cooking in the oven.

BAKED SAVOURY SOUFFLÉS

Basic Soufflé Mixture (e.g. for ham, chicken, and fish)

Yield: 4 portions
Cooking time: 35 – 45 min
Cooking temperature: 175°C (350°F)

Unit	Ingredient	Metric	Imperial
1	Main cooked flavouring (finely minced)	200 g	8 oz
1	Whole egg (separate yolks from whites)	200 g	8 oz
$\frac{3}{4}$	Béchamel	150 ml	6 fl oz
$\frac{1}{4}$	Melted butter	50 g	2 oz
	Seasonings		

Method

Brush soufflé mould liberally with melted butter (enables soufflé to rise without sticking). Moisten main flavouring with béchamel sauce, liquidize or rub through a very fine sieve to form a light purée. Heat this mixture in a saucepan and add the melted butter, seasoning and any additional flavouring (*see* chart). Remove from heat and carefully blend in the egg yolks. Beat egg whites to a stiff snow and blend in a quarter of the whites to the basic mixture. Fold in the remaining whites gently until they are evenly distributed throughout the mixture. Three-quarters fill the prepared soufflé mould, place on to a baking sheet and bake in the pre-heated oven until risen, cooked, and firm to the touch. Serve immediately.

Soufflés Prepared Using the Above Formula

English term	*Main and additional flavourings*	*French term*
Chicken soufflé	Cooked chicken, squeeze of lemon juice, pinch of nutmeg, teaspoon of chicken glaze	Soufflé à la Reine
Ham soufflé	Cooked ham	Soufflé de Jambon
Fish soufflé	Cooked fish (poached in white wine), squeeze of lemon juice, teaspoon or fish glaze. Smoked or strong-flavoured fish are also used.	Soufflé de Poisson

N.B. *See* cooking soufflés 'en bain marie' prior to baking.

25

The Principle and Practice of Grilling

To Grill
Griller

Grilling may be defined as a speedy and dry method of cooking by radiant heat. The food is placed near to the source of heat, which acts to cook each item quickly. This method is ideally suited for use with tender cuts of butcher's meat, offal, poultry, fish and vegetables. At the commencement of cooking the surface of food is sealed to assist in retaining the food's juices and flavour. Grilled products remain a common feature on the menu in both traditional and modern catering units.

Traditionally grilling was carried out on bars over an open, ventilated charcoal fire but modern grills also employ the use of gas and electrically heated appliances.

Grilling may therefore be described as:

1. cooking over radiant heat, e.g. over heated charcoal;
2. cooking under radiant heat, e.g. under gas/electric salamanders;
3. cooking between heat, e.g. electrically heated ridged plates/contact grills.

Broiling is an alternative term used in America to denote grilling.

Points for Consideration

Items for grilling are seasoned with salt and milled pepper just before cooking in order to improve their flavour. In some cases foods are sprinkled with fresh herbs or placed into a marinade to enhance flavour, and in the case of a marinade to aid tenderization. Examples include kebabs in marinade, grilled lamb flavoured with rosemary and garlic.

Prior to grilling certain items are lightly coated in flour, which acts to improve the colour and texture of the cooked product. During cooking the flour browns and crispens, e.g. grilled fish. In all cases foods prepared for grilling are best brushed with oil or melted butter, which keeps them moist and prevents their sticking to grilling bars or trays.

Organization and Preparation

Where a traditional kitchen brigade is employed the following staff are involved with the preparation for and the cooking of grilled products:

Chef Garde-manger   — basic preparation of meat and fish, etc.
Chef Entremettier   — basic preparation of vegetables
Chef Grillardin   — grilling of most products.

Other Chefs de Partie are involved with the preparation of accompanying garnishes and sauces.

In order to ensure speedy and efficient cooking the grilling appliance must be preheated and the grilling bars and trays brushed with a light film of oil to prevent foods sticking during cooking. If a smooth operation is to be achieved advance organization of materials, service and cooking equipment, garnishes and sauces is essential.

Care During Cooking

Most grilling appliances are designed to allow for varying degrees of heat. This is achieved by the use of sloping bars and fuel regulators. As a result food may commence and continue cooking at different degrees of heat, e.g. a steak may be sealed in a hot part of the grill then moved to cook more slowly at a lower temperature.

Grilling tongs are often used to move and turn items during cooking, and are designed to enable the grill chef to turn food safely without having to reach under or over the intense heat. On no account should meat be pierced during grilling as juices escape resulting in less succulent food.

Slices and palette knives are used to turn fish portions or foods that are placed on trays for grilling. Because of the delicate structure of fish, extra care is required to prevent it from flaking and breaking up.

Browning/Gratinating Foods

The salamander is frequently used to colour or glaze foods for service, e.g. fish and vegetable products.

Grilled Butcher's Meat, Offal, Poultry   *Viande Grillée, Abats Grillés, Volaille Grillée*

Grilling is employed in the cooking of a wide variety of butcher's meat, offal and poultry, most of which are prepared into small cuts. Generally speaking only the choice tender cuts are suitable for this method of cookery.

Beef   Boeuf

Sirloin
Fillet
T-bone

Sirloin of Beef on the Bone (Cuts)   Aloyau de Boeuf

English term	French term	Yield for 4 portions	Explanation and illustration
T-Bone steak or Porterhouse steak (U.S.A.)		4 × 400 g (1 lb)	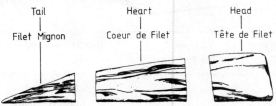 A steak cut across whole sirloin on the bone including the fillet of beef A cut from wing-end of sirloin on the bone excluding the fillet
Club steak (U.S.A.)		4 × 300 g (12 oz)	

Fillet of Beef (Tenderloin – U.S.A.)   Filet de Boeuf

Tail — Filet Mignon   Heart — Coeur de Filet   Head — Tête de Filet

Cuts in Common Use

English term	French term	Yield for 4 portions	Explanation and illustration
	Chateaubriand	2 × 400 g (1 lb) large steaks	A large cut from head of fillet lightly batted to form large steak
Fillet steak	Filet de Boeuf	4 × 200 g (8 oz) steaks	A cut from the head or the heart of the fillet

Tournedos	4 × 150 g (6 oz)		A neat cut from heart of fillet often lightly secured with string to retain round shape

Filet Mignon de Boeuf	7 × 75 g (3 oz) pieces		Small cuts from tail of fillet often used as part of a mixed grill but may be served in their own right

Strip Loin of Beef

Contrefilet de Boeuf
(Boned-out sirloin)

English term	French term	Yield for 4 portions	Explanation and illustration
Double sirloin steak	Entrecôte Double	4 × 300 g (12 oz) steaks	A large cut from boned out sirloin
Sirloin steak	Entrecôte	4 × 200 g (8 oz) steaks	A cut from boned out sirloin
Minute steak	Entrecôte Minute	4 × 150 g (6 oz) steaks	As above but batted out thinly

Rump of Beef
Culotte de Boeuf

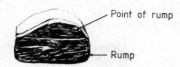

Boned-out Rump

English term	French term	Yield for 4 portions	Explanation and illustration
Point steaks	—	4 × 200 g (8 oz)	A steak cut from point of rump 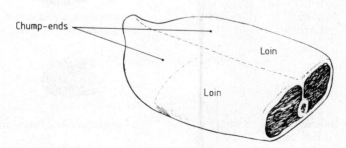
Rump steaks	—	4 × 200 g (8 oz)	A steak from main piece of rump

Lamb
Agneau

Saddle of Lamb (Cuts)
Selle d'Agneau

Saddle on the Bone

English term	French term	Yield for 4 portions	Explanation and illustration
English lamb chop-Barnsley chop	Chop d'Agneau à l'Anglaise	4 × 250 g (10 oz) double chops	A double chop cut across saddle on the bone with kidney skewered in
Lamb chop	Chop d'Agneau	4 × 150 g (6 oz)	A cut across loin of lamb on bone
Chump chop	Chop d'Agneau	4 × 200g (8 oz)	A cut across chump end of lamb on the bone
	Noisette d'Agneau	8 × 75 g (3 oz)	A slanted cut across boned out trimmed loin
	Rosette/ Médaillon d'Agneau	8 × 75 g (3 oz)	A cut across rolled boned out loin
Fillet of lamb	Filet Mignon	4 to 8 lamb fillets fillets according to size	Whole fillets bone out from under saddle of lamb

Best-End of Lamb (Cuts)   Carré d'Agneau

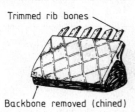

Trimmed rib bones

Backbone removed (chined)

English term	French term	Yield for 4 portions	Explanation and illustration
			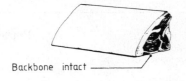
Lamb cutlet	Côtelette d'Agneau	8 × 75 g (3 oz)	A cut across best-end between rib bones
			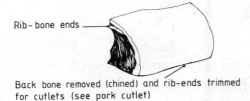
Double lamb cutlet	Côtelette d'Agneau Double	4 × 150 g (6 oz)	As above to include two rib bones

Pork   Porc

Backbone intact

Pork Loin (Cuts)   Longe de Porc

Rib-bone ends

Back bone removed (chined) and rib-ends trimmed
for cutlets (see pork cutlet)

Best-End of Pork (Cuts)   Carré de Porc

English term	French term	Yield for 4 portions	Explanation and illustration
Pork chop	Côte de Porc	4 × 200 g (8 oz)	A cut across the loin of pork on the bone
Pork cutlet	Côtelette/côte de Porc	4 × 200 g (8 oz)	A cut across best-end between rib bones

Offal of Butcher's Meat   Abats de Viande

English term	French term	Yield for 4 portions	Explanation
Lamb ⎫ Calves ⎬liver Pigs' ⎭	Foie d'Agneau Foie de Veau Foie de Porc	400 g (1 lb)	Skin and slice thinly
Lambs' ⎫ ⎬kidney	Rognon d'Agneau	8 kidneys	Skin, slit open and skewer
Calves' ⎬kidney	Rognon de Veau	4 kidneys	Skin, slice and skewer
Pigs' ⎭	Rognon de Porc	8 kidneys	Skin, slit open and skewer

Grilled Chicken   Poulet Grillé

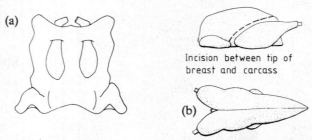

(a)

Incision between tip of breast and carcass

(b)

Chickens are generally prepared in one of two ways in readiness for grilling:

(a) Spatchcock (spread-eagled—English style)
(b) Crapaudine (toad-like—French style).

Smaller chicken cuts may be grilled if required, but it is more common to cook them by shallow or deep frying.

English term	French term	Yield for 4 portions	Explanation and illustration
Chicken Spatchcock (spread-eagled)	Poulet en Spatchcock	2 × 800 g (2 lb) or 4 × 400 (1 lb) chickens	Trim chicken, split down backbone, open and bat. Remove rib cage and backbone. May be skewered to help retain shape when grilling
Chicken cut to toad shape	Poulet en Crapaudine	2 × 800 g (2 lb) or 4 × 400 g (1 lb) chicken	Remove winglets then incise chicken between tip of breast and carcass base to the wing joints. Open out and lightly bat to give toad like appearance

Grilling of Butcher's Meat, Offal and Poultry

Method

Lightly season meat with salt and milled pepper. Brush with oil or melted butter and place on pre-heated grill or trays and commence grilling. Once sealed and brown turn and continue grilling until required degree of cooking is attained. Remove from grill and garnish as required (*see* chart).

N.B.   Liver is passed through seasoned flour then lightly oiled prior to grilling.

For service the ends of cutlet bones are dressed with cutlet frills.

Degrees of Cooking

The following usually apply to cuts of beef but on occasion lamb or offal grills may be served slightly underdone according to customer's wishes. Pork/poultry grills should be cooked thoroughly but not allowed to become dry by over-grilling.

Degrees:

Au Bleu	Blue or very rare
Saignant (bleeding)	Rare or underdone
à Point	Medium or just done
Bien Cuit	Well done

The grilling times taken to achieve the required degree of cooking will vary according to:

(a) thickness and quality of the food being grilled
(b) heat of the grilling appliance
(c) customer's requirements.

Due to these factors it is difficult to specify exact grilling times as these are best judged by the grill cook.

Garnishes for Grilled Butcher's Meat and Offal: Garnish and Sauce for 4 Portions

Name	Unit	Ingredient	Metric	Imperial	Examples of uses
à la Maison (in the style of the house	1 1 1	French-fried onions Straw potatoes (cooked) Cooked mushrooms 4 Grilled tomatoes 4 Small bunches of watercress Garnish as required	100 g 100 g 100 g	4 oz 4 oz 4 oz	Grills of beef, lamb pork, chicken
Bouquetière	1	Béarnaise sauce Bouquets of cooked assorted vegetables (*see* p. 274). Garnish as required and serve sauce separately	250 ml	10 fl oz	Chateaubriand
Henri IV	1	Pont-Neuf Potatoes 4 Small bunches of watercress Surround with potatoes and watercress	200 g	8 oz	Grills of beef cuts
Maître d'Hôtel	1 ½	Straw potatoes Parsley butter 4 Small bunches of watercress Decorate with watercress and potatoes Finish with slices of parsley butter	100 g 50 g	4 oz 2 oz	Grills of beef, lamb, pork
Mirabeau	1	Anchovy butter 12 Anchovy fillets (cut into thin strips) 8 Olives 4 Small bunches of watercress Decorate grilled meat with anchovy fillets, surround with watercress and olives. Finish with slices of anchovy butter on service	50 g	2 oz	Grilled entrecôtes

Name	Unit	Ingredient	Metric	Imperial	Examples of uses
au Lard		4 Slices grilled bacon			Grilled liver
Tyrolienne	1 $^1/_2$	French fried onions Tomato concassé 4 Small bunches of watercress Place tomato on grilled meat, surround with onion and watercress	200 g 100 g	8 oz 4 oz	Grills of beef and lamb
Vert Pré	1	Straw potatoes (cooked) 4 Small bunches of watercress Surround with garnish	100 g	4 oz	Grills of beef, lamb, pork, offal and poultry

Garnishes for Grilled Chicken: Garnish and Sauce for 4 Portions

Name	Method of Cutting	Unit	Ingredient	Metric	Imperial
Poulet Grillé Diable (grilled chicken with devilled sauce)	Spatchcock	1 $^2/_5$ $^2/_5$ $^2/_5$	Devilled Sauce Straw potatoes (cooked) Melted butter White breadcrumbs Diluted English mustard 4 Small bunches of watercress Half-way through grilling brush chicken with mustard, melted butter and sprinkle with breadcrumbs. Continue grilling under salamander until golden brown and cooked. Garnish with straw potatoes, water- cress and accompany with devilled sauce	250 ml 100 g 100 g 100 g	10 fl oz 4 oz 4 oz 4 oz
Poulet Grillé Américaine (grilled chicken American style)	Spatchcock		As for Poulet Grillé Diable but garnished with the addition of: 8 Grilled mushrooms 4 Grilled tomatoes 4 Slices of grilled bacon		

Name	Method of Cutting	Unit	Ingredient	Metric	Imperial
Poulet Grillé à l'Anglaise (chicken spatchcock)	Spatchcock		As for Poulet Grillé Diable but omitting mustard. Garnish with addition of: 8 Fanned gherkins		
Poulet Grillé Crapaudine (grilled chicken in the shape of a toad)	Crapaudine		Cooked and served as for Poulet Grillé Diable but omitting mustard		

Other Grilled Meats in Common Use

Gammon Steaks

Yield: 4 × 200 g (8 oz) steaks

Method

Omit seasoning (gammon has been previously cured with salt), and proceed as for grilled meats.
May be garnished with:

(a) shallow-fried eggs;
(b) glazed pineapple rings;
(c) glazed peaches;
(d) vert-pré, etc.

Grilled Hamburgers (see p. 326)

Yield: 4 portions

Method

Cook as for grilled meats. May be garnished and presented in a variety of ways including:

(a) à la Maison;
(b) Tyrolienne;
(c) with fried eggs;
(d) with sauce charcutière, etc.

In popular catering hamburgers are often grilled and served sandwiched in bread rolls with various salads, sauces, and relishes.

Grilled Bacon/Sausages/Bacon Rolls

Yield: 4 portions 400 g (1 lb) sausages
     4 portions 200 g (8 oz) bacon slices (trimmed)
     4 portions 200 g (8 oz) bacon slices (rolled) may be skewered for grilling.

Method

Place on to lightly greased grilling trays, put to grill under pre-heated salamander and cook on one side. Turn to complete cooking. Use as required.

N.B.   Used as main-course items for breakfasts, lunch and high teas or to complete other preparations.

Mixed Grill

Selection of grilled meat, which may vary according to the establishment's requirements.
Yield: 4 portions

4 Grilled lamb cutlets (with frills)
4 Grilled lamb's kidneys
4 Grilled slices of bacon (trimmed)
4 Grilled slices of liver
4 Grilled sausages

Garnish with:

4 Grilled mushrooms
4 Grilled tomatoes
4 Small bunches of watercress
4 Small portions straw potatoes

GRILLING ON SKEWERS

En Brochette
Kebab (Turkish)

Yield: 4 portions
Cooking time: 10 – 15 min

Unit	Ingredient	Metric	Imperial
1	Selected meat cut in 2 cm [(³/₄ in cubes)]	600 g	1¹/₄ lb
¹/₅	Onion (large dice)	120 g	4 oz
¹/₅	Oil	120 ml	4 fl oz
¹/₂₀	Lemon juice	30 ml	1 fl oz
	Bay leaves and thyme		
	Salt and milled pepper		

Preparation

Lightly season meat and place in a bowl with remaining ingredients. Mix thoroughly, cover with cartouche and allow to stand for a few hours to marinade before use. Place meat on skewers interspersed with onion and herbs.

Method of Grilling

Proceed as for grilled meats (*see* p. 425) or place on grilling trays and cook under the salamander turning to complete cooking. Serve presented on a bed of braised rice (*see* p. 244) accompanied with a suitable sauce (*see* chart).

Extensions of Above Formula: Additional Garnish in Relation to 1 unit 600 g (1¼ lb) meat

Name	Main ingredient	Unit	Ingredient	Metric (g)	Imperial (oz)	Suggested Accompanying Sauce
Brochette de foie de Volaille (chicken livers grilled on the skewer)	Chicken livers					Mádeira sauce
Brochette de Rognon (kidneys grilled on the skewer)	Lamb ⎱ kidneys Veal ⎰					Madeira or devilled sauce
Shish kebab or Kebab à la Turque (lamb grilled on a skewer Turkish style)	Fillet of lamb	⅕	Button mushrooms Marinade with meat and intersperse on skewer for grilling	120	4	Jus lié or Madeira sauce
Brochette à la Maison (skewered grilled meats after the style of the house)	e.g. Pork Kidney Liver Bacon	⅕ ⅕	Button mushrooms Peppers (large dice) 4 Small tomatoes (halved) Marinade with meat and intersperse on skewer for grilling	120 120	4 4	Sweet and sour sauce

Grilled Fish   Poisson Grillé

The grilling technique is used in the cooking of a wide variety of fish and shellfish, some of which are prepared into cuts, whilst others are left whole. Those in *common* use are outlined below.

Whole Fish

Gutted and trimmed. Small round fish are also lightly scored (ciseler) in order to aid cooking and prevent the skin from bursting. Burst skin impairs the appearance of the finished product.

English term	French term	Yield for 4 Portions
Herring	Hareng	4 × 200 g (8 oz)
Kippers	Craquelot	4 × 200 g (8 oz)
Mackerel	Maquereau	4 × 200 g (8 oz)
Red mullet	Rouget	4 × 200 g (8 oz)
Sole (Dover)	Sole Douvres	4 × 300 g (12 oz)
Trout	Truite	4 × 200 g (8 oz)
Whiting	Merlan	4 × 200 g (8 oz)
Shellfish		
Lobster	Homard	2 × 500 g (1¼ lb)
Scampi	Langoustine	400 g (1 lb) shelled weight

Fish that are Commonly Prepared as Small Cuts for Grilling

English term	French term	Common cuts for grilling
Cod	Cabillaud	Filet—Suprême—Darne
Dover sole	Sole Douvres	Filet
Haddock	Aigrefin	Filet—Suprême—Darne
Hake	Colin	Filet—Suprême—Darne
Halibut	Flétan	Tronçon
Lemon sole	Sole Limande	Filet
Plaice	Plie	Filet
Salmon	Saumon	Darne
Whiting	Merlan	Filet

Illustrated Fish Cuts used for Grilling

English term	French term	Yield for 4 portions	Explanation and illustration
Fillet	le Filet	4 to 8 fillets according to size, and requirements	A cut of fish free from bone. Flat fish yields 4; round fish yields 2
Supreme	le Suprême	4 × 125 g (5 oz) portions	A slanted cut from large fish fillets.

English term	French term	Yield for 4 portions	Explanation and illustration
Steak of round fish	la Darne	4 × 150 g (6 oz) portions	A cut of round fish on the bone
Steak of flat fish	le Tronçon	4 × 150 g (6 oz) portions	A steak of flat fish on the bone

Preparation for Grilling

Fish may be prepared for grilling in one of the following ways:

1. Dry the fish, lightly season and rub with lemon juice, pass through seasoned flour, oil or melted butter and place on prepared grilling trays. For kippers omit flour and lemon juice.
2. Dry the fish, lightly season and rub with lemon juice, pass through melted butter and white breadcrumbs, lightly pat to remove excess crumbs. Place on prepared grilling trays. Sprinkle with few drops of melted butter.
3. When grilling *live lobster* split in half lengthways remove sack from head and waste cord from tail. Crack the claws. Lightly season and brush flesh and claws liberally with melted butter. Place on prepared grilling trays.

Method

Place trays of fish/shellfish under pre-heated salamander and grill until cooked and golden brown. Throughout grilling moisten lightly with melted butter or oil to aid even and moist cooking. When grilling whole fish or thick cuts of fish, e.g. darnes it is necessary to grill fish on both sides. However, with thin cuts, e.g. fillets, the intense heat should be sufficient to cook the fish through and therefore turning may not be required.

Once cooked arrange fish portions neatly on to lightly buttered service dishes, moisten with some cooking liquor and garnish with picked parsley and a wedge of lemon. Serve with accompanying sauce and any additional garnish.

N.B. Before serving grilled fish steaks remove centre bone, outside skin and trimmings.

Before serving lobster remove the cooked meat from the claw shell and place in carapace (head) cavity.

Name of dish	Method of preparation	Grilling time (min) (approximately)	Additional garnish and accompanying sauce
Poisson Grillé (grilled fish)	1	3 – 10 according to size and thickness of fish	A variety of sauces may be used e.g. sole with parsley butter, herrings with mustard sauce, mackerel with anchovy butter, red mullet with shrimp butter, etc.
Filet/Suprême de Poisson St. Germain	2	3 – 10 according to size and thickness of fish	Noisette potatoes and Sauce Béarnaise
Merlan Entier St. Germain	2	8 – 12	Noisette potatoes and Sauce Béarnaise
Filet de Poisson Caprice	2	3 – 5	Grilled banana halves and Sauce Robert. N.B. Bananas crumbed as for fish
Langoustine en Brochette (scampi on a skewer)	1 or 2	5	Selected hard butter sauce or Sauce Diable
Langoustine en Brochette au Lard (scampi on a skewer wrapped in bacon)	1	5 – 8	Pilaff of rice and sweet and sour sauce
Homard Grillé (grilled lobster)	3	10	Lobster butter

N.B.　Many other fish may be cooked by this method and served with an appropriate sauce.

Grilled Vegetables　　　　　　　　　　　Légumes

Few vegetables are cooked by the grilling method although many are glazed or gratinated under the salamander in readiness for service. The main exceptions are tomatoes and mushrooms.

Grilled Tomatoes　　　　　　　　　　Tomates Grillées

Yield: 4 portions—8 medium tomatoes
Cooking time: 3 – 5 min

Method

Remove eye from tomatoes and lightly score rounded surface in a criss-cross fashion. Place on lightly greased grilling tray, season with salt and pepper, brush with oil and grill steadily under salamander until cooked. Present for service brushed with melted butter and garnished with sprig of parsley.

N.B.   Tomatoes may be skinned, left whole or cut into halves prior to grilling.

Grilled Mushrooms   Champignons Grillés

Yield: 4 portions 200 g (8 oz)
Cooking time: 3 – 5 min

Method

Remove stalks and peel if necessary. Place on lightly greased grilling tray and continue as for grilled tomatoes.

26

Combined Methods of Cookery: Meat and Fish

Extensions Involving a Combination of Cookery Principles as Applied to Meat and Fish Products

The aim of this study is to outline those products, which due to their mode of production, cannot be strictly classified under any one specific principle of cookery. These items are mainly produced by employing a combination of cookery methods. The more common examples are covered in this study and many of these preparations could be classified as rechauffé products.

Poultry

CHICKEN PIE (USING COOKED CHICKEN)   Volaille

Yield: 4 portions
Cooking time: 20 – 30 min
Cooking temperature: 205°C (400°F)

Unit	Ingredient	Metric	Imperial
1	Cooked chicken (large dice) (free from bone)	500 g	$1\frac{1}{4}$ lb
$\frac{3}{5}$	Chicken velouté	300 ml	12 fl oz
$\frac{1}{5}$	Cream	100 ml	4 fl oz
$\frac{1}{10}$	Onion medium dice	50 g	2 oz
$\frac{1}{20}$	Butter	25 g	1 oz
	Salt and pepper to taste		
★	Puff pastry		

★ Sufficient puff pastry for 4 portions approximately 200 g (8 oz) prepared weight.

Method

Sweat onions in butter without colour, add chicken, lightly season, moisten with sauce and cream. Bring to the boil, adjust seasoning and consistency then place filling into earthenware pie dish. Roll out puff pastry 3 mm (⅛ in) thick, moisten edge of pie dish and line with a strip of pastry. Moisten pastry edge and cover pie with remaining pastry. Take care not to stretch the pastry otherwise it will shrink and slide into pie dish during baking. Seal well, trim and decorate with pastry trimmings as required. Rest before baking to allow pastry to relax (avoids excess shrinkage during baking). Egg-wash for baking. Bake in oven until cooked and golden brown. Once cooked clean edges of pie dish and surround with pie collar for service.

Extensions of Chicken Pies: Added Ingredients to 1 Unit – 500 g (1¼ lb) of Cooked Chicken

Name of dish	Unit	Ingredient	Metric (g)	Imperial (oz)
Chicken and mushroom pie	⅕	Sliced sweated mushrooms Add to filling	100	4
Chicken and ham pie	⅕	Cooked ham (large dice) Add to filling	100	4
Chicken, ham and mushroom pie	⅕ ⅕	Sliced sweated mushrooms Cooked ham (large dice) Add to filling	100 100	4 4

N.B.   The above pies may also be prepared with cooked turkey.

For service single portions are often prepared in individual earthenware pots.

SALPICON OF CHICKEN   Salpicon de Volaille

Yield: 4 portions

Unit	Ingredient	Metric	Imperial
1	Cooked chicken (medium dice) (free from bone)	400 g	1 lb
⅝	Suprême or Madeira sauce (as required)	250 ml	10 fl oz
1/16	Butter	25 g	1 oz
	Salt and pepper to taste		

Method

Toss chicken in melted butter, lightly season and moisten with sauce. Bring to boil, correct seasoning and consistency, use as required.

Chicken Vol-au-Vent   Vol-au-Vent de Volaille

Method

Fill four baked hot vol-au-vent cases with hot chicken salpicon using suprême or Madeira sauce. Garnish as required.

Chicken Vol-au-Vent with Asparagus   Vol-au-Vent de Volaille Princesse

As above using suprême sauce and garnished with hot buttered asparagus tips.

Chicken and Mushroom Vol-au-Vent   Vol-au-Vent de Volaille et Champignon

As for chicken vol-au-vent with the addition of $1/5$ unit [(50 g (2 oz)] button mushrooms à blanc.

N.B.   Many other varieties may be prepared, e.g. chicken and ham.

CHICKEN PANCAKES   Crêpes de Volaille

Yield: 4 portions
Cooking time: 5 – 8 min
Cooking temperature: 205°C (400°F)

Unit	Ingredient	Metric	Imperial
1	Cooked chicken (medium dice free from bone)	400 g	1 lb
1	Suprême sauce	400 ml	16 fl oz
$1/16$	Butter	25 g	1 oz
	8 pancakes		
	Salt and pepper to taste		

Method

Sweat chicken quickly in melted butter, lightly season and moisten with half of the sauce to form a hot salpicon. Season to taste.

Stuff pancakes with salpicon, roll to cigar shape and lay in a lightly buttered gratin dish. Brush with melted butter and place in oven to heat thoroughly. Serve accompanied with a sauceboat of sauce suprême.

Chicken Pancakes with Asparagus   Crêpes de Volaille Princesse

As above but garnish pancakes with buttered asparagus tips.

Chicken and Mushroom Pancakes   Crêpes de Volaille et Champignon

As for chicken pancakes with addition of $1/5$ unit [50 g (2 oz)] sliced sweated mushrooms added to basic salpicon.

N.B.   Many other varieties of chicken pancakes can be prepared using different sauces and garnishes, e.g. curred chicken pancakes.

CHICKEN À LA KING

Émincé de Volaille à la King

Yield: 4 portions
Cooking time: 20 – 30 min

Unit	Ingredient	Metric	Imperial
1	Cooked chicken (cut into large dice on slant, free from bone)	500 g	1¼ lb
1	Sauce suprême (*see* p. 179)	500 ml	1 pt
¹/₅	Button mushroom (white)	100 g	4 oz
¹/₁₀	Pimentoes (diced)	50 g	2 oz
¹/₁₀	Butter	50 g	2 oz
¹/₂₀ 1	Egg yolk	25 g	1 oz
/₂₀	Sherry	25 g	1 oz
	Salt and pepper		
★	Rice pilaff		

★ Sufficient pilaff for 4 portions (*see* p. 244).

Method

Sweat peppers in butter without colour. Add mushrooms and continue sweating until cooked. Add chicken, lightly season, moisten with sherry and sauce suprême. Bring to the boil, correct seasoning and consistency, simmer to heat the chicken thoroughly, remove from heat and add egg yolk. Present for service with rice pilaff.

Turkey à La King

Émincé de Dinde à la King

As above but replace chicken with cooked white turkey meat.

CHICKEN IN CURRY SAUCE (USING COOKED CHICKEN)

Cari de Volaille

Yield: 4 portions
Cooking time: 15 – 20 min

Unit	Ingredient	Metric	Imperial
1	Cooked chicken (large dice on slant, free from bone)	500 g	1¼ lb
1	Curry sauce (*see* p. 193)	500 ml	1 pt
¹/₁₀	Butter	50 g	2 oz
	Salt to season		
★	Plain boiled rice		

★ Sufficient boiled rice for 4 portions (*see* p. 243).

Method

Sweat chicken in melted butter without colour. Add sauce, bring to the boil, simmer to heat the chicken thoroughly, adjust seasoning and consistency. Serve accompanied with plain boiled rice and traditional curry accompaniments (*see* p. 345).

Beef   Boeuf

BASIC COOKED FILLING FOR STEAK PIES OR PUDDINGS

Yield: 4 portions
Cooking time: $1\frac{1}{2} - 2$ hr

Unit	Ingredient	Metric (g)	Imperial (oz)
1	Stewing beef ($1\frac{1}{2}$ cm ($\frac{3}{4}$ in) dice)	600	20
$\frac{1}{5}$	Onion (diced)	120	4
$\frac{1}{20}$	Flour	30	• 1
$\frac{1}{20}$			
	Dripping	30	1
$\frac{1}{40}$	Tomato purée	15	$\frac{1}{2}$
	Salt and pepper to taste		
★	Brown stock		

★ Sufficient to cover meat during cooking and form a lightly thickened sauce.

Method

Lightly season the meat and seal quickly in heated dripping, add onions and cook until light brown. Add flour to form a light brown roux, cool slightly and add tomato purée. Moisten with stock to cover meat, bring to boil to form a lightly thickened sauce. Cover with lid and simmer gently on stove top until meat is tender. Correct seasoning and consistency and use as required.

N.B.   During cooking stir periodically to prevent meat sticking to saucepan.
Cooking may be achieved by oven stewing in moderate heat.

Beefsteak Pies (using cooked filling)

Yield: Use 200 g (8 oz) of puff pastry
         or 200 g (8 oz) of flour prepared into short pastry for 4 portions
Baking time: 20 – 30 min
Cooking temperature: 205°C (400°F)

Method

Place filling in earthenware pie dish. Roll out pastry 3 mm ($\frac{1}{8}$ in) thick and proceed as for chicken pies (*see* p. 435).

Beefsteak Puddings (using cooked filling)

Yield: Use 200 g (8 oz) of flour prepared into suet pastry for 4 portions
Steaming time: 1 hr

Method

Roll out two-thirds of suet pastry and line greased pudding basin. Place filling into lined basin, roll out remaining pastry and form a sealed lid. Cover with greased greaseproof paper and pudding cloth. Set to steam until pastry is cooked. Once cooked clean basin, surround with clean serviette and present for service.

Extensions of Cooked Filling for Steak Pies or Puddings: Added Ingredients to 1 – Unit 600 g (1¼ lb) of meat

Name of dish	Unit	Ingredient	Metric (g)	Imperial (oz)
Steak and mushroom pie/pudding	⅕	Sliced, sweated mushrooms Add to cooked filling	120	4
Steak and kidney pie/pudding	⅕	Diced ox-kidney Seal and cook with beef	120	4
Steak, kidney and mushroom pie/pudding	⅕ ⅕	Diced ox-kidney Sliced, sweated mushrooms Seal and cook kidney with beef and add mushrooms to cooked filling	120 120	4 4

BEEFSTEAK AND POTATO PIE

Yield: 4 portions
Stewing time: 1½ – 2 hr
Baking time: 20 – 30 min
Baking temperature: 205° (400°F)

Unit	Ingredient	Metric (g)	Imperial (oz)
1	Stewing beef (medium dice)	400	16
1	Potatoes (medium dice)	400	16
½	Onion (medium dice)	200	8
	Salt and pepper to taste		
⋆	White beef stock		
†	Short pastry		

⋆ Sufficient stock to cover meat and potatoes during cooking.
† Sufficient short pastry to cover pie during baking 200 g (8 oz) flour prepared into short pastry.

Method

Place onions and meat in saucepan and lightly season. Cover with stock, bring to boil, skim, cover with tight-fitting lid and stew gently on stove top until threequarters cooked. Add potatoes and continue cooking until meat is cooked and potatoes begin to fall. Correct seasoning and consistency. Place filling into earthenware pie dish, roll out pastry 3 mm (⅛ in) thick and proceed as for chicken pie (*see* p. 435).

COTTAGE PIE

Yield: 4 portions
Baking time: 30 min
Baking temperature: 205°C (400°F)

Unit	Ingredient	Metric (g)	Imperial (oz)
1	Cooked beef (coarsely minced)	400	16
1	Duchess potatoes (prepared)	400	16
¼	Onion (brunoise)	100	4
¹/₁₆	Butter	25	1
	Salt and pepper to taste		
★	Jus lié		

★ Sufficient jus lié to moisten the meat.

Method

Sweat onion in butter until light brown. Add cooked meat, moisten with jus lié, bring to boil and simmer to heat thoroughly. Adjust seasoning and consistency. Place in pie dish, decorate surface with piped duchess potato and place in oven to bake until thoroughly heated and golden brown. Remove from oven, clean dish and surround with pie collar for service.

MIROTON OF BEEF   Miroton de Boeuf

Yield: 4 portions
Cooking time: 20 min
Cooking temperature: 205°C (400°F)

Unit	Ingredient	Metric	Imperial
1	Sliced cooked beef	400	1 lb
⅝	Sauce lyonnaise (*see* p. 95)	250 ml	10 fl oz
¼	Onions (shredded)	100 g	4 oz
⅛	Butter	50 g	2 oz
⅛	White breadcrumbs	50 g	2 oz
	Salt and pepper to taste		
	Chopped parsley		

Method

Sweat onions in butter to golden brown, and lay in gratin dish. Arrange meat in neat overlapping slices on onions, lightly season and cover with heated sauce lyonnaise. Sprinkle with breadcrumbs and place in oven to heat thoroughly and gratinate for service. Once gratinated, present for service garnished with chopped parsley.

CORNED BEEF HASH CAKE

Yield: 4 portions
Cooking time: 8 – 10 min

Unit	Ingredient	Metric (g)	Imperial (oz)
1	Corned beef (coarsely chopped)	200	8
1	Dry mashed potatoes	200	8
1/4	Onion brunoise (sweated)	50	2
1/8	Egg yolk	25	1
	Salt and pepper to season		
	Chopped parsley		

Method

Combine all ingredients together and season to taste. Shape into small cakes and shallow fry in oil on both sides until golden brown.

  N.B.   This dish may also be prepared as a large cake in a frying pan.

When shaping use dusting flour to facilitate handling.

Lamb and Mutton   Agneau et Mouton

Shepherd's Pie

As for Cottage Pie (*see* p. 441) but replace cooked beef with cooked lamb or mutton.

MOUSSAKA

Yield: 4 portions
Baking time: 30 min/1 hr
Cooking temperature: 205°C (400°F)

Unit	Ingredient	Metric	Imperial
	2 Large aubergines (peeled and thinly sliced)		
1	Cooked lamb or mutton (coarsely minced)	500 g	1 1/4 lb
2/5	Tomatoes (sliced)	200 g	8 oz

$\frac{1}{5}$	Sauce jus lié or demi-glace	100 ml	4 fl oz
$\frac{1}{5}$	Onion brunoise	100 g	4 oz
$\frac{1}{10}$	Oil	50 ml	2 fl oz
$\frac{1}{10}$	Butter	50 g	2 oz
$\frac{1}{10}$	Grated cheese or white breadcrumbs	50 g	2 oz
$\frac{1}{20}$	Seasoned flour	25 g	1 oz
$\frac{1}{40}$	Tomato purée	12.5 g	1 oz
	Hint of garlic		
	Salt and pepper to taste		

Method

Preparation of Filling　Sweat onions in butter without colour, add meat, moisten with sauce, add tomato purée and hint of garlic, bring to boil and season to taste. Simmer for a few minutes to re-heat thoroughly.

Preparation of Aubergines　Pass sliced aubergines through seasoned flour and shallow fry quickly in hot oil on both sides then drain well.

Completion of Moussaka　Method 1. Arrange layer of aubergines on base of buttered fireproof dish. Cover with the filling, arrange a neat layer of sliced tomatoes and aubergine to cover the filling. Sprinkle with grated cheese or white breadcrumbs and bake in hot oven to heat thoroughly and gratinate.

　　N.B.　Alternatively the moussaka may be lightly coated with a layer of thin mornay sauce prior to baking.

　　Method 2. Arrange alternating layers of aubergine, tomatoes and meat filling in a greased mould, finishing with a layer of aubergine. Bake en bain-marie for approximately 1 hour and turn out of mould for service.

EPIGRAMMES OF LAMB'S BREAST　Poitrine d'Agneau en Épigrammes

Yield: 4 portions
Cooking time: $1\frac{1}{2}$ hr
Frying time: 5 – 10 min

Unit	Ingredient	Metric	Imperial
1	Breast of lamb (skinned and trimmed)	600 g	$1\frac{1}{4}$ lb
$\frac{1}{5}$	Mirepoix (left whole)	120 g	4 oz
$\frac{1}{10}$	Oil	60 ml	2 fl oz
	Bouquet garni		
	Seasoning		
	Seasoned flour		
	Egg-wash		
	Breadcrumbs for pané		
★	White stock		

★ Sufficient stock to cover meat during boiling of lamb.

Method

Place meat and vegetables into cooking vessel and cover with white stock. Bring to boil, skim, add bouquet garni and seasoning. Cover with lid and simmer until lamb is tender approximately 1½ hours. Once cooked remove lamb from stock, bone out and press under light weight until cold and set. Cut into selected shape e.g. squares or diamonds, pané and shallow fry in oil until thoroughly re-heated and golden brown on both sides. Present and serve as for panéed lamb cutlets (p. 316). Traditionally épigrammes are served with lamb cutlets as an integral part of the dish.

Pork   Porc

SCOTCH EGGS

Yield: 4 portions
Frying time: 8 – 10 min
Frying temperature: 175 – 190°C (350 – 375°F)

Unit	Ingredient	Metric	Imperial
1	4 Hard-boiled eggs (shelled) Pork sausagemeat Seasoned flour Eggwash Breadcrumbs for pané	400 g	1 lb

Method

Pass eggs through seasoned flour, envelop each egg in sausage meat and seal well. Pané, deep fry until thoroughly cooked and golden brown. Serve hot on flat with dish paper.
    N.B.   May be served cold with salad.

GRILLED PIG'S TROTTERS WITH DEVILLED SAUCE   Pieds de Porc Grillés Diable

Yield: 4 portions
Grilling time: 8 – 10 min

Unit	Ingredient	Metric	Imperial
	4 Pig's trotters (boiled *see* p. 262)		
1	Sauce diable	250 ml	10 fl oz
⅕	Melted butter	50 g	2 oz
⅒	White breadcrumbs	25 g	1 oz
	Diluted English mustard		
	Salt and pepper to taste		

Method

Lightly season trotters, brush with mustard, melted butter and roll in breadcrumbs. Place on to prepared grilling tray and grill under salamander turning to heat thoroughly and colour golden brown. Arrange on service flat and accompany with devilled sauce.

BRAISED HAM (Gammons are often used) WITH MADEIRA
Jambon Braisé au Madère

Applied to whole hams or gammons
Yield: 600 g (1½ lb) raw wt off bone ⎫
             800 g (2 lb) raw wt on bone ⎬ = 4 portions
Boiling time: 20 min per 400 g (1 lb)
Braising time: 45 – 60 min
Oven temperature: 190°C (375°F)

Unit	Ingredient	Metric	Imperial
	Whole ham or gammon (as required)		
1	Madeira	250 ml	10 fl oz
⅕	Soft brown sugar	50 g	2 oz
★	Demi-glace		

★ Allow ¼ l (½ pt) for every four portions.

Method

Boil selected joint until almost cooked. Remove from cooking liquor and trim away skin and excess fat. Score and place into braising vessel, moisten with Madeira and sprinkle surface of joint with sugar. Place in oven to complete cooking. Baste frequently with Madeira to form a glaze with sugar. Once cooked and glazed remove joint from oven and allow to set for carving. To form sauce add demi-glace to cooking liquor, degrease then adjust seasoning and consistency. Pass through fine chinois. For service carve ham into thin slices, place on to service dish and lightly coat with sauce.

Braised Ham with Madeira and Spinach
Jambon Braisé Florentine

As above but place carved ham slices on to a bed of buttered, cooked leaf spinach before coating lightly with sauce.

Baked Ham in Pastry
Jambon en Croûte

Boil selected ham or gammon joint until cooked (*see* p. 259). Remove from cooking liquor, trim away skin and excess fat and allow surface of joint to cool. Envelop joint in rolled out short or puff pastry and place pastry join/seal down on to a greased baking sheet. Decorate with pastry trimmings, brush liberally with egg wash and cut out small steam vent. Bake until pastry is golden brown and cooked. For service, carve ham and serve accompanied with a piece of pastry and a suitable sauce, e.g. madeira.
N.B.   As a guide use 50 g (2 oz) prepared pastry per portion.

Sugar Baked Hams

Method

Boil selected ham or gammon joint until cooked (*see* p. 259), remove from cooking liquor, trim away skin and excess fat. Score criss-cross fashion and stud with cloves. Sprinkle with soft brown sugar, place into cooking vessel and bake in hot oven (205°C(400°F)) until glazed to rich golden-brown colour. Remove joint from oven and allow to set for carving.

Sugar Baked Ham with Peaches or Pineapple

Serve carved ham with a portion of glazed peach or pineapple and accompany with suitable sauce, e.g. Madeira, hot Cumberland sauce, sweet and sour sauce, etc.

N.B.   *To glaze fruit* Dust poached peach halves or pineapple rings with icing sugar and glaze under salamander.

Alternative Method of Glazing Hams

Combine soft brown sugar with a little flour, moisten with a few drops of cold water to form a paste. Spread paste over surface of ham before glazing in a hot oven.

Deep-Fried Cooked Meats

BASIC COOKED FORCEMEAT

Yield: 4 portions
Cooking time: 4 – 6 min
Frying temperature: 175 – 190°C (350 – 375°F)

Unit	Ingredient	Metric	Imperial
1	Selected cooked meat (coarsley minced or small dice)	250 g	10 oz
$^1/_2$	Chicken velouté or béchamel (to bind)	125 ml	5 fl oz
$^1/_{10}$	Egg yolk	25 g	1 oz
	Chopped parsley		
	Nutmeg (pinch)		
	Salt and pepper		

Method

Place meat in a cooking vessel, bind with velouté, bring to the boil to form a stiff mixture. Remove from heat, add yolks, nutmeg, parsley and season to taste. Spread mixture on to a buttered tray, allow to cool and set. When set, scale off to required weight, mould into required shape, pané then re-shape neatly. Deep fry until thoroughly re-heated and golden brown. Serve garnished with deep fried parsley and accompany with selected sauce (see chart).

Examples of Shapes

(a) *Croquettes* — small cylinders (2 per portion)

(b) *Cutlets – Côtelettes* – mould into cutlet shape, insert blanched macaroni to imitate a cutlet bone. Once fried garnish with 'mock' bone and dress with cutlet frill (1 – 2 per portion).

(c) *Balls* – moulded into neat spheres (2 per portion).

Examples of Dishes Prepared Using Above Formula

English term	Main meat and added ingredients	Example of sauces to accompany	French term
Beef croquettes	Cooked beef	Devilled sauce/Sauce Diable	Croquettes de Boeuf
Chicken cutlets/ Croquettes	Cooked chicken	Piquant sauce/Sauce Piquante	Côtelettes/Croquettes de Volaille
Chicken and ham cutlets/Croquettes	Equal quantities of cooked chicken and ham	Chasseur sauce/Sauce Chasseur	Côtelettes/Croquettes de Volaille et Jambon
Chicken and mushroom cutlets/ Croquettes	Cooked chicken plus $\frac{1}{5}$ unit 50 g (2 oz) sweated chopped mushroom	Madeira sauce/Sauce Madère	Côtelettes/Croquettes de Volaille et Champignon
Game cutlets/ Croquettes	Cooked game	Port wine sauce and redcurrant jelly/ Sauce au Porto	Côtelettes/Croquettes de Gibier

N.B. Drain deep-fried products well and place on dish papers to absorb any excess grease. The above cutlets may be shallow fried.

Kromeskis Russian Style   Cromesquis à la Russe

Prepare basic cooked forcemeat (p. 446) using a combination of cooked *chicken* and cooked *tongue*, use a quarter the amount of tongue to chicken. Shape into croquettes and wrap each one in a thin slice of *streaky bacon*. Pass through seasoned flour and batter, deep fry until thoroughly heated and golden brown. Garnish with deep-fried parsley and serve accompanied with suitable sauce, e.g. Sauce Smitane, Sauce Tomate.

DURHAM CUTLETS

Yield: 4 portions
Cooking time: 4 – 6 min
Frying temperature: 175 – 190°C (350 – 375°F)

Unit	Ingredient	Metric (g)	Imperial (oz)
1	Cooked beef (minced)	200	8
$\frac{1}{2}$	Dry mashed potato	100	4
$\frac{1}{4}$	Onion (brunoise, sweated)	50	2
$\frac{1}{8}$	Egg yolk	25	1
	Chopped parsley		
	Seasoning		

Method

Combine all ingredients thoroughly to form a stable mixture, season to taste. Divide into four portions and shape into cutlets. Pané, reshape, insert blanched macaroni to imitate a cutlet bone. Deep fry until thoroughly heated and golden brown. Serve garnished with deep fried picked parsley. Accompany with a suitable sauce, e.g. jus lié.
   N.B.   May be shallow fried.

RISSOLES

Yield: 4 portions
Cooking time: 5 – 8 min
Frying temperature: 175 – 190°C (350 – 375°F)

Unit	Ingredient	Metric (g)	Imperial (oz)
1*	Cooked meat (coarsely minced)	100	4
$\frac{1}{4}$	Whole egg (beaten)	25	1
$\frac{1}{4}$	Onion brunoise (sweated without colour)	25	1
	Chopped parsley/picked parsley		
	Seasoning		
†	Puff pastry (trimmings may be used)		

* Cooked beef is often used but a variety of cooked meats is acceptable.
† Sufficient pastry for 4 portions, i.e. 200 g (8 oz) at prepared weight.

Method

Combine meat, onion, egg, chopped parsley, and seasoning to form a stable mixture. Divide into four portions. Roll out pastry thinly and cut into four 11 cm (4½ in) squares approximately. Water wash edges, place filling in centre and fold corner to corner to form a triangular shape. Seal edges well. Deep fry until pastry is cooked and golden brown. Drain well and serve garnished with deep fried picked parsley. Accompany with suitable sauce, e.g. jus lié.

RUSSIAN FISH PIE   Coulibiac de Saumon à la Russe

Yield: 4 portions
Cooking time: 30 – 40 min
Cooking temperature: 205°C (400°F)

Unit	Ingredient	Metric	Imperial
1	Cooked salmon	300 g	12 oz
¼*	Rice pilaff	75 g	3 oz
¼	Sliced mushrooms (sweated without colour)	75 g	3 oz
¼	Fish velouté	75 ml	3 fl oz
⅛	Vesiga	37.5 g	1½ oz
	1 Chopped hard boiled egg		
	Chopped parsley		
	Seasoning		
†	Puff pastry		

* Indicates amount of raw rice used to prepare pilaff.
† Sufficient for 4 portions, i.e. 250 g (10 oz) approximately, at prepared weight.

Method

Soak vesiga overnight in cold water, boil in lightly salted water for 2 – 3 hours until tender. Refresh and cut into medium dice ready for use. Roll out pastry into a rectangle of approximately 40 cm × 25 cm × 3 mm (15 in × 10 in × ⅛ in). Combine together rice,

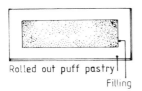

Rolled out puff pastry
Filling

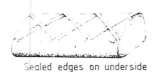

Sealed edges on underside

mushrooms, vesiga, hard boiled egg, chopped parsley, velouté and season to taste. Place half of this mixture along the centre of the rolled out pastry. Follow with the salmon and complete with a layer of the rice mixture. Moisten pastry edges and fold the pastry over to totally enclose the filling. Place on to lightly greased baking sheet with sealed edges underneath. Decorate with pastry trimmings, egg wash and rest before baking. Bake until cooked and golden brown and serve accompanied with a suitable sauce, e.g. beurre fondue, sauce hollandaise.

N.B.   Classically this product is prepared using brioche pastry, *see* p. 543.

Russian Chicken Pie   Coulibiac de Volaille à la Russe

Prepared in the same manner as for Russian fish pie (*see* p. 449) but substitute cooked salmon with diced cooked chicken, and fish velouté with chicken velouté.

Fish   Poisson

FISH PIE

Yield: 4 portions
Cooking time: 30 minutes
Cooking temperature: 205°C (400°F)

Unit	Ingredient	Metric	Imperial
1	Cooked flaked fish (free from bone and skin)	400 g	1 lb
1	Duchess potatoes (prepared)	400 g	1 lb
5/8	Béchamel or fish velouté	250 ml	10 fl oz
1/10	Melted butter	25 g	1 oz
	Chopped parsley		
	Salt and pepper to taste		

Method

Lightly butter pie-dish. Boil sauce, correct seasoning and consistency and add chopped parsley to garnish and flavour. Coat base of pie dish with layer of sauce, add flaked fish, lightly season and moisten with remaining sauce. Pipe duchess potatoes over surface to cover the fish. Sprinkle with melted butter and bake in oven until thoroughly heated and golden brown for service.

Salpicon of Fish   Salpicon de Poisson

A term used to define a single or variety of cooked flaked fish cohered with a selected sauce to form a moist fish filling. Such preparations are used when preparing vol-au-vents, savoury pancakes and coquilles, etc. The sauces commonly used are fish based, e.g. fish velouté derivatives.

Yield: 4 portions

Unit	Ingredient	Metric	Imperial
1	Selected flaked cooked fish	400 g	1 lb
5/8	Selected sauce (fish velouté based)	250 ml	10 fl oz
	Butter		
	Seasoning		

Method

Re-heat fish in melted butter, season and moisten with sauce, bring to boil, correct seasoning and consistency. Use as required.

Fish Vol-au-Vents   Vol-au-Vent de Poisson

Method

Fill four baked hot vol-au-vent cases with hot salpicon of fish, garnish as required and serve immediately.

Fish Vol-au-Vent with Asparagus   Vol-au-Vent de Poisson Princesse

Method

As above garnished with buttered asparagus tips.

Seafood Vol-au-Vent   Vol-au-Vent de Fruits de Mer

Method

As for Vol-au-Vent de Poisson using a selection of fish and shellfish.

N.B. Many varieties of Vol-au-Vent may be prepared using selected fish/shellfish and a suitable sauce.

FISH IN SCALLOP SHELL   Coquilles de Poisson
(use four scallop shells)

Yield: 4 portions
Cooking time: 8 – 10 min
Cooking temperature: 205°C (400°F)

Unit	Ingredient	Metric	Imperial
1	Selected flaked cooked fish	400 g	1 lb
1	Fish velouté	400 ml	16 fl oz
³/₄	Duchess potatoes (prepared)	300 g	12 oz
¹/₈	Cream	50 ml	2 fl oz
¹/₁₆	Egg yolk	25 g	1 oz
	Seasoning		

Method

Pipe border of duchess potatoes around the edge of the scallop shells. Place under salamander to set potatoes and lightly colour. Form a salpicon with fish and half of the sauce, season to taste. Fill shells with salpicon, add yolk and cream to remaining sauce and napper fish. Place in oven to heat thoroughly and glaze brown. Present for service on flat with dish paper.

N.B. Adjust coating sauce to light-coating consistency for use.

Fish in Scallop Shell with Cheese   Coquilles de Poisson Mornay

As above but using fish mornay sauce.

Seafood in Scallop Shell   Coquilles de Fruits de Mer

As for Coquilles de Poisson using a selection of fish and shellfish.
   N.B.   Other varieties of coquilles may be prepared using selected fish/shellfish and a
suitable sauce.

SAVOURY PANCAKE BATTER   Appareil à Crêpe

Yield: 4 portions (8 pancakes)

Unit	Ingredient	Metric	Imperial
1	Milk	250 ml	10 fl oz
$2/_5$	Flour	100 g	4 oz
$1/_5$	Whole egg (beaten)	50 g	2 oz
$1/_{20}$	Oil	12.5 ml	$1/_2$ fl oz
	Seasoning		
	Chopped parsley		

Method

Sift flour and seasoning into mixing bowl. Form a well, pour in beaten egg and milk.
Whisk ingredients together to form a smooth pancake batter. Add chopped parsley and
whisk in the oil.

Cooking of Pancakes   Coat base of pancake pan with film of oil and heat on stove top.
Pour off excess oil and add sufficient batter to form a thin pancake. Cook pancake on both
sides to golden brown. Turn out ready for use.

FISH PANCAKES   Crêpes de Poisson

Yield: 4 portions
Cooking time: 10 min
Cooking temperature: 205°C (400°F)

Unit	Ingredient	Metric	Imperial
1	Fish velouté	500 ml	1 pt
$4/_5$	Selected, flaked cooked fish	400 g	1 lb
$1/_{20}$	Egg yolk	25 g	1 oz
$1/_{20}$	Cream	25 ml	1 fl oz
	8 Pancakes		
	Salt and pepper to taste		

Method

Form hot salpicon with fish and half of the sauce, season to taste. Stuff pancakes, roll cigar shape and lay into lightly buttered gratin dish. Adjust seasoning and consistency of remaining sauce, add egg yolk, cream and mask pancakes. Place in oven to heat thoroughly and glaze brown for service.

Fish Pancakes with Bercy Sauce   Crêpes de Poisson Bercy

As for Crêpes de Poisson using Sauce Bercy.

Crab Pancakes with Thermidor Sauce   Crêpes de Crabe Thermidor

As for Crêpes de Poisson but using a salpicon of crab with Sauce Thermidor. Gratinate with grated parmesan.

N.B. Other varieties of pancakes may be prepared using selected fish/shellfish and suitable sauce.

CURRIED PRAWNS   Cari de Crevettes Roses

Yield: 4 portions
Cooking time: 5 min

Unit	Ingredient	Metric	Imperial
1	Peel cooked prawns	300 g	10 oz
1	Curry sauce (*see* p. 193)	300 ml	10 oz
1	Boiled rice	300 g	10 oz
$1/_{10}$	Butter	30 g	1 oz

Method

Sauté prawns in butter, add curry sauce and simmer for a few minutes to thoroughly heat. Serve accompanied with plain boiled rice.

FISH KEDGEREE

Yield: 4 portions
Cooking time: 25 min

Unit	Ingredient	Metric	Imperial
1	Selected flaked cooked fish	400 g	1 lb
1	Curry sauce (heated)	400 ml	16 fl oz
	2 Hard boiled egg (quartered)		
$1/_8$	Butter	50 g	2 oz
	Salt to taste		
★	Rice pilaff		

★ Sufficient for 4 portions (*see* p. 244)

Method

Sauté flaked fish quickly in melted butter, add rice and heat thoroughly. Present in buttered service dish and decorate with egg. Serve accompanied with a sauceboat of heated curry sauce.

LOBSTER IN CHEESE SAUCE   Homard Mornay

Yield: 4 portions
Cooking time: 8 – 10 min

Unit	Ingredient	Metric	Imperial
	2 Boiled lobsters (medium sized)		
1	Fish mornay sauce	500 ml	1 pt
$\frac{1}{10}$	Butter	50 g	2 oz
	Salt and cayenne pepper to taste		
	Grated parmesan to gratinate		
	Four sprigs of parsley		

Method

Split lobsters lengthways and remove flesh from tail and claws, slice tail meat leaving claw meat whole. Clean shell and dry for use. Sweat lobster meat in butter without colour, lightly season and cohere with a little mornay sauce, remove from heat. Pour a little sauce into base of lobster shells, add lobster placing claw meat into the head cavity. Napper with remaining sauce, sprinkle with grated parmesan and gratinate until golden brown. Present for service on a dish paper and flat, garnished with picked parsley.

LOBSTER NEWBURG   Homard Newburg

Yield: 4 portions
Cooking time: 5 – 8 min

Unit	Ingredient	Metric	Imperial
	2 Boiled lobsters (medium sized)		
1	Cream (double)	250 ml	10 fl oz
$\frac{1}{5}$	Butter	50 g	2 oz
$\frac{1}{5}$	Madeira	50 ml	2 fl oz
$\frac{1}{10}$	Brandy	25 ml	1 fl oz
	Salt and pepper to taste		
★	Rice pilaff		
	Salt and pepper to taste		

★ Sufficient rice pilaff for 4 portions (p. 244)

Method

Mix egg yolk with a little of the cream to form a liaison and put aside. Remove lobster meat from tail and claws. Cut tail into thick pieces, leaving claw meat whole. Gently sweat lobster in butter, lightly season, flame with brandy, add Madeira and reduce by a half. Pour on the cream, bring to boil and simmer briskly to coating consistency. Correct seasoning, remove from heat, stir in liaison and do not reboil.

Where possible serve rice and lobster in separate timbales decorating lobster with head and tail shell. N.B. Lobster Newburg may be garnished with slices of truffle flavoured with brandy.

Lobster in Thermidor Sauce   Homard Thermidor

Proceed as for Homard Mornay using thermidor sauce (p. 182), garnish with the addition of 4 truffle slices.

LOBSTER CARDINAL   Homard Cardinal

Yield: 4 portions
Cooking time: 8 – 10 min

Unit	Ingredient	Metric	Imperial
	2 Boiled lobsters (medium sized)		
1	Lobster sauce (*see* p. 196)	250 ml	10 fl oz
1/5	Butter	50 g	2 oz
1/5	Mushrooms (cooked small dice)	50 g	2 oz
1/5	Cream } liaison	50 ml	2 fl oz
1/5	Egg yolk }	50 g	2 oz
1/10	Brandy	25 ml	1 oz
1/10	Parmesan (grated)	25 g	1 oz
	Picked parsley		
	Pinch of salt and pepper		
	4 slices of truffle		

Method

Split lobsters lengthways and remove flesh from tail and claws, slice tail meat and leave claw meat whole. Clean shell and dry for use. Re-heat lobster meat and mushrooms in butter without colour, lightly season, flame with brandy and cohere with a little of the lobster sauce to form a salpicon. Bring remaining lobster sauce to the boil, remove from heat, add liaison of egg yolks/cream and correct seasoning. Moisten base of lobster shells with sauce, fill with salpicon of lobster and mushrooms, placing claw meat into the head cavity. Napper with remaining sauce, sprinkle with grated parmesan and gratinate to golden brown. Present for service on a dish paper and service flat, garnished with truffle and picked parsley.

DEEP-FRIED FISH CAKES   Médaillons de Poisson Frits

Yield: 4 portions
Cooking time: 4 – 6 min
Frying temperature: 175 – 190°C (350 – 375°F)

Unit	Ingredient	Metric (g)	Imperial (oz)
1	Cooked white fish (free from bone and skin)	200	8
3/4	Dry mashed potato (cooked weight)	150	6
1/8	Whole egg (beaten)	25	1
	Chopped parsley		
	Anchovy essence		
	Seasoning		

Method

Flake fish and mix with potato. Add parsley, few drops anchovy essence, bind with egg and season to taste. Divide into four equal pieces, shape in médallions, pané and deep fry until thoroughly reheated and golden brown. Serve accompanied with a suitable sauce, e.g. tomato, tartare or parsley sauce, etc.

Deep-Fried Salmon Fish Cakes   Médaillons de Saumon Frits

As above but substitute white cooked fish with cooked salmon.
  N.B.   Fish cakes may be shallow fried.

Snails   Escargots

Cooked snails are readily available in a canned form. The shells are packed separately and sold with each tin of snails. These commercial snails are ideal for use in the kitchen.

Snails with Garlic Butter   Escargots au Beurre d'Ail

Yield: 6 snails per portion

Method

Place snails into shells and fill with garlic butter (*see* p. 201). Place on to snail dish with shell cavity facing upwards. Quickly heat through in a hot oven [205°C (400°F)] for a few minutes. Present for service.

27

Combined Methods of Cookery: Vegetables and Potatoes

Introduction

The aim of this study is to outline those vegetable products, which due to their mode of production, cannot be strictly classified under any one specific principle of cookery. These items are produced by employing a combination of cookery methods. The more common examples are covered.

DUCHESS POTATO MIXTURE

This is a basic potato mixture, which is used to prepare a wide variety of potato products. Yield: 4 portions

Unit	Ingredient	Metric	Imperial
1	Snow potatoes (well dried p.186)	400 g	1 lb
$1/_{16}$	Butter	25 g	1 oz
$1/_{16}$	Egg yolk	25 g	1 oz
	Seasoning		
	Pinch of nutmeg		

Method

Combine all ingredients, mix thoroughly, season to taste and use as required.

Extensions of Duchess Potatoes: Preparation and Added Ingredients in Relation to 1 Unit i.e. 400 g (1 lb) Duchess Mixture

Baked varieties into 4 portions

English term	Unit	Ingredient	Metric	Imperial	French term
Duchess potatoes		Fill piping bag and star tube with basic mixture. Pipe 5 cm (2 in) cones on to lightly greased baking sheets. Set in moderately hot oven 205°C (400°F) for a few minutes, egg wash and continue baking until golden brown and thoroughly heated (approximately 5–8 min)			Pommes Duchesse
Rosette potatoes		As for duchess but pipe into small rosettes			Pommes Rosette
Brioche potatoes		Mould basic mixture into spheres and form into small cottage loaf shapes. Proceed as for duchess potatoes			Pommes Brioche
Marquise potatoes	$\frac{1}{4}$	Tomates concassées	100 g	4 oz	Pommes Marquise
		Using a piping bag and star tube, pipe potato nests directly on to a greased baking sheet. Fill centre of nests with tomates concassées and proceed as for duchess potatoes			
Chester potatoes	$\frac{1}{8}$	Grated Cheshire cheese	50 g	2 oz	Pommes Chester
		4 Thin slices Cheshire cheese			
		Combine grated cheese with basic duchess potato mixture and shape into small round potato cakes [1 cm (³⁄₈ in) thick]. Place on to lightly greased baking sheet and brush with beaten egg. Lay cheese slices on to potato cakes, bake in moderately hot oven [205°C (400°F)] until golden brown and thoroughly heated (approximately 5–8 min)			

Deep-Fried Varieties

Croquette potatoes		Shape basic duchess mixture into small cylinders, pané and deep fry for service			Pommes Croquettes

Almond potatoes		Divide basic duchess mixture and shape into eight small pears. Pané with a mixture of almonds and breadcrumbs. Decorate top of potato with whole almonds and deep fry for service			Pommes Amandines
Berny potatoes		Combine a garnish of finely chopped truffle with basic duchess mixture. Proceed as for Pommes Amandine but shape mixture into small apricots. Decorate with a piece of parsley stem to represent apricot stalk. Deep fry for service			Pommes Berny
Royal or St. Florentine potatoes	$^1/_4$	Finely chopped cooked ham	100 g	4 oz	Pommes Royale/St. Florentin
		Combine ham with basic duchesse mixture, shape into small rectangles and pané with a mixture of breadcrumbs and pasta vermicelli. Deep fry for service			
Dauphine potatoes	$^1/_2$	Choux pastry (net wt)	200 g	8 oz	Pommes Dauphine
		Combine pastry with basic duchess mixture. Mould into small balls or shape oval with oiled tablespoons. Deep fry for service. N.B. May be placed on to strips of oiled greaseproof paper to store prior to frying			
Lorette potatoes	$^1/_2$	Choux pastry (net wt)	200 g	8 oz	Pommes Lorette
	$^1/_{16}$	Grated parmesan	25 g	1 oz	
		Combine choux pastry and cheese with duchess mixture. Mould into cigar shapes and proceed as for pommes dauphine			
Elizabeth potatoes	$^1/_2$	Choux pastry net wt)	200 g	8 oz	Pommes Elisabeth
	$^1/_8$	Cooked spinach (dry)	50 g	2 oz	
		Combine pastry with basic duchess mixture and shape into small balls. Depress to form a cavity. Fill with spinach and reshape to seal. Proceed as for dauphine potatoes			

Shallow-Fried Varieties

Galette potatoes		Shape basic duchess mixture into small potato cakes. Shallow fry on both sides and serve			Pommes Galette

Extensions of Boiled/Steamed Potatoes in Jackets: Preparation and Added Ingredients in Relation to 1 Unit i.e. 400 g (1 lb) Boiled Potatoes

Yield: 400 g (1 lb) 4 portions
Cooking time: 15–20 min

Method
Boil/steam scrubbed jacket potatoes until almost cooked, drain well, cool and peel for use.

English term	*Unit*	*Ingredient*	*Metric*	*Imperial*	*French term*
Shallow-fried potatoes		Cut cooked potatoes into ¹/₂ cm (¹/₈ in) thick slices. Shallow fry in hot fat and toss to brown evenly. Season to taste, then sprinkle with chopped parsley for service			Pommes Sautées
Garlic-flavoured shallow-fried potatoes		As for Pommes Sautées but flavour with chopped garlic during cooking. Brush lightly with garlic butter and sprinkle with chopped parsley for service			Pommes Provençale
Shallow-fried potatoes with onions	¹/₂	Onions (sliced and sautéed)	200 g	8 oz	Pommes Lyonnaise
		Proceed as for Pommes Sautées, when potatoes are almost cooked add sautéed onions and toss to mix. Season to taste, then sprinkle with chopped parsley for service			
		Thinly slice/coarsely grate cooked potatoes. Lightly season and place into a buttered omelet pan to form a loose textured cake. Shallow fry to colour both sides and until thoroughly heated. Serve as required.			Pommes Roesti

Extension of Plain Boiled Potatoes: 1 unit 400 g (1 lb) boiled potatoes

English term	*Method of cooking*	*French term*
Shallow-fried turned potatoes	Select the plain boiled turned potatoes and drain well. Shallow fry in hot fat and toss to brown evenly. Season to taste. Sprinkle with chopped parsley for service	Pommes Rissolées
Shallow-fried new potatoes	As above using plain boiled new potatoes	Pommes Nouvelles Rissolées

Vegetables Tossed in Butter   Légumes Sautées au Beurre

Boiled and refreshed vegetables are lightly seasoned then quickly shallow-fried in butter to re-heat for service. In some instances the vegetables take on faint brown tinge as a result of this process.

Vegetables commonly reheated by this method are listed below.

English term	*French term*
Artichoke bottoms (à blanc)	Fonds d'Artichauts Sautés au Beurre
Beans (French)	Haricots Verts Sautés au Beurre
Brussels sprouts	Choux de Bruxelles Sautés au Beurre
Cauliflower	Chou-fleur Sauté au Beurre
Celeriac	Céleri-rave Sauté au Beurre
Oyster plant/salsify	Salsifis Sauté au Beurre
Parsnips	Panais Sautés au Beurre
Spinach (leaf)	Épinard en Branche Sauté au Beurre

During shallow frying the flavour of the vegetables may be enhanced by the addition of other ingredients. These ingredients may also improve the appearance of the finished product. Common examples include the following.

Vegetables Tossed in Butter with Herbs   Légumes Sautés aux Fines Herbes

During cooking sprinkle vegetable with fine herbs.
   Suitable for use with: artichoke bottoms, cauliflower, salsify, parsnips, celeriac, etc.

Vegetables Tossed in Butter with Chestnuts   Légumes Sautés Limousine

During cooking add pieces of cooked chestnuts (p. 376).
   Suitable for use with: artichoke bottoms and Brussels sprouts.

Vegetables Tossed in Butter Polonesian Style   Légumes Sautés Polonaise

During cooking sprinkle the vegetable with sieved hard-boiled egg, chopped parsley and fried breadcrumbs and finish with beurre noisette.
   Suitable for use with: Brussels sprouts and cauliflower.

Independent Vegetable Preparations Involving Combined Methods

STUFFED ARTICHOKE BOTTOMS WITH CHEESE   Fonds d'Artichauts Farcis au Gratin

Yield: 4 portions
Baking time: 5 – 8 min
Cooking temperature: 175°C (350°F)

Unit	Ingredient	Metric	Imperial
	4 large or 8 small cooked artichoke bottoms (à blanc)		
1	Cheese sauce	250 ml	10 fl oz
⁴/₅	Duxelle	200 g	8 oz
¹/₅	Grated cheese	50 g	2 oz
	Seasoning		

Method

Season artichoke bottoms and place in buttered gratin dish. Fill with duxelle, coat with cheese sauce and sprinkle with grated cheese. Bake in oven to reheat thoroughly and glaze. Serve as required.

Artichoke Bottoms Stuffed with Spinach   Fonds d'Artichauts Florentine

As above but replace duxelle with dry spinach purée.

STUFFED EGG PLANT   Aubergine Farcie au Gratin

Yield: 4 portions
Baking time: 8 – 10 min
Cooking temperature: 175°C (350°F)

Unit	Ingredient	Metric	Imperial
	2 Medium egg plants		
1	Duxelle	200 g	8 oz
¹/₈	White breadcrumbs	25 g	1 oz
	Seasoning		

Method

Cut aubergines into halves lengthways, score the pulp criss-cross fashion and shallow or deep fry in hot oil until the pulp softens. Remove the pulp leaving the skin intact, chop pulp and combine with duxelle. Adjust seasoning and fill skins with mixture. Sprinkle with breadcrumbs, place into a buttered gratin dish, bake in oven to thoroughly reheat and gratinate. Serve as required.

SHALLOW-FRIED CORN CAKES   Galettes de Maïs Sautées

Yield: 4 portions
Cooking time: 3 – 5 min

Unit	Ingredient	Metric (g)	Imperial (oz)
1	Corn kernels (boiled)	200	8
¼	Egg	50	2
⅛	Flour	25	1
	Seasoning		

Method

Beat egg, mix with corn and lightly season. Add flour and mix thoroughly to form a cohered mixture.
Drop small portions of mixture into frying pan and lightly press to form corn cakes. Fry on both sides until cooked and golden brown. Serve as required.
    N.B. Tinned or frozen corn kernels may be used.

BUBBLE AND SQUEAK

Yield: 4 portions
Cooking time: 8 – 10 min

Unit	Ingredient	Metric	Imperial
1	Cabbage (cooked and chopped)	200 g	8 oz
1	Mash potatoes (dry)	200 g	8 oz
¼	Melted bacon fat	50 ml	2 fl oz
	Pinch of salt and pepper		

Method

Combine cabbage, potato and season to taste. Shape in small cakes and shallow fry in bacon fat on both sides until golden brown. Often served at breakfast time.
    N.B. This product may also be prepared by forming a large cake in a frying pan.

28

Savouries and Hot Hors D'Oeuvres

In English cookery savouries denote a range of products that are served near the end of a meal. These items have never gained the popularity on the continent, which they enjoy on English menus and in the United States of America.

Mainly they are comprised of various preparations (fish, meat, cheese, eggs, etc.), carefully prepared and neatly served on croûtes of toasted bread or in pastry cases. As they are served near the end of the meal they are of a light nature, and in the main highly seasoned, often being prepared with the addition of mustard, cayenne pepper and Worcester sauce, etc.

In addition, these products may be served prior to the main meal as hot hors d'oeuvres or hot canapés (see below). They are also becoming increasingly popular for use in the more modern type of fast-food operation, e.g. snack bar, bistro, motorway operation. In these instances they can be served as a snack 24 hours a day and in many cases are cooked to order.

Where a traditional kitchen brigade is employed the following Chefs de Partie are involved:

Chef Garde-Manger   —   basic preparation of fish, meats, etc.
Chef Rôtisseur   —   cooking and service of most savouries.

Savouries are usually cooked to order to ensure freshness. They are widely employed when planning à la carte, luncheon and dinner menus. For service savouries are dressed neatly on flats with dish papers and may be garnished with bunches of picked parsley where appropriate.

The savouries listed in this study are examples of those that are most commonly employed when compiling modern menus. It must be noted, however, that many other such products may be prepared, this being dependent upon local needs as well as the cook's flair and creative ability.

Hot Hors d'Oeuvres and Hot Canapés

These products may be defined as small savoury items prepared from a wide range of foods, which are cooked and presented in a variety of ways.

In addition to the canapés listed in this study, other examples of hot hors d'oeuvres may include the following: deep-fried goujons of fish, pork or chicken fritots, deep-fried savoury croquettes, vegetable fritters, savoury bouchées and choux pastry cases. Such preparations are served for hot finger buffets and also at cocktail and reception parties. They may be accompanied with a selection of hot and cold sauces in the form of 'dips'.

Examples of Savouries in Common Use

The following savouries are served on hot buttered toast which is usually cut into rectangular shapes. The size and shape of these canapés or croûtes will be determined by the preparations being placed upon them for service. Examples of alternative shapes include squares, triangles, diamonds, and circles.

Ingredients and Method for Four Portions:

Name of dish	Unit		Metric	Imperial
Anges à Cheval [Angels on horseback (oysters in bacon on toast)]		4 Prepared croûtes 8 Oysters 8 Rashers of streaky bacon Salt and pepper to season		
	Season and wrap the oysters in bacon and secure on skewers . Grill gently until cooked, dress on croûtes for service			
Canapé aux Champignons (mushrooms on toast)	1 ¼	4 prepared croûtes Grilling mushrooms (flat) Melted butter Salt and pepper to season	200 g 50 g	8 oz 2 oz
	Wash and peel mushrooms. Season, brush with melted butter and grill until cooked. Dress on croûtes for service			
Canapé des Gourmets (ham with mustard on toast)	1 1	4 Prepared croûtes Cooked ham (fine dice) Mustard butter (*see* p. 202)	200 g 50 g	8 oz 2 oz
	Mix ham and butter together, spread evenly on to croûtes and place under grill to heat for service			
Canapé Hollandaise (smoked haddock and egg on toast)	1	4 Prepared croûtes Smoked haddock (poached in milk) 2 Hard boiled eggs Salt and cayenne pepper to season	200 g	8 oz
	Flake the poached haddock removing any skin and bone. Place on to croûtes and decorate with sliced or quartered hard boiled eggs. Season the egg, brush with butter and reheat under the grill for service.			

Name of dish	Unit		Metric	Imperial
Canapé Ivanhoë (creamed haddock on toast with mushrooms)	1	4 Prepared croûtes Smoked haddock (poached in milk)	200 g	8 oz
	¼	Béchamel	50 ml	2 fl oz
	⅛	Cream	25 ml	1 fl oz
		4 Grilled mushrooms		
		Cayenne pepper to season		

Flake the poached haddock removing any skin and bone, combine with the béchamel and cream. Reheat, season with cayenne and place on to croûtes, decorate with grilled mushrooms for service

Canapé Ritchie (creamed haddock on toast with cheese)	1	4 Prepared croûtes Smoked haddock	200 g	8 oz
	¼	Béchamel	50 ml	2 fl oz
	¼	Grated cheese	50 g	2 oz
	⅛	Cream	25 ml	1 fl oz
		Cayenne pepper to season		

Proceed as for Canapé Ivanhoë mixing half the cheese with haddock mixture. Place mixture on to croûtes, sprinkle with remaining cheese and brown under the grill for service

Croûte Quo Vadis (soft herring roes and mushrooms on toast)	1	4 Prepared croûtes Soft herring roes	200 g	8 oz
		4 Grilled mushrooms		
		Seasoned flour		
		Melted butter		

Wash the roes, pass through seasoned flour and place on to a buttered grilling tray. Brush with butter and grill until cooked. Place on to croûtes and decorate with grilled mushrooms for service

Croûte Anchois (anchovy fillets on toast)	1	4 Prepared croûtes Anchovy fillets	100 g	4 oz
		Melted butter		
		Squeeze of lemon juice		
		Picked parsley		

Place the anchovy fillets on to croûtes, sprinkle with lemon juice, brush with melted butter and grill to reheat. Serve decorated with picked parsley

| Croûte Baron (mushrooms, bacon and meat marrow on toast) | | 4 Prepared croûtes
8 Grilled mushrooms
8 Slices of poached beef marrow
4 Slices of grilled bacon
Salt and pepper to season | | |

Place the grilled bacon on to croûtes, arrange the grilled mushrooms and poached beef marrow on top. Season and reheat under the grill for service

| Croûte Derby (creamed ham on toast with pickled walnut) | 1
¼
⅛ | 4 Prepared croûtes
Cooked ham (fine dice)
Béchamel
Cream
4 Slices of pickled walnut
Cayenne pepper to season | 200 g
50 ml
25 ml | 8 oz
2 fl oz
1 fl oz |

Mix together the ham, béchamel, cream and boil to reheat, season with cayenne. Spread mixture on to croûtes and garnish with pickled walnut for service

| Croûte/Canapé Diane (chicken livers and bacon on toast) | | 4 Prepared croûtes
4 Trimmed chicken livers
8 Slices of streaky bacon
Salt and cayenne pepper to season | | |

Cut the chicken livers in half, season and wrap in bacon, secure with skewers. Grill on both sides until cooked, arrange on to croûtes for service

| Croûte Windsor (creamed ham on toast with mushrooms) | Proceed as for Croûte Derby, replace the pickled walnuts with four grilled mushrooms |

| Diables à Cheval (devils on horseback prunes in bacon on toast) | 1 | 4 Prepared croûtes
Chutney
8 Rashers of streaky bacon
8 Stewed prunes (*see* p. 556)
Salt and pepper to season | 50 g | 2 oz |

Remove the stones from the prunes and stuff with chutney. Season, wrap in bacon and secure on skewers. Grill gently until cooked and dress on croûtes for service

| Laitances sur Croûtes (soft herring roes on toast) | Proceed as for Croûte Quo Vadis, omit the grilled mushrooms |

Name of dish	*Unit*		*Metric*	*Imperial*
Moelle sur Croûtes (meat marrow on toast)		4 Prepared croûtes		
	1	Poached beef marrow	200 g	8 oz
		Chopped parsley		
		Salt and pepper to season		
	Slice the marrow into ½ cm (¼ in) slices, arrange on to croûtes, season and reheat under the grill. Sprinkle with chopped parsley for service			
Scotch Woodcock (scrambled eggs on toast with anchovies and capers)		4 Prepared croûtes		
	1	Scrambled eggs	200 g	8 oz
	⅛	Capers	25 g	1 oz
		8 Anchovy fillets		
	Dress scrambled eggs on to croûtes and decorate with strips of anchovy fillet and capers			
Sardines sur Croûtes (sardines on toast)		4 Prepared croûtes		
		8 Sardines in oil (canned)		
		Melted butter		
		Squeeze of lemon juice		
		Salt and pepper to season		
	Skin the sardines and remove bone if required. Dress on to croûtes, season, sprinkle with lemon juice and brush with melted butter. Heat under the grill for service. N.B. May also be prepared with fresh grilled sardines when available			
Welsh Rarebit (flavoured cheese on toast)		4 Prepared croûtes		
	1	Béchamel	125 ml	5 fl oz
	⅘	Grated cheese	100 g	4 oz
	⅗	Beer	75 ml	3 fl oz
	⅕	Egg yolk	25 g	1 oz
		Seasonings: diluted English mustard Worcester sauce salt and cayenne pepper		
	Reduce the beer by half, add the béchamel and reboil. Add cheese and simmer until melted. Remove from heat, add egg yolk, seasonings, mix thoroughly, and cool ready for use. Spread on to croûtes and heat under the grill until golden brown and serve.			
Buck Rarebit (flavoured cheese on toast with poached eggs)	Proceed as for Welsh Rarebit and top each portion with a poached egg			

N.B. The above savouries are served on flats dressed with dish papers and may be garnished with bunches of picked parsley where appropriate.

Other Savouries and Savoury Preparations in Common Use

Cheese or Crab Fritters   Beignets de Fromage/Crabe

Choux pastry flavoured with crab or cheese, shaped with spoons and deep fried. See study on deep frying (*see* p. 304).

PUFF PASTRY CASES FILLED WITH CURRIED SHRIMPS Bouchées à l'Indienne

Yield: 4 portions
Cooking time: 5 – 8 min

Unit	Ingredient	Metric	Imperial
	8 Small bouchées (baked)		
1	Shrimps (picked)	200 g	8 oz
1	Curry sauce (*see* p. 193)	200 ml	8 fl oz
1/8	Butter	25 g	1 oz
	Salt and pepper to season		

Method

Melt the butter in a saucepan, add the shrimps, season and sweat without colour. Add the curry sauce and simmer gently for 2 – 3 minutes. Heat the bouchées and fill with the curried shrimps, dress on flats with dish papers for service.

CHEESE AND HAM WITH BREAD (shallow fried)   Croque-Monsieur

Yield: 4 portions
Cooking time: 5 – 6 min

Unit	Ingredient	Metric (g)	Imperial (oz)
	8 Slices (plain bread)		
1	Gruyère cheese (thinly sliced)	100	4
1	Cooked ham (thinly sliced)	100	4
	Clarified butter (for frying)		

Method

Place ham between slices of cheese then sandwich with bread, press firmly together. Cut out with a round cutter or into rectangular shapes as required. Shallow fry gently in clarified butter on both sides until golden brown. Dress on flats with dish papers and serve immediately.

Savoury Flans   Quiches

Open flans garnished with various fillings. They may be prepared in flan rings to serve four people or in small individual pastry cases. *See* Chapter 24.

Cheese Soufflé   Soufflé au Parmesan/au Fromage

Baked savoury soufflés which may be prepared in large or individual soufflé moulds for service (*see* p. 415).

29

Breakfast Cookery

Meals at breakfast time take a variety of forms, but may be broadly classified as English or Continental. The English breakfast is a substantial meal at which a variety of hot and cold courses is offered. The Continental breakfast, however, is a lighter meal consisting mainly of a selection of bread rolls, croissant, toast, butter, preserves and beverages.

Where the English breakfast is offered a breakfast cook is responsible for preparing and cooking breakfast dishes. In some establishments, however, other members of the kitchen brigade are involved in preparing and cooking items for the breakfast menu, e.g. stewed fruits prepared by the pastry chef.

Examples of breakfast dishes shown on the menus below, along with other suitable items are outlined in the respective studies (*see* index).

Breakfast   Good Morning

Continental – Café Complet

Chilled Juices   Orange   Grapefruit   Tomato

Croissants   Brioche   Toast   Brown and White Rolls with Butter   Preserves
Marmalades   Honey (clear or cloudy).

Tea   Coffee   Chocolate   Milk

Breakfast   Good Morning

English — Petit Déjeuner

Chilled Grapefruit   Spanish Melon
Oranges   Apples
Chilled Juices: Orange Grapefruit Tomato
Compotes: Figs Plums Pineapple Apples Prunes

French Onion Soup

Oatmeal Porridge   Alpen   Rolled Oats
Rice Krispies   Bran Flakes   Shredded Wheat
Puffed Wheat   Special K   Corn Flakes   Sugar Puffs

Kedgeree
Fried Fillet of plaice with Lemon
Grilled Kippers
Poached Haddock Monte Carlo

Eggs: Fried Turned Scrambled Poached Boiled
Omelettes: Plain Tomato Cheese Ham Prawn

Grilled Lamb's Kidneys   Black Pudding   Grilled Bacon
Lyonnaise Potatoes

To order:

Pork Sausages   Baked Tomatoes   Grilled Gammon

Cold Meat   Green Salad

Spiced Scones

Griddle Cakes with Honey or Maple Syrup

Rolls: White   Energen Breads: Brown, Hovis
Toasts: White Brown Raisin Melba   To Order: French Toast
Muffins   Biscuit Ryvita

Waffles with Demerara Sugar

Croissants   Danish Pastries   Brioches

Preserves   Marmalades   Honey (Clear or Cloudy)

Teas: Ceylon China Russian Mint

Coffee: Cona Nescafé Sanka

Cocoa   Chocolate

N.B. *French Toast*
Dip slices of selected bread into beaten egg then shallow fry until crisp and golden brown.
If required the beaten egg may be lightly sweetened and flavoured with a pinch of allspice
or nutmeg.

SECTION FOUR
Pastry work

30

Basic Pastries

Basic pastries are among the most versatile preparations utilized throughout practical cookery. At some time or another, the principal kitchen departments will use one or other of the pastries in the formation of respective culinary products. Folklore has it that the traditional pastries originated from the simple flour and water paste primarily used to envelop the historic spit-roasts enjoyed by earlier generations. The pastry, it is said, absorbed flavour/moisture/fat from the meat, thus becoming a tasty product in its own right. Even today some joints may be wrapped in a similar dough-pastry before being baked, typically hams and gammons.

Modern day pastries, however, commonly appear in the cook's repertoire of basic preparations. Throughout this text a varied and interesting use of pastries is well documented within sections showing how pastries are used to enclose, cover, accompany, decorate, hold, protect and generally enhance food products.

Basic Pastry Classifications

Most pastries can be classified using four main headings:

1. Shortcrust pastries (including variations).
2. Puff pastries.
3. Raised pastries.
4. Miscellaneous pastries.

Short Pastry Varieties

Short pastries are not always appreciated by customers as in many instances the quality of the pastry items on offer is often diminished by the poor texture of the finished product. When correctly produced however, short pastries provide a splendid eating experience.

Within bakery terminology the word '*short*' refers to a pastry which is easily broken and one that is *not* tough, resilient or elastic.

Short pastry can be a mixture of flour, fat, sugar, salt, water, egg and milk and, as such, appear in a variety of ways. For example, the pastry may be made plain (without sugar) or sweetened; the fats used as a shortening agent could include either lard, margarine, butter or a combination of these, as is also the case with the moistening agents previously listed.

For reasons which will be made clear, any flour chosen to make short pastries should be of *low protein* (gluten forming) produced from weak wheats.

Ingredient Principles: Short Pastries

Soft Flour

Dependent upon which type of wheat is milled, flour will have a *strong, medium* or *weak* gluten potential. When water is combined with insoluble wheat proteins (found in milled wheat flour), an elastic substance known as '*gluten*' is formed (e.g. the gluten test).

The measure of the flour strength is mainly based upon the strength/quality of the gluten. Strong flours have a high gluten potential and are used to prepare the more resilient doughs and pastries which require a good deal of working and handling – e.g. bread dough, puff pastry. *Soft* flours, on the other hand (those low in gluten potential), are chosen for the production of the less resilient pastries which require minimal handling and working such as the short pastry varieties. Soft flour therefore, allows for less resilience, toughness and elasticity.

Shortening Agents

Shortening agents or fats, namely *lard, margarine, butter compound or combinations* of these, reduce the elasticity in pastries making them 'shorter'. When dispersed evenly throughout flour, fats act to insulate the protein particles from the liquid content. Because it is a combination of insoluble proteins and liquid which produce gluten, the greater the fat content/distribution throughout the flour, the more extensive the insulation. As a consequence, less gluten (elasticity) is developed and the 'shorter' the final basic product.

Liquids

Namely water, milk, egg act as moistening and binding agents.

In the making of short pastry, small amounts of liquid to flour are generally used minimizing elasticity within the basic product.

Sugar

Besides its sweetening quality, sugar in solution (dissolved sugar) acts to soften any gluten present. Therefore in short pastry recipes fine-grained sugar is advocated, e.g. caster to ensure that it dissolves more easily in the liquid. Coarse grained sugar (granulated) may not dissolve so easily, the crystals then remain in the pastry and do not therefore help to soften the gluten but carmelize during baking appearing as dark spots on the surface of the cooked pastry. To aid the dissolving process any sugar is either mixed with the liquid before adding to the flour or creamed into the fat to prevent it from remaining as crystals.

Production Factors for Consideration

If short pastries are to remain light and free from toughness, precautions other than those associated directly with ingredient selection must be observed.

Over-working/handling of the pastry during its mixing and subsequent rolling can develop the gluten and toughen the pastry. This is probably owing to a breaking down of the 'fat barrier' during these processes.

Working-in scraps – *cuttings* – an excess use of scraps or cuttings of pastry results in over-working handling with the same results as described above.

Over-dusting with flour – too much dusting with flour also causes toughening due to any hydration of the additional protein present.

To summarize – when producing short pastries

Ingredients $\longrightarrow$
- Use soft flour
- Use soft caster sugar
- Use small amounts of liquid

Preparation and pre-cooking procedures $\longrightarrow$
- Rub the fat in thoroughly/evenly
- Apply minimal handling/working
- Use very little dusting flour
- Do not over-work scraps
- Dissolve sugar into liquid before adding the flour (where applicable)
- Before baking rest/relax pastry in a cold place and under-cover to reduce shrinkage factor on cooking

Fault-Finding Chart for Shortcrust Pastries

The reasons for the faults in the finished shortcrust pastries are outlined below:

Shrinkage of shortcrust $\longrightarrow$
- Over-rolled/handled pastry
- Pastry stretched during rolling
- Dough over-mixed
- Flour too strong
- Inadequate mixing of fat and flour
- Fat too hard to coat flour grains
- Inadequate resting before baking

Shortcrust tough/hard $\longrightarrow$
- Too much liquid used
- Oven too cool during baking
- Over-baking
- Fat was too hard to coat flour grains
- Over-handling of pastry

Blistered shortcrust $\longrightarrow$
- Inadequate/uneven mixing of ingredients
- Too much liquid
- Oven too hot

Speckled shortcrust $\longrightarrow$
- Sugar used is too coarse
- Sugar incorrectly added in the method
- Oven too hot in conjunction with above

Shortcrust of rough texture appearance $\longrightarrow$ Fat and flour insufficiently mixed

Soggy shortcrust $\longrightarrow$
- Excess fat used
- Baking at too cool temperature
- Insufficient baking
- Too much liquid used

Varieties of Short Pastry: Ingredients in Relation to 400 g (1 lb) Flour

English	Unit	Ingredient	Metric	Imperial	French
Short pastry (ordinary)	1	Flour (soft)	400 g	1 lb	Pâte à foncer ordinaire
	¼	Lard	100 g	4 oz	
	¼	Margarine	100 g	4 oz	
	⅛	Water (approx.)	50 ml	2 fl oz	
		Pinch of salt			
Short pastry (rich)	1	Flour (soft)	400 g	1 lb	Pâte à foncer
	½	Butter	200 g	8 oz	
	⅛	Water (approx.)	50 ml	2 fl oz	
		Pinch of salt			
Short pastry (French)	1	Flour (soft)	400 g	1 lb	Pâte à brisée
	½	Butter	200 g	8 oz	
	⅛	Egg yolk	50 g	2 oz	
	⅛	Water	50 g	2 fl oz	
		Pinch of salt			
Sweet short pastry	1	Flour (soft)	400 g	1 lb	Pate à foncer sucrée
	½	Butter or margarine	200 g	8 oz	
	⅛	Caster sugar	50 g	2 oz	
	⅛	Water	50 ml	2 fl oz	
		Pinch of salt			
Sweet pastry	1	Flour (soft)	400 g	1 lb	Pâte à sucrée
	½	Butter or margarine	200 g	8 oz	
	¼	Caster sugar	100 g	4 oz	
	¼	Egg (whole/beaten)	100 ml	4 fl oz	
		Pinch of salt			
Flan pastry	1	Flour (soft)	400 g	1 lb	Pâte à flan
	¾	Butter or margarine	300 g	12 oz	
	¼	Caster sugar	100 g	4 oz	
	¼	Egg (whole/beaten)	100 ml	4 fl oz	
		Pinch of salt			
Raised pie paste (cold)	1	Flour (medium)	400 g	1 lb	Pâte à pate
	¼	Butter or margarine	100 g	4 oz	
	¼	Lard	100 g	4 oz	
	¼	Water (cold)	100 ml	4 fl oz	
	⅛	Egg (whole/beaten)	50 ml	2 fl oz	
		Pinch of salt			

Method 1: for savoury short pastries

Sift flour and salt together. Rub in the fat to form a sandy texture. Form a well, add sufficient liquid (water or water and egg) to bind and form a smooth short pastry.

Method 2: for sweetened short pastries

Sift flour and salt together. Rub in the fat to form a sandy texture. Form a well, dissolve sugar in liquid and pour into the well. Combine all ingredients to form a smooth short pastry.

   N.B.   Liquid content in pastries may vary according to the water absorption rate of the flour.

Short Pastry Based Products

FRUIT PIES

Preparation of fruit

Apples:
Wash, peel, quarter and remove the core, cut into even slices.

Cherries, damsons, greengages, plums:
Remove the stalks, wash. Halve and remove the stone, if required.
N.B.   Cherries may be stoned and left whole.

Blackberries, raspberries, red currants, black currants:
Remove the stalks, wash and drain well.

Gooseberries:
Remove the top and tails, wash.

Rhubarb:
Remove leaves, trim ends and cut into 2 cm (1 in) pieces, wash well. If rhubarb is green or stringy, peel away the skin.

Tinned fruit:
Drain any excess fruit juice.
N.B.   Tinned fruits are often already sweetened, in these cases they will require no further sweetening during pie production.

Dried Fruit:
Soak fruit in water for several hours. Wash and drain ready for use.

Production of fruit pies (in a pie dish)

Yield: 4–6 portions
Cooking time: 30–40 min
Cooking temperature: 205°C (400°F)

Unit	Ingredients	Metric	Imperial
1	Selected prepared fruit (see above)	400 g	1 lb
½	Short pastry	200 g	8 oz
★	Caster sugar		

★ Sufficient to sweeten selected fruit to taste.

Method

Place prepared fruit in a pie dish, add sugar. Roll out the pastry 3 mm (⅛ in) thick, moisten edge of pie dish and line with a strip of pastry. Moisten edge and cover with remaining pastry, taking care not to stretch the pastry otherwise it will shrink and slide into pie dish during baking. Seal well and decorate edge of pastry. Brush evenly with milk and sprinkle with caster sugar, make a slit in the centre of the pie to allow steam to escape during baking. Rest pie to allow the pastry to relax (avoids excess shrinkage during baking). Bake in oven until pastry is golden brown and fruit is cooked. Clean edge of pie dish and surround with a pie collar for service.

ENGLISH PLATE PIES

Yield: 4–6 portions
Cooking time: 30–40 min
Cooking temperature: 205°C (400°F)

Unit	Ingredient.	Metric	Imperial
1	Selected prepared fruit (see above)	400 g	1 lb
¾	Short pastry	300 g	12 oz
*	Caster sugar		

* Sufficient to sweeten selected fruit to taste.

Method

Take half the pastry, roll out 3 mm (⅛ in) thick and line an ovenproof pie plate. Place fruit on to the pastry taking care not to get juice around the edges, sweeten fruit with sugar and moisten edges of pastry. Cover with remaining pastry then proceed as for fruit pies made in a pie dish. Place pie on a service flat with doily, serve.

   N.B.   Fruit pies may be served hot or cold accompanied with custard, fresh cream or ice cream.

Dutch Apple Pie

Proceed as for an English plate pie but sweeten with demerara sugar, add 30 g (1 oz) of washed picked sultanas to the apples and flavour with a pinch of cinnamon. Filling may be par-cooked before adding to pie if required.

FLANS   Pâte à sucrée or Pâte à flan

Pastry

Allow approximately 25 g (1 oz) of flour per portion when preparing pastry.

Method

Roll out the pastry 3 mm (⅛ in) thick and 2 cm (1 in) larger than the flan ring. Pick up pastry by carefully wrapping around rolling pin. Lay pastry over flan ring and gently ease into ring to cover base and sides. Ensure any air is expelled and that pastry is an even thickness. Trim surplus pastry from top edge, decorate with pastry tweezers or with fingers and thumb. Allow to set/rest in a cool place for 30 minutes to reduce excess shrinkage during baking.

Baking a flan blind

Dock the pastry at the base of the flan ring, place a circle of greaseproof paper in the ring and fill with baking beans or peas. Bake at 215°C (420°F) until the pastry has set (approximately 10 minutes). Carefully remove the baking beans and greaseproof paper from the flan and lift off the flan ring. Brush the outside of the pastry case with egg wash and continue baking until golden brown and completely cooked.

(a) Fruit Flans Prepared Using Blind-Baked Pastry Cases

SOFT AND TINNED/POACHED FRUIT FLANS

Allow 50 g (2 oz) fruit per portion.

Method

Half fill the baked flan with pastry cream (*see* p. 649), arrange fruit (sliced or whole) onto the surface to form an attractive design. Mask with fruit glaze or apricot glaze.

Examples of Soft and Tinned/Poached Fruit Flans

	English name	French name
Fresh fruits	Banana flan	Flan aux bananes
	Raspberry flan	Flan aux framboises
	Strawberry flan	Flan aux fraises
Tinned/poached fruits	Cherry flan	Flan aux cerises
	Peach flan	Flan aux peches
	Pear flan	Flan aux poires
	Pineapple flan	Flan aux ananas
	Mandarin flan	Flan aux mandarines
	Mixed fruit flan	Flan aux fruits

(b) Fruit Flans Prepared with Raw Fruit Baked Within a Raw Pastry Case

Allow 75 g (3 oz) prepared raw fruit per portion.
Preparation of fruit for flans: see fruit pies, p. 479.

Method

Line a flan ring with selected pastry and rest for 20 minutes. Carefully arrange the fruit in the base of the flan case and sprinkle with sufficient sugar to sweeten. Bake at 200°C (405°F) until the fruit is cooked and the pastry is golden brown. Mask with fruit/apricot glaze to finish.

Examples of Fresh Fruit Flans

	English name	French name
	Apple flan*	Flan aux pommes
	Apricot flan	Flan aux abricots
	Cherry flan	Flan aux cerises
	Gooseberry flan	Flan aux groseilles
	Plum flan	Flan aux prunes
	Rhubarb flan	Flan au rhubarbe

* For this flan use 100 g (4 oz) of prepared fruit per portion.

Fruit Tartlets and Barquettes

These are made in the same manner as fruit flans. Small tartlet tins or barquettes are lined with pastry. They are baked blind or filled with fruit and then baked dependent upon the fruit selected. Prior to service, they are masked with apricot glaze or fruit glaze.

APPLE FLAN   Flan aux pommes

Yield: 6–8 portions
Cooking time: 20–30 min
Cooking temperature: 205°C (400°F)

Unit	Ingredient	Metric	Imperial
*	Sweet or flan pastry		
1	Cooking apples	800 g	2 lb
¼	Caster sugar	200 g	8 oz
¹⁄₁₆	Apricot glaze	60 g	2 oz
¹⁄₃₂	Butter or margarine	25 g	1 oz

* Sufficient to line a 20 cm (8 in) flan ring.

Method

Line a flan ring with pastry and bake blind. Put aside two medium-sized apples. Take remaining apples, peel, core and slice. Place in a saucepan, add the sugar and butter, cook over a gentle heat until the apples are soft, liquidize or pass through a sieve. Allow to cool, then place into base of flan. Peel, core and neatly slice remaining apples, arrange neatly on top of apple purée overlapping to form a circle. Sprinkle with sugar. Bake until top layer of sliced apples is cooked (approximately 10 min), remove from oven and mask with apricot glaze.

N.B.   Cooked apple purée is known as marmalade de pomme.

APPLE MERINGUE FLAN

Flan aux pommes meringuées

Yield: 6–8 portions
Cooking time: 30–40 min
Cooking temperature: 205°C (400°F)
Prepare an apple flan omitting the sliced apples on top.
Added ingredients:

Unit	Ingredient	Metric	Imperial
1	Caster sugar	100 g	4 oz
½	Egg whites	50 ml	2 fl oz

Method

Beat the egg whites until stiff, add half the sugar and continue whisking. When the meringue is stiff, stir in the remaining sugar. Pipe the meringue on to the flan using a star tube. Place in the oven and bake until meringue is set and coloured.

BAKEWELL TART

Yield: 6–8 portions
Cooking time: 30–40 min
Cooking temperature: 205°C (400°F)

Unit	Ingredient	Metric	Imperial
*	Sweet or flan pastry		
1	Frangipane filling (p. 649)	480 g	1 lb
⅛	Raspberry jam	60 g	2 oz
⅛	Water icing (p. 646)	60 ml	2 fl oz

* Sufficient to line a 20 cm (8 in) flan ring.

Method

Line flan ring with pastry and dock the base. Spread a thin layer of raspberry jam across the bottom, then fill with frangipan mixture, ensuring top surface is level. Roll out the pastry scraps and cut into 8 mm (⅜ in) wide strips. Arrange strips on top of frangipan to form a lattice pattern. Rest for 20–30 minutes then bake to a golden brown. When cool, finish with a thin layer of water icing.

BAKED EGG CUSTARD FLAN

Yield: 6–8 portions
Cooking time: 30–40 min
Cooking temperature: 175°C (350°F)

Unit	Ingredient	Metric	Imperial
★	Short pastry		
1	Milk	400 g	1 pt
	4 Eggs		
¹/₁₀	Caster sugar	40 g	2 oz
	Vanilla essence		
	Pinch of nutmeg		

★ Sufficient to line a 20 cm (8 in) flan ring.

Method

Line flan ring with pastry, do not dock the base. Warm the milk, add sugar and eggs. Whisk to mix thoroughly and dissolve the sugar, flavour with vanilla essence. Pass custard through a fine strainer into pastry case, sprinkle with nutmeg. Bake until custard is set and pastry is cooked. Allow to cool, then remove from flan ring and serve as required.

BAKED EGG CUSTARD TARTLET

Proceed as for custard tart but line small deep tartlet tins with pastry.

LEMON MERINGUE PIE   Flan aux citrons meringuées

Yield: 6–8 portions
Cooking time: 30–40 min
Cooking temperature: 205°C (400°F)

Unit	Ingredient	Metric	Imperial
★	Sweet or flan pastry		
1	Water	250 ml	10 fl oz
	Lemon juice/fresh/strained	50 ml	2 fl oz
¹/₅	Sugar	50 g	2 oz
¹/₁₀	Cornflour	25 g	1 oz
¹/₂₀	Butter	12.5 g	½ oz
	2 Egg yolks		
	Finely grated lemon zest of lemons used		

★ Sufficient to line a 20 cm (8 in) flan ring.

Method

Line flan ring with pastry and bake blind. Combine sugar, three-quarters of the water, zest and bring to the boil. Mix and dilute cornflour with remaining cold water. Working off the boil, blend the cornflour solution into the hot syrup and whisk/stir thoroughly through the boil to thicken and gelatinise. Incorporate lemon juice, butter and egg yolks to form a smooth lemon filling (at this point taste for flavour and adjust accordingly). Pour into baked pastry case and finish as for apple meringue (p. 483).

N.B.   Extra lemon juice/sugar may be added to the filling to adjust flavour as required.

MINCEMEAT PIE (Plate)

Yield: 6–8 portions
Cooking time: 30 min
Cooking temperature: 205°C (400°F)

Unit	Ingredient	Metric	Imperial
1	Short pastry	300 g	12 oz
1	Mincemeat	300 g	12 oz

Method

Proceed as for English fruit plate pie, but replace fruit filling and sugar with mincemeat.

MINCEMEAT PIES (individuals in small tartlet tins)

Proceed as for mincemeat pie but produce in small tartlet tins.

OPEN SYRUP TART

Yield: 6–8 portions
Cooking time: 20–30 min
Cooking temperature: 205°C (400°F)

Unit	Ingredient	Metric	Imperial
*	Short pastry		
1	Golden syrup	200 g	8 oz
¼	White breadcrumbs	50 g	2 oz
⅛	Lemon juice	25 g	1 oz

* Sufficient to line a baking plate.

Method

Line ovenproof baking plate with pastry. Warm the syrup, add breadcrumbs, lemon juice and blend together. Spread evenly over the pastry. Roll out the pastry scraps and cut into 8 mm (⅜ in) strips. Arrange strips on top of syrup to form a lattice pattern. Rest for 20 minutes then bake until golden brown. Serve hot or cold.

SYRUP TARTLETS

Proceed as for syrup tart but line small tartlet tins with pastry.

JAM, LEMON CURD TART AND TARTLETS

Proceed as for syrup tart or tartlet but fill with jam or lemon curd prior to baking.

BAKED APPLE DUMPLINGS

Yield: 4 portions
Cooking time: 30 min
Cooking temperature: 205°C (400°F)

Unit	Ingredient	Metric	Imperial
	4 Small cooking apples		
1	Short pastry	480 g	1 lb
⅛	Sugar	60 g	2 oz
	4 Cloves		

Method

Peel and core apples, fill centres with sugar and a clove. Roll out pastry 2 mm (⅛ in) thick, cut into four even sized squares. Moisten edges of squares with water. Place a stuffed apple in the centre of each square and bring the pastry together to completely enclose the apples, ensure all edges are sealed. Roll out any scraps of pastry, cut into small circles 2 cm (1 in) diameter and place on top of each apple. Brush with milk and place on a greased baking sheet. Rest for 20 minutes then bake until pastry is golden brown and apple is cooked. Serve accompanied with custard.

BAKED JAM ROLL

Yield: 4 portions
Cooking time: 30–40 min
Cooking temperature: 205°C (400°F)

Unit	Ingredient	Metric	Imperial
1	Short pastry	300 g	12 oz
⅓	Jam	100 g	4 oz
1/10	Caster sugar	30 g	1 oz
1/24	Baking powder	15 g	½ oz

Method

Before producing pastry, sift baking powder with soft flour. Roll out pastry to form a rectangle 30 × 20 cm (12 × 8 in). Spread the jam evenly onto the pastry leaving 1 cm (½ in) clear on all edges. Brush edges with eggwash. Fold over the two shorter edges towards the centre to seal in the jam. Then roll up loosely towards the longer edge, seal and place onto a greased baking sheet with the sealed edge down. Brush with water and sprinkle with caster sugar. Rest for 20 minutes then bake until golden brown. Serve accompanied with a sauceboat of custard or jam sauce.

N.B. As an alternative, baked short pastry roll may be filled with mincemeat, lemon curd, date and apple or syrup.

FRUIT CRUMBLES (Apple, gooseberries, rhubarb, plum, etc.)

Unit	Ingredient	Metric	Imperial
1	Flour (soft)	200 g	8 oz
½	Margarine or butter	100 g	4 oz
¼	Caster sugar	50 g	2 oz
	Pinch of salt		

Method

Sift flour and salt together. Rub in the fat to form a sandy texture. Add sugar and mix well.
Preparation of fruit for crumbles: see fruit pies.
Preparation of fruit crumbles:
Yield: 4–6 portions
Cooking time: 30–40 min
Cooking temperature: 205°C (400°F)

Unit	Ingredient	Metric	Imperial
1	Crumble mixture (see above)	350 g	14 oz
1	Selected prepared fruit	350 g	14 oz
★	Caster sugar		

★ Sufficient to sweeten selected fruit.

Method

Place fruit in a buttered pie dish, add sugar. Cover with crumble mixture. Bake until fruit is cooked and the crumble is light brown.

　N.B.　Fruit crumbles may be varied by the addition of cinnamon, mixed spice, sultanas, demerara sugar, etc. according to taste.

Choux Pastry

Choux pastry is not always recognized for its culinary versatility yet it is widely used throughout the professional kitchen in the preparation of both sweet and savoury products. This easily made robust pastry is successfully baked, deep fried and poached for the production of many well known gourmet favourites.

Ingredient Principles: Choux Pastry

Typically, strong flour is used for the production of choux pastry. However, it is interesting to note that the gluten in the panada will have lost its extensibility during the initial cooking and gelatinization will have taken place before the raw eggs are added. The incorporation of *uncoagulated* films of egg albumen throughout the basic panada is vital if sufficient volume is to be achieved during subsequent cooking. The correct water/moisture content facilitates the gelatinization of starch and the generation of steam during cooking resulting in a light stable product. The fat/butter content acts mainly as a shortening agent, thus improving the overall eating quality of the finished products.

Aeration/Volume Criteria

Mechanical aeration takes place as the raw eggs are gradually beaten into the *pre-cooled/* cooked panada. When the prepared choux pastry undergoes the baking process, the trapped air expands and the moisture in the pastry changes into steam. Essentially the expanding air and steam are enclosed securely within the pastry by the non-coagulated films of egg albumen present. In the early stages of baking, the albumen extends and inflates because of the internal pressure created by expanding air and steam. The choux pastry, therefore, increases in volume until the egg albumen coagulates/sets and stabilises in the latter stages of baking. Any sugars present caramelise to give the pastry its golden brown colour.

CHOUX PASTRY   Pâte à Choux

Cooking time: 15–20 min

Unit	Ingredient	Metric	Imperial
1	Water	125 ml	5 fl oz
⅘	Flour (strong)	100 g	4 oz
⅖	Butter/margarine	50 g	2 oz
	3 Eggs★		
	Salt to season		

★ Sufficient egg to form a smooth pipeable mixture.

Method

Combine water and butter, bring to the boil, add sifted flour, stir continuously and thoroughly to the boil. Continue cooking until mixture (panada) clears the sides of the saucepan and is of a smooth texture (this ensures adequate cooking of the starch). Allow to cool, then beat in the eggs gradually until a smooth pipeable mixture is produced. Use as required.

    N.B.   All the egg may not be required as quantities required vary marginally according to the strength of the flour used.

CHOUX PASTRY PRODUCTS

Examples of choux pastry products prepared using amounts specified in basic recipe.

CREAM BUNS   Choux à la Crème

Yield: 12
Baking time: 20–30 min
Cooking temperature: 215°C (420°F)

Method

Using a piping bag and star tube, pipe choux pastry on to a greased baking sheet to form rosettes approximately 5 cm (2 in) diameter. Sprinkle with nibbed almonds. Bake in a hot oven until crisp and light brown. Allow to cool, split open and fill with crème chantilly. Dust liberally with icing sugar.

PROFITEROLES WITH CHOCOLATE SAUCE

Profiteroles
au Chocolat

Yield: 8 portions
Baking time: 15–20 min
Cooking temperature: 215°C (420°F)

Method

Proceed as for cream buns but pipe profiteroles 2.5 cm (1 in) diameter. Bake in a hot oven until crisp and light brown. Allow to cool. Either split open or make a hole in the base of the bun and fill with crème chantilly. Place in a service dish and dust liberally with icing sugar. Serve accompanied with a sauce boat of hot chocolate sauce (*see* p. 641).

ECLAIRS

Eclairs

Yield: 16
Baking time: 20–25 min
Cooking temperature: 215°C (420°F)

Method

Using a piping bag and plain 1.5 cm (½ in) tube, pipe choux pastry on to a greased baking sheet to form fingers approximately 10 cm (4 in) long. Bake in a hot oven until crisp and light brown. Allow to cool, split open and fill with crème chantilly. Dip the top of the eclair in:

Chocolate couverture or baker's chocolate	Eclairs au chocolat
Chocolate flavoured fondant	Eclairs au chocolat
Coffee flavoured fondant	Eclairs au café

SMALL PARIS BREST

Petite Paris-Brest

Yield: 12
Baking time: 20–25 min
Cooking temperature: 215°C (420°F)

Method

Using a piping bag and plain 1.5 cm (½ in) tube, pipe choux pastry on to a greased baking sheet to form rings approximately 8 cm (3 in) diameter. Sprinkle with nibbed almonds. Bake in a hot oven until crisp and light brown. Allow to cool, cut in half horizontally and fill base with crème chantilly flavoured with praline (*see* p. 649). Replace the lid and dust liberally with icing sugar.

SWANS
Cygnes

Yield: 12
Baking time: 20–30 min
Cooking temperature: 215°C (420°F)

Method

Using a piping bag and star tube, pipe choux pastry on to a greased baking sheet to form twelve oval bulbs (these represent the bodies of the swans). Place the remaining choux pastry in a paper piping bag, cut a small aperture and pipe shapes on to a separate greased baking sheet to represent the necks of the swans. Bake in a hot oven until crisp and light brown. Allow to cool, cut the bodies horizontally across the top and fill base with crème chantilly. Cut the top pastry in to half vertically to represent two wings. Position the wings and neck to form a swan. Dust liberally with icing sugar.

N.B.   Other fillings can be used, e.g. crème chantilly combined with strawberry/raspberry purée, etc.

CHOUX FRITTERS
Beignets Soufflés

Yield: 8 portions
Frying time: 5–8 min
Frying temperature: 175–190°C (350–375°F)

Method

Shape pastry into ovals using dessert spoons, place on to a lightly oiled paper. Place into the friture and fry steadily until fritters soufflé become crisp and golden brown. Drain well and dust with caster or icing sugar. Place on a service flat with a doily and serve accompanied with hot apricot sauce.

Savoury Fritters

HOT BOILED WATER PASTRY

Unit	Ingredient	Metric	Imperial
1	Medium flour	400 g	1 lb
3/8	Lard	150 g	6 oz
5/16 ★	Water	125 ml	5 fl oz
	Pinch of salt		

★ Water content may vary according to the water absorption rate of the flour.

Method 1, Hot water pastry:

Boil the water. Sift flour and salt together and place in a basin. Rub in the lard to form a sandy texture. Form a well, add sufficient boiling water to bind and form a smooth pastry.

Method 2, Boiled water pastry:

Boil the water and lard together. Sift flour and salt and place in a basin. Form a well, add sufficient boiling liquid to bind and form a smooth pastry.

N.B. Both the above pastries are best used whilst warm.

Puff Pastry

Puff pastry is generally described as being '*full or three-quarters puff*' a description based upon the amount of fat to flour content; and by mode of production, namely: *English, Continental (French)* or *Scotch*. The difference between these three methods relates to the technique used to incorporate the bulk of the fat content into the pastry dough during the early stages of production.

Ingredient principles:

Pastry fat is a product specifically manufactured for use with puff pastry production. It is produced from oils/fats which have high melting points enabling kitchen staff handling facility at various working temperatures, its malleability and stability being important characteristics.

Butter on the other hand produces a product of superior eating quality but lacks the handling qualities of pastry fat. Consequently, when utilizing butter in recipes careful manipulation and adequate storage/resting in cool conditions are essential. The recommended butter for puff pastry production is one of a waxy texture used in conjunction with a softer pastry dough.

Strong flour with a high gluten potential is recommended to produce an elastic and resilient pastry dough. Such a preparation needs to withstand the 'extensive handling' required to build-up the laminated structure of puff pastry. Furthermore, the high gluten content formed will facilitate 'lift and stability'. Any *acid content* in the recipe will increase the extensibility of the gluten.

Water content acts to bind the dry ingredients, provide moisture vapour development within the gluten and to assist starch gelatinization during the cooking process.

Production factors:

Turns/folds: the number of turns given during production provides laminations of between 700 and 1500 fat layers in the pastry. The process of lamination is *usually* achieved by one of the following *folding* methods:

(a) Folding into *thirds* (associated with the English method *see* p. 493)
(b) Folding into 'book folds'
(c) Using a combination of 'thirds and book folds' (not commonly used).

During this process of rolling/folding, it is essential that the layers be evenly laminated/insulated and that an adequate number of layers are formed. However, too many layers or too few layers will result in an inferior product of minimum and uneven lift (*see* faults chart, p. 492).

Rolling-out: the pastry should be evenly rolled to a uniform shape/dimension. Care must be taken *not* to roll-out too thinly as this could adversely affect the lamination structure (*see* faults chart, p. 492).

Resting: it is essential to rest the pastry between turns to facilitate the rolling-out procedures, product quality, correct volume and shape.

N.B.   During the 'resting' periods the pastry is rapped in polythene to prevent skinning then it is stored in a cool place.

Scraps/trimmings: puff pastry scraps/trimmings can be used exclusively for products in their own right, e.g. cheese straws, eccles cakes, but alternatively may be incorporated with best quality (virgin) puff pastry. When puff pastry goods are being produced, it is useful, therefore, to include some items which can be produced directly from the trimmings.

N.B.   The scraps of pastry are evenly layered, beneath the top fold of virgin puff pastry before the final rolling is implemented prior to production.

Baking/cooking: as a guiding rule, puff pastries are *baked* in a hot oven, namely, '215°C (420°F) for sugared varieties' and '230°C (450°F) for egg-washed varieties'. Of course, variations around these temperatures exist by recipe specification. Puff pastry is also cooked by the *deep-frying method*, e.g. savoury rissoles and in these instances the general frying temperature gradients are used.

Lift: 'Virgin' puff pastry is used where maximum lift is the requirement. The volume of lift will depend upon product quality, the number of laminations built-up during production and the effect of heat. Where less than maximum lift is required, whilst yet maintaining a flaky texture, strips or virgin pastry plus scraps and/or the 'docking' technique can be employed.

Lift occurs during cooking as a result of the laminated structure (hundreds of leafy fat layers sandwiched between thin layers of dough), working in conjunction with the steam generated from moisture content in the pastry. On heating, the fat melts, the generated steam invades the spaces between the layers which lift/move apart as the product expands. This process continues until the pastry goods become cooked, stable and of a flaky light texture; a result of protein coagulation and starch gelatinization.

Storage: puff pastry can be stored long term deep frozen, or short term on refrigeration. In either case, the product must be wrapped in polythene to prevent any surface skinning.

N.B.   Deep frozen pastry must be allowed to thaw completely before use.

	Fault-finding chart
Faults	*Reason*
Lack of volume (lift)	Flour too soft
	Dough insufficiently developed
	Gluten not developed
	Laminations broken down when rolling out
	Fat penetrating the dough layers
	Insufficient resting between turns
	Fat too soft, causing difficulties in lamination
	Too few or too many turns
	Too low a baking temperature
	Fat too hard preventing build-up of laminations
Misshapen goods	Insufficient resting
	Final roll (before cutting) too thick
	Inaccurate and incorrect folding
	Incorrect cutting procedures
Poor eating quality	Using flour that is too strong
	Baking at too low a temperature
	Excessive use of dusting flour
	Failure to brush flour from the dough

PUFF PASTRY: ENGLISH/FRENCH METHOD
(using equal fat to flour, i.e. 'full puff')

Pâte Feuilletée
(Feuilletage)

Yield:

Unit	Ingredient	Metric	Imperial
1	Strong flour	400 g	1 lb
7/8	Pastry fat	350 g	14 oz
5/8 ★	Water/cold	250 ml	10 fl oz
1/8	Butter/margarine	50 g	2 oz
	Squeeze of lemon juice		
	Pinch of salt to taste		

★ Water content varies marginally according to the flour absorption rate. As a guide, use 225 ml (9 fl oz) per 400 g (1 lb) flour and increase to recipe quantity if needed.

Method

Sift flour, add butter/margarine and rub into the flour. Dissolve salt into cold water and add squeeze of lemon juice. (N.B. pinch of cream of tartare may be used to replace lemon juice.) Form a bay with flour mixture, add water and mix to form a dough. Thoroughly develop to a smooth, clear, tough dough. Cover the dough and allow to rest/relax for 15 minutes. Once rested, the main pastry fat can be added by the English or French method.

English Method

1. Roll out the dough to a rectangle approximately three times as long as wide. Ensure the corners are kept square.

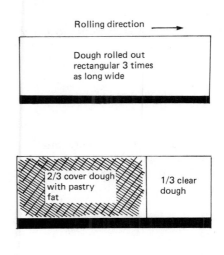

2. Shape the pastry fat into a rectangle two thirds the size of the dough and place onto the rolled-out pastry as shown.

3. Fold uncovered/clear one third of dough over onto the fat.

4. Now fold in half to give
   2 layers of pastry fat and
   3 layers of dough.

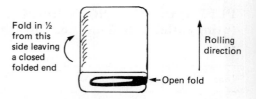

Fold in ½ from this side leaving a closed folded end

Rolling direction

←Open fold

5. After resting the pastry for 30 minutes, it is ready for rolling-out by 'turns' which can be either *half turns* (a total of 6) or *book turns* (a total of 4) *see* p. 495 for instructions.

French Method

1. Take a ball of rested dough and cut criss-cross about half-way through.

2. From the centre pull out each cut/quarter to form a rough star leaving the centre fairly thick.

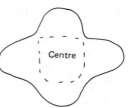

Centre

3. Now roll-out each corner to *quarter* the thickness of the centre.

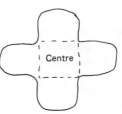

Centre

4. Form the pastry fat evenly into the same shape as the centre and place onto the central thick portion of the dough as indicated.

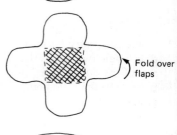

Fold over flaps

5. Fold-over all the flaps to fully enclose the fat, making sure that *each flap* fully encloses the fat.

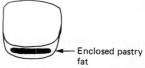

←Enclosed pastry fat

6. After resting the pastry for 30 minutes, it is ready for rolling out by *turns* which can be either *half turns* (a total of 6) or *book turns* (a total of 4) *see* p. 495 for instructions.

Puff Pastry Production

'Half turns' method

Total number of *half turns* given is 6.

1. Roll out the rested dough (which now has pastry fat enclosed within) to a rectangle approximately three times as long as wide.

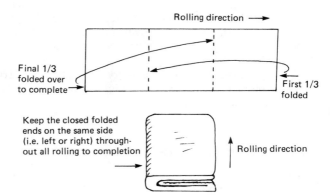

Rolling direction →

Final 1/3 folded over to complete→

First 1/3 folded

2. Now fold into three as indicated by arrows in diagram 1. At this point, *one half turn* has been completed. Rest pastry for 1 hour.

Keep the closed folded ends on the same side (i.e. left or right) throughout all rolling to completion →

↑ Rolling direction

N.B. In all, *six half turns* are required so that is *4* more half turns are given with appropriate rests between (rest between each *two* half turns for $\frac{1}{2}$ hour) then *one half turn* only will be required before pastry is ready for working-off.

In every case, ensure that the closed-folded edge is on the same side when pinning-out for each one of the turns, namely to the 'left or right', but *not* either. During the rolling ensure that the corners are kept square, that rolling is even and the pastry is never rolled too thin (this will result in breakdown of the layers) and that all 'dusting flour' is brushed off before folding. Often the pastry is produced to the fifth half turn and then rested overnight before completion the next day.

During all resting periods the pastry should be covered (polythene) and allowed to stand in a cool place. Covering prevents skinning of the pastry's surface and a cool temperature facilitates subsequent handling.

'Book turns' method

1. Roll-out the rested dough (which now has pastry-fat enclosed within) to a rectangle approximately *4* times as long as wide.

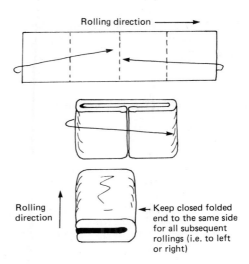

Rolling direction →

2. Now fold both ends to the centre as indicated by arrows in diagram 1.

3. To complete fold one end to the other to give the finished '*book fold*' giving '*one completed book turn*' at this point. Rest for 1 hour at this stage.

Rolling direction ↑

← Keep closed folded end to the same side for all subsequent rollings (i.e. to left or right)

N.B.   In all *4 book turns* are required so that if 2 more book-turns are given with appropriate rests between each ($\frac{1}{2}$ hour between each) then only one book turn will be required before the pastry is ready for working-off.

In every case, ensure that the closed-folded edge is on the same side when pinning out each one of the book turns, namely to the 'right or left' but *not* either. During rolling ensure that all corners are kept square, that rolling is even and the pastry never rolled too thin (this will result in a breakdown of the layers) and that all 'dusting flour' is brushed-off before folding. Often pastry is produced to the 'third book turn' stage then rested overnight for completion the next day.

During all resting periods, the pastry should be covered (polythene) and allowed to stand in a cool place. Covering prevents skinning on the pastry's surface and a cool temperature facilitates subsequent handling.

SCOTCH OR ROUGH PUFF PASTRY

Yield

Unit	Ingredient	Metric	Imperial
1	Strong flour	400 g	1 lb
¾	Pastry fat	300 g	12 oz
⅝*	Water/cold	250 ml	10 fl oz
	Squeeze lemon juice		
	Pinch of salt to taste		

* Water content varies marginally according to the flour absorption rate. As a guide, therefore, use *225 ml (9 fl oz) per 400 g (1 lb)* flour and increase to recipe quantity if needed.

Method

Sift flour, chop all fat into 2.5 cm (1 in) cubes and mix water with lemon juice and salt to dissolve. Lightly incorporate cubes of fat throughout the sifted dry flour. Make a bay with this mixture, add water and form a dough, keeping the cubes of fat in-tact. From this point half or book turns can be used to produce the rough puff pastry.

N.B.   Rough puff pastry is generally best used for goods which would normally be produced from puff pastry scraps.

ECCLES CAKES/BANBURY CAKES

Yield: 8 cakes approximately
Baking time: 15–20 min
Baking temperature: 215°C (420°F)

Unit	Ingredient	Metric	Imperial
1	Puff pastry scraps (well rested)	400 g	1 lb
¼	Selected filling (*see* chart below)	100 g	4 oz
	Water-wash or egg whites/caster sugar		
	to finish		

Method

Roll-out the pastry into a sheet of 3 mm (⅛ in) thick and cut-out into 10 cm (4 in) circles using a pastry cutter. Place 15 g (½ oz) filling into the centre of each circle. Bring outside edges of pastry together and fully enclose the filling. Seal firmly, shape and roll-out as indicated in the chart below. Wash each cake with egg white or water, dip in caster sugar, then place onto prepared baking sheet. Incise the top of the paste with a knife or scraper forming two or three slits. Rest and bake to golden brown. On completion, remove onto cooling wires.

Name	Filling	Additional directions
Eccles cakes	10 g (4 oz) Currants Brown sugar to sweeten Pinch mixed spice Melted butter to moisten	Once sealed, turn eccles cake over and pin-out to approx. 75 mm (3 in) diameter
Banbury cakes	As above	Once sealed, shape into boat-shapes and flatten-down ensuring no filling escapes. Roll-out to 6 mm (¼ in) thick

TURNOVERS   Chaussons

Yield: approx. 12
Baking time: 20 min
Baking temperature: 215°C (420°F)

Unit	Ingredient	Metric	Imperial
1	Puff pastry scraps (well rested)	400 g	1 lb
½/¾*	Selected filling (*see* chart below) Water wash or egg whites/caster sugar to finish	200–300 g	8–12 oz

* Quantity dependent upon type of filling being used. For *apple turnovers* 300 g (12 oz) will be required but for *jam turnovers* only 200 g (8 oz) needed.

Method

Roll pastry into an even sheet of 2.5 mm (⅒ in) thick and cut out approximately 12 circles using a 10 cm (4 in) fluted/plain cutter. Using a rolling pin, slightly elongate each pastry disc from the centre leaving the centres slightly thinner than the edges. Moisten half-way around with water and deposit selected filling (*see* chart below) in the centres keeping the edges clear. Fold over to form a half-moon type shape and seal the edges well. Wash with water or egg-whites, dip into caster sugar, place onto prepared baking sheet, incise each turnover to allow for a steam vent. Rest for 30 minutes, bake until crisp and golden.

   N.B.   A 10 cm (4 in) square shape can be used with the turnovers having a finished triangular appearance.

Types of Turnovers

Name	Selected filling	French term
Apple turnover	Sweetened apple purée flavoured with cinnamon or clove	Chausson aux pommes
Jam turnover	Selected jam	Chausson aux confiture

CREAM PUFFS

Yield: approx. 16
Baking time: 15–20 min
Baking temperature: 215°C (420°F)

Unit	Ingredient	Metric	Imperial
1	Puff pastry	400 g	1 lb
5/8	Whipped cream/fresh (sweetened)	250 ml	10 fl oz
1/4	Raspberry jam	100 g	4 oz
	Water wash or egg whites/caster sugar to finish		

Method

Roll out pastry to large even rectangle of 3 mm (⅛ in) thick and prick surface thoroughly with a spiked docker or fork. Cut the rolled out pastry in approximately 16 × 8 cm (3 in) squares/circles. Wash with either water or egg white, dip into caster sugar, place products onto a prepared baking sheet and rest for 30 minutes. Bake in a hot oven for 15–20 minutes or until baked and golden. Remove from oven and place onto cooling wires. When cold, split each shape into two (leaving a base and a top), pipe a portion of jam onto the bottom piece, follow with a generous bulb of sweetened whipped cream and replace the top. Leave plain or dust with icing sugar and present on fancy doily for service.

PALMIERS

Yield: 16 sandwiched palmiers
Baking time: 15–20 min
Baking temperature: 215°C (450°F)

Unit	Ingredient	Metric	Imperial
1	Puff pastry scraps (well rested)	400 g	1 lb
5/8	Whipped cream/fresh (sweetened)	250 ml	10 fl oz
1/8	Raspberry jam	50 g	2 oz
1/8	Caster sugar	50 g	2 oz

Method

Roll out pastry evenly to a rectangular strip of approximately 20 cm (8 in) wide of 3 mm (⅛ in) thick. Water wash the surface and sprinkle liberally with caster sugar. Fold each of the long edges towards the centre *3* times giving an even width to each fold. Flatten the centre line slightly with the rolling pin, lightly egg wash the centre then fold inwards and press together to seal lightly giving a long strip of approximately 12 mm (½ in) thick by 6 cm (2½ in) wide. Now cut the strip into 12 mm (½ in) sections (32 approximately and space out on prepared baking sheet with the 'cut folds' uppermost (provide 8 cm (3 in) spacing between each one). Rest the goods for 30 minutes. Bake in hot oven until barely golden, turn each palmier over using a palette knife and complete baking until cooked, golden and lightly caramelized. Remove from oven and place on cooling wires. Once cold, sandwich in pairs with a little raspberry jam and a portion of whipped sweetened fresh cream. Present for service on fancy doily.

SLICES

Yield: 16 slices
Baking time
Baking temperature: 226°C (440°F)

Unit	Ingredient	Metric	Imperial
1	Puff pastry scraps (well rested)	400 g	1 lb
⅛	Selected filling (*see* chart below)	250 ml	10 oz
	Raspberry jam	50 g	2 oz
	Hot apricot purée/warm fondant/ decoration to finish		

Method

Roll out pastry in an even rectangle of 10 cm (4 in) width by 3 mm (⅛ in) thick. Place onto a prepared baking sheet and 'dock' well all over. Rest for 30 minutes. Bake until crisp and lightly golden in colour. Avoid dark colouration. On completion of baking and cooling, divide into two lengthways giving top and bottom pieces. Use the flat bottomed piece for the top giving an even topped surface for finish and decoration. Spread the remaining piece with raspberry jam followed by an even generous layer of freshly whipped sweetened cream or confectioner's custard.

Spread the flat surface of the top with hot apricot purée then selected warm fondant and allow to set. Once set cut the top into equal sized slices of approximately 5 cm (2 in) wide. Place the slices on top of the prepared base and complete by cutting through the base to form individual portions. Decorate with browned desiccated coconut/browned nibbed almonds and present on fancy doily for service.

Typical Examples

Name	Filling	Finish
Vanilla slices	Vanilla flavoured pastry cream *see* p. 648	Fondant as shown above and browned nibbed almonds
Cream slices	Cream Chantilly *see* p. 647	Fondant as shown above and browned desiccated coconut

CREAM HORNS

Cornets à la Crème

Yield: approx. 16
Baking time: 15–20 min
Baking temperature: 215°C (420°F)

Unit	Ingredient	Metric	Imperial
1	Puff pastry	400 g	1 lb
⅝	Whipped cream/fresh (sweetened)	250 ml	10 fl oz
⅛	Raspberry jam	50 g	2 oz
⅛	Caster sugar	50 g	2 oz
	Water-wash for dampening/finish		

Method

Roll out pastry into a sheet of 2 mm (¹⁄₁₆ in) thick and trim to neaten the edges. Cut into strips of 2.5 cm (1 in) wide × 42 cm (15 in) long and dampen with water. Using prepared moulds, and starting at the pointed end, roll the strips around the mould allowing each roll to overlap the previous one (take care not to pull and stretch the paste during this process). Trim off the end of the pastry so that it finishes underneath on the flattened side at the open end of the mould (lightly dampen the pastry at this end and make secure). Waterwash presentation side, dip in caster sugar, place on baking sheet sealed side downwards and rest for 30 minutes. Bake in a pre-heated oven until crisp and golden brown. Remove from oven and whilst warm separate baked horns from their moulds (a gentle twist facilitates removal) and place onto cooling wires. Once cooled, fill each one with a small bulb of jam and piped whipped cream. Finish open end with a piped rosette of whipped cream.

MINCE PIES

Yield: approx. 12
Baking time: 20–25 min
Baking temperature: 232°C (450°F)

Unit	Ingredient	Metric	Imperial
1	Puff pastry	400 g	1 lb
⅜	Mincemeat	150 g	6 oz
	Water-wash/egg-wash/icing sugar to finish		

Method

Roll out the pastry to approximately 2.5 cm (¹⁄₁₀ in) thick. Using a fancy cutter of 6.5 cm (2½ in) cut out *eight* fluted discs for the bases and another *eight* using a 8 cm (3 in) fancy cutter for the tops. Arrange the eight bases onto a prepared baking sheet and brush the edges of each one lightly with water to dampen. Place a good teaspoon of mincemeat onto the centre of each of the pastry bases forming small mounds. Now cover each prepared base with the tops and seal using an *inverted* pastry cutter (5 cm (2 in) size). Brush each pie carefully with egg-wash, prick with a fork/knife to provide a steam vent facility and rest for

30 minutes. Bake in a hot oven until crisp and golden brown. Remove from oven, place on cooling wires, dust with icing sugar and serve warm/hot with brandy butter presented on service tray with fancy doily.

N.B.   May be served as a hot sweet with crème anglaise or brandy sauce.

FRUIT BAND: 1 (using blind-baked pastry band)   Bande aux Fruits

Yield: 4–8 portions to size
Baking time: approx. 15 min
Baking temperature: 226°C (440°F)

Unit	Ingredient	Metric	Imperial
1	Puff pastry	300 g	12 oz
1	Pastry cream	300 ml	12 fl oz
1	Selected fruit (*see* chart)	300 g	12 oz
*	Whipped cream/fresh (sweetened/ optional)		
	Egg-wash/apricot or clear fruit glaze to finish as required		

* For decoration purposes only approximately 100 ml (4 fl oz) for above recipe.

Method

Roll out pastry evenly to 3 mm (⅛ in) thick × 15 cm (6 in) wide × 35 cm (14 in) long and cut *two* evenly trimmed strips lengthways by 1¼ cm (½ in) wide. Put aside to rest. Pin-out the remaining pastry to 1.5 mm ¹⁄₁₆ in) thick and cut out 12 cm (4½ in) wide trimmed strip lengthways for the base. Place base onto prepared baking sheet and lightly egg wash both edges lengthways. Arrange the two prepared strips along each edge carefully and press down lightly to seal. Flute the long edges with the back of a knife to decorate and egg wash (edges only). Dock the centre base and rest for 30 minutes prior to baking. Bake in pre-heated oven until crisp and golden brown. On completion remove from oven and place onto a cooling wire. Once cool, fill the cavity with a layer of pastry cream and arranged fruit (*see* chart below). Glaze appropriately with hot apricot or fruit glaze. Once cool decorate with the appropriate number of cream rosettes. Slice between cream rosettes into portions and present on service tray with fancy doily.

N.B.   May be presented whole.

Typical Fruit Bands (prepared using above formula)

Name	Main fruit/preparation	French term
Apricot band	Tinned/poached apricots. Drain well, slice and arrange neatly. Apricot glaze to finish	Bande aux abricot
Banana band	Fresh banana/skinned/sliced. Flavour banana slices with lemon juice and arrange neatly. Apricot glaze to finish	Bande aux bananes

Name	Main fruit/preparation	French term
Cherry band	Tinned/poached cherries. Stone, drain well, slice and arrange neatly. Cherry glaze to finish	Bande aux cerises
Mandarin band	Tinned mandarins/well drained. Arrange neatly and finish with mandarin glaze	Bande aux mandarines
Peach band	Tinned/poached peaches well drained. Slice, arrange neatly and finish with peach glaze	Bande aux pêche
Pear band	Tinned/poached pears, well drained. Slice, arrange neatly and finish with pear glaze	Bande aux poires
Pineapple band	Tinned/fresh prepared pineapple. Drain well, cut into thin half rings or chunks, arrange neatly and finish with apricot glaze	Bande aux ananas
Strawberry/raspberry band	Prepared fresh strawberries/raspberries. Leave whole, arrange neatly and finish with red fruit glaze N.B. Pastry cream is often replaced with fresh strawberry/raspberry puree (sweetened) or respective jams	Bande aux frais/framboises
Fruit band	Use selected fruit variety. Arrange/finish appropriately	Bande aux fruits

FRUIT BAND: 2 (complete-baked method)   Bande aux Fruits

Yield: 4–8 portions to size
Baking time: approx. 30 min
Baking temperature: 215°C (420°F)

Unit	Ingredient	Metric	Imperial
1*	Selected fruit (see chart below)	400 g	1 lb
½	Puff pastry	200 g	8 oz
¼	Pastry cream or frangipane	100 g	4 oz
	Whipped fresh cream for decoration/accompaniment		
	Egg-wash/apricot or clear fruit glaze to finish		

* Quantity varies with type of fruit used 400 g (1 lb) being the maximum.

Method

Proceed as for *fruit band*: 1 up to the point just before baking. At this stage, spread the pastry cream *or* frangipan down the centre of the band. Arrange the selected prepared fruit (*see* chart below) to fill the cavity between the edges of the band and bake until cooked/

golden in colour. Remove from the oven, place onto cooling wires and finish with the appropriate glaze. When cold, decorate with the appropriate numbers of cream rosettes to portion. Slice between rosettes and present on service tray with fancy doily.

N.B.   May be presented whole.

Typical Fruit Bands (prepared using the above formula)

Name	Main fruit/preparation	French term
Apple band	*Fresh* peeled and cored thinly slice. Arrange neatly overlapping. Finish with apricot glaze	Bande aux pommes
Gooseberry band	*Fresh* prepared gooseberries. Arrange neatly to fill the band. Finish with clear fruit glaze	Bande aux groseilles vertes
Peach band	*Fresh* stoned, peeled peaches. Slice and arrange neatly, overlapping to fill band. Finish with clear fruit glaze	Bande aux pêche
Pineapple band	*Fresh* peeled and cored pineapple. Cut into thin half rings or chunks. Arrange neatly overlapping to fill the band. Finish with apricot glaze	Bande aux ananas
Rhubarb band	Peeled *fresh* rhubarb. Cut into small neat 2.5 cm (1 in) sections. Arrange neatly to fill the band. Finish with red or clear fruit glaze	Bande aux rhubarde

N.B.   Other fruit may be used including tinned varieties. In this case, the fruit must be exceedingly well drained.

JALOUSIE AND D'ARTOIS

Yield: 8 portions
Baking time: approx. 30 min
Baking temperature: 215°C (420°F)

Unit	Ingredient	Metric	Imperial
1	Puff pastry	300 g	12 oz
⅔★	Selected filling (*see* chart below)	200 g	8 oz
	Egg or water wash/icing sugar to finish		

★   May increase in the case of apple filling to 1 unit 300 g (12 oz).

Method

Roll out pastry into oblong shape approximately 30 cm (12 in) long × 25 cm (10 in) wide × 2.5 mm (¹⁄₁₀ in) thick. Cut *one* 12.5 cm (5 in) wide strip lengthways for the top and put aside to rest. Roll out remaining pastry to 1.5 mm ($\frac{1}{16}$ in) thick and cut a piece the same width and length as the top for the base piece. Place the base onto a prepared baking sheet and dock well all over. Moisten all around the edges of the base lightly with egg-wash and spread the selected filling evenly to within 2.5 cm (1 in) of the edges of the base. Fold the rolled out pastry top in half lengthways and incise small slits slantwise along the fold at 6 mm ($\frac{1}{4}$ in) intervals and to within 2.5 cm (1 in) of each end. Whilst folded lay the top onto the filling with the cut fold in the centre, unfold carefully, enclose the filling completely and press edges to seal. Trim and decorate the edges as required. Egg-wash *or* water-wash and sprinkle with caster sugar. Rest for 30 minutes before baking. Bake in pre-heated oven until crisp and golden brown (if only egg-washed dust with icing sugar during baking to give a glazed finish). Remove from oven and serve hot/cold with suitable sauce, e.g. apricot, custard or whipped fresh cream (sweetened).

Typical Jalousie/D'Artois (prepared using above formula)

Name	Main selected filling	French term
Apple jalousie	Partially cooked peeled/and cored sliced apples (sweated butter with sugar to sweeten and cinnamon to flavour)	Jalousie aux pommes
Jam jalousie	Strawberry/raspberry jam	Jalousie à la confiture
Mincemeat jalousie	Mincemeat	Jalousie à la noël
Almond slice	Frangipane N.B. Before applying frangipane filling spread base of pastry with a thin layer of apricot jam	D'Artois aux amandes

PITHIVIER

Yield: 8 portions
Baking time: approx. 30 min
Baking temperature: 215°C (420°F)

Unit	Ingredient	Metric	Imperial
1	Puff pastry	300 g	12 oz
$\frac{2}{3}$	Frangipane filling	200 g	8 oz
$\frac{1}{8}$	Apricot jam Water-wash/egg-wash/icing sugar for dusting/glazing purposes	25 g	1 oz

Method

Roll out half of the puff pastry evenly to a circular shape of 1.5 mm ($\frac{1}{16}$ in) thick. Cut out a disc-shape of approximately 20 cm (8 in) diameter. Turn over and place onto a prepared baking sheet, dock well and lightly water-wash all around the circular edge. Spread the apricot jam evenly to within 2.5 cm (1 in) of the surrounding edge then layer-in the frangipane filling evenly to cover the jam. Roll out the remaining half of the pastry to a uniform circular shape of 3 mm (⅛ in) thickness and cut out to a disc-shape slightly larger than the base of approximately 21 cm (8½ in) diameter to form a top. Turn the top over, carefully cover the base to enclose the filling, seal, decorate the edge and egg-wash the top thoroughly. Now carefully incise eight evenly spaced curved slits *into but not completely through the top*, working from the centre and to within 2.5 cm (1 in) of the edge. Rest for 30 minutes and bake in pre-heated oven until cooked and light golden in colour. Whilst hot, dust liberally with icing sugar and continue in oven for a few seconds longer to glaze. Remove from oven and allow to cool. Present on service dish with fancy doily.

SAUSAGE ROLLS

Yield: Standard = 12   Cocktail = 24
Baking time: 15–20 min
Baking temperature: 230°C (450°F)

Unit	Ingredient	Metric	Imperial
1	Puff pastry (scraps or Scotch, well rested)	400 g	1 lb
1	Selected sausagemeat (pork/beef/spiced, etc.)	400 g	1 lb
	Water-wash/egg-wash for sealing/glazing purposes		

Method

Roll out pastry into an even rectangle of 2.5 mm (1/10 in) thick. Cut the rectangle into 11.5 cm (4½ in) strips. Mould/pipe the selected sausagemeat into ropes of 2–2.5 cm (¾–1 in) diameter, lay onto the prepared pastry strips and water-wash the clear edge of the pastry strips to lightly moisten. Fold/roll pastry around the sausagemeat and seal firmly to enclose. Mark/decorate the presentation surface with the back of a knife and cut into the required sizes namely, *standard 7.5–10 cm (3–4 in)* or *cocktail 3.5 cm (1½ in)*. Egg-wash to glaze, place onto a prepared baking tray and rest 30 minutes. Bake in a pre-heated oven until crisp and of a light golden colour. Remove from oven, place onto cooling wires and serve as required.

N.B.   May be presented hot or cold. Offered on service dish with plain doily.

PUFF PASTRY CRESCENTS   Fleûrons

Roll out well rested puff pastry trimmings evenly to 3 mm (⅛ in) thickness. Take a 6–8 cm (2½–3 in) plain/fancy round cutter and cut out neat crescent shapes of approximately 2 cm (¾ in) wide across the central section. Place onto prepared baking tray, egg-wash carefully to glaze, rest for 30 minutes and bake until crisp and golden in colour at 230°C (450°F) 10–15 minutes. Remove from oven, place onto cooling wires and use as required.

N.B.   Used as a garnish with many poached fish/shellfish items and other entrées.

Puff Pastry Cases (Vol-au-vents/Bouchées)

These products are best described as open baked pastry cases. *Vol-au-vents* are *round* or *oval* in shape and quite large in size, ranging from approximately 8 cm (3 in) diameter to larger varieties around 15 cm (6 in) dimensions. Bouchées, on the other hand, are usually *small* and *round* in shape of approximately 2.5 cm (1 in) to 5 cm (2 in) diameter. Modern cookery features other shapes for pastry cases, e.g. fish shapes/small rectangles, etc.

VOL-AU-VENTS/BOUCHÉES/CASES

Yield: 6 vol-au-vents/16 bouchées
Baking time: approx. 15–20 min
Baking temperature: 226°C (440°F)

Unit	Ingredient	Metric	Imperial
1	Puff pastry (virgin) Water-wash/egg-wash for sealing/glazing purposes	400 g	1 lb

Method 1: two piece technique for individual vol-au-vent cases

Roll out pastry to 3 mm (⅛ in) thick and form an even rectangle. Mark a half-way line (do not cut but just mark lightly). On one half mark out lightly the number of cases using a 8 cm (3 in) plain cutter. In the centre of the marked areas cut out a central piece using a 5 cm (2 in) cutter of the same shape, namely round or oval as required. Put the cut-out discs aside. Lightly water-wash the half with the cut out holes and lay the plain half carefully over and onto the 'cut out side'. Gently press to seal. Reverse the whole sheet so that the *cut out side* is now *uppermost*. Take a 8 cm (3 in) cutter of correct shape, place around the holes (keeping the hole central) and cut through the pastry to give individual cases. Place onto the prepared baking trays, prick the central base of each and carefully egg-wash the top surrounding edge of each case (the cut-out discs may be egg-washed, baked and used as lids with the final products).

Rest the prepared cases for 30 minutes, place in pre-heated oven and bake until crisp and golden brown. On completion, remove from oven and place onto cooling wires. Use as required.

Method 2: single piece technique for individual vol-au-vent cases

Roll out the pastry to 6 mm (¼ in) thick and form an even rectangle. Cut out using a 8 cm (3 in) plain cutter and place up-side down onto prepared baking trays. Carefully egg-wash each one. Whilst still moist, cut half-way down/through using a 5 cm (2 in) cutter. Rest for 30 minutes and bake in pre-heated oven until crisp and gold brown. Remove from oven and remove the central lids giving open cases. Place lids and cases on cooling wires in readiness for use.

N.B.   For bouchées use same methods but smaller cutters as indicated in the introduction above.

Suet Pastry

Suet pastry is widely used throughout the professional kitchen when preparing sweet and savoury dishes. It is readily prepared and ideally suited to the preparation of popular British steamed favourites from the menu, e.g. steak and kidney pudding, steamed apple pudding, savoury dumplings, etc.

Ingredient principles:

Medium strength flour is used for the production of suet pastry because sufficient gluten is needed to ensure that the steamed pastry retains its shape and stability. At the same time, the cooked pastry must be soft, palatable and without undue toughness or elasticity.

The shortening agent incorporated is beef suet, available commercially in ready for use form. However, a superior pastry can be prepared using fresh beef suet. In this instance, the suet is picked to remove any sinew/skin, mixed with a little flour and chopped finely ensuring the suet particles remain separate. The suet is kept refrigerated in order to maintain its fresh crisp texture.

The water content for suet pastry is greater than for short pastries because suet does not have the same insulating properties as other shortening agents. Hence more water is required to form a soft pliable dough.

Aeration/chemical:

To ensure that suet pastry does not become heavy and stodgy during the steaming process baking powder is incorporated as an aerating agent. When heated in moist conditions baking powder produces carbon dioxide gas which aerates the pastry. The result is a light palatable product which may be used to line pudding basins to form a pastry case for various fillings; or as a foundation for sweets in their own right, e.g. roly poly puddings, etc.

SUET PASTRY   Pâte à Graisse

Unit	Ingredient	Metric	Imperial
1	Flour (medium strong)	200 g	8 oz
$\frac{1}{2}$	Beef suet (finely chopped)	100 g	4 oz
$\frac{1}{2}$	Water (cold)	100 ml	4 fl oz
$\frac{1}{16}$	Baking powder	12.5 g	$\frac{1}{2}$ oz
	Pinch of salt to taste		

N.B.   If using fresh beef suet, remove sinew and skin, mix with a little flour, chop finely.

Method

Sift flour, salt and baking powder together. Add suet and mix thoroughly. Form a well, add sufficient water to bind and form a pastry dough.

STEAMED FRUIT PUDDINGS

Yield: 6 portions
Cooking time: 2 hr

Unit	Ingredient	Metric	Imperial
1	Selected prepared fruit (*see* chart)	500 g	20 oz
⅕	Sugar	100 g	4 oz
⅒	Water	50 ml	2 fl oz
★	Suet pastry		

★ Sufficient for 6 portions, approximately 150 g (6 oz) flour prepared into suet pastry (*see* p. 507).

Method

Roll out two-thirds of suet pastry and line a greased pudding basin. Place selected prepared fruit into lined basin, add sugar to sweeten and moisten with water. Roll out remaining pastry to form a lid. Place lid in position and seal edges. Cover with greased greaseproof paper and pudding cloth. Set to steam until cooked. Once cooked, clean the basin, surround with clean serviette and present for service accompanied with custard sauce.

Examples of Steamed Fruit Puddings Prepared Using 1 Unit (500 g (1¼ lb)) Prepared Fruit

Pudding	Unit	Selected fruit	Metric	Imperial
Steamed apple pudding	1	Apples	500 g	20 oz
Steamed apple and blackberry pudding	½ ½	Apples Blackberries	250 g 250 g	10 oz 10 oz
Steamed apple and redcurrant pudding	½ ½	Apples Redcurrants	250 g 250 g	10 oz 10 oz
Steamed gooseberry pudding	1	Gooseberries	500 g	20 oz
Steamed plum pudding	1	Plums	500 g	20 oz
Steamed rhubarb pudding	1	Rhubarb	500 g	20 oz
Steamed rhubarb and apple pudding	½ ½	Rhubarb Apples	250 g 250 g	10 oz 10 oz

For preparation of fresh fruit see fruit pies (p. 479).

N.B.   When preparing fruit puddings using sharp flavoured fruit, e.g. rhubarb, gooseberries, etc., it may be necessary to add extra sugar to ensure sufficient sweetness.

STEAMED JAM ROLL/JAM ROLY POLY PUDDING

Yield: 4–6 portions
Cooking time: 1¼–1½ hr

Unit	Ingredient	Metric	Imperial
1	Suet pastry	300 g	12 oz
¼	Jam	75 g	3 oz

Method

Roll out pastry to form a rectangle 30 cm × 20 cm (12 in × 8 in). Spread the jam evenly on to the pastry leaving 1 cm (½ in) clear on all edges. Brush edges with water. Fold over the two shorter edges towards the centre to seal in the jam. Then roll up loosely towards the longer edge, seal the ends. Place in a well greased pudding sleeve and steam until cooked. Turn and serve accompanied with a sauce boat of custard or jam sauce. As an alternative, the roll may be placed into a well greased paper then wrapped in a pudding cloth prior to steaming.

   N.B.   Steamed suet pastry rolls may be filled with mincemeat, lemon curd, date and apple or syrup, as required.

STEAMED FRUIT ROLL

Yield: 4–6 portions
Cooking time: 1¼–1½ hr

Unit	Ingredient	Metric	Imperial
1	Flour (medium strength)	200 g	8 oz
½	Beef suet (finely chopped)	100 g	4 oz
½	Water or milk	100 ml	4 fl oz
½	Selected fruit (*see* chart below)	100 g	4 oz
¼	Caster sugar	50 g	2 oz
1/16	Baking powder	12.5 g	½ oz
	Pinch of salt		

Method

Sift flour, salt and baking powder together. Add suet, caster sugar, selected fruit and mix thoroughly. Form a well, add sufficient liquid to bind and form a dough. Roll out to form a rectangle 30 cm × 20 cm (12 in × 8 in). Brush edges with water. Roll up loosely towards the longer edge, seal the ends. Place in a well-greased pudding sleeve and steam until cooked. Serve accompanied with a sauce boat of custard. As an alternative, the roll may be placed in a well-greased greaseproof paper then wrapped in a pudding cloth prior to steaming.

Examples of Steamed Fruit Rolls Prepared Using the Above Formula

Steamed roll	Unit	Selected fruit	Metric	Imperial
Steamed currant roll	¼	Currants	100 g	4 oz
Steamed currant and sultana roll	⅛ ⅛	Currants Sultanas	50 g 50 g	2 oz 2 oz
Steamed date roll	¼	Chopped dates	100 g	4 oz
Sultana roll	¼	Sultanas	100 g	4 oz

Suet Dumplings

Scale off suet pastry into 25 g (1 oz) balls and simmer in stock for approximately 15–20 minutes. Alternatively when being served with a brown stew they may be cooked in the stew's sauce 15–20 minutes before required for service.

31

Cakes, Biscuits, Gateaux and Torten

This section deals with a mixed variety of flour confectionery goods. Non-fermented aerated items such as cakes, gateaux, torten, morning goods and others are featured, and the fundamental ingredient production principles outlined.

Aeration Factors for Non-Fermented Goods

In addition to the organic fermentation process using yeast, two other methods of aeration are commonly used for culinary products. Typically, the *mechanical* and *chemical* aeration processes are employed independently or simultaneously in recipe formulations to aerate and lighten confectionery products.

Chemical Aeration

Chemical aeration generally denotes the use of baking powder as a raising agent. *Baking powder* is essentially produced from two chemicals, *cream of tartare (an acid)* and *bicarbonate of soda (an alkali)*. The baking powder composition being 2 parts acid to 1 part alkali.

In the presence of *moisture and heat*, the chemicals react to produce carbon dioxide gas (CO_2) which becomes entangled in the protein framework of flour confectionery goods (e.g. scones, cakes, etc.) during the early stages of baking. As baking continues, the heat penetrates, the CO_2 gas expands to raise/lighten the product until the structure of the confection sets changing from a relatively soft structure at the commencement of the process to a more rigid form on completion. These changes in structure are brought about during baking by the coagulation of proteins and gelatinisation of starch within the aerated product; hence aerated goods which do not readily collapse.

Conditions Suitable for Chemical Aeration

Chemical raising agents need specific conditions if they are to be successfully applied. These favourable conditions require the presence of moisture, warmth and heat, a correct recipe balance (proportion of raising agent to other ingredients), a thorough/even distribution of the raising agent throughout the mixture and correct handling throughout the production process. When such conditions prevail, and even when the products are formed cold in readiness for baking, some gas is produced and given off. It is important, therefore, that such chemically aerated goods should not stand too long before reaching the oven.

If used in excess, baking powder will cause cooked products to collapse or break-up as illustrated in collapsed cakes/suet dumplings. Alternatively, if insufficient baking powder is used the resultant product will show a close, heavy texture; hence the importance of recipe balance.

N.B.   *Bicarbonate of soda* (alkali) is sometimes used on its own as a chemical raising agent forming CO_2 gas when suitable conditions prevail. However, its use in this way is limited because of its residual objectionable taste and discolouring characteristic. Furthermore, when used in isolation (i.e. without acid) bicarbonate of soda is less efficient as a producer of carbon dioxide gas. It is generally used, therefore, in such products as ginger cakes – parkin, in which the spices and other ingredients dominate flavour, where a dark colour is required and where a slower generation of CO_2 gas is not a disadvantage.

Mechanical Aeration (related to baked products)

Whether achieved manually or by machine, the two commonly used types of mechanical aeration are *whisking* and *creaming*.

Whisking process	Air is incorporated mechanically when whole egg/sugar or egg white/sugar undergo the whisking process. In all cases egg albumen (white) expands rapidly during whisking and air is taken-in, dispersed and held throughout the network of stretched albumen (protein)
Creaming or sugar batter process	Air is incorporated mechanically when given quantities of fat/sugar are creamed/beaten together to form a soft, light and fluffy mixture. During creaming, the mixture takes-in and retains air. Eggs are then beaten-in carefully, incorporating more air to form a stable aerated emulsion of fat, sugar and eggs.

Combined Mechanical/Chemical Aeration

Sometimes a combination of methods is recommended for specific flour confectionery goods. In most cases, mechanical aeration is the underlying aerating technique, but baking powder is also added to provide further 'lightness' and a more open texture.

Ingredients Criteria

In addition to chemical raising agents, the nature and role of the ingredients present in flour confectionery recipes is worthy of note. Throughout preparation and cooking the various reactions and interactions that take place within mixtures are critical to product quality. The objective when producing aerated flour confectionery goods being to provide items (cakes, morning goods, etc.) which are suitably aerated/raised by volume, which have a stable structure yet light/soft textured eating quality, which have the correct flavour/taste; and when applicable offer adequate keeping qualities/shelf life without any undue deterioration.

Types/Role of Flour

Because of their relatively *low* protein content, *soft flour* is typically used (sometimes medium strength flour is used, *see* p. 515) to produce the types of flour confectionery goods outlined in this section. The fine texture of such flours and their characteristically low gluten-forming capacity ideally meets the flour's role toward providing *fine textured aerated confectionery goods of a soft/short crumb*. As flour is the main ingredient in flour confectionery items, the starch protein contents present act to stabilize (firm-up) the structure of the baked finished goods: a result of starch gelatinization and protein coagulation. Furthermore, food scientists suggest that the finer and more even the flour granules, the better the end result as fine-textured soft flours tend to form a relatively soft gluten structure which does not toughen on mixing. Plain cake/soft flours are the norm for these products, but occasions arise when medium strength, self-raising or wholemeal flours are used.

Types/Role of Fat

The functions of fat in flour confectionery recipe formula involves one or more of the following roles, namely to act as a shortening/tenderizing agent, to take-in and trap air during mechanical creaming/beating and to introduce flavour/colour where appropriate. During various mixing processes such as rubbing-in/sugar batter methods fat envelops and separates flour particles thus preventing the formation of long gluten strands once the moisture is added. The shortening/tenderizing of the starch/gluten contents results in a better quality product of a soft short crumb. When the sugar batter/creaming method is applied to cake-making, the fat content takes in and traps air during the creaming/beating process, thereby aerating the mixture (mechanical aeration), *see* p. 512. Certain fats will influence flavour/colour to a lesser or greater extent. Butter/butter compositions are good examples. The characteristic flavour/colour of butter has a noticeable effect on flavour/colour when it is included in recipe formula. However, the disadvantage of using butter is related to its low-creaming quality and its relatively high cost compared with hydrogenated shortening agents/fats. A number of fats/shortenings, therefore, can be used for flour confectionery goods; fats of either a pleasing or bland flavour are acceptable. As a rule, plastic rather than hard fats are more suitable because of their high-creaming quality. Many such suitable proprietary brands of vegetable shortenings are available which are often hydrogenated thus improving their keeping and creaming qualities. Generally these proprietary shortenings are very similar in texture (plastic), taste (bland), and in their suitability for use throughout flour confectionery products. However, using all bland fat/shortening is not flavour-enriching and it is better to use a blend of suitable fats including some butter for flavour. Butter, margarine, fats, shortenings, etc. offer suitable selections for blending which besides affecting flavour may also reduce costs. As a rule using 'all butter or margarine' is not recommended for the inclusion of even a small amount of 'pure fat' will improve the texture of the finished goods.

N.B. Lard has *no acceptable creaming quality* and is, therefore, not used in the sugar-batter creaming method.

Types/Role of Sugar

Besides sweetening, the presence of sugar in flour confectionery recipes has marked effects upon the texture, colour and flavour of finished articles. Sugar tenderizes gluten and egg proteins in accordance with the quantity of sugar used in the recipe. As a general guide increased sugar, within the bounds of recipe balance, leads to an increase in these tenderizing effects. Obviously the inclusion of sugar affects taste and crumb-colour both of which are directly affected by increases/decreases of this commodity. White and brown, fine and coarse sugars, syrups (honey/golden) may be used within the realms of flour confectionery. As a guide, finely grained sugar blends more fully with other ingredients providing fine textured products, coarser sugar, however, generally means a coarser textured product of less volume. The use of syrup can lead to heavy, close, moist textures; which in specific cases is desirable. When using the sugar-batter/creaming method, the fine/sharp caster sugar granules also assist in the aerating function as air is incorporated into the mixture.

The Role of Eggs

Because of their structure/composition, eggs have a number of important roles in flour confectionery processes. They can be used to shorten, aerate, stabilise, emulsify, moisten, flavour, colour and increase the food value of many confections. Beaten egg whites/whole eggs *incorporate and hold-in air* to varying degrees during basic cake-making processes, whilst the egg yolk protein lecithin, when incorporated acts as an emulsifier.

As a guiding rule, and taking into account the principles of recipe balance, whole egg is said to *raise/moisten* its own weight of flour (even in the presence of fat/sugar). At given temperatures egg proteins *coagulate/stabilize* to assist in the structural formation typical of flour confectionery items. Additionally, eggs provide both flavour, colour (yellow pigmentation of yolk) and nutritive value making them an invaluable ingredient.

In the absence of fat/sugar, eggs are said to 'raise' double their weight in flour, e.g. Yorkshire pudding batter.

The Role of Liquids/Moistening Agents

The liquid content in flour confectionery goods is needed for any one or more of a number of reasons. Typically liquid serves to hydrate gluten forming proteins/starch particles and provide a medium in which salt/sugar/chemical raising agents can be readily dissolved whilst also providing moistness within given mixtures. A *shortage* of moistening will result in over-dry textures whilst an excess of liquid has an adverse effect upon volume and at the same time results in an over-moist product.

Liquids used in flour confectionery goods (in addition to the moisture provided by such ingredients as eggs/some fats) may include milk, fruit juices, essences and the like, with milk the most common. Moisture is also an essential ingredient towards the processes of chemical aeration and starch gelatinization during baking/cooking.

Summary

Essentially the types of ingredients used in flour confectionery goods and the proportions/balance outlined in recipe formulations are so designed as to allow the shortening/tenderizing ingredients, such as fats, egg yolks, sugar to offset the potentially toughening/stabilizing/binding processes attributed to flour, egg whites and liquids.

Basic Production Methods Used in Mechanically/Chemically Aerated Goods

A variety of basic production methods can be used for these types of goods. The *rubbed-in method* (with chemical aeration), *sugar batter method* and *whisked sponge method* are common processes, and the ones featured specifically in this and other sections. Methods such as the *flour batter method* are more specialized and readers should consult detailed bakery/patisserie texts for more technical information.

The rubbed-in method (with chemical aeration) is typified in the making of scones/raspberry buns, p. 516, the sugar batter method is outlined in the making of Victoria sandwich/steamed/baked sponges, p. 518 and the whisked sponge method applied in the making of swiss roll, fatless sponge, genoese, sponge fingers, etc. p. 520 respectively.

SCONES (White)

Yield: 16 × 60 g (2 oz) individual scones
Baking time: 15–20 min
Baking temperature: 204°C (400°F)

Unit	Ingredient	Metric	Imperial
1	Medium flour/white plain	480 g	1 lb
½*	Milk	240 ml	'8 fl oz
¼	Shortening	120 g	4 oz
¼	Caster sugar	120 g	4 oz
⅛	Egg/beaten	60 ml	2 fl oz
¹⁄₁₆	Baking powder	60 g	1 oz
	Pinch of salt		

* May vary slightly according to absorption rate of the flour.

Method

Lightly grease a baking sheet and put aside. Combine baking powder, flour, salt and sift two or three times to distribute evenly. Add shortening and rub in to form a light crumbly texture. Whisk together milk, beaten egg, sugar and incorporate/dissolve thoroughly. Form a bay with the dry ingredients and pour in the prepared liquid. Working gently with minimum handling/mixing, bring ingredients together to form a soft, smooth, cleared scone dough. Do not toughen by over mixing. Rest the dough for 10 minutes, then roll-out 1.5 cm (½ in) thick. Cut out scones with a 6.5 cm (2½ in) cutter, place onto prepared greased baking sheets, egg-wash the tops only (*see* N.B. below) and rest for 10 minutes. Bake in oven at 204°C (400°F) for approximately 15–20 minutes until the tops are golden and the sides white.

N.B.   Plain scones do not require to be egg-washed, but once filled with jam and cream are dusted with icing sugar.

Scones Prepared Using Above Formula: Ingredient Amounts in Relation to 1 Unit, i.e. 480 g/1 lb Flour

Name	Unit	Added ingredients	Metric	Imperial
Plain scones		As above but omit egg-washing procedure Dust cooled scones with icing sugar to finish		
Fruit scones	¼	Sultanas Mix with rubbed-in ingredients before forming the bay	120 g	4 oz
Whole/wheatmeal scones		Replace white flour totally or by 50% with wholemeal/wheatmeal flour as required Increase milk content by approximately 30 ml (1 fl oz)		

RASPBERRY BUNS

Yield: 16 × 50 g (2 oz) buns
Baking time: 15–20 min
Baking temperature: 225°C (440°F)

Unit	Ingredient	Metric	Imperial
1	Soft flour/white	400 g	1 lb
½	Milk	200 ml	8 fl oz
¼	Caster sugar	100 g	4 oz
⅛	Shortening	50 g	2 oz
⅛	Margarine	50 g	2 oz
⅛	Egg/beaten	50 ml	2 fl oz
1/16	Baking powder	25 g	1 oz

Method

Prepare a greased baking tray and put aside. Combine flour/baking powder and sift together two or three times for even distribution. Add shortening/margarine and rub-in to form a crumbly texture. Blend together egg, milk and sugar to dissolve. Now make a bay with dry ingredients, pour sweetened liquid into bay and with the minimum of handling form a clear, soft, smooth dough. Using a little dusting flour, scale-off into 50 g (2 oz) pieces, mould into balls, milk wash, dip into caster sugar and place onto greased baking sheet. Depress each bun to form a dent in the centre, pipe-in a tiny bulb of raspberry jam and bake at 225°C (440°F) for 15–20 minutes.

Rock cakes: As above, but incorporate ⅛ *unit, i.e. 50 g (2 oz) currants* and 1/16 *unit, i.e. 25 g (1 oz) mixed peel* by sprinkling around the bay before liquid is added. Form the dough with fruit, scale-off into 50 g (2 oz) cakes, place onto greased tray, sprinkle with granulated sugar and bake as above.

SHORTBREAD

Yield: according to size/shapes produced (approximately 700 g (1½ lb) of shortbread biscuits)
Baking time: 10–15 min
Baking temperature: 193°C (380°F)

Unit	Ingredients	Metric	Imperial
1	Soft flour/white	360 g	12 oz
⅔	Butter	240 g	8 oz
⅓	Caster sugar	120 g	4 oz

Method

Prepare lightly greased baking tray and put aside. Sift flour, put aside and thoroughly cream together butter/caster sugar. Fold flour carefully through the creamed mixture and bring to a smooth paste. If necessary, wrap and store in a refrigerator in readiness for rolling/moulding.

1. Shortbread Fingers

Place shortbread paste onto cooking surface and roll into a rectangular shape of 1 cm (½ in) thick. Transfer to prepared baking sheet, dock evenly all-over (facilitates baking process) and trim edges. Mark into fingers cutting half-way through only. Bake until cooked and golden brown. Remove from oven, dredge with fine caster sugar whilst hot and divide into fingers.

2. Medium Shortbread Rounds/Moulded

Weigh off the required amount of shortbread paste and gently press into a flattened disc in the shape of the shortbread mould. Dust the mould with rice flour, press the shortbread paste firmly into the mould and level off. Reverse the mould over the prepared baking sheet, knock the edges of the mould allowing the paste to drop-out onto prepared baking tray, with the pattern uppermost. Dock, if appropriate, then bake until cooked and golden brown. Remove from oven and whilst hot dredge with fine caster sugar.

3. Shortbread Rounds/Non-moulded

Weigh-off required amount of shortbread paste, mould into a ball then roll-out to 12 mm (½ in) thick circular shape. Place onto baking sheet, dock evenly all over, crimp edges and bake until cooked and golden brown. Once cooked, remove from oven and whilst hot dredge with fine caster sugar.

VIENNESE (piped)

Yield: 16 units
Baking time: approx. 15–20 min
Baking temperature: 204°C (400°F)

Unit	Ingredients	Metric	Imperial
1	Soft flour/white	200 g	8 oz
1	Margarine	200 g	8 oz
¼	Icing sugar	50 g	2 oz
	Vanilla essence to flavour		

Method

Combine icing sugar/margarine and cream to a light mixture. At this stage, incorporate vanilla essence to flavour. Sift the flour, and *cream* half of it into the already creamed sugar/margarine mixture. Now incorporate remaining flour in the same manner to form a soft piping mixture.

1. Viennese Fingers

Prepare a lightly greased/floured baking tray. Using a piping bag and 12 mm (½ in) star tube, pipe 7.5 cm (3 in) biscuits onto the tray. Bake until golden around the edges, but pale in the centre. Remove from oven to cool. For presentation, sandwich together with jam/buttercream and dip/decorate ends with chocolate (melted).

2. Viennese Tarts (rose tarts)

Place paper cases into custard tins and pipe-in a small rose bowl with piping bag and 12 mm (½ in) star tube. Bake until golden, remove from oven and remove paper cups with viennese from the tins. Dust with icing sugar and pipe a small bulb of red jam in the centre of each.

VICTORIA SPONGE SANDWICH

Yield: 1 Victoria sandwich
Baking time: approx. 25 min
Baking temperature: 182°C (360°F)

Unit	Ingredients	Metric	Imperial
1	Butter	120 g	4 oz
1	Caster sugar	120 g	4 oz
1	Whole egg	120 g	4 oz
1	Soft white flour	120 g	4 oz
¹⁄₁₆	Baking powder	7.5 g	¼ oz

Method

Grease/flour two 15 cm (6 in) sandwich pans/tins, sift flour and baking powder two or three times and put aside. Bring all ingredients to room temperature. Place butter/caster sugar in mixing bowl and beat together until light and creamy (scrape down sides of mixing bowl from time to time during beating process). Beat-in quarter of the egg gradually, clear and scrape down. Continue to add each quarter of egg, clearing/scraping down each time until all the egg is fully incorporated. Carefully fold in and incorporate the sifted flour mixture. *Do not overmix.* Divide equally into prepared sandwich pans/tins, bake at 182°C (360°F) for 25 minutes until baked and golden brown. Remove from oven, turn-out onto cooling wires and allow to cool. Sandwich cooked sponges with raspberry jam and dust with icing sugar for service.

GENOESE (Butter Sponge)   Génoise

Yield: Dependent upon shape and size of tin used
Baking time: 30–35 min
Baking temperature: 205°C (400°F) (on a dropping oven)

Unit	Ingredients	Metric	Imperial
1	Whole egg	300 g	10 oz
⁴/₅	Caster sugar	240 g	8 oz
⁴/₅	Soft white flour	240 g	8 oz
⅕	Butter/melted	60 ml	2 fl oz

Method

Grease/flour the cake pans/tins, sift soft flour and put aside. Place eggs/caster sugar in mixing bowl and place over warm bain-marie. Whisk (preferably by machine) on top speed for 10 minutes/medium speed for 10 minutes to thick ribbon stage and until mixture doubles in volume. Remove from the machine and gradually/evenly fold in the sifted flour (and cocoa for chocolate *see* below) by hand until half clear. At this stage, slowly pour-in the melted butter and fold in gently to clear both butter and flour. *Do not overmix.* Scale mixture into prepared pans and bake at 205°C (400°F) in a dropping oven for approximately 30 minutes until baked and golden. Remove from oven and turn-out onto cooling wires and allow to cool. Use as required *see* p. 524 for applications.

CHOCOLATE GENOESE (Génoise au Chocolat)

Replace ⅛, i.e. 30 g (1 oz) soft flour with cocoa. Incorporate cocoa with soft flour in formula.

PLAIN FATLESS SPONGE

Yield: 2 × 15 cm (6 in) pans/tins
Baking time: approx. 30 min
Baking temperature: 205°C (400°F)

Unit	Ingredients	Metric	Imperial
1	Whole egg	150 g	5 oz
⁴/₅	Caster sugar	120 g	4 oz
⁴/₅	Soft white flour	120 g	4 oz

Method

Grease/flour the baking tins and put aside. Combine whole egg/caster sugar in a scrupulously clean bowl/whisk. Place over warm bain-marie, whisk to thick ribbon stage and until the mixture doubles in volume. Pass flour through fine sieve and blend/fold carefully/evenly through the whisked preparation. Gently divide/scale-off equally into prepared tins ensuring the mixture is level. Bake until golden in colour and resilient to the touch. Remove from the oven, allow to stand for a few minutes, then turn-out onto cooling wires.

Sponge Sandwich

When cool, sandwich the two together with jam or jam and whipped cream.

Sponge Flan

Use sponge/flan tins to replace plain tins and continue as above. When cool, brush inside cavity with hot apricot purée. Fill with prepared selected fruit (neatly arranged) and finish with a light coating of apricot glaze. Serve accompanied with Chantilly cream.

Cup Cakes

Pipe mixture into greaseproof cases and place in tart pans for baking. If so desired sprinkle with currants or glace cherry prior to baking. When cool, finish as required.

JAM SWISS ROLL

Yield: 2 medium rolls
Baking time: approx. 8 min
Baking temperature: 232°C (450°F)

Unit	Ingredient	Metric	Imperial
1	Whole egg/beaten	200 g	8 oz
½	Caster sugar	100 g	4 oz
½	Soft flour/white	100 g	4 oz

Method

Line selected baking sheet with greaseproof paper and put aside. Combine beaten egg and caster sugar in mixing bowl and whisk together over warm bain-marie to the thick ribbon stage and until the mixture doubles in volume. Pass the flour through a fine sieve and blend/fold carefully/evenly through the whisked preparation. Place/spread the sponge evenly in the prepared baking sheets approximately 45 cm × 23 cm (18 in × 12 in). Bake at 230°C (450°F) for approximately 8 minutes, remove immediately from the oven and reverse sponge onto sugared cloth/paper, leaving baking tray in position. Allow to cool slightly, remove tray and greaseproof paper from sponge. Spread the sponge lightly with selected jam and roll up lightly in cloth/paper. When cool and ready for service remove paper/cloth and serve as required.

CHOCOLATE SWISS ROLL

As above but replace quarter of flour with cocoa powder (sift cocoa powder with the flour) and fill with chocolate butter-cream or freshly whipped Chantilly cream to replace jam filling.

   N.B.   The filling is applied/incorporated after the sponge has been rolled plain, allowed to cool, unrolled, filled then re-rolled.

CHOCOLATE LOG

As for chocolate swiss roll filled and decoratively masked with chocolate buttercream along the length of the roll and at each end with a thin spread of white buttercream decorated with a piped thin spiral of chocolate circles to resemble the normal swiss roll finish. Garnish the log lightly with some holly.

   N.B.   Small swiss rolls are prepared specifically for lining/decoration purposes.

SPONGE FINGERS   Biscuits à la Cuillère

Yield: 20–30 according to size produced
Baking time: 4–5 min
Baking temperature: 232°C (450°F)

Unit	Ingredient	Metric	Imperial
4	Whole eggs		
1	Caster sugar	120 g	4 oz
1	Soft white flour	120 g	4 oz
	Few drops vanilla essence		

Method

Line baking sheet with a sheet of greaseproof paper and put aside. Place egg yolks, sugar and vanilla essence in a bowl, whisk to a thick ribbon stage, until the mixture doubles in volume. Pass flour through a fine sieve and whisk egg whites until stiff. Fold one third of the whites into the egg yolk mixture, then carefully fold in one third of the flour. Repeat process until all egg white and flour is incorporated. Place mixture in piping bag with 12 mm (½ in) plain tube and pipe even sized sponge fingers onto sheets of greaseproof on a flat working surface. Sprinkle the piped fingers liberally with caster sugar and lift the paper with piped fingers vertically allowing for removal of loose excess sugar. Now place the greaseproof with fingers onto prepared baking sheet. Bake at 232°C (450°F) for approximately 4–5 minutes to a light golden colour. Remove from oven, allow to cool and use as required.

CATS' TONGUES   Langues du Chat

Yield: 60–80 according to size produced
Baking temperature: 215°C (420°F)

Unit	Ingredient	Metric	Imperial
1	Butter	120 g	4 oz
1	Sugar/icing or caster	120 g	4 oz
1	Egg whites	120 g	4 oz
1	Flour/soft/sifted	120 g	4 oz
	Few drops of vanilla essence to flavour		

Method

Lightly grease baking sheet and put aside. Cream together butter/icing sugar, gradually whisk in the egg whites (unwhipped) to incorporate, flavour with few drops of vanilla essence and finally fold-in the sifted flour to form a piping mixture. Transfer mixture to piping bag with 6 mm (¼ in) tube and pipe out spaced fingers of 6 cm (2½ in) long leaving room for the mixture to spread. Bake in oven at 215°C (420°F) until the edges of the biscuits take-on a pale golden colour. Remove from oven, transfer to tray, allow to cool and use as required.

N.B.   Whilst in a hot state the biscuits are sufficiently malleable and can be shaped around a piece of dowel to form hollow tubular shapes. On cooling the shape will be retained.

BRANDY SNAPS

Yield: 36
Baking temperature: 160°C (320°F)

Unit	Ingredient	Metric	Imperial
1	Caster sugar	240 g	8 oz
½	Butter	120 g	4 oz
½	Golden syrup	120 g	4 oz
½	Soft white flour	120 g	4 oz
	Good pinch of ground ginger		

Method

Liberally grease a clean baking sheet and put aside. Sift flour/ginger, combine with remaining ingredients and mix thoroughly to a paste then put aside to stand for 20 minutes. Roll out the paste into a rope and cut into small 15 g (½ oz) pieces. Place each onto the prepared baking sheet allowing plenty of space between each for spreading. Flatten each piece with fork, place in oven and bake at 160°C (320°F) until brown, flat and of a perforated appearance. Remove, allow to cool *slightly*, remove with a palette knife, shape as required (*see* below), allow to set/cool, remove and store in biscuit tin for use.

Examples of Shapes

1. Cigarettes: roll around 12 mm (½ in) dowelling sticks
2. Cornets: shape around cream horn tins (size to suit requirements).

GÂTEAUX AND TORTEN

The difference between gâteaux and torten is often one of individual interpretation. Generally a large gâteaux, divided into slices, which are in turn individually decorated, is termed a torten. The composition of tortens is extensive and the creative pâtissier will use all his/her skills to produce appetising and varied selections. Frequently the gâteaux/torten is named after the main flavouring or decoration used, e.g. Kirsch Torte, Walnut Torte, Orange gâteaux.

Composition of Torten

Torten is usually prepared using a genoese sponge presented on a base of japonaise, sweet pastry or shortbread. The sponge may be sandwiched/soaked with flavoured stock syrup then filled with cream, buttercream, fruit, etc. prior to external decoration.

Assembly of Torten

Spread selected base (japonaise, sweet pastry, etc.) with jam and cut sponge horizontally into two discs. Place a sponge disc onto the base and sprinkle liberally with flavoured stock syrup. Spread with buttercream and arrange filling (fruit, chocolate, nuts, etc.) neatly over the surface. Spread with another layer of buttercream. Add final layer of sponge and sprinkle liberally with flavoured stock syrup. Mask the top and sides with whipped cream or buttercream, then coat the sides with nibbed/flaked nuts/chocolate vermicelle, etc. Place onto a cake board and mark the top with a torten divider. Decorate each individual section/portion uniformly for presentation purposes.

Examples of Ingredients for Preparation/Assembly of Torten

Bases	Shortbread, japonaise, puff pastry, sweet pastry
Sponge	Genoese, chocolate genoese
Soaking liquors	Stock syrup and fruit juices flavoured with: rum, brandy, kirsch, curacao, etc.
Filling, decoration creams	Butter cream, whipped double cream flavoured with: essences, spirits, etc.
Selected fillings	Various fruits: cherries, orange segments, pineapple, etc.
	Various nuts: hazel nuts, almonds, walnuts, etc.
	Flaked/grated chocolate, meringue, non-churned ice-cream mixtures, chopped praline, Bavarian cream
Coatings for sides	Nibbed/flaked nuts, plain, coloured or roasted
	Chocolate vermicelle, chocolate shapes
	Sponge fingers, biscuits, marzipan
Decoration	Fresh/tinned fruit slices and segments
	Chocolate shapes
	Praline shapes
	Marzipan flowers, models
	Whole/half/nibbed nuts
	Glace fruits, e.g. cherries, angelica
	Piped cream/butter cream

Examples of Gâteaux Prepared Using Genoese Sponge Base

English term	Ingredient and method	French term
Chocolate gâteau	Chocolate flavoured genoese sponge Chocolate buttercream Melted chocolate Chocolate vermicelle Chocolate squares	Gâteau au Chocolat

Cut cake in half horizontally. Spread base with chocolate butter cream, sandwich two halves together. Mask sides with butter cream and coat with chocolate vermicelle. Coat top of gâteau with melted chocolate, allow to set. Decorate with piped buttercream and chocolate curls/cut-outs or finely piped chocolate shapes

Coffee gâteau	Genoese sponge Coffee flavoured buttercream Toasted nibbed almonds	Gâteau Moka

Cut cake in half horizontally. Spread base with coffee buttercream. Sandwich two halves together. Mask sides with buttercream and coat with toasted nibbed almonds. Coat top with buttercream. Using a small plain tube and bag filled with buttercream, pipe the word 'moka' across the centre of the gâteau

Spring gâteau	Genoese sponge Vanilla buttercream Pale green buttercream Pale pink buttercream Nibbed almonds	Gâteau Printanière

Cut the cake into three slices horizontally. Spread base with green buttercream. Add middle slice of genoese and spread with pink buttercream. Place top slice of genoese in position, mask sides with vanilla buttercream and coat with nibbed almonds. Mask the top with vanilla buttercream and mark with the back of a knife into six or eight equal wedges to represent portions. Fill each wedge with small piped buttercream stars, alternating the colours around the gâteau

Black forest gâteau	Chocolate flavoured genoese sponge Crème Chantilly Chocolate shavings Black cherries (tinned or fresh/stoned) Kirsch	Gâteau Forêt Noir

Cut the cake in half horizontally. Sprinkle the base with kirsch then spread with Crème Chantilly. Arrange well drained cherries neatly on the cream. Spread with another layer of Crème Chantilly. Place top in position and sprinkle with kirsch. Mask top and sides with Crème Chantilly. Coat the sides with chocolate shavings and decorate the top with rosettes of cream and black cherries

Ice-cream gâteau	Genoese sponge Liqueur syrup (selected liqueur to suit) Iced-bombe mixtures (selected to suit) Whipped cream Selected coating for sides Selected decoration materials, e.g. glacé fruits/ nuts/chocolate	Gâteau Glacé

Cut the cake in half horizontally and moisten base with liqueur syrup. Cover with one or more even layers of selected ice-bombe mixtures, cap with remaining genoese and freeze. For service decorate sides/top as required

N.B. A japonaise base can be used to replace the sponge.

Examples of Gâteaux Prepared Using Miscellaneous Bases

English term	Ingredient and method	French term
	24–30 Small choux buns or profiteroles Crème Chantilly Boiled sugar, hard crack (155°C (310°F)) Spun sugar Circle of baked shortbread (18 cm (7 in) diameter) Crystallized violets	Croquembouche

Dip the tops of the baked profiteroles in boiled sugar. Allow to cool and set hard. Build a pyramid (around a cardboard or metal cone) with the profiteroles, sticking them together with boiled sugar. Allow to set, then remove cone. Fill centre of cone with Crème Chantilly, then place onto shortbread base and decorate with crystallized violets. Just prior to service, place a nest of spun sugar on the top to highlight

N.B. Alternatively the centre of the croquembouche may be filled with flavoured bavarois

	Strawberry flavoured bavarois 2 circles of baked shortbread (18 cm (7 in) diameter) Icing sugar Red piping jelly	Gâteau MacMahon

Mark shortbread circles into eight equal wedges prior to baking. Place a circle of shortbread into a flan ring/cake hoop of equal diameter. Fill with bavarois and allow to set. Divide remaining shortbread into 8 wedges. Sprinkle 4 wedges with icing sugar and spread 4 wedges with red piping jelly. Remove flan ring or hoop and arrange wedges of shortbread on top of the bavarois alternating the colours

	Choux pastry Puff pastry Crème St Honoré Crème Chantilly 12 small choux buns or profiteroles Boiled sugar, hard crack (155°C (310°F)) Spun sugar Glacé cherries Angelica	Gâteau St Honoré

Roll out puff pastry to form a circle 21 cm (8 in) diameter and prick all over with a fork or docker. Using a plain 14 mm (½ in) tube, pipe a ring of choux pastry on the edge of the puff pastry. Allow to rest, bake in a hot oven (215°C (420°F)) then cool. Fill choux buns with Crème Chantilly, then dip the tops in boiled sugar and position closely around the choux pastry ring securing with a blob of boiled sugar to form a crown. Fill centre of gateau with Crème St Honoré. Decorate buns with glacé cherries/angelica and finish with a nest of spun sugar in the centre of the gâteau

English term	*Ingredient and method*	*French term*
	1 Choux bun	Gâteau Religieuse
	10 Choux paste eclairs (10 cm (4 in) long, tapered)	
	Crème Chantilly	
	Chocolate bavarois (prepared in a bombe mould)	
	Circle of baked shortbread (18 cm (7 in) diameter)	
	Chocolate fondant	
	Coffee fondant	

Place shortbread on service dish. Demould bavarois and position in centre of shortbread. Fill eclairs and choux bun with Crème Chantilly, dip tops in fondant (5 eclairs chocolate/5 eclairs coffee/choux bun chocolate). Position eclairs upright around the bavarois, alternating the colours. Pipe Crème Chantilly between each eclair, pipe a large rosette of Crème Chantilly on top of the gâteau and decorate the top with the chocolate choux bun

32

Steamed and Baked Puddings

The plethora of popular British steamed/baked puddings which form an indispensible part of our indigenous diet are internationally renowned. As these puddings are of a substantial and warming nature, they are ideally suited to service on winter luncheon menus. Nutritionally they can be an important high-energy food for growing children and manually active adults. Choices range from simple steamed/baked sponge puddings to the more complex traditional Christmas pudding.

Ingredient/Production Principles

Essentially, two distinct types emerge, namely those produced by:

(a) Creamed/sugar batter mode of production, e.g. jam sponge pudding
(b) Rubbed in mode of production, e.g. steamed suet college pudding.

Sponge Puddings

Sponge-based steamed/baked puddings are aerated by a *combination* of mechanical (sugar batter methods) and chemical (baking powder) processes. Mechanical aeration denotes the incorporation of air when whisking or beating during the creaming of butter/sugar and incorporation of egg. As a guide, the egg content in the given recipe will aerate its own weight in flour. Chemical aeration involves the utilization of baking powder in moist/hot conditions to produce carbon dioxide gas (CO_2). The gas is trapped within the protein framework of the sponge batter and during cooking it expands causing the batter to rise/aerate until the product structure is set and of a light texture. The firm non-collapsible structure is essentially a result of protein coagulation and starch gelatinization within the product during the cooking process.

Soft flour is used because of its low gluten content. A flour of high gluten content would produce a tough coarse textured sponge.

In addition to the egg content, milk is also incorporated to produce a raw sponge batter of soft dropping consistency. Sufficient liquid is needed to allow for maximum aeration, to produce a light textured sponge and assist in the process of starch gelatinization.

Suet Puddings

Suet puddings based on the recipe given on p. 530 should be rich and relatively light. This type of pudding is mainly aerated by chemical means generally using baking powder (*see* sponge puddings above for detailed explanation). The introduction of fresh breadcrumbs serves to lighten the mixture by reducing the overall gluten content prior to cooking. The factors concerning the use of soft flour, the quantity of overall moisture used apply as for sponge puddings (*see* above).

Pudding Moulds/Basins/Sleeves/Dishes

The choice of respective cooking container will depend upon volume being produced, portion control requirements, style of service and equipment available. For types and preparation *see* pp. 528–9.

BASIC SPONGE PUDDING MIXTURE
(Sugar batter method/steamed or baked)

Yield: 8 portions
Steaming times: basins/sleeves 1½–2 hr/small dariole 30 min
Baking time: 30–40 min

Unit	Ingredient	Metric	Imperial
1	Soft flour	200 g	8 oz
⅝	Butter/margarine	125 g	5 oz
⅝	Caster sugar	125 g	5 oz
⅝	Whole egg/beaten (strained)	125 ml	5 fl oz
¼	Milk	50 ml	2 fl oz
1/16	Baking powder	12.5 g	½ oz

Method

Beat fat/sugar together to a light creamy texture (having the ingredients at room temperature facilitates this process) and scrape down. Now beat in a quarter of the egg until clear and scrape down. Continue to beat in each quarter of egg as above until fully incorporated and clear (scrape down after each beating). Sift flour and baking powder together *3* times to distribute and blend together evenly. Carefully *fold* sifted flour into the creamed sugar batter and *do not overmix*. At this stage incorporate sufficient milk to form a soft dropping consistency.

1. For steamed sponges only

Basins: Grease well, three-quarters fill with respective mixture, cover to secure with pleated greased greaseproof paper and steam for 1½ to 2 hours as required.
Sleeves: Grease well, line base of sleeve with a strip of greased greaseproof paper, three-quarters fill with respective mixture, enclose with sleeve lid and steam 1½–2 hours.
Darioles: Grease well, three-quarters fill with respective mixture, cover with sheet of greased greaseproof paper to protect fully and steam for 30–40 minutes.
Service of steamed sponges: Turn out onto hot service vessel whole or portioned with appropriate accompanying sauce (*see* chart below).

2. For baked sponges only

Pie dishes: Grease well, three-quarters fill with respective mixture and bake until cooked and golden. Turn out if required according to recipe, portion and serve with appropriate accompanying sauce (*see* chart below).

Steamed/Baked Sponge Puddings Using Above Formula: Added Ingredients in Relation to 1 Unit 240 g (8 oz) Soft Flour

Pudding	Unit	Ingredient	Metric	Imperial	Sauce/hot
Vanilla		1 Teaspoon vanilla essence Add to basic mixture to flavour			Vanilla or custard
Lemon/castle		Juice/finely grated zest of 2 lemons Incorporate thoroughly with the basic mixture			Lemon
Orange		As for lemon but using orange zest/juice			Orange
Chocolate	¼	Cocoa powder Substitute 50 g (2 oz) of flour with cocoa powder	50 g	2 oz	Chocolate
Ginger	⅛ ¹⁄₁₆	Preserved ginger/finely diced Powdered ginger Sift powdered ginger with flour. Add diced preserved ginger just before placing mix into mould	25 g 12.5 g	1 oz ½ oz	Custard
Coconut	¼	Desiccated coconut Fold-in to basic mixture after the flour and adjust to dropping consistency with the milk	50 g	2 oz	Jam
Fruit	½	Currants/sultanas/raisins (washed and dried) Roll fruit lightly through some flour and fold-in to basic mixture just before moulding N.B. If using raisins chop into small pieces	100 g	4 oz	Custard
Cherry	½	Glacé cherries/chopped almond essence to taste Flavour basic mixture with a few drops of almond essence and fold-in cherries just before moulding	100 g	4 oz	Almond or custard
Pineapple	¼	Pineapple/chopped Place an even layer of pineapple over the base of the pudding moulds before filling with basic sponge mix	50 g	2 oz	Custard or pineapple

Pudding	Unit	Ingredient	Metric	Imperial	Sauce/hot
Jam		Selected jam Spread a layer of jam evenly over the bottom of the pudding moulds before filling with the basic sponge mix			Jam
Golden		Golden syrup Spread a layer of syrup evenly over the bottom of the pudding moulds before filling with the basic sponge mix			Golden syrup
Canary		Lemon curd Spread a layer of lemon curd evenly over the bottom of the pudding moulds before filling with the basic sponge mix			Custard (lemon flavoured)

Eve's Pudding (baked)

Yield: 8 portions
Baking time: 40 min
Baking temperature: 190°C (375°F)

Method

Cover the base of a buttered pie dish generously with a filling made up of prepared sliced baking apples which have been flavoured with lemon juice/finely grated rind, and sweetened with apricot jam. Fill the remainder of the pie dish with basic sponge mixture, *see* p. 528, making sure to completely cover the apple preparation. Bake until cooked and golden, remove from oven, clean edge of pie dish, dust with icing sugar, surround with pie collar and present for service with hot custard sauce.

BASIC STEAMED SUET PUDDING MIXTURE (rubbed-in method)

Yield: 6–8 portions
Steaming times: 2–2½ hr

Unit	Ingredient	Metric	Imperial
1*	Soft flour and fresh breadcrumbs (equal flour to breadcrumbs)	200 g	8 oz
⅝†	Milk	125 ml	5 fl oz
½	Suet/prepared chopped	100 g	4 oz
¼	Caster sugar	50 g	2 oz
¼	Whole egg/beaten	50 g	2 oz
¹⁄₁₆	Baking powder	10 g	½ oz

* The combination of equal parts flour and fresh breadcrumbs produces a lighter pudding than when using flour only.

† Sufficient to form a mixture of dropping consistency.

Method

Sift flour, salt, baking powder two or three times for even distribution and place into a mixing bowl. Add all remaining *dry* ingredients as applicable (see chart below for additional ingredients/instructions). Moisten with beaten egg and sufficient milk to form a mixture of dropping consistency.

PUDDING BASINS/SLEEVES: prepared as for basic sponge pudding mixture, p. 528

Steamed Suet Puddings Using Above Formula: Added Ingredients in Relation to 1 Unit 200 g (8 oz) Flour/Breadcrumbs

Pudding	Unit	Ingredient	Metric	Imperial	Sauce
Coconut	¼	Coconut/desiccated Combine with dry ingredients	50 g	2 oz	Jam

College	¼
	¼
	¹⁄₁₆
		Raisins
		Sultanas
		Candied peel/chopped level
		   teaspoon mixed spice
		Sift mixed spice with flour, etc. and combine
		   fruit with dry ingredients
			50 g
			50 g
			10 g
				2 oz
				2 oz
				½ oz
					Custard

Date	½	Dates/stoned and chopped
		1 Tablespoon golden syrup
		Pinched mixed spice
		Sift mixed spice with flour, etc. Add dates with
		   dry ingredients
		Warm syrup and add with egg/milk
		N.B. Soft brown sugar may be used to replace
		   caster sugar
			10 g	2 oz	Custard

Golden layered		Golden syrup as required
		Layer base of pudding basin/sleeve with syrup,
		   add half basic mixture and repeat finishing
		   with the mixture
					Syrup

Jam layered		Selected jam As for golden layered pudding but using jam			Jam
Lemon or Orange		Grated rind of 1 lemon/orange Combine with dry ingredients			Lemon or orange
Fig	½	Dried figs/chopped Pinch ground ginger Grated rind of 1 small lemon Sift ginger with flour, etc. Combine with all dry ingredients	100 g	4 oz	Custard or syrup

Pudding	Unit	Ingredient	Metric	Imperial	Sauce
Fruit	¼	Raisins	50 g	2 oz	Custard
	¼	Sultanas	50 g	2 oz	
		Combine with dry ingredients			
Ginger	⅛	Golden syrup or treacle	25 ml	1 fl oz	Syrup
		1 Teaspoon ground ginger			
		Sift ground ginger with flour, etc. to incorporate			
		Warm the syrup or treacle and mix with the beaten egg and milk			

N.B.   Other suitable puddings can be created from the basic formula, e.g. marmalade, lemon curd, etc.

CHRISTMAS PUDDING   Pouding Noël

Yield: 25 portions
Steaming times: 450 g (1 lb) for 4 hr
                800 g (2 lb) for 6 hr
                1.6 g (4 lb) for 8 hr

Unit	Ingredient	Metric	Imperial
	Dry:		
1	Sultanas, raisins, currants, chopped peel	1 kg	2½ lb
¼	Beef suet/chopped	250 g	10 oz
¼	Breadcrumbs	250 g	10 oz
¼	Apples/peeled/chopped	250 g	10 oz
⅕	Brown sugar	200 g	8 oz
⅛	Plain flour	125 g	5 oz
¹⁄₄₀	Ground almonds	25 g	1 oz
¹⁄₄₀	Crystallised ginger	25 g	1 oz
	1 Teaspoon mixed spice to flavour		
	1 Level teaspoon salt to taste		
	Moist:		
⅛	Stout ale	125 ml	5 fl oz
⅛	Whole egg/beaten	125 ml	5 fl oz
¹⁄₄₀	Rum/Brandy	25 ml	1 fl oz
¹⁄₄₀	Madeira	25 ml	1 fl oz
¹⁄₄₀	Sherry	25 ml	1 fl oz
	Juice/zest of 1 orange and 1 lemon		

Method

Sift flour, salt and mixed spice together two or three times. Combine with all remaining dry ingredients, mix well and form a bay. Combine all moist ingredients and mix well. Pour the prepared liquid into the bay of dry materials and stir thoroughly to form a uniform mixture. Allow the mixture to stand at least overnight or for approximately 1 week to develop flavour and mature.

Prepare some well-greased pudding basins and fill with the pudding mixture. Cover with greased greaseproof paper, then with foil or pudding cloth. Secure with string. Steam for 4–8 hours according to size of pudding (*see* above for times). On completion remove from the steamer, allow to cool, remove cloth/foil, clean basin then using clean pudding cloth or foil tie-up as before. Store in a cool dry clean place for safe hygienic storage.

Re-heating and service: Steam for a further 2–3 hours as required by weight of pudding, turn-out onto presentation dish, flame with rum or brandy and serve with appropriate sauce, e.g. rum sauce, brandy sauce, custard sauce, sabayon sauce.

Individual portions of pudding can be readily re-heated via the microwave oven according to manufacturers' guidelines. In this case the second steaming/reheating process can be ignored.

33

Fermented/Fermented Laminated Goods

A basic understanding of commodities, processes and methods is required in order to produce quality fermented goods. The following notes outline some of the basic principles.

Commodity Factors

Strong flour is typically used in the production of fermented goods because of its high *gluten* forming potential (formed in conjunction with the proteins when the water component is added). The development of this gluten provides the required elasticity in the dough. During bulk fermentation, the dough stretches as the carbon dioxide gas produced is trapped within the expanding structure. On cooking, the protein gluten eventually coagulates, ceases to expand and sets to form a shaped/stable product.

Yeast is a living unicellular fungi plant/micro-organism which under suitable conditions reproduces rapidly, converting sugars into carbon dioxide gas and alcohol. This form of organic (panary) aeration is used to great advantage in the production of a wide variety of fermented goods. When used in excess, yeast can adversely affect both flavour and texture by leading to yeasty porous products.

Temperature gradients are also critical for reproduction/growth of yeast during fermentation. Cold temperatures inhibit growth, whereas high temperatures, e.g. 49°C (120°F) kill off/destroy active yeast.

Reproduction Factors

To reproduce itself and give off CO_2/alcohol yeast requires four conditions:

1. Warmth. Ideal temperatures for reproduction/fermentation purposes are 25–28°C (76–82°F).
2. Sugar. Sugar is the principal food required by yeast. This is obtained by direct addition in recipes and by the ability of yeast to convert the starch present into sugar.
3. Moisture. Present in the recipe in the form of water/milk/eggs.
4. Oxygen. Essentially introduced during mixing and knocking-back stages to invigorate the yeast and allow fermentation to continue.

Salt is commonly present in recipes as a seasoning/flavouring agent. However, in the case of fermented goods it also acts to regulate the fermentation process and strengthen/stabilize the gluten content.

N.B. Excessive amounts of salt will retard the reproduction of yeast resulting in inedible and poorly aerated goods.

Fat has a shortening effect upon gluten which helps produce a fine textured crumb in finished products; fat used in excess leads to crumbliness. Where recipes require a relatively high content (as for example in savarin dough) the fat component is generally added after bulk fermentation has taken place so as not to inhibit gluten development or fermentation.

Production Factors

Throughout the making of bread and other fermented yeast goods, specific technical jargon is used to describe the various stages of production. Each stage plays an important role in the production cycle. The principal stages are briefly explained and outlined in the notes following:

Stage	*Functions*

1. *Dough-making, mixing and kneading*	(a) To develop even dough temperature/O.T. throughout (approximately 27°C (80°F)) to encourage yeast fermentation.
	 (b) To aid in the development/formation of gluten; during mixing the soluble ingredients combine with water whilst the insoluble proteins in the flour become hydrated and form *gluten*.
	 (c) Mixing and kneading aid in:
	   (i) Gluten development (dough elasticity).
	   (ii) Texture development (dough becomes softer and smooth).
	   (iii) Development of CO_2 gas and alcohol formed from the naturally present sugars.
	   (iv) The incorporation of gas into the dough.
	   (v) The even distribution of yeast and other ingredients throughout the dough which allows for a maximum supply of food for the yeast.
	   (vi) The even distribution of salt throughout the dough helps to give a measure of stability to dough structure because of the salt's stabilising effects on gluten.

2. *B.F.T. (bulk fermentation time)* The dough approximately doubles its original size during rising If over-fermented at this stage the dough will collapse. B.F.T. is carried out in warm, moist conditions	(a) Produce CO_2 which *aerates* the dough during the fermentation process. (b) To aid the development of *dough* 'quality' before the baking takes place. Enzymic action brings this about during fermentation as the yeast feeds off the natural sugars present together with sugars from the starch. The yeast then produces CO_2 and alcohol. (c) To provide and generate warm conditions ideal for multiplication of yeast cells and enzymic action throughout the dough during B.F.T. *see* p. 534. (d) To improve the elasticity of the dough by further developing and softening of the gluten content.

Stage	Functions
K.B. (knocking-back) This process is carried out half-way through B.F.T. If over-done, the dough structure can be irreparably damaged and the gluten's resilience lost. After the K.B. period, the dough is allowed to relax and become inflated with gas again ready for the next stages	(a) To expel the CO_2 which escapes as the dough structure collapses. (b) To *reduce* the *volume* of the dough and provide a dough of *closer texture* by reducing the size of aerated pockets within the dough structure. (c) To develop an even temperature throughout the dough. (d) To maintain dough quality and gluten development. (e) To allow for the entry of air to invigorate the yeast.
3. *Scaling off and moulding*	(a) To weigh-off goods at required product weight. (b) To shape the goods to a given specification. (c) To cause partial expulsion of the CO_2 gas, a closing of the dough texture by reducing the dough volume and assist in the final crumb structure.
4. *Proving* This stage is carried out in controlled warm and moist conditions	(a) To allow the dough pieces to expand before baking. (b) To provide ideal conditions for a rapid generation of CO_2. (c) To develop the correct shape, volume and texture in the dough pieces prior to baking. (d) To prevent skinning, surface defects, dulled appearance, uneven expansion and mis-shapen goods. (e) To allow the gluten structure to recover from the stresses and strains of moulding.
5. *Baking*	(a) To cause an initial rapid increase in yeast and enzyme activity. (b) To destroy the yeast activity around $49°C$ ($120°F$) (c) To encourage further enzyme activity/sugar production which in turn sweetens the crumb and also caramelizes at the surface to effect crust colour and appearance. (d) To generate steam/alcohol vapour pressure which aids expansion within the gluten structure. (e) To enable starch to gelatinise (gel) and proteins to coagulate thus providing a digestible (cooked) product of a stable structure.
6. *Cooling*	(a) To allow rapid cooling and prevent formation of moulds and *rope*. (b) To allow for evaporation of steam from the baked item. (c) To encourage the development of rigidity in the final texture.

Another stage may be involved according to the methods used and the products being made, namely:

A ferment, where liquid is added to the yeast, often with other ingredients, under conditions designed to encourage a rapid fermentation (a ferment) before the addition of the bulk of the flour in the mixing. A ferment has the appearance of a light fermenting batter. This technique can be applied when producing rich dough mixtures, e.g. bun dough.

BREAD ROLLS

Yield: 16–18 at 50 g (2 oz) scale-off
Bulk fermentation time: 1 hr
Baking time: 10–15 min
Baking temperature: 232°C (450°F)

Unit	Ingredient.	Metric	Imperial
1	Strong flour	600 g	20 oz
$\frac{5}{8}$	Water 27°C (80°F)★	375 ml	12½ fl oz
$\frac{1}{20}$	Yeast	30 g	1 oz
$\frac{1}{40}$	Lard	15 g	½ oz
$\frac{1}{40}$	Milk powder	15 g	½ oz
$\frac{1}{40}$	Sugar	15 g	½ oz
$\frac{1}{80}$	Salt (good pinch)	8 g	¼ oz
	Egg wash		

★ The amount of water may vary slightly according to the water absorption rate of the flour.

Method (straight dough)

Sift flour, salt, milk powder together, rub in the fat content and form a bay. Combine yeast with three-quarters of the water, add sugar and mix until dissolved. Pour into bay and commence mixing/forming the dough whilst adding the remaining water as required. Knead thoroughly to form a smooth elastic well developed dough. Cover with a damp cloth and stand in a warm place for the required B.F.T. period. Halfway through B.F.T. knock-back (knead) gently then allow fermentation to continue until dough has doubled in size. Knock-back, divide into 50 g (2 oz) pieces, mould round and place onto slightly greased baking sheets. Prove in a warm, moist atmosphere until doubled in size, brush with egg-wash then bake in a pre-heated oven. Remove from oven and cool on a wire rack.

BROWN BREAD ROLLS

Proceed as for white bread rolls but make up the 1 unit flour (i.e. 600 g (20 oz)) with equal quantities of strong white and wholemeal flours, namely 300 g (10 oz) strong white flour combined with 300 g (10 oz) wholemeal flour.

N.B. For even distribution blend flours together thoroughly once the white flour, salt and milk powder have been first sifted together as indicated in the method.

BUN DOUGH

Yield: 16–18 buns at 50 g (2 oz) scale-off
Bulk fermentation time: 1 hr
Cooking time: 10–20 min
Baking temperature: 225°C (440°F)
Frying temperature: (dough nuts) 195°C (380°F)

Unit	Ingredients	Metric	Imperial
1	Strong flour	400 g	1 lb
$\frac{5}{8}$	Milk	250 ml	10 fl oz
$\frac{1}{8}$	Butter	50 g	2 oz
$\frac{1}{8}$	Egg	50 ml	2 fl oz
$\frac{1}{16}$	Caster sugar	25 g	1 oz
$\frac{1}{16}$	Yeast	25 g	1 oz
$\frac{1}{64}$	Salt (good pinch)	6 g	$\frac{1}{4}$ oz

Method (straight dough)

Prepare dough as for bread rolls, *see* p. 537. Cover with a damp cloth and stand in a warm place for the required B.F.T. period. Halfway through B.F.T. knock-back (knead) gently, then allow fermentation to continue until dough has doubled in size. Use as required (*see* chart below).

Extensions of Bun Dough: Added Ingredients in Relation to 1 Unit, 400 g (1 lb) flour

Name	Unit	Ingredient	Metric	Imperial
Bath buns	$\frac{1}{4}$	Sultanas	100 g	4 oz
	$\frac{1}{8}$	Mixed peel	50 g	2 oz
	$\frac{1}{8}$	Nib sugar	50 g	2 oz
	★	Bun glaze/wash		

Add sultanas and mixed peel to basic mixture. After final knock-back, scale-off into 50 g (2 oz) pieces and shape into rough rounds. Place onto a lightly greased baking sheet, sprinkle with nib sugar. Prove in a warm, moist atmosphere, then bake in a pre-heated oven. Remove from oven and whilst still hot brush with bun glaze

Chelsea buns	$\frac{1}{4}$	Caster sugar	100 g	4 oz
	$\frac{1}{4}$	Sultanas	100 g	4 oz
	$\frac{1}{8}$	Currants	50 g	2 oz
	$\frac{1}{8}$	Mixed peel	50 g	2 oz
	$\frac{1}{8}$	Butter (melted)	50 g	2 oz
		Ground nutmeg to flavour		
	★	Bun wash/glaze		

Roll out basic bun dough to form a rectangle approximately 60 cm (24 in) by 30 cm (12 in). Sprinkle with a mixture of caster sugar/nutmeg, sultanas, currants, mixed peel. Roll up swiss-roll fashion, brush with butter, then cut into sixteen 3.5 cm ($1\frac{1}{2}$ in) slices. Place onto a lightly greased baking sheet, prove, bake and finish as for bath buns

Cream buns/Devonshire splits		Double cream/whipped		
		Strawberry jam		
		Icing sugar		

Divide dough into 50 g (2 oz) pieces, mould round and place onto a lightly greased baking sheet. Prove/bake as for bath buns and allow to cool. Split open, pipe in a bulb of strawberry jam, fill with whipped fresh cream and dust with icing sugar

Name	Unit	Ingredient	Metric	Imperial
Doughnuts		Raspberry jam		
		Caster sugar		
		Cinnamon		

Divide dough into 50 g (2 oz) pieces, mould round. Insert thumb and form a centre cavity, fill cavity with raspberry jam, seal and re-mould to round shape. Prove on a well oiled tray and in a warm, moist atmosphere. Deep fry until cooked and golden brown. Drain well, allow to cool then roll in caster sugar flavoured with a pinch of cinnamon

Name	Unit	Ingredient	Metric	Imperial
Fruit buns	⅛	Currants	50 g	2 oz
	⅛	Sultanas	50 g	2 oz
	⅛	Mixed peel	50 g	2 oz
		Mixed spice (good pinch)		
	*	Bun glaze/wash		

Add mixed spice, peel, currants and sultanas to basic mixture. After final knock-back, divide into 50 g (2 oz) pieces, mould round and place onto a lightly greased baking sheet. Prove in a warm, moist atmosphere then bake in a pre-heated oven. Remove from oven and brush with bun glaze/wash whilst still hot

Name	Unit	Ingredient	Metric	Imperial
Currant buns	¼	Currants	100 g	4 oz
	*	Bun glaze/wash		

Add currants to basic mixture, then proceed as for fruit buns

Name	Unit	Ingredient	Metric	Imperial
Hot cross buns	⅛	Flour	50 g	2 oz
	⅛	Currants	50 g	2 oz
	⅛	Sultanas	50 g	2 oz
	⅛	Mixed peel	50 g	2 oz
		Mixed spice (good pinch)		
	*	Bun glaze/wash		

Proceed as for fruit buns. Mix sufficient water with the flour to form a piping batter. Prior to proving, pipe a cross on each bun. Prove, bake and finish as for fruit buns

Name	Unit	Ingredient	Metric	Imperial
Swiss/iced buns		Water icing (*see* p. 646)		

Divide dough into 50 g (2 oz) pieces, mould to form finger shapes 10 cm (4 in) long. Prove and bake as for fruit buns. Allow to cool then dip tops in water icing
N.B.   Water icing may be coloured and/or flavoured as required

* Bun glaze/wash boil together equal quantities of sugar and water to form a light syrup. Brush buns whilst still hot to glaze.

DANISH PASTRY   Pâte Danoise

Yield: approx. 30 pieces
Baking time: 10–15 min
Baking temperature: 232°C (450°F)

Unit	Ingredient	Metric	Imperial
1	Medium flour	400 g	1 lb
⅝	Butter	250 g	10 oz
⅜	Milk	150 g	6 oz
¼	Egg	100 g	4 oz
¹⁄₁₆	Yeast	25 g	1 oz
¹⁄₁₆	Sugar	25 g	1 oz
	Good pinch salt		
	Apricot glaze		
	Water icing		

Method

Sift flour and salt together, combine yeast with liquid (egg and milk), add sugar and mix until dissolved. Combine flour and liquid to form a dough, do not over mix/toughen. Roll out dough 1 cm (⅜ in) thick and twice as long as wide, keeping the corners square. Disperse butter evenly over two-thirds of rolled-out dough. Leave outer edges and remaining one-third of dough clear. Fold the clear one-third onto half of covered portion and fold over once more to form two fat and three dough layers. Press down to secure edges. Roll out and fold again into three as previously described. At this stage, one half-turn has been completed. Repeat rolling and folding process twice more (3 half-turns in total) allowing pastry to rest and relax between each turn. Rest pastry for 20–30 minutes before use.

N.B. *See* p. 495 for illustrated diagrams showing folding techniques.

Prepare Danish pastries (*see* chart below), place onto baking sheets and prove in a warm, moist atmosphere until doubled in size. Bake in a pre-heated oven until cooked. Remove from the oven, brush with hot apricot glaze and water icing to decorate.

DANISH PASTRIES (typical basic examples):

Crème pâtissiere (*see* p. 648)
Mincemeat
Frangipane (*see* p. 648)
Chopped ginger (peel and chop)
Sliced apple (peel, core, slice)
Mixed dried fruit (currants, sultanas, mixed peel, chopped glace cherries)

Examples of Danish Pastries Prepared Using Basic Pastry and Various Selected Fillings: Prove, Bake and Finish as in Method Above

Name	Selected filling and added ingredients
Danish custards	Crème pâtisserie

Roll-out pastry to form a rectangle 6 mm (¼ in) thick and cut into 10 cm (4 in) *squares*. Fold two opposite corners into the centre thus forming two pockets. Prior to proving/baking fill each open-end with a bulb of creme pâtisserie

Name	Selected filling and added ingredients
Pin wheels	Mixed dried fruit Cinnamon

Roll-out the pastry to form a rectangle 6 mm (¼ in) thick and 25 cm (10 in) wide. Sprinkle with mixed dried fruit and cinnamon. Roll up swiss-roll fashion, cut into slices approximately 2.5 cm (1 in) thick

1. Flatten slightly and place disc-like onto a baking sheet (Catherine wheels)
2. Make one cut horizontally through the slice leaving the outer layer of pastry intact, then open-up like a fan
3. Make two cuts horizontally through the slice leaving the outer layer of dough intact, then open-up like a fan

Crescents	Mincemeat or frangipane

Roll out the pastry to form a strip 6 mm (¼ in) thick and 20 cm (8 in) wide. Cut the strip into triangles with a 10 cm (4 in) base. Place filling onto the base edge, then roll the triangle up to enclose the filling and form a crescent-like cigar shape (as for croissants, *see* p. 542).

Danish apple slice	Sliced apple Egg-wash Caster sugar

Roll out the pastry to form a strip 6 mm (¼ in) thick and 10 cm (4 in) wide. Cut into 4 cm (1½ in) fingers. Brush with egg-wash then arrange overlapping apple slices on top of each finger. Sprinkle with caster sugar

Bears' paws	Mincemeat or frangipane Nibbed almonds Egg-wash

Roll out the pastry to form a rectangle 6 mm (¼ in) thick and 8 cm (3¼ in) wide. Place filling along the centre of the strip. Egg-wash along one edge, then fold over and seal. Cut into 8 cm (3¼ in) lengths. Make incisions along the sealed edge at 6 mm (¼ in) intervals to form paws. Shape like a crescent so that the incisions/paws open. Brush with egg-wash and sprinkle with nibbed almonds

Ginger cuts	Chopped ginger Caster sugar Nibbed almonds Egg-wash

Roll out the pastry to form a rectangle 6 mm (¼ in) thick and 8 cm (3¼ in) wide. Brush with egg-wash then sprinkle with caster sugar and ginger along the length of the strip. Fold over and seal, cut into 8 cm (3¼ in) lengths, brush with egg-wash and sprinkle with nibbed almonds

Almond slice	Frangipane Nibbed almonds Egg-wash

Proceed as for ginger cuts, but fill with frangipane

Many other varieties of Danish pastry can be prepared according to requirements.

CROISSANTS

Yield: 18
Cooking time: 10–15 min
Cooking temperature: 232°C (450°F)

Unit	Ingredient	Metric	Imperial
1	Flour/medium	400 g	1 lb
5/8	Water	250 ml	10 fl oz
1/2	Butter/Pastry margarine	200 g	8 oz
1/16	Yeast	25 g	1 oz
1/16	Milk powder	25 g	1 oz
1/32	Sugar	12 g	1/2 oz
1/64	Salt (good pinch)	6 g	1/4 oz

Method

Sift flour, salt and milk powder together and form a bay. Combine yeast with water, add sugar and mix until fully dissolved. Pour into bay, combine/mix ingredients together and knead thoroughly to form a smooth elastic well-developed dough. Cover with a damp cloth and allow to rest for 15–20 minutes. Proceed as for Danish pastry dough until 3 half-turns have been completed and allow to rest for 20–30 minutes.

Roll-out pastry into a strip 6 mm (¼ in) thick and 20 cm (8 in) wide. Cut the strip into triangles with a 10 cm (4 in) base. Starting at the base, roll the triangles into cigar-like forms then shape into crescents. Place onto baking sheets, brush with egg-wash and prove in a warm moist atmosphere until doubled in size. Bake in a pre-heated oven until cooked, remove and place onto a wire rack to cool.

BRIDGE ROLLS

Yield: approx. 25/30 at 25 g (1 oz) scale-off
Bulk fermentation time: 1 hr
Baking time: 10–12 min
Baking temperature: 232°C (450°F)

Unit	Ingredient	Metric	Imperial
1	Strong flour	400 g	1 lb
5/10	Milk (27°C (80°F))	125 ml	5 fl oz
1/4	Egg	100 ml	4 fl oz
1/8	Butter	50 g	2 oz
1/16	Yeast	25 g	1 oz
1/32	Sugar	12.5 g	1/2 oz
1/64	Salt (good pinch)	6 g	1/4 oz

Method (straight dough)

Prepare dough as for bread rolls, *see* p. 537. Cover with a damp cloth and stand in a warm place for one hour (B.F.T.). Halfway through the B.F.T. knock-back (knead) gently, then allow fermentation to continue until dough has doubled in size. Knock-back gently, scale-off into 25 g (1 oz) pieces and mould into cigar shapes. Place onto a lightly greased baking sheet and prove in a warm moist atmosphere until doubled in size. Brush with egg-wash, bake in a pre-heated oven, remove and cool on wire rack.

BRIOCHE

Yield: approx. 25 at 25 g (1 oz) scale-off
Bulk fermentation time: 5–6 hr
Baking time: 10–15 min
Baking temperature: 235°C (450°F)

Unit	Ingredient	Metric	Imperial
1	Strong flour	250 g	10 oz
$^6/_{10}$	Egg/beaten lightly	150 g	6 oz
$^1/_2$	Butter/soft	125 g	5 oz
$^2/_{10}$	Milk (27°C (80°F))	50 ml	2 fl oz
$^1/_{10}$	Yeast	25 g	1 oz
$^1/_{20}$	Sugar	12 g	$^1/_2$ oz
$^1/_{40}$	Salt (good pinch)	6 g	$^1/_4$ oz

Method

Dissolve yeast in the warm milk, add 25 g (1 oz) of the flour, mix to form a batter and allow to ferment in a warm place. Combine the remaining flour, salt, sugar and sieve together into a mixing bowl. Add the ferment (yeast batter), beaten eggs and mix thoroughly to form a smooth dough. Now fully incorporate/beat-in the softened butter, cover with a damp cloth and stand in a *very cool* place for 5–6 hours (B.F.T.). Knock-back gently, divide into 25 g (1 oz) pieces and mould each to represent small cottage loaves.

Place into well-buttered/floured brioche or fluted cake tins and prove in a warm moist atmosphere until doubled in size. Brush with egg-wash, bake in a pre-heated oven, remove and turn-out to cool on wire rack.

SAVARIN PASTE   Pâte à Savarin

Yield: 2 (according to size of mould)
Bulk fermentation time: 45 min
Baking time: 10–30 min
Baking temperature: 232°C (450°F)

Unit	Ingredient	Metric	Imperial
1	Strong flour	200 g	8 oz
$^5/_8$	Egg/beaten lightly	125 g	5 oz
$^1/_2$	Butter (melted)	100 g	4 oz
$^1/_4$	Milk	25 ml	1 fl oz
$^1/_{16}$	Yeast	12.5 g	$^1/_2$ oz
$^1/_{16}$	Caster sugar	12.5 g	$^1/_2$ oz
$^1/_{32}$	Salt (good pinch)	6 g	$^1/_4$ oz
	Apricot glaze*		
	Syrup for savarins/babas*, *see* pp. 646–7		

* Sufficient to dip and glaze the finished products.

Method

Sift flour and salt together, blend yeast with liquid (egg, milk), add sugar and mix until dissolved. Combine ingredients together and beat well to form a smooth/soft elastic dough. Cover with a damp cloth and stand in a warm place for 40 minutes (B.F.T.). Now beat-in the melted butter and pipe dough into well greased/floured moulds to third full. Allow to prove in a warm atmosphere until doubled in size, then bake in a pre-heated oven. Remove from oven, de-mould and allow to cool. When cold, soak in hot flavoured stock syrup, *see* p. 646–7 to fully moisten, allow to cool and brush with apricot glaze. Decorate for service as required (*see* chart below).

Examples of Sweets Prepared Using Savarin Paste

Name	Unit	Added ingredients	Metric	Imperial
Baba au Rhum	¼	Currants	50 g	2 oz
Rum baba	⅛	Dark rum	25 ml	1 fl oz
		Crème Chantilly		
		Glacé cherries		
		Angelica		

Add currants to savarin paste. Third fill well greased dariole moulds and bake as above. Soak in hot syrup that has been flavoured with rum, *see* p. 647. Allow to cool, brush with apricot glaze, decorate with piped Crème Chantilly, glacé cherries and angelica

Croûtes aux Fruits		Fruit salad		
Fruit croûtes		(*see* p. 627)		
		Icing sugar		
		Crème Chantilly		
		Glacé cherries		
		Angelica		

Bake savarin paste in a well greased charlotte mould or bread tin. When cold, cut into even slices 1 cm (½ in) thick, dust liberally with icing sugar and glaze in a hot oven or under the salamander. Arrange the slices in an overlapping fashion around service dish, fill the centre with fruit salad and brush fruit with apricot glaze. Decorate with piped Crème Chantilly, glacé cherries and angelica

Croûtes a l'Ananas		8 Slices fresh/tinned		
Pineapple croûtes		pineapple		
		Icing sugar		
		Crème Chantilly		
		Glace cherries		
		Angelica		

Bake, slice and glaze with icing sugar as for fruit croûtes (*see* above). Decorate each croûte with a slice of pineapple and arrange in overlapping fashion on the presentation dish. Brush with apricot glaze, decorate with piped crème Chantilly, glacé cherries and angelica
N.B.   Other fruit croûtes may be prepared, e.g. peach, banana, apricot, etc.

Marignans Chantilly		Crème Chantilly		
		Glacé cherries		
		Angelica		

Name	Unit	Added ingredients	Metric	Imperial

Bake savarin paste in small well greased barquette (boat-shaped) moulds. When cold soak in hot flavoured syrup, *see* pp. 646–7 to moisten fully, slit top of marignan open and brush with apricot glaze. Fill with piped Crème Chantilly, decorate with glacé cherries and angelica

Marignans au Rhum

Proceed as for Marignans Chantilly, but soak in hot, rum flavoured syrup, *see* p. 647 to moisten fully prior to glazing and decorating

Savarin aux Fruits	Fruit salad
Fruit savarin	Crème Chantilly

Bake paste in a savarin mould. When cold, soak in hot flavoured syrup, *see* pp. 646–7 to fully moisten and brush with apricot glaze. Place on a round service dish and fill centre cavity with fruit salad. Brush fruit with apricot glaze and decorate with piped Crème Chantilly

34

Milk Puddings

Hot milk pudding varieties are a popular substantial sweet whether served in their own right or when presented with other appropriate ingredients such as stewed fruits or jam. Milk of course adds considerably to the nutritive value of the starch-rich (cereal based) milk puddings in terms of added protein, calcium and vitamins. These puddings are enjoyed at all levels of catering, by all age groups and in all walks of life from growing children to grandparents.

Ingredient/Production Principles

The starch, rich cereals and pasta used for milk puddings, namely rice, tapioca, sago, semolina, short macaroni and vermicelle are typically bland in flavour. However when blended and cooked with other ingredients such as milk, sugar, vanilla essence, nutmeg and butter, these basic materials take on agreeable pleasant flavours. The smooth, moderately thickened consistency of the puddings is largely due to the gelatinization of starch which takes place during cooking. Liquid penetration and the generation of steam within the cereal causes the starch granules to swell, burst and release their starch content; this in turn proportionately thickens the liquid milk content. As a rule 1 unit milk will be adequately thickened by $\frac{1}{8}/\frac{1}{10}$ unit cereal/pasta for milk puddings but adjustments can be made to consistency during the final stages of the cooking process. It is worth noting also that short grained carolina rice is preferred for the making of rice pudding as it releases its starch readily, and has a high liquid absorbing capacity.

Baking and boiling methods are used in the production of these types of pudding for both small and large-scale proportions. When the boiling method is adopted the pudding must be stirred frequently to prevent clogging/sticking and burning. Cooking in a double boiler is a technique sometimes used to minimize these problems. Egg yolks which are sometimes added to enrich milk puddings are incorporated just before serving/glazing.

BAKED RICE PUDDING   Pouding au Riz à l'Anglaise

Yield: 4 portions
Cooking time: 1½–2 hr
Cooking temperature: 150°C (300°F)

Unit	Ingredient	Metric	Imperial
1	Milk	600 ml	20 fl oz
$\frac{1}{10}$	Carolina rice (short grain)	60 g	2 oz
$\frac{1}{10}$	Caster sugar	60 g	2 oz
$\frac{1}{20}$	Butter	30 g	1 oz
	Vanilla essence		
	Pinch of nutmeg		

Method

Wash rice and place in a pie dish. Add the sugar, milk and mix well. Flavour with vanilla essence, sprinkle with nutmeg and finish with knobs of butter. Bake in a moderate oven until the rice is cooked and the top is golden brown. Clean the rim of the pie dish and present on a service flat with doily.

BOILED CEREAL/PASTA MILK PUDDINGS

Yield: 4 portions
Cooking time: 45 min–1 hr

Unit	Ingredient	Metric	Imperial
1	Milk	600 ml	20 fl oz
$\frac{1}{10}$	Selected cereal/pasta	60 g	2 oz
$\frac{1}{10}$	Caster sugar	60 g	2 oz
$\frac{1}{20}$	Butter	30 g	1 oz
	Vanilla essence		
	Pinch of nutmeg		

Method

Place milk in a thick-bottomed saucepan and bring to the boil. Stir in the cereal/pasta ensuring the grains do not clog together, and stir to the boil. Simmer gently, stirring frequently until the cereal/pasta is cooked and the mixture becomes fairly thick. Add sugar, pinch of nutmeg, vanilla essence and adjust consistency if required. Pour into a pie dish, add knobs of butter and brown in a hot oven or alternatively brown under a salamander. Clean the rim of the pie dish and present on a service flat with doily.

Examples of Cereal/Pasta Milk Puddings Using Above Formula:
Ingredients in Relation to 1 Unit (600 ml (20 fl oz)) Milk

Pudding	Unit	Selected cereal or pasta	Metric	Imperial
Ground rice pudding (Pouding crème de riz)	$\frac{1}{10}$	Ground rice	60 g	2 oz
Macaroni pudding (Pouding au macaroni)	$\frac{1}{10}$	Macaroni (short cut)	60 g	2 oz

Pudding	Unit	Selected cereal or pasta	Metric	Imperial
Rice pudding (Pouding au riz)	$\frac{1}{10}$	Carolina rice (short grain)	60 g	2 oz
Sago pudding (Pouding au sagou)	$\frac{1}{10}$	Sago	60 g	2 oz
Semolina pudding (Pouding au semoule)	$\frac{1}{10}$	Semolina	60 g	2 oz
Tapioca pudding (Pouding au tapioca)	$\frac{1}{10}$	Tapioca	60 g	2 oz
Vermicelle pudding (Pouding au vermicelli)	$\frac{1}{10}$	Pasta vermicelle	60 g	2 oz

FRENCH RICE PUDDING   Pouding au Riz à la Française

Prepare boiled rice pudding as above, prior to browning in the oven blend 2 egg yolks into the basic mixture. Beat the remaining egg whites until stiff and fold-in. Pour mixture into a buttered pie dish and bake in bain-marie or in the oven until risen, cooked and golden brown. Serve immediately.

35

Baked Egg Custard Sweets

Hot and cold baked egg custard sweets retain their popular status as part of the pastry cook's repertoire. The items produced from the basic mixture are both extensive and varied in composition. Such variety provides sweets which can be of light/heavy texture, readily digestible and nutritious.

Ingredient/Production Principles

Baked egg custard varieties are oven-baked en bain-marie at a low temperature around 160°C (320°F), and without agitation/stirring. The use of the bain-marie moderates the temperature preventing the custard over-heating around the sides, whilst the heat transfers through to the centre to cook and set the custard.

During cooking the egg white albumen (protein) coagulates at approximately 60°C (140°F), closely followed by the yolks. This coagulation property is responsible for setting baked egg custard products. If the custard is allowed to over-heat during the cooking process, the protein will curdle/contract leading to weeping (a separation of solids/liquid content). This adversely affects the appearance/texture and eating quality of the finished sweets.

During the preparation of the basic raw mixture, it is essential to strain and de-froth the custard prior to use in order to remove any broken egg shell and chalaza. De-frothing prevents any undue aeration at the surface.

Prior to filling, moulds can be brushed with a film of light syrup or water to prevent sticking. On completion of cooking/cooling, as applicable, the top surface edge is carefully loosened to facilitate de-moulding. Those items which need chilling for service are held on refrigeration (following cooling) until required.

EGG CUSTARD MIXTURE AND EXTENSIONS

Yield: 4–6 portions
Cooking time: 40 min–1 hr
Cooking temperature: 160°C (320°F) *see* chart

Unit	Ingredient	Metric	Imperial
1	Milk/scalded	600 ml	1 pt
$\frac{2}{5}$★	Whole egg	240 ml	8 fl oz
$\frac{1}{10}$	Caster sugar	60 g	2 oz
	Vanilla essence to flavour		

★ Whole egg content may be reduced to $\frac{3}{10}$ unit (180 ml (6 fl oz)) and $\frac{1}{5}$ egg yolk (120 g (4 oz)) introduced to compensate and enrichen.

Method

Whisk together egg content, caster sugar and vanilla flavouring. Whisk the hot milk into the egg mixture and incorporate thoroughly. Strain the whole preparation to remove any shell or balancers and skim away the surface froth. The raw egg custard mixture is now ready for use.

Egg Custard-Based Products Prepared Using Above Formula: Added Ingredients in Relation to 600 ml (1 pt) Milk

Name	Unit	Ingredient	Metric	Imperial
Baked egg custard		Grated nutmeg to flavour		
		Pour the basic egg custard mixture into a suitable pie dish. Sprinkle surface of custard with grated nutmeg. Cook en bain-marie in oven 40 minutes–1 hour at 160°C (320°F) until set. Remove from oven, clean edges of pie dish and surround with lace collar for service. Serve hot or cold		
Crème renversée (reversed creams)		Brush darioles/charlotte mould with light syrup or water and fill up with basic mixture. Cook en bain-marie in oven 40 minutes–1 hour at 160°C (320°F). Once set, remove from oven, allow to cool thoroughly and turn out for service		
Crème caramel (Caramel cream)	$\frac{1}{4}$	Prepared caramel (*see* p. 651)	150 ml	5 fl oz
		Brush darioles with light syrup or water. Cover base of moulds with caramel. (Single darioles or suitable charlotte mould) Fill up moulds with basic mixture and cook en bain-marie in oven 40 minutes to 1 hour at 160°C (320°F) until set. Allow to cool thoroughly and turn out for service surrounded with remaining caramel		

Name	Unit	Ingredient	Metric	Imperial
Crème viennoise (Viennese creams)	¼	Prepared caramel (p. 651)	150 ml	5 fl oz

Brush darioles or charlotte mould with light syrup or water. *Alter milk and sugar* content in basic mixture to 480 ml (¾ pt) and 60 g (2 oz) respectively. Allow the hot caramel to cool yet remain in a free-running state. Now whisk the caramel into the basic mixture to flavour
Fill up the individual darioles/charlotte mould with the custard mixture and cook en bain-marie in oven 40 minutes–1 hour at 160°C (320°F) until set. Allow to cool thoroughly and turn out for service

Name	Unit	Ingredient	Metric	Imperial
Crème à la florentine	¼	Chantilly cream (flavoured with kirsch)	150 ml	5 fl oz
		Crushed praline to flavour		
		Pistachios to decorate		

As for Crème Renversée but flavour basic custard with a little crushed praline. Decorate with rosettes of Chantilly cream and pistachios

Name	Unit	Ingredient	Metric	Imperial
Crème beau-rivage	¼	Prepared caramel (p. 651)	150 ml	5 fl oz
	¼	Chantilly cream	150 ml	5 fl oz
		6 Cornets (pp. 521–2)		

As for Crème Caramel but use border/savarin mould. Pour caramel into base and fill up with basic egg mixture. Cook en bain-marie in oven for 40 minutes–1 hour at 160°C (320°F) until set. Allow to cool thoroughly and turn out onto service vessel. Fill centre with piped Chantilly cream and decorate with Chantilly cream-filled cornets

Name	Unit	Ingredient	Metric	Imperial
Crème opéra	⅖	Fresh strawberries (macerated in kirsch-flavoured syrup)	240 g	8 oz
	¼	Crème Caprice (p. 648)	150 ml	5 fl oz
		Crushed praline to flavour		
		Spun sugar to decorate		

Brush mould with light syrup or water
Flavour basic custard with a little crushed praline and fill border/savarin mould. Cook en bain-marie in oven 40 minutes–1 hour at 160°C (320°F) until set. Allow to cool thoroughly, turn out onto service dish, fill centre with dome of Crème Caprice, surround with crown of macerated strawberries and present with a veil of spun sugar

Name	Unit	Ingredient	Metric	Imperial
Pouding au pain à l'anglaise (Bread and butter pudding)	¹⁄₁₀	Sultanas 4 Thin slices buttered bread* Caster sugar to glaze Grated nutmeg to flavour Custard or apricot sauce to accompany	60 g	2 oz

Trim crusts from bread and cut into triangles. Neatly arrange alternative layers of bread and sultanas in a well buttered pie dish/container, finishing with a final surface layer of bread. Now barely cover with basic custard and allow to stand/soak for 20 minutes. Just prior to cooking, dredge with caster sugar and sprinkle with nutmeg to flavour. Cook en bain-marie in oven 40 minutes–1 hour at 160°C (320°F) until set and golden brown. Remove from oven, clean edges of pie dish and surround with pie collar for service

* If using stale sliced, stale French bread or sliced stale bread rolls, the crusts may be retained and not removed. In these instances, additional slices are required to make up a sufficient amount of bread.

Name	Unit	Ingredient	Metric	Imperial
Pouding à la reine (Queen of puddings)	¹⁄₅ ¹⁄₂₀	Cake/bread crumbs Red jam (warmed) Grated lemon rind to flavour Sufficient ordinary meringue to decorate (whipped to stiff snow)	120 g 30 g	4 oz 1 oz

Place crumbs and lemon rind in a well-buttered pie dish. Pour on basic egg custard to barely cover and allow to stand/soak approximately 20 minutes. Cook en bain-marie in oven 40 minutes–1 hour until set. Remove from oven and allow to cool. Spread warmed jam over the surface of set pudding and decorate with the prepared meringue (use piping bag and star tube). Now flash pudding in hot oven to colour the meringue. Remove from oven, clean edges of pie dish, surround with pie collar and present for service

Name	Unit	Ingredient	Metric	Imperial
Pouding de cabinet (Cabinet pudding)	¹⁄₅ ¹⁄₈ chopped	Plain sponge cake/diced Glace cherries Angelica Sultanas Currants Sauce anglaise/hot apricot sauce/ sabayon (pp. 641–4)	120 g 75 g	4 oz 2½ oz

Butter and sugar darioles or charlotte mould as appropriate. Combine diced sponge/chopped fruit and mix together evenly. Half fill the mould/s with the mixture. Now fill up the mould/s with basic custard and allow to stand 20 minutes. Cook en bain-marie in oven 40 minutes– 1 hour at 160°C (320°F) until set. Remove from oven, allow to stand for a few minutes then turn out hot and present for service. Serve accompanied with sauce anglaise, sauce sabayon or apricot sauce

Name	Unit	Ingredient		Metric	Imperial
Pouding diplomat (Diplomat pudding)		As for cabinet pudding above but macerate fruit with kirsch and maraschino Generally served cold. May be coated, surrounded or accompanied with Melba sauce			

LITTLE CREAM POTS   Petits Pots de Crème

Yield: 4–6 portions
Cooking time: approx. 20 min
Cooking temperature: 160°C (320°F)

Unit	Ingredient	Metric	Imperial
1	Milk/scalded	600 ml	1 pt
$\frac{1}{5}$	Caster sugar	120 g	4 oz
$\frac{1}{8}$	Whole egg	75 g	$2\frac{1}{2}$ oz
$\frac{1}{10}$	Egg yolk	60 g	2 oz
	Vanilla essence to flavour		

Method

Whisk together egg content, caster sugar and vanilla flavouring. Pour in the hot milk and incorporate by whisking gently. Strain the whole preparation to remove any shell or balancers and skim away any surface froth. The raw petits pots mixture is now ready for use, *see* chart below.

Petits Pots de Crème Prepared Using Above Formula: Added Ingredients in Relation to 600 ml/1 pt Milk

Name	Unit	Ingredient		Metric	Imperial
Petits Pots à la Vanille (Vanilla cream pots)		Pour the above basic mixture carefully into individual earthenware/china pots to fill. Remove any remaining surface froth. Cook en bain-marie in oven at 160°C (320°F) for approximately 20 minutes until just set (cover during cooking but without allowing cover to touch the pots) and without colour. Allow to cool, and present for service in the original pots. Optionally may be decorated with a rosette of fresh whipped cream			
Petits pots au café (Coffee cream pots)		Coffee essence to flavour As for vanilla cream pots but flavour basic custard with coffee essence to taste			

Name	*Unit*	*Ingredient*	*Metric*	*Imperial*
Petits Pots au chocolat (Chocolate cream pots)	¹⁄₁₀	Cocoa powder Chantilly cream to decorate	60 g	2 oz
		Infuse milk with cocoa powder when making basic custard. Continue as for coffee cream pots. Decorate with rosettes of Chantilly cream		

36

Poached and Stewed Fruits

The objectives when poaching/stewing various fruits are to aid digestibility, to retain fruit shape and relatively firm texture as applicable, and to conserve *as far as is possible* flavour, colour and nutritive value. All fruits for poaching/stewing should be of good quality and not overripe or too soft.

Ingredients/Production Criteria

Generally poached/stewed fruit are *either* cooked in a little water with the sugar being added as required once the fruit has softened, e.g. for fruit sauces and fruit purées; or in sugar syrups of varying densities when it is important to retain both the shape and texture of the fruit as in compotes. It is important to note that the composition of fruits directly affects the length of the cooking time, the amount of liquid (water) required and the way in which sugar is incorporated into the process. Soft fruits, for example, have a low cellulose content and will soften/fall quickly when cooked in small amounts of water/syrup. On the other hand, hard fruits, such as apples/pears require more water/syrup and cooking time to soften their cellulose framework.

Cooking Fruit in Stock Syrup

Many *fresh* fruits are cooked in stock syrup so that they retain their normal shape, relatively firm texture and in order to develop a sweet flavour. During cooking, the cellular walls of the fruit become more porous, the water present within the fruit migrates to the more dense syrup, whilst sugar transfers into the fruit cells by absorption. This process helps retain the natural shape of the fruit. The physical changes which take place when cooking by this method prove beneficial to the quality of the finished product. It must be noted that the density of the stock syrups used varies accordingly with the type of fruit being poached/stewed, its composition, structure and texture. As a general guide, softer fruits require a heavier syrup than the harder varieties.

Dried fruits are also cooked/stewed in this fashion. As a general rule, these varieties require washing and overnight soaking before being cooked/stewed in the syrup. In some cases, less soaking time is needed and the fruit is cooked/stewed essentially in water without sugar. The sugar is added at a later stage to sweeten.

Applications

Poached and stewed fruits appear in many guises throughout culinary preparations. Break-fast menus often feature stewed/poached fruits in their own right as compotes of apples, prunes, plums, etc. Likewise stewed/poached fruits form part of various hot/cold sweets offered at other meal services; typical are iced coupes, fruit flans, compotes, fruit pies/tartlets.

Stewed/Poached Fruits   Compote des Fruits

Preparation of dried fruits

Prunes (Pruneaux)
Figs (Figues)   } Soak overnight before cooking
Apricots (Abricots)   } Wash well and drain
Apples, etc. (Pommes)

Preparation of fresh fruits

Apples (Pommes)   } Either peel and quarter or peel and leave whole
Pears (Poires)   }

Apricots (Abricots)
Blackcurrants (Cassis)
Gooseberries (Groseilles vertes)
Greengages (Reins Cloudes)   } Remove stalks and tail, when applicable
Prunes (Pruneaux)   } Wash well and drain
Plums (Prunes)
Raspberries (Framboises)
Redcurrants (Groseilles Rouge)
Strawberries (Fraises)

Peaches (Pêche)   Blanch, skin, halve or leave whole

Cherries (Cerises) } Remove stalks and stones
                   } Wash well and drain

Rhubarb (Rhubarbe) } Top and tail. Peel if necessary
                   } Cut into 5 cm (2 in) lengths

STEWED FRUITS   Compote des Fruits

Yield: 4 portions
400 g (1 lb) prepared fruit
Cooking time: 1–15 min (depending on fruit)

Unit	Ingredient		Metric	Imperial
	Selected fruit			
1	Water		500 ml	1 pt
⅕/²⁄₅*	Sugar	} Stock syrup	100–200 g	4–8 oz
	Cinnamon stick			
	Lemon juice (squeeze of)			

* Will vary according to the type/sweetness of fruit being cooked.

Method

Boil water, sugar, lemon and cinnamon stick together for 10–15 minutes to form stock syrup. Place prepared fruit into stock syrup and stew gently on stove top until fruit is tender. Allow to cool in liquor.

POACHED FRUITS   Compote des Fruits

Yield: 4 portions
400 g (1 lb) prepared fruit
Cooking time: 1–10 min (depending on fruit)

Unit	Ingredient		Metric	Imperial
	Selected fruit			
1	Water	⎫	500 ml	1 pt
⅕	Sugar	⎪	200 g	8 oz
	Lemon juice	⎬ Stock syrup		
	(squeeze of)	⎪		
	Cinnamon stick	⎭		

Method

Boil water, sugar, lemon and cinnamon stick together for 10–15 minutes to form stock syrup. Place prepared fruit in deep poaching dish. Cover with stock syrup and a cartouche. Poach gently in the oven until tender, keeping fruit whole. Do not allow to boil. Put aside to cool in the liquor/syrup ready for use.

  N.B. When preparing raspberries/strawberries pour boiling stock syrup over fruit, then allow to cool in liquor. No cooking time is necessary.

Pears in Red Wine   Poires au Vin Rouge

Proceed as for poached whole pears but replace half of the water content in the syrup with full bodied red wine. During the cooking process, the pears take-on a red colour and are used as a sweet in their own right or as a part of more complex products.

Fruit Purées   Purées des Fruits

Method

Pass the stewed/poached/drained or fresh fruit (as applicable) through a medium sieve/moule and use as required.

  N.B. Fruit may be liquidised prior to being sieved. Obviously the stewed/poached fruit is already sweetened and would not require any additional sugar.

37

Pancakes, Fritters and Sweet Omelets

A number of common features characterize the basic products outlined in this section. Typically all are speedily cooked by quick-heat methods such as shallow frying, griddling or deep-frying. Furthermore, the products rely on the processes of protein coagulation and/or starch gelatinization for their shape, texture and flavour, which are developed during the short cooking period.

Batters and batter production

The production of pancakes and certain fritters involves the use of basic batter preparations. The word batter is derived from the French word *battre* 'to beat' which infers that batters are produced using the 'beating' technique. A degree of beating or whisking is required to blend the ingredients into a smooth lump-free mixture of the correct consistency. The batter may be light and free running for pancakes, or of a heavier coating consistency for fritters. Whichever, the batter will have undergone a period of beating, and in the case of fritter batter, additional aeration. Batters are produced essentially from a blended mixture of plain white flour, milk/water, eggs, seasoning/sugar, which may also be flavoured with butter and further aerated for lightness. Aeration is generally achieved mechanically, chemically or organically, or by using a combination of methods, e.g. egg batter, baking powder batter, yeast batter are typical examples. As a rule batters are whisked or beaten thoroughly to make them light. However, in the case of pancakes less beating is required as excessive beating, even when using soft flour, could lead to a toughening of the gluten present resulting in rubbery textured pancakes. All batters, however, are allowed to stand prior to cooking to facilitate the softening of the starch grains in the flour which in turn acts to lighten and soften the cooked products.

Pancakes
Crêpes

Pancakes are featured on the menu in both sweet and savoury (for savoury pancakes, *see* p. 437) guise. In France they are extremely popular, crêperie restaurants, cafés and street corner food vendors specialize in their preparation and presentation. Many different and varied fillings are offered, e.g. seafood, various meats and sausage, sweet sauces, fruits, ice creams and jams, etc.

Production Factors

Pancakes are usually prepared in special 'crêpe pans', (*see* p. 26) made of heavy black wrought steel; alternatively omelet pans may be used. In either case the pans should be well proven prior to use (*see* p. 238). A common French innovation employs the use of large round griddle plates for cooking crêpes.

Storage

When not for immediate service, pancakes may be prepared, cooled on a clean flat surface, stacked on plates, covered with cling film and refrigerated until required.

Reheating

1. Spread the pancake with required filling, roll up, sprinkle with sugar and reheat in a microwave or hot oven.
2. Reheat in a lightly greased pancake pan and fill/fold as required.
3. Reheat on a griddle plate just prior to service.

Service

Pancakes are served on lightly buttered service dishes, and are usually sprinkled with sugar. Alternatively, the appearance of the pancakes can be enhanced by dusting with icing sugar and glazing. To glaze: either finish under hot salamander or brand trellis fashion with hot poker/branding iron.

SWEET PANCAKE BATTER   Appareil à Crêpe

Yield: 4 portions (8 pancakes)

Unit	Ingredient	Metric	Imperial
1	Milk	250 ml	10 fl oz
$\frac{2}{5}$	Flour	100 g	4 oz
$\frac{1}{5}$	Whole egg (beaten)	50 g	2 oz
$\frac{1}{10}$	Sugar	25 g	1 oz
$\frac{1}{20}$	Butter	12.5 g	$\frac{1}{2}$ oz
	Seasoning		

Method

Sift flour and seasoning into mixing bowl. Form a well, pour in beaten egg, milk and sugar. Whisk ingredients together to form a smooth pancake batter. Melt butter, add to batter and whisk thoroughly.

Cooking of pancakes: Coat base of pancake pan with film of oil and heat on stove top. Pour off excess oil and add sufficient batter to form a thin pancake. Cook pancake on both sides to a golden brown. Turn out ready for use.

Examples of Dishes Using Above Formula: Added Ingredients for 8 Prepared Pancakes (4 portions)

Name	Unit	Ingredient	Metric	Imperial
Apple pancakes (Crêpes Normande)	1	Apple purée	250 g	10 oz
		Caster sugar	50 g	2 oz
Spread pancakes with apple purée, roll up. Sprinkle with caster sugar and reheat in the oven				
Pineapple pancakes (Crêpes créole)	1	Crème pâtissière	150 g	6 oz
	½	Diced pineapple	75 g	3 oz
	⅓	Caster sugar	50 g	2 oz
	⅙	Rum	25 g	1 oz
Mix together, crème pâtissière, rum and pineapple. Spread pancakes with mixture, roll up. Sprinkle with caster sugar and reheat in the oven				
Jam pancakes (Crêpes à la Confiture)	1	Jam	100 g	4 oz
	½	Caster sugar	50 g	2 oz
Spread pancakes with jam, roll up. Sprinkle with caster sugar and reheat in the oven				
Pancakes with lemon (Crêpes au citron)		8 Lemon wedges		
	1	Caster sugar	50 g	2 oz
Reheat pancakes, sprinkle with caster sugar and fold into quarters. Serve accompanied with lemon wedges				
Pancakes with orange (Crêpes à l'orange)		8 Orange wedges		
	1	Caster sugar	50 g	2 oz
Proceed as for pancakes with lemon				
Pancakes with pears (Crêpes couvent)	1	Poached pears (*see* p. 557)	200 g	8 oz
	¼	Caster sugar	50 g	2 oz
Cut pears into small dice, add to pancake batter before preparing pancakes. Prepare pancakes in normal manner. Serve flat sprinkled with caster sugar				
Pancakes with pineapple (Crêpes georgette)	1	Pineapple	200 g	8 oz
	¼	Caster sugar	50 g	2 oz
	⅛	Kirsch	25 g	1 oz
Trim pineapple and cut into small dice, soak in kirsch. Add pineapple and kirsch to batter before preparing pancakes. Prepare pancakes in normal manner. Serve flat sprinkled with caster sugar				

N.B. Pancakes are often accompanied with suitable sweet sauces/syrups and/or ice creams.

SOUFFLÉ PANCAKES

Crêpe Soufflé

Yield: 1 portion
Cooking time: 4–5 min

Unit	Ingredient	Metric	Imperial
	2 Eggs		
1	Caster sugar	30 g	1 oz
½	Butter	15 g	½ oz
½	Icing sugar	15 g	½ oz

Method

Separate the egg yolks and whites, place into basins. Add the caster sugar to the egg yolks and beat until thick and creamy. Whisk the egg whites briskly until stiff. Fold carefully into egg yolks and distribute evenly. Heat omelet pan over a direct heat, add butter and allow to melt. Pour in the egg mixture. Cook until the bottom of the pancake is lightly browned. Place in a hot oven to complete cooking. Carefully fold in half and turn out onto a hot buttered service dish. Sprinkle pancake with icing sugar and brand trellis fashion with a red hot poker. Serve immediately.

Examples of Soufflé/Pancakes: Ingredients for 1 Portion (2 eggs per pancake)

English term	Unit	Ingredient	Metric	Imperial	French term
Soufflé pancake Jamaican style	1 1	Dark rum Black treacle	25 ml 25 g	1 fl oz 1 oz	Crêpe soufflé Jamaique
	Spread soufflé omelet with treacle prior to folding. Flambée at the table with rum				
Soufflé pancake with rum	1	Dark rum	25 ml	1 fl oz	Crêpe soufflé au rhum
	Flambée basic soufflé omelet with rum just prior to service				
Soufflé pancake Viennoise	1	Jam	25 g	1 oz	Crêpe soufflé Viennoise
	Spread omelet with jam prior to folding				

N.B. Other liqueurs may be used to flambée pancakes, e.g. Calvados, Brandy, Whisky, Grand Marnier, etc.

Fritters

Beignets

Fritters are popular in sweet and savoury form. They may be prepared from various fruits, vegetables, cooked rice, choux pastry, etc. (for savoury fritters, *see* pp. 302, 305). In most instances fritters are covered with a protective coating of thick aerated batter or bread-crumbs. However, some varieties of fritters require no protective coating, namely choux pastry based products, e.g. beignet soufflé, crab fritters, cheese fritters, etc.

When deep-frying fritters, great care must be taken to ensure a crisp golden brown finish and that the fruit/filling is thoroughly cooked/reheated. (For notes on frying and safety factors, *see* pp. 293–5.)

Savoury fritters may appear on the menu as hot canapés, starter courses or savouries. Fruit fritters however, are offered as a dessert selection or are utilized as a garnish for some savoury dishes. When offered for dessert they are presented on service flats with a doily accompanied with apricot sauce or custard.

YEAST BATTER   Pâte à Frire

Yield: approx. 1 (2 pt)

Unit	Ingredient	Metric	Imperial
1	Water (tepid)	500 ml	1 pt
⁴⁄₅	Flour	400 g	1 lb
¹⁄₄₀	Yeast	12.5 g	½ oz
	Pinch of salt		

Method

Sift flour and salt into basin and form a well. Cream yeast in water thoroughly and pour into the well. Gradually beat in the flour to form a smooth batter. Cover with a damp cloth and allow to ferment in a warm place for approximately 45 minutes–1 hour. Before use beat thoroughly and adjust to light coating consistency.

FRUIT FRITTERS   Beignets des Fruits

Cooking time: 3–5 min
Frying temperature: 175–190°C (350–375°F)

Mise en place for fruit fritters:

Flour/batter: sufficient to coat food for frying.
Selected fruit: *see* chart below.
Icing sugar: to glaze fruit after frying.
Hot apricot sauce: to accompany the fritters.

Method

Flour and batter selected fruit, drain surplus batter, deep fry until crisp and golden brown. Drain well. Sprinkle with icing sugar and glaze under the salamander. Present on a service flat with doily, accompanied with a sauce boat of hot apricot sauce.

N.B.   As an alternative ice-cream may be served with sweet beignets.

Examples of Dishes Prepared Using Above Formula

Dish	Preparation of fruit	Yield
Apple fritters (Beignets de pommes)	Peel and core apples, cut into ½ cm (¼ in) rings. Sprinkle with sugar and cinnamon, allow to stand for 20 minutes before deep frying	2 Slices of apple per portion
Apricot fritters (Beignets d'abricot)	Cut apricots in half, remove the stone	5–5 Fritters per portion
Banana fritters (Beignets de bananes)	Peel banana just prior to frying. Cut into 2 or 3 wedges	1 Banana per portion
Pineapple fritters (Beignets d'ananas)	Canned fruit: drain fruit of any syrup	2 Fritters per portion

RICE AND APRICOT FRITTERS   Beignets d'Abricot Colbert

Cooking time: 3–4 min
Frying temperature: 175–190°C (350–375°F)

Unit	Ingredient	Metric	Imperial
1	Rice pudding, cold (prepared as for condé, *see* p. 576) 24 Apricot halves	400 g	1 lb

Method

Form rice into 12 even sized balls. Take 2 apricot halves and place on either side of balls, mould to reshape apricots. Pass through flour, egg-wash and breadcrumbs. Deep fry until crisp and golden brown. Serve on a service dish with doily, accompanied with a sauceboat of hot apricot sauce.

CHOUX FRITTERS   Beignet Soufflés

See study Basic Pastries (*see* p. 490).

Sweet Omelets

Sweet omelets are prepared in the traditional manner. They are, however, filled with jam, syrup, fruit/purées, etc., before folding. They are generally dusted with icing sugar, branded trellis fashion prior to service, and on occasions flamed with spirits or liqueurs in the restaurant. The shape, texture, and taste of the omelet is determined by the controlled coagulation of the egg proteins during cooking coupled with the manipulative skills of the cook.

   N.B.   For general points concerning omelet preparation *see* p. 238.

SWEET OMELETS

Yield: 2 eggs (1 portion)
Cooking time: approx. 1–2 min

Method

Break eggs into a bowl, add a pinch of sugar and beat with a fork. Heat omelet pan over a direct heat, add a knob of butter and allow to melt. Pour in the eggs, shake pan briskly whilst gently stirring with the fork to distribute egg evenly around base of the pan.

Once egg begins to set, remove pan from heat, loosen around edge with a fork. Place selected filling in the centre of the omelet. Tilt pan downwards slightly, fold nearside of omelet to centre, tap pan handle briskly to move omelet to far edge of pan. Fold far side of omelet to centre to form a cigar (oval) shape. Seal quickly with fork and turn onto a buttered service dish. Sprinkle omelet with icing sugar and mark trellis fashion with a red hot poker. Serve immediately.

N.B.   Prior to service some sweet omelets are flamed at the table with an appropriate liqueur (*see* chart below for examples).

Examples of Sweet Omelets: Ingredients for 1 Portion (2 eggs per omelet)

English term	Unit	Ingredient	Metric	Imperial	French term
Omelet with calvados	1	Calvados	25 ml	1 fl oz	Omelette au calvados
		Flambée basic omelet with calvados just prior to service			
Omelet with fruit (purée)	1	Selected fruit purée (apple, gooseberries, raspberries, strawberries, etc.)	50 g	2 oz	Omelette aux fruits
		Heat fruit purée, sweeten to taste, place in omelet prior to folding			
Omelet with Grand Marnier	1	Grand Marnier	25 ml	1 fl oz	Omelette au Grand Marnier
		Proceed as for omelette aux Calvados			
Jam omelet	1	Jam	25 g	1 oz	Omelette au confiture
		Heat jam, place in omelet prior to folding			
Omelet with Mandarine Napoléon	1	Mandarine Napoléon	25 ml	1 fl oz	Omelette au Mandarine Napoléon
		Proceed as for omelette aux calvados			

English term	Unit	Ingredient	Metric	Imperial	French term
Raspberry omelet	1	Raspberries (whole)	50 g	2 oz	Omelette aux
	½	Kirsch	25 ml	1 fl oz	framboises
	Sweeten raspberries to taste, place in omelet before folding. Flambée with kirsch just prior to service					
Rum omelet	1	Dark rum	25 ml	1 fl oz	Omelette au
	Proceed as for omelette aux calvados				rhum

38

Hot Sweet Soufflés

Two distinct types of hot sweet (starch-based) soufflé are commonly prepared in the professional kitchen, although other types of hot sweet soufflés are also featured in this book (*see* p. 601 for typical examples). This introduction is concerned with the two basic types, namely *dry* baked soufflé and pudding soufflé varieties which are *baked in a water bath*/bain marie.

Dry baked varieties are light oven-baked soufflés served in or from single or multi-portioned soufflé dishes as appropriate. Traditionally, the soufflés are served *without* an accompanying sauce, but contemporary practice encourages the reverse; hence the list of suggested sauce accompaniments in the chart.

Soufflé puddings differ in texture, method of baking and service in that they are generally more dense in texture, they are oven-baked within a water-bath, and are always turned-out for service accompanied with a suitable sauce. Pudding soufflés are cooked in individual dariole or multiportioned charlotte moulds.

Ingredients Criteria

The composition of both types of soufflé involves a starch-thickend base which may be prepared using the roux, crème pâtissière/panada method. Once cooled, the starch thickened base is flavoured/enriched according to the method used and finally softened, lightened and aerated with a given quantity of whipped egg whites. On heating, the trapped air expands throughout the mixture giving 'lift' until the soufflé is a cooked, light textured and 'relatively' stable; essentially a result of starch gelatinization and protein coagulation. If insufficiently cooked, soufflés will collapse quickly. Furthermore, when baked soufflés cool, the trapped air within contracts causing some shrinkage; hence the need to serve the cooked soufflé immediately it is removed from the oven. For further details on cooking soufflés, *see* pp. 567, 570.

Lightness in soufflés is dependent upon the volume of whipped egg white in relation to the bulk/consistency of the starch thickened base. Texture and lightness, therefore, can be altered by increasing the volume of whites or reducing the amount of starch or using a combination of both techniques in given formula.

BAKED SWEET SOUFFLÉS/DRY BAKED

Yield: 8 portions
Baking time: approx. 35 min
Baking temperature: 175°C (350°F)

Unit	Ingredient	Metric	Imperial
1	Milk/scalded	240 ml	8 fl oz
¾	Whole egg (approx. 3 eggs/separate yolks from whites)	180 g	6 oz
¼	Caster sugar	60 g	2 oz
⅛	Egg white (approx. 1 white)	30 g	1 oz
⅛	Butter	30 g	1 oz
⅛	Flour	30 g	1 oz
	Flavouring/*see* chart below		
	Melted butter/caster sugar for preparing soufflé dishes		

Method

Butter/sugar soufflé dishes and put aside. Using a heavy-based saucepan, form a white roux with butter/flour, add milk (flavoured if applicable, *see* chart below), bring to the boil, stir continuously and form a thickened smooth sauce panada. At this stage, if applicable, incorporate the flavouring (*see* chart below for details), yolks and caster sugar and mix to a smooth texture. Transfer into a mixing bowl and allow to cool. Beat/whisk egg whites until stiff and blend a quarter of the foam into the basic mixture to soften. Fold in the remaining whites carefully and evenly throughout to form a light mixture. Three-quarters fill the soufflé dishes, place onto a baking tray in a pre-heated oven at 175°C (350°F) and bake for approximately 35 minutes (time will vary according to size of soufflé dish/dishes used). When almost baked, remove from oven, dust with icing sugar and return to oven to glaze. Serve immediately in the soufflé dish with under doily/napkin and accompany with an appropriate sauce (optional see chart).

Hot Sweet Soufflés Prepared Using Above Formula: Flavouring Amounts in Relation to 1 Unit 300 ml (½ pt) Milk

Name	Unit	Main flavouring	Metric	Imperial	Sauce
Vanilla soufflé (Soufflé a la vanille)		Vanilla essence Blend with milk to flavour			Vanilla or Anglaise
Coffee soufflé (Soufflé au café)		Coffee essence Blend with milk to flavour			Vanilla or Anglaise
Chocolate soufflé (Soufflé au Chocolat)	¼	Grated/melted chocolate Add to hot milk and allow to melt/blend thoroughly	60 g	2 oz	Chocolate or Anglaise

Name	Unit	Main flavouring	Metric	Imperial	Sauce
Lemon soufflé (Soufflé au citron)		Finely grated zest of 2 lemons Add to the panada on removal from heat and prior to yolks/sugar			Lemon
Orange soufflé (Soufflé à l'orange)		Finely grated zest of 2 oranges. Few drops of orange colouring Add to panada on removal from heat and prior to yolks/sugar			Orange
Rum Soufflé (Soufflé au rhum)	⅛	Dark/golden rum Add to panada on removal from heat and prior to yolks/sugar	30 ml	1 fl oz	Anglaise or rum
Grand Marnier soufflé (Soufflé Grand Marnier)	⅛	Grand Marnier Add to panada on removal from heat and prior to yolks/sugar	30 ml	1 fl oz	Orange or sabayon
Maraschino soufflé (Soufflé au maraschino)	⅛	Maraschino Add to panada on removal from heat and prior to yolks/sugar	30 ml	1 fl oz	Almond
Curaçao soufflé (Soufflé au Curaçao)	⅛	Curaçao Add to panada on removal from heat and prior to yolks/sugar	30 ml	1 fl oz	Orange or sabayon
Cherry soufflé (Soufflé montmorency)	¼	Finely diced glacé cherries (soaked in Kirsch) Fold into creamed panada just before incorporating whipped whites	60 g	2 oz	Almond or Anglaise or apricot
Rothschild soufflé (Soufflé Rothschild)	¼	Finely diced candied fruits (soaked in Kirsch) Fold into creamed panada just before incorporating whipped whites	60 g	2 oz	Almond or Anglaise or apricot
Pineapple soufflé (Soufflé ananas)	¼	Finely diced pineapple (soaked in Kirsch) Fold into creamed panada just before incorporating whipped whites	60 g	2 oz	Apricot or sabayon

Name	Unit	Main flavouring	Metric	Imperial	Sauce
Praliné soufflé (Soufflé praliné)	½	Crushed praliné Fold into creamed panada just before incorporating whipped whites	120 g	4 oz	Caramel or Maple Syrup

N.B. The term 'creamed panada' refers to the panada following the addition of egg yolks/sugar and before the incorporation of egg white foam.

Harlequin Soufflé/Soufflé Arlequin

Place a plastic pastry scraper or other suitable article vertically across the diameter of the prepared mould to divide into two halves. With the scraper remaining, fill one half with *vanilla* soufflé mixture, the other with *chocolate* soufflé mixture, remove the scraper and bake as for basic recipe. Serve accompanied with sauce Anglaise.

BAKED SOUFFLÉ PUDDINGS/BAKED IN WATER-BATH
Pouding Soufflés

Yield: 8 portions
Baking time: approx. 30 min
Baking temperature: 150°C (300°F)

Unit	Ingredient	Metric	Imperial
1	Milk	300 ml	½ pt
⅘	Whole egg (approx. 4 eggs/ separate yolks from whites)	240 g	8 oz
⅕	Butter	60 g	2 oz
⅕	Caster sugar	60 g	2 oz
⅕	Flour	60 g	2 oz
	Flavouring (*see* chart below)		
	Melted butter/caster sugar for preparing dariole moulds		

Method

Butter/sugar the required dariole/charlotte moulds and put aside. Place butter in a basin and cream to a softened pommade. Add caster sugar/flour and incorporate to form a creamed mixture. Bring milk to boiling point (with selected flavouring, if appropriate, *see* chart below), pour/whisk into the creamed mixture and blend thoroughly. Return the mixture into a clean heavy-based saucepan and stir continually to the boil to form a smooth thickened panada. Remove from the heat and, if applicable, add the main flavouring (*see* chart below). Now incorporate the egg yolks beating them in one at a time to form a smooth mixture (at this point, if applicable, add the main flavouring see chart). Now whisk egg whites to a stiff snow and blend a little of the stiff whites into the flavoured panada base to soften its texture. At this point, carefully/evenly fold-in the remaining bulk of the whipped whites. Three-quarters fill the prepared moulds with the mixture, place on stove-top en bain marie, bring to boil gently cooking the soufflés for 5 minutes. Now place in oven (en bain marie) for 20 minutes to complete cooking. Turn-out and serve immediately as required accompanied with appropriate sauce (*see* chart).

Soufflé Puddings Prepared Using Above Formula: Amount of Main Flavouring in Relation to 1 Unit 300 ml (½ pt) Milk

Name	Unit	Main flavouring	Metric	Imperial	Sauce
Vanilla soufflé pudding (Pouding soufflé à la vanille)		Vanilla essence to taste Blend with milk to flavour			Anglaise
Lemon soufflé pudding (Pouding soufflé saxone/au citron)		Finely grated zest 2 small lemons Add to panada on removal from the heat and prior to incorporation of egg yolks			Lemon or sabayon
Orange soufflé pudding (Pouding soufflé à l'orange)		Finely grated zest 2 small oranges Add to panada on removal from the heat and prior to incorporation of egg yolks			Orange or sabayon
Coffee soufflé pudding (Pouding soufflé au café)		Coffee essence to flavour Blend with milk to flavour			Anglaise
Chocolate soufflé pudding (Pouding soufflé au chocolat)	⅕	Grated/melted chocolate Add to hot milk and allow to melt/blend thoroughly	60 g	2 oz	Chocolate or Anglaise
Rum soufflé pudding (Pouding soufflé au rhum)	⅒	Dark or Golden rum Add to panada on removal from heat and prior to incorporation of egg yolks	30 ml	1 fl oz	Anglaise or sabayon
Cherry soufflé pudding (Pouding soufflé montmorency)	⅕	Finely diced glacé cherries (soaked in Kirsch) Fold into creamed panada just before incorporating the whipped egg whites	60 g	2 oz	Almond or Anglaise or apricot

Name	Unit	Main flavouring	Metric	Imperial	Sauce
Rothschild soufflé pudding (Pouding soufflé Rothschild)	⅕	Finely diced candied fruit (soaked in Kirsch) Fold into creamed panada just before incorporating egg whites	60 g	2 oz	Anglaise or apricot
Praline soufflé pudding (Pouding soufflé praliné)	⅖	Crushed praline Fold before incorporating whipped egg whites	120 g	4 oz	Caramel or maple syrup

N.B.   The term 'creamed panada' refers to the panada following the addition of egg yolks and before the incorporation of egg white foam.

Miscellaneous Hot Sweet Soufflés

These soufflés may vary slightly in composition from one to another. Certain recipe formula include a small proportion of 'starch' in the form of confectioner's custard, whilst others feature no starch content whatever. In all cases, however, 'lift, lightness and texture' are essentially a result of the expansion of trapped air (incorporated throughout the mixtures by means of whipped egg white) and protein coagulation during cooking. The reduced or eliminated starch content allows for the production of very light delicious hot soufflés.

FRUIT SOUFFLÉS   Soufflé aux Fruits

Yield: 4
Baking time: approx. 20 min
Baking temperature: 175°C (350°F)

Unit	Ingredient	Metric	Imperial
1	Selected fruit purée/thick (unsweetened/*see* chart below)	240 g	8 oz
¾	Granulated sugar	180 g	6 oz
½	Cold water	120 ml	4 fl oz
½	Egg whites	120 g	4 oz
	Vanilla essence to flavour		
	Melted butter/caster sugar for preparing soufflé dishes		

Method

Lightly butter/sugar soufflé dishes and put aside. Combine granulated sugar/water and boil to soft crack 132–138°C (270–280°F). Do not stir whilst boiling/brush insides of saucepan with little cold water to prevent formation of sugar crystals. Blend hot syrup with selected fruit purée and re-boil to hard ball degree 121°C (250°F) if necessary. Whip whites, vanilla essence quickly to a stiff snow. Gently combine hot fruit mixture with egg white, fill soufflé dish/es, dry-bake at 175°C (350°F) for approximately 20 minutes. Once cooked, present for service immediately (*see* chart).

Fruit Soufflés Prepared Using Above Formula

Name	*Selected fruit purée thick*	*Directions*
Raspberry soufflé (Soufflé aux framboises)	Raspberry purée/thick (unsweetened and flavoured with Kirsch to taste)	Liquidize raspberries, rub through fine sieve and reduce over heat until thick. Use hot
Strawberry soufflé (Soufflé aux frais)	Strawberry purée/thick (unsweetened and flavoured with Kirsch to taste)	Liquidize strawberries, rub through fine sieve and reduce over heat until thick. Use hot
Apricot soufflé (Soufflé aux abricots)	Apricot purée/thick (unsweetened and flavoured with Kirsch to taste)	Liquidize skinned/stoned ripe apricots, rub through a fine sieve and reduce over heat until thick. Use hot
Peach soufflé (Soufflé aux pêches)	Peach purée/thick (unsweetened and flavoured with Kirsch to taste)	Liquidize skinned/stoned ripe peaches, rub through a fine sieve and reduce over heat until thick. Use hot

APPLE SOUFFLÉ   Soufflé aux Pommes

Yield: 4
Cooking time: approx. 20 min
Cooking temperature: 175°C (350°F)

Unit	*Ingredient*	*Metric*	*Imperial*
1	Apple purée/very sweet (thick/flavoured with Calvados to taste)	240 g	8 oz
¼	Egg yolks	60 g	2 oz
¼	Egg whites	60 g	2 oz
¼	Pastry cream Melted butter/caster sugar for preparing soufflé dishes	60 g	2 oz

Method

Butter/sugar soufflé dishes and put aside. Bind apple purée with pastry cream to form a thick base, then blend-in egg yolks. Whisk egg whites to stiff snow and fold into the thick apple base. Fill prepared dishes with soufflé mixture, bake in oven at 175°C (350°F) for approximately 20 minutes. Once cooked present for service immediately.

39

Sweet Flambés

Sweet flambés denote dishes that are flamed and flavoured with appropriate spirits: a form of cooking/presentation carried out in front of the customer. This process usually takes place on a guéridon (trolley table) with the aid of a spirit or gas lamp. As a form of presentation it is extremely dramatic, of great impact often leading to an increase in the sale of sweet dishes at the end of the meal.

Many items, e.g. fruit flambés, are completely cooked at the table. Other sweets, however, are essentially prepared in the kitchen and later flamed by food service personnel in the dining room. Examples include:

Dish	Spirit used
Christmas pudding	Rum or Brandy
Crêpe Normande	Brandy or Calvados
Jam omelet	Rum or Brandy
Rum omelet	Dark Rum

It should be noted that when cooking or finishing dishes at the table high standards of hygiene must be adhered to. Additionally, all foods, seasonings, cooking utensils, service equipment, etc. should be at hand to facilitate a skilled professional presentation for the diner.

Flambéing Techniques

When the product in the chafing dish is ready for flaming, add the selected spirit, heat gently, tilt the pan and catch the open flame. The spirit will ignite resulting in a controlled blue flame. Take care not to over-heat the cooking vessel/contents during this process in order to avoid a flash of flame which is dangerous and uncontrollable.

FRUIT FLAMBÉS   Flambées des Fruits

Yield: 1 portion
Cooking time: 4–5 min

Unit	Ingredient	Metric	Imperial
	Selected fruit (*see* below)		
1*	Light stock syrup	75 ml	3 fl oz
⅓	Caster sugar	25 g	1 oz
⅓	Selected liquor	25 ml	1 fl oz

* Stock syrup may be lightly thickened with arrowroot if required.

Preparation of fresh fruit:

Apricot, peach	Wash, cut in half and remove the stone.
Cherries	Wash and remove stone.
Pear	Wash, peel, cut in half and remove the core, poach.
Pineapple	Top and tail, trim away outer skin, cut a thick slice and remove centre core.

N.B.   Tinned fruit may be used when fresh fruit is not available.

Method

Heat the syrup in a pan. Add the fruit and heat whilst basting continuously. When the syrup has reduced by half, sprinkle with caster sugar, reduce to form a light caramel. Add the selected liquor, flame and serve on hot sweet plate.

Fruit flambés may be plated at the guéridon or served from the pan at the table, in the latter case care must be taken to ensure the liquor has stopped flaming.

Examples of Fruit Flambés Prepared Using the Above Formula: Ingredients in Relation to 1 Portion

Dish	Unit	Ingredient	Metric	Imperial
Abricots flambées		3/4 Apricots		
	1	Stock syrup	75 ml	3 fl oz
	⅓	Brandy	25 ml	1 fl oz
Cerises flambées		Cherries (100 g (4 oz) per portion)		
	1	Stock syrup	75 ml	3 fl oz
	⅓	Kirsch	25 ml	1 fl oz
Pêche flambée		1 Peach		
	1	Stock syrup	75 ml	3 fl oz
	⅓	Brandy	25 ml	1 fl oz
Poire flambée		1 Pear		
	1	Stock syrup	75 ml	3 fl oz
	⅓	Brandy	25 ml	1 fl oz

Dish	Unit	Ingredient	Metric	Imperial
Ananas flambé		1 Thick slice pineapple		
	1	Stock syrup	75 ml	3 fl oz
	⅓	Brandy	25 ml	1 fl oz

BANANE FLAMBÉE

Yield: 1 portion
Cooking time: 4–5 min

Unit	Ingredient	Metric	Imperial
	1 Banana		
1	Unsalted butter	30 g	1 oz
1	Demerara sugar	30 g	1 oz
1	Dark rum	30 ml	1 fl oz

Method

Remove banana from skin and cut in half lengthways. Melt butter in pan. Add banana and heat quickly. Sprinkle on the sugar, when sugar begins to caramelise add the rum and flame. Serve on a hot sweet plate.

CRÊPES SUZETTE

Yield: 2 portions
Cooking time: 4–5 min

Unit	Ingredient	Metric	Imperial
	4 Pancakes (*see* p. 559)		
1	Caster sugar	60 ml	2 fl oz
1	Unsalted butter	60 g	2 oz
½	Curaçao	30 ml	1 fl oz
½	Brandy	30 ml	1 fl oz
	1 Orange (zest and juice)		
	½ Lemon (zest and juice)		

Method

Cream together the butter, sugar, orange zest and lemon zest. Melt the butter mixture in a pan, add the orange juice, lemon juice, curaçao, bring to the boil. Add the pancakes one at a time, baste with cooking liquor and fold into triangles. Reduce cooking liquor by half. Flame with brandy and serve immediately on hot sweet plates.

N.B. Cubes of sugar may be impregnated with the zest and flavour of oranges and lemons by rubbing them over the outer skin of the fruit. In this instance the impregnated sugar lumps are dissolved in the cooking liquor or ground and added to the butter mixture prior to melting.

40

Rice Based Cold Sweets

A variety of cold rice-based sweets can be offered on menus. They are typically substantial because of their starch base content which is often enriched with egg yolks and fresh cream. However, interesting combinations using fruits and glazes result in appetising sweet selections for both luncheon and dinner occasions.

Ingredient/Production Principles

Essentially the capacity of short-grained rice to absorb liquid, to act as a cohesive agent and undergo the process of starch gelatinisation on cooking, provides the setting quality associated with cold rice-based sweets. In some recipes gelatine is also introduced in small quantities to provide increased stability; a useful technique when preparing such sweets for de-moulding, e.g. riz à l'imperatrice.

Additional ingredients, namely eggs, cream, sugar and essences, act to enrichen, sweeten, and flavour, and in the case of sugar also soften the texture of the starch gel. Throughout, the rice should be cooked slowly and stirred frequently to avoid any sticking/burning at the base of the cooking vessel. Care must also be taken to ensure that the rice is fully cooked and of a heavy thickened consistency before cooling.

When gelatine is used in the recipe it is added at the completion of cooking and before cooling takes place, as is also the case with yolks of egg and sugar. Alternatively, whipped cream/egg white where applicable are introduced just prior to setting when the basic mixture is cool.

RICE FOR CONDÉ

Yield: 600 ml (1 pt)
Cooking time: 45 min–1 hr

Unit	Ingredient	Metric	Imperial
1	Milk	600 ml	1 pt
¼	Double cream (softly whipped)	150 ml	5 fl oz
⅛	Carolina rice (short grain)	75 ml	2½ oz
1/20	Caster sugar	30 g	1 oz
	Vanilla essence		

N.B. Egg yolk (1 yolk per 600 ml (1 pt) milk) may be added at completion of cooking to enrichen the mixture.

Method

Place milk in a thick-bottomed saucepan and bring to the boil. Stir in the rice ensuring the grains do not clog together, stir to the boil. Simmer gently stirring frequently until the rice is cooked and the mixture becomes thick. Add sugar, vanilla essence to taste. Allow to cool stirring occasionally to prevent a skin forming. Fold in the whipped cream when the rice is sufficiently cool and near setting.

Rice condé (Riz condé) can be served as a sweet in its own right. Pour mixture into dariole moulds that have been brushed with water. Refrigerate until set. Turn out and serve accompanied with a sauce boat of cold jam sauce.

FRUIT CONDÉ

Yield: 4 portions

Unit	Ingredient	Metric	Imperial
	Selected poached/fresh fruit		
1	Rice condé mixture (*see* p. 576)	600 ml	1 pt
⅕	Apricot glazé, hot (*see* p. 645)	120 ml	4 fl oz
	4 Glacé cherries		
	Angelica (sufficient to decorate)		

Method

Pour rice condé mixture into individual coupes. Allow to set. Arrange selected fruit neatly on top of the rice. Coat with apricot glaze, decorate with glacé cherries and angelica.

Alternatively, pour rice condé mixture into flan ring on a service flat and allow to cool/set. Remove the flan ring and proceed as above.

Examples of Fruit Condés Using Above Formula: Selected Fruit for 4 Portions

Menu term	Selected poached/fresh fruit	Preparation
Pomme condé (Apple condé)	2 Poached dessert apples	Remove any core and slice
Abricot condé (Apricot condé)	8 Poached apricots	Cut in half, remove stone
Banane condé (Banana condé)	2 Bananas	Peel and slice
Pêche condé (Peach condé)	2 Fresh peaches	Skin if required. Cut in half, remove stone, slice
Poire condé (Pear condé)	2 Poached pears	Cut in half, remove core, slice
Ananas condé (Pineapple condé)	2 Thick slices fresh pineapple	Trim, remove core and slice

N.B.   Canned fruit may be used as required or when fresh fruit is not available.

RICE EMPRESS STYLE — Riz à l'Impératrice

Yield: 6 portions

Unit	*Ingredient*	*Metric*	*Imperial*
1	Rice condé mixture (*see* p. 576)	300 ml	½ pt
1	Basic bavarois mixture, (*see* p. 581)	300 ml	½ pt
1/5	Crystallized fruit: glacé cherries angelica candied peel	60 g	2 oz
1/10	Apricot jam	30 g	1 oz
1/10	Kirsch	30 ml	1 fl oz
	Red jelly*		

* Sufficient to line the base of a charlotte mould.

Method

Pour the jelly into a charlotte mould to 0.5 cm (¼ in) thickness, allow to set. Cut the crystallized fruits into small dice and macerate in Kirsch. Combine together the crystallized fruits, Kirsch, hot apricot jam and rice condé mixture. Gently fold in the bavarois mixture. Pour into charlotte mould and refrigerate until set. Place charlotte mould in hot water for a few seconds to loosen filling. Turn out onto a round salver ready for service.

N.B. May be surrounded with a decorative border of piped Chantilly cream and/or served accompanied with Melba sauce.

Extensions of Riz à L'Impératrice Using Above Formula: Added Ingredients in Relation to 1 Unit Rice Condé Mixture 300 ml (½ pt)

Menu term	*Unit*	*Ingredient and method*	*Metric*	*Imperial*
Riz à l'impératrice aux ananas		6 Thin slices trimmed fresh pineapple Decorate riz à l'impératrice with slices of pineapple		
		3 Oranges (zest, segments)		
Riz à la maltaise	1/10	Orange curaçao Blanch zest. Add curaçao and zest to basic rice mixture before adding bavarois, prepare as above. Turn out and decorate with orange segments	30 ml	1 fl oz
Riz à la palerme	½	Double cream (whipped)	150 ml	5 fl oz
	½	Strawberries/fresh Prepare as for Riz à l'impératrice but in a Savarin mould. Turn out, fill centre with sweetened whipped cream and decorate with fresh strawberries	150 g	5 oz

N.B. Other fresh fruit may be used to decorate/accompany riz à l'impératrice, e.g. raspberries, bananas, peaches, etc.

PINEAPPLE CRÉOLE   Ananas Créole

Yield: 6 portions

Unit	Ingredient	Metric	Imperial
	6 Thin slices of trimmed fresh pineapple		
1	Basic rice condé mixture, (*see* p. 576)	600 ml	1 pt
$\frac{1}{20}$	Egg yolk	30 ml	1 fl oz
$\frac{1}{40}$	Leaf gelatine	15 g	$\frac{1}{2}$ oz
	Angelica to decorate		
	Apricot glaze*		

* Sufficient to glaze finished dish.

Method

Soak gelatine in cold water until soft. Add gelatine and egg yolk to hot rice condé mixture and incorporate evenly. Allow to cool until almost setting. Place onto an oval flat and mould to represent a pineapple. Cut pineapple slices in half, arrange neatly onto moulded rice and brush with hot apricot glaze. Cut angelica into strips and place at one end of créole to represent the top of a pineapple. Refrigerate ready for service.

BANANA CRÉOLE   Banane Créole

Proceed as for pineapple créole, but place rice mixture into banana skins which have been kept whole with just a strip removed lengthways (1 banana per portion). Slice banana and arrange neatly on top of the rice, brush with hot apricot glaze and refrigerate for service.

41

Bavarois (Bavarian Creams)

The term bavarois denotes a lightly set smooth textured cold Bavarian cream that has been pre-set with gelatine in a selected mould, which is then turned out and decorated for service. Bavarois of differing flavours are made by incorporating essences, fruit purées, fruit juices and the like. Furthermore, respective moulds may be chilled/lined with jellies, sponge fingers, swiss rolls, etc. prior to filling with the bavarois mixture. In these instances, the individual sweets are respectively known as fruit chartreuse or charlottes.

Ingredient Principles

Two methods of producing bavarois may be used:

1. *Custard-based*, essentially using:
   - Creme anglaise
   - Gelatine
   - Selected flavouring
   - Whipped cream
2. *Syrup-based*, essentially using:
   - Stock syrup
   - Gelatine
   - Selected fruit purée
   - Whipped cream

N.B. Modern commercial practice also may include the incorporation of whipped egg white which reduces the cream content, whilst maintaining bulk, thereby producing a less expensive product.

Custard-Based Bavarois

Fresh egg custard sauce (essentially vanilla flavoured milk thickened with fresh egg yolks and sweetened with sugar) forms the basis of custard-based bavarian creams. During cooking the egg custard must not be allowed to overheat, otherwise it will curdle; consequently the custard is removed from the heat when it lightly coats the back of a spatula/spoon. The custard thickens at around 71°C (160°F) but if held for too long at this temperature the preparation will curdle due to excessive coagulation of the proteins present. The resultant curdled custard cannot be readily rectified.

Gelatine

The setting agent, gelatine, is thoroughly/evenly dissolved throughout the prepared hot custard which when cold causes the completed bavarois to set. During cooling, the basic custard (with gelatine) is stirred frequently until it begins to thicken, prior to setting. At this stage, the other ingredients are incorporated, the mixture then moulded and stored on refrigeration to set.

Whipped cream

The addition of half-whipped cream (and sometimes whipped egg whites) acts to enrich and lighten the finished sweet. Care must be taken to ensure that the cooled custard has started to thicken for setting before folding-in the whipped cream/whites; otherwise the bavarois will lose some volume and may separate whilst in the mould.

Flavourings

Some flavourings are introduced when preparing the hot custard, e.g. vanilla essence, coffee essence, cocoa powder, etc. whilst others are blended with the cooled custard before the addition of the cream, e.g. fruit purées.

Syrup-Based Bavarois

In these types of bavarois, the syrup, which is blended with gelatine and fruit purée, replaces the basic custard preparation to become the main moistening/sweetening medium within the formula.

Moulds and Service

A variety of moulds are suitable for use with bavarois mixtures. Typically charlotte/bavarois, jelly, border or dariole moulds. The moulds, whether plain, lined or chemised are filled with the chosen bavarois mixture, then refrigerated until thoroughly cold and set. For presentation/service, the sweets are de-moulded onto/into an appropriate service dish, e.g. glass bowls/salvers/plates and suitably decorated.

Moulding and Modern Practices

Bavarian creams are often poured into various types of mould for setting. Typical are bomb moulds, fancy decorative moulds, glass moulds, hooped rings, etc. In some cases lining materials such as sponge fingers, swiss rolls are placed into position after the mould has been removed, e.g. hooped ringed moulds.

BAVARIAN CREAM (custard-based)   Bavarois

Yield: 4 portions

Unit	Ingredient		Metric	Imperial
1	Double cream (half whipped)		250 ml	½ pt
1	Milk	Sauce	250 ml	½ pt
⅕	Caster sugar	Anglaise	50 g	2 oz
⅕	Egg yolk		50 g	2 oz
¹⁄₂₀	Leaf gelatine		12–15 g	½ oz
	Crème Chantilly to decorate			

Method

Cream egg yolks and sugar together. Heat the milk, pour onto egg yolks and sugar, whisking continuously. Strain mixture through chinois into a thick bottomed pan. Return to the heat and stir continuously until the mixture thickens sufficiently to coat the back of a wooden spoon/spatula. Do not allow the custard to boil as the egg yolk content will coagulate/curdle. Remove from heat. Soak the gelatine in cold water until soft, add gelatine to the hot custard, stir until dissolved and allow to cool. When mixture begins to thicken, fold in the softly whipped cream, pour into bavarois/charlotte mould and refrigerate until completely set. To de-mould, dip exterior of mould into hot water for a few seconds in order to loosen sides of bavarois. Turn out into/onto presentation dish and decorate with Crème Chantilly for service.

    N.B.   Different flavours of bavarois may require specific decorations, e.g. strawberries with strawberry bavarois (see chart below for details).

Examples of Bavarois (Custard-based): Added Ingredients in Relation to Above Formula

Menu term	Unit	Added ingredient	Metric	Imperial
Banana chartreuse (Chartreuse de Bananes)		2 Bananas (thinly sliced) Lemon jelly (Sufficient to chemise/line a charlotte mould)* Vanilla essence		

Flavour sauce anglaise with vanilla essence before preparing bavarois. Chemise charlotte mould with jelly and line completely with thin slices of banana which have been lightly dipped in jelly. Refrigerate to set. Fill prepared mould with vanilla bavarois, allow to set, turn out for service

N.B.   Other fruits and jellies may be used when preparing Chartreuse, e.g. sliced strawberries strawberry jelly/Chartreuse aux Fraises

Chocolate bavarois (Bavarois au chocolat)	⅕	Chocolate couverture Chocolate cut-outs to decorate	50 g	2 oz

Melt chocolate in milk before preparing bavarian cream. Decorate de-moulded bavarois with chocolate cut-outs, e.g. squares, triangles, etc.

Coffee bavarois (Bavarois au café)		Coffee essence (to taste)		

Add coffee essence to milk before preparing bavarois

Lemon bavarois (Bavarois au citron)		1 Lemon (juice and zest)		

Infuse lemon zest in milk. When custard has cooled, mix in the lemon juice (strained)

* Chemising/lining mould with jelly. Place selected mould in a bowl of crushed ice and water. Fill mould with cool free-running jelly and allow to set on the sides/bottom of mould to 1 cm (¼ in) thickness. Remove mould from ice/water, tip away excess jelly and refrigerate to set firm before use.

Menu term	Unit	Added ingredient	Metric	Imperial
Moscovite charlotte (Charlotte muscovite)	1/5	Sponge finger biscuits (Sufficient to line a charlotte mould) Raspberry jelly Vanilla essence (to taste)	50 ml	2 fl oz

Flavour sauce anglaise with vanilla essence before preparing bavarois. Cover base of charlotte mould with jelly and allow to set. Line sides of mould with sponge finger biscuits. Fill prepared mould with vanilla bavarois, allow to set, then turn-out for service

| Orange bavarois
(Bavarois a l'orange) | | 1 Orange (juice and zest)
1 Orange (segments, julienne of
zest/blanched) | | |

Infuse orange zest in milk. When custard has cooled, mix orange juice. Decorate de-moulded bavarois with orange segments and *blanched* julienne of zest

| Praline bavarois
(Bavarois au praline) | 1/5 | Crushed praline (*see* p.649)
8 Praline leaves/shapes | 50 g | 2 oz |

Blend crushed praline with bavarian cream just prior to addition of softly whipped cream. Decorate de-moulded bavarois with praline leaves/shapes

| Raspberry bavarois
(Bavarois aux
  framboises) | 4/5 | Raspberry purée (raw)
Sugar to sweeten raspberries (to taste) | 200 g | 8 oz |

Reduce milk content by half when preparing basic bavarois. Sweeten raspberry purée to taste and add to basic bavarois just prior to addition of half-whipped cream. De-moulded bavarois may be decorated with whole raspberries

| Ribboned bavarois
(Bavarois rubané) | | | | |

Fill charlotte mould with alternating layers of different flavours and colours of bavarian creams. Allow each ribbon to set for layering, e.g.

Vanilla/coffee
Vanilla/strawberry
Orange/lemon, etc.

| Royal charlotte
(Charlotte royale) | | Small swiss rolls (*see* p. 520–1)
(Sufficient to line a charlotte mould)
Vanilla essence | | |

Flavour sauce anglaise with vanilla essence before preparing bavarian cream. Line base and sides of charlotte mould with thin slices of swiss roll. Fill prepared mould with vanilla bavarois, allow to set. Turn out for service

| Russian charlotte
(Charlotte russe) | | Sponge fingers biscuits (*see* p. 521)
(Sufficient to line a charlotte mould)
Vanilla essence | | |

Proceed as for charlotte royale, but line base and sides of mould with sponge finger biscuits. Fill prepared mould with vanilla bavarois

Menu term	Unit	Added ingredient	Metric	Imperial
Strawberry bavarois (Bavarois aux fraises)	⅘	Strawberry purée (raw) Sugar to sweeten	200 g	8 oz

Proceed as for raspberry bavarois but replace raspberry purée with strawberry purée. De-moulded bavarois may be decorated with whole or sliced strawberries

Vanilla bavarois (Bavarois vanille)		Vanilla essence Glacé cherries/angelica to decorate		

Flavour sauce anglaise with vanilla essence before preparing bavarois. Decorate de-moulded bavarois with glacé cherries/angelica

N.B.   A vanilla pod may be used in place of essence. In this instance, add vanilla pod to milk prior to boiling. Bring to the boil, strain through a chinois ready for use

BAVARIAN CREAM (syrup-based)   Bavarois

Yield: 4 portions

Unit	Ingredient	Metric	Imperial
1	Selected fruit purée (*see* chart below)	240 ml	8 fl oz
1	Double cream (half-whipped)	240 ml	8 fl oz
½	Stock syrup★	120 ml	4 fl oz
1/16	Leaf gelatine Crème Chantilly for decoration	15 g	½ oz

★ The strength of the prepared stock syrup is equal quantities of sugar to water. Boil together to dissolve sugar, allow to cool ready for use.

Method

Bring the stock syrup to the boil. Soak the gelatine in cold water until soft. Add gelatine to the syrup and stir until dissolved. Combine syrup with fruit purée, mix well and allow to cool. When mixture begins to thicken, fold in the half-whipped cream, pour into bavarois/ charlotte mould and refrigerate until completely set.

To de-mould, dip into hot water for a few seconds to loosen sides of bavarois. Turn out into/onto presentation dish and decorate with Chantilly cream for service.

N.B.   When applicable, the selected fruit may be used to decorate the finished bavarois, e.g. whole strawberries/raspberries.

Examples of Bavarois (Syrup-based) Using the Above Formula

English term	Selected purée	French term
Apricot bavarian cream	Stewed apricot purée	Bavarois aux abricots
Gooseberry bavarian cream	Stewed gooseberry sauce★	Bavarois aux groiseilles vertes

English term	Selected purée	French term
Raspberry bavarian cream	Raspberry purée (raw)	Bavarois aux framboises
Rhubarb bavarian cream	Stewed rhubarb purée*	Bavarois au rhubarbe
Strawberry bavarian cream	Strawberry purée (raw)	Bavarois aux fraises

* When preparing gooseberry/rhubarb bavarois, it may be necessary to add extra sugar when preparing fruit purée.

42

Cold Sweet Soufflés, Mousses and Fools

Cold sweet soufflés, fools and mousse provide the pâtissier with ample opportunity to utilize many fresh fruits when preparing these popular and delicious concoctions. The cold sweets detailed are to some extent variations upon a theme differing marginally in ingredient composition and texture.

Ingredients/Production Criteria

Typically the ingredients used to prepare such cold sweet variations include combinations of eggs, sugar, fruit/flavourings, cream, custard and, in some instances, the setting agent gelatine. All three products are relatively rich in composition, but lightened to varying degrees by mechanical/manual aeration and the incorporation of aerated ingredients during production. Essentially the whisking of cream, egg whites and egg yolks throughout the various stages acts to trap and incorporate air thus providing lightness in finished textures. Combinations of cooked and raw ingredients are featured being subsequently assembled to form stable pâtisserie products.

Using Gelatine

Gelatine (a form of protein) is of little significance in its own right. In terms of flavour/colour, it has little to offer in culinary preparations. However, its characteristic gelling/setting property which takes place at given temperatures make it an ideal ingredient for use as a setting/stabilizing agent for *cold* products. Such items often need to maintain their moulded shape and relatively firm texture without becoming tough/rubbery and unacceptable to customers. Before being dispersed throughout mixtures gelatine is firstly soaked in cold liquid (usually water) causing the granules/leaves to take-up water, soften and swell. It is then melted separate from or within heated mixtures facilitating its thorough and even distribution during production. On cooling the gelatine which remains dispersed acts to set the mixture to the required degree whilst still maintaining product shape. Once set the prepared items are able to hold their shape/texture at room temperature to adequately meet the needs of service periods. Modern chilled display units, however, have virtually eliminated this time factor problem. Obviously recipe balance plays a critical role in the effective use of this setting agent (*see* recipe formula for guidelines). When used in cold sweet *soufflé/mousse* and indeed bavarois (*see* p. 580), the gelatine is dissolved/dispersed through a flavoured base which on cooling and before setting point is enriched/lightened by the careful incorporation of half-whipped cream and egg white foam. Cold sweet soufflé and some mousse are moulded prior to setting and the mousse demoulded for service once set.

Fruit fool mixtures, however, are of a softer texture being based upon a combination of cream and fruit purée or cream, fruit purée and custard. They do not require any gelatine for setting purposes as they rely mainly on the holding quality of the whipped cream and starch thickened custard as applicable by recipe. Furthermore, fruit fools are generally presented in coupes/glassware and do not need 'turning-out' for service.

Moulds Used

The moulds/dishes used include soufflé dishes enlarged with a paper collar as described on p. 587 (typically for the cold sweet soufflés). These may be as single- or multi-portioned dishes. Cold sweet mousse can be prepared/set in all manner of moulds in readiness for demoulding: Charlotte moulds, dariole moulds, fancy moulds all feature. Alternatively mousse mixtures can be presented in coupes/glassware for service in the same way as fruit fools.

Holding/Storage

Once prepared cold sweets are held/stored on refrigeration to facilitate any setting requirements and to keep such products hygienically safe prior to service. Often those sweets which contain gelatine are held until thoroughly set then served as soon as possible thereafter.

COLD SWEET SOUFFLÉS/CITRUS FRUITS

Yield: 6–8 portions

Unit	Ingredient	Metric	Imperial
1	Cream/double or whipping	300 ml	10 fl oz
⁴/₅	Caster sugar	240 g	8 oz
⁴/₅	Whole egg/separated	240 g	8 oz
¹/₂₀	Gelatine powder	15 g	½ oz
	Citrus juice/strained/grated zest		
	(*see* chart below for details)		
	Decoration materials		
	(*see* chart below for details)		

Method

Surround selected soufflé dishes with high collar of greaseproof/thin cardboard, secure with string and put aside to chill. Half-whip cream and put aside. Add gelatine to citrus juice and dissolve over low heat. Place egg yolks, caster sugar, gelatine solution and finely grated rind in a mixing bowl and whisk vigorously over bain-marie, to the thick ribbon stage and until the contents have doubled in volume. Remove from bain-marie, continue whisking until the mixture cools and put aside. Place egg whites into clean mixing bowl and whisk to a peaked foam (not too stiff). Ensure that the whisked egg mixture is cold/smooth/not set then carefully fold-in the whipped cream. Finally incorporate the egg white foam evenly throughout to lighten. Pour immediately into the prepared dishes to 3 cm (1½ in) above the rim and refrigerate to set. For service remove paper collar, decorate appropriately and present as required.

Cold Sweet Soufflés Prepared Using Above Formula

Name	Selected citrus juice/zest	Decoration
Lemon soufflé (Soufflé milanaise)	Juice of 2½ large juice-rich lemons/ strained Finely grated zest 2 lemons	Top with rosettes whipped cream and blanched julienne of lemon zest. Sides with toasted nibbed almonds
Lime soufflé (Soufflé au citron vert)	Juice of 4 juice-rich limes/strained Finely grated zest 2 limes Few drops green colouring (pale green)	Top with rosettes whipped cream and blanched julienne of lemon zest. Sides plain
Orange soufflé* (Soufflé a l'orange)	Juice of 2 juice-rich oranges/½ lemon strained Finely grated zest 1 orange Few drops of orange colouring (pale orange)	Top with rosettes whipped cream, blanched julienne of orange zest/orange fillets. Sides plain

* Sugar content can be lowered to taste in this case.

COLD SWEET SOUFFLÉ/FRUIT PURÉES

Yield: 6–8 portions

Unit	Ingredient	Metric	Imperial
1	Cream/double or whipping	300 ml	10 fl oz
1*	Selected fruit purée/cold (see chart below for details)	300 g	10 oz
⁴/₅	Whole egg/separate yolk	240 g	8 oz
¹/₁₀ *	Caster sugar	30 g	1 oz
¹/₂₀	Gelatine	15 g	½ oz
	Cold water to soak/dissolve gelatine		
	Juice of half lemon/strained		

* As a guide 480 g (1 lb) fresh fruit will yield 300 g (10 oz) prepared sweetened purée, see p. 557. Sugar content may be adjusted to taste and approximately 60 ml (2 fl oz) cold water to soak/dissolve gelatine.

Method

Surround selected soufflé dishes with a high collar of greaseproof/thin cardboard, secure with string and put aside to chill. Pour cream in mixing bowl, whisk to the half-whipped stage and put aside. Add gelatine to lemon juice/cold water and dissolve over gentle heat. Place egg yolks, caster sugar, gelatine solution in mixing bowl and whisk briskly over a heated bain-marie to the thick ribbon stage and until the mixture doubles in volume. Remove from the bain-marie, incorporate selected fruit purée and stir until cool but not set. Place egg whites in mixing bowl, whisk to a peaked foam (not too stiff) and put aside. Make sure the basic egg/fruit mixture is cold, smooth and not set then carefully fold-in the half-whipped cream followed by the egg white foam. Transfer the mixture immediately into the chilled dishes to 3 cm (1½ in) above the rim then place on refrigeration to set. For service remove paper collar, decorate appropriately and present as required (*see* chart for details).

Cold Fruit Purée Soufflés Prepared Using Above Formula

Name	*Selected fruit purée*	*Top decoration*
Apricot soufflé (Soufflé a l'abricots)	Apricot purée/cold sweetened (*see* p. 557)	Rosettes of whipped cream/ chopped pistachios
Gooseberry soufflé (Soufflé aux crosseilles vertes)	Gooseberry purée/cold sweetened (*see* p. 557)	Rosettes of whipped cream
Raspberry soufflé (Soufflé aux framboises)	Raspberry purée/cold sweetened (*see* p. 557)	Rosettes of whipped cream/ sugared fresh raspberries
Strawberry soufflé (Soufflé aux frais)	Strawberry purée/cold sweetened (*see* p. 557)	Rosettes of whipped cream/ sugared fresh strawberries

COLD SWEET SOUFFLÉ/MISCELLANEOUS FLAVOURS

Yield: 4 portions

Unit	*Ingredient*	*Metric*	*Imperial*
1	Cream/double or whipping	300 ml	10 fl oz
⅘	Whole egg/separate yolks from whites	240 g	8 oz
⅕	Caster sugar	60 g	2 oz
1/20	Gelatine powder	15 g	½ oz
	Main selected flavourings (*see* chart below for details)		
	Cold water to soak gelatine*		
	Vanilla essence/juice of half lemon strained		

* Approximately 60 ml (2 fl oz) cold water to soak/dissolve gelatine.

Method

Surround selected soufflé dishes with a high collar of greaseproof/thin cardboard, secure with string and put aside to chill. Pour cream into mixing bowl, whisk to the half-whipped stage and put aside. Add gelatine to lemon juice/cold water and dissolve over low heat. Place egg yolks, caster sugar, vanilla essence, gelatine solution into mixing bowl and whisk briskly over a heated bain-marie to the thick ribbon stage and until the mixture doubles in volume. Remove from bain-marie, incorporate selected flavourings and stir until cool but not set. Place egg whites into mixing bowl and whisk to a peaked foam (not too stiff) and put aside. Make sure the basic egg mixture is cold, smooth and not set then fold-in the half-whipped cream followed by the egg white foam. Transfer the mixture into the prepared soufflé dishes to approximately 3 cm (1½ in) above the rim then place on refrigeration to set. For service remove paper collar, decorate appropriately and present as required (*see* chart for details).

Cold Sweet Soufflés Prepared Using Above Formula: Added Ingredients to 1 Unit, i.e. 300 ml (10 fl oz) Cream

Menu term	Unit	Main flavourings	Metric	Imperial
Chocolate soufflé	⅖	Chocolate couverture/melted	120 g	4 oz
(Soufflé au	¹⁄₁₀	Dark or golden rum	30 ml	1 fl oz
chocolat)		Chantilly cream/decorative chocolate piped shapes for decoration purposes		
		Incorporate melted chocolate/rum into prepared egg base (*see* method). Decorate set soufflé with rosettes of whipped cream and chocolate shapes		
Coffee soufflé		Coffee essence/flavouring to taste		
(Soufflé cafe)	¹⁄₁₀	Tia Maria	30 ml	1 fl oz
		Chantilly cream/roasted nibbed almonds for decoration purposes		
		Incorporate coffee essence/flavouring and Tia Maria into prepared egg base (*see* method). Decorate set soufflé with rosettes of whipped cream finished with roasted nibbed almonds		
Peppermint soufflé		Peppermint essence to taste		
(Soufflé crème de	¹⁄₁₀	Crème de menthe	30 ml	1 fl oz
Menthe)		Few drops green colouring to pale green		
		Chantilly cream/decorative chocolate piped shapes for decoration purposes		
		Incorporate peppermint essence/Crème de Menthe into prepared egg base (see method)		
		Decorate set soufflé with whipped cream and chocolate shapes		

COLD SWEET MOUSSE: Soft Fruits (Moulded)

Yield: 8 portions

Unit	Ingredient	Metric	Imperial
1*	Selected fruit purée/cold/sweetened (*see* chart below for details)	300 g	10 oz
⅘	Whole egg/separate yolks from whites	240 g	8 oz
½	Cream/double or whipping	150 ml	5 fl oz

Unit	Ingredient	Metric	Imperial
$\frac{1}{10}$	Caster sugar	30 g	1 oz
$\frac{1}{20}$	Gelatine	15 g	$\frac{1}{2}$ oz
	Juice of half lemon/strained		
†	Cold water to soak/dissolve gelatine		
	Sponge fingers to accompany		

* As a guide 480 g (1 lb) fresh fruit will yield 300 g (10 oz) prepared sweetened purée.
† Approximately 60 ml (2 fl oz) cold water to soak/dissolve gelatine.

Method

Place selected moulds on refrigeration to chill. Pour cream into a mixing bowl, whisk to the half-whipped stage and put aside. Combine gelatine, lemon juice, cold water and dissolve over gentle heat. Place egg yolks, caster sugar, gelatine solution in mixing bowl and whisk briskly over heated bain-marie to the thick ribbon stage and until the mixture doubles in volume. Remove from bain-marie, incorporate selected fruit purée and stir until cool but not set. Place egg whites in mixing bowl, whisk to a peaked foam (not too stiff) and put aside. Make sure the basic egg/fruit mixture is cold, smooth and not set then carefully fold-in the whipped cream followed by the egg white foam. Transfer the mixture immediately into the selected chilled moulds and place on refrigeration to set. De-mould (if required) onto service dishes, decorate appropriately (*see* chart below) and present accompanied with sponge fingers.

Cold Sweet Mousses Prepared Using Above Formula

Name	Selected fruit purée	Decoration/accompaniments
Raspberry mousse (Mousse aux framboises)	Raspberry purée/cold sweetened (*see* p. 557)	Top with fresh raspberries soaked in Kirsch and accompany with sauceboat of lightly whipped cream/ sponge fingers
Strawberry mousse (Mousse aux frais)	Strawberry purée/cold sweetened (*see* (p. 557)	Surround with crown of fresh strawberries soaked in Kirsch and accompany with a sauceboat of lightly whipped cream/sponge fingers
Summer mousse (Mousse estivale)	Summer fruit purée/cold sweetened (*see* p. 557) (Typically raspberries, strawberries, redcurrants, blackcurrants)	Mask with Melba sauce and serve accompanied with sauceboat of lightly whipped cream/sponge fingers
Gooseberry mousse (Mousse de groseilles vertes)	Gooseberry purée/cold sweetened (*see* p. 557)	Top with small langue du chat filled with Chantilly cream or gooseberry fool mixture

COLD CHOCOLATE MOUSSE (moulded)   Mousse au Chocolat Froid

Yield: 8 portions

Unit	Ingredient	Metric	Imperial
1	Cream/double or whipping	300 ml	10 fl oz
1	Chocolate couverture/melted	300 g	10 oz
⅕	Egg white (approx. 2 whites)	60 g	2 oz
⅒	Egg yolk (approx. 2 yolks)	30 g	1 oz
⅒	Dark rum	30 ml	1 fl oz
1/20	Caster sugar	15 g	½ oz
1/40	Gelatine	7.5 g	¼ oz
	Juice of a half lemon/strained		
	Cold water to soak/dissolve gelatine*		
	Chantilly cream/walnuts/fined piped		
	chocolate shapes for decoration		

* Sufficient cold water to soak/dissolve gelatine approximately 60 ml (2 fl oz).

Method

Place selected moulds on refrigeration to chill. Pour cream into mixing bowl, whisk to half-whipped stage and put aside. Combine gelatine with cold water, lemon juice and dissolve over gentle heat. Place egg yolks, caster sugar, gelatine solution in mixing bowl and whisk briskly over heated bain-marie to the thick ribbon stage and until the mixture doubles in volume. Remove from bain-marie, incorporate rum and stir until cool but not set. Place egg whites in mixing bowl, whisk to peaked foam (not too stiff) and put aside. Make sure the basic egg mixture is cold, smooth and not set then carefully fold-in the whipped cream followed by the egg white foam. Transfer mixture immediately into the chilled moulds and place on refrigeration to set. De-mould (if required) onto service dishes, decorate appropriately and present for service.

CHOCOLATE MOUSSE (non-moulded)   Mousse au Chocolat

Yield: 6–8 portions

Unit	Ingredient	Metric	Imperial
1	Cream/whipping or double*	500 ml	1 pt
¼	Chocolate couvertue/melted	125 g	5 oz
⅒	Caster sugar	50 g	2 oz
1/20	Dark rum	25 ml	1 fl oz
	Chantilly cream for decoration		

* When a more economical product is required, replace double cream with whipping or synthetic cream.

Method

Grate the chocolate into a pan and place in double boiler to melt. Whisk cream until stiff, add the sugar, rum, melted chocolate and blend together. Pipe mixture into individual glasses or coupes, decorate with a rosette of crème chantilly and chill for service.

BAVARIAN CREAM-BASED COLD SOUFFLÉ/MOUSSE

Any of the bavarois-based products can be adapted for service as cold soufflées or mousse by adding/incorporating whipped egg white. The whites are whisked to a peaked foam (not too stiff) and folded-in following the cream *see* p. 581 for details.

FRUIT FOOLS 1

Yield: 4 portions

Unit	Ingredient	Metric	Imperial
1*	Selected fruit purée/sweetened (*see* chart below for details)	240 g	8 oz
1	Cream/whipped stiff (double or whipping cream)	240 ml	8 fl oz
	Juice of a half lemon/strained		
	Colouring if appropriate (*see* chart)		
	Whipped cream to decorate		
	Sponge fingers to accompany		

Method

Select individual service dishes (coupes, glassware) and put aside to chill. Flavour fruit purée with lemon juice, pass through medium sieve (to remove any seeds/skins) into a mixing bowl, and blend-in a few drops of colouring if appropriate. Finally, fold-in the whipped cream to form a smooth flavoursome fruit fool. Transfer into chilled service dishes, decorate as appropriate and present accompanied with sponge fingers.

FRUIT FOOLS 2

Yield: 4 portions

Unit	Ingredient	Metric	Imperial
1*	Selected fruit purée/sweetened (*see* chart for details)	150 g	5 oz
1	Thick custard/cold *see* p. 643 (starch thickened)	150 ml	5 fl oz
1	Cream/whipped stiff (double or whipping)	150 ml	5 fl oz
	Squeeze lemon juice/strained		
	Colouring if required/see chart		
	Sponge fingers to accompany		

Method

Select individual service dishes (coupes, glassware) and put aside to chill. Flavour fruit purée with lemon juice, pass through a medium sieve (to remove any seeds/skins) into a mixing bowl and blend-in any colouring if appropriate. Whisk cold custard to a soft smooth texture, incorporate carefully with the fruit purée then fold through the whipped cream to form a smooth flavoursome fruit fool. Transfer into chilled service dishes, decorate as appropriate and present accompanied with sponge fingers.

N.B.   When preparing fruit purées allow *double* the weight of *raw fruit* to arrive at the amount required, i.e. 480 g (1 lb) raw fruit will yield approximately 240 g (8 oz) of the finished purée.

Fruit Fools Prepared Using Above Formula 1 and 2

Name	Selected fruit purée	Top decoration
Apple fool	Stewed apple purée sweetened/cold, *see* p. 557	Rosettes of whipped cream
Apricot fool	Stewed apricot purée sweetened/cold, *see* p. 557	Rosettes of whipped cream
Gooseberry fool	Stewed gooseberry purée sweetened/cold, *see* p. 557	Rosettes of whipped cream
Rhubarb fool	Stewed rhubarb purée sweetened/cold, *see* p. 557	Rosettes of whipped cream
Raspberry fool	Poached raspberry purée sweetened/cold, *see* p. 557	Rosettes of whipped cream/sugared fresh raspberries
Strawberry fool	Poached strawberry purée sweetened/cold, *see* p. 557 Few drops red colouring to pale colour	Rosettes of whipped cream/sugared fresh strawberries

N.B.   Tinned and frozen fruits, well drained, liquidized/sieved to a purée are ideally suited to the preparation of fruit fools. Other suitable fruits may be used.

Fruit Fool-Based Mousse/Non-Moulded

Fruit mousse can also be prepared by incorporating whipped egg white into the various fruit fool mixtures: whipped egg white foam is folded-in to provide a mousse-like texture. The mousse is then presented in coupes in the same way as fruit fools with an accompaniment of sponge fingers. Fruit fool recipe 1, p. 593 is ideally suited to this method.

N.B.   Use approximately 3–4 whites per 480 g (1 lb) of completed fruit fool mixture.

43

Meringue and Meringue Based Sweets

Food scientists use the word 'foam' to describe egg whites whisked to a stiff snow. Once mixed with a given quantity of caster sugar, the foam is more commonly known as meringue. In this form the meringue preparation is used for a wide variety of culinary products. Typically the meringue may be utilized as a product in its own right, e.g. meringue glace/Chantilly or alternatively as part of the more complex sweets such as lemon meringue pie, light sorbets or baked alaskas.

Ingredient Principles

Stiffly whipped egg whites can be aptly described as air dispersed evenly throughout a network of egg albumen. During the whisking process, the egg white protein albumen stretches into a thin film which in turn encloses tiny pockets of air; the build-up of air pockets results in a fairly stable and expanded foam-like preparation. On heating over a given period the protein coagulates and a more or less rigid/stable structure is then formed.

A number of ingredient characteristics can affect the strength/stability of ordinary cold meringue. First, the *egg whites* used should be of a viscous nature indicating a strong albumen content; indeed shelled egg whites are often placed into an appropriate vessel, held in a cool place for a few hours prior to use allowing a percentage of the water within the whites to evaporate. This produces a more concentrated albumen content. Weak, watery egg whites are not recommended because the albumen framework is generally too weak to contain the air as it is incorporated during the whisking process. Egg whites of a stronger albumen content whisk/whip more easily readily enclosing the air during the production process. However, when using 'watery' whites a leakage of air takes place through the already weakened albumen framework and because of the presence of additional water which also breaks down the foam's structure.

The presence of *oil/fat* will also prevent the formation of a quality meringue preparation. The grease inhibits the development of air pockets within the albumen network resulting in a continual lack of incorporated air, which in turn causes the foam to collapse. Conversely, the addition of small quantities of acid/alkali, in the forms of cream of tartare or lemon juice/vinegar and salt when correctly used will actually act to strengthen the foam and assist peaking.

The addition of *caster sugar* provides a more dense, smooth and stable foam/meringue that is able to retain its structure and not easily/quickly collapse and leak moisture.

Over-whisking the whites, particularly without the presence of sugar can cause a foam to break down and drain; clearly seen when a poor quality meringue collapses into a curdled appearance with the liquid drained out at the bottom of the mixing bowl.

Technical Factors Summarized

Egg white | When using separated, shell eggs use whites without any trace of yolk as the fatty yolks prevent formation of a quality meringue.
Spray-dried/frozen whites are often employed.
Where applicable, allow the whites to stand in a cool place for a few hours before use. This allows for a percentage loss of water through evaporation and a subsequent strengthening of the egg white albumen.

Acid/alkali | Add a pinch of cream of tartare or good squeeze of lemon juice and pinch of salt just before whisking in order to further strengthen the albumen framework.

Sugar | Add given 'staged' amounts of caster sugar as indicated by the recipes to strengthen the framework of the developing foam.

Grease | Avoid the presence of fat/grease/oil from any source. Ensure all equipment used is scalded, grease-free, and that hands likewise are free from any greasiness.

Whisking | Avoid over-whisking particularly without the presence of sugar as this may result in a breakdown of the foam indicated by a separated product (fluffy whites float on the drained liquid).

Types of Meringue Foam

Three distinct types of meringue preparation are encountered in the professional kitchen, namely ordinary, Italian and Swiss. However, the types most commonly used are cold ordinary meringue and hot Italian meringue. Whipped egg whites are also used extensively throughout cookery to lighten and aerate many products.

Common Meringue Mixtures

1. *Ordinary cold meringue* (meringue ordinaire) which is made-up essentially using:
   Egg whites
   Caster sugar
   Cream of tartare/lemon juice
2. *Hot Italian meringue* (meringue Italienne) which is made-up essentially using:
   Egg whites
   Boiled syrup 118°C (245°F)
   Cream of tartare/lemon juice

N.B.   For amounts and production methods *see* recipes following.

Notes on Italian meringue

When incorporating the hot boiled sugar syrup to the egg white foam, the pockets of air already trapped within the albumen network become heated, expand and further increase the volume of the foam/meringue. The boiled sugar syrup is *whisked/incorporated* into the *already whipped whites* which have reached the stiff snow stage, before the syrup is introduced. The hot boiled sugar syrup 118°C (245°F) is added as a fine slow stream whilst whisking continues. As the internal temperature of the forming meringue gradually increases, so the trapped air continues to expand, resulting in increased volume and lightness. By the time all the hot syrup has been incorporated, partial coagulation of the albumen framework has taken place to further stabilize the formed Italian meringue. The finished result is a high volume, light and stable product that will stand for a considerable time before any signs of collapse appear. Hence its suitability for sweets which require advanced preparation and holding qualities, e.g. baked alaska and omelet soufflés, etc. *see* recipes.

Notes on Swiss meringue

Swiss meringue is prepared by using the same ingredients as for ordinary meringue. Whites with sugar are then whisked in a bowl over a hot bain-marie until the mixture becomes warm, thick and smooth. The bowl is then removed from the bain-marie and whisking continued until the mixture cools and thickens.

An alternative method of production can be used by:

1. Warming the sugar on tray in the oven.
2. Whisking the whites to a stiff snow.
3. Adding the warmed sugar to the foam whilst continuing to whisk the whites until the mixture becomes stiff.

   Swiss meringue is used to a lesser extent than its two common counterparts; its main utility being associated with the preparation of certain petits fours. The principles of production for Swiss meringue are similar to those already outlined in the preceding notes.

ORDINARY MERINGUE   Meringue Ordinaire

Unit	Ingredient	Metric	Imperial
1	Caster sugar	240 g	8 oz
½	Egg whites	120 g	4 oz
	Pinch cream of tartare or		
	squeeze lemon juice		
	Flavouring if required		

Method

Scald all working utensils to remove any grease and ensure all ingredients are grease/egg yolk free. Preferably machine-whisk the whites with acid to form a stiff foam. Once the foam peaks continue to whisk at medium speed and at the same time add half the sugar and flavouring. Whisk for a further 2 to 3 minutes and form a smooth dense stiff meringue. Finally, remove from the machine, and using a spoon/spatula, *carefully stir/fold-in* the remaining sugar. Once ready, ordinary meringue needs to be used quickly as it only remains stable for approximately 15 minutes.

ITALIAN MERINGUE
Meringue Italienne

Unit	Ingredient	Metric	Imperial
1	Granulated sugar	240 g	8 oz
½	Egg whites	120 g	4 oz
*	Water		
	Pinch cream of tartare		
	Colouring/flavouring if required		

* Sufficient *water* to *dissolve* sugar and form a syrup approximately ⅓ unit (80 ml (2½ fl oz)).

Method

Place sugar, water, cream of tartare in boiling pan, and dissolve the sugar. Heat to the soft ball 118°C (245°F) removing any scum and brushing down sides of pan with clean water to prevent crystallization. When syrup is boiling to temperature, whisk the egg whites to stiff/peaked foam. Continue whisking and gradually pour-in a fine steady stream of the hot syrup to fully incorporate. Continue whisking until a stable and light meringue is formed.

   N.B.   If required add colouring/flavouring once syrup is fully incorporated.

Sweets Typically Produced Using Ordinary Meringue

MERINGUE SHELLS

Yield: 10 portions (20 shells)
Baking/drying temperature: 110°C (230°F)
Baking/drying time: 2–2½ hr

Unit	Ingredient	Metric	Imperial
1	Ordinary meringue mix recipe (ready prepared weight)	360 g	12 oz

Method

Using 12 mm (½ in) piping tube/bag, pipe oval mound-shaped meringue shells onto baking sheet covered with greaseproof paper. Place into low oven at 110°C (230°F) for approximately 2½ hours to dry the shells (leave door of the oven slightly open to allow any steam escape). Once adequately set/dry, remove from oven/baking sheet and store on trays in a dry-airy place ready for use.

   N.B.   As an alternative to oven-drying, the meringue shells may be set/dried-out in a kitchen hot-cupboard but because of a lower temperature the process takes approximately 5 hours.

Sweets Prepared Using Dried Meringue Shells (2 shells per portion)

Name	Ingredient/directions	French term
Cream meringue	Chantilly cream Glacé cherries/angelica Sandwich portion of Chantilly cream between two shells to hold. Place onto presentation dish and decorate top with rosette of Chantilly cream, half glacé cherry and angelica	Meringue chantilly
Ice-cream meringue	Selected ice-cream Sandwich portion of scooped ice-cream between two shells to hold. Present for service	Meringue glacée
Ice-cream and cream meringue	Selected ice-cream Chantilly cream Glacé cherries/angelica As above but decorate with rosette of cream, half glacé cherry and angelica	Meringue glacée chantilly
Chocolate ice-cream meringue	Chocolate ice-cream Chocolate flakes to decorate Sandwich a portion of scooped chocolate ice-cream between two shells to hold. Present for service decorated with flaked chocolate	Meringue glacé suchard

BUILT-UP MERINGUE NESTS/CASES FOR VACHARINS

Yield: 16 single nests *or* 2 × 20 cm (7 in) diameter large vacharin cases
Baking/drying temperature: 110°C (230°F)
Baking/drying time: 2½ hr approx.

Unit	Ingredient	Metric	Imperial
1	Ordinary meringue mixture (ready prepared weight)	360 g	12 oz

Small Single Portioned Nest/Cases 1

Using 12 mm (½ in) plain tube/piping bag, pipe round-shaped meringue nests of approximately 7.5 cm (3 ½ in) diameter onto a baking sheet lined with greaseproof paper.
    N.B.   The nests should be sufficiently built-up to receive an adequate single portion of any selected filling.

Place into a low oven at 110°C (230°F) to cook/dry for approximately 2½ hours (leave oven door slightly ajar to allow any steam/moisture escape). Once adequately set/dry remove from oven/baking sheet and store on trays in a dry-airy place ready for use.

N.B.   As an alternative to oven-drying, the meringue shells may be set/dried-out in a kitchen hot-cupboard but because of the lower temperature the drying process takes approximately 5 hours.

Small Single Portioned Nests/Cases 2

Pencil spaced outline circles approximately 7.5 cm (3 in) diameter onto a sheet of grease-proof paper and place onto a baking sheet. Using a 12 mm (½ in) plain tube/piping bag, pipe single meringue rings following the pencilled circles as a guide. Fill-in a required number of the circles with meringue to form some basis. Set/dry-out and store as above.

Built-up Cases for Large Multi-Portioned Vacharin

Pencil large circles, squares or other shapes onto sheets of greaseproof (approximately 20 cm (7–8 in) diameter/dimension) and place onto baking sheets. Using a ½ in plain tube and piping bag, pipe the shapes required following the pencilled lines as a guide. Fill-in a required number of the shapes with piped meringue for the bases, finishing each base with a single-layered piped border.

N.B.   Double piped building layers can be produced saving both space/time, but the drying-out/setting time may increase slightly. Set/dry-out and store as above.

To Build-up the Vacharin Case

Whether for small single or larger multi-portioned cases, the technique used is the same:

1. Place the selected dried meringue base onto the working surface.
2. Take sufficient dried meringue building rings to build-up to 4 layers (approximately 5.5 cm (2 in).
3. Using either raw whipped meringue or whipped cream as the 'bonding medium', build-up vacharin cases in readiness for use.
4. Pipe a little whipped cream into base of case, fill-up with selected fruit filling, glaze if required, decorate with rosettes of cream and present cold.

Selected Vacharin Sweets (small or large varieties)

Name	Filling/directions	Quantity	Portions	French term
Cherry vacharin	Stoned tinned cherries/well drained Whipped cream for base/decoration Red fruit glaze to finish	480 g (1 lb) 300 ml (½ pt)	4 to 8	Vacharin montmorency
Mixed fruit vacharin	Selected cocktail of fruits (well drained/small pieces) Chantilly cream Combine fruit with cream and use to fill cases	480 g (1 lb) 300 ml (½ pt)	4 to 8	Vacharin aux fruits

Name	Filling/directions	Quantity	Portions	French term
Strawberry vacharin	Fresh strawberries Whipped cream for base/decoration Melba sauce to glaze/finish	480 g (1 lb) 300 ml (½ pt)	4 to 8	Vacharin aux frais
Raspberry vacharin	Fresh raspberries Whipped cream for base/decoration Melba sauce to glaze/finish	480 g (1 lb) 300 ml (½ pt)	4 to 8	Vacharin aux framboises

N.B.   Different fruits and other suitable fillings can be used to create further interesting vacharin sweets.

Meringue Shapes: Using Ordinary Meringue Mixture

Meringue mushrooms

Using a meringue-filled piping bag with 12 mm (½ in) plain tube/baking trays lined with greaseproof pipe small round domes to represent mushroom heads and small, fat, pointed pyramids to represent the mushroom stalks. Dust the heads finely with cocoa powder and place all shapes in very low oven/hot cupboard to bake/dry 110°C (230°F). Once dry, re-move from oven to cool.

To assemble

Prepare a hollow/indentation in underside of mushroom heads, fill with whipped cream and insert the mushroom stalk.

Fancy meringue shapes

Using a meringue filled piping bag with 12 mm (½ in) star tube, pipe out a selection of shapes onto a baking tray lined with greaseproof paper. Decorate with glace fruit/nuts, etc. Bake/dry as above and remove to cool.

N.B.   The shapes are often finished with chocolate (dipped/finely piped) and used as required, e.g. as meringue fancies or as part of other sweets.

Sweets Typically Prepared Using Italian Meringue

SURPRISE SOUFFLÉ OMELETS   Omelettes Soufflées en Surprise

Yield: 4 portions
Oven temperature: 232°C (450°F)
Flash time: 2 min

Unit	Ingredient	Metric	Imperial
1	Italian meringue (ready prepared weight)	480 g	1 lb
1	Selected ice-cream/filling/*see* chart Sheet sponge base (circular 20 cm (8 in)	480 g	1 lb

Unit	Ingredient	Metric	Imperial
	diameter × 2 cm (¾ in) thick or rectangular 20 cm (8 in) long × 7.5 cm (3 in) wide × 2 cm (¾ in) thick, as required) Fruit syrup/liqueur to moisten sponge base Caster sugar for glazing purposes		

Method

Place sheet sponge onto oven-proof presentation dish/flat and moisten with a light fruit syrup and kirsch. Cover top of sponge base with selected ice-creams (*see* chart below). Smother quickly with prepared meringue, neatly flatten/smooth with palette knife to an oval or round shape and decorate with more piped meringue using a fancy tube/piping bag. Now sprinkle lightly with caster sugar, clear rim of service dish of any sugar, flash in hot oven to golden brown for approximately 2 minutes at 232°C (450°F) then serve immediately.

N.B.   If not required for immediate service, the prepared surprise soufflés can be frozen successfully, withdrawn as needed and immediately finished in a hot oven for service as described above.

Soufflé Omelets Prepared Using Above Formula

Name	Selected ice/filling	Shape	French term
Surprise soufflé omelet	Vanilla and strawberry ice-creams	Oval	Omelette soufflée en surprise
Norwegian surprise soufflé omelet	Vanilla/strawberry ice-creams and fruit salad	Oval	Omelette soufflée en surprise norvegienne
Alaskan surprise soufflé omelet	Vanilla ice-cream	Oval	Omelette soufflée en surprise alaksa
Mandarian surprise soufflé omelet	Tangarine ice-cream	Oval	Omelette soufflée en surprise aux mandarins
Cherry surprise soufflé omelet	Raspberry and cherry ice-creams N.B. Present surrounded with poached stoned cherries in brandy. Surround also with some Kirsch and 'flame' for presentation	Oval	Omelette soufflée en surprise aux cerises
Island surprise soufflé omelet	Chocolate ice-cream (other flavours may be used) N.B. Present the glazed omelet with 4 small dry meringue cases on the top filled/flamed with rum	Round	Omelette soufflé en surprise islandaise

N.B.   Many other surprise soufflé omelets can be prepared/created using a variety of suitable ice-creams/fruit fillings.

BAKED ALASKA (single portions)

Yield: 4 portions

Oven flash time/temperature: 2 min at 232°C (450°F)

Unit	Ingredient	Metric	Imperial
1	Italian meringue/ready prepared	480 g	1 lb
1	Selected ice-cream	480 g	1 lb
*	4 Selected fruit portions		
	4 Sponge discs/bases 1 cm (½ in) thick		
	Fruit syrup/liqueur to moisten		
	Caster sugar for glazing		

* Sponge discs of sufficient diameter to hold fruit portions. Fruits typically used include poached peaches/pears.

Method

Place sponge discs onto oven-proof service dishes or baking tray and moisten lightly with fruit syrup/liqueur. Mount fruit and ice-cream portions onto the prepared sponge discs, cover quickly and decoratively with meringue, sprinkle with caster sugar and flash in hot oven to golden brown. Remove from oven and serve immediately.

N.B. The 'Alaskas' can be held on deep-freeze in prepared form (prior to the oven-flash process) then withdrawn as needed and immediately finished in the hot oven as required for service.

SNOW EGGS   Oeufs à la Neige

Yield: 4 portions

Unit	Ingredient	Metric	Imperial
1	Fresh milk	500 ml	1 pt
³/₅*	Ordinary meringue/ready prepared	300 ml	12 oz
¹/₅*	Egg yolks	100 g	4 oz
¹/₁₀	Caster sugar	50 g	2 oz
	Vanilla essence to flavour		
	Flaked/lightly roasted almonds		

* The egg whites/yolks in the above formula make-up the requirements for both the meringue and fresh custard.

Method

Blend milk, vanilla essence, caster sugar together, pour into a suitable poaching vessel and bring to near boiling. Using two tablespoons, prepare smooth oval shapes from the meringue mixture, gently place into the hot milk and poach on both sides until set (the meringue shapes will require careful turning during poaching in order to cook/set them on both sides). Once set, remove the meringues using a perforated spoon and put aside to drain well. Continue shaping, poaching and draining the meringue mixture in this way until the mixture is fully utilized. Now using the poaching milk, prepare a fresh custard sauce/sauce anglaise *see* p. 643 and put aside to cool. Arrange the drained/set/cooled oval meringue shapes/portions in the deep service dishes, pour over the custard and allow to cool/chill. Present for service sprinkled with roasted flaked almonds.

JAPONAISE MIXTURE FOR JAP BASES

Yield: According to size
Baking time: approx. 45 min
Baking temperature: 120°C (250°F)

Unit	Ingredient	Metric	Imperial
1	Caster sugar	480 g	1 lb
⅝	Egg whites	300 g	10 oz
½	Ground almonds/sieved	240 g	8 oz
1/16	Cornflour	30 g	1 oz

Method

Line a baking sheet with rice paper and set aside. Whisk whites to a stiff peak then beat-in half of the caster sugar. Mix and sieve together remaining caster sugar, almonds and corn-flour twice. Gently fold the sieved mixture into the meringue to incorporate evenly, but avoid excessive handling. Using a piping bag (12 mm (½ in)) plain tube, pipe closed flat circular bases of 20 cm (8 in) diameter. Bake in oven at 120°C (250°F) for approximately 45 minutes until cooked, crisp and golden. Allow to cool and use as required.

N.B.   See Chapter 31, for use with gateaux.

44

House Made Ices, Sorbets and Iced Sweets

Fresh house-produced ices and iced concoctions are a welcome and delightful feature on any bill of fare. Discerning customers recognize and appreciate the characteristic flavours, colours, textures and nutritive value of fresh quality ices as opposed to the many standardized mass-produced commercial varieties.

Classification

House-made ice-cream varieties are essentially produced by one of two methods, namely *churn-freezing* or *still-freezing*. During *churn-freezing*, the mixture is gradually frozen whilst in motion within a purpose-designed rotary freezer (manual or mechanical); whereas with *still-freezing* the mixture is blended then moulded as required, placed into a freezer cabinet and allowed to freeze/set firm without any further agitation. The chart below provides a breakdown of the various iced preparations by description and mode of production.

Ices

Churn-frozen varieties	*Still-frozen varieties*
Cream ices (custard/crème anglaise based)	Iced bombes
Water ices (syrup-based)	Iced parfaits
Sorbets (syrup-based lightened with Italian meringue)	Iced bricks
Granites/Marquises (sorbet type derivatives)	Iced soufflés
	Iced mousses
	Cassatas
	(All the above types are produced using rich mixtures made-up from various combinations of egg yolks and/or whites/cream, sugar/stock syrups, milk and flavourings)

Ingredients/Production Criteria

Ice-cream quality is judged in terms of flavour, consistency and stability. The specific importance of each factor closely relates to the type of ice-cream being made. The guidelines outlined below provide a general summary concerning the influence of ingredients and production method upon quality.

Flavour

Custard-based churn-frozen and rich still-frozen ice-cream mixtures should have delicate flavours achieved by the careful selection, balance and blending of the ingredients used. The main flavour should be obvious without predominating and the combined fine flavour of the other ingredients discernible in the background. A quality flavour requires the use of sound untainted fresh ingredients.

In the case of water-ices and sorbets, however, the main flavour is more predominant and refreshing. Indeed, the traditional function of the sorbet on classic menus of refreshing the palate between courses (after the entrée and before the roast) serves to illustrate these characteristics.

It will be noted that in all recipe formulae for ices, the *sugar* and *flavouring* contents can be relatively high, although not excessive. The proportions used counter-balance any adverse effects of low temperatures upon the taste buds (low temperatures dull taste buds).

Consistency Texture

The texture of iced products is largely determined by the nature/blending of the ingredients used, and the subsequent formation of the ice-crystals within the mixture during the freezing process. Quality ices, particularly the churned cream ice varieties and still-frozen varieties require smooth, rich consistencies and the water ices/sorbets, although less rich in texture, should nevertheless be pleasing to the palate.

Fat-rich ingredients, such as egg yolks/cream provide body/substance, whilst sugar in solution/syrup adds smoothness. These ingredients along with the incorporation of air encourage a desirable formation/arrangement of small even-shaped ice-crystals throughout the mixture during freezing.

The sugar solution and all the other ingredients, therefore, act to separate-out the forming ice-crystals keeping them small and even, resulting in a desirable finely textured product. Lumpiness, and the formation of large ice-crystals are undesirable and such formations must be guarded against. Faulty or intermittent churning can lead to both problems, quick freezing as opposed to slow freezing leads to fine rather than large ice-crystal formation. Incorrect recipe balance can lead to sugar crystallization, a result of excess sugar density which can be prevented by the saccharometer test (*see* recipes) before freezing takes place.

Stability

Obviously, it is desirable that ice-creams do not melt too quickly before they can be sampled and enjoyed for their taste, temperature and texture. Stability varies marginally with the richer mixtures (because of their fat content) being more stable than the lighter water-ices and sorbets. Stability in freezing can also be affected by the presence of *sugar* and *alcohol*. Too much of either can adversely affect freezing and, therefore, texture, consistency and stability. Consequently, in some of the formulae sugar density is tested (using a saccharometer) for a satisfactory reading which can be corrected as required before freezing takes place (*see* water-ices and sorbets pp. 607–13) for typical examples.

Freezing Techniques

The two principal methods used to freeze iced products are *churn-freezing* and *still-freezing*. When freezing any mixture, the objective is to achieve a product which is as stable and smooth textured as is possible, characteristics directly linked to the ingredients used and the size, shape and dispersion of ice-crystals within the mixture. Freezing can only take place when the water/liquid content changes from a liquid to a solid state, a result of heat loss from food caused by the use of a surrounding refrigerant, be it chopped ice and salt or other built-in substance.

Churn-Freezers

These take the form of hand-tub freezers, electric tub-freezers (which require a mixture of chopped-ice and salt around the container for cooling/freezing purposes, or purpose-designed power operated ice-cream machines cooled by a built-in refrigerant. The process of churning, however, is a common feature in all types. The mixture for churn-freezing is poured into a metal container which comes equipped with a connecting paddle/mechanism designed to fit/rotate inside the covered container. During churning, the sharp edges of the paddle cut/scrape and disperse the forming ice-crystals from the sides of the container, prevents the formation of large ice-crystals by continual uninterrupted agitation, moves the mixture constantly so that none remains static/unfrozen at the centre and at the same time introduces air to lighten and increase volume.

N.B.   Salt lowers the freezing point of water, hence its use with chopped ice when using hand or electric tub-freezers. A successful ratio is approximately $\frac{1}{5}$ unit salt to 1 unit chopped ice (i.e. 400 g (1 lb) salt to 2 kg (5 lb) chopped ice).

Still-Freezing

This technique is carried out in normal freezer cabinets. The mixtures used are (as previously discussed) rich in composition and of a high fat content. Any air, lightness and volume is incorporated during the whisking/blending processes before the mixtures are moulded for still-freezing. Once moulded, no further agitation is carried out and the product is allowed sufficient time to freeze and become stable.

Hygiene Factors and Legislation

Ice-creams because of their moist and nutrient-rich characteristics, in suitable conditions, are an ideal environment for the growth of harmful pathogenic bacteria. Great care, therefore, needs to be exercised at all stages from preparation to storage and service. Production and service equipment must be scrupulously clean and, where applicable, sterilised before, during and after use.

The production of on-site ice-creams, excluding traditional water-ices and sorbets, are subject to the same legal requirements as their commercial counterparts. The Ice-Cream Regulations 1967 tabulates the permitted minimum contents for specific ice-creams with which the caterer must conform. The Ice-Creams (Heat Treatment) Regulations (1959 and 1963) are concerned with the initial pasteurization or sterilization of ingredients and the cooling of the mixture to below 7.1°C (45°F) within a 1½ hour time span and until frozen.

At this point ice-cream *must* be held frozen at less than −2.2°C (28°F). If during production any of the above temperatures are not adhered to, the total ingredients must be re-pasteurized or sterilized once again.

Storage/Service or Ice-Cream Products

The above products should be held frozen at a temperature not higher than −20°C (−5°F). Obviously at these low temperatures the various products are very hard and difficult to handle for service. A technique used to facilitate the service of ice-cream and related concoctions is to transfer the hard frozen product from the very low temperature deep-freeze into a cabinet (ice-cream conservator) at a higher temperature −12°C to −6°C (10°F to 20°F) on the day before service.

CHURN-FROZEN CREAM ICES

These relatively rich ice-creams are based upon the preparation of a rich fresh custard known as 'Crème Anglaise'. The process and underlying principle of producing the initial custard is the same as for making sauce Anglaise referred to in Chapter 47, p. 643, but involve increased proportions of egg yolk for added richness and consistency. The resultant Crème Anglaise is then strained, allowed to cool before being finished with cream (optional) and the required flavouring. Creamed ices are characterized by smooth rich textures and delicate flavours.

Crème Anglaise-based ice-creams
VANILLA ICE-CREAM   Glacé à la Vanille
Yield: dependent upon flavour of ice produced, 1 l (1 qt)

Unit	Ingredient	Metric	Imperial
1	Milk	500 ml	1 pt
½	Cream/double	250 ml	10 fl oz
¼	Caster sugar	120 g	5 oz
¼	Egg yolks	120 g	5 oz
	Vanilla essence to flavour		

Method

Whisk together egg yolks, caster sugar and vanilla essence to a smooth cream. Bring milk to the boil, pour/whisk into the mixture and thoroughly incorporate. Return to a clean thick-bottomed saucepan and stir over heat continuously without boiling until the custard (sauce Anglaise) coats the back of the spoon/spatula. Immediately pass the custard through a fine sieve into a clean bowl and put aside to cool. Once cooled, blend-in the cream and machine-churn. When smooth and sufficiently firm, transfer ice-cream into a scrupulously clean covered ice-cream container and store on deep-freeze at no less than −20°C (−5°F) until required for service (*see* notes on ice-cream storage and serving, *see* p. 608).

Ice-Creams Prepared Using Above Formula: Added Ingredient Amounts in Relation to 1 Unit, i.e. 500 ml (1 pt) Milk

Name	Unit	Ingredient	Metric	Imperial
Chocolate ice-cream (Glacé au chocolat)	⅕ ⅕	Chocolate couverture Milk Grate couverture into milk and heat until chocolate is thoroughly melted. Add to the prepared hot custard (sauce anglaise)	100 g 100 ml	4 oz 4 fl oz
Coffee ice-cream (Glacé au café)	¹⁄₄₀	Instant coffee Add to hot milk to infuse before making custard	12.5 g	½ oz
Praline ice-cream (Glacé au praliné)	¹⁄₁₀	Praline/crushed Add to ice-cream during rotary freezing just before the ice-cream sets	50 g	2 oz
Caramel ice-cream (Glacé au caramel)		Form a caramel with caster sugar (from basic formulae), and little by little blend carefully with the hot milk before forming basic custard		
Orange ice-cream (Glacé à l'orange)		Finely grated zest of 2 oranges Yellow/red colouring for orange colour Add zest to infuse hot milk and flavour the custard		
Strawberry or raspberry ice (Glacé aux fraises/ framboises)	½ ¹⁄₁₀	Strawberry *or* raspberry purée Caster sugar Red colouring (few drops) Sweeten purée with sugar, pass through fine sieve and blend with basic custard before adding cream, adjust colour of finished cream before churning	250 g 50 g	10 oz 2 oz
Banana ice-cream (Glacé de bananes)	⅘	Banana purée (flavoured with juice of ½ lemon) Blend with basic custard before adding cream	400 g	1 lb

Churn-Frozen Water Ices

This type of iced preparation is based upon the combination/blending of stock syrup, fruit juices, liqueurs and/or fruit purées lightened/modified with partially whipped egg white. The high water content and absence of fat-rich ingredients produces a less rich product than the crème Anglaise based ices. However, water-ices are generally characterized by predominant refreshing flavours and relatively smooth textures. The incorporation of the partially whipped egg white acts to bind, lighten and modify the mixture, thus enhancing the texture/quality of the finished water-ice.

Sugar content/density

The amount of sugar in the mixture to be frozen is critical. Too sweet a mixture will not freeze, whereas too little sugar content results in a hard, tasteless ice. Consequently the required sugar density is given in the recipe formula and the use of a saccharometer recommended. Additionally, it is beneficial to taste the cooled mixture before freezing commences as the flavour of iced preparations is weakened by the freezing process. Keeping on the sweet side, therefore, at this point, and without going above the recommended density is a useful guide.

WATER ICES (Citrus fruits based) Glacé a l'Eau

Yield: approx. 1 l (1 qt)

Unit	Ingredient	Metric	Imperial
1	Water	600 ml	1 pt
½	Granulated sugar	300 g	10 oz
½₀	Egg white/partially whipped	30 g	1 oz
*	Selected citrus fruit flavouring (*see* chart below for details) Colouring (*see* chart below)		

* Varies according to type of ingredients used, *see* chart below.

Method

Combine water/sugar together in heavy-based saucepan, boil for a few minutes to form a light clear syrup. Pour hot syrup onto extracted citrus juices/finely grated zest (*see* chart below for details) and put aside to cool thoroughly. Test sugar density with saccharometer for a reading of 18°–20° Baume. If the reading is *less* add sufficient sugar to correct, if *over* dilute with water to achieve required reading.

Once thoroughly cooled, pass through fine conical strainer, incorporate partially whipped egg white, pour into rotary freezer, churn-freeze until firm and smooth. Transfer to appropriate container, cover/seal and store in deep-freeze at –5°C (–20°F). Present for service in pre-chilled service dishes with wafers/finger biscuits.

Citrus Water Ices Prepared Using Above Formula: Added Ingredients in Relation to 1 Unit, i.e. 600 ml (1 pt) Water

Name	Ingredient	Directions
Lemon water ice (Glacé au citron)	Zest of 2 lemons Juice of 4 lemons	Zest finely grated Juice extracted/strained
Lime water ice (Glacé au citron vert)	Zest of 2 limes Juice of 4 limes Green colouring	Zest finely grated Juice extracted/strained A few drops to pale green

Name	Ingredient	Directions
Orange water ice (Glacé à l'orange)	Zest of 2 oranges Juice of 3 oranges/1 lemon Red/yellow colouring	Zest finely grated Juice extracted/strained Few drops colouring to orange
Tangerine water ice (Glacé aux mandarins)	Zest of 2 tangerines Juice 4 tangerines/1 lemon Red/yellow colouring	Zest finely grated Juice extracted/strained Few drops colouring to orange

WATER ICES (fruit purée based)　　　　　　　　　Glacé a l'Eau

Yield: approx. 1 l (2 pt)

Unit	Ingredient	Metric	Imperial
1	Stock syrup/cold, *see* p. 647	600 ml	1 pt
1	Selected fruit purée (*see* chart below for details)	600 g	1 pt
$\frac{1}{20}$	Egg white/partially whipped Flavourings/colourings (*see* chart below for details)	30 g	1 oz

Method

Blend together cold syrup, prepared fruit purée, any additional flavourings/colourings and place on refrigeration to chill thoroughly. Test sugar density with saccharometer for a reading of 18°–20° Baume. If the reading is *less* add more stock syrup to correct, if *over* dilute with water to achieve required reading. Fold through the partially whipped egg white, pour into rotary freezer, churn-freeze until firm and smooth. Transfer to appropriate container, cover/seal and store in deep-freeze at −5°C (−20°F). Present for service in pre-chilled service dishes with wafers/finger biscuits.

Fruit Purée-Based Water Ices Prepared Using Above Formula

Name	Selected fruit purée flavouring	Directions
Apricot water ice (Glacé à l'abricots)	Apricot purée/ripe unsweetened Juice of 1 lemon/1 orange	Liquidize/sieve apricot flesh 　for purée Extracted and strained
Mango water ice (Glacé au mangue)	Mango purée/ripe/unsweetened Juice of 1 lemon	Liquidize/sieve mango flesh 　for purée Extracted and strained
Melon water ice (Glacé au melon)	Melon purée/ripe/lightly flavoured 　with ginger syrup from jar of 　preserved ginger Juice of 1 orange/1 lemon	Liquidize/sieve melon flesh 　with ginger syrup for 　purée Extracted and strained

Name	Selected fruit purée flavouring	Directions
Pineapple water ice (Glacé à l'ananas)	Pineapple purée/ripe lightly flavoured with Kirsch	Liquidize/sieve pineapple flesh for purée and flavour with Kirsch
Redcurrant or blackcurrant water ice (Glacé aux groseilles rouges/glacé aux cassis)	Redcurrant or blackcurrant purée/ unsweetened Juice of 1 orange	Liquidize/sieve redcurrants/ blackcurrants for purée Extracted and strained
Strawberry or raspberry water ice Glacé au frais/framboises)	Strawberry or raspberry purée/ unsweetened Juice of 1 orange/½ lemon Red colouring	Liquidize/sieve strawberries/ raspberries for purée Extracted and strained Few drops if required

Churn-Frozen Sorbets

Sorbets can best be described as very light, barely frozen ices, traditionally served during formal banquets to refresh guests' palates after the entrée and before the roast. Stock syrup, main flavourings (typically fruit juices, wines, liqueurs) and Italian meringue form the basis for these light refreshing ices. As with water-ices, *see* p. 609, the incorporation of whipped egg white in the form of Italian meringue lightens and modifies the mixture improving the final texture and quality of the finished product.

Sugar Content/Density

The underlying principles outlined under water-ices, *see* p. 609–10 regarding sugar content apply also to sorbets, except that the traditional sorbets are *less* sweet and generally require a lower reading on the saccharometer before freezing. Obviously the less sweet flavour suits the palate refreshing/cleansing function of these ices.

SORBETS

Yield: Dependent upon flavour of sorbet produced

Unit	Ingredient	Metric	Imperial
1	Stock syrup, *see* p. 647	600 ml	1 pt
⅛	Italian meringue/prepared weight	75 g	2½ oz
	Main flavourings (*see* chart below for details)		

Method

Bring syrup to boiling point, pour onto any citrus juices/grated zest and put aside to cool allowing for full extraction/blending of the flavours. Once cool, pass through a fine strainer, blend-in any wine/champagne (not liqueurs) and put in refrigerator to cool thoroughly. Test sugar density with saccharometer for a reading of 15° Baume (except when making liqueur sorbets (*see* note below chart). If the reading is less than required add more cold stock syrup to correct, if reading over dilute with cold water to correct. Pour mixture into churn-freeze machine and commence churn-freezing process until mixture thickens. At this point, incorporate Italian meringue and liqueur if appropriate and continue until a firm light barely frozen sorbet is formed. Spoon barely frozen cone-shaped into pre-chilled glassware.

N.B. When serving liqueur or wine sorbets moisten/flavour with a small spoonful of liqueur/wine as the sorbet goes out for service. To store sorbets, transfer frozen mixture into an appropriate covered container and hold in deep-freeze until required.

Sorbets Prepared Using Above Formula: Added Ingredient Amounts in Relation to 1 Unit, i.e. 600 ml (1 pt) Stock Syrup

Name	Unit	Ingredient	Metric	Imperial
Lemon sorbet (Sorbet au citron)		Finely grated zest and juice of 4 juice-rich lemons		
Orange sorbet (Sorbet à l'orange)		Finely grated zest and juice of 5 juice-rich oranges/1 lemon		
Lime sorbet (Sorbet au citron vert)		Finely grated zest and juice of 4 juice-rich limes Few drops green colouring		
White wine sorbet (Sorbet au vin blanc)	½	Dry white wine Juice and zest of ½ lemon to flavour	300 ml	10 fl oz
Champagne sorbet (Sorbet champagne)	½	Dry champagne Juice and zest of ½ lemon to flavour	300 ml	10 fl oz
Roman punch sorbet (Punch à la romaine)	¼	Dry champagne Juice and zest of 2 oranges Juice and zest of 1 lemon Rum for *service only* (*see* N.B. in method)	150 ml	5 fl oz

Liqueur Sorbets

When preparing liqueur sorbets, the selected liqueur is added *after the Italian meringue and just before the mixture freezes*. The amount of liqueur used is $\frac{1}{10}$ unit liqueur to 1 unit stock syrup 60 ml (2 fl oz) liqueur per 600 ml (1 pt) stock syrup). The juice/zest of lemons/oranges may well be appropriate, additional ingredients with some liqueurs, e.g. orange with Grand Marnier, and these are added as indicated in the method. For these sorbets the cooled stock syrup with any added fruit juice/wine should register 18° Baume before freezing commences.

Churn-Frozen Granités/Marquises

Granités are similar to sorbets/water-ices in composition but excluding the use of Italian meringue or whipped egg white; consequently the frozen granités are characterized by light grainy textures. Granités are essentially made using acidic fruit juices and stock syrup with a sugar density of not more than 14° Baume. Traditionally, granités are used in the same way as sorbets, namely as a means of refreshing the diner's palate between courses. Typical examples lemon, lime, orange granités.

Marquises

Marquises are made using a Kirsch sorbet base (*excluding the Italian meringue content*). This is then churn-frozen to a firm granular texture. At the point of service, flavoured Chantilly cream is incorporated with the frozen mixture. The flavours typically incorporated with the whipped cream include strawberries (purée) and pineapple (purée). The proportion of flavoured cream is approximately ½ unit flavoured Chantilly cream to 1 unit Kirsch sorbet. A plain Kirsch flavoured marquise would require that the Chantilly cream be also flavoured with Kirsch. Marquises are generally served as iced sweets.

Still-Frozen Iced Bombes

These are generally prepared using two distinct types of ice-cream preparations: one (the hard-scoop churned variety) is used and ideally suited for lining the mould, whilst other non-churned varieties (bombe mixtures/mousses) are used for the filling. In some instances, alternate layering techniques are used to produce specific ice-cream bombes of many flavours.

Lining/Filling Bombe Moulds (see p. 29 for illustration of bombe moulds)

1. Chill the bombe mould thoroughly in freezer and/or crushed ice.
2. Line the bottom and sides of the bombe mould with a thin 12 mm (½ in) even layer of selected ordinary hard-scoop ice-cream up to the rim. This can be achieved by using the back of a spoon.
3. Immediately fill the centre up to the top with the selected bombe mixture/filling, cover with a round of greaseproof paper and seal with the mould lid/cover.
4. Place in cabinet to still-freeze.

De-Moulding Ice-Cream Bombes

Dip mould into warm water for a few seconds only and wipe-dry. Remove lid, paper, base plug and allow the bombe to slide out. Decorate/serve immediately.

BASIC BOMBE MIXTURE   Pâte à Bombe

Yield: approx. ½ l (1 pt)

Unit	Ingredient	Metric	Imperial
1	Whipped cream	240 ml	8 fl oz
½	Granulated sugar	120 g	4 oz
½	Egg yolks	120 g	4 oz
⅜	Water	90 ml	3 fl oz
*	Flavouring, *see* chart below		

* An abundance of suitable flavourings may be used in both single and combined forms. The chart below outlines just a few typical examples.

Method

Combine sugar with water in a thick-bottomed saucepan, boil to 118°C (245°F) and put aside to cool slightly. Place yolks into a mixing bowl and whisk well for a few minutes. Gradually whisk hot syrup into the yolks to the thick ribbon stage and until the yolks have doubled in volume. Continue to whisk until the mixture becomes cold. Blend-in the flavouring, fold through the whipped cream and mould as required.

Bombe Filling Prepared Using Above Formula: Added Ingredient Amounts in Relation to 1 Unit, i.e. 240 ml (8 fl oz) Whipped Cream

Name/bombe filling	Unit	Ingredient	Metric	Imperial
Vanilla		Vanilla essence to flavour		
Coffee		Coffee essence and Tia Maria to flavour		
Liqueur/spirit		Selected liqueur or spirit to flavour, e.g. rum/Grand Marnier/Crème de Menthe		
Strawberry/raspberry	⅝	Strawberry/raspberry purée	150 ml	¼ pt
Praline	¼	Crushed praline	60 g	2 oz
Maraschino	¼	Maraschino cherries/chopped (soaked in Kirsch)	60 g	2 oz
Chocolate	½	Chocolate couverture (melt with hot syrup)	120 g	4 oz

Ice-Cream Bombes: Typical Examples

Name	Lining ice-cream	Bombe filling	Decoration
Bombe Africaine	Chocolate	Vanilla	To suit
Bombe Alhambra	Vanilla	Strawberry	Strawberries soaked in Kirsch
Bombe Ceylan	Coffee	Rum	To suit
Bombe Coppelia	Coffee	Praline	To suit
Bombe Maraschino	Vanilla	Maraschino	To suit
Bombe Zamora	Coffee	Curaçao	To suit

Still-Frozen Iced Parfaits

Parfaits are similar in composition and mode of production to the basic bombe mixture except that they are frozen without a lining and always of one flavour only. The formula below also incorporates egg whites to provide more lightness. Once ready, the mixture is used to completely fill the selected parfait mould then placed in the cabinet to still-freeze. Various shaped moulds are now used for parfaits, including the bombe shaped mould previously noted. A recent trend is to freeze the parfait mixture in individual service coupes (glass or metal) and present the individual parfaits suitably decorated for service.

BASIC PARFAIT MIXTURE

Yield: approx. ½ l (1 pt)

Unit	Ingredient	Metric	Imperial
1	Basic bombe mixture, *see* p. 614 (plain no flavouring)	300 ml	1 pt
⅕	Egg whites/whipped stiff snow	120 g	4 oz
*	Selected flavouring (*see* chart below)		

* One distinct flavour only is used for each parfait.

Method

Chill parfait moulds and hold chilled in readiness for moulding. Combine flavouring with cold bombe mixture, fold through whipped whites and fill the prepared moulds (if using parfait moulds/cake tins for turning-out, cover top with a piece of genoese cut to fit exactly). If applicable, turn-out as for bombes, decorate and serve.

Ice-Cream Parfaits Prepared Using Above Formula: Added Ingredient Amounts in Relation to 1 Unit, i.e. 600 ml (1 pt) Basic Bombe Mixture

Name	Unit	Ingredient	Metric	Imperial
Coffee parfait (Parfait au moka)		Coffee essence to taste		
Liqueur parfaits (Parfait aux liqueurs)		Selected liqueur to taste		
Praline parfait (Parfait praliné)	⅒	Crushed praline	60 g	2 oz

Still-Frozen Iced Bricks (Biscuits Glaces)

Denotes ice-cream mixtures which are frozen in brick-shaped moulds. The type of mixtures generally used are of the non-churned still-frozen varieties. In addition to the mixture outlined below, the basic bombe and parfait formulas can also be used. The moulds are brick-shaped with removable tops/bottoms. When preparing the mould, the removable base is lined generously with greaseproof paper (overhanging the edges) before being pressed back into position. The mould is then filled with the ice-cream mixture and the top lid secured with greaseproof in exactly the same way as the base, and the bricks still-frozen.

De-moulding/Service

The mould is dipped into warm water, the top and base removed, the contents loosened around the edges with a knife, if required, allowing the ice-brick to slowly slide out. The iced-brick is then cut into slices, each slice placed onto a wafer biscuit and held in deep-freeze. On service, each slice can be decorated to taste using rosettes of Chantilly cream and other ingredients applicable to the main flavour of the specific iced-brick.

BASIC BISCUIT GLACÉ MIXTURE

Yield: Dependent upon flavour produced

Unit	Ingredient	Metric	Imperial
1	Whipped cream	600 ml	1 pt
²/₅	Caster sugar	240 g	8 oz
¼	Egg yolks	150 g	5 oz
⅕	Italian meringue (ready prepared)	120 g	4 oz
	Selected flavouring (*see* chart below)		

Method

Prepare biscuit glace moulds and hold chilled for filling (*see* notes above). Place caster sugar in heavy-based saucepan with a little water (approximately 150 ml (5 fl oz) and form a syrup at 118°C (245°F). Put aside to cool slightly. Place egg yolks in mixing bowl and whisk well for a few minutes. Gradually whisk the hot syrup into the yolks to the thick ribbon stage and until the mixture has doubled in volume. Continue whisking until the mixture becomes cold. Blend-in the selected flavouring, fold through the whipped cream and Italian meringue. Fill the prepared mould and still-freeze. Turn-out from mould (*see* notes above), cut into thick slices, place onto wafers (optional) and return to freezer. For service, remove from freezer, decorate quickly and serve immediately.

Ice-Bricks Prepared Using Above Formula: Ingredient Amounts in Relation to 1 Unit, i.e. 600 ml (1 pt) Whipped Cream

Name	Unit	Ingredient	Metric	Imperial
Apricot iced-brick (Biscuit glacé à l'abricot)	½	Apricot purée Apricot brandy to flavour	300 ml	½ pt

Name	Unit	Ingredient	Metric	Imperial
Liqueur iced-brick (Biscuit glacé aux liqueurs)	⅛	Selected liqueur	75 ml	2½ fl oz
Coffee and praline iced-brick (Biscuit glacé au café praliné)	⅛	Crushed sieved praline Coffee essence to taste	75 g	2½ oz
Pistachio iced-brick (Biscuit glacé aux pistaches)	⅛	Kirsch flavoured pistachio purée	75 g	2½ oz

Still-Frozen Iced Soufflés

Iced soufflés can be identified by the way in which they are made. Generally two distinct methods are employed according to the nature of the ingredients used. *Method I, see* p. 618 which is typically suited to fruit purée varieties incorporates selected fruit purées with Italian meringue/whipped cream to lighten and enrich. Alternatively, Method II, *see* p. 619 which is based upon the use of a rich cream mousse mixture of *whisked sweetened yolks* enriched and lightened with *whipped cream/egg whites* is ideally suited to the more delicate flavours of vanilla, coffee, chocolate, liqueurs, etc.

Moulding and Still-Freezing Iced Soufflés

Large or small individual soufflé dishes/timbales are similarly prepared:

Surround the outside of the moulds with a high collar of greaseproof paper or thin cardboard 4 cm (1½ in) above edge of soufflé mould) and make secure. Fill the moulds with mixture to approximately 3 cm (1 in) above the edge of the mould (held-in by the collar) and place in the deep-freeze cabinet to still-freeze. To serve, remove from freezer, decorate appropriately, remove paper collar carefully and serve immediately on flat with serviette or on a block of sculptured ice.

ICED SOUFFLÉS: 1 (fruit purée flavoured)   Soufflés Glacés

Yield: 8 covers

Unit	Ingredient	Metric	Imperial
1	Whipped cream	450 ml	15 fl oz
⅔	Selected fruit purée/cold (*see* chart below)	300 ml	10 oz
⅔	Caster sugar	300 g	10 oz
⅓	Egg whites	150 g	5 oz
⅕	Water	90 ml	3 fl oz

Method

Surround selected soufflé moulds with a high collar of greaseproof/thin cardboard, secure with string and put aside to chill. Place sugar/water in heavy-based saucepan and boil to 118°C (245°F) removing any scum and brush down sides with clean water as required. Meanwhile, whisk the egg whites to a stiff peak, continue whisking and gradually pour-in the hot syrup in a fine steam. Continue whisking until the syrup is fully incorporated and the formed Italian meringue cold. At this stage, blend the cold fruit purée into the mixture and finally fold-in the whipped cream. Fill the prepared mould with the mixture at around 5 cm (2 in) above edge (held-in by collar). Place in cabinet to still-freeze. For service, decorate appropriately, remove paper surround and serve immediately.

Iced Fruit Purée Soufflés Prepared Using Above Formula

Name	Selected fruit purée	Decoration
Iced raspberry soufflé (Soufflé glacé aux framboises)	Raspberry purée/sieved	Dust finely with cocoa powder/ icing sugar
Iced strawberry soufflé (Soufflé glacé aux frais)	Strawberry purée/sieved	Dust finely with cocoa powder and icing sugar
Iced apricot soufflé (Soufflé glacé aux abricots)	Apricot purée/sieved Flavoured with Kirsch	Dust finely with cocoa powder and icing sugar

N.B. Other fruits suitable for 'pulping' can be used.

ICED SOUFFLÉS: 2   Soufflés Glacés

Yield: 8 portions

Unit	Ingredient	Metric	Imperial
1	Whipped cream	600 ml	1 pt
¼	Caster sugar	150 g	5 oz
⅕	Egg yolks	120 g	4 oz
⅕	Egg whites	120 g	4 oz
	Selected flavouring (*see* chart below for details)		

Method

Surround selected soufflé moulds with a high collar of greaseproof/thin cardboard, secure with string and put aside. Combine yolks/sugar in mixing bowl, add a teaspoon warm water and whisk over a low-heat bain-marie to the thick creamy ribbon stage and until the yolks have doubled in volume. Remove from the bain-marie and continue to whisk until the mixture becomes cold. Add selected flavouring and put aside. Whisk egg whites to a snow, carefully incorporate into the mixture and finally fold-in the whipped cream to form a light smooth texture. Fill the prepared moulds with the mixture to around 4 cm (1½ in) above the edge (held-in by collar). Place in cabinet and still-freeze. For service decorate appropriately, remove collar and serve immediately.

Iced Soufflés Prepared Using Above Formula

Name	Selected flavouring	Decoration
Iced vanilla soufflé (Soufflé glacé à la vanille)	Vanilla essence to taste	Dust finely with cocoa powder and icing sugar
Iced coffee soufflé (Soufflé glacé au café)	Coffee essence to taste	Dust finely with cocoa powder and icing sugar
Iced chocolate soufflé (Soufflé glacé au chocolat)	Melted chocolate/cool to flavour and taste (60–120 g (2–4 oz))	Dust finely with cocoa powder and icing sugar
Iced liqueur soufflé (Soufflé glacé aux liqueurs)	Selected liqueur to flavour	Dust finely with cocoa powder and icing sugar
Iced praline soufflé (Soufflé glacé praliné)	Crushed praline to flavour (60–120 g (2–4 oz))	Sprinkle with crushed praline and dust finely with icing sugar

N.B. Other suitable flavours can be used singly or in combinations, e.g. pistachio, almond, rum and chocolate.

Still-Frozen Iced Mousses

Iced mousses can be identified by the way in which they are made. Generally two distinct methods are employed according to the nature of the ingredients used. Method 1, *see* p. 621, is best suited to the fruit purée varieties and incorporates selected fruit purée with stock syrup and whipped cream to form a smooth mousse preparation. Method 2, *see* p. 621 is prepared using a flavoured thick custard (crème Anglaise) further enriched with whipped cream. Flavours typically suited to this method include vanilla, coffee, orange, chocolate and the like.

N.B. Ice mousse preparations besides being used in their own right as iced sweets are untilized as fillings for iced bombes, *see* pp. 614–15 in the same way as iced bombe fillings.

Moulding and Serving Iced Mousses

Chilled charlotte moulds are typically used for iced-mousse mixtures.

Pour the mixture into the chilled charlotte mould, fill completely, cover to protect surface, place in freezer cabinet and still-freeze. To serve, remove from freezer, carefully strip away the protective cover, dip exterior of mould in warm water, turn-out onto service dish, decorate to suit and serve immediately.

ICED MOUSSES: 1 (fruit purée flavoured)   Mousses Glacées

Yield: 8 portions

Unit	Ingredient	Metric	Imperial
1	Whipped cream	600 ml	1 pt
½	Stock syrup/cold, *see* p. 646	300 ml	10 fl oz
½	Selected fruit purée	300 ml	10 fl oz
	(*see* chart below for details)		

Method

Take charlotte mould and hold ready chilled for filling. Incorporate fruit purée/flavouring into the cold syrup, add whipped cream and fold-in carefully to form a mousse-like mixture. Pour mixture into the chilled moulds, place in cabinet and still-freeze. For service, dip outside of mould in warm water, turn-out onto service dish, decorate to suit and serve immediately.

Iced Mousses Prepared Using Above Formula

Name	Selected fruit purée/flavouring
Iced apricot mousse (Mousse glacées aux abricots)	Apricot purée lightly flavoured with Kirsch
Iced banana mousse (Mousse glacées aux bananes)	Banana purée lightly flavoured with dark rum
Iced raspberry mousse (Mousse glacées aux framboises)	Raspberry purée lightly flavoured with lemon juice
Iced strawberry mousse (Mousse glacées aux frais)	Strawberry purée lightly flavoured with lemon juice

N.B.   Citrus fruits are *not* suitable for this type of iced mixture.

ICED MOUSSES: 2   Mousses Glacées

Yield: 8 portions

Unit	Ingredient	Metric	Imperial
1	Whipped cream	600 ml	1 pt
½ ★	Thick custard cold (crème Anglaise)	300 ml	½ pt
	Selected flavouring/colouring (*see* chart below for details)		

★ *See* sauces, p. 643 for thick crème Anglaise.

Method

Take charlotte moulds and hold ready chilled for filling. Blend selected flavouring/colouring with the chilled custard as applicable, carefully fold-in the whipped cream to form a smooth mixture. Pour into chilled moulds, fill completely, cover to protect surface, place into freezer cabinet and still-freeze. For service, carefully remove cover, dip exterior in warm water, turn-out onto service dish, decorate to suit and serve immediately.

Iced Mousses Prepared Using Above Formula: Added Ingredient Amounts in Relation to 1 Unit, i.e. 600 ml (1 pt) Whipped Cream

Name	Unit	Ingredient	Metric	Imperial
Coffee iced mousse (Mousse glacée au café)		Coffee essence to flavour		
Chocolate iced mousse (Mousse glacée au chocolat)	⅕	Melted chocolate/cool Dark rum to lightly flavour	120 g	4 oz
Vanilla iced mousse (Mousse glacée à la vanille)		Vanilla essence to flavour		
Praline iced mousse (Mousse glacée praliné	⅕	Crushed praline (add to milk when making custard)	120 g	4 oz
Orange iced mousse (Mousse glacée à l'orange)		Juice of 1 orange strained (added to cold custard) Zest of 1 orange (infused with milk when making thick custard) Yellow colouring/few drops		

N.B.   *Liqueur iced mousses:* When preparing liqueur iced mousses, add 1–2 measures of selected liqueur to flavour and any other flavouring/colouring as appropriate, e.g. peppermint/green colouring with Crème de Menthe, zest/juice of orange with Grand Marnier, etc.

STILL-FROZEN CASSATAS

Cassatas are produced still-frozen in shallow round, oval moulds including bombe moulds. The mould is initially lined with *three* different types of ice-cream mixtures of the still-frozen types, *see* p. 614–18 then filled at the centre with a blended mixture of 1 unit Italian meringue to ½ unit whipped cream, liberally garnished with glace fruits soaked in an appropriate liqueur.

ICED COUPES

Iced coupes denote concoctions of decorated/garnished ice-creams presented for service in chilled glass or metal *cups known as coupes*. Served as a sweet course, ice coupes are *prepared to order* providing a most delicious/refreshing product. This is particularly so when fresh home-made ice-creams and fresh seasonal fruits/sauces, etc. are available. The chart below provides a minimum list of the more common concoctions.

Name	Ice-creams	Fruit	Sauce	Suggested presentation
Coupe abricotine	Apricot	Apricot halves/ prepared lightly poached	Apricot/cold	Place ice-cream in base of coupe, cover with apricot halves, coat with sauce, decorate with border whipped cream
Couple belle Helene★	Vanilla	Pear halves/ prepared lightly poached	Chocolate (hot) served separately in sauce-boat	Place ice-cream in base of coupe, cover with pear halves
Coupe Edna May	Vanilla	Compote of red cherries (stoned)	Raspberry purée (sweetened)	Cherries in base of coupe, top with ice-cream, cover with raspberry purée, decorate rosette whipped cream
Coupe Jacques	Lemon and strawberry (equal parts)	Macédoine of fruits flavoured with Kirsch	—	Macédoine in base of coupe, cover with ices, finish with rosette whipped cream, decorate with fresh grapes (halved and de-pipped)
Coupe Jamaica	Coffee	Diced pineapple flavoured with rum	—	Pineapple in base of coupe, cover with ice-cream and finish with rosette whipped cream
Coupe Marie Louise	Vanilla	Raspberries/ lightly sweetened	Raspberry	Raspberries in base of coupe, cover with ice-cream, mask with sauce and decorate with border of whipped cream
Coupe Melba★	Vanilla	Peach or pear/ prepared lightly poached or strawberries	Melba	Place ice-cream in base of coupe, cover with selected fruit, mask with melba sauce

★ Classically Peach Melba and Poire Belle Helene are served in timbales over ice, but the coupe-type presentations are more commonly featured in the majority of establishments.

N.B.   A more extensive repertoire of iced coupes can be prepared using either classical or innovatory interpretations.

Iced sundaes are made-up using the same type of ingredient compositions as iced coupes (often decorated liberally with whipped cream, fruit and nuts, etc.). The contemporary practice of serving sundaes in *shallow dishes* allows more space for attractive arrangements of ingredients on presentation.

45

Miscellaneous Sweets

The aim of this study is to outline examples of popular sweets, which owing to their mode of production and presentation cannot be classified under a specific heading.

APPLE CHARLOTTE
Charlotte aux Pommes

Yield: 4 portions
Cooking time: 30–40 min
Cooking temperature: 232°C (450°F)

Unit	Ingredient	Metric	Imperial
1	Cooking apples	400 g	1 lb
1	Stale bread	400 g	1 lb
¼	Butter	100 g	4 oz
★	Sugar		

★ Sufficient to sweeten the cooked apples.

Method

Cut the bread into 5 mm (¼ in) slices and remove the crusts. Cut two circles of bread to fit the base of a charlotte mould, then cut sufficient fingers to line the sides. Melt 75 g (3 oz) of the butter, dip one side of the circles and fingers in the butter. Line the base and sides of a charlotte mould with the dipped sides of bread touching the mould. Retain the second circle of bread to act as a lid after the lined mould is filled with apple.

Peel, core and quarter the apples. Cut into slices and place into a thick bottomed pan with the remaining butter. Cover with a lid and stew gently until the apples begin to fall, remove from heat and sweeten to taste. Fill the mould with apples, place second circle of bread in position and bake in a hot oven until the bread is crisp and brown. Remove from oven and allow to stand for 2–3 minutes. Turn out and serve accompanied with a sauce boat of apricot sauce or custard.

N.B. When individual portions are required prepare in dariole moulds. On occasions the apple purée may be very wet and soft which will result in the finished sweet collapsing. In this instance it is advisable to add some stale white breadcrumbs to the purée before baking.

Apple Strudel   Apfelstrudel

Yield: 6–8 portions
Cooking time: 30–35 min
Cooking temperature: 175–190°C (350°–375°F)

STRUDEL PASTE

Unit	Ingredient	Metric	Imperial
1	Flour	200 g	8 oz
³/₈ ★	Water	75 g	3 oz
¼	Egg	50 g	2 oz
⅛	Butter (melted)	25 g	1 oz
	Pinch of salt		

★ Amount of water may vary according to water absorption rate of flour.

Method

Sift flour and salt into a bowl, form a bay. Whisk together the egg, melted butter and water, pour into bay. Combine ingredients to form a smooth, soft well developed dough. Cover with a damp cloth and rest for 30–45 minutes before use.

STRUDEL FILLING

Unit	Ingredient	Metric	Imperial
1	Cooking apples	400 g	1 lb
¼	Brown sugar	100 g	4 oz
⅛	White breadcrumbs	50 g	2 oz
⅛	Sultanas	50 g	2 oz
⅛	Apricot jam	50 g	2 oz
⅛	Butter	50 g	2 oz
¹/₁₆	Lemon juice	25 ml	1 fl oz
	Cinnamon (good pinch)		
	Melted butter		
	Icing sugar		

Method

Melt the butter in a thick bottomed pan, add breadcrumbs and fry gently until light brown, put aside to cool. Peel, core and quarter the apples, slice thinly into a bowl. Add the brown sugar, fried breadcrumbs, sultanas, apricot jam, lemon juice, pinch of cinnamon and mix well.

Preparation of Strudel

Roll out the paste to form a large rectangle. Place onto a clean, floured tea towel, then stretch the paste until it becomes very thin and transparent, trim the edges. Sprinkle the apple filling over the paste leaving a 3 cm (1¼ in) border clear on all edges. Using the tea towel roll up swiss roll fashion. Place onto a lightly greased baking sheet, brush with melted butter and bake until pastry is crisp and apples are cooked. Trim edges, dust with icing sugar and serve hot accompanied with apricot sauce. This sweet may also be served cold accompanied with a sauceboat of cream.

BLANCMANGE

Yield: 4 portions
Cooking time: 5–10 min

Unit	Ingredient	Metric	Imperial
1	Milk	600 ml	1¼ pt
¹⁄₁₀	Caster sugar	60 g	2 oz
¹⁄₁₀	Cornflour	60 g	2 oz
¼	Butter	15 g	½ oz
	Colour and flavourings (*see* chart below)		

Method

Blend cornflour with a little of the milk. Boil remaining milk, then pour onto cornflour mixing continuously. Return to heat, stir to the boil and simmer for 2–3 minutes stirring continuously. Remove from heat, stir in the sugar, butter and required flavouring/colouring. Dampen a fluted mould with water and pour in the mixture. Leave to cool and set. Loosen blancmange from sides of mould, turn out into a glass bowl and serve accompanied with cold jam sauce.

Examples of Blancmange Using the Above Formula

Blancmange	Method and added colourings/flavourings
Almond blancmange	Almond essence Green colour Add colouring and essence to basic mixture prior to pouring into mould
Strawberry blancmange	Strawberry essence Pink colour Proceed as for almond blancmange
Vanilla blancmange	Vanilla essence Proceed as for almond blancmange
Neopolitan blancmange	Take equal parts of almond, strawberry and vanilla blancmange. Set three different layers in mould, allowing each layer to set before adding the next

BURNT CREAM   Crème Brulée

Yield: 4 portions
Cooking time: 8–10 min

Unit	Ingredient	Metric	Imperial
1	Double cream	500 ml	1 pt
¼	Egg yolk	125 g	5 oz
¹⁄₁₀	Sugar	50 g	2 oz
★	Brown sugar		

★ Sufficient to glaze finished product.

Method

Place egg yolks/sugar into mixing bowl and whisk together. Scald the cream, pour gradually onto yolks/sugar and whisk continually to incorporate. Place mixture over a hot bain-marie or transfer into a double boiler and stir continuously until the mixture thickens sufficiently to coat back of wooden spoon. Pour into soufflé moulds, allow to cool and refrigerate overnight until set. For service sprinkle surface with brown sugar and glaze under salamander serve chilled.

FRESH FRUIT SALAD   Salade des Fruits

Yield: 4 portions

Ingredient		Preparation notes
250 ml (½ pt)	Stock syrup	Prepare and allow to cool (*see* p. 646)
50 g (2 oz)	Grapes	Wash, halve and remove seeds
50 g (2 oz)	Cherries	Wash, halve and stone
50 g (2 oz)	Strawberries	Remove stalk, wash and halve
2	Kiwi fruit	Peel and slice
2	Pineapple slices	Remove any peel/core. Cut fruit into small pieces
1	Melon wedge	Remove any peel and cut fruit into small pieces
1	Peach	Halve, stone, quarter, peel and cut fruit into small pieces
1	Orange	Peel, depith/segment. Retain surplus juice (strained)
1	Dessert apple	Quarter, peel, core and cut into small pieces
1	Dessert pear	Quarter, peel, core and cut into small pieces
1	Banana	Peel and slice just on service for inclusion
1	Lemon	Halve, obtain juice (strained)

Method

Place stock syrup into a bowl, flavour with lemon/orange juices to taste and allow to cool. As fruit is prepared place into cooled syrup (beginning with hard fruits leaving banana until last as banana discolours quickly). Carefully stir to ensure the various fruits are evenly distributed and hold in refrigerator to chill. Present for service plain or accompanied with a sauceboat of lightly whipped cream.

   N.B.   The amount of stock syrup used will vary in accordance with the selection of fresh fruits available at any one time.

Jelly

Gelée

Yield: 6–8 portions

Unit	Ingredient	Metric	Imperial
1	Orange juice and zest		
1	Lemon juice and zest		
1	Water	1 l	2 pt
$\frac{1}{10}$	Sugar	100 g	4 oz
$\frac{1}{20}$	Egg white	50 g	2 oz
$\frac{1}{20}$	Gelatine	50 g	2 oz
	Cinnamon stick		

Method

Place all the ingredients into a thick bottomed pan, mix well to distribute the egg whites. Bring to the boil slowly stirring occasionally. Once boiling point is reached remove from the heat, cover with a lid and allow to stand for 30 minutes without further stirring or undue agitation. Strain carefully through a jelly bag, pour jelly into required mould and refrigerate until set. Demould by placing mould into hot water for 1–2 seconds, turn out into a glass dish.

N.B.   Jelly may be flavoured with various wines/liqueurs in which case reduce the water content in proportion to the amount of wine/liqueur used when preparing the jelly.

Fruit Jelly

Gelée aux fruits

Prepare required fresh fruit as for fruit salad. Arrange neatly in bottom of mould before adding jelly. Turn out and decorate with rosettes of Crème Chantilly.

Russian Jelly

Gelée à la Russe

Whisk liquid jelly briskly over ice until it begins to set. Pour into mould and serve as for fruit jelly.

CHILLED MELON SURPRISE

Melon en Surprise Frappé

Yield: 4–8 portions

Ingredient	Preparation notes
1 large ripe melon/8 portions	Cut off melon tops quarter way down, retain tops for presentation. A plain or serrated type cut may be used.
1 medium ripe melon/4 portions	Remove all seeds gouge out ripe melon fruit into balls using large parisienne cut. Put melon balls aside in
4 small ripe melons/4 portions	basin, sprinkle inside of melon shell with caster sugar and refrigerate both shell and melon balls
Fresh fruit salad for 4–8 portions	Fully prepared (*see* p. 627)

N.B.   Other ways of cutting melons include halving either vertically/horizontally or into baskets.

Method

Combine melon balls with fruit salad and use this fruit mixture to fill melon cavity. If applicable/desirable replace melon-top for presentation. Serve surrounded with crushed ice.

ORANGES IN CARAMEL SAUCE

Orange au Caramel

Yield: 4 portions

Unit	Ingredient	Metric	Imperial
4	Oranges		
1	Caramel sauce (*see* p. 640)	250 ml	10 fl oz

Method

Using a potato peeler remove the zest from two of the oranges. Cut zest into julienne, then blanch and refresh. Cut the top and bottom off the fruit, place onto a chopping board. Using a sharp stainless steel knife, remove skin/pith. Cut fruit into slices horizontally, discarding any pips. Reassemble to form oranges and secure with cocktail sticks. Place into a glass bowl and sprinkle with julienne of zest. Pour over caramel sauce and refrigerate for service.

STRAWBERRIES/RASPBERRIES AND CREAM

Fraises/Framboises à la Crème

Yield: 400 g (1 lb) prepared fruit (4 portions)

Method

Pick fruit to remove stalks. Wash then drain carefully. Serve in a glass bowl accompanied with caster sugar and double cream.

STRAWBERRY SHORTBREAD

Yield: 4 portions

Unit	Ingredient	Metric	Imperial
4	Circles cooked shortbread (9 cm (3½ in) diameter)		
1	Strawberries	300 g	12 oz
	Crème Chantilly		

Method

Pick fruit to remove stalks. Wash fruit and drain carefully. Cut in half vertically. Pipe whipped cream onto shortbread to form a large rosette. Decorate with strawberries. Serve accompanied with caster sugar.

STRAWBERRIES/RASPBERRIES
ROMANOFF   Fraises/Framboises Romanoff

Yield: 400 g (1 lb) prepared fruit (4 portions)

Unit	Ingredient	Metric	Imperial
1	Strawberries or raspberries	300 g	12 oz
1/6	Orange juice	50 ml	2 fl oz
1/12	Curaçao	25 ml	1 fl oz
★	Crème Chantilly		

*Sufficient to decorate.

Method

Pick fruit to remove stalks. Wash then drain carefully. Place fruit into a glass bowl. Pour over orange juice and curaçao. Refrigerate and leave to macerate until ice cold. Decorate with rosettes of Crème Chantilly.

   N.B.   Cut strawberries into quarters prior to macerating.

SUMMER PUDDING

Yield: 6–8 portions
Preparation time: 10–12 hr

Unit	Ingredient	Metric	Imperial
1	Fresh strawberries	150 g	6 oz
1	Fresh raspberries	150 g	6 oz
1	Redcurrants (stewed)	150 g	6 oz
1	Blackcurrants (stewed)	150 g	6 oz
6	Slices white bread (free from crust)		
★	Caster sugar		

★ Sufficient to sweeten fruit.

Method

Put aside one slice of bread and use the remainder to line a 1 l (2 pt) pudding basin/mould. Pick the raspberries and strawberries to remove stalks. Wash fruit then drain carefully. Cut strawberries into quarters then combine with raspberries, redcurrants and blackcurrants. Sweeten to taste. Place fruit into bread-lined mould and place remaining slice of bread on top. Cover with a disc of greaseproof paper onto which place a small plate and a 1 kg (2 lb) weight. Refrigerate for 10–12 hours. Demould just prior to service and present in a glass bowl accompanied with a sauceboat of cream.

SYLLABUB

Yield: 4 portions

Unit	Ingredient	Metric	Imperial
1	Double cream	250 ml	½ pt
½	Sweet white wine	125 ml	¼ pt
⅕	Caster sugar	50 g	2 oz
⅕	Lemon juice	50 ml	2 fl oz
⅒	Brandy	25 ml	1 fl oz

Method

Place cream in a basin and whisk gently. When cream begins to thicken add the lemon juice and wine, continue whisking until the mixture thickens. Add the sugar, brandy and blend together. Pour into individual glasses and chill well before service.

TRIFLES

Yield: 8 portions

Unit	Ingredient	Metric	Imperial
1★	Hot custard sauce (of light pouring consistency)	600 ml	1 pt
³⁄₁₀	Plain sponge	180 g	6 oz
¹⁄₂₀	Jam	30 g	1 oz
	Fruit syrup for moistening purposes		
	Flavouring, *see* chart below		

★ Sauce Anglaise can be used to produce an excellent product.

Method

Sandwich the plain sponge with jam, cut into small dice and place into service dish/coupes. Soak sponge with some of the fruit syrup and add the chosen flavouring (*see* chart below). Pour custard over the prepared sponge/filling and allow to cool/set. When cold decorate with whipped cream (using a savoy bag and star tube) cherries and angelica. Hold on refrigeration for service.

Trifles Prepared Using Above Formula: Amounts in Relation to 1 unit i.e. 600 ml (1 pt) Custard Sauce

Name	Unit	Ingredient	Metric	Imperial
Fruit trifle	³⁄₅	Selected tinned fruit	360 g	12 oz
		Cut fruit into small pieces and add to sponge filling		

Name	Unit	Ingredient	Metric	Imperial
Sherry trifle		Cooking sherry Flavour sponge filling with sherry to taste		
Fruit and sherry trifle	⅗	Selected tinned fruit Cooking sherry to taste Cut fruit into small pieces, flavour sponge with sherry to taste and add fruit	360 g	12 oz

ZABAGLIONE

Yield: 4 portions
Cooking time: 6–8 min

Unit	Ingredient	Metric	Imperial
1	Egg yolks	150 g	6 oz
1	Caster sugar	150 g	6 oz
1	Marsala	150 ml	6 fl oz

Method

Place all the ingredients into a mixing bowl. Whisk over a bain-marie until thick, creamy and doubled in volume. Pour into glasses and serve immediately accompanied with biscuits à la cuillère.

46

Petits Fours
(a basic introduction)

Petits fours translated means small ovens, perhaps a reference to the small seventeenth century ovens used to bake these delectable confection or to the practice of baking petits fours in slow ovens once the larger products had gone through, and when the oven temperature had fallen considerably.

Whatever, these small and often baked items can become a star attraction during the final stages of the meal experience. Characteristically petits fours should be small and dainty, freshly prepared and attractively presented; the intention being to tempt the appetite with one more mouthful at the finale of a sumptuous meal when perhaps the diner's appetite is beginning to wane.

The selection of petits fours offered should be well balanced offering to the guest a varied and interesting sample made up of both dry and glazed items. From a culinary viewpoint and for the purposes of classification two broad categories of petits fours are produced, namely sec (dry) and glazed varieties which involve the application of many culinary skills and techniques.

Petits fours sec describes items which are left essentially plan/dry for presentation. In some cases dry petits fours are decorated with chocolate or finished with a solution of gum arabic to enhance appearance.

Petits fours glacées refers to those products which are typically glazed/coated with fondant or boiled sugar.

Petits fours are served at the end of the meal alongside the coffee and liqueurs. The sec varieties are offered, displayed plainly on the presentation dish (with fancy doily) whilst the glacées varieties are placed into small paper cases before being arranged similarly.

The products outlined in this section form only a basic outline of relatively simple petits fours and is therefore limited. Specialist patisserie texts provide a more comprehensive selection for those seeking more than a basic selection.

ENGLISH ROUT BISCUITS (moulding consistency)

Yield: 18
Baking temperature: 249°C (480°F)
Baking time: 5 min

Unit	Ingredient	Metric	Imperial
1	Ground almonds	120 g	4 oz
1	Caster sugar	120 g	4 oz
1*	Egg yolks	30 g	1 oz
	Few drops vanilla essence		
	Egg-wash/decoration (*see* chart)		

* Sufficient to produce a dough-like moulding mixture is required. The amount shown above is a guide and may require slight adjustment.

Method

Line a baking sheet with rice paper and dust lightly with ground rice. Put aside. Combine/blend all ingredients (omit egg-wash/decoration) to form a dough-like moulding paste. Prepare into small varied shapes (*see* chart below). Place onto prepared baking sheet, brush with egg-wash, decorate and stand/dry for 12 hours or over-night. Bake in oven at 249°C (480°F) until tinged to a light golden colour. Remove from oven, allow to cool and serve fresh.

Shapes Prepared Using Above Mixture

Shapes	Directions/decoration
Small plain/fancy discs	Roll-out paste 12 mm (½ in) thick. Cut-out plain or fancy discs using small cutters. Decorate with nuts/glacé fruits as appropriate
Tiny dumplings (slightly depressed)	Mould mixture into tiny dumplings, depress slightly with fork and mark top criss-cross fashion with small sharp knife
Small cottage loaf	Mould mixture into two tiny dumpling shapes one larger than the other. Join together and depress the centre of the small dumpling to join-up with the larger to form a cottage-loaf shape
Small pear	Mould mixture into tiny pear-shapes and insert fine strip of angelica to represent the stalk

N.B.   Other attractive petits fours shapes can be created in miniature using the above mixture.

FRENCH ROUT BISCUITS (piping consistency)

Yield: approx. 18
Baking temperature: 249°C (480°F)
Baking time: 5 min

Unit	Ingredient	Metric	Imperial
1	Ground almonds	120 g	4 oz
1	Caster sugar	120 g	4 oz
¼★	Egg white	30 g	1 oz
	Squeeze of lemon juice		
	Decoration: blanched almonds, glacé cherries/fruits, candied peel, nuts		

★ Sufficient to obtain a mixture of firm piping consistency is required. The amount shown above is a guide and may require slight adjustment.

Method

Line a baking sheet with rice paper and lightly dust with ground rice. Put aside. Combine and blend all ingredients (omit decoration) to form a smooth paste for piping. Transfer mixture into piping bag with appropriately sized star/fancy tube and pipe the fancy shapes (small rounds, fingers, ovals, etc.) onto the prepared baking sheet and decorate appropriately using the materials listed.

Allow the biscuits to stand/dry for approximately 12 hours or overnight.

Bake in an oven at 249°C (480°F) for approximately 5 minutes until the edges are tinged brown. Remove from oven and brush lightly with gum arabic solution (gum arabic melted in a little water) to enhance appearance.

Allow to cool and serve fresh.

MACAROONS   Macarons

Yield: 15
Baking temperature: 160°C (320°F)
Baking time: 30 min

Unit	Ingredient	Metric	Imperial
1	Caster sugar	240 g	8 oz
½	Ground almonds	120 g	4 oz
¼★	Egg white	60 g	2 oz
	Few drops almond essence		

★ Sufficient to obtain a mixture of piping quality is required. The amount shown above is a basic guide and may require slight adjustment to achieve the consistency needed.

Method

Line a baking sheet with non-greased greaseproof paper and put aside. Mix all ingredients together to form a mixture of piping consistency. Using piping bag and 12 mm (½ in) plain tube pipe (well spaced) small round bulbs of 18 mm (¾ in) diameter size. Brush surface of macaroons very lightly with water dampen/moisten.

Bake in oven at 160°C (320°F) for approximately 30 minutes until light brown in colour. Remove from oven, allow to cool, carefully turn sheet of greaseproof over with macaroons attached so they can become free and easy to remove. Serve fresh.

N.B.   Before baking the macaroons can be decorated with split almonds, walnuts, glacé cherries, angelica, candied peel as required.

PIPED SHORTBREAD   Sablé à la Poche

Yield: 10
Baking temperature: 191°C (375°F)
Baking time: approx. 10 min

Unit	Ingredient	Metric	Imperial
1	Soft flour/sifted	240 g	8 oz
¾	Butter	180 g	6 oz
½	Caster sugar	120 g	4 oz
⅛	Whole egg/beaten	30 g	1 oz
¹⁄₁₆	Egg yolk	15 g	½ oz
	A few drops vanilla essence		

Method

Prepare a lightly greased/floured baking sheet and put aside. Cream together butter/sugar until soft and light. Gradually beat in egg yolk/whole beaten egg to incorporate. Blend in sifted flour and finally vanilla essence and mix to a smooth piping paste. Transfer mixture into a piping bag with 12 mm (½ in) star tube and pipe small (well spaced) rosettes onto the prepared baking sheet. Decorate centre of each rosette with quarter of glacé cherry and bake in oven at 191°C (375°F) for approximately 10 minutes until pale golden in colour. Remove from oven, allow to cool and service fresh.

SMALL SHORTBREADS   Petits Sablés

Roll-out shortbread paste (*see* p. 517) to 6 mm (¼ in) thick and cut into small and varied shapes, e.g. fingers, fancy discs, triangles etc. Decorate with pieces of glacé cherries/angelica/fine indented lines, place on lightly greased baking tray and bake/finish as for shortbreads (*see* p. 517).
Serve fresh.

RUM TRUFFLES

Flavour cake crumbs with dark rum then moisten with sufficient boiling apricot purée to bind and form a smooth pliable paste. Mould into small balls, dip in melted dark chocolate then roll in chocolate vermicelli. Allow chocolate to set then present for service in petit four cases.

MARZIPAN FRUITS

Colour the marzipan as required then mould to represent small fruits e.g. bananas, lemons, apples, peaches, oranges etc. Allow to dry for several hours then paint or spray with edible colour.

Examples of Marzipan Fruits

Fruit	Colour of marzipan	Finish
Apples	Green	Paint or spray a red or yellow bloom
Bananas	Yellow	Paint lines along the banana using brown colouring
Oranges	Orange	Decorate with a small green marzipan leaf
Lemon	Yellow	As for oranges
Peaches	Yellow	Spray lightly with red colour

MARZIPAN CUT OUTS/CHOCOLATES

Colour the marzipan as required (yellow, green, red etc.) then pin out 1 cm (½ in) thickness using icing sugar as the dusting agent. Cut out using small fancy cutters. Serve dusted with icing sugar or dip in melted chocolate.

FONDANT CREAMS

Unit	Ingredient	Metric	Imperial
1	Fondant	120 g	4 oz
½	Icing sugar	60 g	2 oz
⅛	Glycerine	15 g	½ oz
	Colour and flavourings		

Method

Warm the fondant until it becomes soft and pliable. Remove from the heat, add the glycerine, required colour and flavouring then allow to cool. Add the icing sugar and knead to form a smooth pliable paste. Pin out to 1 cm (½ in) thickness using icing sugar as the dusting agent. Cut into various shapes using small fancy cutters. Serve dusted with icing sugar or dip in melted chocolate.

Examples of Fondant Creams

Name	Colour and flavouring	Finish
Peppermint creams	Green colour and peppermint essence	Dust with icing sugar
Chocolate peppermint creams	As above	Dip in melted chocolate
Strawberry creams	Pink colour and strawberry essence	Dust with icing sugar
Chocolate strawberry creams	As above	Dip in melted chocolate
Orange creams	Orange colouring and essence	Dust with icing sugar
Chocolate orange creams	As above	Dip in melted chocolate

GENOISE FONDANT DIPS

Sandwich together two thin slices of genoise with butter cream. Brush the top with boiling apricot glaze and cover with a thin sheet of marzipan. Cut into various shapes e.g. squares, mounds, triangles, oblongs, etc.

1. Coat with appropriately coloured fondant and decorate as required, e.g. piped fondant or chocolate, glacé fruits, marzipan shapes, nuts etc.
2. Brush marzipan with boiling apricot glaze onto which place small marzipan fruits, nuts, glacé cherries etc. Coat with appropriately coloured fondant and decorate as required.

Present for service in petit four cases.

DIPPED CARAMELLED FRUITS

Preparation of fruit

Dates:	Cut a slit lengthwise and remove the stone. Stuff with coloured marzipan
Grapes:	Using scissors cut into pairs held together by a cross section of stalk
Oranges, mandarins, satsumas:	Peel then divide into segments without breaking the membrane that surrounds the fruit
Strawberries:	Wash carefully, dry with absorbent paper leaving the stalk intact
Kumquats:	Wash, dry with absorbent paper leaving the stalk intact

Method

Allow fruit to dry for several hours then dip into boiled sugar at 157–160°C (315–320°F) (hard crack). Drain carefully then place onto a lightly oiled marble slab. When set, place in petit four cases for service.

N.B.   Caramelled fruits have a short shelf life and should be serviced within 2–3 hours of preparation.

DIPPED CHOCOLATE FRUITS

Prepare fruit as for caramelled fruits (*see* p. 638) but dip in melted plain or milk chocolate. Present for service in petit four cases.

SMALL CORNETS   Petits Cornets

Using the cats tongues mixture (*see* p. 521) and using a piping bag with 6 mm (¼ in) plain tube, pipe tiny bulbs (well spaced) onto a lightly greased baking sheet and bake as for cats tongues. Remove from oven and whilst still hot shape the malleable discs into some cream horn tins to form small cornets. Allow to cool/set, remove and store in closed biscuit tin. When required fill cornets with liqueur flavoured pastry cream or ganathe.
Serve fresh.

SMALL BRANDY SNAPS

Using recipe (*see* p. 522) prepare small brandy snaps and serve plain or fill with Chantilly cream (*see* p. 647) just prior to service. Present fresh.

SMALL CHOUX PASTRY GOODS (*see* pp. 488–90)

Pipe/shape/bake/cool tiny eclairs, profiterols, swans, fill appropriately, e.g. flavoured cream, pastry cream, dust lightly with icing sugar and serve fresh. Other finishes such as fondants can be used.

47

Sauces, Glazes/Syrups, Fillings and Miscellaneous Preparations

This section includes those items which form the basic mise-en-place of most well run pastry departments. These preparations enable the pastry chef to present sweets, gateau, ices, etc. for service with the minimum of difficulty, correctly flavoured and with suitable accompanying sauces. As such the quality of ingredients used and the excellence of their preparation contribute enormously to the armoury of the pastry chef.

Sweet Sauces

CARAMEL SAUCE   Sauce Caramel

Yield: approx. 500 ml (1 pt)
Cooking time: 12–15 min

Unit	Ingredient	Metric	Imperial
1	Sugar	400 g	1 lb
¾	Water	300 ml	12 fl oz

Method

Place the sugar and 200 ml (8 fl oz) of the water into a thick bottomed pan, bring to the boil and allow to boil gently without agitating the pan. Continue simmering until the sugar cooks to a golden brown, add the remaining water (stand back to avoid initial steam) and re-boil until sugar crystals dissolve. Allow sauce to cool. If it is too thick add a little water. To thicken re-boil until the required consistency is reached.

DARK CHOCOLATE SAUCE

Sauce au Chocolat

Yield: 500 ml (1 pt)
Cooking time: 3–4 min

Unit	Ingredient	Imperial
1	Single cream	12 fl oz
⅔	Dark chocolate (bakers or couverture)	8 oz

Method

Melt the chocolate in a double pan. Meanwhile, heat the cream. Add melted chocolate to cream stirring continuously. Serve hot or cold.

N.B. When melting chocolate do not allow temperature to exceed 40°C (100°F).

GOLDEN SYRUP SAUCE

Sauce au Sirop Doré

Yield: ½ l (1 pt)
Cooking time: 2–3 min

Unit	Ingredient	Metric	Imperial
1	Water	250 ml	½ pt
1	Golden syrup	250 g	10 oz
¹⁄₁₀	Arrowroot or cornflour	25 g	1 oz
	1 Lemon (juice and zest)		

Method

Place sugar, water, lemon juice and zest of lemon into a saucepan, bring to the boil stirring occasionally. Simmer for 2–3 minutes then thicken with diluted cornflour or arrowroot. Strain through a fine chinois, use as required.

JAM SAUCE

Sauce à la Confiture

Yield: 750 ml (1½ pt)
Cooking time: 3–4 min

Unit	Ingredient	Metric	Imperial
1	Selected jam	500 g	1¼ lb
½	Water	250 g	10 fl oz
	Arrowroot or cornflour*		

*Sufficient to thicken sauce if required

Method

Place jam and water in a thick bottomed pan, bring to the boil stirring occasionally. Simmer for 3–4 minutes, adjust consistency with diluted cornflour or arrowroot. Strain through a chinois, use as required.

Examples of Jam Sauces Using the Above Formula

Apricot jam sauce (Sauce abricot)
Raspberry jam sauce (Sauce à la confiture)
Strawberry jam sauce (Sauce à la confiture)

LEMON/ORANGE SAUCE　　　　　　　　　Sauce au Citron/à l'Orange

Yield: approx. ¾ l (1½ pt)
Cooking time: 2–3 min

Unit	Ingredient	Metric	Imperial
1	2 Lemons or 2 oranges (juice and zest)		
1	Water	500 ml	1 pt
	Sugar	125 g	4 oz
¹⁄₂₀	Arrowroot or cornflour	25 g	1 oz

Method

Place sugar, water, fruit juice and zest in a saucepan, bring to the boil stirring occasionally. Simmer for 2–3 minutes then thicken with diluted cornflour or arrowroot. Strain through a fine chinois, use as required.

SWEET MILK BASED SAUCES

Yield: approx. ½ l (1 pt)
Cooking time: 4–5 min

Unit	Ingredient	Metric	Imperial
1	Milk	500 ml	1 pt
¹⁄₁₀	Sugar	50 g	2 oz
¹⁄₂₀	Butter	25 g	1 oz
¹⁄₂₀	Cornflour	25 g	1 oz
¹⁄₂₀	Selected spirit (rum, brandy) or essence/flavouring	25 ml	1 fl oz

Method

Mix the cornflour with a little cold milk in a basin. Boil the remaining milk with the sugar then pour onto the diluted cornflour, whisking constantly. Return to the pan and bring to the boil stirring continuously with a wooden spoon. Add the butter and selected spirit or essence to flavour. Strain through a fine chinois and use as required.

Examples of Sauces Prepared Using Above Formula

English term	Spirit, essence or flavouring	French term
Almond sauce	Almond essence	Sauce amandes
Brandy sauce	Brandy	
Chocolate sauce	Cocoa powder	Sauce au chocolat
Dissolve cocoa powder with cornflour and milk when preparing sauce		
Rum sauce	Dark rum	
Whisky sauce	Whisky	

CUSTARD

Yield: ½ l (1 pt)
Cooking time: 4–5 min

Unit	Ingredient	Metric	Imperial
1	Milk	500 ml	1 pt
$\frac{1}{10}$	Caster sugar	50 g	2 oz
$\frac{1}{20}$	Custard powder	25 g	1 oz

Method

Mix the custard powder with a little cold milk in a basin. Boil the remaining milk with the sugar then pour onto the diluted custard powder whisking constantly. Return to the pan and bring to the boil stirring continuously with a wooden spoon. Strain through a fine chinois, use as required.

FRESH EGG CUSTARD   Sauce Anglaise

Yield: 650 ml (1¼ pt)
Cooking time: 5–6 min

Unit	Ingredient	Metric	Imperial
1	Milk	500 ml	1 pt
$\frac{1}{5}$★	Egg yolk	100 g	4 oz
$\frac{1}{10}$	Caster sugar	50 g	2 oz
	Vanilla		

★The number of yolks used will vary according to size of eggs used. As a guide, egg yolks weigh from 15–21 g (½–¾ oz). For a thick sauce Anglaise double quantity of egg yolk i.e. 200 g/8 oz yolk

Method

Place the vanilla pod and milk into a thick bottomed pan, bring to the boil, remove from heat and allow to stand for 2–3 minutes. Meanwhile whisk the egg yolks and sugar in a basin. Strain the milk through a fine chinois, pour onto the egg yolks and sugar whisking continuously. Return to saucepan and stir over a low heat until the sauce thickens sufficiently to coat the back of a wooden spoon. Strain through a fine chinois and use as required.

MELBA SAUCE   Sauce Melba

Yield: 650 ml (1¼ pt)
Cooking time: 10–15 min

Unit	Ingredient	Metric	Imperial
1	Fresh or frozen raspberries	400 g	1 lb
½	Sugar	200 g	8 oz
⅛	Water	50 ml	2 fl oz
	1 Lemon (juice and zest)		

Method

Place all the ingredients into a thick bottomed pan, bring to the boil stirring occasionally. Simmer for 10–15 minutes then strain through a fine chinois, cool and use as required.

   N.B.   When a cheaper version of sauce Melba is required use raspberry jam sauce. In this case it may be flavoured with lemon juice and zest.

SABAYON SAUCE   Sauce Sabayon

Yield: 4–6 portions
Cooking time: 6–8 min

Unit	Ingredient	Metric	Imperial
1	Caster sugar	100 g	4 oz
¾	Egg yolk	75 g	3 oz
¾	White wine	75 ml	3 fl oz
	Juice from ½ lemon		

Method

Place all ingredients into a mixing bowl. Whisk over a bain-marie until thick, creamy and doubled in volume. Pour into a sauceboat and serve immediately.

Examples of Sauces Derived from Sauce Sabayon: Added Ingredients in Relation to Basic Recipe

Name of sauce	Unit	Added ingredient	Metric	Imperial
Lemon sabayon (Sabayon au citron)		1 Lemon (juice and zest)		
Orange sabayon		1 Orange (juice and zest)		

Name of sauce	Unit	Added ingredient	Metric	Imperial
Marsala sabayon (Sabayon au marsala)	½	Marsala	50 ml	2 fl oz
Rum sabayon (Sabayon au rhum)	¼	Dark rum	25 ml	1 fl oz
Cognac sabayon (Sabayon au cognac)	¼	Cognac	25 ml	1 fl oz

Glazes and Syrups

APRICOT GLAZE/RED GLAZE

Yield: approx. ½ l (1 pt)
Cooking time: 3–4 min

Unit	Ingredient	Metric	Imperial
1	Apricot jam or red jam (raspberry, strawberry)	300 g	12 oz
¼–½	Water	150–300 ml	3–6 fl oz

Method

Place jam and half the water in a thick bottomed pan, bring to the boil stirring occasionally. Simmer for 3–4 minutes, adjust consistency with remaining water, re-boil and strain through a fine chinois. Use hot.

ARROWROOT GLAZE

Yield: ½ l (1 pt)
Cooking time: 3–4 min

Unit	Ingredient	Metric	Imperial
1*	Fruit juice	500 ml	1 pt
1/20	Arrowroot	25 g	1 oz
	Sugar and colouring if required		

*Fruit juice/syrup from tinned/canned fruit is ideal for this glaze.

Method

Place fruit juice into a thick bottomed pan, bring to the boil stirring occasionally. Sweeten to taste. Adjust consistency with diluted arrowroot, colour if required and strain through a fine chinois. Use hot.

WATER ICING

Yield: 475 g (1 lb 3 oz)

Unit	Ingredient	Metric	Imperial
1	Icing sugar	400 g	1 lb
3/20	Warm water (100°C/50°C)	75 ml	3 fl oz
	Colour and flavourings		

Method

Sieve the icing sugar into a bowl. Gradually add the warm water to form a smooth icing. Colour and flavour as required.

STOCK SYRUP

Yield: 1 l (2 pt)
Cooking time: 4–5 min

Unit	Ingredient	Metric	Imperial
1	Water	500 ml	1 pt
1	Sugar	500 g	20 oz

Method

Place sugar and water in a thick bottomed pan, bring to the boil stirring occasionally. Simmer for 2–3 minutes, drain to remove any scum then cool and store in a refrigerator ready for use.

BUN GLAZE

Proceed as for stock syrup.

SAVARIN SYRUP   Sirop à Savarin

Yield: 1 l (2 pt)
Cooking time: 3–4 min

Unit	Ingredient	Metric	Imperial
1	Water	500 ml	1 pt
4/5	Sugar	400 g	1 lb
	1 Orange (zest and juice)		
	1 Lemon (zest and juice)		
	1 Cinnamon stick		
	2 Cloves		

Method

Place all the ingredients into a thick bottomed pan, bring to the boil stirring occasionally. Simmer for 3–4 minutes, skim to remove any scum then strain through a fine chinois. Use whilst still hot.

BABA SYRUP

Sirop à Baba

Proceed as for savarin syrup but replace 50 ml (2 fl oz) of the water content with dark rum.

Fillings and Creams
BUTTERCREAM

Yield: 400 g (1 lb)

Unit	Ingredient	Metric	Imperial
1	Unsalted butter	200 g	8 oz
1	Icing sugar	200 g	8 oz
1/10	Stock syrup or flavouring	50 g	2 oz

Method

Place butter in a bowl and cream together. Sieve icing sugar and gradually add to butter beating continually, add stock syrup or flavouring and beat until light and fluffy.

BRANDY BUTTER

Replace stock syrup with brandy when preparing buttercream.

RUM BUTTER

Replace stock syrup with rum when preparing buttercream.

WHISKY BUTTER

Replace stock syrup with whisky when preparing buttercream.

SWEETENED WHIPPED CREAM 1

Crème Chantilly

Unit	Ingredient	Metric	Imperial
1	Double/whipping cream	500 g	1 pt
1/10	Caster sugar	50 g	2 oz
	Vanilla essence (few drops)		

Method

Place all the ingredients into a bowl. Whisk over ice until sufficiently stiff for piping. Keep on refrigeration for use on day of preparation.

SWEETENED WHIPPED CREAM 2   Crème Caprice

Method

Prepare Crème Chantilly omitting the sugar content. When stiffly whipped fold in ⅕ unit, 100 g (4 oz) of crushed/broken pieces of meringue. Keep on refrigeration for use on day of preparation.

FRANGIPANE

Yield: 400 g (1 lb)

Unit	Ingredient	Metric	Imperial
1	Butter or margarine	100 g	4 oz
1	Caster sugar	100 g	4 oz
1	Egg	100 g	4 oz
½	Ground almonds	50 g	2 oz
½	Cakecrumbs	50 g	2 oz
	Almond essence (few drops)		

Method

Place the butter/margarine and sugar in a bowl and cream together. Gradually add egg beating continually, flavour with almond essence. Mix together the cake crumbs and ground almonds, then fold into the creamed butter and sugar mixture. Use as required.
    N.B.   Frangipane may be stored refrigerated for 2–3 days if not for immediate use.

PASTRY CREAM   Crème Pâtissière

Yield: 750 ml (1½ pt)
Cooking time: 8–10 min

Unit	Ingredient	Metric	Imperial
1	Milk	500 ml	1 pt
⅕	Caster sugar	100 g	4 oz
⅕	Egg yolks	100 g	4 oz
⅒	Flour	50 g	2 oz
	Vanilla essence		

Method

Whisk the egg yolks and sugar together until the ribbon stage, blend in the flour. Flavour milk with vanilla essence, bring to the boil then pour onto the egg yolk mixture stirring continuously. Return to pan and stir to the boil with a wooden spoon. When the pastry cream has thickened use immediately or pour into a bowl and cover with a buttered grease-proof paper ready for use.

CRÈME ST HONORÉ/CRÈME CHIBOUST

Unit	Ingredient	Metric	Imperial
1	Pastry cream	500 ml	1 pt
$\frac{1}{5}$	Egg white	100 g	4 oz
$\frac{1}{10}$	Caster sugar	50 g	2 oz
$\frac{1}{40}$	Leaf gelatine	12–13 g	$\frac{1}{2}$ oz

Method

Soak leaf gelatine in cold water until soft, add to pastry cream and bring to the boil. Whisk egg whites until very stiff, gradually add the sugar whisking continually. Fold beaten egg whites into boiling hot pastry cream. Use whilst still hot.

Miscellaneous Preparations

GANACHE

Ganache

Cooking time: 6–8 min

Unit	Ingredient	Metric	Imperial
1	Chocolate couverture (milk or plain)	375 g	15 oz
$\frac{2}{3}$	Whipping cream	250 ml	10 fl oz

Method

Melt the chocolate in a double pan. Meanwhile boil the cream. Pour the cream into a bowl and add the melted chocolate stirring continuously. Beat until smooth.

Uses

Hot for coating gateau, torten etc.
Warm piping or as a filling cream.
Cold modelling, sweets, etc.

PRALINE

Praliné

Yield: approx. 600 g ($1\frac{1}{2}$ lb)
Preparation time: 30–40 min

Unit	Ingredient	Metric	Imperial
1	Caster sugar	400 g	1 lb
$\frac{1}{4}$	Water	100 g	4 oz
$\frac{1}{4}$	Hazelnuts skinned and roasted	100 g	4 oz
$\frac{1}{4}$	Almonds skinned and roasted	100 g	4 oz
$\frac{1}{4}$	Glucose	100 g	4 oz
	Lemon juice (few drops)		

Method

Place the water, sugar, glucose and lemon juice into a thick bottomed pan. Bring to the boil and cook without undue agitation until golden brown. Add the nuts then pour mixture onto a marble slab. Allow to cool then crush with a rolling pin, store in an airtight container and use as required.

BOILED SUGAR

Unit	Ingredient	Metric	Imperial
1	Cube or granulated sugar	500 g	20 oz
⅖	Water	200 ml	8 fl oz
	Cream of tartar (pinch)		
	Sugar thermometer for guidance		

Method

Place sugar and water in a thick bottomed or copper pan. Slowly bring to the boil stirring occasionally to dissolve the sugar. Moisten the cream of tartar with a few drops of water and add to the sugar mixture. Clean the sides of the pan with a clean moist brush. Place sugar thermometer in the sugar solution then boil quickly without further agitation. When the required temperature is reached place the base of the pan into cold water to prevent further cooking.

A Guide to Sugar Temperatures

Degree of cooking	°C	°F
Soft boil	116–118	240–245
Hard boil	121	250
Soft crack	132–138	270–280
Crack	154	310
Hard crack	157–160	315–320
Caramel	177	350

SPUN SUGAR

Boil sugar to 157°C (315°F) then plunge the base of the pan into cold water to prevent further cooking. Support two oiled sticks between two tables, then dip a fork into the sugar solution and throw strands of sugar across the sticks. Repeat the process until you have sufficient spun sugar. Remove from sticks and carefully shape as required. Use immediately as spun sugar has poor keeping qualities in moist conditions, e.g. busy kitchen.

CARAMEL

Unit	Ingredient	Metric	Imperial
1	Sugar	200 g	8 oz
⅝	Water	125 ml	5 fl oz

Method

Place sugar and 100 ml (4 fl oz) of the water into a thick bottomed or copper pan. Cook as for boiled sugar (*see* p. 650) until golden brown. Add the remaining water and reboil until caramel is completely mixed. Use as required.

N.B.   When adding water to golden brown syrup beware of steam.

Glossary of Culinary Terms

Abats Offal e.g. hearts, liver, kidney, etc. of butcher's meats and giblets of poultry, etc.

à blanc To keep white

à brun To make brown

Aboyeur 'Barker' – the person responsible for shouting out the customer's order to the kitchen departments

Adjunct (vegetable) A vegetable flavouring used when a full mirepoix is unsuitable, e.g. onion flavouring in curry sauce

Aiguillette Small long strips of cooked meat, e.g. aiguillettes of duck

Ail Garlic

Aile Wing of poultry

Aileron Winglet of poultry

Airelles cousinettes Cranberries

à la In the style of . . . e.g. à l'Anglaise (English style)
  à la Française (French style)
  à la Maison (style of the house, etc.)

à la carte Dishes prepared or cooked to order, which are separately priced

al dente Used to describe Italian pasta cooked 'with a bite'

Aloyau de boeuf Whole sirloin of beef on the bone

Appareil A mixture of different foods for the preparation of a dish

à point Just cooked

Aromates Herbs and spices used for flavouring

Aspic A clear savoury jelly

Assaisonner To season, or season to taste

Assiette Anglaise A selection of cold sliced meat, e.g. ham, tongue, beef, chicken, etc.

au beurre With butter

au bleu Beef steaks cooked 'blue' or very underdone, also a method for cooking live trout

au four Oven baked

au gratin Foods sprinkled with grated cheese or breadcrumbs and browned under salamander or in a hot oven

au vin blanc With white wine

au vin rouge With red wine

Bain-marie   Mary's bath, an open water bath in which sauces/soups, etc. are stored in bain-marie pans to keep hot

Ballotine   Boned leg of poultry, stuffed and rolled prior to cooking

Barder   To cover pieces of meat, poultry, game, etc. with strips of fat in order to keep them moist, protect from scorching and prevent excess shrinkage

Baron   Double loin of beef or saddle of mutton/lamb with legs attached

Barquettes   Boat-shaped tin moulds used when preparing boat-shaped pastry cases

Baste   The process of moistening foods with the cooking juices and fats throughout cooking, e.g. basting roast meats

Bâtons   Foods cut into small, neat rectangles, e.g. bâton shape or neat sticks of French bread

Bavarois   A lightly set, smooth textured, cold Bavarian cream

Baveuse   A term used to describe omelets with a soft texture and moist centre

Beard (to)   Removing the beard from oysters and mussels

Beignets   Deep-fried savoury or sweet fritters

Beurre manié   A mixture of butter and flour manipulated to a smooth paste and used as a thickening agent

Bien cuit   Well cooked

Blanc   A specially prepared cooking medium of water, flour, lemon juice, and seasoning in which certain vegetables are cooked in order to prevent them discolouring

Blanc de volaille   Breast of chicken

Blanch (to)   (a)   Blanched meat – meat and bones brought to the boil, then refreshed in
(Blanchir)   cold water to remove scum;

          (b)   Blanched vegetables – brought to boil, refreshed in cold water then drained. This process helps to retain colour, softens vegetable fibres to facilitate shaping when braising and aids to retain vitamin C by eliminating destructive enzyme action;

          (c)   Deep-fried potatoes, to par-cook certain potato dishes, keep them white in readiness for further cooking;

          (d)   Blanched tomatoes, plunging tomatoes into boiling water for a few seconds to facilitate removal of skin.

Blanquette   A type of white stew (*see* p. 341)

Bombe   Different flavours of ice-cream set in a bombe mould

Bouchées   Small baked puff pastry cases

Bouillabaisse   A French Mediterranean fish stew or soup

Bouillon   A type of stock, e.g. chicken, or broth-type soup

Bouquet garni   A neat bundle of herbs used to flavour culinary products during cooking

Brochet   The French term for the fish 'Pike'

Broche (en)   Spit roasting

Brochette (en)   Cooking on a skewer

Broil   An American term to denote grilling

Brunoise   A cut of very fine dice

Budding   A term used to describe the opening of shellfish (molluscs)

Bulk fermentation time (B.F.T.)   Initial fermentation time for yeast goods prior to moulding

Canapé   Various cooked shapes of bread used as a base for hors d'oeuvre and savoury dishes

Carapace   The body/head shell of lobster

Cartouche   A piece of greased paper to cover foods in cooking or storage

Cassata Neapolitan ice-cream speciality, often liberally garnished with glacé fruits

Casserole A type of stewing vessel made of earthenware or metal

Chapelure Brown breadcrumbs

Charlotte A hot or cold dessert prepared in a charlotte mould, e.g. apple charlotte, charlotte royal

Chateaubriand A large steak cut from the head of the beef fillet

Chauffant A vessel of seasoned boiling water used in the re-heating of vegetables

Chiffonade Finely shredded lettuce or sorrel used to garnish and flavour soups

Chinois fine/coarse (fin/gros) conical strainer

Ciseler To make small incisions e.g. scoring small round fish prior to grilling. Also finely shredding of vegetables

Civet A brown stew of furred game, e.g. Civet de Lièvre (hare), Civet de Venaison (venison)

Clarification A process used to make soup, jellies and butter, etc. of clear appearance

Clouté Studded or to insert nail-shaped pieces of food into various preparations e.g. onion clouté, an onion studded with cloves or ham studded with cloves

Cocotte Large and small fireproof earthenware cooking vessels

Cohere Moistening and light binding of fish meat or vegetables with a sauce

Collops Thin, small, round cuts of meat and fish, etc., e.g. collops of lobster

Compote Stewed fruit

Concassé Roughly chopped

Contrefilet Boned-out sirloin e.g. strip loin

Coquilles Mollusc shells

Corbeille Basket, e.g. corbeille de fruits, a basket of fresh fruit

Court-bouillon A flavoured cooking liquor used in the cooking of fish and some offal, e.g. brains

Cordon Ribbon, indicates a thread or ribbon of sauce used to flavour and garnish culinary products

Correcting A term used to denote the adjusting of colour, flavour, and consistency of culinary preparations

Côte Rib or chop, e.g. rib of beef, pork chop

Côtelette Cutlet, e.g. lamb cutlet

Coupe Service dish used in which individual ice-cream desserts are served.

Crapaudine A term denoting a raw chicken prepared for grilling, cut and shaped to represent a 'toad'

Crêpes Pancakes

Croquettes Cooked forcemeats of meat, fish or cooked vegetables, shaped and prepared for frying

Croûtes Various shapes of fried/toasted bread on which various foods are presented

Croûtons Various shapes of fried bread used as a garnish with culinary preparations, e.g. soup croûtons, heart-shaped croûtons

Cru Raw or uncooked

Crustaceans A classification of certain shellfish, e.g. lobster, prawns, crabs, scampi, etc.

Cuisse Leg, e.g. cuisse (of chicken), Cuisse de Nymphes/Grenouilles (frogs legs)

Dariole Small, tin lined copper or aluminium mould

Darne A steak of round fish on the bone, e.g. darne (of salmon)

Daube A type of oven stew cooked in a special vessel (daubière)

Daubière A type of casserole made of earthenware

Déglacer To remove food sediment from a cooking vessel by 'swilling out' with a suitable liquid, e.g. wine or stock. To deglaze

Dégraisser   To skim away fat

Déjeuner   Luncheon

Devilled   To highly season with a hot flavouring, e.g. cayenne pepper

Dish paper   Plain absorbent paper used on service dishes to absorb excess grease from foods

Doily   A decorative paper base used on service flats to enhance the appearance of pastry goods

Doré   Gilded or golden in golour, e.g. gilded fish (*see* p. 329)

Duxelle   A basic preparation of cooked finely chopped mushrooms, flavoured with shallots and seasonings

Écumé   Skimmed

Egg wash   Beaten egg used when breadcrumbing foods or brushing foods to facilitate browning during cooking

Émincer   To cut into thin slices

En papillote   Cooking and serving foods in a paper bag

En-tasse   Served in a cup, e.g. consommé en tasse

Entier   Entire or whole

Entrecôte   Steak cut from boned out sirloin (strip loin)

Entremets   Desserts

Escalopes   Thin slices, usually applied to meats, e.g. escalopes of veal

Escargot   Edible snails

Estouffade   A rich brown stock

Faggot   As for bouquet garni

Farce   A stuffing

Fécule   A type of starch thickening

Feuilletage   Puff pastry

Fines herbes   Selected herbs comprised of parsley, chervil, chives, and tarragon

Flamber   To flame a dish with spirits/liqueur. Dishes are often flamed at the table by food service personnel

Fleurons   Cooked crescents of puff pastry

Flûtes   Toasted, thin slices of French bread sticks, usually served as an accompaniment with certain soups

Fonds   Foundations, e.g. stocks

Fourrer   To stuff

Frappe   To serve chilled on crushed ice

Friandise   Petits fours

Fricassée   A type of white stew (*see* p. 253)

Fruits de Mer   Assortment of sea food

Fumé   Smoked

Fumet   Essence of fish stock

Galette   Small, flat cake of potato, vegetables, etc.

Gastric   A mixture of sugar and vinegar used to sharpen the flavour of tomato sauce or soup

Gateau   A decorated cake often divided into portions. May be served as a dessert or an afternoon tea snack

Gibier   Game

Glace   Ice-cream

Glaze to   To brown products under the salamander

Gluten Protein present in wheat

Gourmet An epicure, a connoisseur of food

Gratinate To sprinkle foods with grated cheese or breadcrumbs to be browned under the salamander

Gras de Cuisse Chicken thigh

Grenouilles Frogs

Hacher To mince or finely chop

Hâtelette Elaborately adorned skewer

Haute Cuisine High class cookery

Hors d'Oeuvre Selection of first courses featured on the menu, usually cold

Indienne (à la) Indian style, often denotes use of curry flavourings

Italienne (à la) Italian style

Jardinière A term used to denote vegetables cut into bâtons

Julienne A term used to denote foods cut into thin strips

Jus (au) With juice or gravy

Jus lié Thickened gravy

Jus rôti Roast gravy, unthickened

Jus rôti lié Roast gravy, thickened

Larder The insertion of strips of bacon or pork fat into meats, poultry and game in order to keep them moist during cooking, and prevent excess shrinkage

Lardons Bâtons of streaky bacon, blanched and sautéd, used as a garnish

Liasion Mixture of egg yolks and cream used to thicken and enrich culinary products, e.g. soups and sauces

Macédoine Various foods cut into neat cubes or dice

Macerate To soak in liqueur in order to soften and add flavour. Often applied to fresh fruits, e.g. strawberries macerated in curaçao

Mandolin A special vegetable slicer

Manié To manipulate or knead

Maraschino A liqueur prepared from black cherries

Mar-For slicer Manual vegetable slicer

Marinade A preparation used to flavour and tenderise butcher's meats, poultry, game and fish. Often comprised of oil, wine or lemon juice, vegetables and aromates

Marmite Stock pot, or earthenware pot in which soups may be cooked and served

Mask A term used to denote coating foods with a sauce

Matelot A type of French fish stew

Médaillon A round shaped portion of meat or fish

Menu Bill of fare

Mignonette pepper Milled peppercorns

Mijoter To simmer

Minute (à la) Cooked very quickly 'in a minute'

Mirepoix A vegetable flavouring, roughly cut to various sizes according to requirements

Mise-en-place Put in place, in culinary jargon refers to advanced preparation

Molluscs A classification of shellfish, e.g. oysters, mussels, scallops, etc.

Monter au beurre Mount with butter, adding butter to sauce preparations to enhance flavour, appearance and improve consistency

Mouli (légume) A manual or mechanical vegetable mill, used to purée vegetables and soups

Mousse A lightly textured sweet or savoury dish which may be served hot or cold

Napper　To coat items with sauce
Nature (au)　Natural
Navarin　A brown lamb stew
Noisette d'Agneau　A small, trimmed cut of lamb taken from the boned loin

Paillettes au fromage　Cheese straws
Panaché　Mixture
Panada　A term used to describe types of binding agent
Paner　To pass ingredients through seasoned flour, egg wash and breadcrumbs (pané)
Pannequets　Small pancakes
Parfait　Speciality single flavoured ice-cream set in a mould
Paw paw　A tropical fruit similar to a small green melon
Paupiette　A stuffed portion of meat/fish rolled into a cylindrical shape
Paysanne (à la)　Peasant style, also indicates the use of particular shapes, i.e. circles, squares, and triangles (*see* p. 165)
Petit déjeuner　Breakfast
Petits fours　Selection of after dinner sweet items, e.g. marzipan fruits, fondant chocolates
Pilon　Drumstick, e.g. pilon de cuisse (chicken drumstick)
Piquant　Sharp flavour
Piquer　Foods studded with fat, cloves, garlic, truffle etc.
Plat à sauter　A shallow frying vessel
Plat du jour　Suggested dish of the day
Pré-sale　Lamb or mutton, reared and bred on salty meadows
Primeurs　Spring vegetables
Printanier　Spring vegetables
Prosciutto　Italian Parma ham
Proving　A second fermentation period for yeast goods following moulding and prior to cooking
Provençale (à la)　Regional or provincial style
Pulse　Dried or fresh podded vegetables
Purée　Pulped foods

Quenelles　Various shapes of fine forcemeats produced from veal, chicken, fish, and game
Queue　Tail, e.g. ox-tail

Râble (de lièvre)　Saddle of hare
Ragoût　A stew
Raspings　As for chapelure
Ravier　A small dish in which hors d'oeuvres are served, manufactured in a variety of materials e.g. glass, plastic, stainless steel, earthenware etc.
Réchauffé　Reheated
Refresh　To plunge hot foods into cold water in order to halt cooking and cool quickly before draining for use or storage
Rennet　A preparation obtained from a calves stomach. Used as a setting agent when preparing junket
Rissoler　Shallow fry quickly in hot fat/oil to golden brown
Rondeau　A large round shallow cooking vessel
Roux　A mixture of fat/oil and flour, cooked to varying degrees and used as a thickening agent

Sabayon   A mixture of egg yolks and a few drops of water cooked and whisked en bain-marie to ribbon stage. Used to thicken, enrichen, and improve appearance of culinary products

Sacchrometer   Used to measure the density of sugar/syrup solutions

Saignant   Rare or underdone (bleeding)

Salamander   Overhead grilling appliances

Salmis   A brown stew of feathered game

Salpicon   A mixture of foods cohered with a sauce and used as a filling

Sauteuse   A shallow cooking vessel with sloping sides (*see* p. 25)

Sauter   To shallow fry or toss over heat in a plat à sauter

Score   To incise the surface of foods

Sec   Dry, not sweet

Shredded   Sliced finely

Singer   To colour brown

Sippets   Small shallow fried soup croûtons

Sorbet   Frozen ices lightened by the addition of Italian meringue

Soufflé   A very light sweet or savoury product

Spatchcock   A term denoting a raw chicken split down the back-down and 'spreadeagled for grilling (*see* p. 424)

Spatula   A flat wooden spoon

Sundaes   Ice-cream desserts with whipped cream, fruits, nuts, sauces, etc. Served in oval, shallow glass dishes

Suprême   Denotes use of delicate cuts taken from breast of poultry or game. Also a cut of fish on the slant, free from bone

Sweat   Initial cooking of foods in fat/oil under cover, without significant colour change

Table d'hôte   Inclusive menu at a set price

Tammis   Very fine sieve

Tammiser   To pass sauces through a fine cloth to remove particles and give a fine, smooth sauce

Timbale   A drum-shaped serving vessel

Tomatéd   Significantly flavoured and coloured with tomato

Tomates concassées   Chopped tomato flesh cooked in butter/oil with small amount of onion and garlic

Tomato concassé   Chopped tomato flesh

Torten   A large decorated cake divided into portions

Tourné   To turn or trim with a sharp knife to required shape, e.g. vegetables turned barrel-shape, turned (fluted) mushrooms, etc.

Tournedos   Small cuts taken from centre of beef fillet

Tranche   A slice or cut

Trancher   To carve or cut

Tranchelard   A French carving knife

Tronçon   A cut of flat fish on the bone

Truffle   A fungus used in cookery to garnish and flavour

Truss   To secure foods with string, e.g. poultry

Vert-pré   Indicates use of a green garnish or colour, e.g. watercress to garnish grills

Vesiga   Dried spinal marrow of the sturgeon used mainly in the preparation of 'coulibiac' a type of Russian fish pie

Vin   Wine

Vol-au-Vent   Large puff pastry case

Xérès Sherry

Zabaglione A sweet of Italian origin, prepared using egg yolks, caster sugar and marsala cooked to a sabayon

Zest Orange or lemon rind

Index

All dishes are listed under their 'umbrella' ingredient e.g. all vegetables under V, all meat under M, all fish under F etc.

Aeration, 511–12
Anchovy, *see* Sauces and savouries
Apple, Charlotte, 624
  strudel, 625–6
  see also Sauces
Apricot fool, 594
Artichokes, *see* Vegetables
Asparagus, *see* Vegetables
Aspic jelly, basic, 156–7
  fish, 157
Avocado pear, *see* Fruit

Batters, frying, 295–6
  for pancakes, 558–9
  savoury pancake, 452
  yeast, 562
Bavarois, 580–5
  custard-based:
    banana Chartreuse, 582
    chocolate, 582
    coffee, 582
    lemon, 582
    Moscovite Charlotte, 583
    orange, 583
    praline, 583
    raspberry, 583
    ribboned, 583
    Royal Charlotte, 583
    Russian, 583
    strawberry, 584
    vanilla, 584
  syrup-based:
    apricot, 584
    gooseberry, 584

    raspberry, 585
    rhubarb, 585
    strawberry, 585
Beans, *see* Vegetables
Beef, *see* Meats
Beetroot, *see* Vegetables
Beignets (fritters), 561–2
  banana, 304
  crabe, 304
  fromage, 304
  fruits, 304
Beurre manié, 172
Binding agents, 72
Biscuits:
  à la cuillère, 521
  brandy snaps, 522, 638
  English rout, 634
  French rout, 634–5
  glacés, 616–18
    apricot, 617
    coffee and praline, 618
    liqueur, 618
    pistachio, 618
  langues du chat, 521–2, 638
  macaroons, 635–6
  shortbread, 517
    piped, 636
    small, 636
  Viennese, 517–18
Bitoks, 326
  see also Meats
Blanc, 268
Blancmange, 626
Blanquette, 341–4
  see also Meats

Bombes, 614–15
  chocolate, 615
  coffee, 615
  liqueur, 615
  maraschino, 615
  praline, 615
  strawberry, 615
  vanilla, 615
Bouchées, *see* Savouries
Bouillabaisse, 354–5
Bouquet garni, 161–2
Brains, poached, 280–1
  see also Meats
Bratt pan, 51–2
Bread rolls, 537
  bridge, 542–3
Breadcrumbs, 168
Breakfast, 471–2
Brioche, 543
Broccoli, *see* Vegetables
Brochettes, 429–30
  see also Meats
Brussels sprouts, *see* Vegetables
Bubble and squeak, 463
Buns:
  Bath, 538
  Chelsea, 538
  cream, 538
  currant, 539
  dough for, 537–8
  fruit, 539
  hot cross, 539
  raspberry, 516
  Swiss/iced, 539
Butter, clarified, 168
  sauces, 200–2

Cabbage, *see* Vegetables
Cakes:
  chocolate log, 521
  Genoese, 519
    chocolate, 519
  plain fatless sponge, 519–20
  sponge fingers, 521
  Swiss roll, jam, 520
    chocolate, 521
  Victoria sponge sandwich, 518–19
  see also Gâteaux
Canard, *see* Meats
Canneloni, 252–3

Carbonnade, 362–3
Carrots, *see* Vegetables
Cassatas, 622
Cauliflower, *see* Vegetables
Celeriac, *see* Vegetables
Celery, *see* Vegetables
Cheese straws, 202
Chef's knives, 13–16
Chestnuts, braised, 376
  see also Vegetables
Chicken, à la King, 438
  in curry sauce, 438–9
  see also Meats
Chicory, *see* Vegetables
Chili con carne, 346–7
Choucroûte (sauerkraut), 377, 378
Civets, *see* Meats
Condé, fruit, 577
  apple, 577
  apricot, 577
  banana, 577
  peach, 577
  pear, 577
  pineapple, 577
Convection ovens, 42–4
Convenience products, 6
Cooking vessels, 21–9
  dishes, 29–32
  metals used, 21–3
  vessels, 23–9
Coq au vin, 347–8
Corn, cakes, 463
  see also Vegetables
Corned beef hash cake, 442
Cornish pasties, 406
Court-bouillon, 264–5
Crème brûlée, 627
Crêpes, Suzette, 575
  see also Pancakes
Croissants, 542
Cucumber, *see* Vegetables
Curly Kale, *see* Vegetables
Curried meats, 344–5
  see also Meats
Curried prawns, 453
Custard, 643
  baked egg, 549–50
  crème, à la florentine, 551
    beau-rivage, 551
    caramel, 550

Custard—*continued*
  opéra, 551
  renversée, 550
  viennoise, 551
  fresh egg, 643–4
  petits pots de crème, 553
    à la vanille, 553
    au café, 553
    au chocolat, 554
  pouding, à la reine, 552
    au pain à l'anglaise, 552
    de cabinet, 552
    diplomat, 553
  savoury egg, 203

Daube de boeuf, 363–4
Dips, avocado, 89
  soured cream, 88–9
Doughnuts, 539
Dressings, mayonnaise, 85–7, 191–2
  sour cream, 84–5
  vinaigrette, 87–8
Dripping, 168
Duck, *see* Meats
Dumplings, baked apple, 486
  cornmeal, 249
  Paris style, 248
  potato, 248–9
  Roman style, 247–8
  tiny, 246
Durham cutlets, 448
Duxelle, 163–4

Eclairs, 489
Egg, batter, 296
  mayonnaise, 115–18
Eggs, *see* also Omelets
  dur, 230–1
    à la coque, 231
    à la tripe, 231
    aurore, 231
    Bombay or Indienne, 231
    Chimay, 231
    mollet, 231
  en cocotte, 232–3
    à la creme, 232
    à la Reine, 233
    bérgère, 232
    Bordelaise, 232
    jus lié, 233

    Périgourdine, 233
    petit-duc, 233
    Portugaise, 233
    soubise, 233
  fried:
    deep, 236
    shallow, 236
  poached (pochés), 228–30
    à la Reine, 230
    Argenteuil, 229
    Bénédictine, 229
    Florentine, 230
    Indienne (Bombay), 230
    Mornay, 230
    moulés, 229
    Washington, 230
  scrambled (brouillés), 236–7
    Archiduchesse, 237
    aux champignons, 237
    aux croûtons, 237
    aux foies de volaille, 237
    grand'mère, 237
    Portugaise, 237
  sur le plat, 234–5
    à la creme, 235
    Américaine, 234
    au lard, 235
    aux crevettes grises, 235
    Bercy, 234
    chasseur, 235
    florentine, 235
    Lorraine, 235
Emulsification, 72–6
Entrées and relevés, 77–9
Enzymic browning, 63–4
Epigrammes of lamb, 443–4
Escargots, 456
Essences, 171
Estouffade, 170

Farce, à la florentine, 251–2
  Italienne, 252
Fennel, *see* Vegetables
Fermented goods, 534–6
Fillings and creams, 647–9
  brandy butter, 647
  butter cream, 647
  crème St Honoré/chiboust, 649
  frangipane, 648
  pastry cream, 648

Fillings and creams—*continued*
  rum butter, 647
  whipped cream, 647–8
  whisky, 647
Fish:
  aspic jelly, 157
  baked, 407–8
  braised, 373
  coquilles de poisson, 451
    Mornay, 452
  coquilles de fruit de mer, 452
  crab, 122
  deep fried, 298–301
    à la française, 300
    à l'anglaise, 300
    à l'orly, 300
    cakes, 456
    Colbert (sole), 300
    en colère, 300
    fish and cuts, 298–9
    fritto misto mare, 301
    whitebait, 301
  eel stew, 353–4
  grilled, 430–3
    Caprice, 433
    fish and cuts, 431–2
    homard, 433
    langoustine en brochette, 433
    au lard, 433
    merlan entier St Germain, 433
    method, 432
    preparation, 432
  kedgeree, 453–4
  lobster (homard)
    américaine, 355–6
    Cardinal, 455
    Mornay, 454
    Newburg, 356–7, 454–5
    Thermidor, 455
  moules, à la crème, 357
    à la poulette, 357
    marinière, 357
  pie, 450
    Russian, 449
  poached, 281–8
    Bercy, 285
    bonne femme, 285
    Bréval/d'Antin, 285
    Cubat, 285
    dieppoise, 284

    Dugléré, 284
    florentine, 286
    Granville, 284
    Mornay, 285
    Polignac, 284
    St Valéry, 285
    Suchet, 284
    Véronique, 285
    vin blanc, 284
    Walewska, 286
  potted, 121–2
  shallow fried (meunière), 327–32
    amandine, 330
    belle meunière, 330
    bretonne, 330
    Cléopâtra, 330
    cuts, 328
    Doria, 330
    grenobloise, 330
    method of cooking, 329
    Murat, 330
    scampi/scallops, 331
      Newburg, 331
      Thermidor, 332
  skate (raie) au beurre noir, 266
  soufflé, 416
  soup, 222–3
  soused, 120–1
  stewed:
    bouillabaisse, 354–5
    matelote d'anguille, 353–4
    matelote de poisson, 353
  trout (truite) au bleu, 266–7
Flambés, 573–5
  banane, 575
  crêpes Suzette, 575
  fruit, 574–5
Flans, 480–4
  apple, 482
    meringue, 483
  baked egg custard, 483–4
  fruit, 481–2
Flour, browned, 168
  strong, 534
Fondant creams, 637–8
Food, colour changes, 63–6
  effect of cooking on, 57–66
  flavour and odour changes, 63
  texture changes, 60–3
French toast, 472

Fricassées, 343–4
Fritters, 561–2
  banana, 304
  cheese, 304
  choux, 490
  choux pastry bread, 304
  crab, 304
  fruit, 304, 562–3
  rice and apricot, 563
Fruit:
  avocado pear, 114
  band, 501–3
  cocktails, 110–13
  crumbles, 487
  deep-fried, 304
  flambés, 574–5
  fools, 593–4
    apple, 594
    apricot, 594
    gooseberry, 594
    raspberry, 594
    rhubarb, 594
  fritters, 562–3
  omelet with, 564
  pies, 479–80
  pudding, steamed, 508
  purées, 557
  roll, steamed, 509
  salad, fresh, 627
  soufflés, 571–2
Fruits:
  dipped caramelled, 638
    chocolate, 638
  pears in red wine, 557
  poached, 556, 557
  stewed, 556–7
Fryers, computerized, 53–4
Frying, deep, 293–304
  shallow, 304–34
Fumet de poisson, 171

Galantine, 139–41
  chicken, 145–6
Game, *see* Meats
Gammon, grilled, 428
Ganache, 649
Garlic pellets, 163
Garnishes, 164–8
Gâteaux, 523–6
  au chocolat, 524

croquembouche, 525
forêt noir, 524
glacé, 524–5
Macmahon, 525
moka, 524
printanière, 524
religieuse, 526
St Honoré, 525
Gelatine, 586–7
Gelatinization, 72
Glazes, 171, 645
Glossary, 652–9
Gnocchi, 246
  Parisienne, 248
  piémontaise, 248–9
  polenta, 249
  romaine, 247–8
Goulash, 345–6
Granités/marquises, 613–14

Ham, *see* Meats
Heat transfer, 55–6
Homard, 355–7, 433, 454–5

Iced coupes, 622–3
  abricotine, 623
  belle Hélène, 623
  Edna May, 623
  Jacques, 623
  Jamaica, 623
  Marie Louise, 623
  Melba, 623
Ices, 605–12
  churn-frozen cream, 608–9
    banana, 609
    caramel, 609
    chocolate, 609
    coffee, 609
    orange, 609
    praline, 609
    strawberry, 609
    vanilla, 608
  churn-frozen water, 609–12
    apricot, 611
    fruit purée, 611
    lemon, 610
    lime, 610
    mango, 611
    melon, 611
    orange, 611
    pineapple, 612

Ices—*continued*
    redcurrant, 612
    strawberry, 612
    tangerine, 611
    criteria, 606–7
    hygiene factors, 607–8
    techniques, 607
Icing, water, 646
Ingredients criteria for cakes, 512–15
Irish stew, 352–3
Italian stuffing, 252

Jam, omelet, 564
    roll, baked, 486
        steamed, 509
    Swiss roll, 520
Jelly, 628
Jerusalem artichokes, *see* Vegetables

Kale, *see* Vegetables
Kebabs, 430
Kedgeree, 453–4
Kidneys, *see* Meats
Kitchen, brigade, 33–6
    clothing for, 11–13
    modified, 36–7
    small equipment, 16–20
Kohlrabi, *see* Vegetables
Kromeskis, 448

Lady fingers (okra), *see* Vegetables
Lamb, *see* Meats
Lasagne, 254
Leeks, *see* Vegetables
Lentils, *see* Vegetables
Lettuce, *see* Vegetables
Liaisons, 173
Liquidizer, 49
Liver, *see* Meats
Lobster, Américaine, 355–6
    Newburg, 356–7
    see also Fish

Macaroni, *see* Pasta
Maillard browning, 66
Marinade (red wine), 349
Marrow, *see* Vegetables
Marzipan, cut outs/chocolates, 637
    fruits, 636–7

Mayonnaise, 85–7, 191–2
    seafood, 118
    shellfish with, 119
Meats, baked, 401–16
    beef:
        steak pies, 402–3
        fillet in puff pastry, 405–6
    game:
        pigeon pie, 404
        rabbit pie, 404
    ham:
        en croûte, 445
        sugar baked, 446
        with peaches or pineapple, 446
    lamb:
        Cornish pasties, 406
    poultry:
        chicken pie, 404
    toad in the hole, 406–7
    veal and ham pie, 405
Meats, boiled, 258–9
    beef:
        à l'anglaise, 260
        à la française, 260
    ham:
        à sauce persil, 260
    mutton:
        sauce aux câpres, 260
    offal:
        langue de boeuf à l'anglaise, 260
        langue de boeuf à sauce madère, 260
        langue de boeuf florentine, 260
    pig's trotters, 262
    poultry:
        à la stanley, 263
        argenteuil, 263
        aux sauce champignons, 263
        hongroise, 263
        sauce suprême, 263
    tete de veau vinaigrette, 261
Meats, braised, 360–72
    beef:
        carbonnade de boeuf, 362–3
        daube de boeuf, 363–4
    beef joints:
        pièce de boeuf braisé, 368
        pièce de boeuf braisé à la mode, 368
        pièce de boeuf braisé au vin rouge, 368
        pièce de boeuf braisé bourgeoise, 368

Meats, braised—*continued*
  pièce de boeuf braisé bourguignonne, 368
  beef, small cuts, 361
    au vin rouge, 362
    bourgeoise, 362
    jardinière, 362
    paysanne, 362
    printanier, 362
  ham:
    au madère, 445
    florentine, 445
  lamb small cuts:
    chops d'agneau braisés, 361–2
  mutton:
    daube de mouton, 363–4
  offal:
    coeur d'agneau braisé, 364–5
    coeur de boeuf braisé, 369
    langues d'agneau braisées, 366
    langues d'agneau braisées florentine, 366
    langue de boeuf braisée, 369
    liver and onions, 365–6
    queue de boeuf braisée, 364
    ris à blanc, 370–1
    ris à brun, 366–7
  poultry:
    ballotines de volaille, 362
    caneton braisé à l'orange, 369–70
  veal joints:
    l'epaule farcie braisée, 369
    pièce braisé à blanc, 371–2
    poitrine farcie, 369
  veal small cuts:
    chops de veau braisés, 361–2
    paupiettes de veau braisés, 362
Meats, deep fried, 446
  beef:
    croquettes de boeuf, 447
    Durham cutlets, 448
  game:
    côtelettes de gibier, 447
    croquettes de gibier, 447
  poultry:
    chicken southern style, 297
    côtelettes de volaille, 447
    croquettes de volaille, 447
    fritots de volaille/pork, 297
    pilon de volaille frit, 297

    suprême de volaille cordon bleu, 297
    suprême de volaille Kiev, 297
    Wiener Schnitzel, 298
Meats, grilled, 417–30
  cuts:
    beef, 418–21
    chicken, 424–5
    lamb, 421–3
    offal, 424
    pork, 423–4
  degrees of cooking, 425
  garnishes, 426–7
    à la maison, 426
    américaine, 427
    crapaudine, 428
    diable, 427
  miscellaneous:
    bacon/sausages, 428–9
    brochettes à la maison, 430
    brochettes de rognon, 430
    brochettes de volaille, 430
    gammon, 428
    hamburgers, 428
    mixed grill, 429
    on skewers, 429
    shish kebab, 430
Meats, poached:
  offal:
    cervelles au beurre noir, 280
    cervelles au beurre noisette, 280
  poultry:
    suprême de volaille aux sauce champignons, 280
    suprême de volaille florentine, 279
    suprême de volaille Polignac, 280
    suprême de volaille princesse, 280
Meats, poêle:
  agneau (lamb):
    Clamart, 400
    Dubarry, 400
  boeuf (beef) and garnishes:
    Mercédès, 400
    niçoise, 400
    Richelieu, 400
  canard (duck):
    à l'orange, 399
    aux cerises, 399
  faisan (pheasant), 400
  hare (râble de lièvre), 400

Meats, poêle—*continued*
  poulet (chicken) en cocotte:
    aux chipolata, 399
    bonne femme, 399
    Champeaux, 399
    fermière, 399
    grand'mère, 399
    paysanne, 399
  preparation of meats, 397
  veau (veal):
    noix de veau Mercédès, 400
Meats, sauté:
  beef:
    bitoks, 326
    cuts of beef, 312
    sautés, de boeuf
      a l'estragon, 314
      au beurre noisette, 313
      au poivre à la crème, 313
      aux champignons, 313
      bordelaise, 313
      chasseur, 314
      fleuriste, 314
      hongroise, 314
      marchand de vin, 314
      périgourdine, 314
      Rossini, 314
      Strogonoff, 315
  lamb:
    cuts of lamb, 315–16
    methods of cooking, 316
    sautés of lamb:
      à l'anglaise, 317
      chasseur, 317
      Clamart, 317
      fleuriste, 317
      hongroise, 317
      maréchale, 317
      niçoise, 317
      Reform, 317
  offal:
    foie de volaille à sauce madère, 324
    foie sauté au lard, 323
    foie sauté lyonnaise, 323
    rognons, 323
      au madère, 324
      chasseur, 324
      turbigo, 324
  poultry:
    cuts of chicken, 306–7

  poulet sauté:
    archiduc, 307–8
    Bercy, 308
    bonne femme, 308
    bourguignonne, 308
    Champeaux, 309
    chasseur, 309
    Duroc, 309
    hongroise, 309
    portugaise, 309
    provençale, 310
    pojarski de volaille, 327
  suprême de volaille garnishes:
    archiduc, 310
    à la crème, 310
    aux champignons, 311
    Doria, 311
    hongroise, 311
    maréchale, 311
    Maryland, 311
    Sandeman, 311
  veal/pork sautés:
    bitoks, 326
    cuts of veal, 318–19
    garnishes:
      à l'anglaise, 319
      à la crème, 320
      au madère, 320
      au marsala, 321
      aux champignons, 320
      cordon bleu, 320
      Holstein, 320
      italienne, 320
      maréchale, 320
      milanaise, 320
      napolitaine, 321
      viennoise, 321
    methods of cooking, 319
    pojarski de veau, 327
  venison:
    cuts, 321–2
      au porto, 322
      aux cerises, 322
      chasseur, 322
      smitane, 322
Meats, roasted, 382–95
  accompaniments, 390–1
  carving, 391–4
  gravies, 389
  preparation, 383–5

Meats, roasted—*continued*
  stuffings, 386–8
Meats, steamed, 289–90
  beef steak pudding, 291
Meats, stewed:
  beef:
    boeuf bourguignonne, 340
    goulache de boeuf, 345
    hachis de boeuf, 340
    kari de boeuf, 344
    ragoût de boeuf, 339
  game:
    blanquette de lapin, 341
    civet de gibier, 350–1
    fricassée de lapin, 342
    ragoût de lapin, 340
    salmis de gibier, 348–9
  lamb:
    blanquette d'agneau, 341
    chop d'agneau Champvallon, 352
    goulache d'agneau, 345
    Irish stew, 352–3
    kari d'agneau, 344
    Lancashire hot pot, 351
    navarin d'agneau, 339
  mutton:
    goulache de mouton, 345
    kari de mouton, 344
  offal:
    ragoût de rognon, 340
    tripe and onions, 353
  pork:
    blanquette de porc, 343
    fricassée de porc, 343
    goulache de porc, 345
  poultry:
    coq au vin, 347–8
    fricassée de volaille, 342, 343
  veal:
    blanquette de veau, 341
    fricassée de veau, 343
    goulache de veau, 344
    kari de veau, 344
    oss-bucco milanaise, 347
    ragoût de veau, 340
    ragoût de veau au vin blanc, 340
    ragoût de veau Marengo, 340
Melon surprise, chilled, 628–9
Meringue, 595–604
  baked Alaska, 603

Italian, 596–7, 598
Japonaise mixture, 604
mushrooms, 601
nests, 599–600
ordinary, 597
shells, 598
  chocolate ice-cream, 599
  cream, 599
  ice-cream, 599
  ice-cream and cream, 599
snow eggs, 603
surprise soufflé omelets, 601–2
  Alaskan, 602
  cherry, 602
  island, 602
  mandarin, 602
  Norwegian, 602
Swiss, 597
vacharins, 600–1
Metrication, 2, 4–5
Micro-Aire ovens, 40–1
Microwave cooking, 41–2
Microwave ovens, 38–40
Milk puddings:
  baked rice, 546–7
  blancmange, 626
  boiled cereal/pasta, 547
  French rice, 548
  ground rice, 547
  macaroni, 547
  rice, 548
  sago, 548
  semolina, 548
  tapioca, 548
  vermicelli, 548
Mirepoix, 162–3
Miroton of beef, 441–2
Mixed grill, 429
Moules marinière, 357
Moussaka, 442–3
Mousses:
  chocolate (moulded), 592
    (non-moulded), 592
  cold sweet, 590–3
  fruit purée:
    apricot, 621
    banana, 621
    raspberry, 621
    strawberry, 621
  gooseberry, 591

Mousses—*continued*
 iced, 620–2
  chocolate, 622
  coffee, 622
  orange, 622
  praline, 622
  vanilla, 622
 raspberry, 591
 soft fruits, 590–1
 strawberry, 591
 summer, 591
Mutton, *see* Meats

Noodle, dough, 250–1
 see also Pasta
Okra, *see* Vegetables
Omelets, 238–41
 à la turque, 240
 Arnold Bennet, 240, 241
 au fromage, 241
 au jambon, 241
 aux champignons, 241
 aux crevettes, 240
 aux tomates, 241
 espagnole, 239
 fermière, 240
 fines herbes, 241
 limousine, 241
 Lorraine, 241
 paysanne, 240
 parmentier, 240
 savoury soufflé, 241
 surprise, soufflé, 601–2
 sweet, 563–5
  jam, 564
  raspberry, 564
  rum, 564
  with Calvados, 564
  with fruit, 564
  with Grand Marnier, 564
  with Mandarine Napoleon, 564
Onion, clouté, 162
 see also Vegetables
Oranges in caramel sauce, 629
Osso-buco, 347
Oven temperature guide, 6–7

Paella, 246
Panadas, 173

Pancakes, 558–9
 apple, 560
 crab, 453
 de volaille, 437
  et champignons, 437
  Princesse, 437
 fish, 452–3
 jam, 560
 purée, 560
 soufflé, 561
  Jamaican, 561
  Viennoise, 561
  with rum, 561
 with lemon, 560
 with orange, 560
 with pears, 560
 with pineapple, 560
Parfaits, 616
Parsnips, *see* Vegetables
Pasta, 246–56
 salad, 99–100
Pastries:
 choux à la crème, 488–9
 cream horns, 500
 cream puffs, 498
 Danish, 539–41
  almond slice, 541
  apple slice, 541
  bear's paws, 541
  crescents, 541
  custards, 540
  ginger cuts, 541
  pin wheels, 541
 Eccles cakes/Banbury cakes, 496–7
 eclairs, 489
 fruit band, 501–3
 jalousie and d'artois, 503–4
 palmiers, 498–9
 pithivier, 504–5
 profiteroles, 489
 slices, 499
 small Paris Brest, 489
 swans, 490
 turnovers, 497–8
Pastry, 475–80
 choux, 247, 487–8
 hot boiled water, 490–2
 puff, 493–6
 rough puff, 496
 short, 475–80

Pastry—*continued*
  strudel, 625
  suet, 507
Pâte a choux, 247
Pâté, 139–41, 143–5
Peas, *see* Vegetables
Pepper salad, 100–1
Pies, 435–6
  chicken, 435–6
    and ham, 436
    and mushroom, 436
    ham and mushroom, 436
    Russian, 450
  cold, 134–6
    English layered, 136–7
    raised, 137–8
  English plate, 480
  fish, 450
  fruit, 479–80
  lemon meringue, 484
  mincemeat, 485, 500–1
  steak, 439–41
Pig's trotters, grilled, 444–5
Pizzas, 412–13
Poisson, *see* Fish
Pojarski, 327
Potato:
  and watercress salad, 102
  dumplings, 248–9
  salad, 102
Potatoes:
  baked, 409–11
    Anna, 411
    arlie, 410
    Byron, 411
    Darphin, 411
    gratinées, 410
    Macaire, 410
    ménagère, 410
    Nana, 411
    Robert, 410
    surprise, 410
    voison, 411
  boiled, 274–6, 460
    à la crème, 275
    à la neige, 275
      Biarritz, 276
      en robe de chambre, 275, 276
      maitre d'hotel, 275
      mousseline, 276

    nature, 275
    nouvelle, 276
    nouvelles à la menthe, 276
    nouvelles persillées, 276
    persillées, 275
    purée, 275
    purée à la crème, 275
    purée au gratin, 276
    quelin, 275
  braised, 378–81
    au lard, 379
    berrichonne, 378
    boulangère, 379
    bretonne, 379
    champignol, 381
    cretan, 381
    Dauphinoise, 380
    Delmonico, 380–1
    fondant, 381
    hongroise, 379
    savoyarde, 379–80
  deep fried, 302–3
    alumettes, 303
    bataille, 303
    chips (crisps), 302
    frites (chipped), 303
    gauffrettes, 303
    mignonette, 303
    pailles, 303
    pont neuf, 303
    soufflé, 303
  duchesse extensions, 457–9
    amandine, 459
    Berny, 459
    brioche, 458
    Chester, 458
    croquettes, 458
    Dauphine, 459
    Elizabeth, 459
    galette, 459
    Lorrette, 459
    marquise, 458
    rosette, 458
    royale/St Florentin, 459
  sautées extensions, 460
    lyonnaise, 460
    provençale, 460
    rissolées, 460
    roesti, 460
  shallow fried, 333–4

Potatoes—*continued*
  à cru, 334
  cocotte, 334
  columbine, 334
  noisette, 334
  parisienne, 334
  parmentier, 334
  sablées, 334
Potiron provençale, 349
Poultry, *see* Meats
Praline, 649–50
Profiteroles, 489
Proprietory products, 123–6
Protein, gelation and coagulation, 72
Pudding:
  bread and butter, 552
  cabinet, 552
  Christmas, 532–3
  diplomat, 553
  Eve's, 530
  milk, 546–8
  Queen of, 552
  sponge, 527, 528–9
  sponge (steamed):
    canary, 530
    cherry, 529
    chocolate, 529
    coconut, 529
    fruit, 529
    ginger, 529
    golden, 530
    jam, 530
    lemon/castle, 529
    orange, 529
    pineapple, 529
    vanilla, 529
  steak, 439–40
  steamed fruit, 508
  suet, 528
  suet (steamed), 530–1
    coconut, 531
    college, 531
    date, 531
    fig, 531
    fruit, 532
    ginger, 532
    golden layered, 531
    jam layered, 531
    lemon or orange, 531
  summer, 630

Pumpkin *see* Vegetables
Quiches, 413–15, 470
  au fromage, 414
  aux oignons, 414
  forestière, 414
  fruits de mer, 414
  lorraine, 414

Raie au beurre noir, 266
Ravioli, 251–4
Régéthermic oven, 52–3
Rice, 242–5
  au foie de volaille, 245
  au jambon, 245
  à volaille, 245
  aux champignons, 245
  aux crevettes roses, 245
  créole, 245
  Empress style, 578
  fried, 243
  italienne, 245
  milanaise, 245
  nature, 243
  paella, 246
  piémontaise, 245
  rissotto/pilaff, 244
Rissoles, 448–9
Royale, 203
Rum, baba, 544
  truffles, 636

Salad:
  celeriac, 101
  chicken liver, 104–5
  coleslaw, 103
  exotic, 95
  Florida, 97
  japonaise, 96
  meat, 98
  mimosa, 97
  mixed green, 97
  mixed potato, 102
  mushroom, 104
  niçoise, 103
  pasta, 99–100
  pepper, 100–1
  potato and watercress, 102
  rice, 100
  seafood, 99
  vegetable, 101–2
  Waldorf, 96

Salads:
  classification, 92
  rules for, 91–2
  simple, 93–5
Salmis de gibier, 348–9
Salpicon, chicken, 436
  fish, 450–51
Salsify, *see* Vegetables
Sandwiches, 127–31
  bookmaker, 132
  club, 131
  croque monsieur, 132–3
  hot pitta bread, 133
Sauce:
  allemande, 180
  américaine, 196
  anchovy, 177
  apple, 198
  aurore, 179
  béarnaise, 189
  béchamel, 177
  Bercy, 181, 183
  beurre fondue, 200
  beurre meunière, 200
  beurre noir, 200
  beurre noir aux câpres, 200
  beurre noisette, 200
  bigarade, 195
  bolognaise, 197
  bordelaise, 184
  bourguignonne, 184
  bread, 198
  caper, 180
  caramel, 640
  champignon, 180, 181, 187
  charcutière, 187
  chasseur, 185
  Chateaubriand, 184
  chaudfroid, 155–6
  cheese, 177, 181
  chocolate, dark, 641
  Choron, 190
  cranberry, 199
  crapaudine, 184
  cream, 177
  crevettes, 181
  Cumberland, 199
  curry, 179, 193
  demi-glace, 183
  devilled, 185

diable, 185
divine, 188
egg, 178
espagnole, 182
estragon, 187
Foyot, 190
golden syrup, 641
gravy, 192
Granville, 181
guacamole, 90
hollandaise, 188
homard, 196
hongroise, 180, 182
indienne, 179
italienne, 185
Ivoire, 180
jam, 641–2
jus lié, 192
kari, 193
lemon/orange, 642
lobster, 196
lyonnaise, 185
madeira, 186
maltaise, 189
marchand de vin, 186
mayonnaise, 85–7, 191
melba, 644
melted butter, 200
mint, 199
Mornay, 177, 181
mousseline, 189
moutarde, 178
mushroom, 180, 181, 187
mustard, 178
noisette, 189
oeufs, 178
onion, 178, 185
orange, 195
paprika, 180, 182
parsley, 178
Périgueux, 186
piquant, 186
poivrade, 186
porto, 187
portugaise, 194–5
poulette, 180
prawn, 181
provençale, 194–5
Reform, 187
rémoulade, 191

Sauce—*continued*
  Robert, 187
  sabayon, 644–5
  sherry, 187
  shrimp, 181
  smitane, 197
  soubise, 178
  suprême, 179
  sweet and sour, 195–6
  sweet milk, 642–3
  tartare, 191
  Thermidor, 182
  tomate, 179, 193–4
  tomatoed demi-glace, 187
  Valoise, 190
  velouté, 178–9
  vin blanc, 181
  white wine, 181
  xérès, 187
Sauces, 173–203
  basic, 173–5
  butter, 200–2
  emulsified, 174–5
  independent, 175
  non-derivative, 175
Sauerkraut, 377, 378
  Sausage rolls, 505
  Savarin, aux fruits,
    545
  fruit croûtes, 544
  marignans, Chantilly, 544–5
    au rhum, 545
  paste, 543–4
  rum baba, 544
Savouries, 464–70
  canapés:
    aux champignons, 465
    gourmets, 465
    hollandaise, 465
    Ivanhoe, 466
    Richie, 466
  croûtes:
    anchois, 466
    anges à cheval, 465
    baron, 467
    beignets de crabe, 469
    beignets de fromage, 469
    bouchées à l'indienne, 469
    buck rarebit, 468
    Croque Monsieur, 469
    Derby, 467

    diables à cheval, 467
    Diane, 467
    laitances, 467
    moelle, 468
    Quo Vadis, 466
    sardines, 468
    Scotch woodcock, 468
    Welsh rarebit, 468
    Windsor, 467
Scones, 515–16
Scotch eggs, 444
Sea kale, *see* Vegetables
Snails, 456
Sorbets, 612–13
  champagne, 613
  lemon, 613
  lime, 613
  liqueur, 613
  orange, 613
  Roman punch, 613
  white wine, 613
Soufflés, 415–16
  baked, in water bath, 569–71
    cherry, 570
    chocolate, 570
    coffee, 570
    lemon, 570
    orange, 570
    praline, 571
    Rothschild, 571
    rum, 570
    vanilla, 570
  cheese, 415–16
  chicken, 416
  cold, sweet, 586–90
    fruit purées, 588–9
      apricot, 589
      gooseberry, 589
      raspberry, 589
      strawberry, 589
    lemon, 588
    lime, 588
    miscellaneous, 589–90
      chocolate, 590
      coffee, 590
      peppermint, 590
    orange, 588
  dry baked, 567–9
    apple, 572
    apricot, 572
    cherry, 568

Soufflés—*continued*
  chocolate, 567
  coffee, 567
  curaçao, 568
  Grand Marnier, 568
  harlequin, 569
  lemon, 568
  Maraschino, 568
  orange, 568
  peach, 572
  pineapple, 569
  praline, 569
  Rothschild, 568
  raspberry, 572
  rum, 568
  strawberry, 572
  vanilla, 567
 fish, 416
 ham, 416
 iced, 618–20
  apricot, 619
  coffee, 620
  chocolate, 620
  liqueur, 620
  praline, 620
  raspberry, 619
  strawberry, 619
  vanilla, 620
 savoury, 416
Soups:
 bisques, 213–14
  crabe, 214
  crevettes, 214
  homard, 214
  recipe, 213–14
 bortsch, 223
 broths, 214–17
  beef, 215
  bonne femme, 216
  chicken, 215
  cocky leeky, 216
  game, 215
  minestrone, 216
  mutton, 215
  paysanne, 216
  recipes, 214
  chowders (fish broths),
   216–17
  clam, 217
  mussel, 217
  oyster, 217

  recipe, 216–17
  scallop, 217
  seafood, 216–17
 consommés, 217–19
  alphabétique, 219
  brunoise, 219
  Célestine, 219
  en tasse, 219
  gelée, 219
  julienne, 219
  madrilène, 219
  porto, 219
  recipe, 218
  royale, 219
  tortue, 219
  vermicelle, 219
  xérès, 219
 creams, 207–9
  argenteuil, 208
  asperge, 208
  carottes, 208
  céleri, 208
  champignon, 209
  cressonière, 209
  crécy, 208
  Doria, 208
  Dubarry, 208
  florentine, 209
  Judic, 208
  Lamballe, 225
  légumes, 209
  Longchamps, 225
  oignon, 209
  poireaux, 208
  portugaise, 221
  recipe, 208
  Solférino, 221–2
  St Cloud, 225
  St Germain, 224–5
  tomate, 221
  Washington, 209
 croûte au pot, 227
 French onion, 220
 gazpacho, 225
 Germiny, 224
 mulligatawny, 220–1
 petite marmite, 226–7
 petite marmite bearnaise,
  227
 purées (aqueous), 206–7
  carottes, 207

Soups—*continued*
  céleri, 207
  cressonière, 207
  Dubarry, 207
  flamande, 207
  légumes, 207
  navet, 207
  oignon, 207
  parmentier, 207
  poireaux, 207
  potiron, 207
  recipe, 206–7
  rutabaga, 207
  purées (pulses), 205–6
  condé, 206
  conti, 206
  égyptienne, 206
  Esaü, 206
  lentilles, 206
  soissonnaise, 206
  St Germain, 206
  soupe de poissons, 222–3
  thickened brown, 212–13
  game, 212
  hare, 213
  kidney, 212
  mock turtle, 213
  oxtail, 212
  pheasant, 213
  tomate, 221
  veloutés, 209–12
  Agnès sorel, 210
  asperge, 211
  champignons, 211
  cressonnière, 211
  dieppoise, 210
  Doria, 211
  huîtres, 210
  poisson, 210
  recipe, 211
  volaille, 210
  vichyssoise, 226
Spaghetti, *see* Pasta
Spetzli, 256
Spinach, *see* Vegetables
Starches, as thickeners, 67–71,
  172–3
  freeze-thaw, 71
Steamers, pressure type, 44–6
  pressureless type, 47–8
Steaming, 289–92

Steaming pressures, 7
Stewing and braising, 335–8
Stocks, 168–71
Strawberry/raspberry cream, 629
Strawberry/raspberry Romanoff, 630
Strawberry shortbread, 629
Stuffings:
  chestnut, 388
  Italian, 252
  lemon, parsley and thyme, 387
  sage and onion, 386–7
  sausagemeat, 388
  spinach, 251–2
Sugar:
  boiled, 650
  caramel, 651
  spun, 650
Summer pudding, 630
Swede, *see* Vegetables
Sweetbreads, *see* Meats
Sweetcorn, *see* Vegetables
Syllabub, 631
Syneresis, 71
Syrups, 646–7
  baba, 647
  savarin, 646–7
  stock, 646

Tart:
  Bakewell, 483
  jam, lemon curd, 485
  open syrup, 485
Tartlets:
  baked egg custard, 484
  jam, lemon curd, 485
  syrup, 485
Temperature guide, 6–7
Tenderizing methods, 61–3
Terrine, 139–41
  duck, 142–3
  house, 141–2
Toad in the hole, 406–7
Tomato concassé, 164
Trifles, 631–2
Tripe and onions, 353
Turnip, *see* Vegetables

Vacharin, 600–1
  cherry, 600
  mixed fruit, 600
  raspberry, 601
  strawberry, 601

Vegetable salad, 101–2
Vegetables, baked, 408–11
  courgettes, 408
  cucumber, 408
  mushrooms, 408
  tomatoes, 409
Vegetables, boiled, 267–76
  artichokes, globe (artichauts):
    au beurre fondue, 271
    boiled, 272
    fonds farcis au gratin, 462
    fonds florentine, 462
    fonds provençale, 462
    fonds sautés au beurre, 461
    hollandaise, 272
  artichokes, Jerusalem (topinambours):
    à la crème, 271
    au beurre, 271
    aux fines herbes, 271
    nature, 271
    persillés, 271
    purée, 271
  asparagus (asperge):
    au beurre, 269
    au beurre fondue, 269
    amandine, 269
    hollandaise, 269
    nature, 269
    purée, 269
  beans broad (fèves):
    à la crème, 269
    à sauce persil, 269
    nature, 269
  beans butter:
    à la menthe, 273
    au beurre, 273
    nature, 273
  beans french (haricots verts fins):
    à la crème, 269
    au beurre, 269
    nature, 269
    tourangelle, 269
  beans haricots blancs:
    au beurre, 273
    bretonne, 273
    nature, 273
  beans kidney (flageolets):
    au beurre, 273
    nature, 273
  beans, panaches, 274

beetroot (betterave):
  à la crème, 271
  au beurre, 271
  nature, 271
broccoli (brocolis):
  amandine, 269
  au beurre, 269
  hollandaise, 269
  milanaise, 269
  Mornay, 269
  nature, 269
  polonaise, 269
brussels sprouts (choux de bruxelles):
  au beurre, 269
  milanaise, 269
  nature, 269
  polonaise, 269
cabbage (chou):
  au beurre, 269
  nature, 269
carrots (carottes):
  à la crème, 271
  au beurre, 271
  glacées, 271
  persillées, 271
  purée, 271
  vichy, 271
cauliflower (choufleur):
  amandine, 269
  au beurre, 269
  aux fines herbes, 269
  hollandaise, 269
  milanaise, 269
  Mornay, 269
  nature, 269
  polonaise, 269
celeriac (céleri-rave):
  à la crème, 271
  au beurre, 271
  aux fines herbes, 271
  nature, 271
chicory (endive):
  à la crème, 269
  au beurre, 269
  Mornay, 269
  nature, 269
  purée, 269
courgette:
  à la crème, 270
  au beurre, 270

Vegetables—*continued*
    aux fines herbes, 270
    Mornay, 270
    nature, 270
    persillée, 270
  cucumber (concombre):
    à la crème, 269
    au beurre, 269
    glacé, 269
    milanaise, 269
    nature, 269
    persillé, 269
  curly kale (chou frisé):
    au beurre, 269
    nature, 269
  fennel (fenouil):
    à la crème, 272
    au beurre, 272
    aux fines herbes, 272
    milanaise, 272
    Mornay, 272
    nature, 272
    persillées, 272
    poulette, 272
  gumbo (okra):
    au beurre, 269
    hollandaise, 269
    nature, 269
  kale sea (chou de mer):
    à la crème, 270
    au beurre, 270
    hollandaise, 270
    nature, 270
  kohlrabi:
    à la crème, 271
    au beurre, 271
    nature, 271
    persillé, 271
  leeks (poireaux):
    à la crème, 270
    au beurre, 270
    Mornay, 270
    nature, 270
  lentile (lentilles):
    purée, 273
    purée à la crème, 273
  marrow (courge):
    à la crème, 270
    au beurre, 270
    aux fines herbes, 270

    Mornay, 270
    nature, 270
    persilleé, 270
  onions (oignons):
    à la crème, 272
    nature, 272
  parsnips (panais):
    à la crème, 272
    au beurre, 272
    nature, 272
    persillé, 272
    purée, 272
  peas (mange tout):
    au beurre, 270
    glacés, 270
    hollandaise, 270
    nature, 270
  peas (petits pois):
    à la menthe, 270
    au beurre, 270
    flamande, 270
    nature, 270
    purée, 270
  peas marrowfat:
    à la menthe, 273
    au beurre, 273
    nature, 273
  ratatouille, 359–60
  salsify (salsifi):
    à la crème, 272
    au beurre, 272
    aux fines herbes, 272
    nature, 272
    persillés, 272
    poulette, 272
    tourangelle, 272
  spinach (épinards):
    à la crème, 270
    au beurre, 270
    Mornay, 270
    nature, 270
    purée, 270
  swedes (rutabaga):
    au beurre, 272
    nature, 272
    persillés, 272
    purée, 272
  sweetcorn (maïs) off the cob:
    à la crème, 270
    au beurre, 270

Vegetables—*continued*
  nature, 270
  sweetcorn (maïs) on the cob:
    au beurre fondu, 270
    nature, 270
  turnips (navets):
    au beurre, 272
    nature, 272
    persillés, 272
    purée, 272
Vegetables braised, 373–81
  cabbage, 374, 377
  celery, 374
  endive, 374
  fennel, 374
  leek, 374
  lettuce, 374
  onion, 374
  peppers, 374
  recipe, 374
Vegetables deep fried, 301–3
  aubergine frite, 301
  beignets de choufleur, 302
  beignets de panais, 302
  champignons frites, 302
  courgettes frites, 302
  oignons frites, 302
Vegetables grilled, 433–4
  mushrooms, 434
  tomatoes, 433–4
Vegetables roasted, 395
Vegetables sautées au beurre, 461
  artichoke bottoms (fonds), 461
    aux fines herbes, 461
    limousine, 461
  beans (haricots verts fins), 461
  brussels sprouts (choux de bruxelles),
    461
    limousine, 461

    polonaise, 461
  cauliflower (choufleur), 461
    aux fines herbes, 461
    polonaise, 461
  celeriac (céleri-rave), 461
    aux fines herbes, 461
  parsnips (panais), 461
    aux fines herbes, 461
  salsify (salsifi), 461
    aux fines herbes, 461
  spinach (épinards), 461
Vegetables shallow fried, 332–4
  aubergines provençale, 332
  champignons sautés, 333
  courgettes provençale, 332
  oignons boutons sautés, 333
  oignons sautés, 333
Vegetables stewed, 358–60
  courge (marrow) provençale, 359
  petits pois (peas)
    à la française, 358
    bonne femme, 358
    paysanne, 358
  potiron (pumpkin) provençale, 359
  ratatouille, 359–60
Venison, *see* Meats
Vertical cutter/mixer, 49–51
Vol au vent, 437
  cases, 506
  de fruits de mer, 451
  de poisson, 451
    Princesse, 451
  de volaille, 437
    et champignons, 437
    Princesse, 437

Yeast, 534
  batter, 295–6, 562
Yorkshire pudding, 389

Zabaglione, 632

THE NEW WINE COMPANION
David Burroughs and Norman Bezzant
Published on behalf of the Wine and Spirit Education Trust

From vine to palate, here is a complete introduction to wine and the wine trade. The authors have extensively revised, updated, and expanded their earlier *Wine Trade Student's Companion,* adding among much else a section on cider and perry and frequent suggestions for suitable foods to accompany various wines. This version begins with a brief history of the origin and spread of wine-making, followed by profiles of the principal types of wines and spirits, their methods of production, and their use. Sections on sparkling wines, fortified wines, spirits, liqueurs, and beers are included. The book's concluding chapters deal with the trade itself and its products as presented to the consumer. Finally there are seven appendixes — covering everything from pests and diseases to cocktail recipes — and a glossary with pronunciation guide. All chapters are thoroughly illustrated with maps, diagrams, and appropriate decorative drawings. The running question-and-answer footnotes, originally designed as an aid for students will also serve as a valuable checklist for other readers.

0 434 09867-224 pp

WINE REGIONS OF THE WORLD
Second edition
David Burroughs and Norman Bezzant
Published on behalf of the Wine and Spirit Education Trust

This book is a comprehensive guide to the main wine and spirit-producing areas of the world (there is also an additional section on cigars).

As well as being a key text for the Wine and Spirit Education Trust Higher Certificate, Wine Regions will be of value for the City and Guilds of London Institute course 707-3 — Food Service, those seeking HCIMA qualifications, and BTEC certificates and diplomas in Catering Technology. It is a useful source of background information for the shipping, manufacturing, distribution, restaurant and hotel, and publicity fields.

0 434 90174 1 336 pp

FOOD COMMODITIES
Second edition

Bernard Davis

A complete, up-to-date study of all the major foods used in the Hotel and Catering Industry

Designed to provide students and caterers with a basic knowledge of foods as commodities used in catering, Bernard Davis methodically classifies each food group, their characteristics, methods of production, varieties available, catering uses, storage requirements and scientific and nutritional aspects so that readers can readily identify those areas in which they should be conversant.

The book covers the requirements of students preparing for the following examinations: City and Guilds of London Institute Examinations in Cookery, BTEC Diploma in Hotel and Catering Operations, Institutional Housekeeping and Catering, BTEC Diploma in Hotel and Catering Administration-Institutional Management, Degree courses in Hotel and Catering Administration-Management.

It will also be suitable for students following home economics and domestic science courses or sitting for the Royal Society of Health Examinations in Food Inspection. The book will be of special interest to practising caterers and hotelkeepers actively engaged in food purchasing.

'Bernard Davis is to be congratulated in producing a book of character the use of which will add substantially to our knowledge of food commodities.' *HCIMA Journal.*

0 434 90306 x 384 pp